Lexical Representation and Process

Lexical Representation and Process

edited by
William Marslen-Wilson

A Bradford Book
The MIT Press
Cambridge, Massachusetts
London, England

First MIT Press paperback edition, 1992

This book was set in Times Roman by Asco Trade Typesetting Ltd. in Hong Kong and printed and bound in the United States of America.

Library of Congress Cataloging-in-Publication Data

Lexical representation and process / edited by William Marslen-Wilson.
   p. cm.
  Papers from a conference on lexical representation and process held in Nijmegen, the Netherlands, from June 30 to July 4, 1986, under the joint sponsorship of the Max-Planck-Institut für Psycholinguistik and the Inter-facultaire Werkgroep Taal- en Spraakgedrag of the University of Nijmegen.
  "A Bradford book."
  Bibliography: p.
  Includes index.
  ISBN 0-262-13240-0 (hb), 0-262-63142-3 (pb)
  1. Lexicology—Congresses. 2. Psycholinguistics—Congresses.
I. Marslen-Wilson, William. II. Max Planck Institut für Psycholinguistik (Nijmegen, Netherlands) III. Katholieke Universiteit Nijmegen. Interfacultaire Werkgroep Taal- en Spraakgedrag.
P326.L39 1989
413'.028—dc19   88-36787
                                             CIP

Contents

Contents

Preface

This book is based on a set of beliefs about what are the important issues in the study of human language comprehension and production. These beliefs situate the mental lexicon as the central link in language processing. The lexicon serves, on the one hand, to relate the speech signal to mental representations of lexical form, and, on the other, to relate lexical contents to the syntactic and semantic interpretation of the message being communicated. This means that the proper psycholinguistic study of the lexicon requires us to combine theories of the form and content of lexical representation with theories of lexical processing—of how lexically stored knowledge is brought to bear during the on-line processes of comprehension and production.

These themes are realized in four different ways in the four parts of the book. Part I presents some general, process-oriented accounts of lexical processing. Marslen-Wilson (chapter 1), Seidenberg (chapter 2), and Forster (chapter 3) look at the structure of the comprehension process; Butterworth (chapter 4) and Dell (chapter 5) examine the production process. In each case, the emphasis is on the properties of the lexical system viewed from a primarily psychological process perspective—a perspective that varies radically from the distributed connectionist approach of Seidenberg to the more traditional symbolic approaches of Forster and Butterworth.

Part II, which still focuses more on process than on representation, looks at the nature of the input to the lexical processing system. The questions asked here are questions about the nature of the processing relationship that holds between lexical form representations and the sensory input. Klatt (chapter 6) and Elman (chapter 7) look at the immediate processing of speech, asking how the speech signal, in all its variability, is mapped onto mental representations of lexical form. Rayner and Balota (chapter 8) and Besner and Johnston (chapter 9) look at the somewhat different issues raised by access processes in the visual domain.

Part III looks much more explicitly at theories of lexical representation and at their consequences for theories of lexical process. Frauenfelder and Lahiri (chapter 10) and Cutler (chapter 11) work out some of the intriguing consequences of modern phonological theory—both for psycholinguistic theories of lexical representation and for models of the processes that map from the speech input onto these representations. The next two chapters focus on another aspect of linguistic form—the morphological structure of complex word forms—and on its consequences for readers and listeners. Henderson (chapter 12) surveys current psychological approaches to morphology in the visual domain; Hankamer (chapter 13) examines some of the psycholinguistic implications of a morphological parser for Turkish (which is vastly different in its morphological properties from English, to which most research in morphology has been restricted). Schreuder and Flores D'Arcais (chapter 14) turn their attention to semantic representations in the lexicon and to current psycholinguistic views of this domain.

Part IV focuses on the role of lexical representations in the processes of syntactic parsing and semantic interpretation. What kinds of structural information are coded in the lexicon, and how is this information deployed over time as the speech is heard or the text is read? This is a richly controversial area, and the controversy is reflected in the four chapters here. Frazier (chapter 17) assigns a somewhat different and more limited role to lexical information in structuring the immediate analysis process than Tyler (chapter 15), Steedman (chapter 16), or Tanenhaus and Carlson (chapter 18). Tyler focuses primarily on the process aspects of the relationship between lexical representations and higher-level processes, whereas Steedman examines the role of the lexicon from the perspective of an incremental parser based on categorial grammar. Tanenhaus and Carlson argue for the value of the linguistic concept of thematic role, stored lexically, in illuminating the on-line process of parsing and interpretation.

The overall structure of the book reflects, then, the basic structure of the lexical processing system, with a central core of lexical representations of sounds and meanings looking both outward toward the signal and inward toward the message. But the book also reflects a field in the throes of transition. On the one hand, linguistic concepts have reappeared as a crucial input to psycholinguistic models; on the other, the radical alternative of a reborn associationism offers quite different ways of representing regularity and structure in lexical representations and processes. We live in interesting times.

Acknowledgments

This book grew out of a conference on Lexical Representation and Process held in Nijmegen, The Netherlands, under the joint sponsorship of the Max-Planck-Institut für Psycholinguistik and the Interfacultaire Werkgroep Taal en Spraakgedrag of the University of Nijmegen. I thank my colleagues in the MPI Language Comprehension Group, in particular Uli Frauenfelder and Aditi Lahiri, for their help in organizing the conference, which we did in collaboration with Rob Schreuder of the University of Nijmegen—whose help I also gratefully acknowledge. I am especially grateful to Edith Sjoerdsma for the cheerful efficiency with which she handled the vast amounts of paperwork and organizational detail involved in running an international meeting. I also thank Mr. Koenig, head of the MPI Administration, for the effective and flexible support that he provided throughout—not forgetting the excellent party that he and his staff organized at the end of the conference. My fellow directors, Pim Levelt and Wolfgang Klein, were generous in their advice and support right from the beginning of this project.

I am most grateful for the further efforts of Edith Sjoerdsma and for the help and support of the MRC Applied Psychology Unit in the preparation of the manuscript. I also thank Robert Bolick of The MIT Press for his advice and encouragement. And best thanks, finally, to Lolly Tyler, who bore up pretty well through all of this.

William Marslen-Wilson

PART I
Psychological Models of Lexical Processing

Chapter 1

Access and Integration: Projecting Sound onto Meaning	William Marslen-Wilson

The role of the mental lexicon in human speech comprehension is to mediate between two fundamentally distinct representational and computational domains: the acoustic-phonetic analysis of the incoming speech signal, and the syntactic and semantic interpretation of the message being communicated. My purpose in this chapter is to describe the consequences of this duality of representation and function for the organization of the mental lexicon as an information-processing system–that is, for the way the system is organized to manage the on-line projection of sound onto meaning. I will do so in terms of the two major processing functions that the lexicon needs to fulfill, which correspond to the two processing domains in which it participates.

The first of these, the *access* function, concerns the relationship of the lexical processing system to the sensory input—what I will refer to as the domain of *form-based functions and processes*. The system must provide the basis for a mapping of the speech signal onto the representations of word forms in the mental lexicon. If one assumes some form of acoustic-phonetic analysis of the speech input, it is a representation of the input in these terms that is projected onto the mental lexicon.

The *integration* function, conversely, concerns the relationship of the lexical processing system to the higher-level representation of the utterance. In order to complete the recognition process, the system must provide the basis for the integration, into this higher level of representation, of the syntactic and semantic information associated with the word that is being recognized. This is the domain of *content-based functions and processes.*

The general problem for a processing theory of the mental lexicon is to understand the nature of the process that links these two functional domains. The specific and immediate puzzle is to understand how the system is able to solve this problem—to project sound onto meaning—

with the speed and the seamless continuity that is evidenced by our subjective experience and by experimental research.

Our phenomenological experience of speech is that we understand it as we hear it. We do not, under normal conditions of language use, hear speech as episodes of uninterpreted sensory input followed at some delay by bursts of meaningful interpretation. Instead, our immediate experience is of a process of unbroken and continuous interpretation.[1] This subjective impression is borne out in many different experimental studies conducted over the past 15 years. These studies confirm that the speech signal is continuously and immediately projected not only onto the lexical level but also onto levels of semantic and pragmatic interpretation. In fact, the projection from signal to message seems to be carried out just about as fast as is either neurally plausible or informationally possible.

If we look, for example, at the performance of *close shadowers*, we see a direct illustration of the quantitative and qualitative properties of the basic transfer function of the system (Marslen-Wilson 1973, 1975, 1985; Marslen-Wilson and Welsh 1978). Close shadowers are individuals who are able to repeat back connected discourse at repetition delays averaging around 250 msec (measured from the onset of a word as they hear it to the onset of the same word as they repeat it). At delays as short as this, the shadowers seem to be operating near the limits of the ability of the speech signal to deliver information. Nonetheless, in a wide variety of tests, it is clear that even at these extreme temporal limits they are repeating back the speech input in the context of its ongoing interpretation, not just at the lexical level but also in terms of the syntactic and semantic constraints provided by the current utterance context (Marslen-Wilson 1975).

The picture of human speech processing revealed in close-shadowing performance is corroborated in many other studies, which confirm (on the one hand) the speed with which the speech signal is projected onto the lexicon and (on the other) the earliness with which it starts to have consequences for higher-level interpretation. (For detailed discussions of this research, see Marslen-Wilson 1984, 1987 and Marslen-Wilson and Tyler 1980, 1981, 1987.) I take these basic performance characteristics of the lexical processing system as the starting point for the present discussion.

1 Speed and Parallelism in Access and Integration

The problem of lexical processing is viewed, classically, as a problem of *selection*. How, given a particular sensory input, does the listener select the word form that best matches this input? How far, furthermore, is this selection process purely a form-based access process? Is the outcome of the recognition process determined solely by goodness of fit in the form domain, or does it also involve goodness of fit in the content domain?

Cast in the context of the speed and immediacy of lexical processing, the answer to these questions reveals a close interdependence between the domains of form and content in the on-line processing of spoken language. This is because the evidence for the speed of speech comprehension is also evidence for what I have called *early selection* (Marslen-Wilson 1987)—that is, the identification of spoken words, in normal utterance contexts, before sufficient acoustic-phonetic information has accumulated to allow the identification decision to be made on this basis alone. Numerous studies, using shadowing (Marslen-Wilson 1973, 1975, 1985), monitoring (Marslen-Wilson and Tyler 1975, 1980; Marslen-Wilson, Brown, and Tyler, 1988), and gating techniques (Tyler 1984; Tyler and Wessels 1983, 1985), show not only that words are, on average, recognized in context about 200 msec from word onset, but also that the sensory information available at that point is normally quite insufficient by itself to allow the correct identification of the word being heard (Marslen-Wilson 1984, 1987).[2]

This means that the on-line selection process cannot be just a matter of form-based processing. Discrimination between lexical forms cannot be treated purely in terms of information derived from the sensory input. Instead, the perceptual process involves the intersection of two sets of constraints—sensory and contextual—involving not just access but also integration. The sensory constraints derive from the goodness of fit of different word forms to the incoming acoustic-phonetic analysis of the speech signal; the contextual constraints derive from the goodness of fit of different lexical contents to the current utterance and discourse context. Neither of these kinds of constraints is, by itself, adequate to uniquely specify the correct word candidate at the observed moment of successful selection in normal processing. Together, however, they converge to define a unique intercept—to define the single correct path between sound and meaning.

This on-line processing dependency between form-based and content-based processing domains closely determines the basic functional structure of the lexical processing system. Specifically, it requires that the system be able to combine *multiple access* of lexical forms with *multiple assessment* of the contextual appropriateness of the lexical contents associated with these forms.

Multiple access is the accessing of multiple candidates in the mapping of the acoustic-phonetic input onto the mental representations of lexical form. The sensory input defines a class of potential word forms, all of which (in principle) must be made available for assessment against the current utterance and discourse context. Multiple assessment is the corollary of multiple access. If the input generates multiple candidates, then it must be possible for the system to assess all these candidates for their contextual appropriateness.

In postulating a system capable of realizing these capacities, we need, finally, to bear in mind the constraints imposed by the observed real-time performance of the human selection process—that is, by the fact that sensory and contextual constraints converge on their target, on average, within about 200 msec from word onset. The effect of this is to rule out strictly serial models of access and selection. It requires, instead, as I have argued in detail elsewhere, a processing model that embodies some form of functional parallelism (Marslen-Wilson 1987; Marslen-Wilson and Tyler 1981; Marslen-Wilson and Welsh 1978).

This gives a basic outline of the processing solution that the mental lexicon finds to the problem of how to relate information in the form domain to information in the content domain. What I am concerned with in the rest of this chapter is the additional constraints that can be placed on the model of this solution. I will begin by considering how the performance of the system in the access domain, as it projects the sensory input onto mental representations of lexical form, can be further specified. It is convenient to do this in the context of a more concrete model of the form-based access process, and I will use for this purpose the *cohort model* of spoken-word recognition.

2 The Cohort Model and the Contingency of Perceptual Choice

With the details of any specific implementation left aside, the cohort model rather straightforwardly captures the requirements for functional parallelism in the process of lexical access. For present purposes, its general properties can be laid out as follows:

• It assumes discrete, computationally independent recognition elements for each lexical unit, where each such unit represents the functional coordination of the bundle of phonological, morphological, syntactic, and semantic properties defining a given lexical entry.

• Each recognition element can be directly and independently activated by the appropriate patterns in the sensory input.

• The level of activation of each element increases as a function of the goodness of fit of the input pattern to the form specifications for each element. When the input pattern fails to match, the level of activation immediately starts to decay.[3]

These assumptions, taken together, lead to the characteristic cohort view of the form-based access and selection process, as specified for words heard in isolation. The process begins with the multiple access of word candidates as the first one or two segments of the word are heard. All the words in the listener's mental lexicon that share this onset sequence are assumed to be activated. This initial pool of active word candidates constitutes the *word-initial cohort*, which represents the primary decision space within which the subsequent process of selection will take place. The selection decision itself is based on a process of successive reduction of the active membership of the cohort of competitors. As more of the word is heard, the accumulating input pattern will diverge from the form specifications of an increasingly high proportion of the cohort's membership. This process of reduction continues until there remains only one candidate that still matches the sensory input—in activation terms, until the level of activation of one recognition element is criterially discriminable from the level of activation of its competitors. At this point the form-based selection process is complete, and the word form that best matches the speech input can be identified.

This is a very approximate and underspecified view of the process of access and selection, but it does make explicit one very important claim about the nature of perceptual processing in the speech domain: the claim for what I have labeled the *contingency of perceptual choice* (Marslen-Wilson 1987). The identification of any given word does not depend simply on the information that this word is present. It also depends on the information that other words are *not* present, since it is only at this point that the unique candidate emerges from among its competitors. This means that the outcome and the timing of the selection process are determined by the properties of the *complete ensemble* of perceptual possibilities open to the listener.

These claims for the contingency of perceptual choice are intimately bound up with the notion of *recognition point*. This is the claim, deriving from the cohort analysis of the recognition process, that the point at which a word can be recognized is a function not just of the word itself but also of its nearest competitors. The concept of recognition point is central to the cohort model, and it is this that makes the model empirically powerful. It gives us the ability to take *any* word and to predict when it can be recognized. By looking at the word and at its cohort of competitors, we can predict the point at which the word will become unique, and, therefore, the point at which it can be recognized. It is difficult to take seriously theories of spoken-word recognition that are not able to make word-specific predictions of this kind, especially in view of the accumulating evidence for the psycholinguistic validity in on-line processing of the notion of recognition point (Marslen-Wilson 1984, 1987; Tyler and Wessels 1983).

The notion of contingent perceptual choice is also central to the new generation of parallel distributed processing models of the lexicon (Elman, this volume; Rumelhart et al. 1986; Seidenberg, this volume). Whether one is looking at localist models (such as TRACE; see Elman in this volume and McClelland and Elman 1986) or at genuinely distributed models derived by using back-propagation learning algorithms, in each case the system's response to a given input is contingent on the properties of the ensemble of simultaneous perceptual possibilities in the context of which the input is being analyzed. This holds true whether the effects of the ensemble are pre-compiled into the system as a result of its learning experience (as in the Seidenberg-McClelland pronunciation model; see Seidenberg in this volume) or whether these effects emerge on-line through the competition between different candidates (as in models such as TRACE, or as in the early interactive activation models of visual-word recognition [see, e.g., McClelland and Rumelhart 1981]).

TRACE, in fact, was originally designed as a realization of the performance characteristics embodied in the cohort model (Elman and McClelland 1984), and can be taken as a demonstration of the computational feasibility of this type of functionally parallel processing system—though this is not to say (as Elman points out in his chapter below) that this is the only type of model that can exhibit cohort-like behavior.

3 Continuity of Information Uptake in Form-Based Access

Not only does the cohort approach to form-based processing bring out the contingent nature of perceptual analysis; it also brings into focus its *continuous* and *sequential* nature. The cohort model has standardly taken a strong position on the continuity and the sequentiality of access and selection, assuming that the system takes maximal advantage of stimulus information as it becomes available over time. This position was supported by earlier findings (Marslen-Wilson 1978, 1980, 1984) that projection onto the lexicon was continuous at least down to the segment. There was no evidence—for example, from non-word detection tasks—that access to the lexicon was in terms of processing units as large as syllables. More recent research (Warren and Marslen-Wilson 1987, 1988), which I will now discuss in more detail, shows that the claims for continuous projection hold even under a maximally fine-grained analysis of the relationship between variation in the signal and decisions at the lexical level.

The salient feature of the speech signal, considered as an information channel, is that it is based on a continuous sequence of articulatory gestures, which result in a continuous modulation of the signal. Cues to any individual phonetic segment are distributed over time, and, in particular, they overlap with cues to adjacent segments. This means that the speech signal is rich in what we can call *partial information*—that is, anticipatory cues to the identity of an upcoming segment. As the listener hears one segment, he will also hear partial cues to the identity of the next. An example of this is the presence of cues to the place of articulation of a word-final plosive in the formant structure of the preceding vowel. Thus, in the word *scoop* the lips may move toward closure for /p/ during the vowel, whereas in *scoot* the tip and body of the tongue are brought forward to form closure for the /t/. Both movements, conditioned by the place feature of the consonants, produce differences in the formant frequency patterns toward the end of the vowel.

The question that has been asked in recent research is whether this type of partial information is made available at the lexical level. How far is the on-line process of lexical access and selection sensitive to the continuous nature of information transmission in the speech signal, and to the availability of partial information as it accumulates over time? We have investigated this question in a number of studies, carried out in English and in Bengali (Lahiri and Marslen-Wilson 1988; Warren and Marslen-Wilson 1987, 1988), in which the speech gating task has been used to trace the temporal microstructure of acoustic-phonetic uptake during spoken-word recognition. I will focus here on the English studies, looking at the uptake at the lexical level of partial cues to word-final place and voice in CVC monosyllables.

In these experiments, listeners heard gated fragments of CVCs drawn from pairs contrasting in place (e.g. *scoop/scoot*) or in voice (e.g. *log/lock*). The words were presented in increments of 25 msec, with special emphasis on the 125 msec leading up to the closure of the vowel. Gate 0 in figure 1 represents the gate at which the vowel terminated. The subjects were required at each increment to say what they thought the word was or what it was going to become.

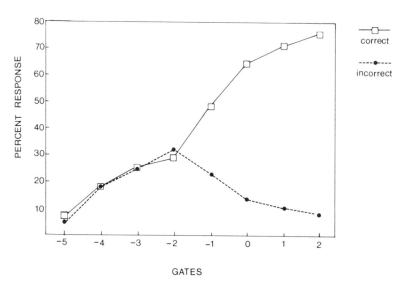

Figure 1
Lexical responses to pairs of CVCs contrasting in word-final place. Correct
responses are cases where subjects responded with the member of the pair having
the correct place (e.g. *scoop*); incorrect responses are cases where they responded
with the other member of the pair (e.g. *scoot*). The gates increment by 25 msec,
with vowel closure set at gate 0.

For the place contrasts, primarily involving CVCs ending in voiceless
plosives and matched for frequency, partial information as to place of
articulation was conveyed by the changing spectral properties of the vowel
as it approached closure. The question at issue was whether this would
affect lexical access and selection, as reflected in the subjects' responses at
each gate. If so, then their responses should have started to diverge before
vowel closure (i.e., before gate 0), and certainly before they heard the plosive
release (which fell 80–100 msec after closure). The results, summarized in
figure 1, clearly show this early divergence, with a strong preference at gate
0 for the word with the correct place of articulation.

For the voicing contrasts we were asking similar questions, but now we
were looking at a durational cue. (Vowel length is a powerful cue to voicing
in English.) In the gating task, listeners heard the vowel slowly increasing
in length over successive gates. Our question was whether they would
exploit this information as it became available. Figure 2 (where gate 0 again
represents vowel closure) shows that, after an initial period in which voiceless responses predominate, listeners start to successfully discriminate
voiced words from voiceless words as soon as the length of the vowel starts

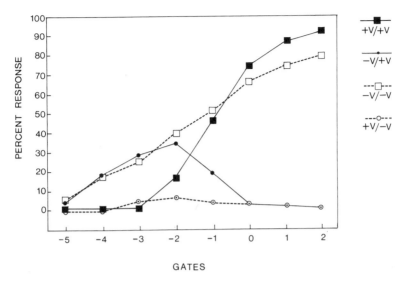

Figure 2
Lexical responses to pairs of CVCs contrasting in word-final voice (such as *dog–dock*). Correct responses are labeled + V/ + V for voiced stimuli and − V/ − V for unvoiced stimuli. Incorrect responses are cases where listeners gave the unvoiced member of a pair in response to the voiced item (labeled − V/ + V) or the voiced item in response to the unvoiced item (labeled + V/ − V). The gates increment by 25 msec, with vowel closure set at gate 0.

to exceed the durational criterion (around 135 msec from vowel onset for this particular stimulus set).

Figures 1 and 2 provide clear evidence for the immediate uptake of accumulating acoustic information. There do not appear to be any discontinuities in the projection of the speech input onto the lexical level. The speech signal is continuously modulated as the utterance is produced, and this continuous modulation is faithfully tracked by the processes responsible for lexical access and selection. As the spectrum of a vowel starts to shift toward the place of articulation of a subsequent consonant, this is reflected in a shift in listeners' lexical choices, which becomes apparent about 25–50 msec before closure. As the duration of a vowel increases, the listener produces lexical choices that reflect these changes in duration, shifting from voiceless to voiced as the durational criterion is reached and surpassed (at about 50–75 msec before closure). There is immediate use of partial durational cues, just as there is immediate use of partial spectral cues.

This is evidence for continuity of projection onto the lexical level, at as fine a grain of temporal and informational analysis as the speech signal seems to permit. It does not, however, give a complete answer to the question of directionality and sequentiality of access and selection processes. The next section describes some recent research that addresses this issue more directly.

4 Directionality in Lexical Access

The cohort model—especially in its earlier versions (Marslen-Wilson and Welsh 1978; Marslen-Wilson and Tyler 1980)—has made strong claims for the intrinsic directionality of the access process, arguing that the on-line decision space for lexical choice is entirely defined by the beginnings of words. The speech input at the beginning of a word defines the membership of the word-initial cohort, and the subsequent process of word recognition is determined by the way in which different sources of constraint—both sensory and contextual—operate on the membership of this set. The corollary of this is that *late entry* into the decision space is prohibited. Candidates cannot be considered by the system unless they match from word onset.

This emphasis on the beginnings of words has been widely disputed, and for two kinds of reasons—first, on the grounds that the sensory input in fluent speech cannot guarantee the system reliable information about word onsets. A cohort-based recognition process would run into trouble whenever the information at word beginnings was inadequate, and this would happen far too often for such a system to be workable. The second line of criticism derives from models of the mapping process in which the directionality of the mapping is less crucial. These are, in particular, models in the connectionist tradition, where what is most important is the total amount of overlap between the input and a given lexical representation, relative to the overlap with other potential candidates, and where directionality *per se* does not play a major role. A model like TRACE (Elman, this volume), for example, will recognize "bleasant" as "pleasant", since the degree of overlap with the form representation of "pleasant" is high and since there is no other word form in the lexicon to which "bleasant" is a better fit (McClelland and Elman 1986).

However, these two lines of criticism, as well as the original claims of the cohort model, were developed in the absence of any direct evidence about the actual importance of word onsets in determining what can or cannot be accessed during on-line speech processing. In some recent research

(Marslen-Wilson and Zwitserlood 1989) we have attempted to remedy this, asking whether or not there is a strong temporal directionality in lexical access and whether the on-line decision process does tolerate the late entry of potential word candidates. We did this by investigating the relative effectiveness of two kinds of *partial* primes in activating their target lexical representations. In particular, we contrasted cases where the primes matched their targets from word onset with cases where the primes rhymed with their targets but mismatched word-initially.

We already had information from earlier research (Marslen-Wilson, Brown, and Zwitserlood, manuscript; Zwitserlood 1985) about the effects of word-initial partial primes. Using cross-modal priming tasks, we showed that stimuli of this type were very effective in activating lexical representations. Listeners heard incomplete sequences, such as the string [kapit], which is compatible both with the word *kapitein* and with the word *kapitaal* (meaning *captain* and *capital*, respectively, in Dutch). At the onset, for example, of the [t] in [kapit], the listeners saw cross-model visual probes. This probe was associatively related either to *kapitein* (e.g., BOOT, meaning *ship*) or to *kapitaal* (e.g., GELD, meaning *money*). Reaction times to make lexical decisions to these visual probes were compared with response times to the same probes presented in the middle of control words to which they were not associatively related. The probes were also presented at the end of the critical words and their controls. The results showed that responses to both probes were facilitated, relative to the control condition, when they were presented in the middle of the spoken word. Both GELD and BOOT, for example, were facilitated when they were presented during the [t] of [kapit]. In contrast, when the probes were presented at the end of the word, only the probe related to the word actually presented was facilitated. Thus, at the end of *kapitein*, BOOT is facilitated, but not GELD.

This research was originally conducted to provide evidence for the multiple activation of semantic codes early in the word-recognition process. For current purposes, what it demonstrates is that *partial* word-initial overlap is sufficient to activate lexical representations to the degree necessary to produce priming in a cross-modal task of this nature—and, furthermore, that the size of the priming effects is almost as large as the effect for the complete word. In her version of this experiment (looking at the results for her neutral context condition), Zwitserlood obtained a 40-msec priming effect for end-of-word probes and a mean of 33 msec for mid-word probes (following partial primes like [kapit]).

In the second set of experiments, we looked at the effectiveness of *rhyme primes* in activating the words with which they rhymed, using both real-word and nonword primes. Again working in Dutch, we compared facilitation to a cross-modal visual probe (such as *BIJ*, meaning *bee*) following either the original complete word (such as *honing*, meaning *honey*) or rhyme primes (such as the real word *woning*, meaning *dwelling*, or the nonsense word *foning*). Here we got a quite different pattern of results. The complete overlap condition (*honing*–BIJ) produced significant facilitation, relative to the control condition, of 32 msec, which is comparable to the effect for full primes in other experiments. But neither of the rhyme prime conditions showed any significant effects. The real-word rhyme (*woning*–BIJ) was facilitated by 11 msec, whereas the effect for the nonword rhymes (*foning*–BIJ) was only 4 msec. In contrast to the onset primes, rhyme primes were notably ineffective in priming their targets. And though there may be theoretical reasons for not expecting the real-word rhymes to be fully effective in priming other real words,[4] there is no reason, on a nondirectional story, not to expect nonword rhymes to map effectively onto their targets.

This failure of effective rhyme priming cannot be attributed to insufficient amounts of stimulus overlap between primes and targets. (Overlap is estimated here in terms of the number of shared segments; the prime *foning*, for example, has four segments in common with its target, *honing*.) In fact, the amount of overlap (at 4.5 segments) was considerably larger in the rhyme-prime experiment than in the onset-prime experiment, where the average amount of overlap was only 3.1 segments, counting from word onset. In general, what seemed to be important was not the simple amount of input that matched a given form representation but whether it did so from word onset. Rhyme primes failed to facilitate their targets even for very large amounts of overlap. Sequences up to three syllables long, where only the first consonant was mismatching, still showed no significant priming effect.

This suggests that there is indeed a strong directionality to the access process. Primes that do not share word onsets with their targets are always significantly less effective than primes that do. Perceptually, sequences that mismatch at word onset do not seem to enter normally into the on-line decision space. In particular, and contrary to what strongly interactive models would predict, the rhyme prime is never treated as if it *were* the original word. Although the listener may well be able to determine, on line, that the nonword *bleasant* is intended as a token of the string *pleasant*, this does not mean that the perceptual experience of *pleasant* is substituted for the percept of the mispronounced token, nor does it mean that this overriding of the original mispronunciation is without cost for the processor.

This discussion of lexical-context effects in the interpretation of the speech input forms a natural transition to the final sections of this chapter, where we need to consider the role of still higher levels of potential contextual constraint in the access and selection processes.

5   Access and Integration

In the previous three sections I have concentrated on the properties of form-based selection processes. I now turn to the question of the relationship between these processes and the domain of content-based processes, where lexical contents are integrated with higher-level representations and interpretations.

I argued at the beginning of the chapter that there is a basic processing dependency between access and integration in determining the outcome of lexical processing. Words are recognized in context before sufficient sensory information has accumulated to allow correct recognition on this basis alone. How is the system organized to do this, and what forms of interchange does it permit between contextual constraints and operations in the form-based domain?

I will begin by summarizing the evidence for multiple access of phonological and semantic codes early in the selection process, since these provide the processing basis for contextual effects in on-line lexical processing. Starting with form-based processes, there is a certain amount of evidence for the multiple access of different phonological forms. The pattern of responses, for example, over the early gates in standard gating studies, suggests the availability of multiple possibilities activated by the speech input (Tyler 1984; Tyler and Wessels 1985). More directly, cross-modal form priming studies (Tyler, Warren, and Brown, unpublished research) show how partial inputs map onto multiple representations. If listeners hear the initial consonant and vowel of stimuli such as *crate*, one finds significant facilitation of lexical decisions not only to the word CRATE, presented as a cross-modal probe at vowel offset, but also to other words, such as CRANE, that are still compatible with the available input.

In regard to the activation of lexical contents, there is now extensive evidence for the multiple activation of semantic codes early in the access process. This evidence comes from the research cited earlier (Marslen-Wilson et al., manuscript; Zwitserlood 1985) showing how ambiguous word fragments, such as the initial sequence [kapit], significantly prime lexical decisions to visual probes associated with both of the words with which this sequence is compatible (i.e., *kapitein* and *kapitaal*). Another set of experiments that are consistent with this, originated by Swinney (1979) and widely continued since then (Lucas 1987; Onifer and Swinney 1981; Seidenberg, Tanenhaus, Leiman, and Bienkowski 1982), demonstrate the multiple activation of the different meanings associated with a homophone —in Swinney's classic study, the spoken word *bank* facilitates concurrent cross-modal probes associated both with its "river" reading and its "money" reading.

Evidence from monitoring and shadowing tasks (Marslen-Wilson 1975; Marslen-Wilson and Tyler 1975, 1980) suggests that the activation of semantic codes associated with a word follows very closely on—if it is not simultaneous with—the activation of phonological codes. We found, for example, in a comparison of Rhyme Monitoring with Category Monitoring tasks—which draw respectively, on phonological and on semantic properties of lexical representations—that there was no significant difference in the timing with which these tasks could be carried out. The evidence for early selection undoubtedly requires an access process where semantic codes are activated very early in processing.

Given this evidence for the early and multiple access of lexical forms and contents, what can we say about the way in which sentential constraints allow the listener to achieve early selection from among this welter of competing alternatives? In answering this question it is important to keep distinct two separate sets of issues involved in characterizing the role of context in a perceptual process. The first of these concerns the *timing* and the *location* of the effects of context: Do these effects operate in a top-down manner to affect the early stages of form-based access and selection, or do they operate later in the process, affecting decision stages at higher levels of the system? The second set of issues concern the *type* of effect that contextual constraints can have, independent of whether these effects operate from the top down. Do contextual constraints have inhibitory or facilitatory effects—or indeed both? In particular, can they override or suppress the perceptual hypotheses deriving from the sensory signal?

We can evaluate these issues with respect to the different points in the recognition process at which context could potentially have an effect. The first set of contrasts involves the question of *contextual preselection*: Can context operate, in advance of any sensory input, to change the properties of the primary form-based access process? Before any of the word has been heard, is the processing system already in some way predisposed to favor word candidates with a particular subset of syntactic and semantic properties? There are a number of ways in which it could do this. One is by preselecting a subset of contextually favored items, which then constitute the decision space within which the sensory input needs to discriminate. Another possibility is that context could change in advance the activation level of recognition units. This was the mechanism proposed in the logogen model (Morton 1969), where context operated to raise the activation level of contextually favored candidates, so that they would then need less sensory input, relative to contextually inappropriate candidates, to reach threshold.

Both these proposals, and indeed the concept of contextual preselection in general, are rejected by the cohort model, which has always emphasized the priority, in lexical access and selection, of the sensory input to the system. This principle of *bottom-up priority* expresses itself, first of all, as a prohibition on contextual preselection (Marslen-Wilson and Tyler 1980, 1981; Marslen-Wilson and Welsh 1978). The original arguments against contextual preselection (Marslen-Wilson and Welsh 1978) were made on *a priori* grounds—in particular, that the recognition process would operate more efficiently and with less error if it were the sensory input that first circumscribed the universe of possible readings. Although there is plenty of evidence to support the general notion of bottom-up priority in form-based access and selection, there is relatively little evidence bearing on the specific issue of top-down preselection.

An exception to this is Zwitserlood's (1985) recent use of a cross-modal priming task to measure the activation of semantic codes as a word is heard in and out of context. Our earlier research (Marslen-Wilson et al., manuscript) demonstrated the multiple activation of semantic codes for ambiguous word fragments (such as [kapit]) heard in isolation. Zwitserlood's study continued this work, probing at the beginning of a word, and at various points through that word, to determine how far contextual constraints affect the activation of different word candidates.

In the condition that is relevant here, listeners heard the entire preceding context, but *none* of the actual target word. A cross-modal visual probe, associatively related to this target word, was presented at the offset of the last word preceding the target word in the context sentence. This tests for possible effects of preselection or preactivation at the lexical level. If a strongly predictive sentential context is available, does this have any consequences for lexical representations even before the arrival of any of the relevant sensory information? The results show that there is no effect of this sort. Response times to the visual probe, even when seen at the offset of a highly constraining context, do not differ at all from responses to the same probe following an unrelated control context.

If we rule out the possibility of contextual preselection, this still leaves open the question of whether contextual constraints can nonetheless operate from the top down to affect later stages of the form-based access and selection process. Once a set of word candidates is activated, can contextual variables affect the state of the recognition elements that compute the basic goodness of fit between the input and lexical representations? The principle of *bottom-up priority* requires that the sensory input be the determining factor in the output of the form-based access and selection process, and there is now a great deal of evidence to support this. In fact, for every experiment I have cited as showing the multiple activation of semantic codes, there is a parallel experiment showing that these early activation processes cannot be suppressed by sentential context.

For instance, in the gating studies reported in Tyler 1984 and in Tyler and Wessels 1983, the availability of strong syntactic and semantic constraints does not prevent the accessing, at early gates, of word candidates that are compatible with the available sensory input but incompatible with the available structural context. Another example is the research on multiple sense activation for homophone inputs, which shows that sentential context is neither able to preselect the appropriate reading of an ambiguous word nor to suppress the activation of inappropriate readings. In Swinney's original study (1979), the facilitation of cross-modal probes associated with contextually inappropriate readings, testing at the offset of the ambiguous word, is just as strong as for probes associated with the contextually appropriate reading.

A different source of evidence for the priority of the signal is the research by Samuel (1981a,b) in which the phoneme-restoration task (Warren 1970) was adapted for use in a signal-detection paradigm. Listeners heard sentences containing a critical word, in which there was a target segment that was either excised from the signal and *replaced* by noise or else remained intact but had noise *added* to it. To the extent that listeners failed to discriminate the two conditions, and reported the replaced stimuli as added, then they were "restoring" the missing segment. The point of interest here is the effects of sentential context on the ratio of added to replaced responses. Samuel's use of the signal-detection paradigm allowed him to separate effects of bias from genuine perceptual effects. Although context does affect performance in this task, it is clear that the effects are primarily bias effects. There is no evidence that sentential context affects the basic discriminability of the sensory input.

A third source of evidence is Zwitserlood's (1985) study. Apart from testing at onset of the critical word, as described above, Zwitserlood also tested at four subsequent points in the word, probing at each test position with a cross-modal target word that was associatively related either to the word actually being heard (such as *kapitein*) or to a competitor word (such as *kapitaal*). This was done either in a neutral context or in a variety of constraining contexts (where the constraints were always in favor of the word actually being heard). The results here also point strongly to a system based on the notion of bottom-up priority. Consistent with Samuel's results, Zwitserlood finds no effects of context on activation levels until the sensory input has started to discriminate between the word actually being heard and its competitor.

At the first two probe positions there is equally strong facilitation of probes related to the actual word as to its competitor. This holds irrespective of context, and replicates the activation pattern that we found previously for words in isolation. Even if the context strongly favored the word actually being heard, so that the competitor word was highly implausible, this had no effect on their relative levels of activation, as measured in the cross-modal semantic priming task.

It is only at Zwitserlood's third probe position that context effects start to emerge. This is the probe position corresponding to the point in the word at which the sensory input starts to differentiate the actual word from its competitor (as established in gating experiments run on these stimuli). This divergence is only weakly reflected in the neutral and weak context conditions. But there is now a very marked effect of context in the conditions where the sentence context is strongly constraining. Context has the effect here of strongly amplifying the cues emerging in the signal, so that activation of the actual word is considerably increased, while activation of the competitor is greatly decreased (relative to the other context conditions).

These results, and those described earlier, suggest two things: First, that sentential context does not function to override perceptual hypotheses based on the sensory input to the system. Significant effects of context only emerge at a point in processing where the sensory input is already starting to point towards one lexical candidate rather than another. Moreover, once a bottom-up hypothesis has been established, context can have both inhibitory and facilitatory effects, amplifying the effects of bottom-up perceptual trends. Second, these results suggest a clear answer to the question of where in the system context has its major effects—of where the candidates generated by the form-based access process first come into functional contact with the sentential context. The evidence from the research of Samuel, Zwitserlood, and others makes it implausible that these effects are located anywhere in the primary mechanisms for form-based access and selection.

If there are top-down effects that penetrate as deeply as this, it is hard to understand why these effects do not affect the access process earlier in the word, and why they do not affect the basic perceptual processing of the sensory input.

This analysis is in any case necessary to explain the marked asymmetry in the timing with which context effects are detectable at different levels of the system. In Zwitserlood's lexical decision task, which seems to be primarily tapping into the activation of lexical representations, we see no effect of context until relatively late in the word, at a point where the correct candidate has begun to be selected by the bottom-up input. But we know from gating tasks, and from comparable experiments using other on-line tasks, that certain effects of context can be detected much earlier than this. The early probe positions in Zwitserlood's study, for example, reflect the points at which the correct candidate begins to be correctly identified when a constraining sentential context is available. This means that there must be another level of the system, a level that has access both to the early output of the form-based access process and to the current sentential context. It is here, rather than at the level of lexical representation tapped into by the cross-modal lexical decision task, that the main business of integration will have to be located.

I conclude, therefore, that the intersection of form-based and content-based constraints does not take place within the primary mechanisms for form-based access and selection. It takes place, instead, at the interface between lexical contents and the current utterance and discourse representation. As I have argued elsewhere (Marslen-Wilson 1987), we can capture the phenomena of early selection by exploiting the capacity of a parallel system for multiple access and multiple assessment. This will lead to a form of on-line competition between the most salient candidates—those best fitting the speech input—to occupy the available sites in the higher-level representation. Once the appropriate senses associated with a given word form have been bound to these sites, we can say that lexical processing is complete—that the interpretation of the signal has moved, via the processes of access and integration, into the domain of understanding and interpretation.

The speed and the earliness of the selection process, therefore, will be a joint function of two variables: the degree to which the bottom-up fit for a given candidate differentiates it from its competitors and the extent to which the contextual match similarly differentiates it. The facilitatory effects of context reflect the tendency of the system to commit itself to a particular interpretation—to close on a particular candidate cluster of semantic and syntactic attributes—even though the sensory input may not have fully differentiated the word form associated with this bundle of attributes. But this early closure, indicating integration before access is complete, does not implicate any form of top-down interaction between the form and the content domains.

In summary, if we combine the analysis of form-based processes presented earlier in this chapter with the current conclusions about the type of processing relationship that holds between access and integration, then this leads to a view of the processes of access and selection that shares many of the functional characteristics of a Fodorian input system (Fodor 1983). This is also a view, as Forster points out in chapter 3 of this volume, that offers interesting possibilities for convergence between models in the auditory domain and the kinds of "activate-and-check" models that have been proposed in the visual modality, ranging from McClelland's (1979) cascade model to the models subsequently proposed by Norris (1981, 1986) and by Forster (this volume) himself. It is also possible that we are starting to understand enough about the access process to be able to start asking the really difficult questions about lexical processing—questions about the nature of lexical representations, and questions about the nature and the time course of the process of integration.

Notes

1. This is not to say that all speech is completely understood as it is heard, but it is to say that we never normally experience speech except in the context of our attempt to meaningfully interpret it.

2. The argument from early sele:tion does not require that *all* words be recognized early in context. It simply requires that this be a potentially dominant mode of operation of the processing system in the perception of fluent speech. The best evidence bearing on this is the recent study by Bard, Shillcock, and Altmann (1987), which shows that, of a very large sample of words in continuous speech, only about 20 percent are not recognized, in a word-by-word gating task, by the time all of the word is heard. "Late" selection seems to be relatively infrequent, and (as the results of Bard et al. also suggest) more likely to affect function words than to affect content words.

3. In earlier versions of the model, mismatch information had an active inhibitory role in the system. Recent research suggests that it may be necessary to allow at least some bottom-up inhibition back into the system (Marslen-Wilson and Zwitserlood 1989).

4. The point here is that in models like TRACE, which allow lateral inhibition between competing nodes within a level of the system, the activation of the real word *woning* by the input *woning* will lead to the inhibition of *honing* by its more successful (because better-matching) competitor. This would obscure any activation

of *honing* by the overlapping segmental input from *woning*. But none of these problems should apply for the nonword rhymes, since these should not cause lateral inhibition at the lexical level in the same way.

References

Bard, E. G., R. C. Shillcock, and G. T. M. Altmann. 1987. The recognition of words after their acoustic offsets in spontaneous speech: Effects of subsequent context. Manuscript, Department of Linguistics, University of Edinburgh.

Elman, J. L., and J. L. McClelland. 1984. Speech perception as a cognitive process: The interactive activation model. In N. Lass (ed.), *Speech and Language*, volume 10. New York: Academic.

Fodor, J. A. 1983. *The Modularity of Mind*. Cambridge, Mass.: MIT Press.

Lahiri, A., and W. D. Marslen-Wilson. 1988. The mental representation of lexical form: A phonological approach to the recognition lexicon. Manuscript, Max-Planck-Institut für Psycholinguistik, Nijmegen.

Levelt, W., and H. Schriefers. 1987. Issues of lexical access in language production. Manuscript, Max-Planck-Institut für Psycholinguistik, Nijmegen.

Lucas, M. M. 1987. Frequency effects on the processing of ambiguous words in sentence contexts. *Language and Speech* 30: 25–46.

Marslen-Wilson, W. D. 1973. Linguistic structure and speech shadowing at very short latencies. *Nature* 244: 522–523.

Marslen-Wilson, W. D. 1975. Sentence perception as an interactive parallel process. *Science* 189: 226–228.

Marslen-Wilson, W. D. 1978. Sequential decision processes during spoken-word recognition. Presented at Nineteenth Annual Meeting of Psychonomic Society, San Antonio, Texas.

Marslen-Wilson, W. D. 1980. Speech understanding as a psychological process. In J. C. Simon (ed.), *Spoken Language Generation and Understanding*. Dordrecht: Reidel.

Marslen-Wilson, W. D. 1984. Function and process in spoken word-recognition. In H. Bouma and D. Bouwhuis (eds.), *Attention and Performance X*. Hillsdale, N.J.: Erlbaum.

Marslen-Wilson, W. D. 1985. Speech shadowing and speech comprehension. *Speech Communication* 4: 55–73.

Marslen-Wilson, W. D. 1987. Functional parallelism in spoken word-recognition. *Cognition* 25: 71–102.

Marslen-Wilson, W. D., and L. K. Tyler. 1975. Processing structure of sentence perception. *Nature* 257: 784–786.

Marslen-Wilson, W. D., and L. K. Tyler. 1980. The temporal structure of spoken language understanding. *Cognition* 8: 1–71.

Marslen-Wilson, W. D., and L. K. Tyler. 1981. Central processes in speech understanding. *Philosophical Transactions of the Royal Society of London* B295: 317–332.

Marslen-Wilson, W. D., and L. K. Tyler. 1987. Against modularity. In J. L. Garfield (ed.), *Modularity in Knowledge Representation and Natural-Language Understanding.* Cambridge, Mass.: MIT Press.

Marslen-Wilson, W. D., and A. Welsh. 1978. Processing interactions and lexical access during word-recognition in continuous speech. *Cognitive Psychology* 10: 29–63.

Marslen-Wilson, W. D., and P. Zwitserlood. 1989. Accessing spoken words: The importance of word onsets. *Journal of Experimental Psychology: Human Perception and Performance,* in press.

Marslen-Wilson, W. D., C. Brown, and L. K. Tyler. 1988. Lexical representations in spoken language comprehension. *Language and Cognitive Processes* 3: 1–21.

Marslen-Wilson, W. D., C. Brown, and P. Zwitserlood. Spoken word-recognition: Early activation of multiple semantic codes. Manuscript, Max-Planck-Institut, Nijmegen.

McClelland, J. L. 1979. On the time relations of mental processes: An examination of systems of processes in cascade. *Psychological Review* 86: 287–330.

McClelland, J. L., and J. L. Elman. 1986. The TRACE model of speech perception. *Cognitive Psychology* 18: 1–86.

McClelland, J. L., and D. E. Rumelhart. 1981. An interactive activation model of context effects in letter perception: Part 1. An account of basic findings. *Psychological Review* 88: 375–407.

Norris, D. 1981. Autonomous processes in comprehension. *Cognition* 11: 97–101.

Norris, D. 1986. Word-recognition: Context effects without priming. *Cognition* 22: 470–476.

Onifer, W., and D. A. Swinney. 1981. Accessing lexical ambiguities during sentence comprehension: Effects of frequency of meaning and contextual bias. *Memory and Cognition* 9: 225–236.

Rumelhart, D. E., J. L. McClelland, and the PDP Research Group. 1986. *Parallel Distributed Processing,* volume 1. Cambridge, Mass.: MIT Press.

Samuel, A. G. 1981a. Phonemic restoration: Insights from a new methodology. *Journal of Experimental Psychology: General* 110: 474–494.

Samuel, A. G. 1981b. The role of bottom-up confirmation in the phonemic restoration illusion. *Journal of Experimental Psychology: Human Perception and Performance* 7: 1124–1131.

Seidenberg, M. S., M. K. Tanenhaus, J. M. Leiman, and M. Bienkowski. 1982. Automatic access of the meanings of ambiguous words in context: Some limitations of knowledge-based processing. *Cognitive Psychology* 14: 489–537.

Swinney, D. 1979. Lexical access during sentence comprehension: (Re)consideration of context effects. *Journal of Verbal Learning and Verbal Behavior* 18: 645–659.

Tyler, L. K. 1984. The structure of the initial cohort. *Perception and Psychophysics* 36: 415–427.

Tyler, L. K., and J. Wessels. 1983. Quantifying contextual contributions to word recognition processes. *Perception and Psychophysics* 34: 409–420.

Tyler, L. K., and J. Wessels. 1985. Is gating an on-line task? Evidence from naming latency data. *Perception and Psychophysics* 38: 217–222.

Warren, R. M. 1970. Perceptual restoration of missing speech sounds. *Science* 167: 392–393.

Warren, P., and W. D. Marslen-Wilson. 1987. Continuous uptake of acoustic cues in spoken word-recognition. *Perception and Psychophysics* 41: 262–275.

Warren, P., and W. D. Marslen-Wilson. 1988. Cues to lexical choice: Discriminating place and choice. *Perception and Psychophysics* 43: 21–30.

Zwitserlood, P. 1985. Activation of word candidates during spoken-word recognition. Paper presented at 26th Annual Meeting of Psychonomic Society, Boston.

Chapter 2

Visual Word Recognition
and Pronunciation:
A Computational Model
and Its Implications

Mark S. Seidenberg

This article discusses a model of visual word recognition and pronunciation that J. L. McClelland and I have developed (Seidenberg and McClelland 1987). The model was developed within the "connectionist" framework that is currently generating broad interest among cognitive scientists. Our goal was to account for some of the types of knowledge and processes that support word-recognition skill, and for their acquisition. With K. E. Patterson, we have also explored the model's implications concerning the impairments characteristic of acquired forms of dyslexia (Patterson, Seidenberg, and McClelland, in press). The model provides a unified account of a broad range of empirical phenomena that reading researchers have studied for the past 10–15 years (see Henderson 1982 and Carr and Pollatsek 1985 for reviews). It also provides an explicit account of the two tasks that have been most widely used in this research: pronouncing a string of letters aloud (naming) and deciding whether a string of letters is a word or nonword (lexical decision).

Aside from what it contributes to our understanding of reading, ours is one of the more fully developed models to have emerged from the connectionist framework. Taken as a case study in connectionist modeling, it provides the basis for an exploration of the utility of this approach. The questions that arise in this regard concern the role of such models in explanatory theories of perception and cognition. The structure of the chapter, then, is as follows: I first give a general overview of the model and then provide examples of some of the phenomena the model explains. The closing sections address some broader issues concerning the interpretation and evaluation of this model and others like it.

1 The Model

We conceive of a lexical-processing module with the general form illustrated in figure 1. The goal is an integrated theory that accounts for several

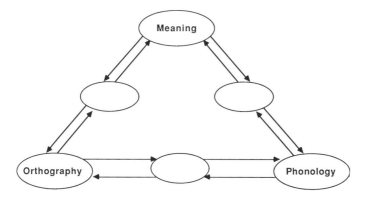

Figure 1
The structure of a general model of lexical processing.

aspects of lexical processing involving orthographic, phonological, and semantic information. The theory is to account for how these types of information are represented in memory, and how they are used in tasks such as deriving the meaning of a word from its written form, deriving the spelling of a word from phonology, and deriving the phonological code from spelling. The implemented model represents the part of figure 1 that is concerned with how readers perceive letter strings and pronounce them aloud. The model consists of a network of interconnected processing units. There are 400 units used to code orthographic information, 200 hidden units, and 460 units used to code phonemic information (figure 2). The connections between units carry weights that govern the spread of activation through the system. There are connections from all orthographic units to all hidden units, and from all hidden units to all phonological units. In addition, there is a set of connections from the hidden units back to the orthographic units. As will become clear below, these weights encode what the model knows about written English—specifically, orthographic redundancy (i.e., the frequency and distribution of letter patterns in the lexicon) and the correspondences between orthography and phonology.

Every letter string can be characterized by patterns of activation across the orthographic and phonological units, which are the model's representations of a string's orthographic and phonological codes. The schemes for representing these codes are described in Seidenberg and McClelland 1987. Two points about these representational schemes should be noted. First, both orthographic and phonological coding schemes make use of local context sensitivity. Each letter in the input is encoded as a grapheme that

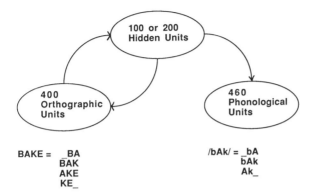

Figure 2
Structure of the implemented model and the context-sensitive coding schemes.

codes letters to the left and to the right (figure 2); the initial consonants in BIKE and BAKE, then, differ in this "Wickelgraph" representation. Similarly, we use the context-sensitive phonemes (Wickelphones) employed by Rumelhart and McClelland (1986), who describe the motivation for this approach; essentially it is an attempt to encode order information without position-specific "slots." Second, these representations are distributed rather than local. Each orthographic unit consists of a $10 \times 10 \times 10$ table of letters. Each table represents 1,000 Wickelgraphs formed by the cross-product of the entries. A unit is activated whenever an input letter string contains one of these 1,000 Wickelgraphs. Each grapheme in a letter string activates about 20 units, meaning that there is no single unit corresponding to a particular letter or Wickelgraph. Similarly, each Wickelphone in a word's pronunciation activates 16 of the units coding phonological output (see McClelland and Rumelhart 1986 for details).

The model works as follows. The input to the system is a string of letters (a word or a nonword), which is encoded as a pattern of activation across the orthographic nodes. The latter string is recoded as a set of Wickelgraphs, and those units whose tables contain these Wickelgraphs are activated. Activation then spreads through the system (see Seidenberg and McClelland 1987 for details); the activation of a unit is a weighted sum of the activations passed along the lines coming into it, and this activation is passed through a nonlinear squashing function to yield a net activation with a value between 0 and 1 (see Rumelhart and McClelland 1986). Two types of output are computed: a pattern of activation across the phonological units and a re-creation of the input pattern across the orthographic nodes. The former can be thought of as the node's computation of a phonological code for an input letter string; the latter can be considered a representation of the orthographic input in a short-term sensory store.

In the model's initial configuration, each connection was assigned a small random weight; hence the model was a *tabula rasa*. Weights on connections were modified during a learning phase, which simulated the acquisition of these types of knowledge. The model was trained on a set of 2,897 English words, including all the uninflected monosyllabic words in the Kucera-Francis (1967) corpus more than two letters long, plus additional items that do not occur in the corpus, minus foreign words and abbreviations. On each learning trial the model was presented with one of these letter patterns. The probability that an item would be selected for training was a function its Kucera-Francis frequency; higher-frequency words were presented more often than lower-frequency words. The word was encoded as a pattern of activation across the orthographic nodes, and both orthographic and phonological output were computed. Initially, of course, the model produced random output. The goal of training was to find a set of weights such that the model produced optimal output for any input string. By "optimal" I mean that the model minimized an error measure governed by the difference between the activation produced at output and that which would be produced if all and only the units corresponding to the input were fully on. The orthographic error score is the sum over all of the orthographic units of the squared differences between actual and obtained output; a similar error score is derived for phonological output. These error terms have two functions. First, they provide measures of the model's performance; error scores for words vary as a function of amount of training, and as a function of lexical variables such as orthographic redundancy, orthographic-phonological regularity, and frequency. Second, the error scores were the input to the back-propagation learning algorithm (Rumelhart, Hinton, and Williams 1986), which was used to modify the weights on connections. The learning algorithm is a means of performing gradient descent in a multi-layer system; it modifies the weights in proportion to their effects on reducing this error.

The model, then, produces output specifying the orthographic and phonological codes of the input string. These codes are used in performing tasks such as naming and lexical decision. We characterize the model's performance in terms of error scores calculated for different types of words after different amounts of training, and relate these to human performance on these tasks.

Because the model contains such a large pool of words, we can perform very close simulations of many empirical phenomena reported in the literature, often using the same stimuli as in a particular lexical-decision or naming experiment; where the stimulus materials were not provided in an experiment, we have utilized items with similar characteristics. Table 1 is a list of some of the phenomena we have simulated; in the cited cases the model's output conformed very closely to the behavioral data (see Seidenberg and McClelland 1987). To illustrate the model's performance, I will focus on two phenomena: frequency and regularity effects in naming, and criterion shifts in lexical decision.

2   Frequency, Regularity, and Naming

Behavioral Phenomena

Words vary in orthographic redundancy and in orthographic-phonological regularity. Many studies have investigated the effects of these variables on performance (see Seidenberg 1985a for a review; see also Brown 1987 and Van Orden 1987). Although many types of words have been studied, here I consider only two: regular and exception words. Regular words contain spelling patterns that recur in a large number of words, always with the same pronunciation. MUST, for example, contains the ending -ust; all monosyllabic words that end in this pattern rhyme (JUST, DUST, etc.). Some theories assume that these words are pronounced by grapheme-phoneme correspondence rules (Coltheart 1978). The words sharing the critical spelling pattern are termed the neighbors of the input string (Glushko 1979; McClelland and Rumelhart 1981). It has generally been assumed that neighbors are defined in terms of word endings or rimes (Treiman and Chafetz 1987), although it is surely the case that other parts matter as well (Taraban and McClelland 1987).

Exception words contain a common spelling pattern that is pronounced irregularly. For example, -ave is usually pronounced as in GAVE and SAVE, but has an irregular pronunciation in the exception word HAVE. In terms of orthographic structure, regular and exception words are similar: Both contain spelling patterns that recur in many words. Whereas regular words are thought to obey the pronunciation "rules" of English, exception words do not.

Performance on regular and exception words provides information concerning the computation of a word's phonological code. These words are similar in terms of orthography, and they can be equated in terms of other

Table 1
Some of the phenomena simulated by the model.

Phenomenon	Reference(s)
Frequency effects, naming	Forster and Chambers 1973; Balota and Chumbley 1985
Frequency effects, LD	Balota and Chumbley 1984
Frequency blocking effects, LD	Gordon 1983; Glanzer and Ehrenreich 1979
Orth-phon regularity effects, naming	Seidenberg et al. 1984; Taraban and McClelland 1987; Brown 1987
Orth-phon regularity effect, LD	Seidenberg et al. 1982; Parkin 1982; Coltheart et al. 1979
Criterion shifts in LD	Waters and Seidenberg 1985
Orthographic redundancy, LD and naming	Waters and Seidenberg 1985; Parkin 1982
Homographs, LD and naming	Seidenberg et al. 1984
Pseudohomophone effects, naming	McCann and Besner 1987
Pseudohomophone effects, LD	Besner and McCann (in press)
Regularity effects in reading acquisition	Backman et al. 1984; Seidenberg et al. 1986
Naming deficits, poor readers	Backman et al. 1984; Bruck et al. 1986
Naming deficits in surface dyslexia	Shallice et al. 1982; Bub et al. 1985
Syllabic effects, naming and LD	Jared and Seidenberg 1987; Seidenberg (in press, a)
Nonword pronunciation	Glushko 1979
Orth/phon priming, naming and LD	Meyer et al. 1974; Hillinger 1980; Taraban and McClelland 1987
Repetition and frequency interaction, LD	Besner and Swan 1982

Table 2
Mean naming latencies (from Seidenberg 1985a).

Type	Example	Latency (msec)	Percent error
High-frequency, regular	NINE	540	0.4
High-frequency, exception	LOSE	541	0.9
Low-frequency, regular	MODE	556	2.3
Low-frequency, exception	DEAF	583	5.1

factors such as length and frequency. Differences between them in terms of processing difficulty must be attributed to the one dimension along which they differ: regularity of spelling-sound correspondences.

The studies examining the processing of such words have yielded fairly coherent results. First, there are frequency effects; higher-frequency words are named at faster latencies than lower-frequency words (Frederiksen and Kroll 1976; Forster and Chambers 1973; Waters and Seidenberg 1985).[1] Second, regularity effects—faster latencies for regular words compared to exceptions—are specific to lower-frequency items (Andrews 1982; Seidenberg et al. 1984; Seidenberg 1985a; Waters and Seidenberg 1985; Taraban and McClelland 1987). In short, there is a frequency by regularity interaction, as exemplified by the results from Seidenberg 1985a presented in table 2.

The number of "higher-frequency" words for which irregular spelling-sound correspondences have little impact on overt naming is likely to be quite large because of the type/token facts about English (Seidenberg 1985a). A relatively small number of word types account for a large number of the tokens that a reader encounters. In the count of Kucera and Francis (1967), for example, the 133 most frequent words in the corpus account for about half of the total number of tokens. Hence, a small number of words recur with very high frequency, and these are the words for which the structural variables have little effect. Moreover, the size of this pool varies as a function of reading skill. In Seidenberg 1985a, I partitioned the data in table 2 according to overall subject naming speed; this yielded fast, medium, and slow reader groups (table 3). Among these subjects, who were McGill University undergraduates, the fastest readers named lower-frequency words more rapidly than the slowest readers named higher-frequency words. Thus, fast readers recognize a larger pool of items without interference from irregular spelling-sound correspondences. In effect, more words are treated as though they are "high-frequency" items.

Table 3
Mean naming latencies (in msec) as a function of decoding speed.

Word type	Subject group		
	Fastest	Medium	Slowest
High-frequency, regular	475	523	621
High-frequency, exception	475	517	631
Difference	0	−6	+10
Low-frequency, regular	500	530	641
Low-frequency, exception	502	562	685
Difference	+2	+32	+44

Phonological Output and Naming

Before characterizing the model's performance, it is necessary to consider a theory of the naming task and how it relates to the output computed by the model. We assume that overt naming involves three cascaded processes (see also Balota and Chumbley 1985). First, the input's phonological code is computed. Second, the computed phonological code is translated into a set of articulatory motor commands. Finally, the articulatory motor code is executed, resulting in the overt response. Only the first of these processes is implemented in the Seidenberg-McClelland model. In practice, however, the phonological output computed by the model is closely related to observed naming latencies.

A word is named by recoding the computed phonological output into a set of articulatory motor commands, which are then executed. Differences in naming latencies derive primarily from differences in the quality of the computed phonological output. Informally speaking, a word that the model "knows" well produces phonological output that more clearly specifies its articulatory motor program than a word that is known less well. Thus, naming latencies are a function of phonological error scores, which index differences between the veridical phonological code and the model's approximation to it.

Differences in naming latencies could also be associated with the execution of the compiled articulatory motor programs. The distributions of phonemes in high- and low-frequency words differ; some phonemes and phoneme sequences occur more often in higher-frequency words than in lower-frequency words, and vice versa (Landauer and Streeter 1973). Phonemes also differ in ease of articulation (Locke 1972); higher-frequency words may contain more of the phonemes that are easier to pronounce, or it may be that the phonemes that are characteristic of high-frequency words are easier to pronounce because they are used more often. Thus, naming latencies for high- and low-frequency words could differ not because frequency influences the computation of phonological output, or the translation of this output into an articulatory code, but because they contain phonemes that differ in ease of articulation. I will ignore this aspect of the naming process for two reasons. First, we have not implemented procedures for producing articulatory output. What is more important, existing studies indicate that the lexical variables of interest—frequency, orthographic-phonological regularity, orthographic redundancy, syllabic structure, etc.—have their primary effects on the computation of phonological output. These effects obtain even when articulatory factors are carefully controlled (McRae, Jared, and Seidenberg 1988).

To illustrate, consider a pair of high- and low-frequency homophones such as *main* and *mane*. The model is trained to produce the same phonological output for both words. After a sufficient amount of training, both words produce output that resembles the correct phonological output more closely than it resembles the phonological output for any other string of phonemes. Because they differ in frequency, however, *main* produces a smaller error score than *mane*; in general, the model performs better on words to which it has been exposed more often. It will be easier, then, to compile the pronunciation of the high-frequency item than to compile that of the low-frequency item. This predicts that they should differ in terms of immediate naming latencies, which they do (McRae et al. 1988). Because the words are homophones, the same articulatory motor program is used to produce overt responses. Hence, if the words are named after a delay, the compilation stage will have been completed and they should produce identical naming latencies, which they do (McRae et al. 1988). If the words had differed in ease of articulation, latency differences would be observed in both immediate and delayed naming (Balota and Chumbley 1985).

Simulations
The 2,897 stimuli ranged in length from 3 to 7 letters and in frequency from 0 to 69,971 on the Kucera-Francis (1967) count. The learning phase consisted of a series of passes through the training set, termed *epochs*. In each epoch, a subset of the 2,897 items were probabilistically selected for learning trials on the basis of their estimated frequencies; 450–550 items were presented per epoch. Connection weights were modified after each learning trial. The performance of the model on all 2,897 items was tested after 5 epochs, after 5 additional epochs, and after subsequent 10-epoch intervals. The data presented below are for 250 learning epochs. The data in these

analyses are the orthographic and phonological error scores for different subsets of words extracted from the entire 2,897-word data set.

Frequency and Regularity Effects

Consider first the model's performance on a subset of words that were used in a study by Taraban and McClelland (1987). Their stimuli included 24 words from each of the 4 categories created by crossing the factors frequency (high, low), and type (exception, regular). Examples are given in table 4. Figure 3 presents the simulation results. Each data point represents the average phonological error term for the 24 items of each type. The learning sequence is characterized by the following trends: Training reduces the error terms for all words in an approximately logarithmic manner. Throughout training, there is a frequency effect; the model performs better on words to which it is exposed more often. Note that although the test stimuli are dichotomized into high- and low-frequency groups, frequency is actually a continuous variable and it has continuous effects in the model. Early in training, there are large regularity effects for both high- and low-frequency items; in both frequency classes, regular words produce smaller error terms than exception words. Additional training reduces the exception effect for higher-frequency words, to the point where it is eliminated by 250 epochs. However, the regularity effect for lower-frequency words remains.

Taraban and McClelland's adult subjects performed as follows. First, lower-frequency words were named more slowly than higher-frequency words. Second, there was a frequency by regularity interaction; exception

Table 4
Examples of regular and exception words in test list.

High-frequency	Low-frequency
Exception	
COME	GROSS
DONE	PINT
FOOT	PEAR
ARE	DEAF
Regular	
CAME	GRAPE
DARK	PEEL
FACT	PUMP
OUT	DEAL

words produced longer naming latencies than regular words only when they were low in frequency. For lower-frequency words, the difference between regular and exception words was 32 msec, which was statistically significant; for higher-frequency words, the difference was 13 msec and nonsignificant. This is the pattern of results produced by the model after 250 epochs. Mean squared errors range from 2.97 to 6.31; the difference between low-frequency regular and exception words was 2.48, and for higher-frequency words it was 0.17. Figure 4 presents the two additional studies of this type, each of which utilized slightly different set of items. Data from experiment 2 of Seidenberg et al. 1984a are in the upper left corner; data from Seidenberg 1985a are in the upper right corner. Below each figure is the model's performance on the same items. Again there are frequency by regularity interactions in both experiments and simulations, with a good fit between the two.

The model is revealing about the behavioral phenomena in two respects. First, it is clear that in the model the frequency by regularity interaction

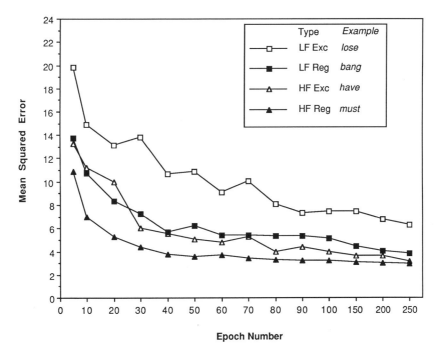

Figure 3
Results of the simulations over 250 learning epochs for the subset of items used by Taraban and McClelland (in press).

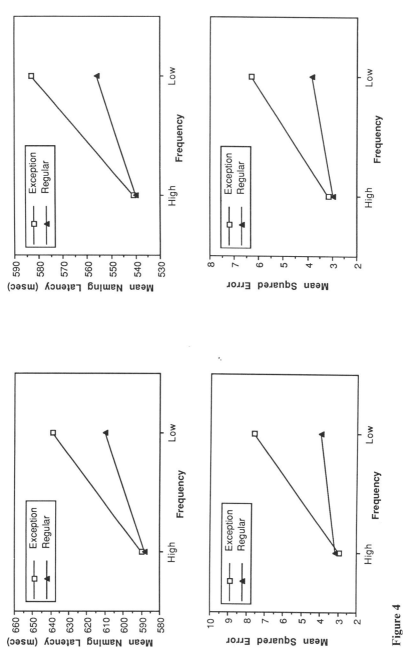

Figure 4

Upper left: Results of the Seidenberg (1985b) experiment. Lower left: Results of the simulation on the same items. Upper right: Results of Seidenberg et al.'s (1984a) experiment 3. Lower right: Results of the simulation on the same items.

results because the output for both types of higher-frequency words approach asymptote before the output for the lower-frequency words. Hence, the difference between the higher-frequency regular and exception words is eliminated whereas the difference between the two types of lower-frequency words remains. This result suggests that the interaction observed in the behavioral data results from a genuine "floor" effect due to the acquisition of a high level of skill in decoding common words. In the model, the differences between the two types of lower-frequency words would also diminish if training were continued for more epochs. This aspect of the model provides an explanation for the finding (Seidenberg 1985a) that there are individual differences among skilled readers in terms of regularity effects. The fastest subjects in this study showed no regularity effect, even for words that are "lower" in frequency according to standard norms. The model suggests that these subjects may have encountered lower-frequency words more often than the slower subjects, with the result that they effectively become "high-frequency" items.

Second, the model provides a theoretical link between effects of frequency and orthographic-phonological regularity. Both result because the patterns that were presented most often during training have more impact on the connection weights than items presented less often, resulting in better performance. Higher-frequency words produce smaller error scores because, by definition, they occur more often in the language, and thus in the training phase, than lower-frequency words. Note, however, that words with regular orthographic-phonological correspondences benefit for the same reason: By definition, they occur more often in the language—and thus in the training set—than exceptional ones. Hence, both "frequency" and "regularity" effects derive from the same source: the effects of repetition on learning.

The model has also yielded very good results in tests on several other types of stimuli that have been used in behavioral studies (see Seidenberg and McClelland 1987). To mention a few just briefly:

• It performs worst on "strange" words, such as BEIGE and AISLE, which contain unusual spelling patterns. This is consistent with the results of Seidenberg and Waters (1985) and Parkin (1982), who termed these *OPD words*.

• There have been several studies of so-called regular inconsistent words, which were thought to be theoretically important because dual-route and analogy models of naming make different predictions about their behavior (Henderson 1982; Patterson and Coltheart 1987). These studies have yielded inconsistent results (Glushko 1979; Seidenberg et al. 1984; Taraban and McClelland 1987; Stanhope and Parkin 1987), with some studies finding longer latencies for regular inconsistent words than for regular words and others finding no difference. Interestingly, where regular inconsistent effects were obtained in an experiment, the model yields effects for the same stimuli; where effects were not obtained, the model also yields no effects. Ironically, there is one exception to this pattern: In the original experiment examining regular inconsistent words, Glushko found an effect whereas the model predicts no difference. However, as Seidenberg et al. (1984a) demonstrated, Glushko's result was due to repetition priming within the experiment. When this priming was eliminated, no effect was obtained.

• The model replicates the results of Brown (1987), which were presented as evidence for a model of the naming process somewhat different from the one developed here. Brown argues that the factor relevant to naming latency is simply the number of times a spelling pattern is associated with a given pronunciation, not regularity defined in terms of number of inconsistent neighbors. On his account, an exception word such as *lose* produces longer naming latencies than a regular word such as *dust* because the rime *-ose* is assigned the "ooze" pronunciation in only one word whereas *-ust* is pronounced "ust" in many words. Brown's main prediction is that words such as *soap*, which he terms "unique," should produce latencies similar to those of exception words. Both unique and exception words contain rimes that occur only in a single item; for example, there are no other *-oap* words in English. Hence, they are equated in terms of the number of times their rimes are associated with a given pronunciation. They differ in terms of number of inconsistent neighbors—*lose* has many, *soap* has none—but this fact is thought to be irrelevant. Brown reported a naming experiment in which unique and exception words produced longer latencies than regular words but did not differ from each other and concluded that his hypothesis is correct.

The model performed as follows on Brown's stimuli. The mean phonological error scores (and standard deviations) after 250 epochs were Unique: 6.645 (5.432); Exception: 6.114 (3.510); Regular: 5.017 (4.196). The model actually does better than these numbers suggest, because Brown's exception words include CLERK, VASE, and TOOTH, which are regular in American English (and in our corpus). When these items are excluded, the mean for the exception words becomes 6.531. Thus, the model replicates Brown's results but, importantly, it does not follow the computational principle he proposed. The model's performance is definitely influenced by the number of times a spelling pattern is associated with a given pronunciation. However, this represents only one of many influences on the connection weights, which reflect the aggregate effects of training on the entire stimulus list. The main influence on the phonological output for a word is the number of times the model was exposed to the word itself. The number of times the model was exposed to closely related words (e.g., similarly spelled rhymes) exerts secondary effects; there are also small effects due to exposure to other words. It is easy to see why the model produces similar results for exception words such as LOSE and unique words such as SOAP. The model is trained on a large number of -ose words, and the weights come to reflect the fact that those words typically rhyme with POSE. It then performs relatively poorly when presented with the exception LOSE. Unique words such as SOAP fare differently. The fact that -oap is pronounced "ope" is not very strongly encoded by the weights, because this pattern is encountered so infrequently. This also means, however, that the model has not been given inconsistent feedback about the pronunciation of this pattern. The tradeoffs between these factors are apparently such that SOAP and LOSE are about equally difficult to name.

Seidenberg and McClelland (1987) also report new behavioral data indicating that consistency of spelling sound correspondences does affect naming, contrary to Brown's (1987) model.

• The model was trained on both alternative pronunciations of homographs such as LEAD and BASS; these words yield high phonological error scores, consistent with the finding that they also produce very long naming latencies (Seidenberg et al. 1984a).

• The model yields plausible output for nonwords derived from various kinds of words; for example, it performs better on nonwords such as NUST and FIKE (derived from regular words) than on nonwords such as MAVE and MOSE (derived from exceptions).

Summary of the Naming Simulations
The model provides a basis for understanding the manner in which knowledge of orthographic-phonological correspondences is represented in memory and used in naming. There have been two standard interpretations of regularity effects. According to the dual-route model of reading (Coltheart 1978), readers attempt to pronounce words by applying rules governing the spelling-sound correspondences of English. Although regular words can be pronounced by rule, exception words cannot. The attempt to pronounce exceptions by rule results in a temporary garden path, producing longer naming latencies than for regular words. Exception words are eventually pronounced correctly by consulting a phonological lexicon

in which the pronunciations of all words are listed. According to a second account (Glushko 1979), words (and nonwords) are pronounced by "lexical analogies." Although Glushko did not propose an explicit "analogy" process, Rumelhart and McClelland (1982) discussed in very general terms how his idea might be realized within their interactive-activation model (which Glushko's work helped to inspire). In their model, the computation of the pronunciation of a word could be influenced by feedback from partially activated "neighboring" words. For example, the pronunciation of HAVE could be affected by feedback from words such as GAVE and SAVE. Thus, inconsistencies among a pool of partially activated neighbors are responsible for regularity effects (see Henderson 1982 for discussion).

Our model differs from both of these accounts. In contrast to the dual-route model, there are no rules specifying the regular spelling-sound correspondences of the language and there is no phonological lexicon in which the pronunciations of all words are listed. All items—regular and irregular, word and nonword—are pronounced using the knowledge encoded by a single set of connections. One of the main contributions of the model is that it demonstrates that pronouncing exception words and pronouncing nonwords do not require separate lexical ("addressed") and nonlexical ("assembled") mechanisms. In contrast to the analogy account, there are no lexical nodes representing individual words and there is no feedback from inconsistent neighbors. In fact, phonological output is computed on a single forward pass through the network. This gives the model a very different character from the interactive-activation model, in which behavioral phenomena result from complex interactions among partially activated words and letters.

Currently, some researchers (e.g., Kay and Bishop [1987]) are attempting to identify the perceptual units relevant to pronunciation, and other research focuses on discovering the correct definition of regularity (Parkin 1982; Parkin and Underwood 1983) or pronunciation neighborhood (Patterson and Coltheart 1987). From the perspective of the model, these questions do not adequately reflect the kinds of knowledge that underlie pronunciation, how this knowledge is represented in memory, or how it influences processing. Connection weights reflect the cumulative effects of many learning trials, each of which imposes small changes on the weights. There is no single "perceptual unit" relevant to pronunciation. The output that the model produces for a given letter string is determined by the properties of *all* the words presented during training. From this perspective, the various definitions of "regularity" or "neighborhood" are simply imperfect generalizations about the nature of the input and its effects on what is learned. These generalizations capture only part of the structure of written English. In testing the model's performance on different types of words, such as regular and exception, we are trying to observe the effects of some aspects of the learning experience against a background of noise provided by all other aspects of this experience. Some such effects (e.g., differences between regular and exception words) can be observed in the model and reliably obtained in behavioral experiments. However, the important generalization is that all such effects emerge from specific learning experiences, which have many other consequences as well.

One other aspect of the naming simulations should be mentioned. The model gives a good account of some of the basic features of children's acquisition of naming skills and differences among good and poor readers. The model provides a characterization of a broad range of phenomena related to skilled visual word recognition and naming. As a learning model, it also speaks to the issue of how these skills are acquired; moreover, it provides an interesting perspective on the kinds of impairments that are characteristic of developmental and acquired dyslexias. Developmental dyslexia could be seen as a failure to acquire the knowledge that underlies word recognition and naming. Acquired dyslexias naturally correspond to impairments following damage to the normal system. Here I will focus on the acquisition of naming skills and their impairment in developmental dyslexia. Our studies of acquired forms of dyslexia are discussed in Patterson, Seidenberg, and McClelland (in press).

Consider the results of an experiment in which we retrained the model with half as many hidden units, 100 instead of 200. In all other respects the training procedure was the same as before. At the start of training, all weights were given small random values. The model was again trained on the 2,897-word vocabulary. Figure 5 gives the mean phonological error scores for regular and exception words in the Taraban-McClelland stimulus set. The upper panel shows the results for 200 hidden units (presented earlier in figure 3); the lower panel shows the results with fewer hidden units. Two main results can be observed. First, from epoch 10 to epoch 250, training with fewer hidden units yields poorer performance for all word types. High-frequency regular words, for example, asymptote at a MSE of about 6 in the 100-unit condition, and at about 4 in the 200-unit condition; other words yield similar results. Second, after 250 epochs exception words produce significantly poorer output than regular words in both high and low frequency ranges in the 100-unit condition; in the 200-unit condition, exception words produce larger error scores only in the lower frequency range.

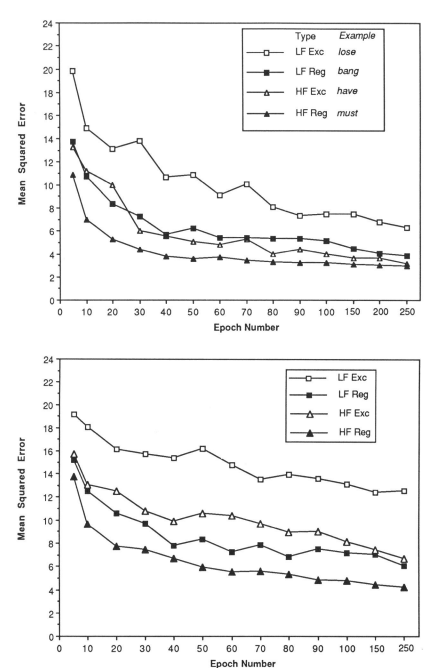

Figure 5
Top: Results of the simulation of the Taraban-McClelland (1987) experiment
(250 epochs, 200 hidden units). Bottom: Results for the same stimuli (100 hidden
units).

It is known that acquiring knowledge of spelling-sound correspondences is a key component of learning to read; disorders in phonological-analysis skills are thought to be a primary source of reading disability, and children who are backward readers (see Backman, Bruck, Hebert, and Seidenberg 1984) or developmental dyslexics (see Seidenberg, Bruck, Fornarolo, and Backman 1986) exhibit relatively poor performance in naming words and nonwords aloud (see Stanovich 1986 for review). One of the primary developmental trends observed in studies such as Backman et al. 1984 is that although children who are acquiring age-expected reading skills initially have more difficulty naming higher-frequency exception words (and other items containing spelling patterns associated with multiple pronunciations) than they have naming regular words, this deficit is eliminated by about Grade 5 (10 years of age). During the first few years of instruction, children learn to name common exception words as efficiently as regular words. Even among skilled adult readers, however, lower-frequency exception words continue to produce longer naming latencies and more errors than lower-frequency regular words. Among both children learning to read and adults, then, differences in naming skill are associated with differences in the number of words read without interference from irregular spelling-sound correspondences.

Both poor readers who are reading below age-expected levels and children who have been diagnosed as developmental dyslexics fail to show this improvement in naming higher-frequency exception words. For example, the naming performance of the poor readers in grades 3 and 4 in the Backman et al. study was like that of good readers in grade 2. Both the younger and poorer readers made more errors on exception words and other items containing spelling patterns associated with multiple pronunciations. Similarly, the naming performance of the children in the Seidenberg et al. (1986) study who were diagnosed as developmental dyslexics was similar to that of age-matched poor readers and to that of younger good readers.

Eliminating half the hidden units, then, produced a general decrement in performance; more important, *higher-frequency* words produced the patterns associated with *lower-frequency* words in the 200-unit simulation, i.e., larger error scores for exception words compared to regular. Even with fewer hidden units the model continued to encode generalizations about the correspondences between spelling and pronunciation; error scores were smaller for regular words than for other types. However, it performed more poorly on words whose pronunciations are not entirely regular.

Apparently, including fewer hidden units makes it more difficult to encode item-specific information concerning pronunciation.

These results capture a key feature of the data obtained in our studies of backward readers: These children continue to perform poorly in naming even higher-frequency exception words. At the same time, their performance shows that they have learned some generalizations about spelling-sound correspondences; for example, they are able to pronounce many nonwords correctly. The main implication of the simulation, of course, is that children who are not achieving age-expected reading skills may in some sense be allocating too few computational resources to the task. There is another important implication, however. Apparently, the architecture of the model determines in an important way its ability to behave like humans. If there are too few units, the model can learn generalizations about the regularities in the writing system; however, it does not have the capacity to encode enough of the word-specific information relevant to exception words to perform as well as humans. We are currently running new simulations to determine how the model will behave with a much larger number of hidden units ("too many"). It seems likely that a substantial increase will result in the model's beginning to dedicate individual units to individual words. This behavior would correspond to learning the pronunciations of words on an item-by-item basis but failing to encode generalizations about spelling-sound regularities. Learning of this sort would lead to poor performance in naming novel stimuli (a characteristic, it should be noted, of "phonological" dyslexia). The important point is that human performance seems to reflect rather subtle constraints concerning computational resources. The nonintuitive idea that impaired performance might result from dedicating too few or too many resources to a task is one that could be pursued in future research.

3 Criterion Shifts in Lexical Decision

I now turn to the model's account of the lexical decision task. The main interest of this account is that lexical decisions can be made despite the fact that there are no word-level units. Moreover, the model suggests that lexical decisions to isolated words are not necessarily made by identifying a letter string as a particular word, common assumptions to the contrary. This aspect of the model will be illustrated by simulating a set of results that have been the source of considerable confusion in the literature. There have been many lexical-decision studies, analogous to the naming studies mentioned above, using regular and exception words (see, e.g., Coltheart,

Besner, Jonasson, and Davelaar 1979; Bauer and Stanovich 1980; Parkin 1982; Parkin and Underwood 1983; Seidenberg et al. 1984a). As in the naming studies, orthographic-phonological regularity has negligible effects on lexical decisions for higher-frequency words. Whereas the naming studies have yielded robust exception effects for lower-frequency words, the results of the lexical-decision experiments have been inconsistent. In some studies, such as those of Coltheart et al. (1979) and Seidenberg et al. (1984a, experiment 3), no effects of orthographic-phonological regularity were observed; in others, such as those of Parkin (1982) and Bauer and Stanovich (1980), they were.

These inconsistent effects have been interpreted as indicating that words can be recognized by either "direct" (visually based) or "mediated" (phonologically based) processes (Carr and Pollatsek; 1985 Seidenberg 1985a). In cases where there were no effects of phonological regularity, it was inferred that recognition is direct; where there were such effects, recognition was thought to be phonologically mediated. Use of these alternative strategies was thought to be under the reader's control (Coltheart 1978). This account left a key question unresolved, however: It did not explain the factors that determined why a particular strategy seemed to be used in a particular experiment. Because the inconsistent results that led to this view involved the same types of stimuli (regular and exception words) used in different experiments, it cannot be the case that direct access is used for one type of word (e.g., exceptions) and mediated access for the other (e.g., regular), as suggested by some versions of the dual-route model.

Waters and Seidenberg (1985) discovered a generalization that accounts for these seemingly inconsistent outcomes. They noted that the lexical-decision results depended on the types of words and nonwords included in a stimulus set. When the stimuli in an experiment contain only regular and exception words and pronounceable nonwords, no exception effect is observed (Waters and Seidenberg 1985; Coltheart et al. 1979). Under these conditions, the effect of irregular spelling-sound correspondences for lower-frequency words obtained with the naming task is eliminated. The situation changes when the stimuli contain a third type of item: the so-called strange words first studied by Seidenberg et al. (1984a). These are items, such as ONCE, AISLE, and BEIGE, that contain unusual spelling patterns. Waters and Seidenberg (1985) showed that an exception effect for lower-frequency words is observed only when these items are included. Under these conditions, the lexical-decision results mimic those obtained with the naming task. This generalization concerning the presence or absence of strange words in the stimuli accounts for the seemingly inconsistent results of previous lexical-decision studies. Thus, phonological effects in lexical decision depend on the composition of the stimuli in the experiment. Importantly, the results on the naming task are not affected by this factor; there are robust exception effects for lower-frequency words whether or not strange words are included (Waters and Seidenberg 1985).

Waters and Seidenberg (1985) proposed the following account of these results: When the stimuli consist of regular and exception words and pronounceable nonwords, subjects based their decisions on the results of orthographic analyses. Hence, no effects of phonological regularity are observed. Including the strange stimuli increases the difficulty of the word/nonword discrimination. Subjects are asked to respond "word" when they see an item with an unfamiliar spelling pattern (such as AISLE) and to respond "nonword" when they encounter stimuli that contain common spelling patterns but are nonetheless not words (e.g., NUST). Making this discrimination on the basis of orthographic information is difficult; thus, subjects change their response strategy, turning to phonological information as the basis for their decisions. In effect, the subject now responds "word" if the stimulus has a familiar pronunciation, and "nonword" if it does not. Under these conditions, the task is much like naming: It requires computing the phonological code. Thus, the results are similar to those in naming, with a regularity effect for lower-frequency words.

In sum, subjects vary the criteria by which lexical decisions are made. In contrast, subjects cannot vary their response strategies when the task is to name words aloud. Naming does not involve discriminating between words and nonwords; rather, it requires the subject to produce the correct pronunciation, which cannot be accomplished until the phonological code has been computed.

Lexical Decisions in the Model
Our account of lexical decision involves the orthographic output that is computed in parallel with phonological output. Orthographic output represents the retention or recycling of orthographic information in a short-term sensory store. We assume that this information is relevant to visual-perceptual aspects of reading that have been widely studied by psychologists, such as the word-superiority effect and feature-integration errors (Treisman and Schmidt 1982; Seidenberg 1987). This part of the model addresses the phenomena that motivated the interactive-activation model of McClelland and Rumelhart (1981). The computed orthographic code also may play an important role in some forms of deep dyslexia, in

which patients access semantic information but are unable to report the identities of words.

After the model has been trained, it can be tested on familiar words and on nonwords. These items produce orthographic output, which can be summarized in terms of error scores. In general, the error scores are smaller for words than for nonwords; the model performs better on familiar stimuli. However, the magnitudes of these scores vary as a function of factors such as orthographic redundancy and length. The word and nonword stimuli in an experiment will yield distributions of orthographic-error scores. Assume that the word stimuli include only regular and exception words (items that do not differ in their orthographic properties), and that the nonwords are standard items, such as RONE or BIST. The word and nonword distributions for these words will overlap very little. Lexical decisions can be modeled as the establishment of decision criteria that operate on the orthographic-error scores. As in a signal-detection paradigm, the subject can establish decision criteria such that scores below the cutoff are judged words and those above it are judged nonwords. Latencies should be a function of distance from the cutoff; words producing very small error scores and nonwords producing very large error scores should yield faster responses than stimuli whose scores are closer to the cutoff. Given these distributions, response criteria can be established which yield low error rates in the range observed in actual experiments.

Including strange items in the stimulus set yields word and nonword distributions with greater overlap; some of the lower-frequency strange items produce error scores as high as or higher than those for nonwords. Lower-frequency strange words, such as BEIGE or FUGUE, have been encountered very rarely, and they contain spelling patterns that do not recur in other items. Nonwords, such as BIST or RONE, are also encountered very rarely (typically never), but they contain spelling patterns that recur in many other words. In many experiments, the nonwords are also somewhat shorter than the word stimuli, which will tend to produce smaller error scores.

The effect of including the strange words in the stimulus set is that subjects can no longer establish response criteria that yield acceptably low error rates. Lexical decisions cannot be based on the discriminibility of words and nonwords in terms of orthographic output; subjects must utilize other information in making their decisions. One strategy might be to consult the results of phonological processing; in that case, response latencies should be like those obtained in the naming task, which is also based on this output.

This account of lexical decision is very similar to one proposed by Balota and Chumbley (1984), who suggest that subjects base their decisions on the familiarity of a stimulus. The model demonstrates that a process of the sort they proposed is computationally feasible; the orthographic-error score provides a simple basis for the proposed familiarity judgment. However, the model differs from Balota and Chumbley's in an important respect. They see lexical decision as a two-stage process involving lexical access and postlexical decision. The orthographic information that provides the basis for the familiarity judgment becomes available as part of the process by which the meaning of a word is accessed. In our model, this information becomes available as a result of feedback processes (from hidden units to orthographic units) that are wholly orthogonal to access of meaning. Thus, under one construal of the term, lexical decisions do not involve lexical access (see below).

Simulation Results
We examined the model's performance on the Waters-Seidenberg word and nonword stimuli, using, as before, the weights from 250 learning epochs. All the word stimuli were included in the 2,897-word training set. Comparable data were obtained for the nonword stimuli using the weights from 250 epochs. The upper panel of figure 6 presents the data for the condition in which the stimuli consist of high- and low-frequency regular and exception words and pronounceable nonwords. The data are skewed because, with 250 epochs of training, there is a minimum error of about 2.4. Inspection suggests that the distributions of orthographic-error scores are such that a decision criterion can be established which yields a low error rate similar to that observed in the actual experiment. Since the decision is based on orthographic output, no effect of phonological regularity is observed. The lower panel of figure 6 presents the same data, but including the high- and low-frequency strange items. Now there is considerable overlap between the word and nonword distributions. This is primarily because the mean orthographic-error score for the lower-frequency strange words is 13.177, whereas the mean for the nonwords is 15.450 with a standard deviation of 5.610. This overlap makes it impossible to establish a decision criterion that yields an acceptably low error rate. Under these circumstances, we argue, subjects begin to look to phonological output. Decision latencies now exhibit the pattern associated with the naming task: longer latencies for lower-frequency exception words versus regular words.

In effect, the orthographic-error scores provide a measure of orthographic redundancy. This measure accounts for other empirical phenomena.

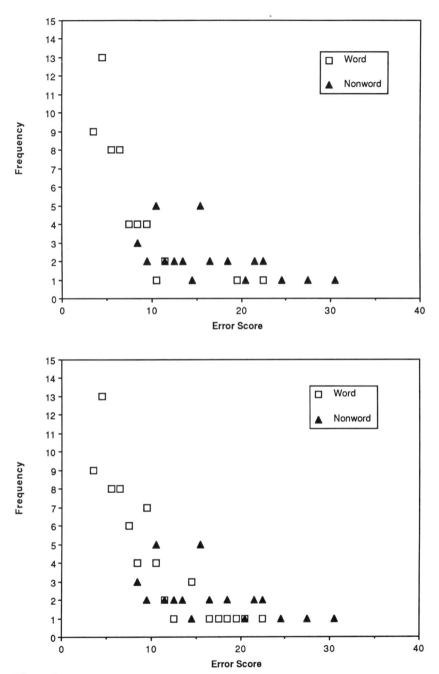

Figure 6
Top: Orthographic error scores (250 epochs) when the stimuli consist of regular and exception words and pronounceable nonwords. Bottom: Orthographic error scores when the stimuli also contain strange words.

For example, Waters and Seidenberg (1985) found that lower-frequency regular and exception words yield similar lexical-decision latencies, whereas strange words yield slower responses. The orthographic-error scores for these words yield the same pattern of results. This measure of orthographic redundancy has intrinsic interest, because it derives from all that the model has encoded about the frequency and distribution of letter patterns in the lexicon. Other measures of orthograhic redundancy have been used in word-recognition experiments (e.g., positional letter frequencies, bigram frequencies, Coltheart's N measure), with mixed results. However, each of these measures reflects only a part of the information encoded in our lexical network.

In sum, the model provides a simple account of observed differences between lexical decision and naming performance. The naming task requires the subject to compute a word's phonological code. Under many conditions, the lexical decision task can be performed on the basis of the output of the orthographic analysis. In these cases, naming produces effects of phonological regularity (for lower-frequency words), but lexical decision does not. However, if the stimuli in a lexical-decision experiment include very wordlike nonwords and very unwordlike words, subjects base their decisions on computed phonological codes. Under these conditions, lexical-decision results are like those that obtain in naming, because both responses are based on the same information.

This model of the lexical-decision process will account for other findings in the literature, including the frequency-blocking effects observed by Gordon (1983) and by Glanzer and Ehrenreich (1979) (see Seidenberg and McClelland 1987).

4   General Discussion: Why the Model Works; What Is Important About It and What Isn't

I hope to have described the model in sufficient detail to provide a clear picture as to how it works and to suggest that its scope—in terms of the range of human behaviors it simulates—is very broad. In the remainder of this article I consider several questions that arise as one attempts to evaluate the model, in terms of its relevance to reading and as an example of a connectionist model.

Why Does the Model Work?
The model clearly produces output that is closely related to measures of human performance, but why? The fact that the model simulates a broad

range of phenomena is important insofar as it suggests that it incorporates key aspects of the problem in its design. What is important, however, is being able to state what those key aspects of the problem are—something that requires going beyond the details of the model itself. The model can be characterized in terms of three general components:

The nature of the input

The model works because it is trained on a significant fragment of written English. The English orthography contains a complex latent structure. Measures of orthographic redundancy (such as positional letter frequencies and bigram frequencies), lists of spelling-sound rules (e.g., Venezky 1970), and definitions of regularity or phonological neighborhood (e.g., Parkin 1982) are crude characterizations of what is actually a very complex correlational structure concerning relations between letters and between letters and phonemes. The model is exposed to this highly elaborated input in the training phase.

The learning rule

This elaborate structure would be of no importance were it not for the fact that at least one learning algorithm is capable of extracting it. The effect of performing gradient descent in weight space is that the weights on connections come to encode regularities encoded in the imput. This is a good thing to be doing if the input does in fact exhibit a rich set of regularities. It is an especially good thing to be doing if the regularities are statistical (as in written English) rather than categorical (as in rules, as they are normally construed). Thus, there is a good match between what the learning algorithm does and what is to be recovered from the input.

The architecture of the system

Although it cannot be determined except through additional experimentation, it seems likely to me that many details of the model are not critical to its operation. It will probably turn out that there is a class of models using different encoding schemes, activation functions, learning rules, etc., all of which produce output that corresponds to behavioral measures about as well as ours does. The important question is: What are the properties common to all of these models, should they exist? These are the aspects that will be relevant to the theory of how humans recognize and pronounce words. If these models are to make a contribution to theory, it will have to be the case that there are only a few such general properties. Our research points to one: In order to capture facts about human behavior, the models apparently have to obey a kind of "Three Bears" principle concerning computational resources. The experiments with the number of hidden units suggest that if there are too few such resources the model will learn regularities but will not be able to cope well enough with exceptions. If there are too many the model will probably assign every word to a single unit, in which case it will cope with the pronunciations of known words but will not encode any regularities, leading to poor generalization. If the number of hidden units is "just right," the model performs about as well as humans do—imperfectly, but well enough to muddle through.[2]

Explicating why this generalization should be true—if in fact it is—turns on having complexity analyses that reveal what kinds of functions can and cannot be computed by systems with differing numbers of units, patterns of connectivity, learning rules, etc. I am afraid it may be a long time before we have much analytical information of this sort. In the meantime, the empirical discovery that something as general as the number of hidden units contributes in specifiable ways to the solution of a problem may be of interest to us as cognitive scientists trying to explain human behavior. This aspect of the model can be seen as providing an example of how biological constraints—the human architecture—constrain what is learnable.

In sum, it will probably turn out that one must have the right amount (and kind) of computational machinery to be able to encode the regularities that are found in the input and extracted by the learning algorithm. There may be other general architectural constraints as well.

This tripartite way of characterizing our model provides a useful framework for thinking about other connectionist models and about behavior in general. It incorporates some of the most important approaches to understanding behavior that have emerged in modern psychology. From Gibson it borrows the emphasis on understanding the structure of the input. From learning theory it borrows the notion of general laws of learning. From Chomsky it takes the emphasis on how biological constraints contribute to what is learnable. Which of these elements contributes most to the solution of a given problem will probably vary. In the case of learning to read and pronounce written English, the biological constraints are probably fairly minimal: The system has to devote the right amount and kind of resources to the problem. The solution is driven largely by the highly structured input and by the power of the learning rule. In language acquisition, where the imput to the system is impoverished relative to what is learned, the learnability problem is thought to be solvable because biology imposes very important constraints on the solution space. Thus, depending upon the nature of the problem, one or another component may contribute disproportionately to its solution; nonetheless, all three need to be considered.

It should be clear from this discussion that I do not consider the "connectionist" approach to be in the least bit incongruent with research on the so-called "logical problem of language acquisition" (e.g., Wexler and Culicover 1979; Berwick and Weinberg 1984). One of the main contributions of the connectionist approach is its concern with neglected issues concerning learning mechanisms. Given a learning mechanism such as the back-propagation algorithm, and some independently motivated assumptions about the nature of the imput to the child and the nature of linguistic representations, it becomes possible to rigorously determine how biological constraints contribute to language learnability. Moreover, I anticipate that work of this sort will contribute to answering questions concerning learning in the absence of direct negative evidence, the child's recovery from overgeneralizations, and other critical problems in language acquisition. More generally, one can imagine how such learning mechanisms might account for the parameter setting intrinsic to the principles-and-parameters approach of Chomsky (1981) and subsequent work in theoretical linguistics (see, e.g., Manzini and Wexler 1987). The connections between these fields have not been widely acknowledged for reasons I take to be largely extrascientific.

Implications Concerning Word Recognition and Naming

Naming

The most important conclusion is that naming of words and nonwords can be accomplished by a single computational mechanism that takes letter strings into phonological output. The model offers a proof by demonstration that a key assumption that motivated earlier theories is invalid. The two pronunciation mechanisms in the "dual-route" model were motivated by the assumption that the naming of exception words and nonwords necessarily required different mechanisms. Exception words cannot be pronounced by rule, only by lookup; nonwords cannot be pronounced by lookup, only by rule. This is perhaps the central dogma that links the different versions of the dual-route theory (Seidenberg, in press, b). We now have a mechanism capable of generating plausible phonological output for both types of stimuli. The model makes good on earlier conjectures (Glushko 1979) that such a "single-route" model would be feasible.

Although the model does not respect the central dogma, it is similar to dual-route models in one respect: The model outlined in figure 1 retains two mechanisms for pronouncing written words. We assume that, in the absence of pathology, readers simply compute pronunciations from orthography, as in the simulations. It might also be possible for readers to compute the meaning of the word on the basis of its orthography, and then compute the pronunciation of the word from its meaning. Thus, naming could be accomplished by utilizing the two remaining sides of the triangle. I think it unlikely that readers normally employ the second of these processes, simply because it is more complex than the direct computation of pronunciation from orthography. Still, it is relevant to cases of deep and phonological dyslexia, in which the normal naming mechanism is disabled.

Since our model incorporates two naming mechanisms, one might conclude that it is simply a variant of the traditional dual-route account. Our model builds upon the dual-route account but differs from it in significant ways. We have preserved what I believe to have been the important insight of the dual-route modelers, namely that there are two naming processes. In other respects, however, the models differ. The dual-route model assumed that one of the pronunciation mechanisms involves grapheme-phoneme correspondence rules, and that it only supports the naming of regular words and nonwords. In our model, the primary naming mechanism utilizes knowledge of spelling-sound correspondences that is encoded by the weights on connections rather than a set of mapping rules; and (critically, because of the manner in which this knowledge is encoded) the naming mechanism is involved in pronouncing all types of stimuli, not merely regular ones. Additionally, in the dual-route account, the second pathway ("lexical" or "addressed" phonology) plays a key role; it is responsible for the naming of all exception words. In our account, the alternative pronunciation pathway through meaning comes into play only in the case of pathology. The key differences between the models, then, turn on the different ways in which knowledge of spelling-sound correspondences are represented. Note that "connections weights" are not simply a notational variant of "spelling-sound rules"; the two types of knowledge have different properties and apply to different types of input.

In sum, the second ("lexical") naming process in the dual-route model was a necessary consequence of the way in which the primary ("nonlexical") mechanism was construed. Readers' knowledge of the correspondences between spelling and pronunciation was assumed to be encoded by a set of mapping rules. By definition, the rules could not cope with the pronunciation of irregular items, meaning that the second process had to exist. Our model suggests that this reasoning is invalid, because the primary naming mechanism can cope with both regular and irregular items. We retain the possibility that words could be named via a second mechanism only as a consequence of general commitments about the architecture of the system.

Lexical decision

Here the model simply provides strong evidence in support of the account of single-word lexical decision developed by Balota and Chumbley (1984), Seidenberg (1985b), Waters and Seidenberg (1985), and others. The main point of this account is that lexical decisions are based on subjects' judgments concerning the discriminability of words and nonwords. The model contradicts the view that lexical decisions are necessarily based on identifying a stimulus as a particular word with a particular meaning. The appropriate generalization appears to be that decision criteria vary as a function of the properties of the stimulus set. We have examined two cases, in which decisions are based on either orthographic or phonological information. These strategies appear to be typical of single-word lexical-decision studies. When the word and nonword stimuli appear in sentence contexts, there is ample evidence that subjects employ a strategy that involves judging the semantic congruence of context and target (Neely 1977; Seidenberg et al. 1984; Burgess, Tanenhaus, and Seidenberg, in press).

One methodological implication of this view is that lexical decision may be a difficult tool to use effectively. Each lexical-decision experiment represents one point in a space defined by the stimuli that happened to have been used. Which point in this space corresponds to the results that would obtain in "normal reading" is unclear.

Lexical access

Though the term "lexical access" is widely used, it (like "word recognition") refers to different things in different theories. My own view is that it is time to retire this term, because it is not consistent with basic properties of activation-type models. The term is something of a holdover from earlier models in which lexical processing was construed in terms of access to different types of information stored in bins or files (see, e.g., Forster 1976). In an activation model, information simply builds up over time; in effect, this represents an increase in the amount of evidence in support of a particular hypothesis (e.g., that the input is a particular word). I do not see any point in terming a specific moment in this process "lexical access." In a model such as Kawamoto's (in press), for example, meaning is represented in terms of semantic features that become activated at different points in time. This view seems consistent with evidence that different semantic features of a word are activated depending upon the context of occurrence (Barsalou 1982; Schwanenflugel and Shoben 1985).

Leaving this issue aside, if we take the term "lexical access" to refer to access of information concerning the meaning(s) of a word, then an implication of our model is that neither naming nor lexical-decision latencies necessarily reflect this process. The model simulates naming and lexical-decision performance even though meaning is not represented at all. Naming simply involves a direct mapping from spelling to pronunciation. Lexical decision simply involves a judgment based on general properties of the word and nonword stimuli. Hence, the results of experiments using these tasks may have no direct bearing on the question of how readers access the meanings of words from print. This is an important conclusion; it suggests that the scores of lexical-decision and naming experiments that were thought to bear on how readers access the meanings of words addressed no such thing at all.

Direct vs. mediated access

Much blood has been spilled among reading researchers in attempting to determine whether access to meaning is "direct" (based on visual information) or "phonologically mediated" (see Henderson 1982 and Carr and Pollatsek 1985 for reviews). Conclusions concerning this issue have been based primarily on the results of lexical-decision and naming experiments, which, I argued above, may have little bearing on the question of meaning access. Our model nonetheless suggests a resolution to this issue. According to the model, access to meaning is direct (for normal, skilled readers, at least). It involves a computation—which we have not yet implemented—that takes letter strings into meaning primitives. It is worth speculating briefly about what this computation might be like. Imagine that the phonological output units employed in our model were actually semantic primitives. Word meaning then corresponds to a pattern of activation across these units. During the learning phase, the connections from hidden units to semantic output units would come to reflect facts about correlations between orthography and meaning. In English, these correlations are not very interesting; English orthography systematically encodes pronunciation, not meaning. The connections between orthographic input and hidden units would likely reflect facts about the distribution of letter patterns in the lexicon—orthographic redundancy. The model will again perform better on familiar, high-frequency items than on unfamiliar ones. The computation from orthography to meaning should then be affected by familiarity, by orthographic redundancy, and (in a minor way) by correlations between orthography and semantics. These are the factors we might expect to influence measures related to silent reading, such as eye-fixation durations.[3]

Our model nonetheless affords the possibility of phonologically mediated access to meaning. Just as pronunciations could be computed by an indirect, meaning-mediated route, meanings could be accessed by an indirect, phonologically mediated route, simply as a consequence of the architecture given in figure 1. As with the indirect pronunciation route, I think the indirect meaning route is likely to be relevant only in rare instances where there is a misfire in the normal orthographic process or in cases of pathology, simply because it involves more processing and therefore is likely to be slower and less accurate. Also, contrary to the dual-route model, phonological mediation will not be associated with one class of words (e.g., regular) and direct access with another (irregular). Still, the possibility of phonologically mediated access (and a race between "direct" and "mediated" processes) is there.

What seems more likely to me is that both the meaning and the pronunciation of a word are normally computed in parallel (see Seidenberg and Tanenhaus 1979; Tanenhaus, Flanagan, and Seidenberg 1980). An orthographic input is encoded, and both of the computations based on orthography are initiated. If we then probe a few moments later (using priming techniques, for example), we find that both meaning-based and sound-based codes have become available. According to our model, these outcomes are the result of two parallel processes. Auditory word recognition works in a similar manner, *mutatis mutandis*. A spoken word is presented to the system, and both sound-to-meaning and sound-to-orthography computations are engaged. We know that listeners assign meanings to utterances. However, if we probe very carefully, we also find that listeners access orthographic information in auditory word-recognition tasks (Seidenberg and Tanenhaus 1979). There is, as we suggested some time ago (Donnenwerth-Nolan, Tanenhaus, and Seidenberg 1981), "multiple code activation" in word recognition, regardless of modality.

According to the model, then, phonological information becomes available in reading, but *not* as a part of the process by which meaning is accessed. It may be a useful by-product of the access of meaning—the phonological code may be useful in retaining information in working memory, facilitating the comprehension process—but it is a by-product nonetheless. This account provides a framework for thinking about the evidence cited in connection with phonological mediation. Researchers from Rubenstein et al. (1971) to Tanenhaus et al. (1980) to Van Orden (1987) have performed clever experiments showing that phonological information becomes available when words are read. For years, researchers have attempted to relate such results to the question of phonologically mediated access (of meaning).

With few exceptions, evidence of phonological *activation* was taken as evidence of phonologically mediated *access of meaning*. It can now be seen that phonological information could become available as a consequence of processes having nothing whatever to do with access of meaning. This point applies to all of the evidence cited by Carr and Polltasek (1985) in support of phonological mediation; none of it distinguishes between phonologically mediated access of meaning and phonological activation in parallel with access of meaning.

It could turn out that these assumptions are simply wrong and that access of meaning is typically phonologically mediated. Two points should be noted, however. First, we now have a coherent proposal concerning the relationship between meaning and phonology in which these codes are accessed by separate processes. This model is consistent with existing evidence. Second, whatever the ultimate fate of this issue, the form of the argument must change from what it has been; evidence that phonological information becomes available in an experiment clearly is not equivalent to evidence that phonological information mediated the access of meaning.[4]

What Is Important about the Model and What Isn't?

Computational modeling contributes to theory development in an idiosyncratic way that is not congenial to many cognitive scientists. Several problems arise. As everyone knows, implementing a computational model involves a raft of compromises; in order to get the model up and running, one must make decisions about issues that are incompletely understood. In our model, the obvious areas of compromise concern the orthographic and phonological encoding schemes, whose limitations have been noted elsewhere (Pinker and Prince 1987). Moreover, limitations on computational resources require that models be restricted in scope, which leads to the familiar charge that they deal with "toy" problems. A model might appear to work as well as it does simply because its scope has been arbitrarily restricted in some way. It is easy to imagine, for example, a model that can cope with the problem of learning to categorize objects as long as the number of categories is less than 3, but fails otherwise. No general principles necessarily follow from the fact that a problem can be solved when it is restricted in this way. In our case, the main restriction is that the training corpus includes only monosyllabic words. Finally, one is invariably forced to characterize the operation of the model in terms of a noncomputational theory stated in English. This is necessary both because the models are so complex and because one needs a description of their behavior that brings out the aspects relevant to understanding a problem rather than burying them in a mass of irrelevant detail (Putnam 1972). If it is necessary to appeal to this higher-level description of what the model does, why bother with the model itself at all?

In light of these observations, it is fair to ask how computational models contribute to an understanding of psychological processes. This issue has been extensively discussed in the literature, and I have little by way of general observations or arguments to add to it. It might be useful, however, to consider the question in regard to a specific, concrete case, namely our model of word recognition.

I assume that computational models involve core aspects (about which theoretical claims are made) and peripheral ones (the repository for all the compromises made along the way to implementation). The boundary between the two is not set *a priori* and may change as understanding of a problem deepens. In our model, the core seems to include the use of distributed representations, multilayer systems, gradient descent, and the Three Bears principle. The periphery includes the orthographic and phonological encoding schemes, the exact size of the vocabulary, the learning rate, etc. The question is whether this division is valid. Some would argue that the compromises that are an inevitable part of computational models vitiate the claims one might want to make about any part of them. Inadequacies in the orthographic and phonological encoding schemes, for example, could invalidate our claims about how knowledge of orthographic-phonological correspondences is represented. This is certainly a realistic concern.

At present, having implemented only one version of the model, we simply cannot determine with any certainty exactly how the compromises that have been made contribute to its behavior. It is possible that this behavior is highly sensitive to—and contingent upon—one or another of its more arbitrary aspects. For example, the scheme used to code phonemes is clearly inadequate; it fails to distinguish between the emphasized phonemes in shin and chin or in zoo and jew. It could be that the model simulates human performance as well as it does only *because* it fails to make relevant distinctions. I think this is highly unlikely; it would be a very cruel world if the model were able to simulate such a broad range of phenomena in close detail only because it uses an inadequate phonological-encoding scheme. Still, this is the risk one takes in developing a computational model, and its consequences can be addressed only through further research on this model and others like it. Already there is one suggestive finding: Sejnowski and Rosenberg's (1986) model, which is similar to ours in many respects, does not use the same encoding scheme; hence it cannot be crucial to this task.

The risk is also tolerable when the benefits are clear. There have been several accounts of naming. Dual-route modelers asserted that words could be pronounced on the basis of spelling-sound rules. Glushko (1979) asserted that nonwords could be pronounced by analogy. I proposed a model of the time course of processing using the vocabulary of the McClelland-Rumelhart (1981) model (Seidenberg 1985b). There is a certain vacuousness to these proposals because, in the absence of a more explicit characterization of the proposed mechanisms, there is no way of knowing whether any of them would actually work. It was only by implementing the model, for example, that we found out that both regular and exception words could in fact be handled by a single mechanism.

I am also fairly confident that ours is not a toy problem. The model has broad scope even if it is restricted to monosyllabic words. In fact, one of the main theoretical claims in our work is that facts about the role of syllables (and morphemes) in visual word recognition do not require the introduction of levels of structure or processing mechanisms specifically related to these units (Seidenberg 1987; in press, a). Specifically, effects of structures such as syllables and morphemes are an emergent consequence of aspects of word structure—orthographic redundancy and orthographic-phonological regularity—*already encoded* by our model on the basis of exposure to monosyllabic words (see Jared and Seidenberg 1987; Seidenberg, in press, a). It follows from our theory that the fact that the model was not trained on multisyllabic words does not matter. This theoretical claim will prove to be either true or false. However, the mere fact that the model has not been trained on multisyllabic words does not invalidate it.

Finally, it is important to keep in mind that details of the model are not as important as the understanding of perceptual or cognitive phenomena to which the model contributes. The simulation results are informative only insofar as they suggest that general principles embodied by the program relate in a systematic way to human performance. The model is useful because it suggests the general principles, but it is not the explanation itself.

Is the Model Falsifiable?
Another issue that arises is whether models of the sort we have developed are falsifiable. These models are thought to amount to a trivial kind of curve fitting, because they can be "tweaked" to fit any pattern of results. It is just a programming trick to take a body of data (concerning, e.g., spelling-sound correspondences) and find a connectionist model that simu-

lates it. On this view, modeling involves a redescription of empirical phenomena in a new and perhaps unwieldy language. The complaint, basically, is that connectionist models are too powerful, with the result that a model could at best achieve descriptive rather than explanatory adequacy. I think these concerns are, again, realistic ones, but that they can only be considered in terms of specific cases. Modeling is a tool, and it is sure to be used in different ways by different people; some models will be more interesting than others.

Perhaps this point is obvious. However, the reactions to our model that I have observed, and the reception of other connectionist models, suggest to me that there are some fairly widespread misconceptions about how such models are developed and how they can be evaluated. Some of these concerns may have arisen in part because of the McClelland-Rumelhart (1981) model, a precursor to the present work that was one of the first connectionist models to have an impact on cognitive psychologists. This model provided a detailed account of a somewhat narrow, though interesting, set of phenomena termed *word-superiority effects*. Two main characteristics of the model have generated concern. One is that it has a large number of parameters (governing, primarily, the spread of activation between and within levels). The other is that, because theirs was not a learning model, the values of the parameters were set by hand to produce the correct output. Because of these properties, it is sometimes surmised that the model can accommodate "any" pattern of results. For example, if the behavioral data had instead revealed a word-inferiority effect, the McClelland-Rumelhart model could accommodate this result if a few parameters were simply changed.

It would be a mistake to overgeneralize from the McClelland-Rumelhart example, however. It is instructive to compare their model with the successor discussed in this chapter. One primary difference between the models is that the number of free parameters has decreased considerably, for two primary reasons. First, our model does not require complex assumptions about the process of spreading activation. We have a homogeneous network in which all connections are of a single type and output is computed on a single pass. Second, the values of the connection weights are not free parameters; they are set by the learning algorithm. As a consequence, the close fit between simulation and behavioral data seen in figure 4 did not come about because we modified the model until it produced the right result. In fact, the reported simulation data are those that the model produced the *first* time it was run using the 2,897-word vocabulary. There were previous runs on a set of 1,200 words, but the model was not changed in any way in moving to the larger set.

It is instructive to note, however, that even the McClelland-Rumelhart model is falsifiable—something that can only be seen by experimenting with it. When a word is presented to the system, activation spreads to several lexical nodes. Incorrect alternative candidates are rapidly eliminated on the basis of information extracted from the bottom-up analysis of the signal. The net result is that the lexical node consistent with the input wins the competition among partially activated alternatives; it passes a threshold level of activation, and the activation of all competitors is inhibited.

Consider now the contrast between words that contain unusual spelling patterns, such as AISLE, ONCE, and BEIGE, and words containing common spelling patterns, such as SPITE, INCH, and TRAIN. As the parameters are set in the original McClelland-Rumelhart paper, their model exhibits the following behavior: Other factors (such as frequency) being equal, strange words reach the threshold level of activation more rapidly than words with common spelling patterns. This is largely a consequence of the fact that the information coming into the system from the bottom up does not activate many lexical candidates, which means that there is less competition at the word level. It follows from the model that words with atypical spelling patterns should be recognized more rapidly than words containing common spelling patterns. This prediction is simply false, however. Among the higher-frequency words in the language, orthographic redundancy has negligible effects on both naming and lexical decision; among the lower-frequency words, items with uncommon spelling patterns (which we termed "strange") produce longer naming and lexical-decision latencies than words with common spelling patterns (Waters and Seidenberg 1985). As the parameters are set in the 1981 paper, then, the McClelland-Rumelhart model makes a prediction that is falsified by the data.

Now the question is this: Could the parameters in the model be changed so as to produce behavior consistent with the empirical evidence? Based on a considerable amount of experimentation with the model, I believe the answer to this question is No. The effects of orthographic redundancy can be eliminated entirely, but the parameters cannot be set so as to provide an advantage for words with common spelling patterns.

The implications of this example should be clear. First, the model can be falsified. One merely has to consider a slightly broader range of phenomena than those that initially motivated it. Second, it cannot be patched up by tweaking the parameters; its behavior is not wholly unconstrained. My guess is that this situation is fairly typical.

One might argue that the problem of falsifiability is more subtle. It is not that individual connectionist models are unfalsifiable; it's that when a particular model is falsified, one can always think of another connectionist model that is capable of accommodating the falsifying data. Having shown that the McClelland-Rumelhart model incorrectly predicts that strange words will be read more rapidly than regular words, it will be possible to develop a new model, within the same framework, that makes precisely the opposite prediction. This is thought to be a bad thing.

It seems to me that there is confusion here between the properties of a theory and the properties of the language in which the theory is stated. Connectionism represents a language or formalism for developing theories of a certain sort. The properties of this formalism—what can and cannot be computed under different assumptions concerning number of nodes, patterns of connectivity, learning algorithms, and the like—are simply unknown at present. Assume for the sake of argument what has not be proven, namely that the connectionist framework is Turing equivalent. It would then be possible to develop a connectionist model of any adequately specified process theory. A particular model could be evaluated in the usual ways, determining whether it achieved descriptive or explanatory adequacy. However, it would be a category error to think that the formalism itself can be evaluated in these ways. If the language has sufficient expressive power, the goal is to evaluate particular theories framed in that language, not to evaluate the language itself.

There is another possibility, however: that the expressive power of this language is restricted in some way. Perhaps there are generalizations that simply cannot be stated within it. I take that to be the main argument of Fodor and Pylyshyn (1987). It will be important to determine more rigorously whether the connectionist formalism is in fact constrained in the ways they suggest. Presumably, to understand why a particular aspect of human behavior can or cannot be captured within a connectionist framework can be seen as one of the important goals of this research, which will yield deeper understanding of the phenomenon.

Finally, it is important to determine whether a given model makes new predictions. The "curve-fitting" criticism implies that the simulation model will account for the data in a sense, but that it will make no new predictions because it does not embody the general principles actually relevant to the problem domain. Again sticking to the case I know best, our model definitely makes testable, nonobvious predictions. For example, the model predicts that there is a class of regular nonwords (such as BLUST and RENK) that should be easier to name than lower-frequency words (such as FUGUE and TYKE). This would contradict the universal finding that words are named faster than nonwords. Similarly, the model makes very specific predictions as to how lexical-decision strategies will be affected by the composition of the stimuli. We should be able to predict when subjects begin basing their decisions on nonorthographic information. These are only simple examples. The model provides a rich source of new insights and predictions concerning reading and naming.

On Rules

The model also sheds some light on current debates concerning the notion that human behavior is governed by rules (Rumelhart and McClelland 1986; Pinker and Prince 1987). It is sometimes asserted that one or another aspect of human behavior can be explained in terms of the rules thought to govern it. A benign view of connectionism is that it simply represents a way to implement rules in terms of computations involving simple, neuron-like processing elements. However, more may be at stake here. Rumelhart and McClelland (1986) note that in many domains human behavior, while regular and orderly, nonetheless exhibits characteristics that are not in keeping with everyday notions of "rule." For example, knowledge of language is sometimes construed as knowledge of a set of rules that, among other things, permit one to distinguish between grammatical and ungrammatical utterances. Human behavior is largely consistent with this hypothesis; most sentences can be clearly judged to be grammatical or ungrammatical. However, there are many unclear cases that yield inconsistent judgments.

It appears that many types of human behavior have a similar character. For example, rational behavior deviates from that expected by rule because it is influenced by frequency and recency of exemplars, by factors correlated with the rule but not a causal part of it, etc. (Tversky and Kahneman 1986). The idea, then, is that "rules" do not adequately express the relevant generalizations about behavior because, on closer inspection, they deviate from what we would expect behavior to be like if it were in fact "rule governed." Behavior is that is systematic but admits of exceptions might be termed "quasi-regular."

It may be that, as Chomsky (1980) has argued, one should simply look to a theory, motivated by independent considerations, to disambiguate unclear cases. However, there is another possibility. Perhaps the unclear cases are providing hints that the rule-based theories are not capturing relevant aspects of phenomena. The important claim of the connectionists is that both the regular and the "anomalous" aspects of "rule-governed" behavior are a consequence of processes at the lower level defined by their models—the so-called microstructure of cognition. In at least some domains, the relevant generalizations about behavior involve this level, not rules. It would be important if it were to be shown that, in some domain, both the seemingly problematical, unclear cases and the regular, "rule-governed" ones are consequences of a certain kind of computation, such as the interactions among simple processing elements. Rumelhart and McClelland (1986) argue that their model of the learning of the past tense of verbs is an example of this sort. Unfortunately, the model is fundamentally flawed (Pinker and Prince 1987): It doesn't achieve observational adequacy in terms of accounting for the facts about verb learning in children, it makes unrealistic assumptions about the input to the child, and so on. The model is so compromised that it cannot be claimed to have captured relevant generalizations that rule-based theories miss.

Our model provides a much more substantive example of this kind of generalization, however. Previously, people attempted to explain the knowledge and use of spelling-sound information in terms "grapheme-phoneme correspondence rules." It is by no means clear how the rules that have been proposed (see, e.g., Venezky 1970; Hanna, Hanna, Hodges, and Rudorf 1968; Wijk 1966) could be employed by what is in fact a highly efficient system; the computational overhead associated with utilizing several thousand overlapping rules is enormous. More important, it is inappropriate to think of the correspondences between spelling and sound in English in terms of rules; written English is a quintessential example of a quasi-regular system. Written English does systematically encode information about pronunciation; however, for a variety of reasons (historical accident, diachronic change in pronunciation, lexical borrowing, etc.), there are numerous violations of these general patterns. These violations appear to be largely unsystematic unless one knows the entire history of the writing system. The exceptions are difficult to reconcile with the notion that the spelling-sound correspondences of English can be characterized by a set of mapping rules. They can be only if one introduces a second mechanism to deal with all the exceptions; hence the dual-route model. This solution is trivializes the notion of rule; *any* system can be considered to be "rule governed" if special mechanisms are introduced to deal with cases where the rules fail.

There is a still more serious problem, however. Even if the vocabulary of English is partitioned into words that are pronounced by rules and those that require special mechanisms, this dichotomy is not rich enough to capture relevant empirical phenomena. For example, there is the celebrated case of regular inconsistent words (Glushko 1979). Words such as PAVE and PAID have pronunciations that are correctly specified by the "rules" of English; hence, they should yield naming latencies similar to those for regular words such as MUST and LIKE. However, PAVE and PAID have "inconsistent neighbors" (the exception words HAVE and SAID), whereas MUST and LIKE do not. Glushko observed that regular inconsistent words yield longer naming latencies than regular words. This outcome is difficult to reconcile with the idea that regular words are pronounced by rule. What kind of rule simultaneously takes into account the generalization that -*ave* is pronounced "aive" and the fact that there is one item in which it is pronounced "av"?

It turns out that Glushko's experiment was flawed and that regular inconsistent words do not, as a class, reliably yield longer naming latencies than regular words (see discussion above). The basic problem is that the pronunciation of a word is influenced by knowledge of a much larger set of words than Glushko assumed. It is not that HAVE has no effect on the pronunciation of PAVE; it's that it is difficult to isolate this effect against the background provided by the effects of many other words. What is correct about Glushko's proposal, I believe, is the idea that the pronunciation of a word is influenced by knowledge of many other words, resulting in an analogue notion of regularity: HAVE is less regular than PAVE, but PAVE is less regular than MUST. This graded notion of regularity is congenial to a system in which weights vary continuously in value; it is not congenial to the notion "rule of pronunciation." I argue, then, that knowledge of the spelling-sound correspondences of English provides a clear case in which relevant generalizations are captured by considering the interactions among neuron-like units that underlie phenomena that at the behavioral level appear to be (almost) "rule governed." There may be others.

Several additional points should be noted:

• Our model may be consistent with a modified notion of "rule." What the model shows is that certain simple, intuitive notions of what is meant by "rule" fail to capture relevant generalizations about naming behavior. One might be able to devise a notational variant of our model employing rules that have other properties. It is valid to ask whether a particular notion of "rule" is adequate as a means of capturing generalizations of a particular sort. This question can be addressed both empirically (Does the rule account for the behavior?) and theoretically (e.g., Does the rule bring out relevant aspects of the problem?). However, it is vacuous to ask whether behavior is rule governed if the notion of "rule" is unconstrained. Much of the debate over "rules" to this point (e.g., Rumelhart and McClelland 1986; Pinker and Prince 1987) has little force because no explicit notion of rule is at stake.

• Although the relevant generalizations about naming behavior fall out of properties of a connectionist system, rather than a set of rules, it is sometimes useful to speak of the model as if it were instantiating rules. This is the "rule as convenient fiction" approach. The reason is simply that the computations that the model performs are very complex and difficult to characterize except in terms of higher-level generalizations that are only approximately true. The fact that it is easier to describe the model in terms of rules or rule-like behavior should not mask the fact that the explanation for the observed empirical phenomena derives from an understanding of how the computation is actually performed. How the knowledge of spelling-sound correspondences is actually encoded and used is critical, not the fact that it is easier to summarize what the model does in language that abstracts away from these characteristics.

Clearly, these higher-level generalizations are important in that they increase our ability to talk about the model. However, their value derives in part from the fact that we know from the implementation how lower-level computations contribute to them. Similarly, the model is useful, but only when coupled with a higher-level theory that abstracts away from its irrelevant aspects. The insight of the connectionist approach is that, at least in some domains, the explanation of behavior involves both levels of description simultaneously.

• Finally, our model demonstrates that there is at least one problem domain in which the explanatory theory involves understanding at McClelland and Rumelhart's (1986) "microstructural" level. The questions that arise are these: What properties are common to the problems for which this type of explanation is appropriate and which of the problems of interest to cognitive scientists are of this type? Addressing these questions seems eminently worthwhile because the answers are by no means obvious. For example, Pinker and Prince (1987) argue that connectionist models are ill suited to explaining the problem of learning the past tenses of verbs (in the sense that they are incapable of capturing relevant generalizations about the process). However, it is not clear whether this problem differs greatly from learning the spelling-sound correspondences of English. Both involve learning quasi-regular systems characterized by a large number of both "rule-governed" cases and exceptions; the exceptions tend to be disproportionately represented among the higher-frequency items, to which the child is exposed first.

Other cases of this sort come readily to mind. For example, it appears that English morphology in general is also quasi-regular. Morphological theories make a distinction between lexical items that can be generated by rule and items that must be "listed" (Aronoff 1976; Mohanon 1981). These theories preserve the notion that morphology is rule governed by introducing a second mechanism to deal with cases where the rules fail. As in the case of accounts of pronunciation in terms of spelling-sound rules, it has been difficult to formulate a felicitous set of morphological rules; as a consequence, there is considerable debate as to which lexical items must be listed. This situation has led Bybee (1985) to formulate a theory of morphological structure that abandons the distinction between "rule governed" and "listed" in favor of a notion of degree of morphological relatedness. It should be clear that this theory is congenial to the approach developed here.

Perhaps, as Fodor and Pylyshyn (1987) argue, there are other types of problems for which connectionist models are ill suited—something that remains to be definitely established. However this issue turns out, I think it is already clear that the models speak in an articulate and informative way to issues of a certain type, and that this type is likely to include a nontrivial subset of the issues of interest to cognitive scientists.

Conclusions

I think that there is reason to believe that in the next few years there will be a model, very much like ours though broader still, that will give an explanatory account of how people read, name, and understand words, how they acquire these skills, and how these skills are impaired in cases of dyslexia and aphasia. If that comes to pass, it will be because of the basic congruence between the nature of connectionist models and the nature of lexical processing. It will also reflect the fact that careful studies of human performance can suggest general processing principles which can then be developed and tested using computational modeling techniques. These developments represent a good example of the power of cognitive science's approaches to understanding behavior.

Acknowledgments

The model described in this paper was developed in collaboration with J. L. McClelland. K. E. Patterson has collaborated on studies of the model's implications concerning dyslexia. Many of the ideas that are expressed emerged in the course of working with them. Although both have influenced the content of this paper in significant ways, they should not be held responsible for it. The paper was completed while I was a visiting scientist at the MRC Applied Psychology Unit, Cambridge, the use of whose facilities I gratefully acknowledge. This research was supported by grants from NIH (HD 18944), NSERC (A7924), and FCAR (Quebec Ministry of Education).

I would also like to acknowledge the important work of Sejnowski and Rosenberg (1986), who have developed a computational model similar to ours in some important respects. Both models simulate the pronunciation of written words, using a multi-layer system and the back-propagation learning algorithm. The two research projects are complementary but not identical. Their model does not contain anything like the orthographic output that is the basis of our account of performance on tasks such as tachistoscopic recognition and lexical decision. We have been much more concerned with relating the model's performance to that of humans, they with sophisticated analyses of what their hidden units encode.

Notes

1. There have been studies that have failed to obtain frequency effects on naming responses (see Waters and Seidenberg 1985 for discussion). At one time the status of these effects was thought to be important. According to some versions of the dual-route model, at least some words can be named on a nonlexical basis, in which case they should not yield frequency effects. There are two related reasons why frequency effects sometimes do not obtain in naming studies. One is that the norms used in designing the relevant kind of experiments are notoriously unreliable as estimates of frequency of occurrence in the language (Gernsbacher 1984), especially in the lower frequency range. When careful estimates of frequency are obtained, there are reliable frequency effects (Waters and Seidenberg 1985). The second point is that the norms are also unreliable as estimates of the frequencies of words for individual subjects. As Seidenberg (1985b) showed, some subjects who are fast readers treat a larger pool of items as "high frequency," perhaps simply because they read more often.

2. Apologies to Wanner and Gleitman (1982), who described a different "Three Bears" principle in learning. Perhaps there is a cognitive universal here.

3. This way of thinking about meaning representation has intrinsic interest. The "meaning" units could be thought of as semantic or conceptual primitives, possibly

innately specified. The idea that their activation levels can vary continuously (between 0 and 1, say) provides an interesting alternative to accounts of meaning in terms of binary features. "Learning the meanings of words" then becomes the task of learning how bundles of features, at different activation levels, are related to the lexical items that happen to occur in a language. Tim Shallice and Geoff Hinton are implementing a semantic-access model of this general sort, although with deep dyslexia rather than acquisition of meaning in mind.

4. This point is relevant to the studies of Serbo-Croatian by the Haskins Laboratories group and their Yugoslavian colleagues (see, e.g., Feldman and Turvey 1983; Lukatela, Popadiç, Ognjenovic, and Turvey 1980). These authors have argued that word recognition in Serbo-Croatian necessarily involves phonological mediation. Their studies show that phonological information affected performance on tasks such as lexical decision. However, they do not show that phonology provided access to meaning.

References

Andrews, S. 1982. Phonological recoding: Is the regularity effect consistent? *Memory and Cognition* 10: 565–575.

Aronoff, M. 1976. *Word Formation in Generative Grammar*. Cambridge, Mass.: MIT Press.

Backman, J., Bruck, M., Hebert, M., and Seidenberg, M. (1984). Acquisition and use of spelling-sound information in reading. *Journal of Experimental Child Psychology* 38: 114–133.

Balota, D., and Chumbley, J. 1984. Are lexical decisions a good measure of lexical access? The role of frequency in the neglected decision stage. *Journal of Experimental Psychology: Human Perception and Performance* 10: 340–357.

Balota, D. A., and Chumbley, J. I. 1985. The locus of the word frequency effect in the pronunciation task: Lexical access and/or production? *Journal of Memory and Language* 24: 89–106.

Barsalou, L. W. 1982. Context-independent and context-dependent information in concepts. *Memory and Cognition* 10: 82–93.

Bauer, D. W., and Stanovich, K. E. 1980. Lexical access and the spelling-to-sound regularity effect. *Memory and Cognition* 8: 424–432.

Berwick, R., and Weinberg, A. 1984. *The Grammatical Basis of Linguistic Performance: Language Use and Acquisition*. Cambridge, Mass.: MIT Press.

Besner, D., and Swan, M. 1982. Models of lexical access in visual word recognition. *Quarterly Journal of Experimental Psychology* 34A: 313–326.

Brown, G. D. A. 1987. Resolving inconsistency: A computational model of word naming. *Journal of Memory and Language* 26: 1–23.

Bub, D., Cancelliere, A., and Kertesz, A. 1985. Whole-word and analytic translation of spelling to sound in a non-semantic reader. In K. E. Patterson, J. C. Marshall, and M. Coltheart (eds.), *Surface Dyslexia*. London: Erlbaum.

Burgess, C., Tanenhaus, M., and Seidenberg, M. In press. Nonword interference and lexical ambiguity resolution. *Journal of Experimental Psychology: Learning, Memory and Cognition.*

Bybee, J. L. 1985. *Morphology: A Study of the Relation between Meaning and Form.* Philadelphia: John Benjamins.

Carr, T. H., and Pollatsek, A. 1985. Recognition of printed words: A look at current models. In D. Besner, T. G. Waller, and G. E. MacKinnon (eds.), *Reading Research: Advances in Theory and Practice, vol. 5.* New York: Academic.

Chomsky, N. 1980. *Rules and Representations.* New York: Columbia University Press.

Chomsky, N. 1981. *Lectures on Government and Binding.* Dordrecht: Foris.

Coltheart, M. 1978. Lexical access in simple reading tasks. In G. Underwood (ed.), *Strategies of Information Processing.* New York: Academic.

Coltheart, M., Besner, D., Jonasson, J., and Davelaar, E. 1979. Phonological recoding in the lexical decision task. *Quarterly Journal of Experimental Psychology,* 31: 489–508.

Donnenwerth-Nolan, S., Tanenhaus, M. K., and Seidenberg, M. S. 1981. Multiple code activation in word recognition: Evidence from rhyme monitoring. *Journal of Experimental Psychology: Human Learning and Memory* 7: 170–180.

Feldman, L. B., and Turvey, M. T. 1980. Word recognition in Serbo-Croatian is phonologically analytic. *Journal of Experimental Psychology: Human Perception and Performance* 9: 288–298.

Fodor, J. A., and Pylyshyn, Z. W. 1987. Connectionism and cognitive architecture: A critical analysis. *Cognition* 28: 3–72.

Forster, K. I. 1976. Accessing the mental lexicon. In R. J. Wales and E. Walker (eds.), *New Approaches to Language Mechanisms.* Amsterdam: North-Holland.

Forster, K. I., and Chambers, S. 1973. Lexical access and naming time. *Journal of Verbal Learning and Verbal Behavior* 12: 627–635.

Frederiksen, J. R., and Kroll, J. F. 1976. Spelling and sound: Approaches to the internal lexicon. *Journal of Experimental Psychology: Human Perception and Performance* 2: 361–379.

Gernsbacher, M. A. 1984. Resolving 20 years of inconsistent interactions between lexical familiarity and orthography, concreteness, and polysemy. *Journal of Experimental Psychology: General* 113: 256–281.

Glanzer, M., and Ehrenreich, S. L. 1979. Structure and search of the internal lexicon. *Journal of Verbal Learning and Verbal Behavior* 18: 381–398.

Glushko, R. J. 1979. The organization and activation of orthographic knowledge in reading aloud. *Journal of Experimental Psychology: Human Perception and Performance* 5: 674–691.

Gordon, B. 1983. Lexical access and lexical decision: Mechanisms of frequency sensitivity. *Journal of Verbal Learning and Verbal Behavior* 22: 24–44.

Hanna, P. R., Hanna, J. S., Hodges, R. E., and Rudorf, E. H. 1966. *Phoneme-Grapheme Correspondences as Cues to Spelling Improvement*. Washington: U.S. Department of Health, Education, and Welfare.

Henderson, L. 1982. *Orthographies and Word Recognition in Reading*. New York: Academic.

Jared, D., and Seidenberg, M. S. 1987. The emergence of syllabic structures in visual word recognition. Manuscript.

Kawamoto, A. In press. Interactive processes in the resolution of lexical ambiguity. In S. Small, G. Cottrell, and M. Tanenhaus (eds.), *Lexical Ambiguity: Computational, Linguistic, and Psycholinguistic Perspectives*. Hillsdale, N.J.: Erlbaum.

Kay, J., and Bishop, D. 1987. Anatomical differences between nose, palm, and foot, or the body in question. In M. Coltheart (ed.), *Attention and Performance XII: Reading*. London: Erlbaum.

Kucera, H., and Francis, W. N. 1967. *Computational Analysis of Present-day American English*. Providence: Brown University Press.

Landauer, T., and Streeter, L. 1973. Structural differences between common and rare words: Failure of equivalence assumptions for theories of word recognition. *Journal of Verbal Learning and Verbal Behavior* 12: 119–131.

Locke, J. L. 1972. Ease of articulation. *Journal of Speech and Hearing Research* 15: 194–200.

Lukatela, G., Popadic, D., Ognjenovic, P., and Turvey, M. T. 1980. Lexical decision in a phonologically shallow orthography. *Memory and Cognition* 8: 124–132.

Manzini, R. M., and Wexler, K. 1987. Parameters, binding theory, and learnability. *Linguistic Inquiry* 18: 413–444.

McCann, R. S., and Besner, D. In press. Reading pseudohomophones: Implications for models of pronunciation assembly and the locus of word frequency effects in naming. *Journal of Experimental Psychology: Human Perception and Performance*.

Meyer, D., Schvaneveldt, R., and Ruddy, M. 1974. Functions of graphemic and phonemic codes in visual word recognition. *Memory and Cognition* 2: 309–321.

Mohanon, K. P. 1981. Lexical Phonology. Doctoral dissertation, MIT.

Neely, J. 1977. Semantic priming and retrieval from lexical memory: Roles of inhibitionless spreading activation and limited-capacity attention. *Journal of Experimental Psychology: General* 106: 225–254.

Parkin, A. J. 1982. Phonological recoding in lexical decision: Effects of spelling-to-sound regularity depend on how regularity is defined. *Memory and Cognition* 10: 43–53.

Parkin, A. J., and Underwood, G. 1983. Orthographic vs. phonological irregularity in lexical decision. *Memory and Cognition* 11: 351–355.

Patterson, K., and Coltheart, V. 1987. Phonological processes in reading: A tutorial review. In M. Coltheart (ed.), *Attention and Performance XII: Reading*. London: Erlbaum.

Patterson, K., Marshall, J., and Coltheart, M. 1985. *Surface Dyslexia*. London: Erlbaum.

Patterson, K., Seidenberg, M., and McClelland, J. In press. Dyslexia in a distributed, developmental model of word recognition. In R. Morris (ed.), *Proceedings of the Oxford Symposium on Parallel Distributed Processing*. Oxford University Press.

Pinker, S., and Prince, A. 1987. On language and connectionism: Analysis of a parallel distributed processing model of language acquisition. *Cognition*, 28: 73–194.

Putnam, H. 1972. Psychology and reduction. *Cognition* 2: 131–146.

Rubenstein, H., Lewis, S. S., and Rubenstein, M. A. 1971. Evidence for phonemic recoding in visual word recognition. *Journal of Verbal Learning and Verbal Behavior* 10: 645–657.

Rumelhart, D., and McClelland, J. 1982. An interactive activation model of context effects in letter perception, Part 2. *Psychological Review* 89: 60–94.

Rumelhart, D., and McClelland, J. L. 1986. On learning the past tenses of English verbs. In J. McClelland et al., *Parallel Distributed Processing*, vol. 2. Cambridge, Mass. MIT Press.

Rumelhart, D., Hinton, G., and Williams, R. 1986. Learning internal representations by error propagation. In D. Rumelhart et al., *Parallel Distributed Processing*, vol. 1. Cambridge, Mass. MIT Press.

Schwanenflugel, P., and Shoben, E. 1985. The influence of sentence constraint on the scope of facilitation for upcoming words. *Journal of Memory and Language* 24: 232–252.

Seidenberg, M. S. 1985a. The time course of phonological code activation in two writing systems. *Cognition* 19: 1–30.

Seidenberg, M. S. 1985b. The time course of information activation and utilization in visual word recognition. In D. Besner, T. Waller, and G. E. MacKinnon (eds.), *Reading Research: Advances in Theory and Practice*, volume 5. New York: Academic.

Seidenberg, M. S. 1987. Sublexical structures in visual word recognition: Access units or orthographic redundancy? In M. Coltheart (ed.), *Attention and Performance XII: Reading*. Hillsdale, N.J.: Erlbaum.

Seidenberg, M. S. In press, a. Reading complex words. In G. Carlson and M. K. Tanenhaus (eds.), *Language Comprehension and Linguistic Theory*. Amsterdam: Reidel.

Seidenberg, M. S. In press b. Cognitive neuropsychology and language: The state of the art. *Cognitive Neuropsychology*.

Seidenberg, M. S., and McClelland, J. L.1987. A distributed, developmental model of visual word recognition and naming. Manuscript.

Seidenberg, M. S., and Tanenhaus, M. K. 1979. Orthographic effects on rhyme monitoring. *Journal of Experimental Psychology: Human Learning and Memory* 5: 546–554.

Seidenberg, M. S., Waters, G. S., Barnes, M. A., and Tanenhaus, M. K. 1984a. When does irregular spelling or pronunciation influence word recognition? *Journal of Verbal Learning and Verbal Behavior* 23: 383–404.

Seidenberg, M. S., Waters, G. S., Sanders, M., and Langer, P. 1984b. Pre- and post-lexical loci of contextual effects on word recognition. *Memory and Cognition* 12: 315–328.

Seidenberg, M. S., Bruck, M., Fornarolo, G., and Backman, J. 1986. Word recognition skills of poor and disabled readers: Do they necessarily differ? *Applied Psycholinguistics* 6: 161–180.

Sejnowski, T., and Rosenberg, C. 1986. NETtalk: A parallel network that learns to read aloud. Technical Report JHU/EECS-86/01, Electrical Engineering and Computer Science Department, Johns Hopkins University.

Shallice, T., Warrington, E. K., and McCarthy, R. 1983. Reading without semantics. *Quarterly Journal of Experimental Psychology* 35A: 111–138.

Stanhope, N., and Parkin, A. J. 1987. Further explorations of the consistency effect in word and nonword pronunciation. *Memory and Cognition* 15: 169–179.

Stanovich, K. E. 1986. Matthew effects in reading: Some consequences of individual differences in the acquisition of literacy. *Reading Research Quarterly* 21: 360–407.

Tanenhaus, M. K., Flanigan, H., Seidenberg, M. S. 1980. Orthographic and phonological code activation in auditory and visual word recognition. *Memory and Cognition* 8: 513–520.

Taraban, R., and McClelland, J. L. 1987. Conspiracy effects in word recognition. *Journal of Memory and Language*, 26: 608–631.

Treiman, R., and Chafetz, J. 1987. Are there onset- and rime-like units in printed words? In M. Coltheart (ed.), *Attention and Performance XII: Reading*. London: Erlbaum.

Treisman, A., and Schmidt, H. 1982. Illusory conjunctions in the perception of objects. *Cognitive Psychology* 14: 107–141.

Tversky, A., and Kahneman, D. 1986. Extensional versus intuitive reasoning: The conjunction fallacy in probability judgment. *Psychological Review* 90: 293–315.

Van Orden, G. C. 1987. A ROWS is a ROSE: Spelling, sound, and reading. *Memory and Cognition* 15: 181–198.

Venezky, R. 1970. *The Structure of English Orthography*. The Hague: Mouton.

Waters, G. S., and Seidenberg, M. S. 1985. Spelling-sound effects in reading: Time course and decision criteria. *Memory and Cognition* 13: 557–572.

Waters, G. S., Seidenberg, M. S., and Bruck, M. 1984. Children's and adults' use of spelling-sound information in three reading tasks. *Memory and Cognition* 12: 293–305.

Wexler, K., and Culicover, P. 1980. *Formal Principles of Language Acquisition*. Cambridge, Mass.: MIT Press.

Wijk, A. 1966. *Rules of Pronunciation for the English Language*. Oxford University Press.

Chapter 3

Basic Issues in Lexical Processing

Kenneth I. Forster

It is now more than twenty years since Oldfield (1966) developed the concept of the mental lexicon, and only slightly less since the pioneering lexical-decision experiments of Rubenstein, Garfield, and Millikan (1970). In that time the lexical decision task has become one of the best-known dependent variables in all of experimental psychology, and the priming paradigm has become a standard technique in many different areas of enquiry. All the signs suggest that the study of lexical access has been productive and stimulating.

Yet there is some disquiet. Surely after all this time we should know all there is to know about the lexical decision and naming tasks. Surely after all the experiments on semantic priming we should know exactly why that effect occurs. But we are still unsure even about whether it has any direct effect on lexical access. As in countless other areas of experimental psychology, most of the progress was probably made during the first six or seven years, when discovering problems could still be counted as progress, and when it was exciting to contemplate the enormous complexity of the system and, at the same time, to be amazed that our techniques could uncover such subtle processes. That stage, of course, is now past. It is time to take stock, to consolidate. Consolidation requires reflection about the fundamental issues, about the areas of agreement and disagreement, and about where we should be headed. This chapter aims to make a small contribution toward that end. In no sense, however, should it be taken as a review of the field.

Distinguishing among the various models of lexical access is becoming increasingly difficult. (See Norris 1986 for the latest general survey.) As the range of phenomena has expanded, the models have become more complex and have split into families of overlapping models. One such family is the activation group. This consists of two main lines: the original logogen theory proposed by Morton (1970), and the more recent parallel-interactive-network model of McClelland and Rumelhart (1981) and its connectionist cousins. Each of these lines breaks down into a series of subfamilies. For example, Morton has offered several revisions of the basic theory (see, e.g., Morton 1979), and the various proponents of logogen theory have all individually offered their own modifications. Similarly, the network family breaks down into a series of models, depending on such considerations as whether one has local or distributed representations (see, e.g., Rumelhart et al. 1986 and McClelland et al. 1986). These theories are tied together by their shared commitment to a totally parallel detector-based system, and to the notion of spreading activation.

The other major contending family is lexical search theory, which consists of a fairly loose assortment of ideas taken from the early Rubenstein random-search model (Rubenstein et al. 1970), the category-search model (Landauer and Freedman 1968), the dictionary-search model (Loftus and Cole 1974), the verification model (Becker 1979), and the two-stage bin model (Forster 1976). What ties these theories together is a collective commitment to the analogy between lexical access and a computer-implemented information-retrieval system, in which variations in access time are interpreted in terms of how information is organized. A better term for this family might be "computational theories of lexical access," since these theories assume that recognition is carried out by a representational system that operates by explicitly manipulating and comparing symbols.[1]

Somewhere between these two major groups lies a third hybrid group, which has features of both. These theories use an activation approach with a detector-based system merely as a front end, which generates a set of likely candidates (i.e., no effort is made to ensure that the only detector to reach threshold is the correct one). These candidates are then submitted to a checking phase, which is designed to select the best candidate. The "activate and check" model proposed by Taft and Hambly (1986) is explicitly designed in this way, with the candidates checked by a frequency-ordered search. Similar models have been proposed by Becker (1979) and by Paap, Newsome, McDonald, and Schvaneveldt (1982). In similar vein, the checking model proposed by Norris (1986) leaves the final selection up to a post-activation checking process, and the latest version of the cohort model (Marslen-Wilson 1987) emphasizes the notions of multiple activation of candidates and a post-activation assessment procedure. A common feature of these models is that the initial selection of candidates is purely form-based, with contextual factors playing a role only at the secondary selection stage.

In light of the variety of models and the range of possible assumptions within each model, it is perhaps not surprising that many feel that it is no longer worth trying to disprove any one of them. There are just too many escape hatches, too many parameters that can be adjusted, or too few restrictions on the types of additional assumptions that can be made. This has led to some disenchantment with the whole enterprise of theory testing. However, I believe that this disenchantment is unwarranted— presumptuous even, since it presupposes that our theories are sufficiently well developed to be tested in the classical manner and that our methods of testing are sufficiently unambiguous. I believe we are still in the process of discovering how to construct useful chains of inference, what kinds of facts are important, and what kinds of theoretical issues are really central. More significant, we are still trying to develop some way to place constraints on the types of explanatory devices that we can or should appeal to.

We have by now (one hopes) abandoned the notion that our battery of reaction-time tasks provides us with straightforward measures of the time taken to perform certain elementary mental operations, and we recognize that even the simplest task may involve a highly complex orchestration of component processes. It might even be the case that this first phase of research in lexical access will have done very little more than establish that this is the case. Our current situation is that we have a proliferation of post-access and post-lexical processes to contend with, and the theoretical debate consists of pushing effects from the "access" column to the "post-access" column and back again. Because of the nature of things, once a variable is placed in the post-access column, it is very hard to get it out again. That is, it is quite easy to find evidence suggesting that an effect *may* be post-access, but very difficult to find evidence that it is definitely not. This leads to the danger that *every* effect will end up in the post-access column, and then we won't need a theory of lexical access at all (see Bradley and Forster 1987).

In short, theory testing has become very difficult and is probably going to become even more so. If history is anything to go by, this will mean that many experimenters will become discouraged and will turn to some new phenomenon for their inspiration. This is just as it should be. In the meantime, those of us remaining need to consider how best to proceed.

It is my belief that the right way to proceed may be to organize our thinking around explanatory devices rather than complete extant theories. For example, rather than asking whether X's 1985 version of logogen theory is better than Y's 1983 version, we should be asking whether the evidence favors a late-selection account of context effects, or whether it is sensible to try to use criterion bias to explain access effects as well as to explain decision effects. It seems highly unlikely (especially now) that any one theorist could possibly have got it all right from the outset, and hence there is no particular interest in showing that each of the extant theories has some crucial defect in one area or another. To be sure, it may be difficult to reach conclusions about explanatory devices in the absence of any details about the rest of the theory; however, the extant theories are not all that detailed anyway, so this may not be an insuperable obstacle.

In this spirit, the present chapter is organized around explanatory devices rather than around theories. Mostly I will do no more than draw attention to ways of thinking about these devices, and possibly to ways in which we might find out something about them. In the early sections, I discuss various issues in the mechanics of access, such as parallel versus serial computation, criterion bias, and the role of context; in the final section I review some new findings that appear to have strong implications for the most basic mechanisms of access.

1   Parallel and Serial Comparisons

What *really* distinguishes an activation model from a search model? Do these two approaches provide genuinely different perspectives, or are propositions expressed in the terms of one approach translatable into the terms of the other? The most obvious way in which the two approaches differ is in the type of comparison process employed. Activation models typically involve parallel comparisons, whereas a search model involves serial comparisons.

A search model of lexical access requires that the stimulus be compared with a set of likely candidates. Implicitly, we have made the assumption that making comparisons requires some special hardware device (e.g., a comparator), which is in short supply, and therefore the candidates need to be queued and fed into the comparator one at a time. Hence we get the notion of serial comparisons.

If there is no reason to use comparators sparingly, we can speed things up considerably by dividing the list of candidates into sublists and submitting each sublist to a separate comparator. This is a parallel system in that the comparators are working in parallel, but it is a serial system in that the candidates are submitted serially. Taking this to the absolute extreme, we could imagine having a separate comparator for every word in the lexicon, so that each sublist has only one member, and hence the serial component of the model vanishes to zero, making it a totally parallel system. This, of course, is what happens in activation theories (see, e.g., Morton 1970 and McClelland and Rumelhart 1981). Each word detector (or logogen, or word node, or its equivalent) is a comparator for a candidate list with one member. In receiving activation from letter detectors and comparing the level of activation with its own internal criterion, each detector essentially compares itself with the input stimulus. Put this way, the difference between a serial-scanning model and an activation model seems fairly minor. The difference is simply the amount of parallel matching that is permitted. However, we should not overlook the fact that the two approaches are based on fundamentally different views of computing architecture. The scanning approach is based on the concept of centralized computation, according to which peripherally stored data must be brought to some central symbol manipulator, whereas the activation approach is modeled on a distributed processing system, according to which symbol manipulators are widely distributed across the system.

Although distributed processing is obviously much faster, it does create control and decision problems. For example, how is it determined which comparator has the best match with the stimulus? One obvious method is to scan all comparators and compare the levels of activation in each, keeping track of which comparator has the highest level of activation. This solution has the effect of making this theory virtually indistinguishable from the serial-scanning model, the only difference being the number of comparisons that are carried out before the scanning process commences (none in the case of the scanning model; all possible comparisons in the case of the activation model). It also introduces the notion of some central executive that carries out the scan, which is just what the parallel-activation scheme was designed to eliminate.

In Morton's logogen model, the solution to this problem was provided by the threshold mechanism. The idea was that each logogen is effectively given the job of deciding whether it is a sufficiently good match to the stimulus to be the *best* match. If the level of activation in one logogen reaches some specified threshold level, then that logogen declares itself the winner and suppresses the activation in all other logogens. This solution would work perfectly well if no logogen could reach the discharge state unless it matched the stimulus perfectly. However, in Morton's model, variations in access time are explained in terms of variations in threshold settings, so it is assumed that thresholds can be set below the level of a perfect match. This obviously creates problems for the correct discrimination of very similar words, and it places enormous weight on which logogen reaches threshold first.

One way to get around this problem is to have each detector not only compare itself with the stimulus but also compare its level of activation with the level of activation in other detectors. This is the approach adopted in network models (McClelland and Rumelhart 1981), where each word detector has inhibitory connections with all other word detectors, so that the most strongly activated detector will eventually suppress activity in all the rest. Once only one detector remains active, access has occurred.

From this discussion, it appears that the crucial difference between activation models and search models has more to do with the type of control system involved in selecting the best solution than with the issue of parallel processing. That is, a search model that can conduct multiple searches in parallel does not appear to take on any of the characteristics of an activation system, but remains essentially a search system. On the other hand, an activation system stripped of its automatic, detector-based control mechanism (either a threshold mechanism or reciprocal inhibition between detectors) starts to look very much like a search system.

From this it follows that it may be more profitable to concentrate our attention on the adequacy of the decision and control mechanisms involved in selecting the best candidate. For the threshold mechanism, it appears that problems arise once the attempt is made to use variations in threshold settings to explain frequency effects (Forster 1976). So, if we take two words that are "neighbors" (differing by one letter) but which differ in frequency (such as BRIGHT and BLIGHT), we must postulate that the higher-frequency word has a lower threshold in order to explain why it is accessed faster. But this means that it is difficult to arrange matters so that the lower-frequency member can be perceived. Whenever BLIGHT is presented, the detector for BRIGHT will also be strongly activated, although not as strongly as the detector for BLIGHT. However, because BRIGHT has a lower threshold, there is a chance that BRIGHT will reach threshold first and suppress activation in the BLIGHT detector.

The situation appears to be much the same for a network model (McClelland and Rumelhart 1981), despite differences in the fundamental assumptions. To explain the frequency effect, we need to assume that the detectors for high-frequency words are more strongly activated than the detectors for low-frequency words, so that, for example, the "initial B" letter detector is connected more strongly to the BRIGHT detector than to the BLIGHT detector. This means that when BLIGHT is the stimulus, the activation level in the BRIGHT detector may well rise more rapidly than that in the BLIGHT detector. The problem now is to prevent the initially more strongly activated BRIGHT detector from driving the activation level in BLIGHT down before the latter has a chance to overtake.

To avoid these problems, we would have to propose a weighting system that guaranteed that the influence of frequency on activation levels could never be enough to compensate for a missing letter. That is, even though the BRIGHT detector gets stronger activation than the BLIGHT detector from five of the six letters in the stimulus, the action of the remaining letter (L) is enough to outweight this difference and to ensure that the BLIGHT detector never falls behind. Of course, we would have to find a set of weights that not only coped with this example, but would also cope with *any* example, so that the contribution of a single letter would always outweigh any effect of frequency—no matter how great the difference in frequency, and no matter how many letters there were in common between the competing words. This latter state of affairs seems particularly difficult to arrange if we assume a linear summation of activation.[2]

These arguments suggest that there are grounds for being suspicious of the mechanisms offered by activation models as ways of deciding between strongly competing alternatives. Both the "first past the post" principle adopted by Morton and the "survival of the fittest" principle adopted by McClelland and Rumelhart run into difficulties when they try to take frequency effects into account. The reason is that they treat the contribution of frequency to the activation process in such a way that its effects become confused with those of the stimulus. (The same can be said for the effects of context.)

Although these cases create difficulties for the pure activation model, one might ask whether a frequency-ordered search model fares any better. Frequency ordering of the candidates means that BRIGHT will be considered as a possible analysis before BLIGHT, which will create the possibility that the stimulus BLIGHT will be misinterpreted. We could avoid this pitfall by insisting on a perfect match before the search stops, but then we could not explain why nonwords that are neighbors of words (e.g., CLIGHT) take longer to reject than nonwords that are not neighbors of words. Obviously, to explain this effect we must postulate that the similarity of CLIGHT to BLIGHT is sufficiently great to fulfill an initial criterion for a match, which means that the search process is temporarily halted or disturbed in some way while this possible interpretation is being checked more fully. So the same thing must happen when the stimulus BLIGHT is compared with the entry for BRIGHT. Their similarity must also be sufficient to halt the search temporarily, only to have the search resume after a more detailed check of the two orthographic patterns, thus making it possible to eventually reach the BLIGHT entry. This predicts that for any pair of orthographic neighbors, recognition of the lower-frequency member will be slowed by the presence of its higher-frequency competitor, whereas recognition of the higher-frequency member will be quite unaffected. (See Forster and Bednall 1976 for evidence supporting this type of argument.)

However, this explanation runs into problems when it is considered that the presence of an orthographic competitor has no effect on lexical decision times for *words*, although it does have an effect for nonwords (Coltheart, Davelaar, Jonasson, and Besner 1977). The explanation offered by Coltheart et al. for this phenomenon was that whenever any logogen is strongly activated, the system extends the deadline for making a "No" decision. Thus, a nonword that resembled other words would take longer to reject, since the system would wait longer before deciding that no logogen was going to fire. For words that resembled other words, however, the "first past the post" principle would mean that a competing neighbor could not affect the time to reach threshold (unless, of course, the neighbor got there first).

But this explanation can readily be adapted to suit the search model as well. Assume that, while searching for a perfect match, the system notes any close matches *en passant*. If a perfect match is eventually found, these close matches can be ignored; however, if no perfect match is found, the close matches need to be evaluated before a "No" decision is made. Hence, the existence of close matches will prolong the decision time for nonwords but will have no effect on words.

Note that in both the activation approach and the scanning approach I am now suggesting essentially the same thing: that an initial stage of processing prepares a list of close matches that need to be evaluated more carefully. It seems, then, that there might be substantial common ground for the activation model and the search model. This is not to say that there is no difference between the models. The activation model still uses an activation system to generate a list of candidates, whereas the search model might use a quite different procedure, such as the "marking" process originally proposed by Rubenstein et al. (1970). I will return to this issue in the final section.

2   Parallel Search Models

I have suggested the possibility that a serial search model need not be restricted to conducting only one search at a time. Is there any benefit in thinking of multiple searches being conducted simultaneously, and how would that be done? My own preference is to think of the lexical processor as having a limited set of comparators, each constantly scanning the members of its sublist, much like a raster scan in a video display (hence the occasional substitution of the term "scan" for "search"). When a lexical input is specified, each comparator immediately begins comparing that input with the members of its sublist, which are still arranged in order of frequency. This is like the original two-stage bin model (Forster 1976), with a bin corresponding to a sublist. However, in this new conception, each bin has its own comparator, and all bins are searched simultaneously. The parallel nature of the system has two consequences. First, it helps to minimize the impact of the "hundred-step rule" (Feldman and Ballard 1982) by minimizing the number of serial steps in the computation. Second, it eliminates the need to calculate which comparator is the best one to try first.

The average bin must be large enough to generate a noticeable frequency effect. In the extreme case of a bin size of 1 (i.e., a totally parallel system), no frequency effect at all would be generated, and some other explanation of the frequency effect would have to be provided. But even a bin size of 2 would create the possibility of a frequency effect, although not a con-tinuously graded effect for each individual subject.

There is one further advantage that might be considered. The original bin model had a hash-coding function that decided which bin a particular orthographic sequence would belong to, if it was a word. This notion runs into problems when we consider nonword interference effects in lexical-decision experiments. For example, suppose we find that XECAUSE takes longer to reject as a word than a suitable control nonword. This means that the entry for BECAUSE must have been encountered, i.e., that the entry for BECAUSE was in the bin that was searched when the subject was given the stimulus XECAUSE. Thus, we would have to say that the hash-code function assigns the same bin number to both XECAUSE and BECAUSE. This suggests that the initial B is irrelevant to the output of the hash code.

Thus, the next thing to do is consider stimuli such as BXCAUSE (to see whether the second letter is important), and then BEXAUSE, BECXUSE, BECAXSE, BECAUXE, and BECAUSX. According to evidence produced in our laboratory many year ago (Amey 1973), we should find exactly the same amount of interference in every case, which leads to the awful con-clusion that *none* of the letters is relevant to the hash-code function.

One way out of this dilemma is to assume that if the target is not located in the first bin, all the other bins are searched in succession until it is established that no bin contains the target. This means that the entry for BECAUSE will eventually be encountered; hence, interference will be generated no matter which bin was searched first. This succeeds in accounting for the interference results, but it creates more problems than it solves. For one thing, we would need to explain why the system so mistrusts the hash-code output. (Why have one if you don't take any notice of it?) For another, it predicts that the average difference between decision times for words and nonwords should be *much* greater than the time to search a single bin. But this is certainly not the case. The latency difference between words and nonwords is usually somewhere around 80 msec, as is our best estimate of the time taken to search a bin (namely, the largest possible frequency effect).

So this account of the insensitivity of interference effects to the position of the changed letter is not particularly satisfying. However, these problems disappear completely if we assume a parallel search model. If there is no hash code, and all bins are searched simultaneously, then the entry for BECAUSE will always be encountered, no matter what stimulus is presented. Further, it becomes clear why the time taken to search a bin was comparable to the word-nonword latency difference, since the time taken to search the whole lexicon is the same as the time taken to search one bin.

To an activation theorist, this kind of proposal might be utterly exasperating. If one is prepared to concede the possibility of parallel comparisons, surely there is no reason not to embrace a fully parallel system with a separate comparator for each lexical entry. What possible reason could one have for postulating a serial component? The answer, I believe, is that a serial component provides the best chance of explaining the frequency effect.

3 Criterion Bias, Context, and Frequency

Whereas search theories attempt to explain variation in access times in terms of the way in which lexical information is organized and the way in which the search is conducted, criterion bias is the fundamental explanatory device for logogen-inspired explanations of most access effects. For example, the frequency effect is attributed either to the lower thresholds for high-frequency logogens or to the higher resting levels of activation. Either way, the effect is the same; less information must be extracted from the stimulus in order for activation to reach threshold level. The same assumption is made for context effects; logogens of words related to the context either have their thresholds lowered or have their activation levels raised.

Is this commitment to a threshold notion in any way central to the activation approach in general, or to the logogen theory in particular? It appears not. There is no reason why this type of explanation should be restricted to word-detector models. For example, a cascade version of a search model could propose that an initial search is begun after only some of the letters have been identified, and that subsequent searches are initiated as further letters become available. To be effective, this requires that the criterion for a match between the stimulus and the entry must be set below a perfect match in at least some cases; otherwise nothing could be accessed on the first search. If the number of matching letters required for recognition is specified separately for each word, then we could propose that high-frequency words have lower criteria than low-frequency words. Thus, a low-frequency word might only be recognized during the search initiated after all letters had been identified, whereas a high-frequency word might be recognized during an earlier search.

But in fact, advocates of search models generally avoid making such an assumption; they prefer to argue that variations in access time reflect characteristics of the search process itself. Just why a search theory should reject the criterion-bias position, which a logogen theory adopts auto-matically, is not altogether clear, since there seems to be nothing preventing either theory from adopting either position. Nor is it the case that logogen theory is committed in any way to criterion bias. The concept of a logogen allows for an interpretation of frequency effects in which the strength of the association between a letter detector and a word detector varies directly with the frequency of the word (the position adopted in connectionist models). In view of this situation, it is not really appropriate to treat evidence in support of criterion bias as if it automatically favored the logogen position (and conversely). It makes more sense to try to approach criterion bias as a separate issue.

The motivating idea behind the criterion-bias proposal appears to be that letter identification is such a time-consuming and drawn-out process that significant gains in efficiency can be obtained if the word-recognition system attempts to "guess" what the word might be as early as possible. Where guesswork is concerned, a frequency bias or a contextual bias is very sensible. But is perception a matter of guesswork? Where degraded inputs are concerned, that seems very plausible. For example, when dealing with handwritten input in which some of the letters are quite indecipherable, the word-recognition system is obviously forced to guess (or else merely pro-vide a list of solutions compatible with the input). When all letters are clearly available, however, this is not so clear—especially if we assume that the letters are processed in parallel, because then (for short words, at least) all letters are available virtually simultaneously.

It could even be suggested that an access system using logogens would work just as well (or even better) without a criterion bias toward high-frequency words. Whether it works better or not depends on the time saved by not having to process the input fully, the cost of making errors, and the frequency of such errors. For example, suppose that the logogen threshold for the very-high-frequency word *have* is set low enough so that it fires even when only three of the letters are present in the stimulus—i.e., so that -AVE, H-VE, HA-E, or HAV- will be sufficient to reach threshold. This implies that whenever any one of the 14 neighbors of *have* occurs, it will be misread as *have*. This might not matter so much for words such as *nave* or *hove*, since these occur so infrequently that the occasional error produced could be overlooked. But it will matter for more common words, such as *gave*, *wave*, and *save*.

One might expect that under these circumstances, high-frequency words would eventually acquire quite distinctive spellings, so that the costs of misidentification could be minimized. That is, overlap in spelling should be confined to the low end of the frequency spectrum. However, as Landauer and Streeter (1973) showed, precisely the reverse is the case, since high-frequency words have more neighbors than low-frequency words. This suggests that spelling patterns have evolved with scant regard for a recognition system with a criterion bias in favor of high-frequency words.

A similar argument against a criterion-bias explanation of frequency effects is provided by the results of our own masked priming experiments (Forster and Davis 1984). A typical trial in this paradigm presents three stimuli in quick succession: a forward mask, a priming stimulus in lower-case letters, and a target item in upper-case letters. The subject's task is lexical decision on the target word. The forward mask and the target are both presented for 500 msec; the prime is presented for only 60 msec. Under these conditions, the prime is virtually invisible for the vast majority of subjects.

When the prime and the target were the same four-letter word, but presented in different format (e.g., *bear*-BEAR), Forster and Davis found that lexical decisions on the target were more rapid than when a completely different word was used as the prime (e.g., *mast*-BEAR). However, this facilitation disappeared entirely once *any* letter was changed (e.g., *wear*-BEAR). Since there was no priming effect for nonword targets, it seems that lexical mediation must be involved—that priming occurs because the prime activates the lexical representation of the target. But if this is the case, then it follows that the detector for words such as *bear* can be activated only by an intact stimulus, since priming stimuli such as *wear*, *boar*, and *bead* have no priming effect on recognition of BEAR. This might be understandable for very-low-frequency words, since they would have very high thresholds, but it would not make sense for high-frequency words. However, the results showed no priming for either high- or low-frequency words once the prime differed from the target by one letter. To explain this result, we would have to propose that the criterion level for four-letter words is set so high that all letters must be identified before access can occur. But this means that we would not expect any frequency effects for such words, since there is no room for criterion bias to operate. Not surprisingly, we obtained clear frequency effects for these words (Forster and Davis 1984); thus, some other explanation of the frequency effect must be found.

However, as Norris (1984) observes, the above argument presupposes that information about words comes in letter-sized quanta, so that the first setting below 4/4 matching letters would have to be 3/4 letters. One might argue instead that the threshold is never set so low that activation in a logogen can reach threshold level when one entire letter in the stimulus has not been processed.[3] That is, for high-frequency four-letter words, the criterion may be set somewhere between a value of 75 percent of features in common (3/4 matching letters) and a value of 100 percent (all letters matching). This means that at least some of the features of each letter must be preserved before threshold is reached.

As Norris observes, this will permit virtually error-free performance, except in the rare cases where the nonmatching letters are nevertheless very similar. This assumption works quite well, except that we now have no particular reason to propose a frequency bias. That is, if it is possible to increase the speed of identification of high-frequency words without producing errors by lowering the threshold slightly, then why not do the same for low-frequency words? With an inherently noisy signal in which some of the letters cannot be identified, it makes sense to be biased in favor of high-frequency words, since this will reduce the overall probability of an error. But it the signal is clear and the probability of error is very low, it makes less sense to have a frequency bias.

A further weakness of this approach is that the powerful frequency effect is now assumed to reflect the savings incurred by not having to extract the last few features of the last letter to be identified. What is it about these features that makes them so expensive to extract? Clearly, this explanation is not particularly compelling without a convincing answer to this question.

Signal-detection theory would seem to be the obvious way to test for criterion-bias effects; however, as Norris (1986) observes, this paradigm can yield rather misleading results when applied to the lexical decision task. Norris shows that an effect of context on criterion bias may appear either as a change in β or as a change in d', depending on the difficulty of the word-nonword discrimination. To detect beta effects, we need to estimate the effect of context on false positives, and to do this we need to compare error rates on nonwords in a "related" condition (e.g., *doctor*-WURSE) and an "unrelated" condition (e.g., *table*-WURSE). However, this procedure is effective only if WURSE is perceived by the subjects to be highly similar to NURSE. If we adopt the suggestion (made above) that the criterion is never lowered enough to make up for a missing letter, then the extent to which WURSE activates the NURSE logogen might not be great enough for the context word *doctor* to induce a false positive response. Even worse is the case where WURSE happens to resemble some totally unrelated word (e.g., PURSE) more closely than it resembles the target (NURSE). In this case, the difference between the related and unrelated conditions disappears altogether, and hence one could hardly expect to detect any evidence for a criterion shift.

A better way to test for criterion-bias effects is to design a task that forces subjects to delay their response until nearly all the stimulus information has been processed. This should have the effect of radically reducing, if not eliminating, any effect that depends on criterion bias. Antos (1979), O'Connor and Forster (1981), and Schvaneveldt and McDonald (1981) have all produced such conditions by using nonwords that closely resemble words, such as FROIT, AMINAL, MOHTER, and ELEPHAHT. The idea is that if criterion bias is involved in semantic priming, then items such as *lion*-TIGAR will show higher error rates than items such as *table*-TIGAR. If subjects adjust their thresholds upward to avoid making such errors, then we would expect no semantic priming effect (or at least a reduced effect) for correctly spelled word pairs, such as *lion*-TIGER. In both the Antos experiment and the Schvaneveldt-McDonald experiment, strong semantic priming effects for correctly spelled words were observed, even though the error rates for nonwords were low and were not affected by context.

Norris (1986) rejects this evidence against criterion bias, appealing again to the argument based on letter-sized quanta. He argues that a "small" difference of one letter might in fact lead to a *large* difference in the number of extracted features. The implication here is that TIGAR is not sufficiently similar to TIGER to lead to increased error rates in the related context condition. However, this argument is less appropriate in the case of the O'Connor-Forster study, since their nonwords evidently *were* sufficiently similar to words to produce such errors. These nonwords were constructed by transposing adjacent letters (e.g., DOTCOR, ENVLEOPE) rather than changing a letter, and this guarantees fairly high similarity to a word (Chambers 1979). In the first O'Connor-Forster experiment, it was shown that in a conventional lexical decision task, misspelled high-frequency words (such as MOHTER) produced higher error rates than misspelled low-frequency words (such as BOHTER), which is exactly what a criterion-bias argument would predict. In a second experiment, O'Connor and Forster showed that primed nonwords (such as *nurse*-DOTCOR) produced more errors than unprimed nonwords (such as *table*-DOTCOR), again in agreement with criterion-bias predictions. In both of these experiments, normal frequency effects and semantic priming effects were observed. But what if subjects were trained *not* to make more errors on high-frequency misspelled words, or on primed nonwords? In this case, criterion-bias models would lead us to expect the frequency effect and the semantic priming effect to disappear altogether, or at the very least to be drastically reduced. The task used by O'Connor and Forster for this purpose was to detect whether an item was a misspelled word. This focuses attention on the misspelling. In responding Yes to ENVLEOPE, a subject indicates awareness that this closely resembles a real word but is not identical to it. For all other items (both correctly spelled words and "normal" nonwords such as NORDLE), No is the correct response.

It seems clear that to correctly classify these items requires very precise information about the constituent letters and their positions. Nevertheless, strong frequency effects and semantic priming effects were obtained. Moreover, the strengths of these effects appeared to be quite normal. One cannot counter this evidence by arguing that these nonwords produced only weak activation in the logogens of the words they resembled, since the evidence from O'Connor and Forster's first two experiments (see also Chambers 1979) shows that this was not the case.

One way of interpreting these results without abandoning the criterion-bias assumption was first suggested to me by Sally Andrews. (A similar proposal is also made in Norris 1986.) The trick is to postulate a post-discharge orthographic checking mechanism. That is, after a logogen with a normal criterion bias discharges, some additional system checks that this was the correct logogen by comparing the stimulus with the orthographic specification appropriate for that logogen. In this way, the aims of the misspelling-detection task can be subverted, since the post-discharge check allows subjects to make a misspelling decision before all the orthographic information has been processed. The logogens are allowed to discharge whenever the normal threshold is reached (before all the features have been processed), and then the decision whether to respond Yes or No can be made by carrying out a post-discharge check of the spelling—if the check reveals a mismatch, the correct response is Yes (i.e., it must be a misspelled word); otherwise the correct response must be No. If no logogen has fired by the time some deadline is reached, the correct response is No.

But there is an obvious weakness in this proposal. In order to find out whether there is a perfect match between the stimulus and the logogen, we would need to have all the features of the stimulus available. Thus, there is no point in attempting to perform such a check immediately after the discharge of a logogen if that logogen fired before all the features had been processed. Once again, it would be necessary to wait until a sufficient proportion of the features had been processed before carrying out the check, and this should eliminate any effects of criterion bias. Nor can the problem be avoided by making a comparison with some relatively low-level input representation, as in Becker's (1979) verification model, since the basic results of the misspelling-detection task are not altered by the use of an unpredictable mixed-case input format (O'Connor and Forster 1981).

However, there is one extra assumption that could save the situation. Suppose that the checking process takes so long to initiate that, by the time the system is ready to carry out the check, all the stimulus information happens to be available. The first thing to note about this explanation is that we are no longer dealing with a pure activation model; instead we have a hybrid activate-and-check model.[4] Furthermore, the explanation depends crucially on the accidental fact that the time required to initiate the post-discharge check happens to be long enough to allow all the information from the stimulus to be extracted before the check begins. While this is certainly a logical possibility, it seems contrived. The original purpose of introducing criterion bias was to speed up the recognition process, yet the postulated checking operation is so slow that we may as well have waited until the stimulus was fully analyzed. Indeed, to produce a frequency effect with this system, the check for a low-frequency word must be delayed until well *after* this point.

So, at the very least, it appears that the arguments in favor of criterion bias could not possibly be described as strong. However, this conclusion applies only to the case of a clearly presented stimulus. As Schvaneveldt and McDonald (1981) have shown, there *is* strong evidence for criterion bias with tachistoscopic exposure. With very brief displays, not all letters may be identified; hence, the identification system is forced to extrapolate, in which case a frequency bias or a contextual bias seems a very sensible strategy. However, it seems that any overt indication of such a strategy disappears with displays of longer duration.

4   Context, Perception, and Inference

A hallmark of the connectionist brand of activation theories (McClelland et al. 1986) has been an unbridled devotion to interactive top-down principles. A mild interactionist might argue that the information supplied by context can assist in the analysis of some input representations, but a connectionist theorist goes further and suggests that the input representation *itself* is modified by context.

Claiming that context has such an effect presupposes a clear distinction between perception and inference. For example, consider the case in which the stimulus is actually X, but the context is heavily biased toward Y, and the subject reports hearing Y. At one extreme, the central system may say: "I know that I *heard* X; but, given the context, I infer that Y was actually spoken, or was at least intended." I imagine nobody would want to claim this state of affairs as evidence for an interactive system, or to argue that this inference about the intended message causes top-down feedback of activation to the Y detector. At the other extreme, the central processor is firmly convinced that it heard Y, since this is what the lexical processor reported, and X was never even considered as a possible interpretation. This is more like a true effect of context on perception.

Somewhere between those extremes lies the boundary between peception and inference. We must survey this boundary before we can make any progress on the question of context effects. In fact, at the moment, the location of this boundary *is* the question. Hence, it is hard to see how theories that either blur the distinction or overlook it entirely can be regarded as making helpful contributions. For example, in discussing the assumption of top-down feedback in a network model, McClelland and Elman (1986, p. 75) make the following remark: "These mechanisms are incredibly simple; yet they appear to buy quite a lot which often gets pushed into unspecified 'decision' and 'postperceptual guessing' processes (e.g., Forster, 1976)." This remark appears to treat "decision" processes as an unnecessary complication—as if a theory that explains context effects without postulating decision processes should be preferred because it is simpler. It certainly *would* be simpler to treat context effects as top-down effects, but it may also be quite wrong. Nobody *wants* to have decision processes as part of their theory—indeed, they may be totally without interest for a theory of the language processor. But while it remains a possibility that such processes may be involved, it seems pointless to proceed as if they did not exist and could safely be treated as excess theoretical baggage.

To be fair, it should be said that McClelland and Elman are really just trying to see how far they can get with what they take to be a very restricted set of assumptions—an understandable reaction to the mush of cognitive psychology in the past twenty years, where theories have become relatively unconstrained. The hope is that we will eventually discover enough pieces of the puzzle to place some constraint on the kinds of theoretical moves that can be made, but for the moment we seem to be well short of the mark.

To return to the main point: Suppose one is presented with the following word fragment, and asked what word it is.

-epre-se-

In the absence of context, it might be difficult to discover what word this corresponds to. But if one is provided with context, the task is much easier. For example:

After his wife died, John became very -epre-se-.

How should this fact be interpreted? We might say that the presented letters activated the detector for DEPRESSED, but not sufficiently strongly to reach threshold or to distinguish the state of this detector from the state of other detectors. But when the context is supplied, the DEPRESSED detector receives further activation (along with the detectors for WITH-DRAWN, etc.), so that the combination of inputs is sufficient to lift the DEPRESSED detector out of the pack.

But should we go further and say that one literally *perceives* the word DEPRESSED? Presumably not, because one could tell whether one saw an incomplete or a complete word in the first place. But what if we presented the fragment very briefly under masking conditions? What if we asked subjects whether they saw an initial d- or not, and some subjects said they did? Wouldn't that start to look like a perceptual effect? If tempted to agree, one should ask why the effect occurs only when the stimulus is masked. The answer might be that top-down feedback can exert a moderating influence on activation patterns only at the lower level. In the case of a clear stimulus, the visual signal is so strong that the top-down feedback is not strong enough to override it (see McClelland 1987 for such an argument). But when the signal is masked, the visual evidence is much weaker. This is certainly a possible interpretation, but by no means the only one. For example, masking may simply make the subject more uncertain about what was actually seen and what was inferred.

Of course, there is a genuinely interesting phenomenon involved here. Somehow the lexical processor is able to combine the information from word fragments and the context, and to select the word that is consistent with both. This system enables us to do crossword puzzles, and to rapidly do things such as name a fruit that begins with P. Now comes the important question: Is this type of processing restricted to those cases of word recognition where the orthographic properties of the target word have been underspecified, or is it crucially involved in all cases?

The interactionist position—that there is only one system—is the simplest. In the most recent defense of this position, McClelland (1987) argues that the evidence apparently favoring a noninteractive view is largely attributable to the relative strengths of the activation from bottom-up and top-down sources. If the bottom-up activation is very strong, then context effects will be weak, but they will still be present.

My own inclination is to argue that two quite different systems may be involved. I would say that the lexical-access module can be used in a "bottom-up" mode or in a "crossword" mode. If the input is too fragmentary for the "bottom-up" mode, then the "crossword" mode must be used as a backup procedure. The strongest version of this dual-mode theory might propose that the lexical-access module cannot be used in both modes simultaneously; a weaker form might relax this constraint and allow for parallel activity in both modes.

Why have two modes? Because the crossword mode would be very inefficient in the absence of a restrictive context. On the other hand, the input may be so ill formed that bottom-up processing is pointless. Hence we need two modes. With speech inputs, it may be much more likely that the crossword mode will prove to be the superior system, since the speech signal is usually fairly noisy and since the temporal distribution of speech dictates that the bottom-up mode must wait until it has a sufficiently large chunk of the input, whereas the crossword mode is free to begin operations when only fragment of the input is available. But with print the entire stimulus is available instantaneously, so there is never a situation in which only a fragment is available (unless some of the letters are missing, ill formed, or degraded). Thus it seems a very real possibility that speech and print will give quite different answers to the question of context effects (see Bradley and Forster 1987).

Recent evidence from Taft (1986) is particularly suggestive here. Previous work with visual inputs has shown that lexical-decision times are slower for letter strings that are not words themselves but which constitute the BOSS (roughly, the initial syllable) of a real word. Thus BLEM (coming from BLEMISH) takes longer to reject than BLEN (coming from BLEND), which is indistinguishable from BLEK (coming from nothing). This is because BLEM is the BOSS of BLEMISH, but BLEN is merely the first four letters of BLEND. However, if the same stimuli are presented acoustically, BLEM and BLEN lead to the same amount of interference relative to BLEK. In other words, the acoustic system generates the possibility of BLEND when given the stimulus BLEN, but the visual system does not.

So the proposal is this: Instead of arguing about whether context effects are perceptual, we should try to look for evidence indicating whether there are two different access modes. To produce relevant evidence, we need to be able to determine whether the bottom-up mode or the crossword mode was influenced by context. This would involve finding an experimental technique that allows this distinction to be made. It might be said that the problem with existing techniques is that the external index of lexical processing is too remote. That is, too many processes intervene between the events that are of interest and the event that controls the subject's response.

I have recently begun work with an alternative technique that may provide useful additional information. The technique depends on the short-term repetition effect discussed above and in Forster and Davis 1984. This effect occurs when the same entry is accessed twice within a short period of time. The short-term effect differs from the long-term repetition effect (Scarborough, Cortese, and Scarborough 1977) in several ways. It is independent of word frequency, and it does not require any special response to be made to the priming stimulus. For our present purposes, the most important feature is that the subject does not need to be consciously aware of the prime in order to show a strong priming effect.

In Forster and Davis 1984 it was proposed that when an entry is accessed, the entry is left in an "open" state for a brief period of time. Open entries are not located any faster (hence the frequency effect remains constant); once they have been located, however, information can be extracted from them faster. This priming phenomenon provides a way of "labeling" which entries were actually accessed, regardless of whether the subject is able to report the words that were presented. Thus it might be proposed that only the entries actually accessed by the bottom-up mode would be labeled.

The first experiment using this technique contrasted plausible and implausible sentences presented under RSVP conditions (60 msec per word). After the last word of the sentence, there was a 300-msec pause; then a target

Table 1
Mean lexical decision times for a target item presented at the conclusion of a rapidly presented sentence.

Condition	Sentence	Target	RT
Plausible			
Repeated	Jim hit his horse with a whip and shouted	WHIP	445
Control	Jim hit his horse with a stick and shouted	WHIP	471
Priming			26
Implausible			
Repeated	Jim sold his drink with a whip and shouted	WHIP	449
Control	Jim sold his drink with a stick and shouted	WHIP	471
Priming			22

item was presented for lexical decision. Table 1 illustrates the design of the experiment and gives the results for the lexical decisions on the target word.

With a total of 60 items and 40 subjects, the priming effect was highly significant: $minF'$ $(1, 87) = 12.72$, $p < 0.001$. However, there was no hint of any interaction between plausibility and priming.

An important feature of the design that should be noted is that in the plausible condition the probe word WHIP was related to the topic of the preceding sentence in both the repeated and the control cases. This is important because in other experiments we have been able to show that "topic" priming occurs. For example, the decision time for WHIP would have been substantially slower than the above control condition if the preceding sentence had been topic-neutral with respect to whips—e.g., *Jim greeted his wife with a kiss and grinned.*

This experiment suggests that the probability of accessing the lexical entry for WHIP is unaffected by the context manipulation. Of course, the probability of *reporting* this word is strongly affected by context, as has been shown repeatedly in other experiments using the RSVP technique with similar types of sentences (e.g., Forster 1974). To check that this is also true in the current situation, an additional group of subjects were presented with exactly the same displays, but were asked to decide whether the target item at the end of the sentence had actually occurred during the sentence. For the plausible contexts, 81 percent of the targets were correctly classified as having been in the sentence; for implausible contexts, 63 percent. Thus it appears that the labeling technique has some promise. Even though information about the presence of a word may be lost by the time the language processor delivers its output to the central processor, the repetition label established during the original processing of the sentence is preserved intact.

But to be effective, the repetition label must be associated with only one kind of processing. If it turns out that the crossword mode also produces the same kind of label, we are no better off. What we need is clear evidence that no label is produced when the presence of a word has to be inferred from context rather than directly perceived. Our initial effort in this direction has not been completely successful. Using the same procedure as in the experiment described above, we measured decision time for the target WHIP after the following sentences:

Jim hit his horse with a whib and shouted.

Jim hit his horse with a flen and shouted.

If labeling is a product of bottom-up processing exclusively, then one might expect no difference in decision times, assuming that the bottom-up processor does not open an entry unless the stimulus matches it perfectly. However, if priming occurs, the interpretation is ambiguous. We can infer either that the entries for closely matching words *are* opened, or that a repetition label will be produced no matter whether the entry is initially accessed by the bottom-up mode or by the crossword mode. The first experiment using this design gave encouraging results, since it showed no repetition priming at all. Unfortunately, what we took to be a straightforward replication with different items showed clear priming effects. How these discrepant results are to be reconciled is not clear at present.

As we shall see in the final section of this chapter, there is strong evidence for the proposal that the bottom-up processor must open entries that match the stimulus only approximately. Thus, in a sense, it does not matter how this issue is resolved. What we need to do instead is study cases where the bottom-up processor could not possibly open the entry, as in the following example, where a highly predictable word is simply omitted:

I was told to brush my every day by the dentist. TEETH

If clear priming effects are also obtained in this case, then we have a clear indication that a repetition label is established by inferential processes as well as by perceptual processes, and we will need to look elsewhere for a suitable diagnostic tool. However, for present purposes, the point still stands that a technique such as repetition labeling at least has the potential to reveal an important distinction, and serves as an illustration of the kinds of techniques that must be developed before any further progress can be made.

5   Cascades and the Output of the Lexical Processor

In the original discussion of cascade processes, McClelland (1979) challenges the notion that the lexical processor provides a single, discrete output for each input item, as would typically be assumed in stage theories. Instead, he proposes that the lexical processor provides a continuous and changing output in the form of a distribution of probabilities across the set of lexical items. This final section will discuss a new line of evidence that leads one to suspect that this idea may be correct.

The evidence concerns the phenomenon of *form priming*. This type of priming occurs when one stimulus facilitates recognition of the other by virtue of similarity of orthographic form. Such an effect would be expected in an activation model, since activation is assumed to be distributed from each letter detector to the detectors of all words containing that letter. So an inescapable consequence of presenting a word is that activation is induced in all its neighbors. Thus the stimulus WAVE must excite the detectors for WADE, WAGE, HAVE, etc. to some degree. Yet, apart from isolated reports (e.g., Hillinger 1980; Evett and Humphreys 1981), the general indication is that evidence for such cross-activation effects is not readily obtained (Bradley, Savage, and Yelland 1983; Colombo 1986).

The early evidence obtained from the masked-priming paradigm discussed above also appeared to support this conclusion. Forster and Davis (1984) found no priming effect unless the prime and the target had exactly the same sequence of letters. That is, a masked presentation of *file* just before a clear presentation of the target TILE had no impact on lexical-decision times for the target. However, prompted by the work of Evett and Humphreys (1981), who obtained clear form priming in a slightly different paradigm, Forster, Davis, Schoknecht, and Carter (1987) went on to consider the matter more closely. For four-letter targets, they obtained exactly the same results as Forster and Davis (1984): no priming unless the prime and target were identical. However, for eight-letter targets strong form-priming effects were obtained. Thus, although the pair *bamp*-CAMP shows no priming, the pair *bontrast*-CONTRAST does. The difference between these cases appears to be a function of neighborhood density rather than one of length *per se*. (A word belongs in a high-density neighborhood if it has many neighbors in the sense of Coltheart et al. 1977.) Long words have very few neighbors, whereas short words usually have many. We (Forster et al. 1987) confirmed this hypothesis by showing that masked form-priming effects could be demonstrated for short targets if both the prime and the target were drawn from low-density neighborhoods (e.g., *sefa*-SOFA).

Although the existence of form priming provides quite dramatic support for an activation approach, it is still necessary to explain why there is no priming at all for items such as *bamp*-CAMP. But perhaps this is no problem if priming is really related to the number of neighbors, since the connectionist versions of activation theory exploit the concept of competition between neighbors. If the prime has many neighbors, it must activate a large number of detectors, which may then reciprocally inhibit one another to the point where no residual activation remains.

It is too early to tell whether this phenomenon is the bonanza it seems for activation theory, since several aspects of the phenomenon are not easy to handle. For example, recent evidence actually suggests that what controls form priming in the four-letter case is the density of the *target* neighborhood, not that of the prime neighborhood (Forster 1987). This does not sit particularly well with the notion of competition among the detectors activated by the prime. In other words, the reason that *file* does not prime TILE is not that *file* has so many neighbors; rather, it is that TILE has so many neighbors.[5] A second problem for the activation account is that the form-priming effect is enhanced if the prime and the target are also related morphologically (Forster et al. 1987). This effect is so strong that *kept* primes KEEP just as well as *keep* does. (Normally, identity primes are much stronger than any other.) This effect cannot be explained in terms of a process that occurs *during* the recognition of the prime, nor can it be described as a form-priming effect. Finally, there is also a problem for activation theory in the fact that the form-priming effect persists across an intervening word (Forster 1987). If the priming effect is seen as the consequence of persisting partial activation in word detectors, then this would mean that the activation level in a given detector reflects not only the properties of the current stimulus but also the properties of the previous stimulus and the one before that. This obviously would add considerable noise to the detector system, and it might even make it quite impossible for the model to discriminate accurately among words.

Another possibility offered within a connectionist system is to drop the idea that priming is the product of persisting activation, and to suggest instead that the weights assigned to the connections between letter detectors and word detectors may be temporarily strengthened. That is, whenever a word is recognized, the active connections are strengthened according to a Hebbian learning rule. This proposal would go a long way toward explaining how priming effects could persist across intervening words, but is quite incapable of explaining any case of form priming. In fact, this approach must predict the exact *opposite* of form priming. For example, consider the case in which the word *presence* is used to prime the target word PRETENCE (British spelling). When the prime is presented, the strength of the connections between each of the active letter detectors and the word detector for *presence* are strengthened. But this means that the connection strengths for these letter detectors (except for the "---s----" detector) and the detector for the word *pretence* must be weakened. Hence we might get priming for identical pairs such as *pretence*-PRETENCE, but only at the expense of pairs such as *presence*-PRETENCE, where we would expect inhibitory effects. Since this is not what happens, some other kind of mechanism must be found.

The Forster-Davis interpretation of priming makes use of an analogy with a disk-operating system. In order to extract information from the lexical entry that has been found to match the stimulus, it must first be "opened." If the lexical entry for the target word has already been "opened" by the prime, then there is a detectable saving. Since the priming effect is independent of frequency (i.e., primed words still show a normal frequency effect), the search for the entry must be carried out in the same way whether the word is primed or unprimed. So it is not the search path to the entry that is changed by the prime; rather it is the state of the entry itself.

This interprets the priming effect as a kind of short-term repetition effect. This works well for cases where the prime and the target are the same word, or even where they are morphologically related words, but not so well when they are quite unrelated, and even worse when the prime is not even a word. Forster et al. (1987) suggest that in these cases we might still have a repetition situation if the prime is (mis)taken to be the target word itself. That is, if *bontrast* primes CONTRAST, then *bontrast* must have been misinterpreted as *contrast*, hence producing an apparent repetition. This seems reasonable if we consider that the lexical processor ought to be able to recover from misspellings. That is, when it is discovered that no entry matches *bontrast* exactly, the system sets about finding the best match. This view would explain why neighborhood density is critical: If many words match the prime, only one may be chosen, and this may not be the target word.[6]

It can be shown, however, that this "best match" hypothesis must be wrong. Consider the priming stimulus *antitude*. The best match for this is either the entry for *aptitude*, that for *attitude*, or that for *altitude*, so it might be expected that all three of these targets would be primed to some degree. But now consider the priming stimulus *aptitude*. The best match for this must be the entry for *aptitude*, and hence we would not expect *aptitude* to prime either ATTITUDE or ALTITUDE. That is, when the prime is *itself* a word, then only one entry should be opened. However, this is not the case. In fact, *aptitude* and *antitude* do equally well in priming ALTITUDE (Forster 1987). This means that the *antitude*-APTITUDE effect is not due to *antitude*'s being mistaken for *aptitude*, and hence it is not a simple repetition effect. This forces a major revision of the search model, since the conclusion must be that a given stimulus must open and/or access several entries rather than just one. The order in which these entries are discovered may still be controlled by frequency, but the search does not terminate when a perfect match is found. Instead, the search must go on to determine whether there are any other entries that match the stimulus sufficiently closely to be included in the set of candidates. This search would, of course, have to be exhaustive, which would normally eliminate any frequency effect (as is argued in Forster and Bednall 1976). In order to avoid undermining the search model's explanation of the frequency effect, it must be assumed that the lexical decision can be triggered by the discovery of the *first* exactly matching entry.

We have already encountered (in section 1) a situation in which the scanning process considered not only perfect matches but also close matches. To explain why Coltheart et al. (1977) found that the number of neighbors affects lexical-decision times for nonwords but not for words, we assumed that some record was kept of close matches. If we now say that the entries for closely matching words are *opened* as they are discovered, then we can use the same mechanism to account for the Coltheart N effect and the masked form-priming effects.

As was noted, to explain the frequency effect we must assume that the system knows immediately when it has found an entry that exactly matches the stimulus. But if this is the case, then why have a list of candidates at all? With hindsight, we can see that this also is not unreasonable. Consider the case of a sentence containing a misspelled word that happens to form another word, as in

This plane usually flies at an attitude of 30,000 feet.

It appears that we are able to recover the intended word *altitude* almost without any effort. This task would be made a lot easier if the entry for *altitude* had also been opened, together with *attitude* and *aptitude*. Thus, when it is discovered that there is something wrong with the phrase *an attitude of 30,000 feet*, an input-error checking routine could ask whether any of the open entries fits the context better than *attitude*.[7] The fact that the input error accidentally formed another word is irrelevant to this process, unless the perceiver believed that in the real world an input error could never form a word.

This interpretation also makes sense of the notion that an entry remains open for some short period of time. What the lexical processor might be doing is "declaring" the possible interpretations of the stimulus at the lexical level, the idea being that higher-level systems, (such as the parser and the interpreter) will use this declaration to extract the necessary information from the lexicon. However, it may not be immediately obvious which interpretation is correct, and hence this declaration should be preserved until it *is* obvious. On this view, a "garden path" sentence is one that delays the point of disambiguation until after the entries have been closed, which forces reprocessing of the input to reopen the required entries. Thus, there is a strong parallel between this view and the proposal that contextually inappropriate readings of an ambiguous word are maintained for a short period of time after the word has been presented (Swinney 1979).

The worst feature of this attempt to explain the form-priming effect (pointed out by Dianne Bradley) is that this elaborate system is postulated just for the purpose of recovery from ill-formed or misrecognized inputs. While this may be important in speech recognition, where the signal may be very noisy, it does not seem quite so essential for recognition of the printed word. True, typographical errors and misspellings abound, but are they common enough to bring about a radical change in the design of the access module? Perhaps not. But perhaps this kind of design *would* be required if the access module were to routinely attempt access without having identified all the letters, as in a cascade model or in Rubenstein's original model (Rubenstein et al. 1970) or in the left-to-right model of Taft and Forster (1976). In this case, the system cannot afford to reject alternatives merely because they do not provide a perfect match with the stimulus. Instead, close matches must be marked as viable candidates, to be more carefully evaluated at a later stage.[8] This, of course, is very much like the criterion-bias position that I argued against above. However, there is a difference. The present view suggests that close matches get marked regardless of their frequency and regardless of whether they fit the context. The only prerequisite is that they should not themselves resemble many words *other* than the input stimulus (which explains the neighborhood-density finding).

There is no doubt that we *are* able to recognize words with missing letters very rapidly. Colin Schoknecht has recently completed a lexical-decision experiment in our laboratory using stimuli such as PA_ENT, _EEKLE,

W_NDER, TELT_R, M_NGLE, and S_RAWL. The subject responds Yes to PA_ENT because inserting R or T will make a word, but responds No to TELT_R because there is no word that can be formed by inserting one letter. The mean lexical-decision time under these conditions for words was 560 msec, compared with 676 msec for nonwords. (The error rates were 10.4 percent and 7.7 percent, respectively.) The most impressive feature is the performance on nonwords. How can we tell so quickly and accurately that there is no word corresponding to BA_ENT? To be absolutely certain, one might imagine that every possible letter would have to be checked, which would take considerable time. But if one is prepared to risk an immediate intuitive response, then a very fast response is possible, and it will be correct 92 percent of the time according to Schoknecht's results. This suggests that the strategy for solving this problem may in fact employ perfectly standard lexical-access routines in which one simply conducts a normal search and then inspects the contents of the candidate list. If the list is empty, a No response is made; otherwise a Yes response is made.[9]

However, this cascade approach creates further problems. If the stimulus is not completely specified, then the initial lexical scan merely establishes a set of candidates which have to be examined further before any decision about the input can be reached. But then we cannot explain the frequency effect by postulating that this initial scan is frequency-ordered. To do this, we need also to assume that the initial scan knows when it has found a perfectly matching entry (as was argued above), and that the details of this entry are immediately made available to other processing systems. But if the stimulus has not been completely specified, then there is no way the system can know whether it has a perfect match.

In short, we would have to look elsewhere for an explanation of frequency effects. One way might be to propose that the frequency effect is introduced during the evaluation process itself, with high-frequency candidates being examined before low-frequency candidates, as in an activate-and-check model. The candidate list is specified before the stimulus is completely coded, but the evaluation process does not begin until the coding is complete. This alternative is certainly viable, except that it predicts that the size of the frequency effect would then depend on the number of entries in the candidate list. Since there are no detectable form-priming effects for short words with many neighbors, we would have to say that the recognition of these words involved candidate lists with only one member, and hence there should be no frequency effects for these words at all. The available evidence offers no encouragement for this view (Forster et al. 1987).

Another possibility that could be revived is the idea that the access system is cyclic. As Rubenstein et al. (1971) proposed, a set of candidates and their evaluation might be marked out within limited frequency bands. The process is carried out first for the highest frequency band; if no solution is found, the process recycles for the next highest frequency band, and so forth. This will produce a graded frequency effect (depending on the bandwidth), even though the initial search that establishes the candidate list is exhaustive. However, this analysis suggests that a word prime would never open the entry for a word neighbor that belonged to a lower frequency band. Our initial efforts to establish such an effect have not been encouraging.

Of course, one could simply give up on the frequency effect altogether, and relegate it to some post-access process, as suggested by Balota and Chumbley (1984). However, this seems half-hearted, especially since the evidence on which Balota and Chumbley base their argument is so weak (see Bradley and Forster 1987). For the moment, it seems far more advisable to use what we know about the frequency effect to constrain our interpretation of the priming effect, rather than the other way around. So, once again for the moment, the best we can do is admit that we cannot see any good reason why the access process should open the close matches as well as the perfect matches, except just to allow for possible errors in the input itself or in the letter-recognition system.

The discovery of a new phenomenon such as the masked priming effect immediately puts the search model under great strain. This seems to be a good thing, since otherwise the experiments would not be telling us anything new. A very obvious development is that the search model is now forced to take on many of the characteristics of the activate-and-check model, and many of the ideas being explored here are echoed in the work of Norris (1986) and Marslen-Wilson (1987). However, it is also quite obvious that the right way to handle the phenomenon has not yet emerged. Our only comfort meantime is the belief that an activation account also becomes unwieldy when one allows activation effects to persist in time. This means that we do not yet have a good idea about the mechanisms underlying form priming. At least, however, we have evidence that something very much like a cascading output system must be involved. The hope is that this new phenomenon will act as a spur for both schools of thought.

Notes

1. Network theorists also discuss their models in terms of neural computation, but it is not clear that the type of computation is the same. Although one might say

that the meaning of a word, for example, could be said to be represented by the activation pattern that it produces in units of a certain type, it is doubtful that this representation is a symbolic representation in the sense required by the notion of a symbol-manipulating system. The fact that neural networks are usually represented as computer programs is completely irrelevant—we might as well say that the weather system is computational because the only way we can hope to understand it is to represent it as a computer program.

2. The point is that we would need to find some fairly deep principle that would explain how this could be the case, not an arbitrary set of values that happen to cover a majority of existing cases. One such possibility is that the weighting function takes neighbors into account. That is, the strength of the connection between the "L in second position" detector and the BLIGHT detector might be stronger than it would otherwise have been if BRIGHT were not a word.

3. Note the echo of the argument in the previous section, where it was suggested that the modification of threshold produced by variation in frequency could never be large enough to compensate for a missing letter.

4. This is not difficult for Norris, since he is proposing a quite different model.

5. A further complication is that this result is not obtained with the paradigm used by Evett and Humphreys (1981), where both the prime and the target are presented briefly in rapid succession under masking conditions and the subject is required to identify the presented word.

6. However, like the activation account, this approach has difficulty with the finding that it is the neighborhood of the target rather than that of the prime that controls the amount of priming.

7. The situation is slightly more complex, since *plane* would also open the entries for *place*, *plate*, *plant*, and *plans* (and even, possibly, *planet*), and *feet* would also have opened *meet*, *feel*, etc.

8. This must certainly be true for object recognition, since we can still recognize objects even though they are partially obscured by other objects.

9. Though not measured specifically in this experiment, the typical word-nonword difference for lexical decision times with intact stimuli would be quite similar to that obtained in the missing-letters task.

References

Amey, T. Word recognition: An investigation of feature analysis and lexical access time. Honors thesis, Monash University, 1973.

Antos, S. J. 1979. Processing facilitation in a lexical decision task. *Journal of Experimental Psychology: Human Perception and Performance* 5: 527–545.

Balota, D. A., and J. I. Chumbley. 1984. Are lexical decisions a good measure of lexical access? The role of word frequency in the neglected decision stage. *Journal of Experimental Psychology: Human Perception and Performance* 10: 340–357.

Becker, C. A. 1979. Semantic context and word frequency effects in visual word recognition. *Journal of Experimental Psychology: Human Perception and Performance* 5: 252–259.

Bradley, D. C., and K. I. Forster. 1987. A reader's view of listening. *Cognition* 25: 103–134.

Bradley, D. C., G. R. Savage, and G. W. Yelland. 1983. Form-Priming or Not? Paper delivered at Fourth Language and Speech Conference, Monash University.

Chambers, S. M. 1979. Letter and order information in lexical access. *Journal of Verbal Learning and Verbal Behavior* 18: 225–241.

Chambers, S. M., and K. I. Forster. 1975. Evidence for lexical access in a simultaneous matching task. *Memory and Cognition* 3: 549–559.

Colombo, L. 1986. Activation and inhibition with orthographically similar words. *Journal of Experimental Psychology: Human Perception and Performance* 12: 226–234.

Coltheart, M., E. Davelaar, J. T. Jonasson, and D. Besner. 1977. Access to the internal lexicon. In S. Dornic (ed.), *Attention and Performance VI*. London: Academic.

Evett, L. J., and. G. W. Humphries. 1981. The use of abstract graphemic information in lexical access. *Quarterly Journal of Experimental Psychology* 33: 325–350.

Feldman, J. A., and F. H. Ballard. 1982. Connectionist models and their properties. *Cognitive Science* 6: 205–254.

Forster, K. I. 1974. The role of semantic hypotheses in sentence processing. In F. Bresson and J. Mehler (eds.), *Current Problems in Psycholinguistics*. Paris: Editions du CNRS.

Forster, K. I. 1976. Accessing the mental lexicon. In R. J. Wales and E. Walker (eds.), *New Approaches to Language Mechanisms*. Amsterdam: North-Holland.

Forster, K. I. 1981. Priming and the effects of sentence and lexical contexts on naming time: Evidence for autonomous lexical processing. *Quarterly Journal of Experimental Psychology* 33: 465–495.

Forster, K. I. 1985. Lexical acquisition and the modular lexicon. *Language and Cognitive Processes* 1: 87–108.

Forster, K. I. 1987. Form-priming with masked primes: The best-match hypothesis. In M. Coltheart (ed.), *Attention and Performance XII*. Hillsdale, N.J.: Erlbaum.

Forster, K. I., and E. S. Bednall. 1976. Terminating and exhaustive search in lexical access. *Memory and Cognition* 4: 53–61.

Forster, K. I. and C. Davis. 1984. Repetition priming and frequency attenuation in lexical access. *Journal of Experimental Psychology: Learning, Memory, and Cognition* 10: 680–698.

Forster, K. I., C. Davis, C. Schoknecht, and R. Carter. 1987. Masked priming with graphemically related forms: Repetition or partial activation? *Quarterly Journal of Experimental Psychology* 39: 211–251.

Hillinger, M. L. 1980. Priming effects with phonemically similar words: The encoding-bias hypothesis reconsidered. *Memory and Cognition* 8: 115–123.

Landauer, T. K., and J. L. Freedman. 1968. Information retrieval from long-term memory: category size and recognition time. *Journal of Verbal Learning and Verbal Behavior* 7: 291–295.

Landauer, T. K., and L. A. Streeter. 1973. Structural differences between common and rare words: Failure of equivalence assumptions for theories of word recognition. *Journal of Verbal Learning and Verbal Behavior* 12: 119–131.

Loftus, E. F., and W. Cole. 1974. Retrieving attribute and name information from semantic memory. *Journal of Experimental Psychology* 102: 1116–1122.

Marslen-Wilson, W. D. 1987. Functional parallelism in spoken word-recognition. *Cognition* 25: 71–102.

Marslen-Wilson, W. D., and A. Welsh. 1978. Processing interactions and lexical access during word recognition in continuous speech. *Cognitive Psychology* 10: 29–63.

McClelland, J. L. 1979. On the time relations of mental processes: An examination of systems of processes in cascade. *Psychological Review* 86: 287–307.

McClelland, J. L. 1987. The case for interactionism in language processing. In M. Coltheart (ed.), *Attention and Performance XII: The Psychology of Reading.* Hove, U.K.: Erlbaum.

McClelland, J. L., and J. L. Elman. 1986. The TRACE model of speech perception. *Cognitive Psychology* 18: 1–86.

McClelland, J. L., and D. E. Rumelhart. 1981. An interactive activation model of context effects in letter perception: Part 1. An account of basic findings. *Psychological Review* 88: 375–407.

McClelland, J. L., D. E. Rumelhart, and the PDP Research Group. 1986. *Parallel Distributed Processing: Explorations in the Microstructures of Cognition. Volume* 2: *Psychological and Biological Models.* Cambridge, Mass.: MIT Press. A Bradford Book.

Morton, J. 1970. A functional model of human memory. In D. A. Norman (ed.), *Models of Human Memory.* New York: Academic.

Morton, J. 1979. Facilitation in word recognition: Experiments causing change in the logogen model. In P. A. Kolers, M. E. Wrolstad, and M. Bouma (eds.), *Processing of Visible Language.* New York: Plenum.

Norris, D. 1984. The mispriming effect: Evidence of an orthographic check in the lexical decision task. *Memory and Cognition* 12: 470–476.

Norris, D. 1986. Word recognition: Context effects without priming. *Cognition* 22: 93–136.

O'Connor, R. E., and K. I. Forster. 1981. Criterion bias and search sequence bias in word recognition. *Memory and Cognition* 9: 78–92.

Oldfield, R. C. 1966. Things, words and the brain. *Quarterly Journal of Experimental Psychology* 18: 340–353.

Paap, K. R., S. L. Newsome, J. E. McDonald, and R. W. Schvaneveldt. 1982. An activation-verification model for letter and word recognition: The word-superiority effect. *Psychological Review* 89: 573–594.

Reicher, G. M. 1969. Perceptual recognition as a function of meaningfulness of stimulus material. *Journal of Experimental Psychology* 81: 275–280.

Rubenstein, H., L. Garfield, and J. A. Millikan. 1970. Homographic entries in the internal lexicon. *Journal of Verbal Learning and Verbal Behavior* 9: 487–494.

Rumelhart, D. E., and J. L. McClelland. 1982. An interactive activation model of context effects in letter perception: Part 2. The contextual enhancement effect and some tests and extensions of the model. *Psychological Review* 89: 60–94.

Rumelhart, D. E., J. L. McClelland, and the PDP Research Group. 1986. *Parallel Distributed Processing: Explorations in the Microstructures of Cognition. Volume 1: Foundations.* Cambridge, Mass.: MIT Press. A Bradford Book.

Scarborough, D. L., C. Cortese, and H. Scarborough. 1977. Frequency and repetition effects in lexical memory. *Journal of Experimental Psychology: Human Perception and Performance* 7: 3–12.

Schvaneveldt, R. W., and J. E. McDonald. 1981. Semantic context and the encoding of words: Evidence for the two modes of stimulus analysis. *Journal of Experimental Psychology: Human Perception and Performance* 7: 673–687.

Swinney, D. A. 1979. Lexical access during sentence comprehension: (Re)Consideration of context effects. *Journal of Verbal Learning and Verbal Behavior* 18: 645–659.

Taft, M. 1986. Lexical access codes in visual and auditory word recognition. *Language and Cognitive Processes* 1: 297–308.

Taft, M., and K. I. Forster. 1976. Lexical storage and retrieval of polymorphemic and polysyllabic words. *Journal of Verbal Learning and Verbal Behavior* 15: 607–620.

Taft, M., and G. Hambly. 1986. Exploring the cohort model of spoken word recognition. *Cognition* 22: 259–282.

Chapter 4

Lexical Access in Speech Production

Brian Butterworth

The problem of lexical access in speech production is, in principle, easy to state: How does the speaker choose one word—a word appropriate to current purposes—from a mental lexicon of many thousands of words? We shall assume that there is indeed in the speaker's head a store of lexical items, each of which, since the relation between sound and meaning in language is largely arbitrary, has to be learned. This is not to say that the mental lexicon, thus construed as a passive store of knowledge, constitutes the whole of the speaker's knowledge of words. He or she doubtless also knows something of the rules for constructing words, which may be deployed when a gap is encountered in lexical search, for example, where some inflected or derived form has not been learned, or cannot for the moment be retrieved. In languages where words can be of arbitrary length (see Hankamer's discussion of Turkish in chapter 13 of this volume), these rules may be used frequently. The nature of the rules and what they can explain has been discussed *in extenso* elsewhere in this volume (see the enlightening chapter by Henderson) and in Butterworth 1983; rather than rehearse well-known arguments about lexical representation, I shall concentrate on issues of *access*, in the hope of throwing some oblique light on questions of representation as well. In particular, I shall focus on evidence from transient troubles in access that arise in normal conversation and from the more long-lasting troubles found in aphasic patients.

Finding a suitable next word in conversational speech, or the name of an object in a naming task, is not a trivial computational problem. The number of words a literate speaker knows is surprisingly large; Oldfield (1963) has estimated the average vocabulary of Oxford undergraduates to be around 75,000 words, with a range of 55,000 to 90,000 words. Given that we speak at 100 to 200 words per minute, this begins to look like a pretty substantial access problem—something of the order of consulting the *Concise Oxford Dictionary*, which has 75,000 entries, two or three times a second. How do we manage it? Clearly, if the store of words were unorganized, an exhaustive search through it for each word spoken would seem incompatible with the known fluency of speech.

Oldfield (1966a, p. 341) suggested that an ideal form of organization would allow "binary, dichotomous search.... The items would each be labeled by a combination of characteristics in such a way that the presence or absence of one of them would enable half the items to be rejected by one decision, half the remainder by a second, and so forth. On this basis we could sort $N = 2^2$ by n decisions.... If N were 7.5×10^4 the number of decisions ... would be about 16.... But in such a system all items would be at the same distance—in terms of decision steps—from the starting point, and all access times would be equal. In practice, this would be a disadvantage because some words are needed more often than others. It might be better to arrange shorter access times for these, even at the expense of longer ones for the rarer words. A good storage system might be one in which the mean access time was minimized." In another paper, Oldfield (1966b) explicitly introduced the idea of "frequency blocking," where words are arranged into sets of similar frequency.

Of course, a basic problem here is the nature of the "characteristics" by which words are classified. Oldfield and Wingfield (1964) mentioned as an analogy, botanical classification, where each word is defined in terms of traditional characteristics of plant morphology. If words were arranged in this way, a thesaurus would be a more helpful analogy than a dictionary, though this assumes that the set of characteristics is ordinarily sufficient to pick out just one word. A real thesaurus usually has several words at the terminal nodes of its classificatory tree, and there is no way to check candidates against search criteria except by cross-checking each word against dictionary definitions.

At the time when Oldfield was elaborating this sequential-decision-tree account, Brown and McNeill (1966) were proposing parallel access to words and their definitions. They modeled their scheme on "keysort cards." On each card was written the pronunciation and definition, *inter alia*, of a single word. "The cards are punched for various features of the words entered.... It is possible to retrieve from the total deck any subset by putting a metal rod through the proper hole.... Perhaps these [features] are the semantic 'markers' that Katz and Fodor postulate.... Metal rods thrust into the holes for each of the [search] features might fish up ... a collection of entries." (Brown and McNeill 1966, p. 333) The desired word can then be selected from among this collection by checking the definition on the card against input search criteria, which presumably contain information beyond that contained in the set of markers.

These two models from the 1960s epitomize two broad classes of account of access that have since been developed by other authors. Fay and Cutler (1977) propose something very like Oldfield and Wingfield's search through a taxonomic tree, and Forster (1976) offers a serial-search model complete with frequency organization. Morton's (1968) "logogen" model gives us parallel access from semantic features and information about current context, without definitional checking but with the added ingredient of variable thresholds on each item.

What all these models have in common is the perfectly natural assumption that lexical access takes place in one stage, with a set of search criteria determining retrieval from a single list of word forms. This is what I think is wrong with them.

1 Two-Stage Models of Lexical Access

In this chapter I shall argue that lexical access in speech production takes place in two temporally distinct stages. In the first stage, the speaker accesses a "semantic lexicon" (henceforth SL). This, in essence, is a trans-coding device that takes as input a semantic code and delivers as output a phonological address. The second stage takes the address as input to another transcoding device—the "phonological lexicon" (henceforth PL)—and delivers a phonological word form as output. The basic form of this two-stage model is sketched in figure 1.

The SL consists of a set of pairs of the form $\langle \ldots, S_i, S_j, \ldots, S_n \rangle \leftrightarrow \langle \ldots, P_i, P_j, \ldots, P_n \rangle$, which associate n-tuples of properties of type S with n-tuples of properties of type P. I shall assume without argument that the S properties S_i, S_j, and S_n denote semantic features of the usual sort,

---

Figure 1   ▶

The basic two-stage model of lexical access in speech production showing how a semantic error ((1a) in the text) could come about. In Stage 1, the semantic search criterion of an n-tuple of semantic features $\langle Sa, Sb, Sc \rangle$ is erroneously matched with a similar n-tuple, $\langle Sa, Sb, Sd \rangle$, in the semantic lexicon. This gives rise to an incorrect address in the phonological lexicon, and thereby to the utterance of a word similar in meaning but different in sound; in this case "like" instead of "hate". Uttering a word that is similar in sound but different in meaning (as (2a) in the text) could occur in Stage 2 if the correct phonological address is erroneously matched to a near neighbor—$\langle Pa, Pb, Pd \rangle$ instead of $\langle Pa, Pb, Pc \rangle$—yielding "bottle" instead of "bottom".

```
                        SEMANTIC SYSTEM


----------------------------------------------------------------
                                        Stage 1: accessing
                                        the semantic lexicon


        <Sa.Sb.Sc>                      semantic search criterion


                    ------------------------
                        SEMANTIC LEXICON

            <Sx,Sy,Sz> <-> <Pf,Pg,Ph>

            <Sa,Sb,Sc> <-> <Pf,Pg,Pi>
            <Sa,Sb,Sd> <-> <Px,Py,Pz>
                        .
                        .
            <Sf,Sg,Sh> <-> <Pa,Pb,Pc>
                    ------------------------

        <Px,Py,Pz>                      address held in buffer
----------------------------------------------------------------
                                        Stage 2: accessing
                                        the phonological lexicon

        <Px,Py,Pz>                      phonological address


                    ----------------------
                        PHONOLOGICAL LEXICON

            <Pf,Pg,Pi> <-> /heit/
                        .
                        .
            <Px,Py,Pz> <-> /laik/
                        .
                        .
            <Pa,Pb,Pc> <-> /botəm/
            <Pa,Pb,Pd> <-> /botl/
                        .

                    ------------------------


            /laik/
                                        word output in buffer
----------------------------------------------------------------
```

described *in extenso* by Miller and Johnson-Laird (1976)—features like TRAVEL, AT, CAUSE, KNOW, MALE, and BROTHER, along with variables and quantifiers, which will have proper ordering. I shall further assume that the P properties P_i, P_j, and P_n denote phonological characteristics such as one syllable, stress on first syllable, onset $/p/$, vowel $/i/$, and coda. This n-tuple of properties represents an address for a word in PL. An n-tuple of S properties constructed by the semantic system constitutes the semantic search criteria for a word. If this is sufficient, then the set of properties it designates will match the S value of a single S-P pair of n-tuples. Following Bock (1982), one can think of this arrangement as a production system, where each item represents a condition-action pair, such that $\langle \ldots, S_i, S_j, \ldots, S_n \rangle$ in SL is the condition that, when satisfied, produces the action $\langle \ldots, P_i, P_j, \ldots, P_n \rangle$. Syntactic conditions can be incorporated into this scheme if necessary, though this will not be discussed here.

One point, however, is that SL is intended as *intermodal*, and is designed to take phonological input to produce an n-tuple of semantic features as output to the semantic system. That is, SL mediates auditory and visual language input as well as language output in both the spoken and written modalities. The role of SL in other language-processing tasks distinguishes it from comparable levels in the models described below. This becomes important when assessing the evidence from aphasia, where independent justification for postulating SL can be found.

In figure 1, the search criterion $\langle S_a, S_b, S_c \rangle$ makes a complete match with $\langle S_a, S_b, S_c \rangle$ in SL, where S_a, S_b, and S_c arbitrarily designate three semantic features. Some criteria might be insufficient to pick out a single pair, if, for example, one property designator is missing. Thus, $\langle S_a, S_b \rangle$ will form an incomplete match with all the pairs from, say, $\langle S_a, S_b, S_c \rangle$ to $\langle S_a, S_b, S_z \rangle$, and hence, instead of just one, several P-type n-tuples, phonological addresses, might become equally activated. It is a consequence of this scheme that items with similar S conditions are accessed by similar semantic-search criteria, and the corresponding words will have similar meanings.

The structure of stage 2 is comparable. PL consists of pairs of the form $\langle P_a, P_b, P_c, \ldots \rangle \leftrightarrow /p_1 p_2 p_3 \ldots /$, where $\langle P_a, P_b, P_c, \ldots \rangle$ is the address output by SL, and $/p_1 p_2 p_3 \ldots /$ is a string of phonemes forming a word known to the speaker. Similar addresses will access similar-sounding words, and incomplete addresses may be consistent with several words.

A critical property of this model is the presence of a buffer in stage 1. Thus the speaker may, but need not, access several items in stage 1 before beginning to access PL in stage 2. This distinguishes the model from proposals by Dell and others (see below) which incorporate levels similar to SL and PL but which do not allow the results of computations at the first SL stage to be held pending a decision to access PL in the second stage. Access is strictly a top-down procedure, with no information flowing back to higher levels apart from the results of checking procedures, which I cannot deal with in detail here. So the semantic system does not know which search criteria will pick out a word in the language. For example, suppose $\langle S_x, S_y \rangle$ specifies "male crow," for which there is no word in English. The fact of the failure to retrieve a single-word output may then be fed back to higher levels, and a new sentence may be constructed in which the object will be denoted by a phrase rather than a single word. The speaker may respond in other ways in such situations—by trying again, in case there was some kind of transient problem, or by attempting to construct a new word ("he-crow") out of known ones, and so on. (See Butterworth 1983 for further discussion.)

The idea of two-stage access in speech, where the first stage is semantically organized and the second is phonologically organized, is not original. Fromkin proposed such a model in 1971, and others have followed in her footsteps. Fromkin based her distinction on two kinds of speech error found in naturally occurring conversations. In the first kind, the speaker substitutes a word that is *similar in meaning* to the target but not similar in sound, as in the following examples from Fromkin 1971 (p. 46):

(1) a. I like to – hate to get up in the morning.

   b. the oral – written part of the exam

In the second kind, the speaker substitutes a word that is *similar in sound* but not in meaning, as in these examples (Fromkin 1971, p. 44):

(2) a. U[tterance]: bottle of page five
      T[arget]:   bottom of page five

   b. while the present – pressure indicates

The independence of the two kinds of error suggested to Fromkin two independent stages (but see Dell 1986). Translating her account into our terminology, the errors in (1) can arise in two ways. First, the semantic search criteria may be defective because of a random error in the semantic system, or because of the speaker's unconscious wishes, or for some other prelinguistic reason. So instead of $\langle S_a, S_b, S_c \rangle$ access is guided by $\langle S_a, S_b, S_d \rangle$ or $\langle S_a, S_b, S_? \rangle$. The address of a word may be retrieved, but it will be of the wrong word, $\langle P_x, P_y, P_z \rangle$ instead of $\langle P_d, P_f, P_g \rangle$, finally producing *like* instead of *hate*. The other possibility is that although $\langle S_a, S_b, S_c \rangle$

($=$ DEF OF HATE) is correctly generated by the semantic system, in stage 1 access matching does not work properly, and $\langle S_a, S_b, S_d \rangle$ ($=$ DEF OF LIKE) is activated.

Fromkin locates the errors in (2) in the access to the phonological lexicon—our stage 2. The correct phonological address has been retrieved (2 syllables, 1 stress, onset /pr/, vowel /e/), but matching goes slightly wrong and a near neighbor is activated instead.

Even within this scheme, other error sources are possible, and we shall discuss some of them in relation to aphasic errors.

One of the best-known versions of the two-stage model has been developed by Garrett over the past ten years (Garrett 1975, 1976, 1980a, 1982). In his model, the first stage of lexical access occurs at what he calls the "functional level," where an abstract characterization of the word is selected (and associated with a specification of its grammatical role); in the second stage, the "positional level," the phonological form of the word is accessed (and inserted into a "planning frame"). However, there are important differences with the model I have outlined. Only nouns, verbs, adjectives, and adverbs are the responsibility of strictly lexical processes: other, closed-class words are the responsibility of syntactic processes. Second, the full form of a word is not accessed by lexical processes (only lexical stems are); inflexional material is added by other processes.

The evidence for these distinctions comes from a careful analysis of the distribution of types of speech errors. Errors involving closed-class items, it is claimed, show systematic differences from those involving lexical stems, and the stems can be involved in error processes without their affixes being involved.

Closed-Class versus Open-Class Words

Sound exchanges, like Spoonerisms, involve open-class words but not closed-class words (Garrett 1975). When a lexical word moves from its intended position, the pattern of sentence accents remains unaffected; thus, in (3) it still falls on the second NP.

(3) U: We have a laboratory in our computer
    T: We have a computer in our laboratory.
    (Accented words underlined. Cited in Cutler and Isard 1980.)

However, movement errors involving closed-class words often take their accent with them, as in (4).

(4) a. U: Can I turn off this.
       T: Can I turn this off.

b. U: Well I <u>much</u> would have preferred the owl.
   T: Well I would have <u>much</u> preferred the owl.
   (From Cutler and Isard 1980.)

Retrieval of Full Form versus Retrieval of Stem

Garrett notes that both closed-class (example 5) and open-class (example 6) words exchange position. (These examples are from Garrett 1980a.)

(5) U: which was parallel, to a certain sense in an experience of
    T: ...in a certain sense, to an experience...

(6) U: Older men choose to tend younger wives.
    T: Older men tend to choose younger wives.

Now, words with affixes do not appear to behave in the same way as the whole-word free forms in (5) and (6). What typically happens is that stems exchange, "stranding" the bound morphemes (i.e., leaving them in their intended sentence positions, but now attached to the wrong stems).

(7) a. U: I'm not in the <u>read</u> for <u>mood</u> ING.
       T: I'm not in the mood for reading.

    b. U: He made a lot money INtelephonING <u>stall</u>S.
       T: He made a lot of money installing telephones
       (Garrett 1975)

    c. U: You have to <u>square</u> it <u>face</u>LY.
       T: You have to face it squarely.

    d. U: I've got a load of <u>cook</u>EN <u>chick</u>ED.
       T: I've got a load of chicken cooked.
       (Garrett 1980a)

Bound morphemes themselves apparently do not exchange, even though final phonemes sometimes do. Garrett uses distributional data to diagnose processing differences, and since stem-movement errors pattern differently from "combined form" (stem + affix) errors, at least some differences in their processing must be involved. The critical difference is that the stem and the affix have different sources, and combined forms are due to lexical insertion into a slot in the "positional frame" which has an affix already attached to it. So it is not surprising that these words come apart at the morphemic seams in movement errors.

I have argued against this view at some length elsewhere (Butterworth 1983), claiming that Garrett's evidence is not decisive against the proposal that words are normally selected as wholes, complete with affixes. One crucial piece of evidence was missing from that argument, as Garrett has forcefully pointed out in a personal communication: If words are selected as wholes, then there should exist at least some errors where they move as wholes. Of course, it is a dangerous dialectical strategy to argue from the nonoccurrence of a certain phenomenon, since a single counterexample will be seriously bad news. As it turns out, there is at least one reported occurrence of such an error:

(8) U: I'm preparing to fill my <u>air</u> with <u>tires</u>.
    T: I'm preparing to fill my tires with air.

Garrett would have to predict that the error would have been

(9) U': I'm preparing to fill my air<u>s</u> with tire_.

This error was reported by Menn, Powelson, Miceli, Williams, and Zurif (1982), who said that it was from the corpus of errors collected by Garrett. Now, it is equally dangerous to argue from a single exemplar—especially in error research, with its well-known problems in hearing reliability and in intepretation (problems which are compounded where the number of examples is small). Nevertheless, this does seem to reopen the argument. And, as Garrett (1980b) admits, some complication of his position is forced by lexically specific allomorphy, which has to apply *after* a stem and an abstract form of the affix have combined. The problem becomes acute when irregular verb forms become involved in errors like (10).

(10) U: I don't know that I'd <u>hear</u> one if I <u>knew</u> it.
    T: I don't know that I'd know one if I'd heard it.

On the simplest form of his model, the error should have been something like

(11) U': I don't know that I'd hear one if I'd know<u>ed</u> it.

There are errors like (11), but there are also other examples of lexically correct irregulars in error positions.

One important recent article (Dell 1986) makes a more complex separation. Derived forms, like *swimm + er*, are represented as wholes at a level corresponding to SL in my scheme, but as two morphemes at PL: *swim + er*. On the other hand, inflectional affixes are independent units at both levels.

In a review of speech-production evidence, Bock (1982, p. 5) is more cautious about this issue, and Stemberger and MacWhinney (1986) have suggested that inflected forms may be produced either by retrieval of the whole form by rule (if the form is regular and frequent) or by rule-based affixation procedures.

A final point on Garrett's model: Closed-class words are involved in exchange errors, but bound morphemes apparently are not. Using distributional differences as a diagnostic for processing loci suggests a distinction between these two types of unit; thus, Dell (1986) locates closed-class *words* in the general lexicon along with open-class words, rather than in a special syntax-related store.

2 Interactive Activation Models

Models of lexical access may have two *levels* without having two stages. In the interactive activation model of Dell (1986) there are two levels of units, corresponding roughly to SL and PL, and information flows bidirectionally between units at both levels quite automatically. Indeed, it is a fundamental assumption of models like Dell's (1986 and this volume) that upward flow helps to determine which lower-level unit is targeted. This is how, for example, Dell explains lexicality effects in segmental speech errors: The activation of phoneme sequences that constitute a word—even the wrong word—feed back to the lexical unit, increasing relative activation in that unit, and then feed forward to the phoneme units, increasing activation in those units, thereby raising the likelihood of production, whereas phonemes not constituting a word cannot feed back to a single lexical unit and mutually increase activation in this way (Dell and Reich 1981). Similarly, there will be feedback as well as feedforward between Dell's "lexicon" (our SL) and the morphological units (roughly our PL, though somewhat more abstracted away from phoneme sequences). Dell does allow for some buffering in the construction of the syntactic representation, which will include the equivalent of SL items; however, the transitory activation of phonological representations, and feedback therefrom, will not be blocked. (See Dell's chapter in this volume for a helpful figure and further discussion.)

The point here is that processes at both levels are inextricably linked in time. In our model, there is no reason to make this assumption, since information flows in one direction only—from the top to the bottom—and we can postulate the completion of retrievals from one stage, which are held in a buffer, before work begins on the next. Some empirical license for this comes from studies of how long it takes speakers to initiate simple descriptions of visual stimuli. In these we find evidence that retrieval of more than one SL item can occur prior to any output.

3 Studies of Picture Description

Many studies of picture-description tasks have found longer latencies to initiate even short and highly stereotyped sentences than to initiate single-word responses. In fact, even nonsentential two-word responses have longer latencies (Kempen and Huijbers 1983). The number and kind of words in the sentence response affects latency. Increasing the set of possible first words, or decreasing their frequency or typicality, produces longer latencies (Lindsley 1975, 1976). And Kempen and Huijbers found that an instruction to use a new verb to describe the same picture produces a quite long-lasting increase in latency, whether the verb is first or second in the sentence (both allowable in Dutch). These findings are explained by Kempen and Huijbers in terms of a two-stage model in which all "lemmas" (equivalent in the relevant respects to our SL items), at least for their two-word sentences, have to be selected before "lexemes" (PL items) can be selected. Utterance of the first word has therefore to wait upon the selection of all lemmas and at least the first lexeme. The second lexeme will be retrieved just before it is needed in the sentence.

Let us take this argument one step further. Suppose that the speaker needs to activate all SL items just for the next clause. Consider then what this would predict for the latency to produce a single-clause sentence with a coordinated noun phrase versus a sentence with coordinated clauses—for example (coordinate NPs), "The square and the circle move up" versus (coordinate clauses) "The square moves up and the circle moves up". It predicts longer latencies for coordinate NPs than for coordinate clauses. This is exactly what Levelt and Maassen (1981) found in a complex and fascinating study of a task that required subjects to describe two moving geometrical shapes in an array. And speakers preferred to use the CNP formulation where both shapes moved in the same direction, so we are not seeing the effects of using an awkward or inappropriate sentence form here.

Levelt and Maassen also examined the effects of word-retrieval *difficulty* on latency. In pretests, the single-word naming latencies for the shapes were established; it turned out that the principal factor in naming latency was the name rather than how long it took to recognize the shape. Shape names could thus be divided into Easy ones (those with short latencies) and Difficult ones (those with long latencies). So in the description task proper, where the speaker has to produce a sentence to describe a two-object array, when the first name is Difficult the latency to begin speaking is reliably 30–40 msec longer than when it is Easy; but the difficulty of the second name has no effect on latency.

Is the effect of Difficulty to be located in accessing SL, or in accessing PL, or in both? If we continue to assume that PL items are retrieved just before they are output, and if Difficulty affects just this stage, then only the Difficulty of the first word should affect latency to initiate (which is the result above) and the difficulty of the second name should have its effect later in the sentence. And this is exactly what Levelt and Maassen found. For both coordinate NP and coordinate clause sentences, the overall duration of the utterance increased reliably when the second name was difficult, wheras the difficulty of the first name had no effect on duration.

Now, this is not Levelt and Maassen's account, though I believe it is consistent with it. There are other data they wish to explain concerning the relation between sentences describing both shapes moving the same way, compared with shapes moving in opposite directions. They argue that these data indicate that a speaker may revise the sentence plan when he encounters difficulties in retrieving the PL item for the second name, given that the SL item has already been successfully accessed and is being held in the buffer. The important point here is that either account involves the temporal separation of the two stages of lexical access.

4 Neuropsychological Evidence for Two Lexical Levels

Another source of evidence for the structure of processes of lexical access in speech (one that has so far been underused) is the breakdown of such access in aphasia. Most if not all aphasic patients suffer from some degree of word-finding difficulty in speech—both in spontaneous conversation and in formal tests of word finding, like naming pictures—but serious cognitive neuropsychological analyses of the processes involved in standard naming tasks are being actively investigated (Howard 1985; Morton 1985; Allport 1985; Ellis 1985). The focus of my discussion of the breakdown and treatment of naming will naturally be on the lexical aspects; I will not consider picture-recognition and representation processes here.

If the processes recruited in picture naming are modular, then deficits brought about by cerebral trauma may be confined to single modules, and the resulting symptom pattern will depend on which module is affected. In the model I am proposing, there are five distinct potential loci of damage (see figure 1), each of which predicts a distinct set of naming problems:

1. Damage to the semantic system itself will lead to incomplete or erroneous semantic specifications of the word to be retrieved. We assume that the semantic system is common to language input as well as language

output processes, so deficits here should lead to semantic errors in comprehension (like selecting a cat in response to the word "dog" in a standard picture-pointing task) as well as to semantic errors (paraphasias) in speech and naming (like calling a dog "a cat".)

2. Impairment in accessing the semantic lexicon from the semantic system, given intact output from the semantic system, will lead to semantic, but not necessarily to phonological, paraphasias in speech and naming; however, word-comprehension problems are not entailed, since access from speech recognition may be intact.

3. Damage to SL itself will lead to the retrieval of incorrect addresses in the phonological lexicon—that is, to semantic paraphasias, but not necessarily phonological paraphasias. Lexically specific semantic priming occurs at this level.

4. Impairments in accessing the phonological lexicon from the semantic lexicon will lead to loss of information about the address in PL, giving rise to phonological but not semantic paraphasias.

5. Damage to PL itself will result in incorrect phonological representations' being in store, or in phonological representations' being abnormally hard to retrieve (or missing; see e.g. Morton and Patterson 1980).

It is not possible to review here all the neuropsychological evidence that bears on each of these postulated levels, but I shall discuss a range of recent work to give a flavor of the kind of inferences that can be made from patient data.

Semantic problems are relatively common in aphasia, and are sometimes worse in one semantic field than the others (Warrington 1975; Hart, Berndt, and Caramazza 1985), but it is frequently difficult to tie them down exclusively to the semantic system itself. Agnosic and perceptual difficulties, and more general questions about access to the semantic system, can complicate the picture. However, naming problems are not invariably associated with semantic deficit. It has long been known that some anomic patients can sometimes use correctly, and describe accurately, objects that they cannot name; and they may also be able to distinguish correct from incorrect names offered by the examiner (Ellis 1985; Kay and Ellis 1987).

A recent study by Howard and Franklin (1989) clearly presents a patient with intact semantics who nevertheless makes numerous naming errors. MK is a fluent Wernicke's aphasic, with fluent and somewhat anomic spontaneous speech. His auditory word comprehension is fair (112/150) on the Peabody Picture Vocabulary Test); his comprehension is slightly better with written presentation (123/150). (See Howard and Franklin 1989 for further details.) The critical test here is one devised by Howard and

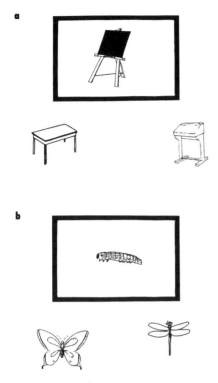

Figure 2
The "Pyramids and Palm Trees" test. Subjects are asked to match the top picture in each triad to one of the bottom two. Note that these are in the same semantic category. (From Howard, personal communication. Reproduced by permission.)

Orchard-Lisle (1984) called the "Pyramid and Palm Trees" test. In this test the patient is presented with three pictures, one above the two others—e.g. a pyramid, a palm tree, and a deciduous tree—and is asked which of the lower pictures goes best with the top picture, the pyramid. The lower pictures are always in the same semantic category; here they are both trees. In order to select the palm tree to go with the pyramid, the subject has to go well beyond the information available in the pictures themselves, and well beyond semantic-category information; he has to use detailed semantic-category information (just TREE is not enough) to make available the fact that it is a *palm* tree, and to derive from this further information: that it grows in tropical climates, that Egypt is tropical, etc. MK was not particularly good at naming these pictures (115/156), typically making the kind of semantically related errors that he made in other contexts. His naming responses to the pictures in figure 2 are given in figure 3.

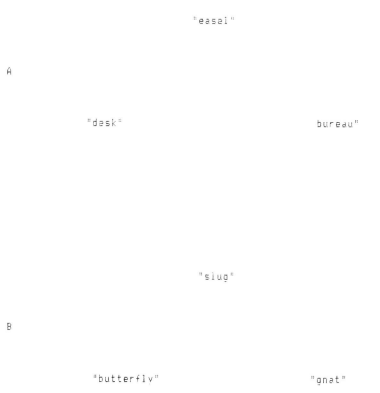

Figure 3
Attempts by an aphasic patient, M.K., to name the pictures in figure 2. He
nevertheless scored 100% on matching a lower picture to the upper one. (From
Howard and Franklin 1989. Reproduced by permission.)

Now, if MK's naming errors were due to impaired semantics, one would
expect his performance on the "Pyramid and Palm Trees" test to show
comparable performance. If he really believed that the bottom left picture
in figure 2a was a desk, then he would likely match that with the easel; and
if he thought the top picture in figure 2b was a slug, he would have no
sensible basis to match it with the butterfly. In fact, he got both of these
trials right, and scored 100 percent on this version of the test—slightly
better than the mean for normals. (Two other versions were administered.
In one, the word "pyramid" was substituted for the picture; in the second,
written words rather than pictures were used. In both, MK scored 100
percent.)

Why then did MK make these naming errors? Within the model assumptions, the errors arise in accessing the semantic lexicon, where (*ex hypothesi*)

words of similar meaning are neighbors, and small access errors should yield semantically related words. This could come about if the search criterion constructed by the semantic system (of the form $\langle \ldots, S_i, S_j, \ldots, S_n \rangle$) were to contain errors, or if some of this information were somehow to be lost in transit between the semantic system and SL, or if the process of matching the criterion to the $S \leftrightarrow P$ pairs were malfunctioning.

Butterworth, Howard, and McLoughlin (1984) found a correlation between patients' semantic naming errors and their semantic comprehension errors. This was not a word-specific effect, since a patient may be able correctly to name a lemon but not to pick it out from an array of fruit. They argued that the cause was not at the level of semantic system but at the level of the SL. They admitted, however, that—although this seems the most plausible account—additional studies of the patients are needed to rule out other candidates. Studies that point more convincingly to the possibility of damage located in SL have used a different technique.

Priming in the Semantic Lexicon
On the principle that if insulin works the patient must have diabetes, it is possible to use the effects of different kinds of treatment to *diagnose* the sources of naming difficulties. Facilitation by priming has recently been revived as an aid and a diagnostic. The time courses of the effects of different kinds of prime turn out to distinguish access levels in our scheme. Patients unable to name a picture can be helped to find the right word by giving them the first phoneme of the target (Patterson, Purell, and Morton 1983). This effect is short-lived; it certainly doesn't last 30 minutes, and it probably lasts only about 5. After that, the patient becomes unable to name the picture again. I assume that the locus of this effect is at the level of the phonological lexicon, which is held to be sensitive to this kind of information.

Semantic primes can be of two types: the target word itself (which, of course, may prime the target at several levels at once) and a semantically related word (for example, an associate of the target). We know there is a very brief effect of semantic primes in a number of tasks, and, within the production system alone, this may have two possible loci, the semantic system or the semantic lexicon, where we might suppose that spreading activation, or something similar, facilitates the retrieval of associated words. On the other hand, semantic primes may work only at one of these levels, and this may support the distinction I have been arguing for.

A second study by Howard and his colleagues (Howard, Patterson, Franklin, Orchard-Lisle, and Morton 1985) throws some dramatic light on this. They tested the effects of target words and associate primes on 20 adult aphasics. In the pretest phase of the experiment, they determined 15 pictures each patient could name and 15 they could not name. The failures were assigned to three categories: *same, associate,* and *control.* In the treatment phase, the patient heard a name and had to point to one of four pictures, with the foils in the same semantic category as the target. The names came from one of three categories: the *same* name as a failure, an *associate* of a failure, or a filler not used in the pretest. Thus, picture names that the subject had failed to retrieve in the pretest would be primed either by the name itself, or by an associate, or by nothing.

There were then three more naming tests: *intermediate naming* following a treatment session of six pointings by about 3 minutes, *Post test 1* about 20 minutes after treatment, and *Post test 2* about 24 hours after treatment. The naming results are shown in figure 4. Hearing the target name and pointing to the picture results in a highly significant improvement in performance. Patients are now getting about 50 percent of the trials right, even at 24 hours. Priming with an associate is the same as no priming at all. Thus, what we find is long-term, lexically specific cross-modal priming. There is no evidence of spreading of activation from associates at this level.

In the semantic system, it must be assumed, semantically related words will be linked to overlapping representations, e.g. the intersection of semantic feature sets. Hence, the activation of an associate will alert features shared with the target at this level, and would thereby surely predict that associates will prime each other. These data then rule out the semantic system as the locus of the effect.

Since the time course of this effect is much longer than that for priming with a phonological cue, we may assume its locus is different, and presumably not at the level where phonological information about the word is made available—i.e., not in accessing PL or in PL itself.

The natural interpretation of these data is, therefore, lexically specific priming in SL.

I suppose a case could be made that we are seeing a combination of semantic priming and phonological priming (though it could not be a simple additive combination, since at 20 minutes, for example, there is neither associate priming nor phonological cueing). Combination effects have been demonstrated, but over much shorter time periods. JCU, a global aphasic described by Howard and Orchard-Lisle (1984), could name only 3 percent of test pictures without help. The first phoneme of the target improved immediate naming to about 50 percent. However, JCU could be induced to produce the semantic coordinate of the target—an incorrect

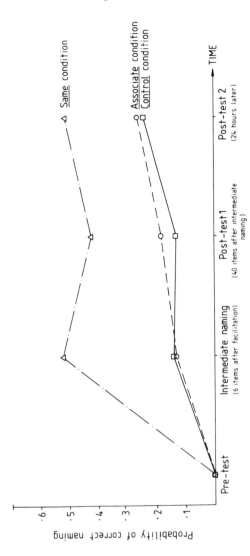

Figure 4

Data on facilitation of naming in aphasic patients. See text for explanation. (From Howard et al. 1985. Reproduced by permission.)

responses, of course—by a misleading phonemic cue. If the target was *lion* and the experimenter offered [tə] as a cue, JCU would say "tiger". The first phoneme of the coordinate usually (57/102) produced no response at all, but it produced 32 semantic paraphasias, and only once the target word. JCU had comparable problems in comprehension of single words—she was likely to accept "tiger" as the correct name for lion, which led Howard and Orchard-Lisle to locate her deficit in the semantics of words. In speech, the deficient representation of the semantics meant that several word candidates would fit the specification, though none very well. The addition of a bit of phonological information would often be sufficient to activate an output from PL, though, as we have seen, not necessarily the correct one.

At the same time, it is possible to find evidence for effects localized at the PL level. Kay and Ellis (1987) describe a patient, EST, who has anomic speech and is poor at object naming whether object presentation is visual, tactile, or by description. He seems to have no perceptual or conceptual problems, and he performs normally on the Pyramids and Palm Trees test. The point of interest is that he has difficulty in retrieving the full phonological form of the target, even though he appears to know what the target is and can often retrieve some phonological information about it. Here is attempt to name stool:

(12) "/stβp/, /stɛp/ ... seat, small seat, round seat, sit on the ... sit on the ... /stə/ /stip/ /stoʊn/ ... it's /stoʊ/ /stei/ /stit/

Notice that the patient is able to find a superordinate (seat) and a functional characterization (sit on the), and several similar-sounding words, and yet he continues trying, apparently unsatisfied with these responses. He often seems to know how many sounds ("letters") are in the target, and he is usually reliable on the first phoneme or phoneme cluster, though Kay and Ellis do not cite figures on positional effects. This is very much like normal people in tip-of-the-tongue (TOT) states (Brown and McNeill 1966).

On Brown and McNeill's model, EST's deficit can be assigned to loss of information about the forms stored in PL. This account makes a further prediction: that cuing by the initial phoneme should not be of much help since, as we have seen, this is already known by the subject. This type of patient seems different from those described above, where it is claimed that (owing to deficits of semantic access) several candidates are activated, which leads to semantic paraphasias. As it happens, EST does not produce errors of this sort.

Kay and Ellis found that the first phoneme helped in 26 percent of the cases where the name was not immediately found spontaneously. And this almost certainly overestimates the effect of cuing, since just giving the subject another chance to name gave 13–20 percent better naming scores without any further help in the study by Howard et al. (1985) (see figure 4 above)—and, of course, results cannot get worse than zero. What is more, cuing with the first phoneme of a coordinate did not lead to the production of the coordinate. Indeed, EST "became quite frustrated by the misleading prompt: given a picture of a *baseball bat* and the cue, 'it's a /rə/' (for *racquet*), he said, 'Doesn't begin with that though, does it? It's a /bə/'!"

One problem with the explanation of the loss of phonological information for low-frequency words in PL is that patients are often able to find the name on one occasion and not on another. This was noticed many years ago by Head (1926), has recently been confirmed more systematically by Howard et al. (1984), and is indeed the case for EST. Moreover, phonological errors in both naming and talking are not consistent over time. Quite different approximations to the target can be elicited; in fact, all the phonemes of the target may be found in these approximations, though not, of course, in any one attempt (Butterworth 1985). This suggests, rather than phonemes being permanently lost from store, that each occasion of access comes up with only (a possibly random) subset of the complete set of phonemes. This doesn't really account for EST's problem; he often makes many attempts to find all the phonemes, and fails (as do normals in TOT states).

An alternative account of these phenomena may lie in how PL is accessed. Recall that SL contains *addresses* of words in PL. Suppose that, for some reason, even though the address is correct, the speaker is unable to retrieve the item at that address. He may give up at that point and produce no response. But he still has some information about what the word sounds like, because he has the address, and neighboring addresses contain similar-sounding words. The addresses bear a systematic relation to their contents, similar addresses pointing to similar-sounding words. So, a determined speaker may try retrieving a neighbor, and may hence come up with a word similar in sound to the target. Or he may employ a fallback procedure that exploits the information contained in the address itself, and deduce that since the address is, say, ⟨one-syllable, onset /st/⟩, it must be a one-syllable word beginning with /st-/. This provides a neat account of both TOT data and EST's results.

The two-stage model thus offers a plausible framework for interpreting some critical neuropsychological data on the varieties of word-finding problems, as well as data from normal speech. These data do not, however, address the distinction I drew earlier between stages and levels. What is needed here is some evidence of temporal disjunction between operations at the different levels. In interactive activation models with two levels roughly corresponding to SL and PL (see, e.g., Dell, this volume), activation of SL nodes automatically feeds down to PL nodes and back up again. You can't stop the process at SL and wait till you are ready to begin activating at PL. To find further evidence for disjunction, we turn to other kinds of data.

4 Evidence for the Temporal Disjunction of Levels

If there really are two lexical-access stages, as opposed to merely two levels, there should be evidence of occasions where the first stage has been completed but the results of its operations have been saved until needed to output the next word, or perhaps saved for checking before going on, as Levelt and Maassen (1981) have suggested.

Temporal Properties of Speech

The natural place to look for temporal disjunction is in the temporal properties of speech. The most studied of these is pausing. Silent pauses in speech typically account for 20–50 percent of total time in conversation, and they seem to be necessary to create time for planning. Reducing planning demands (for example, in reading aloud or in recitation) reduces the proportion of pausing, but it is virtually impossible to talk sense without pausing at least 20 percent of the time. In experimental tasks where simple sentences are produced as quickly as possible under tight grammatical and lexical constraints, the length of the initiation pause depends on what is to be produced, and doubtless on the preplanning needed (Kempen and Huijbers 1983).

In spontaneous speech, we must presume that pauses serve to carry out all the various planning functions needed to produce coherent and appropriate output. Pauses are not distributed evenly, or randomly, through a speaker's output; rather, there is an alternation of hesitant phases with high pause/speech ratios and phases of relatively fluent speech with low pause/speech ratios. A cycle of one hesitant and one fluent phase, lasting 20 seconds on average, corresponds to the expression of an "idea," defined operationally by judges (Butterworth 1975; Petrie 1988, chapter 3), and it would seem that pauses in the hesitant phase are used for outline planning of the whole idea (they will henceforth be called "planning phases," in line with the usual terminology)—the details, including the selection of words, being worked out locally just before output. In fluent (or "execution") phases, pauses are almost exclusively for lexical selection or marking major syntactic boundaries (see Butterworth 1980b and chapters 2 and 3 of Petrie 1988 for reviews of the evidence).

In addition to planning, certain pauses seem to have a specific role in word selection. Goldman-Eisler (1958), in a well-known and much-replicated study, found that words that were unpredictable in context were much more likely to be preceded by a pause than predictable words.

One might argue that "predictability" is an artefact of word frequency, pointing out that unpredictable words tend to have a lower frequency in the language. This would have the desirable consequence of unifying the treatment of delays in conversational output with delays in single-word tasks (e.g., object naming or word naming), which also show frequency effects (see the chapters by Forster, Henderson, and Besner in this volume, and Balota and Chumbley 1985, for reviews of the literature and critical discussions of the locus of frequency effects).

In principle, frequency and predictability are independent, and as a matter of fact, words that are predictable in a given context can be of lower frequency than words that are unpredictable. A rather extreme example makes the point. In

(13) Too many cooks spoil the soup

"soup" is much more frequent than "broth" (in the Kucera-Francis [1970] corpus there are 16 occurrences of "soup" and none of "broth") yet "broth" is more predictable.

Although frequency and predictability are correlated, when they are deconfounded no effect of frequency on pauses is observed independent of predictability (Beattie and Butterworth 1979). This leaves a puzzle that I do not intend to resolve here.

In our model of spontaneous speech, finding a word means accessing first SL and then PL, so lexical pauses may reflect the sum of access times at both levels. Now, one striking finding is that lexical pauses are 50 percent longer in planning phases than in execution phases (0.89 sec vs. 0.57 sec). This is to be expected if, in the planning phase, you select all SL items for the current cycle (in line with the Kempen-Huijbers proposal) saving them in the buffer, but reserving access from PL until you actually need to say the word next. Thus when you choose a word for output during the planning phase, you must carry out access procedures from both SL and PL, whereas by the time you are executing fluently, the SL item has already been selected, and you pause only to carry out access from PL.

.

Gestures

Conversational speech is typically accompanied by hand movements, even in speakers of British English. Simple, repetitive, "batonic" movements are synchronized with the accentuation pattern of the accompanying speech; however, the movements of interest to us here are the more complex "iconic gestures," in which the shape and the dynamics of the movements reflect the meanings of the words they accompany. These are closely tied to the distribution of pauses, rather than accentuation, and to the process of lexical selection.

Seventy percent of iconic gestures (but only 28 percent of batonic movements) accompany those categories of words involved in selection delays, namely nouns, verbs, and adjectives. Interestingly, Butterworth and Beattie (1978) found that the onset of these gestures tends to *precede* the onset of the related lexical item by about 0.8 seconds (*pace* McNeill [1985], who says there is no onset asynchrony). We argued that this is because both gesture and word selection are triggered by the same semantically organized operation, but that gestures are made available more swiftly, perhaps because they are drawn from much smaller ensemble. As a consequence, the onsets of iconic gestures tend to occur in the lexical pauses immediately preceding contextually unpredictable words.

Let us assume that, since they reflect word meanings, iconic gestures are triggered by something semantic and lexically specific, which in our model is an SL item. SL items then trigger both the activation of the gesture and the retrieval of the PL item. In the planning phase, most or all the SL items needed for the whole cycle will be accessed, but only the next PL item. So the pause before next lexical item will reflect successive access to SL and PL for this word and, *at the same time*, the activation of the gesture (if there is one) to accompany that word.

However, in execution phases, where the SL item is already known, the gesture can be elicited more quickly than the retrieval of the phonological word form from PL, perhaps because there are fewer gestures than words, and this will show up as an onset asynchrony, with gesture onset located in the lexical pause. Because we assume that double access occurs only in the planning phase (though not for all words), we predict that the proportion of gesture onsets in pauses should be substantially higher in execution phases, as indeed it is (72 versus 57 percent), even though there is much less pause time in execution phases.

What happens to gestures in aphasic patients with severe word-finding difficulties? According to our account, if the pattern of gestures is normal, we must infer that processes up to and including access from SL are unaffected, and that the problem is to be located in access to PL or thereafter.

We recently described one patient, KC, a fluent jargon aphasic who used neologisms as substitutes to conceal a word-finding problem (Butterworth, Swallow, and Grimston 1981). His speech was grossly abnormal and uninterpretable, but his gestures were quite normal in their shape, in their distribution in relation to word classes, and in the distribution of onsets in relation to pauses. The unusual feature of his gesturing was that many gestures were uncompleted, something we have not observed in normal speakers. When we looked at the location of these incompleted gestures, we found something surprising: They always accompanied symptoms of total word-finding failure. Either KC was aborting the whole sentence and starting again, or he was producing what I have called "device" neologisms, which are quite different in sound from the target and from words in the local context. I have, on the basis of other evidence, argued that these neologisms are produced just when KC fails to find any part of any word candidate at all (in contrast to other neologisms, where he seems to be able to come up with at least part of a word, even if it is the wrong one) (Butterworth 1979). This pattern of gesture and speech is exactly what would be predicted if access to SL is intact but access to PL is grossly disturbed.

Conclusions

A wide range of word-retrieval and related phenomena have natural explanations in a two-stage model of lexical access. More specifically, some of these phenomena indicate a temporal disjunction between stages, which in turn implies a lack of interaction between access stages. Thus, for example, decisions about grammatical relations—which, most agree, are related to Stage 1—may be affected by which item has been accessed from SL, but should not be affected by which word has been accessed from PL. (Some fallback procedure may be invoked on the occasion of word-finding failure; but here there is feedback as to whether a word has been found, not which word has been activated.) There is no space here to interpret some recent experimental findings in detail, but it appears that semantic priming, whose locus must be in the semantic system or in SL, affects word order in sentence-production tasks, but phonological priming does not (Bock 1986). Levelt and Maassen's 1981 study, described above, found no effect of the intrinsic ease of retrieval of words from PL on word order.

I have argued that there is a first stage in lexical access which involves a store of lexically specific items that are not actually words but rather items that pair semantic codes with phonological addresses. One of the properties claimed for this kind of representation is that it is intermodal. It mediates lexical mappings from word input as well as word output, so it is possible to seek independent justification from speech-comprehension tasks; this is what was attempted in the studies of aphasic patients. There is a further natural extension into reading and writing, in which semantic codes will be paired with orthographic addresses. Language users need a way to represent cross-modal mappings between phonological and orthographic word forms and word meanings. This is what the intermodal SL is designed for.

Acknowledgments

I would like to thank David Howard for years of happy collaboration developing these, and other, ideas. The errors in this paper are, of course, mine. My thanks also to Pim Levelt, Gerard Kempen, and Merrill Garrett for useful discussions on the substance of this paper, and to Gary Dell and William Marslen-Wilson for detailed comments on the first draft.

Some of the work by Howard and myself reported here was funded by a MRC Project Grant.

References

Allport, D. A. 1984. Speech production and comprehension: one lexicon or two? In W. Prinz and A. F. Sanders (eds.), *Cognition and Motor Processes.* Berlin: Springer-Verlag.

Balota, D. A., and Chumbley, J. I. 1985. Locus of word frequency effects in the pronunciation: Lexical access and/or production. *Journal of Memory and Language* 24: 89–106.

Beattie, G. W., and Butterworth, B. L. 1979. Contextual probability and word frequency as determinants of pauses in spontaneous speech. *Language and Speech* 22: 201–211.

Bock, J. K. 1982. Toward a cognitive psychology of syntax: Information processing contributions to sentence formulation. *Psychological Review* 89: 1–47.

Bock, J. K. 1986. Meaning, sound and syntax: Lexical priming in sentence production. *Journal of Experimental Psychology: Learning, Memory and Cognition* 12: 575–586.

Brown, R., and McNeill, D. 1966. The "tip of the tongue" phenomenon. *Journal of Verbal Learning and Verbal Behavior* 5: 325–337.

Butterworth, B. L. 1975. Hesitation and semantic planning in speech. *Journal of Psycholinguistic Research* 4: 75–87.

Butterworth, B. L. 1979. Hesitation and the production of verbal paraphasias and neologisms in jargon aphasia. *Brain and Language* 8: 133–161.

Butterworth, B. L. 1980a. Some constraints on models of language production. In B. L. Butterworth (ed.), *Language Production, Volume 1: Speech and Talk*. London: Academic.

Butterworth, B. L. 1980b. Evidence from pauses. In B. L. Butterworth (ed.), *Language Production, Volume 1: Speech and Talk*. London: Academic.

Butterworth, B. L. 1983. Lexical representation. In B. L. Butterworth (ed.), *Language Production, Volume 2: Development, Writing and Other Language Processes*. London: Academic.

Butterworth, B. L. 1985. Jargon aphasia: Processes and strategies. In S. Newman and R. Epstein (eds.), *Current Perspectives in Dysphasia*. Edinburgh: Churchill Livingstone.

Butterworth, B. L., and Beattie, G. W. 1978. Gesture and silence as indicators of planning in speech. In R. Campbell and P. T. Smith (eds.), *Advances in the Psychology of Language–Formal and Experimental Approaches*. New York: Plenum.

Butterworth, B. L., Howard, D., and McLoughlin, P. J. 1984. The semantic deficit in aphasia: The relationship between semantic errors in auditory comprehension and picture naming. *Neuropsychologia* 22: 409–426.

Butterworth, B. L., Swallow, J., and Grimston, M. 1981. Gestures and lexical processes in jargon aphasia. In J. W. Brown (ed.), *Jargonaphasia*. New York: Academic.

Cutler, A., and Isard, S. 1980. The production of prosody. In B. L. Butterworth (ed.), *Language Production, Volume 1: Speech and Talk*. London: Academic.

Dell, G. 1986. A spreading activation theory of retrieval in sentence production. *Psychological Review* 93: 283–321.

Dell, G., and Reich, P. 1981. Stages in sentence production: An analysis of speech error data. *Journal of Verbal Learning and Verbal Behavior* 20: 611–629.

Ellis, A. W. 1985. The production of spoken words: A cognitive neuropsychological perspective. In A. W. Ellis (ed.), *Progress in the Psychology of Language, Volume 2*. London: Erlbaum.

Fay, D., and Cutler, A. 1977. Malapropisms and the structure of the mental lexicon. *Linguistic Inquiry* 8: 505–520.

Forster, K. 1976. Accessing the mental lexicon. In R. J. Wales and E. C. T. Walker (eds.), *New Approaches to Language Mechanisms*. Amsterdam: North-Holland.

Fromkin, V. 1971. The nonanomalous nature of anomalous utterances. *Language* 47: 27–52.

Garrett, M. F. 1975. The analysis of sentence production. In G. H. Bower (ed.), *The Psychology of Learning and Motivation, Volume 9*. New York: Academic.

Garrett, M. F. 1976. Syntactic processes in sentence production. In R. J. Wales and E. C. T. Walker (eds.), *New Approaches to Language Mechanisms*. Amsterdam: North-Holland.

Garrett, M. F. 1980a. Levels of processing in sentence production. In B. L. Butterworth (ed.), *Language Production, Volume 1: Speech and Talk*. London: Academic.

Garrett, M. F. 1980b. The limits of accommodation: Arguments for independent processing levels in sentence production. In V. Fromkin (ed.), *Errors in Linguistic performance: Slips of the Tongue, Ear, Pen and Hand*. New York: Academic.

Garrett, M. F. 1982. Production of speech: Observations from normal and pathological language use. In A. Ellis (ed.), *Normality and Pathology in Cognitive Functions*. New York: Academic.

Goldman-Eisler, F. 1958. Speech production and the predictability of words in context. *Quarterly Journal of Experimental Psychology* 10: 96–106.

Hart, J., Berndt, R. S., and Caramazza, A. 1985. Category-specific naming deficit following cerebral infarction *Nature* 316: 439–440.

Head, H. 1926. *Aphasia and Kindred Disorders of Speech, Volume I*. Cambridge University Press.

Howard, D. 1984. The Semantic Organisation of the Lexicon: Evidence from Aphasia. Ph.D. Thesis, University of London.

Howard, D., and Franklin, S. 1989. *Missing the Meaning*? Cambridge, Mass.: MIT Press.

Howard, D., and Orchard-Lisle, V. M. 1984. On the origin of semantic errors in naming: Evidence from the case of a global aphasic. *Cognitive Neuropsychology* 1: 163–190.

Howard, D., Patterson, K., Franklin, S., Orchard-Lisle, V., and Morton, J. 1984. Consistency and variability in picture naming by aphasic patients. In F. C. Rose (ed.), *Recent Advances in Aphasiology*. New York: Raven.

Howard, D., Patterson, K., Franklin, S., Orchard-Lisle, V., and Morton, J. 1985. The facilitation of picture naming in aphasia. *Cognitive Neuropsychology* 2: 49–80.

Kay, J., and Ellis, A. 1987. A cognitive neuropsychological case study of anomia: Implications for psychological models of word retrieval. *Brain*. 110: 613–629.

Kempen, G., and Huijbers, P. 1983. The lexicalisation process in sentence production and naming: Indirect election of words. *Cognition* 14: 185–209.

Levelt, W. J. M., and Maassen, B. 1981. Lexical search and order of mention in sentence production. In W. Klein and W. Levelt (eds.), *Crossing the Boundaries in Linguistics*. Dordrecht: Reidel.

Lindsley, J. R. 1975. Producing simple utterances: How far do we plan ahead? *Cognitive Psychology* 7: 1–19.

Lindsley, J. R. 1976. Producing simple utterances: Details of the planning process. *Journal of Psycholinguistic Research* 5: 331–354.

Lounsbury, F. G. 1954. Transitional probability, linguistic structure and systems of habit-family hierarchies. In C. E. Osgood and T. Sebeok (eds.), *Psycholinguistics: A Survey of Theory and Research Problems*. Bloomington: Indiana University Press.

McNeill, D. 1985. So you think gentures are nonverbal? *Psychological Review* 92: 350–371.

Menn, L., Powelson, J., Miceli, G., Williams, E., and Zurif, E. 1982. A Psycholinguistic Model for Paragrammatic Speech. Paper presented at B.A.B.B.L.E. Meeting, Niagara Falls, Ontario.

Morton, J. 1968. Considerations of grammar and computation in language behavior. In J. C. Catford (ed.), *Studies in Language and Language Behavior* (Progress Report IV, U.S. Office of Education).

Morton, J. 1985. Naming. In S. Newman and R. Epstein (eds.), *Current Perspectives in Dysphasia*. Edinburgh: Churchill Livingstone.

Morton, J., and Patterson, K. 1980. In M. Coltheart, K. Patterson, and J. C. Marshall (eds.), *Deep Dyslexia*. London: RKP.

Newcombe, F., Oldfield, R. C., and Wingfield, A. 1965. Object naming by dysphasic patients. *Nature* 207: 1217–1218.

Oldfield, R. C. 1963. Individual vocabulary and semantic currency: A preliminary study. *British Journal of Social and Clinical Psychology* 2: 122–130.

Oldfield, R. C. 1966a. Things, words and the brain. *Quarterly Journal of Experimental Psychology* 18: 340–353.

Oldfield, R. C. 1966b. Denomination d'objets et stockage des mots. *Bulletin de Psychologie* 247 (XIX): 733–744.

Oldfield, R. C., and Wingfield, A. 1964. The time it takes to name an object. *Nature* 202: 1031–1032.

Patterson, K., Purell, C., and Morton, J. 1983. The facilitation of word retrieval in aphasia. In C. Code and D. Muller (eds.), *Aphasia Therapy*. London: Arnold.

Petrie, H. 1988. Ph.D. thesis, University of London.

Stemberger, J. P., and MacWhinney, B. 1986. Frequency and the lexical storage of regularly inflected forms. *Memory and Cognition* 14: 17–26.

Warrington, E. K. 1975. The selective impairment of semantic memory. *Quarterly Journal of Experimental Psychology* 27: 635–657.

Chapter 5

The Retrieval of Phonological Forms in Production: Tests of Predictions from a Connectionist Model	Gary S. Dell

Instead of saying "I'll go shut up the barn door", a speaker says "I'll go shut up the <u>darn</u> <u>bore</u>". Why do slips of the tongue like this occur, and what implications do they have for a theory of language production? In this chapter I review a model of retrieval processes in production that makes predictions about the factors influencing these kinds of speech errors (Dell 1986), and summarize some experiments testing these predictions. The approach taken in the model is connectionist. To understand why this approach is useful, one must consider something of the history of research on speech errors and language production.

1 Two Traditions in Studying Speech Errors

Over the last century, slips of the tongue have been examined as scientific evidence within the context of two contrasting traditions, one linguistic and one psychological. The goal of researchers in the linguistic tradition has been to gain insight into the nature of language (Fromkin 1971; Fry 1969; Hockett 1973; Meringer 1908; Meringer and Mayer 1895) and, more recently, the nature of linguistic performance (Berg 1987; Cutler 1981; Dell 1986; Fromkin 1973; Garrett 1975, 1976, 1980; Nooteboom 1969; MacKay 1970, 1972, 1973, 1982; Stemberger 1982, 1985a; Shattuck-Hufnagel 1979, 1983; Shattuck-Hufnagel and Klatt 1979). A characteristic of this tradition is to see errors as the result of the misapplication of linguistic rules; either the wrong rule applies because a constraint on its application is ignored, or the mechanism for applying the rule misfires.[1] Thus, in the case of the <u>darn bore</u> error above, the rules *Onset* → /b/ and *Onset* → /d/ applied at the wrong times.[2]

The emphasis on linguistic regularities within this tradition has led to two related generalities about errors. The first is that errors can be associated with linguistic levels or components. The *darn bore* error can be characterized as phonological because it involves the movement of phonological units (single phonemes, in this case) and, more important, because the kinds of variables that seem to influence these kinds of errors are themselves phonological. For example, the exchanging phonemes in *darn bore* are phonologically similar (they share features) and they occupy phonologically similar positions (both are syllable-initial and word-initial, and both come from stressed syllables). In general, the dimensions of similarity that are correlated with the occurrence of phonemic exchanges are exactly those dimensions that are needed to define phonological acceptability for a string.

The second generality about speech errors that is emphasized in the linguistic tradition is that the major rule systems associated with a linguistic level are usually not violated by an error occurring at that level. At the phonological level, although errors creating nonwords are quite common (e.g., *hollow thud → thollow hud*), the resulting nonwords are nearly always phonologically possible sequences; that is, they adhere to the phonological rules of the language (Fromkin 1971; Wells 1951; for discussions of exceptions see Butterworth and Whitaker 1980 and Stemberger 1983). For errors involving lexical items as a whole, the resulting sequences tend to be syntactically coherent, as in the error *I'm writing a mother to my letter*, in which the exchanging nouns do not upset the syntactic structure of the utterance (Garrett 1975; Stemberger 1985a). Thus, broadly speaking, the work done in the linguistic tradition emphasizes the strong control over errors emanating from the systematicity of language. Furthermore, this systematicity is organized into distinct components, which are assumed to limit the scope of influence of linguistic knowledge over particular types of errors.

Probably the most systematic theory of production to emerge strictly within the linguistic tradition is that of Garrett (1975, 1976, 1980). Garrett and researchers following him (see, e.g., Bock 1986; Bock, in press; Lapointe and Dell, in press; Saffron 1982; Schwartz, in press; Shattuck-Hufnagel 1979) identified two distinct processing levels: a functional level, in which lexical items as whole units are assembled into an underlying syntactic or thematic structure, and a positional level, in which the phonological forms of words are inserted into slots in a surface syntactic/phonological frame. Speech errors are assumed to occur during the construction of the representations associated with each level; hence, each particular error type is associated with one of the levels. The levels are assumed to be independent in that each has access to different kinds of linguistic information, leading to predictions of differential sensitivity of error types to linguistic variables.

For example, a functional-level error, such as the exchange of two words, is predicted to be sensitive to functional-level information, such as the thematic and syntactic properties of the words, and insensitive to positional-level information, such as the phonological form of the words. To a large extent, the theory has been successful in accounting for patterns of speech errors. It has also been applied to aphasia (Saffron 1982) and to other aspects of production (Bock 1986).

The psychological tradition in the study of speech errors is associated with Freud and contrasts sharply with the linguistic tradition. The central notion of the psychological tradition is that speech errors are influenced by factors outside of the intended utterance, and, in general, that slips are products of multiple factors. Several sources of interference can combine in causing a slip. Probably the strongest version of this claim is that unconscious motivation is one of these factors and, in fact, is a necessary one (Freud 1901/1958). Although this Freudian view of speech errors is part of the layman's view of slips, the evidence for it is scanty (Ellis 1980). There is, however, a weaker claim within the psychological tradition that is worthy of attention—a claim that is counter to theories emerging from the linguistic tradition, such as Garrett's (1975). This is that errors occurring at one level of processing can be affected by factors outside that level. So, for example, the *darn bore* error, although clearly an exchange of phonemes, could have been precipitated by nonphonological factors. The fact that *darn* and *bore* are actual words, as opposed to phonologically acceptable nonwords, may have played a role. This possibility, referred to as *lexical bias*, has some empirical support (Baars, Motley, and MacKay 1975; Berg 1983; Dell and Reich 1981; Stemberger 1984a; see, however, Garrett 1976). It is also in the spirit of the psychological tradition to hypothesize that the fact that *darn bore* is itself a meaningful phrase is an important influence. There is some support for this kind of phrasal bias (Motley and Baars 1976; Motley, Baars, and Camden 1982). Finally, one may argue that the person uttering this slip was actually thinking that someone, perhaps the listener, is a "darn bore" and hopes to shut him or her up. This thought, active at the time of speaking, may increase the chance of the phonemes' exchanging (Motley and Baars 1979). The idea that active thoughts may be expressed in phonological errors is quite close to Freud's view, although Freud's claim was stronger. (Freud held that such influences are necessary in slips and that the thoughts in question are unconscious.)

Another class of hypotheses within the psychological tradition deal with the question of multiple relations in word-level slips. These errors include word substitutions, such as *Liszt's second Hungarian restaurant (rhapsody)*, blends, such as *tennis athler (player/athlete)*, and misorderings, such as *He eats yoga (yoghurt) and does yoghurt (yoga)*. In errors of these types the two interacting words are nearly always members of the same syntactic category, a fact that has been emphasized within the linguistic tradition (Fay and Cutler 1977; MacKay 1973; Garrett 1975). However, there appear to be other dimensions of similarity between the interacting words that play a role. Very often, word-level errors will exhibit simultaneously an influence of the interacting words' sound structure and their associative relations to other words. For example, the *restaurant* error above appears to show an associative relation to *Hungarian* and a phonological relation to the target word *rhapsody*. Where such relations have been quantified and examined relative to plausible null hypotheses, the conclusion has emerged that word-level errors are consistently associated with simultaneous multiple relations (Dell and Reich 1981; Harley 1984). One is reminded of Freud's emphasis on multiple causes for slips—a specific case of his principle of overdetermination of behavior—but, again, the finding of multiple relations does not support the orthodox Freudian position, with its necessary unconscious motives; it supports only the weaker claims of the psychological tradition.

Although both the linguistic and the psychological tradition have had influence, the work in the linguistic tradition has held the high ground over the last 20 years. The effects of purely linguistic structure on errors are striking and are often sufficiently strong that they can be characterized as "laws" (Wells 1951). For example, it is true of nearly every phonological slip that it will not create a string that violates the phonological rules of the language. In contrast, the effects that characterize the psychological tradition are more subtle or probabilistic and often need to be demonstrated through controlled experiments or careful statistical analyses of error corpora. Also, the work within the linguistic tradition has the advantage of being grounded in formal theory which has provided a basis for error typology and hypotheses regarding the kinds of influences that should be present in certain kinds of errors (Fromkin 1971; Garrett 1975). The psychological tradition, by itself, lacks a formal theory. Freudian theory provides little more than a set of ideas for interpreting errors in a *post hoc* manner. When hypotheses about multiple influences on errors have been formulated and tested, the purpose has been more to demonstrate the existence of effects than to develop and test predictions from theory.

The contrast between the two traditions has evolved and is really no longer a disagreement between Freudian psychologists and linguists. Rather, it is a debate within psycholinguistic theory about the structure of the processing system. Those theorists emphasizing modular computational processes represent the linguistic tradition, and those stressing interactive processes have inherited the mantle of the psychological tradition. Thus, one approach finds limits on the influence of factors on speech errors of interest, while the other focuses on cases where unexpected diverse influences are at work.

In addition, the two approaches differ on where they place the burden of explanation of speech-error phenomena. In the linguistic tradition, the emphasis has come to be on representations; in the psychological tradition, the processing system itself, rather than the representations that it manipulates, has been the focus. For example, in Garrett's (1975) model the predictions about the sensitivity of error types to linguistic factors derive from the structure of the two hypothesized representations (together with the assumed modularity of the levels associated with each) and not with the ways that the representations are manipulated by psychological processes. Modern work in the psychological tradition, however, typically identifies error effects with particular processes. To explain phrasal biases, Motley and Baars (1976) posited an internal editor that is less likely to detect and correct errors that form coherent phrases. Similarly, to account for multiple influences on word-substitution errors, Dell and Reich (1981) and Harley (1984) discussed the joint effects of top-down and bottom-up processes in lexical retrieval.

The model that I outline here attempts to combine these two traditions and give an account of the kinds of data that each emphasizes. The connectionist or "spreading-activation" framework I adopt allows the interactions among information sources that were the focus of the psychological tradition to be placed within a system of linguistic knowledge. Specifically, much of what is emphasized in the linguistic tradition will be present in the structure of the network, in its units and the connections among them. The effects associated with the psychological tradition will then emerge from the spreading-activation process. I will show both how the model explains existing effects and how it predicts the existence of new effects.

2   A Model of Phonological Retrieval

The model deals with a specific component of the production process: the retrieval of the phonological form of lexical items. That is, given an ordered set of word units (often called *lemmas* in the production literature; see Kempen and Huijbers 1983), it retrieves and orders their segments. Thus one can view the input to the model as the output of a syntactic encoding device which has already selected and ordered words. I will not deal with syntactic encoding here; however, a number of papers have outlined how a connectionist model might implement syntactic encoding decisions in production, and these can be consulted for a discussion of how the current model could be expanded in this direction (Bock, in press; Dell 1986; Lapointe and Dell, in press; MacKay 1982; Stemberger 1982, 1985a).

In assuming that word units have already been selected prior to the retrieval of phonological forms, the model is adopting a two-stage or double-retrieval view of lexical access in production (Fromkin 1971; Garrett 1975; Fay and Cutler 1977; Kempen and Huijbers 1983; Levelt and Schriefers 1985). The evidence from speech errors, speech hesitations, and aphasic syndromes seems to support this view (Butterworth, this volume).

Network Structure
The model's network structure is motivated to a large extent by linguistic theory. The network has two parts: a lexical network and a word-shape network (figure 1). The distinction between the lexical and word-shape networks captures the idea that it is profitable to separate the phonological structure of a word into two components: a frame, or sequence of slots, that specifies the abstract shape of the word and the number and kinds of syllables and phonemes it contains (CVC, CV, etc.), and a separate representation of the actual sounds of the word that are associated with those slots. Shattuck-Hufnagel (1979), Reich (1977), and Stemberger (1984b) have argued persuasively for this separation based on speech-error facts. In addition, phonological theory in linguistics has recognized the need for such a distinction because phonological (and, in some languages, morphological) forms can be elegantly described by making reference only to the frame (or "CV-skeleton") in some cases and only to the sounds (or "melody") in other cases (McCarthy 1981).

The lexical network connects word nodes with their sounds. For ease of exposition, I will assume that the only levels of representation are a word level and a phoneme level (figure 1). The large version of the model (Dell 1986) employs several other levels of representation (features, syllables, etc.); although these appear to be necessary to explain the variety of error phenomena, they are not relevant to the predictions that are explored here. The connections between word and phoneme nodes are excitatory and bidirectional, thus allowing for positive feedback between the levels in much the same way as occurs in the interactive activation model of visual

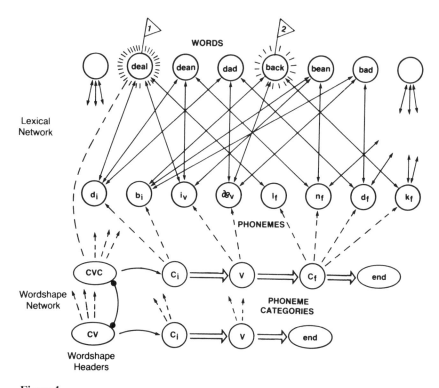

Figure 1

The lexical and word-shape networks in the model. The intended phrase is "deal back", indicated by numbered flags on the word nodes. All connections between nodes in the lexical network are excitatory and two-way. The broken lines indicate connections between the lexical and word-shape networks. The arrows between phoneme category nodes in the word-shape network indicate their sequence of activation.

word identification (McClelland and Rumelhart 1981; Rumelhart and McClelland 1982).

Each word node in the lexical network also connects to a wordshape "header" node—a node representing the pattern of phoneme categories for the word (CVC, CV, etc.)—which, in turn, connects to a sequence of phoneme categories. For example, the CVC header connects to C_i (for pre-vocalic consonant), which connects to V (for vowel), which connects to C_f (for post-vocalic consonant). Each of the phoneme-category nodes then connects back to all possible phoneme nodes of its category. This component of the model, which is based on suggestions by Stemberger (1984b), is a significant modification of the earlier model (Dell 1986). The earlier model had a single canonical syllable shape for CVC that was called into action for all words. For multisyllabic words it was used as often as was necessary, and for non-CVC syllables special null and cluster units in the lexical network were employed. The failure of this model to explain the probabilities of phoneme addition errors (e.g., *blue bug* → *blue blug*) and deletion errors (→ *bue bug*) (Dell 1986; Stemberger and Treiman 1986) motivates the change from the single CVC syllable shape to an approach with several possible wordshapes. However, the wordshape component of the present model—particularly the mechanism for competition among wordshapes—has not been well explored through simulation. Thus, the model that is directly tested here will not deal with predictions related to competing wordshapes. All words will be assumed to have the same CVC shape (see figure 1), which essentially removes the competition issue from consideration.

Processing Assumptions
I will illustrate the model's processing assumptions by walking through the steps involved in phonologically encoding the phrase "deal back". I assume that the syntax has already selected and ordered these words, as is indicated by the numbered flags in figure 1.

Activation of word nodes
The first word, *deal,* is initially the "current word," the word that is currently being phonologically encoded. An arbitrary amount of activation (100 units) is added to that word's node, and upcoming words in the same phrase (*back*) that are already flagged are primed by adding in a lesser amount of activation (50 units).

Spread of activation
Activation spreads in the lexical network by the following rule: During each time step, every node sends some fraction p of its activation to nodes that

it is directly connected to. When activation reaches its destination node, it adds to that node's activation. Also, during each time step each node's activation decays by a factor g toward its resting level. Specifically,

$$\Delta A(j) = \text{Input}(j) - [A(j) - R(j)]q,$$

where $A(j)$ is the activation level of node j at a certain time, $\Delta A(j)$ is the change that this level undergoes in one time step, and $R(j)$ is the node's resting level. The resting level is assumed to be zero for phoneme nodes and to vary with frequency for word nodes. Input(j) is the incoming activation sent to j from its neighbors during a time step; this is given by

$$\text{Input}(j) = p \sum_{i=1}^{k} A(i),$$

where $A(i)$ is the activation level of the ith neighbor of j (of k neighbors) during the time step. Thus, in this model every node has the same decay rate and every connection has the same strength. Only resting levels differ with frequency. The spreading rule is completely linear, and, given that the lexical network has only excitatory connections among its nodes, the model has the characteristics of the networks studied by Shrager, Hogg, and Huberman (1987). In such networks, the decay rate q must be somewhat greater than the spreading rate p to keep the network from entering a phase in which activation levels go haywire. However, when the ratio p/q is small, the network is reasonably well behaved, and it is in this region that the present model operates—specifically, where $p/q < 0.5$.

The spread of activation allows for activated words to retrieve their constituent phonemes in the lexical network. Because activation spreads in both a top-down and a bottom-up fashion, many words and phonemes other than the correct ones become activated to some extent and thus contribute to the retrieval process. We shall see later how the action of these extrinsic nodes influences the retrieval process.

Selection of the most highly activated phonemes
After a certain number of time steps have passed (parameter r, which is determined by the speech rate), the most highly activated phonemes are selected. How many phonemes, what kind of phonemes, and their order depends on the wordshape network. Activated word nodes are assumed to send activation to their respective header wordshape nodes. When it comes time to select phonemes, the most highly activated header wins the right to select a phoneme for each of its category nodes. Selection could be achieved by any of several mechanisms. For example, the phoneme-category nodes could be activated in series (see Jordan 1985 and Shastri and Feldman 1984 for some connectionist serial order devices). When

activated, each node would send an increasing amount of activation to all the phoneme nodes in its category until one of them—the one with the highest activation level to begin with—reached some selection threshold. This kind of categorically triggered selection has been suggested by MacKay (1982) and Stemberger (1985a). In the *deal back* example, the CVC word-shape would be the controlling shape, and so the categories C_i, V, and C_f would then select the most highly activated initial consonant, vowel, and final consonant. In this case, given that the word *deal* controls most of the activation in the lexical network, the selected sounds would be /d/, /i/, and /l/.

Post-selection feedback
In this final stage, the activation levels of the selected phoneme nodes are set to zero (their resting levels). This post-selection inhibition helps prevent unwanted reselection, or stuttering. However, these turned-off phonemes quickly rebound from zero because of other activated nodes in the network connected to them. So, when /d/, /i/, and /l/ are selected and turned off, they rebound because of the highly activated *deal*, *dean*, and other nodes.

The post-selection inhibition is analogous to the checkoff monitor in Shattuck-Hufnagel's (1979) model of speech errors and is very much like the assumed post-activation inhibition in MacKay's (1982) and Rumelhart and Norman's (1982) work. In general, modelers have favored an active device that quickly turns off elements once they are used, rather than relying on a passive decay process to do the job. The advantage of this arrangement will be seen later when exchange errors are examined.

A final aspect of post-selection feedback is the updating of the current word. In this example, the "current" status must change from *deal* to *back*. When this happens, the entire process of activation, spread of activation, and selection repeats itself, and the sounds of *back* are retrieved and selected in proper order.

The Model's Error Mechanism
A phonological speech error happens simply when the wrong phoneme is more active than the correct one of the same phoneme category and is selected.[3] So, if /d/ is more activated than /b/ when the model is encoding *back*, the resulting string is *deal dack*, a phoneme *perseveration* error. Anticipations, such as *beal back*, work in much the same way except that the major source of interference comes from upcoming syllables. Exchanges (*beal dack*) are more complex. By definition, an exchange is first an anticipation (*deal → beal*) and then a perseveration (back → dack) involving the

same sounds. In the model, once a sound (e.g., /b/) has been anticipated, like any selected sound, it is subject to post-selection inhibition. The replaced sound /d/ is still active, however, and is looking for a place to go. If it remains active enough it could be selected the next time its phoneme category comes up because the proper sound (/b/) was turned off in the previous word. Whether an initial anticipatory error (*beal...*) becomes an exchange or an anticipation will depend on several factors, such as the speech rate, the decay rate, and the availability of a suitable alternative slot for the replaced sound. Some predictions regarding these error types are discussed later.

Given that errors arise when the wrong sounds are more active than the right ones, it is only natural to ask what leads to the wrong sounds' being more active. This is where the model shows the advantages of its connectionist nature and its affinity with the psychological tradition in studying speech errors. There are three sources of interference. First, the spreading of activation from intended words creates its own interference by activating many words and phonemes that are not really involved in the utterance at all. Second, previously spoken words and upcoming words in the same phrase are active and therefore are sources of interference, particularly if the speech rate is fast. Third, it is assumed that unintended words are activated by extraneous cognition and perception, which is consistent with the evidence from the speech-error literature (e.g., Motley and Baars 1976; Harley 1984).

The model actually would not make a slip when saying a two-word phrase like *deal back*. Slips are most common when the model tries to say many words quickly (Dell 1986). The various sources of interference then combine and conspire to direct activation to the wrong phonemes at the wrong time. As I turn to specific empirical phenomena in the next section, this should become clear.

3 Empirical Issues

All the data that I discuss in this section come from previously reported and new studies using a specific experimental paradigm that elicits initial consonant exchanges, anticipations, and perseverations. The paradigm is a modification of one used by Baars and Motley (1974); table 1 illustrates the procedure. Subjects see word pairs at a one-per-second rate, with the instruction to prepare to say each pair as they see it. Eventually, they see a series of question marks that signal the subject to speak. They must say aloud the last word pair that they saw. In some of the experiments presented

Table 1
Error-generation procedure.

	Sample list section
	seed reap
Filler stimuli	same rope
	lamb toy
	big dumb
Interference stimuli	bust dog
	bet dart
Critical stimulus	deal back
Signal to speak	??????????
Deadline interval	
	└tone sounds
Subject response	"deal back" or
	"beal dack" or
	"beal back" or
	"deal dack"

here the task was to say the words "as quickly as possible"; and in other experiments subjects were given a deadline (a tone) before which they had to finish speaking. When the deadline was manipulated, it was done in a between-subjects fashion. The reason that slips are obtained at all is that certain critical stimuli (e.g., *deal back* in table 1) are preceded by three to five interference stimuli that bias for a reversal of initial consonants. A final aspect of the procedure is that after saying each prompted stimulus the subjects have to judge whether or not they said what they intended to say, and have to repeat slowly what they intended to say. This allows for errors of reading or memory to be separated from errors of output (true slips of the tongue). Typically, from 80 to 90 percent of the errors obtained are output errors (Dell 1986).

This experimental paradigm is beginning to be used by researchers as an alternative to simply analyzing error collections (Baars et al. 1975; Dell 1984, 1986; Levitt and Healy 1985; Stemberger and Treiman 1986). It enables one to manipulate conditions of interest, to obtain actual error probabilities as opposed to error frequencies, and to eliminate the sampling biases that are known to contaminate error collections. Furthermore, as far as we know, there are no major inconsistencies between the experimental data and the naturalistic data (Stemberger 1985b).

Built-In versus Predicted Empirical Phenomena

In any modeling enterprise it is useful to distinguish between empirical phenomena that are specifically built into the model and phenomena whose existence the model predicts. This is particularly important in connectionist models of the kind being presented here, in which the network structure, both the units and connections, are specified beforehand rather than learned. In the present model, many of the structural and processing features were built in specifically to create known empirical phenomena. As I list these built-in features and effects, I will try to give a feel for the extent to which each feature is motivated. In some cases a feature is present in the model only because of a single empirical effect that needs to be accounted for. Naturally, these built-in devices are neither elegant nor convincing. In other cases, a feature is responsible for a single, known speech-error effect, but it can point to other motivation from outside the speech-error literature. Finally, there are the best cases: those in which a built-in feature is related to several previously known empirical phenomena.

Built-In Features

Anticipatory priming

Upcoming words in the same phrase as the current word are primed. This feature's primary motivation is simply the existence of anticipatory slips. If the feature were not in the model, it would not produce anticipations or exchanges. There is actually good secondary motivation for anticipatory priming; it was discussed by Lashley (1951). The existence of long-distance dependencies in the grammar requires that representations be constructed in advance of the word currently being said. Anticipatory priming is a natural consequence of advance planning in an activation model. However, it is acknowledged that the present model does not deal with these long-distance dependencies.

Syllabic-position encoding of consonants

In the model there are separate phoneme nodes for pre- and post-vocalic consonants, and corresponding C_i and C_f phoneme categories in the word-shape network. The motivation for this is a single speech-error phenomenon: that pre- and post-vocalic consonants almost never slip with one another (MacKay 1970). For example, *cat* would never slip to *tack*. Separating pre-vocalic from post-vocalic versions of a consonant produces the desired effect, but at a considerable cost. The network no longer recognizes the /k/s in *cat* and *tack* as related sounds. The fact that the ultimate phonetic shapes of pre- and post-vocalic versions of the same consonant differ a great deal is little consolation, because phonetic shape is known to be specified *after* the phonological retrieval processes leading to slips of the sort discussed here (Fromkin 1971; Garrett 1975). Thus, the model's mechanism for handling syllable-position effects in errors is not a very satisfactory one.

Selection of phonemes

That *phonemes* are the units that are selected is a built-in feature whose principal motivation is the empirical fact that most phonological speech errors involve the movement, deletion, or addition of single phonemes (70–90 percent of phonological errors; see Dell 1986 and Stemberger 1983). One could argue that linguistic theory provides the necessary additional motivation for the choice of the phoneme, and this argument has some merit. In its use of CV-skeletons, phonological theory makes a strong commitment to phoneme-sized slots to which material is then linked. However, there really is not any reason in linguistic theory that the units linked could not be phonological features of some sort rather than phonemes. The main reason the model selects phonemes rather than features is that phoneme slips are much more common than feature slips (Shattuck-Hufnagel 1979, 1983; Stemberger 1983).[4]

Post-selection inhibition

The turning off of phoneme nodes after they are selected is necessary in the model to produce exchange errors. If selected sounds were not turned off, anticipations (*deal back* → *beal...*) would remain simple anticipations (*beal back*) instead of becoming complete exchanges (*beal dack*). As I mentioned earlier, post-selection inhibition is a feature of many models, and has the added motivation of being necessary to prevent unwanted repetition. Thus, this feature is not built in solely to produce a single error effect.

Frequency-sensitive resting levels

The assumption of higher resting activation levels for more frequent words is built in primarily to account for data showing that low-frequency words are more vulnerable to phonological errors than high-frequency words. Stemberger and MacWhinney (1986) have shown that this is true in natural error collections. In addition, a new experiment (Dell, in preparation [a]) has verified this using the experimental paradigm discussed earlier. Unrelated pairs of low-frequency words (e.g., *vogue pang*) were found to be more vulnerable to initial consonant misordering than high-frequency pairs (e.g., *vote pass*). The percentages of errors were 4.9 and 1.9 for low- and high-frequency stimuli, respectively. The frequency-sensitive resting levels of activation produce this effect simply by giving high-frequency word nodes a head start in activating their phonemes. As a result, when a high-frequency word is the current word, its phonemes reach high levels of activation quickly, and intruding segments from previous or upcoming words have little chance of being selected.

Bottom-up (phoneme-to-word) excitatory connections
There is no necessary reason why phonemes should send activation to words in language production. Only the top-down (word-to-phoneme) connections are really required to effect the retrieval of phonological forms. However, I have argued previously (Dell 1985) that there are good functional and empirical reasons to build bottom-up excitatory connections into a production model, aside from their need to be included for word recognition. In this case, unlike those discussed so far, the built-in feature is responsible for accounting for many empirical phenomena at once. The presence of bottom-up connections allows for interactive positive feedback between the word and phoneme levels. This feedback produces two broad categories of error effects: familiarity biases and similarity effects.

Familiarity biases can be said to occur when errors exhibit tendencies to produce familiar phonemes, strings of phonemes, words, or strings of words. The biases emphasized in the psychological tradition for phonological slips to create words and meaningful phrases are examples. Let us consider the lexical bias effect, the tendency for phonological errors to create words, in more detail. This phenomenon was originally shown by Baars et al. (1975) using the experimental paradigm discussed earlier. Specifically, initial consonant misorderings that created words (e.g., *dean bad → bean dad*) were nearly three times more likely than slips making nonwords (*deal back → beal dack*). The mechanism of lexical bias in the model is the bottom-up flow of activation. When a potential error string has a word node associated with it (e.g., *dean bad → bean*), that node can provide an additional source of activation to the phonemes making up the slip (see figure 2). This is because the *bean* node can capture the bottom-up flow from the /i/ and /n/ of the correct word *dean* together with that from /b/ in *bad*, and create a positive correlation among their activation levels. If the error string has no word node for *deal back → beal*), this correlation cannot be achieved and the slip is less likely. So, in short, lexical bias happens because the interactive flow of activation between words and phonemes ensures that a pattern of activation that corresponds to a single word is a stable pattern. If the pattern corresponds to a nonword, particularly one that does not share properties with many words, it tends to change until it does. An alternative explanation for lexical bias is that the phonological encoding process is overseen by a special lexical editor, an extra

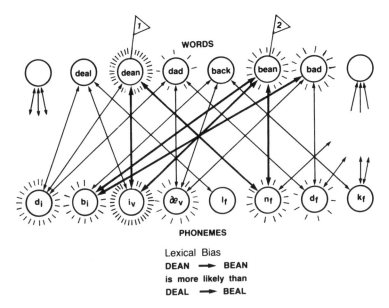

Figure 2
The mechanism for lexical bias in the model. The intended word, *dean*, has a greater chance of slipping to *bean* because of the presence of a *bean* node. The connections primarily responsible for the effect are marked with bold lines.

device that scans potential speech and filters out nonwords (Baars et al. 1975). Because of the model's feedback properties, it automatically filters out some nonword slips without appealing to a special editor.

In addition to providing an explanation for lexical bias, the bottom-up connections also provide for a variety of other familiarity biases that have been found. For example, phonemes that are common in the vocabulary tend to replace those that are less common (Levitt and Healy 1985; Motley and Baars 1975; however, see Shattuck-Hufnagel and Klatt 1979). The model produces this effect because phonemes that are present in many words, particularly in common words, receive additional input as activation reverberates between words and phonemes. The more "Freudian" familiarity biases, such as tendencies to create meaningful and contextually appropriate phrases (e.g., the *darn bore* error), cannot be produced in the present model, because the model does not represent the relevant syntactic, semantic, and pragmatic knowledge. If the model did represent this knowledge—a very big "if"—its connectionist properties would provide a natural mechanism for producing these familiarity biases as well.

The other category of error effects brought about by the model's bottom-up connections concerns the similarity between target and intruding material in errors. An example of this is the repeated-phoneme effect studied by MacKay (1970) and Wickelgren (1969). Two sounds are more likely to participate in an error if their neighboring sounds are identical. Thus, *deal beak* will slip to *beal ...* more than *deal back* will. The repeated /i/ induces the error. This phenomenon has previously been explained by what can be called an adjacency mechanism. The representation of each sound reflects the sounds that are supposed to be adjacent to it (Wickelgren 1969), and thus a sound resists movement into a new context unless the new adjacent sounds are identical to the old ones. The model produces the repeated-phoneme effect differently, through the interactive spread of activation between words and phonemes as shown in figure 3. Consider what happens when the intended phrase is *deal beak*. Both words connect to the same vowel node, /i/. Hence, when *deal* is the current word and *beak* is primed, the node for /i/ will act as a siphon and tend to equalize the activation levels

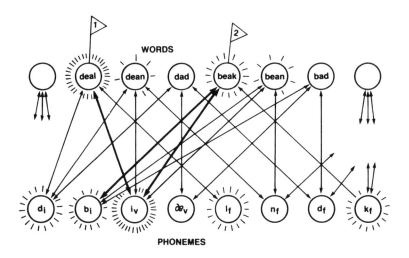

Repeated Phoneme Effect
DEAL BEAK ➡ BEAL....
is more likely than
DEAL BACK ➡ BEAL...

Figure 3
The mechanism for the repeated phoneme effect in the model. The intended words, *deal back*, share the vowel node /i/, which increases the flow of activation between the words, increasing the chance of a slip of *deal* to *beal*. The bold lines indicate the connections that are responsible for the effect.

of *deal* and *beak*. As a result, there is a greater chance of each word's phonemes being selected while the other is being encoded.

This concludes the discussion of the speech-error effects that were previously known and were built into the model's structural and processing assumptions. Next, let us turn to the model's predictions—the effects which can be deduced from the model by simulation, and which had not been previously explored. There are four classes of predictions regarding speech errors that have now been tested to some extent: effects of nonadjacent repeated phonemes, interactions involving changes in the speaking rate, interactions involving error types, and effects of frequency differences in homophonic words. These are discussed in the following section.

Model Predictions

Nonadjacent-repeated-phoneme effects

The model's account of the repeated-phoneme effect predicts that a repeated phoneme can induce nonadjacent phonemes to slip as well as adjacent ones. This is because the effect is mediated by the word nodes rather than by a phonemic-adjacency mechanism. Thus the repeated /l/ in *deal ball* should be effective in leading to misordering of /d/ and /b/, just as the repeated /i/ in *deal beak* should. This prediction was tested experimentally (Dell 1984) using the initial-consonant error-generation paradigm. Critical word pairs in one group either shared a vowel (*mad back*) or did not (*mad bake*), and pairs in a second group either shared a final consonant (*boot coat*) or did not (*boot comb*). Words in the shared-phoneme conditions were rotated with those in the control conditions so that the same words were present in the two conditions within a group. Because the procedure generated initial-consonant slips, the shared vs. control condition in the second group was a test of the prediction that repeated phonemes induce nonadjacent ones to slip. For pairs in group 1, the expected adjacent-repeated-phoneme effect was found in 8.0 percent versus 4.5 percent of initial-consonant misorderings. In group 2, a significant effect was found as well: 6.3 percent versus 2.4 percent. The finding of nonadjacent effects was given additional credibility by an analysis of a collection of initial-consonant exchanges. The adjacent second-position phonemes were found to be identical in 28.6 percent of the errors, and the nonadjacent third-position phonemes were identical nearly as often, (24.1 percent of the errors). By chance, one would expect the phonemes in these positions to be identical less than 10 percent of the time (Dell 1984). The model's

Table 2
Lexical bias as a function of deadline (Dell 1986).

	Deadline (msec)		
Condition	500	700	1000
Word outcome	11.6	12.3	7.7
Nonword outcome	13.9	8.0	4.8

Numbers are percentages of initial consonant misordering errors. The total number of opportunities per condition is 440.

prediction was confirmed, showing that the repeated-phoneme effect is more likely mediated by higher-order units (e.g., syllables or words) than by a phoneme-adjacency mechanism.

Speech-rate interactions
The model makes more slips when it speaks fast—that is, when parameter r, the number of time steps that pass between the encoding of each syllable, is small. By itself, this effect is an uninteresting consequence of the fact that the spreading of activation takes time. When there is less time for retrieval of the correct phonemes, incorrect ones are selected; this leads to slips. What is interesting is that the model predicts different patterns of errors at different rates. The reason for this is that many error effects are due to activation reverberating between levels. Hence, these effects will be time dependent. As an example, consider the prediction that familiarity effects should increase as speech slows. The prediction that the lexical bias effect should depend on the speech rate was tested (Dell 1986). Three deadlines were employed to manipulate the speech rate: 500, 700, and 1,000 msec. Table 2 shows that the lexical bias effect, the difference between word and nonword error outcomes, interacted significantly with the deadline in the predicted direction. Thus, the tendency for slips to create familiar strings seems to depend on some process that takes time. The prediction of a speech-rate interaction has not yet been tested for other familiarity effects, such as the tendency for errors to create meaningful phrases (Motley and Baars 1976), but it clearly could be.

Error-type interactions
Exchanges, anticipations, and perseverations are distinct but related errors according to the model. An exchange, unlike the other two types, is a double error; two erroneous selections have to occur to make an exchange. Because of this, the model makes a class of predictions regarding the differential sensitivity of exchanges and the other error types to various effects. These predictions, developed formally in Dell 1986, can be summarized quite

simply: Any error-causing agent (e.g., high speech rate, low-frequency words, repeated phonemes) should show its influence on exchanges more than on anticipations and perseverations; specifically, the ratio of errors with the agent to errors without the agent should be greater for exchanges than for the other types. Because of their greater complexity, exchanges "need" more error-correlated agents to instigate them. Hence, the effect of any one agent will be revealed more strongly in exchanges. Table 3 shows that results of several experiments testing this claim. In all experiments but one, the manipulated variable had a greater effect on exchange probability than it had on anticipations and perseverations. The one exception involved the lexical-bias variable (Dell 1986). Here the tendency for slips to create words over nonwords was, if anything, more evident in the anticipations and perseverations than in the exchanges. Thus, there may be something about the lexical-bias effect that the model has failed to capture. A reanalysis of the original lexical-bias data of Baars et al. (1975), however, did show the predicted interaction (bottom of table 3), and thus it is possible that the failure to find the effect (Dell 1986) is spurious.

The prediction that error effects should be stronger with exchanges than the other types is not made by the only other model that makes quantitative predictions about these error types, the scan-copy model of Shattuck-Hufnagel (1979). In this model, exchanges do not have a double nature. Rather, a single particular malfunction triggers an exchange. Anticipations and perseverations require this same malfunction plus an additional malfunction to occur. (The nature of the additional malfunction determines whether the error is an anticipation or a perseveration.) It is, therefore, difficult to see how exchanges could be expected to be more sensitive to error agents than anticipations and perseverations in this model. To achieve these effects, one would have to assume that agents that cause the exchange malfunction tend to *prevent* the occurrence of the additional malfunction.

Lack of a frequency effect for homophonic words

As was discussed earlier, the model makes more slips on low-frequency words than on high-frequency words. Thus, for example, the sounds of *woo* would be more likely to slip than the sounds of *we*. What about *wee*, a low-frequency word with a high-frequency homophone? The model predicts that a low-frequency word can "inherit" the relative invulnerability of its high-frequency homophone. This occurs despite the assumption that the low-frequency homophone's word node has a low resting level of activation. The mechanisms responsible for the prediction can be illustrated most easily with the *we-wee* example. Assume that the *we* word node

Table 3
Obtained interactions between conditions and error types.

Deadline (Dell 1986) ($N = 880$ per condition)

Deadline (msec)	Error types	
	Exchanges	Anticipations & perseverations*
500	4.4	8.3
700	3.0	7.2
1,000	0.8	5.5

Deadline (Dell, in preparation [b]) ($N = 792$ per condition)

Deadline (msec)	Error types	
	Exchanges	Anticipations & perseverations
600	1.1	2.8
1,000	0.1	2.5

Repeated phonemes (Dell 1986) ($N = 1,320$ per condition)

Condition	Error types	
	Exchanges	Anticipations & perseverations
Repeated vowels	3.4	6.3
Different vowels	2.0	7.7

Word frequency (Dell in preparation [a]) ($N = 616$ per condition)

Target-word frequency	Error types	
	Exchanges	Anticipations & perseverations
Low ($\log_{10} = 0.35$) (Kucera & Francis)	2.8	2.1
High ($\log_{10} = 2.11$) (Kucera & Francis)	0.3	1.6

Lexical bias (Dell 1986) (700 and 1,000 msec deadlines only, $N = 880$)

Condition	Error types	
	Exchanges	Anticipations & perseverations
Word outcomes	2.2	7.8
Nonword outcomes	1.6	4.8

Lexical bias (Baars et al. 1975) (Experiments 1 and 2 pooled, $N = 350$)

Condition	Error types	
	Exchanges	Anticipations & perseverations
Word outcomes	10.0	9.4
Nonword outcomes	2.9	4.0

*This category also includes incomplete errors such as *deal back—beal* has a resting level of activation appropriate for a common word and that the separate *wee* word node has an appropriately low level. However, because both have the same sounds, they connect to the same lower-level nodes. In the complete model (Dell 1986) this includes syllable nodes as well as phoneme nodes. When *wee* is the intended word it therefore activates the same network structures as *we*. As these feed back to the word nodes, *we* becomes active and thus contributes effectively to the retrieval of the correct phonemes. Figure 4 shows the rate with which the networks illustrated can activate the /w/ phoneme in *we*, *wee*, and *woo*. Clearly, the low-frequency word *wee* has its sounds retrieved nearly as effectively as *we*, even though (for this example) its word node has the same resting level of activation as *woo*.

This prediction was tested by constructing 22 pairs of phrases of the form *we rose/wee rose* and *him to sing/hymn to sing* in which high- and low-frequency members of nonhomographic homophone pairs were placed in contexts suitable for both (Dell, in preparation [b]).[5] Initial consonant exchanges were induced by the error-generation deadline procedure discussed earlier. Despite large differences in printed frequency between the high (mean $\log_{10}$ = 3.30, Kucera and Francis 1967) and low (mean $\log_{10}$ = 1.36) homophones, the initial consonant error rates were identical (3.3%, $N = 792$). This result is, of course, not conclusive. It needs a companion demonstration that a comparable low-frequency nonhomophone would have a higher error rate. So, one would need to compare, for example, *none*, *nun*, and *numb*, and show that the low-frequency word with the high-frequency homophone *nun* has an error rate equal to the high-frequency homophone, *none*, and that both are substantially less than that of the phonologically similar low-frequency word, *numb*.

So far, it has been shown that the model predicts certain error effects and that many of these predictions were confirmed. What would be more convincing would be to show that there is some internal consistency in the way that the model handles all the effects. In other words, are the network structure and the set of parameters needed to produce effect A the same as those required to produce effect B? I have explored this goal only to a small extent. In one experiment (Dell 1986), I varied three factors: the lexical-bias factor (word outcomes vs. nonword outcomes), the repeated-phoneme-effect factor (whether the words shared a vowel or not), and the speech rate (deadlines of 500, 700, and 1,000 msec). For each of these 12 conditions, the probabilities of exchanges, anticipations, and perseverations were assessed. Hence, there were 36 error probabilities to account for. I attempted to fit the model to the data by varying the spreading rate, p, the decay rate, g,

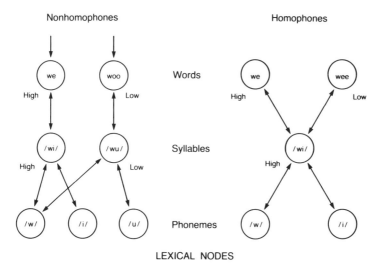

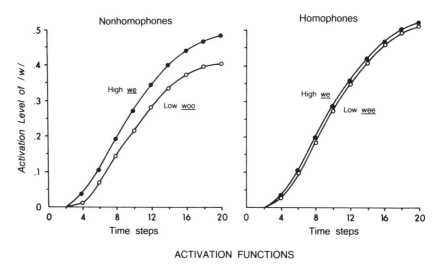

Figure 4

Word, syllable, and phoneme nodes for the homophones *we* and *wee*, contrasted with the nonhomophones *we* and *woo*. The resting level of activation for the low-frequency word nodes *wee* and *woo* is assumed to be −0.1 and 0 for all other nodes. Below are the activation levels of the node for /w/ as a function of time for each network ($p = 0.1$, $q = 0.2$).

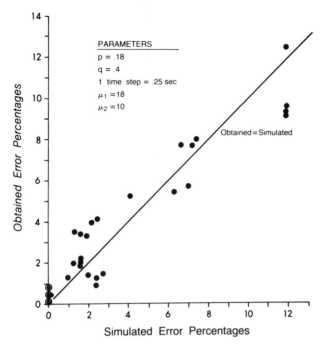

Figure 5
Simulated and obtained error probabilities for data from Dell 1986. Each point represents a given combination of condition and error type. Parameters μ_1, and μ_2 are means of Poisson processes reflecting the strength of the anticipatory and perseveratory biases, respectively, generated by the interference pairs in the error-generating procedure. The other parameters are explained in the text. Circled dots represent multiple points.

the length of a single time step, t, and two additional parameters that reflected the potency of the interference pairs in the experimental procedure (see Dell 1986 for details). Figure 5 shows the relation between the simulated and the obtained error probabilities. At least for these experimental factors, the model appears to be capable of producing the major patterns in the data.

Conclusion

In this overview, I have focused on a class of error phenomena in which the presented model does well, specifically, on familiarity and similarity effects involving initial-consonant misordering errors. There are many phenomena concerning these same error types that the model handles less well. In addition, there are many other phenomena dealing with related error types that the model ought to have something to say about but does not. These have been reviewed elsewhere (Dell 1986). However, to conclude, I will mention one set of particularly troublesome facts about speech errors.

An important aspect of the model is that it encodes the parts of a word in parallel. Word nodes activate all their phonemes at once, and a separate wordshape device imposes serial order on the phonemes.[6] This separation between the highly parallel lexical network and the serial wordshape network is responsible for much of the model's success. However, there are error effects that suggest that the model's indifference to serial order in the lexical network is not correct. Syllable-initial and word-initial consonants are about 5 times as likely to participate in phonological errors than final consonants (Stemberger 1983). The present model does not produce this effect; because of the parallel lexical network, initial and final sounds are equally likely to slip. Other evidence, from studies measuring the time to initiate words, suggests that phonological retrieval is much more serial than the model would have it. Meyer (reported in Bayer and Marslen-Wilson 1986) found that advance knowledge of the phonological properties of a word reduced the time to produce the word only if the knowledge concerned a continuous string of segments including the initial segment. If the initial segment was not known, knowledge of other segments did not speed retrieval. Thus, it appears that initial segments are distinct in some way.

I believe that the model must be changed to accommodate these initialness effects, as they are fundamental to its domain. Thus, despite the support for the model from the tests of its predictions, there is good reason to reject it in its present form. However, the basic approach of combining linguistic assumptions with a connectionist paradigm has been fruitful. The paradigm provides a formalism that allows the linguistic and psychological approaches to language production and speech errors to be brought together to achieve a better understanding of language production.

Acknowledgments

This is a revision of a paper published in *Journal of Memory and Language*. The author wishes to thank Pat O'Seaghdha, Joe Stemberger, and Jay McClelland for comments. Preparation of this manuscript was supported by ONR grant N00014-84-K-655 and NIH grant NS-25502-01.

Notes

1. I am using "rule" in a broad sense, including insertion rules such as N → *girl* and Onset → /bl/ in addition to rules that contain only categories.

2. Actually, explanations of exchange errors in the linguistic tradition are more complex and refer to a variety of information-processing devices other than rules, such frames, buffers, and scanners. (See, e.g., Dell 1986; Fromkin 1971; MacKay 1970; Shattuck-Hufnagel 1979).

3. Stemberger (1984b) has pointed out that the inclusion of wordshapes allows for errors in which the wrong shape is chosen, thus leading to the addition or deletion of sounds.

4. The complete model does contain feature nodes in the lexical network (Dell 1986), and these have the effect of causing similar phonemes—ones sharing features— to be more likely to slip with one another. However, the basic selection processes addresses the phoneme and not the feature nodes.

5. The high-frequency members of the pairs were function words; the low-frequency members were content words. This was because another purpose of the study was to test for a difference in slippability between function and content words, an expectation of the production model of Garrett (1975). The negative finding in this study does not rule out the Garrett model, however, because it is not clear how much syntactic planning is going on in these experimental procedures in which subjects simply recite what they have read.

6. Technically, the model encodes parts of *syllables* in parallel; for multisyllabic words, each syllable must become "current" at separate times.

References

Baars, B. J., and Motley, M. T. 1974. Spoonerisms: Experimental elicitation of human speech errors. In *Catalog of Selected Documents in Psychology*. Journal Supplement Abstract Service.

Baars, B. J., Motley, M. T., and MacKay, D. G. 1975. Output editing for lexical status from artificially elicited slips of the tongue. *Journal of Verbal Learning and Verbal Behavior* 14: 382–391.

Bayer, J., and Marslen-Wilson, W. (eds.) 1986. *Annual Report Nr. 7*. Nijmegen: Max-Planck-Institut für Psycholinguistik.

Berg, T. 1983. Monitoring via Feedback in Language Production: Evidence from Cut-offs. Manuscript.

Berg, T. 1987. The case against accommodation: Evidence from German speech error data. *Journal of Memory and Language* 26: 277–299.

Bock, J. K. 1986. Meaning, sound, and syntax: Lexical priming in sentence production. *Journal of Experimental Psychology: Learning, Memory and Cognition* 12: 575–586.

Bock, J. K. In press. Coordinating words and syntax in speech plans. In A. Ellis (ed.), *Progress in the Psychology of Language*, volume 3. London: Erlbaum.

Butterworth, B. 1983. Lexical representation. In B. Butterworth (ed.), *Language Production*, volume 2. London: Academic.

Butterworth, B., and Whittaker, S. 1980. Peggy Babcock's relatives. In G. E. Stelmuch and J. Requin (eds.), *Tutorials in Motor Behavior*. Amsterdam: North-Holland.

Cutler, A. 1981. The reliability of speech error data. *Linguistics* 19: 561–582.

Dell, G. S. 1984. Representation of serial order in speech: Evidence from the repeated phoneme effect in speech errors. *Journal of Experimental Psychology: Learning, Memory, and Cognition* 10: 222–233.

Dell, G. S. 1985. Positive feedback in hierarchical connectionist models: Applications to language production. *Cognitive Science* 9: 3–24.

Dell, G. S. 1986. A spreading activation theory of retrieval in sentence production. *Psychological Review* 93: 283–321.

Dell, G. S. In preparation [a]. Word-frequency and phonological speech errors.

Dell, G. S. In preparation [b]. Function morphemes and phonological encoding in language production.

Dell, G. S., and Reich, P. A. 1981. Stages in sentence production: An analysis of speech error data. *Journal of Verbal Learning and Verbal Behavior* 20: 611–629.

Ellis, A. W. 1980. On the Freudian theory of speech errors. In V. A. Fromkin (ed.), *Errors in Linguistic Performance: Slips of the Tongue, Ear, Pen, and Hand*. London: Academic.

Fay, D., and Cutler, A. 1977. Malapropisms and the structure of the mental lexicon. *Linguistic Inquiry* 8: 505–520.

Freud, S. 1958. *Psychopathology of Everyday Life* (A. A. Brill, Tr.). New York: New American Library. (Original work published 1901.)

Fromkin, V. A. 1971. The nonanomalous nature of anomalous utterances. *Language* 47: 27–52.

Fromkin, V. A. 1973. Introduction. In V. A. Fromkin (ed.), *Speech Errors as Linguistic Evidence*. The Hague: Mouton.

Fry, D. B. 1969. The linguistic evidence of speech errors. *Brno Studies in English* 8: 69–74.

Garrett, M. F. 1975. The analysis of sentence production. In G. H. Bower (ed.), *The Psychology of Learning and Motivation*. New York: Academic.

Garrett, M. F. 1976. Syntactic processes in sentence production. In R. J. Wales and E. C. T. Walker (eds.), *New Approaches to Language Mechanisms*. Amsterdam: North-Holland.

Garrett, M. F. 1980. Levels of processing in sentence production. In B. Butterworth (ed.), *Language Production*, volume 1. London: Academic.

Harley, T. 1984. A critique of top-down independent levels models of speech production: Evidence from non-plan-internal speech errors. *Cognitive Science* 8: 191–219.

Hockett, C. F. 1973. Where the tongue slips, there slip I. In V. A. Fromkin (ed.), *Speech Errors as Linguistic Evidence*. The Hague: Mouton.

Jordan, M. I. 1986. Attractor dynamics and parallelism in a connectionist sequential machine. In *Proceedings of the Eighth Annual Conference of the Cognitive Science Society*.

Kempen, G., and Huijbers, P. 1983. The lexicalization process in sentence production and naming: Indirect election of words. *Cognition* 14: 185–209.

Lapointe, S. 1975. A theory of verb form use in the speech of agrammatic aphasics. *Brain and Language* 24: 100–155.

Lapointe, S., and Dell, G. S. In press. A synthesis of some recent work in sentence production. In G. Carlson and M. K. Tanenhaus (eds.), *Linguistic Structure in Language Processing*. Dordrecht: Reidel.

Lashley, K. S. 1951. The problem of serial order in behavior. In L. A. Jeffress (ed.), *Cerebral Mechanisms in Behavior*. New York: Wiley.

Levelt, W. J. M., and Schriefers, H. 1985. Issues of lexical access in language production. Paper presented at Workshop on Language Processing, Center for the Study of Language and Information, Stanford, California.

Levitt, A. G., and Healy, A. F. 1985. The roles of phoneme frequency, similarity, and availability in the experimental elicitation of speech errors. *Journal of Memory and Language* 24: 717–733.

MacKay, D. G. 1970. Spoonerisms: The structure of errors in the serial order of speech. *Neuropsychologia* 8: 323–350.

MacKay, D. G. 1972. The structure of words and syllables: Evidence from errors in speech. *Cognitive Psychology* 3: 210–227.

MacKay, D. G. 1973. Complexity in output systems: Evidence from behavioral hybrids. *American Journal of Psychology* 86: 785–806.

MacKay, D. G. 1982. The problems of flexibility, fluency, and speed-accuracy trade-off in skilled behavior. *Psychological Review* 89: 483–506.

McCarthy, J. 1981. A prosodic theory of nonconcatenative morphology. *Linguistic Inquiry* 12: 373–418.

McClelland, J. L., and Rumelhart, D. E. 1981. An interactive activation model of context effects in letter perception: Part 1. An account of basic findings. *Psychological Review* 88: 375–407.

Meringer, R. 1908. *Aus dem Leben der Sprache: Versprechen, Kindersprache, Nachahmungstrieb*. Berlin: Behrs.

Meringer, R., and Mayer, K. 1895. *Versprechen und Verlesen*. Stuttgart: Goschensche.

Motley, M. T., and Baars, B. J. 1975. Encoding sensitivities to phonological markedness and transition probability: Evidence from spoonerisms. *Human Communication Research* 2: 351–361.

Motley, M. T., and Baars, B. J. 1976. Semantic bias effects on the outcomes of verbal slips. *Cognition* 4: 177–188.

Motley, M. T., and Baars, B. J. 1979. Effects of cognitive set upon laboratory induced verbal (Freudian) slips. *Journal of Speech and Hearing Research* 22: 421–432.

Motley, M. T., Baars, B. J., and Camden, C. T. 1982. Syntactic criteria in pre-articulatory editing: Evidence from laboratory-induced slips of the tongue. *Journal of Psycholinguistic Research* 5: 503–522.

Nooteboom, S. G. 1969. The tongue slips into patterns. In A. G. Sciarone, A. J. van Essen, and A. A. Van Raad (eds.), *Leyden Studies in Linguistics and Phonetics*. The Hague: Mouton.

Reich, P. A. 1977. Evidence for a stratal boundary from slips of the tongue. *Forum Linguisticum* 2: 211–217.

Rumelhart, D. W., and McClelland, J. L. 1982. An interactive activation model of context effects in letter perception: Part 2. The contextual enhancement effect and some tests and extensions of the model. *Psychological Review* 89: 60–94.

Rumelhart, D. E., and Norman, D. A. 1982. Simulating a skilled typist: A study of skilled cognitive motor performance. *Cognitive Science* 6: 1–36.

Saffron, E. M. 1982. Neuropsychological approaches to the study of language. *British Journal of Psychology* 73: 317–337.

Schwartz, M. F. In press. Patterns of speech production deficit within and across aphasia syndromes: Applications of a psycholinguistic model. In M. Coltheart, R. Job, and G. Sartori (eds.), *The Cognitive Neuropsyuchology of Language*. London: Erlbaum.

Shastri, L., and Feldman, J. A. 1984. Semantic Networks and Neural Nets. Technical Report 131, University of Rochester Computer Science Department.

Shattuck-Hufnagel, S. 1979. Speech errors as evidence for a serial-ordering mechanism in sentence production. In W. E. Cooper and E. C. T. Walker (eds.), *Sentence Processing: Psycholinguistic Studies Presented to Merrill Garrett*. Hillsdale, N.J.: Erlbaum.

Shattuck-Hufnagel, S. 1983. Sublexical units and suprasegmental structure in speech production planning. In P. F. MacNeilage (ed.), *The Production of Speech*. New York: Springer-Verlag.

Shattuck-Hufnagel, S., and Klatt, D. 1979. The limited use of distinctive features and markedness in speech production: Evidence from speech error data. *Journal of Verbal Learning and Verbal Behavior* 18: 41–55.

Shrager, J., Hogg, T., and Huberman, B. A. 1987. Observations of phase transitions in spreading activation networks. *Science* 236: 1092–1094.

Stemberger, J. P. 1982. The Lexicon in a Model of Language Production. Doctoral dissertation, University of California, San Diego.

Stemberger, J. P. 1983. *Speech Errors and Theoretical Phonology: A Review*. Bloomington: Indiana University Linguistics Club.

Stemberger, J. P. 1984a. Lexical Bias in Errors in Language Production: Interactive Components, Editors, and Perceptual Biases. Manuscript, Carnegie-Mellon University, Pittsburgh.

Stemberger, J. P. 1984b. Wordshape Errors in Language Production. In Research on Speech Perception Progress Report 10, Indiana University Speech Research Laboratory.

Stemberger, J. P. 1985a. An interactive activation model of language production. In A. Ellis (ed.), *Progress in the Psychology of Language*. London: Erlbaum.

Stemberger, J. P. 1985b. The reliability and replicability of naturalistic speech error data: A comparison with experimentally induced errors. In Research on Speech Perception Progress Report 11, Indiana University Speech Research Laboratory.

Stemberger, J. P., and MacWhinney, B. 1986. Frequency and the lexical storage of regularly inflected forms. *Memory and Cognition* 14: 17–26.

Stemberger, J. P., and Treiman, R. 1986. The internal structure of word-initial consonant clusters. *Journal of Memory and Language* 25: 163–180.

Wells, R. 1951. Predicting slips of the tongue. *Yale Scientific Magazine* 3: 9–30.

Wickelgren, W. A. 1969. Context-sensitive coding, associative memory, and serial order in (speech) behavior. *Psychological Review* 76: 1–15.

PART II
The Nature of the Input

Chapter 6

Review of Selected Models of Speech Perception

Dennis H. Klatt

In 1979 I published a theoretical paper concerning the issues confronting models of speech perception and the implications of including lexical access (word identification from acoustic information) in these models (Klatt 1979). The traditional focus of speech-perception theorizing before then had been phonetic perception (Liberman et al. 1967; Studdert-Kennedy 1974, 1980; Darwin 1976; Pisoni 1978, 1985). Drawing on computational strategies created for the ARPA speech-understanding project (Klatt 1977), I proposed a new perceptual model in which all possible acoustic realizations of a word or a sequence of words of the language were precompiled into a decoding network called LAFS (Lexical Access From Spectra). Separate paths and spectral templates are created in the network for alternative pronunciations of each word and for each possible phonetic recoding of word pairs across a word boundary (e.g. "could you" → [kʊjə]).

It was argued that LAFS is computationally superior to any two-stage model involving an intermediate phonetic/phonemic representation of the input because a phonetic representation discards detailed acoustic information that would actually be useful in lexical decisions, and thus induces errors that are hard to correct. It may turn out that, because of memory limitations or other constraints, perceptual strategies must always involve early phonetic decisions; however, from a system-optimization point of view, such a strategy violates the principle of delaying commitment until the discarded information is no longer of any use, and is thus a suboptimal strategy.

What has happened to the field of model building for speech perception since my 1979 review? Since the LAFS model was first described, I made some preliminary attempts to build a simulation, but was discouraged by the behavior of the distance metrics available to compare spectra. These metrics were as sensitive to irrelevant spectral variability as to cues to fine phonetic distinctions—a status that has not changed appreciably even though many new metrics have been proposed (see e.g. Nocerino et al. 1985). This is probably one of the primary reasons why speech-recognition technology has not achieved clear success in such difficult tasks as speaker-independent recognition of the alphabet and of very large vocabularies. While unable to build LAFS, I have made some theoretical extensions in the area of generalized cross-word-boundary processing (Klatt 1986a); I will describe these briefly in a later section. I remain interested in pursuing investigations of the performance potential of such models and their relationship to the way humans recognize spoken sentences.

In another direction, considerable engineering effort has been devoted to trying to improve the abilities of speech-recognition devices. Although progress has been slow, some interesting systems have been built (Cole et al. 1986; Zue 1985; Blomberg et al. 1986; Church 1987; Levinson and Rabiner 1985; Bush and Kopek 1986; Averbuch et al. 1987). Pattern-matching and learning systems involving (e.g.) hidden Markov processes continue to have a performance advantage over systems that attempt explicit phonetic-feature extraction and/or segmental labeling. It is reasonable to take this work seriously and try to determine its implications for models of speech perception. Furthermore, a few new models—such as Trace (Elman and McClelland 1986), an acoustic-gesture model (Marcus 1986), and a perceptual-pointer model (Miller 1982)—have been proposed, and the motor theory has been revised in several directions (Liberman and Mattingly 1986; Fowler and Smith 1986). Stevens has continued his quest for invariant acoustic properties that would simplify the extraction of phonetic-feature information from speech (Blumstein and Stevens 1979), and, more important, has revised his ideas as to the nature and the role of features in models of speech perception (Stevens 1986). The following models will be considered in this review:

• a revised version of the motor theory (Liberman and Mattingly 1986)
• analysis by synthesis using broad phonetic classification for initial lexical search (Zue 1986)
• lexical access from phonetic features (Stevens 1986)
• the LAFS model of spectral sequences for words (Klatt 1979, 1986a)
• auditory front ends that attempt to model the encoding of speech by the peripheral auditory system
• pseudo-neural models and other network models such as Trace (Elman and McClelland 1986)
• phonetic recognition using features as input to a decision strategy involving fuzzy logical prototypes (Massaro 1987)

• the perceptual-pointer "speech is not special" theory (Miller 1982)
• the hidden Markov models that seem to be winning in the speech-recognition competition (Jelinek 1985).

1 A Generic Model of Speech Perception

The young child first exposed to speech presumably learns to recognize words as holistic acoustic patterns. However, this solution is not acceptable if one is going to learn to talk and to execute speech-production plans by manipulating abstract phonemic segments—a view strongly supported by speech-error data (Fromkin 1971; Shattuck-Hufnagel 1979). In this case, the child must learn to associate aspects of the coarticulated acoustic signals in the environment with signals that the child can produce by various fundamental articulatory gestures. This process presumably results in a new way of processing speech during perception so as to recover phonetic segments, syllables, distinctive features, or component articulatory gestures (Jusczyk 1986). The choice between these units (which are not mutually exclusive) is very much up in the air at this point (Pisoni and Luce 1987), but a model must ultimately decide on the code(s) to use to represent words during lexical access and on a way to derive this representation from acoustic data. In LAFS, familiar words are recognized by a process that avoids explicit recognition of any of these below-the-word intermediate representations, but unfamiliar words and names are processed phonetically by a special network that works in parallel with the normal process.

Figure 1 shows a generic model of bottom-up lexical-hypothesis formation. The diagram contains a matcher, an analysis subsystem for delivering appropriate representations of incoming speech samples to the matcher, and a synthesis subsystem for delivering an appropriate representation of some or all of the lexicon to the matcher. The matcher compares the input representation with each proposed lexical representation and derives a score representing the goodness of the match. But what is the detailed nature of the matching process, and exactly what type of representation is being matched? From the vantage point of this figure, it is possible to identify the critical areas of disagreement among the various models of the · process.

Serial vs. Parallel Search
Bradley and Forster (1987) argue that in order to account for the fact that common words are recognized more quickly than unexpected words, one must posit a serial model of lexical matching in which items are ordered

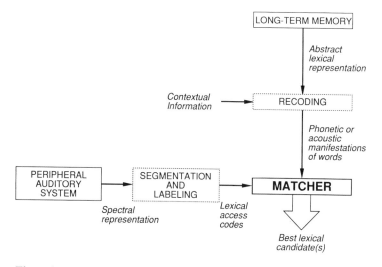

Figure 1
Block diagram of a general model of "bottom-up" lexical hypothesis formation.
Boxes enclosed in dashed lines may not appear in some models of perception.

according to frequency of occurrence in the language. In a model like LAFS, or in the most recent version of the cohort theory (Marslen-Wilson 1987), a parallel search is conducted, and word-frequency effects must be explained in some other way.

Early Access vs. One Final Decision
Reaction-time experiments suggest that listeners can respond before hearing the acoustic end of a word if all other lexical candidates can be ruled out at an earlier point in time (Marslen-Wilson and Welsh 1978). Semantic priming effects (Marslen-Wilson 1987) indicate that a cohort of partially matching words is sent to the lexical-retrieval module even before a unique lexical item has been identified, perhaps on the basis of a match to the first syllable or morpheme. These data present problems for models that have been formulated to provide a single answer when all the acoustic information has been processed, but most models can be recast rather easily to output a cohort of items that are consistent with the input up to that point in time. If the input is noisy, or if the system is designed conservatively to allow for possible imperfect matches to the correct word, then it is conceivable that, in general, many lexical candidates appear at the output of this module. In that case, there must be a mechanism for efficiently selecting from this subset of candidates on the basis of syntactic, semantic,

and pragmatic constraints or on the basis of a return to the acoustic data via analysis by synthesis (Halle and Stevens 1962; Klatt 1979, appendix A) or one form of the motor theory (Liberman et al. 1967).

Matching at an Abstract Phonemic Level vs. at an Input Spectral Level

Many models assume that the matcher deals with a hypothesized phonetic/ phonemic string (Studdert-Kennedy 1974; Pisoni 1978; Stevens 1986), perhaps supplemented by information concerning the syllable structure and the stress pattern (Church 1987). Alternatively, it has been argued that a segmental representation discards too much useful information and also is susceptible to errors whose ultimate correction is difficult (Klatt 1979). One way to avoid making explicit segmentation and labeling decisions is to match at the level of a continuous representation in time/frequency/energy, such as a sequence of spectra (Klatt 1979), or a set of distinctive features represented in a nontraditional way, i.e. by continuously varying time functions (Stevens 1986; Klatt 1986d). In the latter cases, either the lexicon is represented in these terms or the lexical representations must be generated on the fly by rules whose input consists of the more abstract phonological representations of words.

Phonological Recoding in Continuous Speech

Significant recoding can take place when words are embedded in conversational sentences. An optimum decoding strategy would involve a processor capable of computing the expected allophonic variability of a word when given the word's prior context (denoted "contextual information" in figure 1). Alternative models might precompile such information into a decoding network structure (Klatt 1979), or simplify the process by supposing that words are recognized by matching against an ideal context-independent prototype while treating the context-governed recoding as noise that adds to distance scores at this level (Stevens 1986). Another type of model might be proposed in which a words is recognized if any of its alternative phonetic forms appears—whether or not the context is consistent with the observed alternative (Harrington and Johnstone 1987). The latter two models, though theoretically inelegant and unlikely to perform well enough to model human performance, considerably simplify the computations required during perception. Surprisingly, I know of few data bearing on the choice among these three views—except perhaps for the tape-splicing demonstrations that show small reaction-time advantages for words containing coarticulatory cues consistent with the sentence context (Martin and Bunnell 1982; Marslen-Wilson 1987).

Variability and the Inherent Complexity of the Task

If one assumes a model in which a phonetic or phonemic representation is computed prior to lexical search, there are many ways in which the analysis might proceed, and many stumbling blocks in terms of within-speaker and cross-speaker variability in the acoustic manifestations of phonetic segments and features (Perkell and Klatt 1986). I will review the relative advantages of feature-based models, segment-based models, diphone-based models, syllable-based models, strict left-to-right processing strategies, stressed-syllable-focused strategies, emphasis on context-independent cues (invariance models) versus context-dependent cues (encodedness models), use of inferred articulatory shapes and gestures versus the outputs of auditory models (such as spectral cues and their rate of change), and various proposed computational strategies for speaker normalization intended to reduce variability. Variability in the acoustic manifestations of a given utterance is substantial and arises from many sources, including the following:

• recording conditions (background noise, room reverberation, microphone/telephone characteristics)
• within-speaker variability (breathy/creaky voice quality, apparent shifts in formant frequencies due to changes in fundamental frequency of the voice, speaking-rate-related undershoot in articulatory targets, imperfect repetition of the same intended articulatory gesture)
• cross-speaker variability (differences in dialect, vocal-tract length and neutral shape, detailed articulatory habits)
• segment realization variability (degree of articulatory undershoot due to stress or duration requirements; coarticulatory influences of adjacent segments, including a variable amount of feature propagation—such as nasality or rounding—from adjacent sounds, optional deletions/simplifications such as not releasing a final plosive)
• word environment variability in continuous speech (cross-word-boundary coarticulation, phonological and phonetic recoding of words in sentences, changes to the duration of a word as a function of syntactic position or semantic highlighting).

As I pointed out in my original paper, these sources of variability lead to acoustic non-invariance for phonetic segments and features, to a need for time-normalization procedures and/or a way of disregarding temporal variability, to a need for talker normalization procedures and/or a way of dynamically adapting the system to the characteristics of the current talker, to a need to deal with the ambiguity introduced by phonological recoding of words in sentences, and to difficulties in the interpretation of prosodic cues to lexical identity.

2   Recent Models of Speech Perception

Given this framework and this set of issues, we are now prepared to examine critically some of the recent proposals in the area of speech-perception modeling. Do these models provide concrete solutions to the problems listed above?

The Revised Motor Theory

The motor theory of speech perception (figure 2) is an argument in support of a view that speech production and speech perception are intimately related via common processing strategies and representations. Liberman and Mattingly (1986) have recently proposed a revised motor theory consisting of several refinements to the original conceptualization (Liberman et al. 1967). The basic processing units of the new theory are the intended gestures associated with a phonetic segment during speech production. The gestures associated with the lips, the tongue body, the tongue blade, the velum, and the larynx are claimed not only to be natural units for production and perception, but perhaps also to be related in insightful ways to traditional distinctive features (Browman and Goldstein 1985). In perception, a specialized module is provided by genetic design to process acoustic waveforms and to directly perceive these underlying articulatory intentions into a sort of "gestural score" that is related to traditional abstract segments and features.

In the original model, hypotheses were in the form of either phonetic segments ("I think I see a [ta]") or *observed* articulatory gestures. In the new revised theory, it is the *underlying* abstract gestures that are perceived directly (Gibson 1966) by somehow disentangling the acoustic consequences of sequences of semi-independent gestures of different articulators which begin and end at varying times. For example, if nasalization starts earlier or later than usual, we nevertheless "hear" a nasalization gesture that is abstract and somewhat timeless.

The second important aspect of the revised motor theory is the statement that we "directly perceive" these abstract gestures. Through genetic endowment, or whatever, the gestures appear directly and "name themselves" as natural categories. It appears that Liberman and Mattingly mean that a specialized processing system creates labels for a perhaps language-universal set of abstract phonetically useful articulatory gestures. This

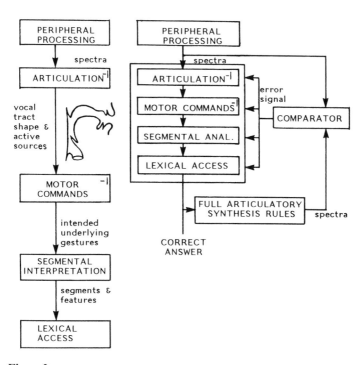

MOTOR THEORY OF SPEECH PERCEPTION

(1) DIRECT FORM   (2) ANALYSIS BY SYNTHESIS

Figure 2

The motor theory of speech perception can take on two forms: a form involving
direct perception of intended articulatory gestures (Liberman and Mattingly
1986) and an analysis-by-synthesis form in which articulatory synthesis rules
play a prominent role (Stevens 1960).

special module knows all the detailed relationships between an intended gesture and its possible acoustic manifestations as a function of phonetic context, stress pattern, and other performance options available to the speaker. Furthermore, the relationship is sufficiently unique to be invertible —that is to say, direct perception of gestures is now believed to be possible without recourse to (e.g.) analysis-by-synthesis verification of several candidate hypotheses that might have been consistent with a given set of local acoustic observations. The theory makes no claims as to how this is accomplished by processing of acoustic data; it claims only that it must logically be true in order to account for certain experimental data of perception.

The revised motor theory of Liberman and Mattingly makes four strong claims: that speech production and perception are linked in such a way as to have a common representation and a common processing strategy; that the basic unit is the underlying *intended* gesture of an articulator associated with a phonetic segment—the underlying unit is not the actual articulatory trajectory implied by the acoustics; that perception is direct—the special-purpose module is capable of interpreting acoustic input[1] in terms of candidate underlying gestures and selecting the correct gesture pattern by a rapid automatic decision process to which we have no conscious access; and that no other model can account for the diverse set of multi-modal, coarticulatory, cue-trading, and duplex perception phenomena that characterize speech. I consider each of these claims in the following paragraphs.

The Link between Production and Perception
In all models of speech perception involving an intermediate phonetic level of representation, one could easily make the case that production shares a similar or identical phonetic representation. Thus, the claim of the revised motor theory that intended gestures are both the input to the production process and the output of a specialized perception module does not demonstrate by itself a unique intimate relationship between production and perception. The case stands or falls on the way that processing for perception is related to processing for production. I do not see any simple way to relate the two processes other than to state that they are in some sense inverses of one another.

Rules for speech production translate desired abstract gestures into patterns of motor commands that will produce acceptable acoustic output with minimal articulatory effort. The only conceivable way to incorporate such rules in a perceptual strategy would be to use them as part of an analysis-by-synthesis module that would test whether there is any way in which a hypothesized underlying gesture complex could have resulted in the observed acoustic pattern, given the timing options available to the speaker. Enumeration and testing of the nearly infinite alternatives that such a model would produce is a far cry from "direct perception," and the approach would not explain the far more difficult step of how to generate reasonable candidate underlying gestures in the first place. Direct perception implies, more or less, that any pattern of speech acoustics that the native speaker can make will be interpreted, either by table lookup or by algorithmic analysis, into the appropriate underlying sequence of gestures. I conclude that production and perception are clearly closely tied in the sense that perceptual strategies must know a great deal about production options and their acoustic manifestations, but they are almost certainly completely different in terms of the processing strategies and the data structures employed.

Observed Articulatory Trajectories and Intended Gestures
The distinction between the actual articulatory gestures implied by acoustic data and the underlying intended gesture is essentially the same as the distinction between a phonetic description of the speech event and its underlying phonological description. The claim, then, is that we hear phonemes, but that we hear them in terms of their component underlying articulatory gestures rather than as unanalyzed beads on a string. The attraction of this view is in the way time (both rate of articulation and timing relationships between articulators) is relegated to representational irrelevance, so that many of the problems associated with the variability of speech in its temporal aspects are avoided. The problem with this view is that the mechanisms employed to achieve this dissociation are not explicated.

Another school of motor-theory proponents (Fowler and Smith 1986) argues that we hear the actual articulatory gestures that the speaker produces. Component gestures of segments are heard in a context-independent way by factoring out coarticulatory influences of adjacent segments, using a sort of perceptual "vector analysis" that is not unlike the stream segregation process observed by Bregman (1978) for sequences of complex tones. How to do this for the more complex case of speech is not further elaborated, but experimental data are provided to argue that listeners compare phonetic qualities of vowels after subtracting away the expected coarticulatory influences of adjacent segments.

Extraction of Intended Gestures from the Speech Signal
Any model in which a detailed account of the cue-trading and gesture-timing options available to the speaker is seriously contemplated faces a

very serious "degrees of freedom" crisis. If only one such factor (e.g. anticipatory lip rounding) is considered, it is not difficult to map out the acoustic consequences of earlier and earlier onset of the lip-rounding gesture on all possible adjacent phonetic segments and to memorize these facts or capture them by a formula. However, when one simultaneously has to worry about variable timing of velar lowering, glottal abduction, etc. within the same phonetic sequence, there seems to be considerable difficulty in regularizing or memorizing the acoustic effects, particularly since the effects are generally not independent. For example, the second formant frequency may be influenced by changes in the shapes of the pharyngeal, oral, and lip regions of the vocal tract. The only hope is that there exists an acoustic-to-vocal-tract-shape transformation which essentially separates the effects into local perturbations in vocal-tract shape over time that can then be interpreted in a much more straightforward manner. In my opinion, the motor theory stands or falls on the existence of this transformation.

Can the speech signal be transformed into a sequence of shapes of a hypothesized vocal tract (Atal 1975)? At present, such a transformation is beyond the capabilities of experts in speech processing, partly because of difficulties in formant tracking and partly because of the difficulty of determining a unique articulatory shape or trajectory from formant data alone (Atal et al. 1978). A given set of formant values can be produced by several different vocal-tract shapes, and there is generally at least one plausible shape for every vocal-tract length one might posit. (Vocal-tract length is not fixed: it varies over time owing to larynx height and lip protrusion gestures.) Quite sophisticated approaches involving simultaneous modeling of the shape of the glottal pulse (Fujisaki and Ljungqvist 1987) or involving the time course of spectral changes (Atal 1983; Marcus 1986) have been tried: their limited success indicates that the most important problem for motor theorists to address is the nature of this transformation. If articulatory shape were available from the signal, the claim that underlying gestures can be extracted would at least be within the realm of plausibility.

Uniqueness of the Motor-Theory Account

A transformation directly from (e.g.) an auditory representation such as spectral sequences into underlying gestures, without an intermediate articulatory shape transformation, is to me no different in kind from other models such as LAFS (Klatt 1979). In LAFS (described below), spectra are mapped directly to words (and SCRIBER maps them into phonetic segments) via a decoding network. In the revised motor theory, spectra could be mapped directly to abstract phonological gestures by a similar structure and a similar process, using hidden learning procedures such as are employed in the IBM speech-recognition device (Jelinek 1985). Thus the revised motor theory, in its unspecified form, is not necessarily a particularly special theory. It has no inherently strong ties to articulation (other than a mapping from spectra to a quasi-articulatory gestural output representation) unless it posits a "vocal-tract shape" intermediate processing stage as an essential component for the interpretation of acoustic data in linguistic terms.

In summary: An attractive motor-theory *philosophy* has been described by Liberman and Mattingly, but we are far from the specification of a motor-theory *model* of speech perception.

Analysis by Synthesis

An analysis-by-synthesis model of phonetic perception (right panel of figure 2) was formulated in the late 1950s in order to account for processing of the complex encodedness of stop consonants (Stevens and Halle 1962). Analysis by synthesis is a "hypothesize and test" technique that was first applied to the speech problem of formant tracking (Bell et al. 1961) and later applied to the problem of lexical hypothesis formation from incomplete or errorful phonetic specifications, as in figure 3. The claim is that, given a lexical hypothesis, it is relatively straightforward to predict and

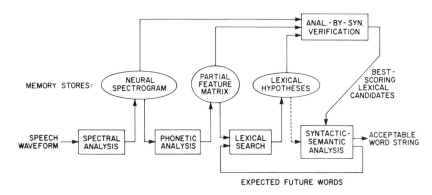

Figure 3
An analysis-by-synthesis model of lexical hypothesis generation and verification. After Klatt (1979).

verify expected acoustic manifestations of the word, whereas the inverse—direct interpretation of acoustic data in phonetic or articulatory terms—involves ambiguities due to uncertainties about phonetic context and reduction of unstressed syllables. However, the analysis-by-synthesis model of speech perception has been criticized on two grounds: that no one has explained satisfactorily how the process gets started (i.e., where the lexical hypotheses come from) and that too much "cognitive processing" (too many sequential decisions per unit time) may be required in such a model (Newell 1979).

Zue (1986) has proposed a method of initial lexical hypothesis generation using robust acoustic features. The complete model involves three stages in the processing of the speech signal: (1) an initial broad phonetic segmentation and classification of the input waveform according to robust acoustic features such as "strong-fricative," "weak-fricative," "front-vowel," "stop," and "stressed-vs.-unstressed syllable" (Huttenlocher and Zue 1984), (2) probing of the lexicon to obtain a (hopefully small) set of words or word candidate coverings of the broad-class phonetic representation for an utterance, and (3) selection among the candidates through a process of detailed analysis-by-synthesis verification of phonetic hypotheses.

Robust Features

Zue argues that the production of a detailed phonetic transcription is extremely difficult, owing in part to context-dependent interpretation of some distinctive features. However, he believes that there exist broad phonetic categories, such as "strong-fricative," whose acoustic properties are robust across phonetic contexts and across speakers. The categories can be identified in running speech with a very high degree of accuracy using relatively simple acoustic properties and relatively simple thresholding decision strategies. There is no need for context-dependent decision strategies that would, for example, require knowing that the segment was a labial in order to make an optimum voicing determination. The idea is appealing, but the performance of a system based on these ideas is not yet very good (Huttenlocher 1986), so fallback procedures may have to be devised for cases where errors are made. Glass and Zue (1987) are exploring a second alternative, which involves using a robust measure of spectral change in the outputs of an auditory model to define alternative signal segmentations, using a clustering technique to label these segments in terms of a set of ten spectral shapes, and redefining lexical entries when linguistic expectations conflict with the analysis results. Improved performance is claimed, but the error rate and the ambiguity of alternative representations may still be too high.

Candidate Reduction

The second claim made by Zue is that there is sufficient constraint in the broad phonetic category labels to severely restrict candidate lexical coverings of the input. This appears to be the case when isolated words are considered; there was a mean of 21 perfectly matching words in many probes of a 20,000-word lexicon. However, in continuous speech, with the multiple alternative starting points for words, and the multiple alternative pronunciations of words created by phonological processes operating across word boundaries, there appear to be far too many lexical candidates for analysis-by-synthesis to deal with, even if one assumes a perfect broad classifier. Harrington and Johnstone (1987) show that there are often millions of alternative parses of a broad-classification transcription of a sentence into words. Even if a perfect *phonemic* transcription that would specify segments to a greater extent than the broad classification features were available, the number of alternative parses of these sentences into words would not be reduced very much. It is not even clear whether a narrow *phonetic* transcription, with its implied constraint on syllable structure and thus on possible word boundary locations (Church 1987), would reduce the search space sufficiently to make analysis by synthesis at a lexical level a practical strategy.

Analysis-by-Synthesis Verification

The theoretical advantages of stating rules in their synthesis form are well known. However, it is a big step to program a complete analysis-by-synthesis verification strategy, and Zue has not yet undertaken this step. Klatt and Cook (1976) used a conventional synthesis-by-rule program to generate speech and then transform it into a sequence of spectra to be matched by a dynamic programming temporal alignment procedure during verification, but this turned out to be less than satisfactory for a speaker-independent application.

In summary: There is serious question whether a broad classifier can provide sufficient constraint to form the initial hypothesizer of an analysis-by-synthesis strategy for continuous speech, even if performing in a highly accurate way, because of the ambiguity caused by multiple lexical parses of the broad-category representation of the input.

A General Feature-Based Model

A literal translation of the phonetic feature concepts implicit in Jakobson, Fant, and Halle 1963 or Chomsky and Halle 1968 to the domain of

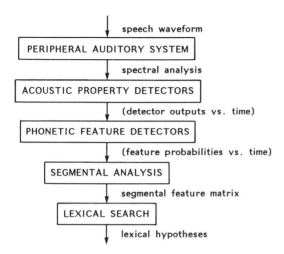

speech waveform

PERIPHERAL AUDITORY SYSTEM

spectral analysis

ACOUSTIC PROPERTY DETECTORS

(detector outputs vs. time)

PHONETIC FEATURE DETECTORS

(feature probabilities vs. time)

SEGMENTAL ANALYSIS

segmental feature matrix

LEXICAL SEARCH

lexical hypotheses

Figure 4
Block diagram of a "literal" phonetic-feature detector model of speech
perception.

perception might result in the procedure outlined in figure 4. Similar
models are discussed in Studdert-Kennedy 1974 and in Pisoni and Luce
1987.

Peripheral Processing
I assume that the peripheral processing stage provides at least two representations of input speech waveforms: an average-firing-rate representation
of the short-time spectrum (Goldhor 1986) and some sort of synchrony
spectrum (Sachs et al. 1982; Allen 1985). Details are not important to the
issues at hand, although there is some hope that a properly designed
simulation of peripheral processing, including critical bands, masking,
adaptation, and synchrony to formant frequencies, will make the task of
later modules easier by enhancing invariant acoustic characteristics of
phonetic features and suppressing irrelevant variability.

Acoustic-Property Detectors
A set of acoustic-property detectors transform this spectral input representation into time functions that characterize the degree to which certain
properties are present in the input at a given instant of time. These property
detectors are assumed to differ from the raw input spectra in that they
compute *relational* attributes of the signal, which tend to be more invariant
and "quantal" (Stevens 1972) across phonetic contexts and across speakers

than are the raw spectra. The acoustic-property detectors are further assumed to differ from *phonetic*-feature detectors (the next stage) in that they compute relatively simple general auditory properties, which are useful for processing other signals as well as speech. Examples of possible auditory properties are onset detectors, spectral-change detectors, spectral-peak detectors, formant-frequency detectors, formant-motion detectors, presence-of-voicing detectors, fundamental-frequency detectors, and nasal-formant detectors. Other authors have proposed detectors employing three-and-a-half bark smoothing (Chistovich 1979, 1985), principal-components analysis (Klein, Plomp, and Pols 1970), formant ratios (Syrdal 1985), and vocal-tract shape estimation (Atal 1974).

Phonetic-Feature Detectors

A phonetic-feature detector has the task of examining an input set of auditory-property values over a chunk of time and making linguistic decisions that are language-specific. Of course, aspects of the speech-production/perception process may constrain these decisions to be similar across languages (Stevens 1972), but I assume that phonetic-feature detectors are not hard-wired universal phonetic transcribers, but are rather tunable to the phonetic contrasts of the language in question. A phonetic-feature detector may make a relatively simple decision based on input from a single acoustic-property detector (the usual case, according to Stevens), or a feature detector may combine information from several different auditory-property detectors.

The decision of a phonetic-feature detector is, in principle, binary—reflecting the presence or absence of the feature at that instant of time. However, in a speech-recognition context, it may be better to think of the detector output as expressing the *probability* of the presence of a particular feature at that time, given the acoustic evidence to date. In this way, one can represent ambiguity and possibly recover later from inevitable errors. The output probability values may spend most of the time around 0 and 1, as a linguist would expect when the acoustic data are clear, but this is certainly not possible in the presence of background noise. Experience with speech-understanding systems has shown the disadvantages of forcing an early decision when, in fact, representations incorporating uncertainty often permit correct resolution in later decision stages (Klatt 1977). Even if phonetic-feature outputs are probabilities, there is still a considerable reduction of information taking place at this stage; only about 12 to 20 or so slowly varying feature "time functions" are present in the model to represent phonetic events.

Segmental Analysis

Up to this point, the object of the computations has been to describe via phonetic features what is actually present in the acoustic signal (or, equivalently, which articulatory gestures were used to generate the observed acoustic data). The segmental analysis stage must temporally "align the columns" of the set of feature-detector outputs that have been computed in parallel so as to produce what can be interpreted as a sequence of discrete segments (the presumed form of the lexical entries). In the spirit of creating as much parsimony with standard linguistic formalism as possible, I have assumed that the segmental representation is basically a feature matrix (Chomsky and Halle 1968), but it can become a lattice of alternative matrices where necessary to describe segmentation ambiguity. One might also argue for additional levels of phonological representation to delimit syllables, onsets and rhymes, etc. (Halle and Vergnaud 1980), or to group features into tiers that need not be temporally perfectly aligned (Clements 1985; Stevens 1986).

Entries in the matrix are, again, probabilities, but this time they indicate the likely presence or absence of more abstract "phonological" features— reflecting the speaker's underlying intentions (to the extent that it is possible to infer such intentions from the acoustic data). For example, when producing /ænt/, a speaker may produce [æ̃t]—a nasalized vowel followed by a [t]—with little or no evidence for a nasal murmur after the vowel; however, this stage of the analysis would postulate a nasal segment between the vowel and the [t], assign the nasality to it, and deduce the probable phonetic quality of the preceding vowel if it had not been nasalized.

Lexical Access

The lexical access module accepts as input the segment matrix (and perhaps prosodic information and syntactic/semantic expectations) in order to seek candidate lexical items. The mechanics of the matching process requires the development of sophisticated scoring strategies to penalize mismatches and deal with missing and extra segments. In general, word boundary locations are not known for certain, so lexical probes may be required at many different potential starting points in an unknown sentence.

This attempt to specify fairly concretely a feature-based model of perception has been undertaken in order to now be able to critically evaluate various components of the standard model. The schematic spectrogram of the utterance [ada] presented in figure 5 illustrates several cues that interact to indicate whether the plosive is voiced or voiceless. Although six cues are identified in the figure (and Lisker [1978] has cataloged sixteen potential

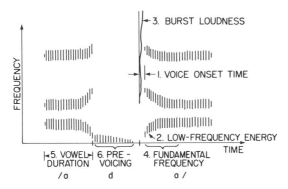

Figure 5
Six acoustic cues to voicing for plosives.

cues), it is by no means clear that the cues correspond to the outputs of six quasi-independent acoustic-feature detectors. Proper analysis of this and other phonetic situations may reveal the existence of integrated detectors that combine at an auditory level some of the cues to voicing listed in the figure. Even if this were true, the task of the voicing-feature detector is a complex one. It is perhaps worthwhile to consider in detail some issues that arise when one is attempting to specify the nature of the transformation from acoustic properties to phonetic feature output for this admittedly complicated case:

• *Feature independence.* If one part of the voicing-feature detector's strategy is to measure voice onset time by determining burst onset followed by voicing onset, the detector should probably be willing to accept a weaker burst as an onset if the plosive is labial than if it is not. Similarly, the VOT boundary between voiced and voiceless is somewhat shorter for labials. Is the voicing feature detector permitted to know the place decision, or is it permitted to compute information required for an optimum voicing decision, or is it forced to make an independent judgement of VOT or duration of aspiration which will be corrected by the next processing level that has available all feature outputs?

• *Time functions vs. event sequences.* The voicing decision involves multiple cues that occur at different times. The temporal location of release relative to closure can vary, making it hard to use fixed measurement points in combining information over time. Are the cues to voicing best thought of as time functions, as has been assumed thus far, or as ordered events that occur in sequence and must be interpreted by a temporally flexible algorithm that produces an output decision only at points where sufficient information has been accumulated? (What is the representation of knowledge and decision flow in a feature detector?)

• *Cue-combination rules.* Ultimately, the voicing feature must combine all the available evidence into a single voicing decision (probability) that is the best decision possible at that given instant of time. How is evidence combined? Is the decision framework basically articulatory and Bayesian (Massaro 1987)?

• *Intended vs. Actual Articulations.* Do the feature-detector outputs represent (e.g.) vowel qualities or articulations actually observed, or do they try to estimate underlying targets by discounting co-articulatory influences of adjacent segments?

• *Phonetic Features or Segments.* Are phonetic features identical in acoustic attributes for different segments? For example, is the place decision for a nasal made in exactly the same way as a place decision for a plosive? If not, would it be better to view perception as the problem of identifying *segments* from the temporal variations in acoustic-property-detector outputs? For example, [t, d, n] share a common place of articulation, and may share a single unifying integrated property, but it is unlikely that they share identical manifestations of place of articulation (Repp 1982). Is there an inherent advantage to features, or is the preference philosophical? An alternative to the feature matrix is a segmental representation or a matrix in which each column lists all possible phonetic segments and an associated probability for each. Suppose we observe a voice onset time that is more compatible with [p, g] than with either [b] or [k]. It would be easy to specify highest probability for [p] and [g] within a segmental representation—and some perceptual data suggest that this is appropriate (Oden and Massaro 1978) —but it is impossible to selectively favor this pair on the basis of feature probabilities alone.[2]

• *Broad vs. narrow phonetic representations.* An intervocalic post-stressed [p] is weakly aspirated, and therefore is somewhat ambiguous in voicing. The phonetic-feature-system representation, as described here, does not permit specifying gradations of VOT, only probability of voicelessness, so this plosive will be represented only as having some moderate probability of being voiceless. There is no way, within the representation chosen, to differentiate between a confident decision of an intermediate degree of aspiration and an uncertain decision of strong aspiration. Since the analysis produces a phonemic decision, an input word-initial highly aspirated [p] will generate more confident [p]-ness probabilities, and thus will better fit all lexical /p/s, including those in post-stressed position. It would be better if it were somehow possible to say that post-stressed /p/s are expected to be less aspirated. This example and many others suggest that it is not a good idea to try to recover phonological segments (phonemes) before probing the lexicon because narrow phonetic information is useful in determining likely word-boundary locations, syllable structure, and stress patterns.[3]

The questions raised as to the detailed nature of feature extraction algorithms have no simple answers. The limited performance of phonetic recognition systems and feature-extraction algorithms reported thus far in the literature is certainly not encouraging. Features may very well be an essential aspect of perception, but strategies for their evaluation are unlikely to be simple. In addition, to the extent that the segmental feature matrix produced by this type of model is broadly phonetic or phonemic, I believe that it is suboptimal for lexical search.

The LAFF (Lexical Access from Features) Model
Can the phonetic-feature-extraction model described above, which was obtained by literal translation of linguistic theory, be modified to address and overcome the problems just enumerated? Stevens (1986) has proposed a modification (figure 6), which involves doing away with the segmental interpretation stage, and therefore accessing the lexicon directly from a set

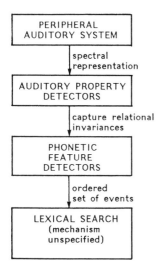

Figure 6
The Stevens LAFF (Lexical Access from Features) model of speech perception, in which lexical access involves a "features as an event sequence" representation that avoids explicit segmental analysis.

Table 1
Tentative (possibly incomplete) list of universal distinctive features for
characterizing + vocalic and − vocalic portions of a syllable. After Stevens (1988).

+ vocalic	− vocalic
high	continuant
low	sonorant
back	consonantal
round	voiced
tense	strident
nasal	coronal
spread glottis	anterior
constricted glottis	distributed
	lateral

of temporally asynchronous distinctive features. Features, which we depicted
as time functions in the generic model, should be viewed in quite another
way according to Stevens. Features are language-universal and binary.
Attributes that are acoustic correlates of the features can be derived from
the signal but are meaningful only in certain information-bearing stretches
of the acoustic stream. Attributes are extracted using an approach in which
events such as the syllabic peak define measurement times for certain
+ vocalic features, tentatively enumerated by Stevens in table 1; other
signal times, characterized by sudden acoustic onsets, offsets, and obstruent
intervals, define measurement points at which certain types of − vocalic
features are to be measured. Thus the features are not defined for all times
in running speech, but more nearly represent an ordered sequence of
"feature-change" events separated by don't-care regions.

The features listed in table 1 are similar to the conventional distinctive
features of Chomsky and Halle (1968), except that care has been taken to
find relatively simple acoustic correlates of each feature (Stevens 1988). In
a few cases, this has required redefinition of the meaning of a feature (e.g.,
− sonorant is now defined by the relative weakness of the first harmonic
in the spectrum, making it necessary to redefine [h] as − sonorant). Which
features to include in this universal set, and how best to define them, are
far from settled at this point.

It is assumed that the lexicon is represented in terms of a special pre-
compiled form of feature matrix that facilitates matching with the sequence
of attributes extracted from the signal for each syllable of running speech.
Aspects of the precompilation process are illustrated in table 2, which
shows the standard lexical entry for the word "pawn" before and after

Table 2
A conventional lexical representation for the English word "pawn", shown at the top, has been modified below to reflect expectations as to the temporal locations within the syllable of acoustic information important to the detection of feature values. In addition, features not specified by plus or minus are deemed not critical to the lexical decision. After Stevens (1988).

Conventional lexical representation

	p	ɔ	n
high	−	−	−
low	−	+	−
back	−	+	−
nasal	−	−	+
spread glottis	+	−	−
sonorant	−	+	+
voiced	−	+	+
strident	−	−	+
consonantal	+	−	+
coronal	−	−	+
anterior	+	−	+
continuant	−	+	−

Modified lexical representation

	p	ɔ	n
high		−	
low		+	
back		+	
nasal			+
spread glottis	+		
sonorant	−		
voiced	−		
strident			
consonantal	+		+
coronal	−		+
anterior	+		+
continuant	−		−

transformation into a special decoding form. Precompilation of a special decoding structure for lexical access is in the same spirit as that proposed for LAFS (Klatt 1979), except that Stevens wishes to retain the theoretical advantages of binary features—those putative advantages being that each feature has a fairly simple acoustic correlate, and that context-conditioned changes in the acoustic realizations of syllables in running speech are nearly always describable as simple changes in one or two features. Features are grouped in tiers, with each tier corresponding to slightly different measurement points with respect to the syllable nucleus and margins. For example, a decision as to whether the initial segment of the syllable has the feature + spread glottis depends on detection of aspiration in the interval between plosive release and voicing onset, so the plus in the modified feature representation is offset to the right of the /p/ column. Similarly, the presence or absence of voicing and aspiration features are examined only when there is a change to or from a −sonorant interval, whereas the features consonantal, coronal, anterior, and continuant are usually determined by spectral properties during the constricted interval for a consonant (and/or just at the release of a plosive). In the special case of a postvocalic nasal consonant, which is sometimes replaced by brief vowel nasalization in running speech, the plus is placed in the interval between the /ɔ/ and the /n/ to indicate that the general requirement for the feature to be detected is an interval of nasalization at the end of the vowel.

The next step is to attempt lexical identification directly from the feature representation. Tentatively, Stevens assumes that the input is matched directly against the modified lexical representation exemplified by table 2. Each feature is weighted according to its importance to the lexical decision process, and unexpected feature values are penalized, using distance metrics which have yet to be worked out. Possible cross-word-boundary recodings are not considered during matching, so there are likely to be (hopefully small) mismatches when words are modified by context. In the LAFS model to be described next, a mechanism is described for precompiling cross-word-boundary phonetic recoding effects into the lexical decoding network instead of treating them as "noise."

The Stevens approach avoids conversion of the input feature representation to a (phonological) segmental representation and the concomitant problems of aligning the columns of the feature matrix. The strengths of the model are in the potential ability of feature detectors to extract relational invariants and quantal properties from speech without having to make phonological or segmental decisions, and in the transformation from continuous time to discrete events, which gets rid of temporal variability to some extent while preserving temporal order requirements of feature changes within words. However, the model does not directly address the other issues raised above concerning feature independence, the nature of cue-combination rules, and the desirability of incorporating degree of feature strength rather than making a binary decision. A cost associated with the modifications proposed by Stevens is the rather inelegant nature of the resulting lexical representations—lexical entries used in perception are not nearly as abstract and phonological as the entries presumably used for speech production.

In summary: Stevens has proposed a departure from the traditional model of feature-based phonetic processing and lexical access that is a radical simplification. It is important that Stevens now elaborate in detail the way that feature computations proceed and the way that distance metrics can be devised to score input feature representations against lexical entries. Since one of the strongest claims of the LAFF model is that a small set of features can represent the acoustic signal with sufficient detail and accuracy during the lexical-access process, it will be necessary to build a simulation that matches human performance in some task domain in order to be convincing. The performance of current speech-recognition devices makes the attainment of such a goal seem remote at this time.

The LAFS (Lexical Access from Spectra) Model

An alternative model of perception, LAFS (Lexical access from spectra) (Klatt 1979, 1986a), proposes that the expected spectral patterns for words and for cross-word-boundary recodings are stored in a very large decoding network of expected sequences of spectra. The LAFS model was born out of a belief that it ought to be possible to modify the Harpy speech-understanding system and related systems (Klatt 1977) into a plausible perceptual model if one could properly generalize three oversimplifying assumptions made in Harpy: that each phonetic segment could be described by a single spectral template, that cross-word-boundary recodings are restricted to single-segment deletions, and that all possible sentences are enumerated in a single finite-state network. The critical assumptions made in formulation of the LAFS model are the following:

• that any phonetic transition can be characterized to an arbitrary degree of accuracy by a sequence of spectra, as in figure 7, or by several alternative spectral sequences

• that matching at the lexical level is done in terms of spectra, so that familiar words in long-term memory must somehow be represented in terms of these spectral templates

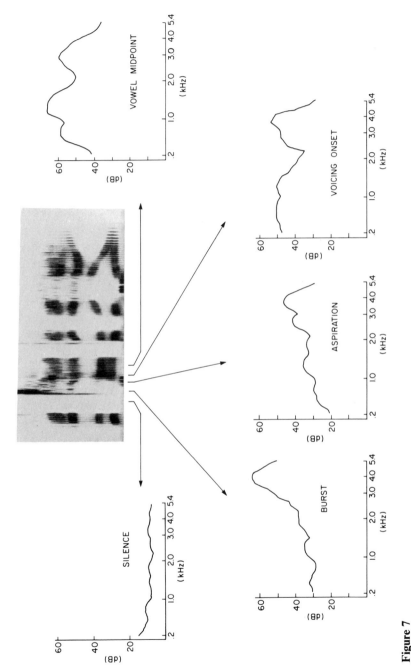

Figure 7
The phonetic transition from the middle of [t] to the middle of [a] in the spectrogram has been approximated by a sequence of five static critical-band spectra.

• that phonetic recoding within words and across word boundaries is best represented by a fully expanded decoding network that enumerates all possible spectral sequences for all possible word combinations of English, as in figure 8

• that a uniform scoring strategy involving a spectral distance metric that computes *phonetic* differences between the input spectrum and each spectral template in the network allows the network to build up matching scores for all possible words in parallel.

The network, as originally conceived as a speech-recognition device (Klatt 1979), is depicted in figure 8. Common initial portions of words can share network templates and paths (e.g. the [kən] portion of "control" and "convert"), but each CV or VC diphone transition is considered a separate pattern, which allows the system to characterize expected variations in the acoustic manifestations of phonetic segments as a function of their phonetic context. Perception consists of finding the best match between the input representation (a sequence of auditory spectra) and paths through the network. The network represents phonetic transitions, but no explicit phonetic feature or segmental decisions are made as long as the system is dealing with familiar words.

The advantages of the LAFS model are these:

• There is no preliminary segmentation, with its potential for error.

• There are no phonetic-feature or phonetic-segment decisions, with their potential for error and their potential for discarding useful information concerning allophonic variants expected in different stress/structural positions.

• There is no assumption of phonetic-feature invariance across segment types and across phonetic environment, so all phonetic sequence possibilities can be effectively treated as separate patterns if necessary.

• The representation for a word (spectral templates) can be modified on the basis of experience, and the tuning is local—there is no danger of overgeneralization.

• The scoring strategy is uniform throughout the network, and is based on the concept of a unified spectral distance function that measures perceived phonetic distance between spectra and that can be related to probability (Jelinek 1985).

• No decisions are made too early, since the first decision is a lexical one.

The disadvantages of the LAFS model are the following:

• It may not be possible to define a spectral distance metric that is powerful enough to make fine phonetic discriminations in the face of the kinds of spectral variability seen in real data.

STEP 1: LEXICAL TREE (PHONEMIC)

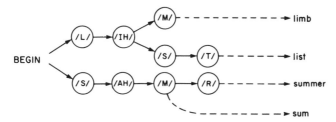

STEP 2: LEXICAL NETWORK (PHONETIC)

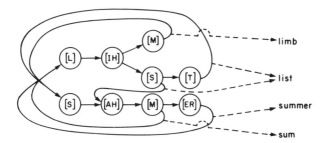

STEP 3: LEXICAL ACCESS FROM SPECTRA (SPECTRAL TEMPLATES)

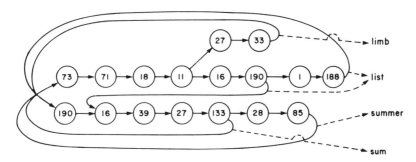

Figure 8
In LAFS, all words (or morphemes) of the lexicon are combined into a phonemic
tree (step 1). Then this tree is converted into a phonetic network by applying
phonetic recording rules specifying alternative pronunciations within and across
word boundaries (step 2). One rule, illustrated in this example, is final [t] deletion
in some cluster environments, e.g., "list some" → [lɪs:ʌm]. Finally, the phonetic
transitions are replaced by subnetworks of expected sequences of spectral
templates of the type shown in figure 7 (step 3).

• It will not be easy to preprocess spectra to normalize out cross-speaker variations associated with differences in vocal-tract length and voicing-source breathiness, or to make dynamic modifications of the type "the current speaker habitually uses a fronted allophone of /a/" (but see Schwartz et al. 1987 for a possible implementation).

• Certain kinds of permitted variability, such as the timing of the onset of nasalization before a nasal consonant, cannot be described except by creating a family of alternative spectral sequences with varying degrees of nasalization, and this solution may be impractical in the face of the vast collection of articulator coordination timing freedoms available to the speaker.

• It is hard to imagine a process whereby cross-word-boundary recodings are discovered and reduplicated at the ends of all relevant words in the decoding network.

I have given some thought to alternatives to the LAFS spectrally based uniform scoring metric. One alternative would be to allow each template in the network to employ an arbitrary metric best suited to the phonetic distinction being made at that node, perhaps even using feature-extraction procedures such as those discussed by Stevens (1986) or Massaro (1987). Conceptually, the alternative has many attractive advantages, but before abandoning the considerably simpler uniform metric (which can nonetheless emphasize different parts of the spectrum depending on input spectral shape by, e.g., using a weighting function to emphasize spectral differences at the locations of the major energy concentrations in a particular input spectrum), I would like to investigate the power of a new class of spectral representations in which both the static spectrum and a highly smoothed estimate of local spectral change are available to the metric. The smoothed spectral change representation has had a dramatic effect on reducing the error rate in many speech-recognition tasks (Rabiner 1987). Other authors have argued for the importance of spectral change information, both on the basis of recognition performance (Marcus 1984) and on the basis of perceptual theory (Stevens 1986).

In LAFS, recoding rules of cross-word-boundary phenomena are fully elaborated (duplicated) at the end of every word in the lexicon. This is done to ensure that a rule discovered in one context is applied in all relevant contexts, but it seems to be a perceptually implausible method of implementation. What, then, are the implications of assuming that there is really only one physical cross-word-boundary subnetwork (Klatt 1986a)? Consider one form that this structure could take in LAFS (figure 9) by assuming for the moment the simplifying assumption that coarticulation across word

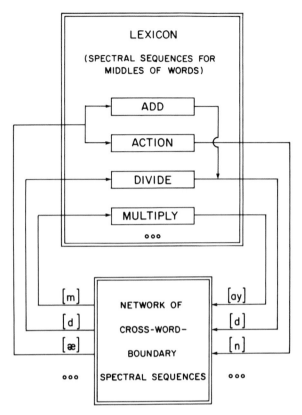

Figure 9
A modified LAFS model of lexical hypothesis generation in which cross-word-boundary coarticulatory and phonological-recoding effects are described by a single separate subnetwork.

boundaries is restricted to the diphone consisting of the last half of the phoneme at the end of the word and the first half of the initial phoneme of all words. Then, instead of creating a large set of paths and states for each word in the lexicon, so as to connect the end of the word to all word beginnings, it suffices to jump to the appropriate place in a single word-boundary network, carrying forward a backpointer to the word that would be recognized if this were to continue to be the best network path. The word-boundary network specifies spectral sequences that must be traversed in order to get to the beginning of words with each possible beginning phoneme.

It is possible to conceive of more general variants of this approach that allow coarticulation and phonological recoding over greater portions of words and that might incorporate into this special part of the network regular suffixes such as plural and past, and might even incorporate the short, highly modifiable function words, such as "to", "and", "a", and "the". The implications of this possibility are worthy of exploration, because it may be the case that short function words are different from other words not only because of their grammatical function and their high frequency of occurrence but also because they are acoustically so modifiable by context that they must be placed in this special cross-word-boundary network.

Issues of tuning to the characteristics of a new speaker and of learning new words and new pronunciation rules in a LAFS model are considered elsewhere (Klatt 1986a).

In summary: Several modifications can be proposed to counter important objections raised concerning the plausibility of LAFS as a perceptual model; however, until such time as a working system is constructed, LAFS is no more convincing than several other candidate models.

Auditory Modeling

In any detailed model of speech perception, the choice of an initial spectral representation can be critical. Some modeling efforts have focused on psychophysical evidence in order to settle issues of filter shapes, bandwidths, and spacing along the frequency axis (Klatt 1976, 1982). Recently, interest has focused on detailed physiological evidence about the encoding of speech-like signals in the auditory periphery (see the special January 1988 issue of the *Journal of Phonetics*, especially the papers by Shamma and Seneff).

The auditory model of Seneff (1988), illustrated in figure 10, includes transformations to effect the filtering process accomplished by basilar

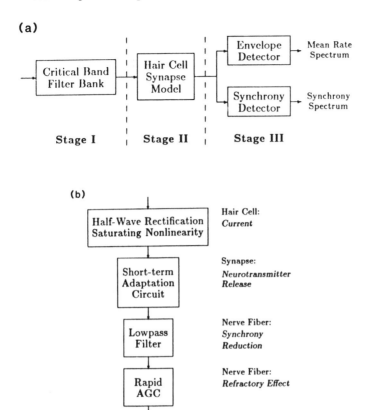

Figure 10
Block diagram of (a) an auditory model that produces two spectral representations of a speech signal and (b) details of the hair cell and synapse actions. After Seneff (1988).

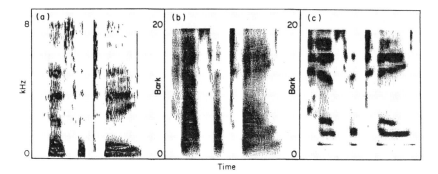

Time

Figure 11
Three spectral representations of the word "hesitate" spoken by a female talker:
(a) conventional broadband spectrogram, (b) mean-rate spectrogram, and (c)
synchrony spectrogram. After Seneff (1988).

membrane mechanics, the transduction process accomplished by the hair
cell and the primary auditory neuron, and the measurement of temporal
synchrony of fiber responses relative to their best frequency (presumably
accomplished by a higher brain center). Two spectral representations are
produced by the model: an average firing rate spectrogram and a synchrony
spectrogram; an example of each is shown in figure 11. Seneff claims that
the rapid adaptation inherent in the transduction process produces an
average firing rate response in which speech onsets and offsets, as well as
rapid spectral changes, are better represented than in a conventional spectrogram. Correspondingly, the synchrony spectrogram is said to bring out
formant spectral peaks and to be far less disrupted by moderate amounts of
background noise than is a conventional spectrogram.

One potential problem with the synchrony spectrogram representation
is that individual harmonics are resolved in the low-frequency region of the
first formant, especially for female voices. Thus there is in general no
spectral peak right at the first formant frequency, and it is up to higher
brain centers to interpret relative amplitudes of individual harmonics to
determine F1 (if formants are perceptual dimensions—a conjecture that is
appealing but of uncertain status). There may be some advantages to a
processing strategy that delays the phonetic interpretation of spectral
details at and below F1, because nasalization and breathiness can have
similar effects on these harmonic amplitudes (Klatt 1987b), and one may
have to base the phonetic interpretation on the presence or absence of
other cues.

The computations required to produce a synchrony spectrogram appear to necessitate neural processing structures that include precise delay lines and correlation computations. Shamma (1988) has formulated an alternative auditory model that takes advantage of the rapid phase change associated with the steep high-frequency skirt of the auditory filter. He shows that it is possible to design a mechanism for emphasizing formant peaks by lateral inhibition networks rather than synchrony detection.

Both the synchrony spectrogram and the Shamma spectrogram are representations that seem to be closer to phonetic category templates. That is, they are representations that are relatively insensitive to spectral tilt and formant bandwidths (peak heights) in the same way that listener judgements of phonetic similarity of vowels are insensitive to these dimensions (Klatt 1982).

Perceptrons, Hidden Units, and Pseudo-Neural Models

Work in artificial intelligence and parallel computation has changed some of the ways in which we view the probable functioning of the human brain. It is now believed that the brain is slow and not very good at logical operations but is ideally suited to massively parallel search, comparison, and classification operations. While it is known that the brain is genetically organized to have a great deal of specialized structure, the hope has been expressed that speech perception might be accomplished by simulated neural networks of relatively simple structure (Elman and McClelland 1986). The idea is to formulate a mechanism whereby network connections are specified in advance by the designer (Elman and McClelland 1986), analogous to genetic determination of structure, or are modified incrementally on the basis of a pattern-learning algorithm (Hebb 1949; Rosenblatt 1962).

The pattern-learning model has been applied to the learning of past forms of verbs (Rumelhart and McClelland 1986) and to the derivation of phonemes from the orthographic representation of a word (Sejnowski and Rosenberg 1986), as in figure 12. These two applications have been heralded as successes for the approach, although a critical evaluation of the performance of Sejnowski and Rosenberg's NETtalk with respect to an alternative pattern-learning strategy calls into question the learning abilities of such networks (Klatt 1987a). There is considerable interest in applying these ideas to speech recognition (Lippmann 1987), but it is too early to predict the ultimate success of such applications.

The first pseudo-neural pattern-matching algorithms (Rosenblatt 1962) could only learn to group together patterns having certain structural

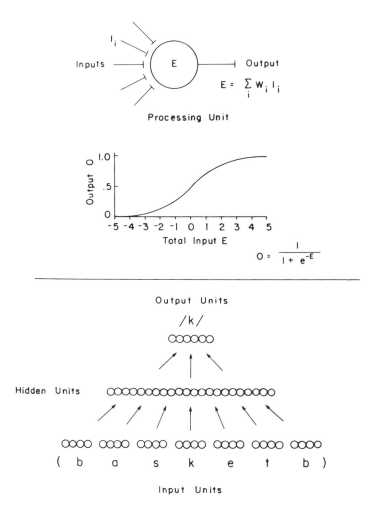

Figure 12
Perceptrons, shown at the top, classify input patterns of activation by adjusting the weights of connections to summating decision units. With a layer of hidden units, shown at the bottom, this kind of model takes on additional computational power.

similarities. The constraint can be characterized mathematically by the statement that the network could learn only first-order predicates (Minsky and Papert 1969). The new models attempt to overcome this limitation by adding one or more layers of "hidden units" between the input representation and the output classification neurons (Rumelhart, Hinton, and Williams 1986), as in figure 12. Input patterns are classified using an error "back-propagation" learning strategy to adjust connection weights. With one layer of hidden units, convex open or closed regions of the pattern space can be associated with output labels; two layers of hidden units allow learning of arbitrarily complex regions (limited by the number of hidden units and the size of the training data set). It has even been shown that a neural network of this type can be configured to simulate the Viterbi decoding algorithm of a hidden Markov approach to speech recognition (Lippmann 1987).

The drawback of the generalized hidden unit approach has been that the learning of complex predicates has been painfully slow and often incomplete. Thus, the application of these models to speech perception, which is the question addressed here, turns crucially on the degree to which speech cues are encoded in ways requiring context-conditioned interpretation. Cues whose interpretation requires contextual information imply processing solutions involving higher-order predicates and large amounts of training data, unless the modeler builds a preprocessing structure that gives speech patterns maximal invariance across phonetic context variation and speaker variation.

Let me give a few examples of complex predicates (context-dependent acoustic cues) that cannot be learned by perceptrons and seem to be learned incompletely or only after exposure to vast amounts of training data in the newer hidden-layer forms of pseudoneural models. Table 3 lists several cases where a given acoustic observation is interpreted differently depending on a complex set of values of other variables. For example, a voice onset time of 25 msec indicates a voiced consonant most of the time, but not if the place of articulation is labial (VOT is shorter before labials), or if the syllable is unstressed (VOT is shorter in unstressed syllables), or if the speaking rate is rapid (VOT is influenced by speaking rate), or if the preceding segment is an /s/ (VOT is shorter than normal in /s/-plosive clusters). The important point is that the simple one-layered network will learn to ignore VOT because it seems to be an unreliable cue, whereas we listeners somehow learn to pay attention to the cue but interpret it with respect to all the other relevant cues. Equally important is the observation that a set of hidden units have no preconceived hypotheses as to what kinds

Table 3
Examples of noninvariance that cause problems for pattern-matching approaches to phonetic recognition but seem not to bother listeners.

1. The voice onset time signaling voiced or voiceless for plosives is nearly equal for /pa/ and /gi/, indicating that the interpretation of a cue to one feature—voicing—depends on values of other features.

2. Rounding anticipation in /s/ spectra make female [sh] spectra before unrounded vowels similar to male [s] spectra before rounded vowels, implying that rounding intrusions and gender are factors to be discounted before classifying fricative spectra.

3. The burst spectra for /g/ before front vowels are similar to burst spectra for /d/ before rounded vowels, requiring that interpretation of burst spectra take into account acoustic aspects of the following vowel.

4. Formant transitions for obstruent consonants tend to obey a locus theory equation; i.e., the observable initial values for formants at voicing onset vary with the identity of the following vowel.

5. There are occasional violations of expected patterns (e.g., F2 and F3 come together in a velar-like way for a syllable such as /od/ for many speakers), but there is no perceptual confusion between "road" and "rogue".

6. Vowel-vowel coarticulation across an intervening obstruent can cause the formant transitions for a CV to vary quite a bit depending on the identity of the vowel preceding the CV (Ohman 1966).

7. Formant values for vowels depend on phonetic environment, where (e.g.) a postvocalic /l/ can drastically affect a lax front vowel.

8. Formant values for vowels depend on vowel duration, which depends in turn on the syntactic position of the word in the sentence, so that interpretation of durational cues to lexical contrasts requires discounting effects of syntax and semantic highlighting.

of higher-order predicates to try, and so must try them all simultaneously (and require incredible amounts of balanced training data to select the correct data correlations)—whereas, if the advocates of the motor theory are right, listeners develop only a narrow set of hypotheses, constrained by what has been learned about the relations between speech-production capabilities and the resulting acoustic output. For me, this motor constraint, which might be construed as the weakest form of a motor theory, has considerable face validity.

In summary: Pseudo-neutral networks have taken the cognitive-science and speech-recognition communities by storm, but it is too early to determine whether present-day neural-network learning strategies are sufficiently powerful to compete with traditional approaches when the task is speech recognition (Lippmann 1987). However, the field is very active, and it may be the case that improved learning strategies and/or network structures will be discovered that will make this approach more attractive

(Waibel et al. 1987). Computationally, it appears that hidden-layer neural networks are not really very different from traditional statistical approaches to recognition. Furthermore, they will probably turn out to be not very realistic models of brain function, either at the microscopic level or as language-learning models that must ultimately account for "one-exposure learning" and other complex aspects of cognition.

The Trace Interactive Activation Model
The Elman-McClelland Trace model of word hypothesization from acoustic data is illustrated in figure 13. A set of feature detectors extract important properties from a spectral representation of the raw speech signal. Higher modes in a network recognize phonemes and then words. The network is highly interconnected with bidirectional facilitory connections between levels that share common properties (e.g., between the features that compose a phoneme and that phoneme, or between the phonemes that compose a word and that word) and inhibitory connections within levels (e.g., if /b/ is activated it will tend to suppress activity for related phonemes, such as /p/). In this critical review, I will be concerned primarily with the problems inherent in going from an input representation to a phonemic representation in Trace.

Elman and McClelland make four strong claims: that a network model of appropriate structure can be tuned to recognize phonemes accurately in continuous speech, that phonemes can be recognized from a set of acoustic features extracted at fixed times relative to one another, that context-dependent constraints can be represented by hard-wired weighting connections between consonants and adjacent vowels, and that connections to and from a lexical level facilitate word recognition and simultaneously cause perceptual biases to hear phoneme sequences that make up English words. Of particular importance is the emphasis they place on the idea that variation in the acoustic manifestations of a consonant depending on the following vowel is not a source of noise, as might be assumed in a model of speech perception stressing invariant cues to phonetic contrasts, but is rather a source of very useful information in an appropriate model. The four claims are examined in the following paragraphs.

The Phoneme as a Unit
Elman and McClelland made no strong commitment to phonemes over syllables or any other linguistic unit, but in order to evaluate this type of model they had to choose some unit in order to see what problems would arise. Tests have been limited to plosive-vowel syllables from one speaker, using only a few vowels. So far, phonemic recognition performance is not

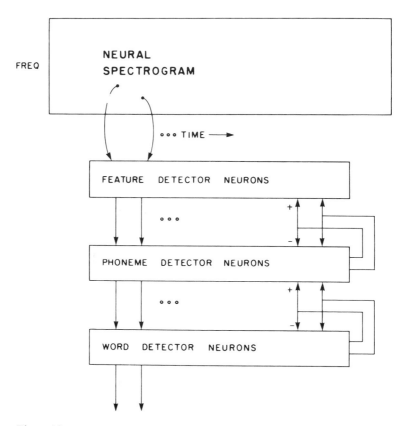

Figure 13

The Trace model of speech perception consists of three layers of nodes connected
to one another by excitation/inhibition paths having adjustable weights. The first
layer of nodes consists of a set of phonetic-feature detectors that read information
off a neural spectrogram. The second layer makes phonemic decisions based
on the strength of various features in the input, as well as being influenced by
activation of words at the next level. Phonemes activate words at the highest
level in the model.

at all impressive (and they haven't tackled the hard problems, such as the multiple-speaker problem, continuous speech, and plosive allophones occurring in unstressed environments or in clusters).

Feature Detectors

In the Trace model, a set of features not unlike the distinctive features described by linguists are extracted from the signal by a set of property detectors. Each detector is represented at many different instants of time in order to allow for temporal variation in the relative locations of different features making up a phoneme. It is up to the experimenter to adjust the weights on connections between these features and phonemes so as to be able to accept natural variations in the timing of acoustic events, yet not get confused by the multiple answers provided by the multiply defined features. I have argued elsewhere (Klatt 1986b) that the time dimension in speech must be treated in a more insightful way to overcome the inherent temporal variability of speech.

Contextual Effects

The fact that the acoustic shape of a stop consonant depends in part on the following vowel is hard-wired into the Elman-McClelland model by providing structure that permits the vowel portion of the signal to influence dynamically the weights applied to the features used for classification of the consonant. For example, if a vowel feature detector detects the presence of a front vowel, all consonantal place-of-articulation feature detectors in a time interval preceding the vowel are inhibited except for those feature detectors expecially designed to recognize consonants before front vowels. Again, the variation in temporal location of long and short vowels makes it difficult to implement such a scheme. When fully elaborated to account for segmental cue-trading and context-dependent interactions such as those shown in figure 5 and listed in table 3, this structural solution to combating context dependencies seems highly implausible and untrainable.

Interactions between Phonemic Level and Word Level

The positive feedback paths between the phonemic level and the lexical level in the Trace model potentially account for aspects of perceptual biases such that we tend to hear phonetic patterns that make up real words (phonotactic constraints) and we can sometimes make early decisions about lexical candidates even though the entire word has not yet been heard. For me, this is the most attractive aspect of the model, but it is far from clear that the details are correct. (For example, perhaps shared stress pattern or allophonic detail associated with syllable structure should count as much as phonemic similarity.)

In summary: The Trace model is structurally similar to the "spreading activation" pseudo-neural learning models, and suffers from the same kinds of limitations. The most difficult problem to solve in this kind of model is how to allow for temporal variability and context-conditioned allophonic variation in a way that does not diminish the ability of the network to make fine phonetic distinctions. Variability in time, frequency, and intensity produces patterns that are not easy to group together on the basis of similarity measures, and articulatory variability is rule-governed in ways that these neural models find it difficult to describe or discover even if provided with vast amounts of balanced training data.

A Feature-Integration Model
Massaro (1987) considers the problem of how information from different feature detectors is combined to make segmental decisions in perception. In Massaro's fuzzy logical model of perception (figure 14), perception of syllables or other phonetic units is based on a two-stage process involving (1) the detection of a set of independent acoustic properties or features from the signal and (2) utilization of a common metric to represent the degree of match of feature strength to that in the prototype specification of the phonetic unit (using fuzzy truth values that range from 0 (property totally mismatched to the expected value in the prototype specification) to 1.0 (property present at expected strength). Multiplication of truth values for all relevant features results in a score for each alternative syllable or phonetic unit of the language, and division by the sum of these scores for all alternative syllables of the language results in a pseudo-probability or confidence in the recognition decision. Perceptual data from a number of different kinds of cue-interaction experiments can be fitted by this type of model (reviewed in Massaro 1987), and the fit is often significantly better than that provided by alternative models. Unfortunately, there are usually a fairly large number of model parameters that must be deduced from the data that is to be described, suggesting that the approach might be profitably constrained in some further way. As yet, there have been few attempts to extrapolate results obtained from one type of cue-interaction experiment to data from another experiment or data from the general phonetic perception situation.

Repp (1987) has questioned the ability of this model to describe the way that two factors interact to signal place of articulation for nasal consonants. A similar type of cue interaction having to do with the cues to nasality and breathiness (Klatt 1987b) could be troublesome; two cues that normally

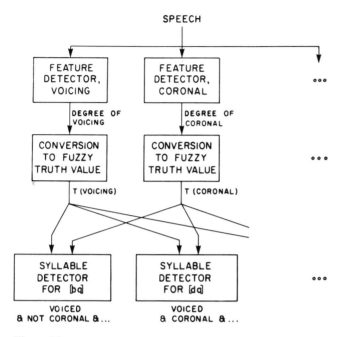

Figure 14
The Massaro (1987) fuzzy logical model of how feature information is combined
in order to identify a syllable. First the relationship between an acoustic
measurement of feature strength and the probability of responding with a plus
or minus feature decision is converted into a fuzzy "truth value"; then these
independent truth values are combined using multiplicative logical predicates
to determine the most likely syllable.

signal nasality in a male voice (increase in the bandwidth of F1 and increase
in the strength of the first harmonic) are reinterpreted as cues to breathiness,
with no tendency to hear nasality, if synthesized in a female voice that is
accompanied by breathiness noise in the frequency region above 2 kHz.
Since breathiness is not a phonemic prototype in English, it may not
be possible to characterize this interaction within the present feature-
integration scheme.

   In summary: The demonstrated success of the Massaro strategy for cue
integration in accounting for perceptual data probably makes it the best
current choice for models employing feature detectors and segmental decisions. However, there are troublesome special cases, and one has no way
of knowing whether the acoustic parameters that one has chosen are in fact
the best set for characterizing human perception.

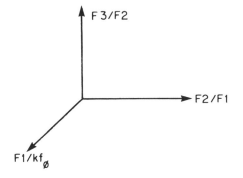

1. Auditory pointer moves about in above space.

2. Perceptual pointer attached by spring to the auditory pointer lags behind due to 60-180 ms time constant.

3. When perceptual pointer "slows down" a phonetic event is recognized, identity determined by nearest "target zone".

Figure 15
A model of speech perception in which a perceptual pointer moves about in a three-dimensional space, slowing down or changing directions at locations corresponding to the phonemes contained in the utterance. After Miller (1982).

An Auditory-Perceptual Pointer Model

Miller (1982) has proposed an auditory-perceptual model of phonetic perception that is simple yet far-reaching in its claimed capabilities. It is a psychoacoustician's response to the encodedness claims and the "speech is special" claims of advocates of the motor theory. The model, illustrated in figure 15, is divided into three components:

• A simulation of the auditory system calculates spectral characteristics of incoming speech, and these are transformed into an auditory-perceptual space of only a few dimensions. For vowels, these dimensions are related to ratios of formant frequencies and the ratio of F1 to a function of average fundamental frequency ($F1/kF0$, $F2/F1$, $F3/F2$). The advantages of such dimensions for speaker normalization have been championed by many researchers (Disner 1980; Nearey 1983; Syrdal 1984), but it is not yet clear whether they can be reliably extracted from natural speech (Bladon 1982; Klatt 1986c). For voiceless sounds, related dimensions are derived from the spectrum.

• A perceptual pointer moves about in this three-dimensional auditory space, reacting to the input vector with a relatively slow time constant of 60–180 msec. A spring attached to the perceptual pointer causes it to overshoot acoustic targets when the input vector changes direction suddenly, and this is intended to have the effect of undoing coarticulatory undershoot. Thus, a rising F2 at the release of /ba/ will cause the perceptual pointer to reach a higher value than the F2 value at vowel midpoint, whereas a falling F2 in /da/ will cause the opposite effect. In this way, we hear /a/ tokens in which the effects of adjacent consonants on vowel formant patterns are automatically undone.

• Whenever the perceptual pointer reaches a low velocity or changes direction, a perceptual event, corresponding to a phonetic segment, is detected. The particular phonetic event depends on the nearest target zone in the space. Target zones are defined during language acquisition.

The model is an attempt to make speech perception simple, direct, and non-"special." It started as a gender-independent model of vowel quality categorization (Miller et al. 1980), and then evolved to encompass consonants in continuous speech (Miller and Jongman 1987). As formulated, the model makes strong claims as to the nature of perceptual processing and the permitted kinds of coarticulatory undershoot and recoding that can be tolerated before misperceptions will occur. These predictions seem to run counter to some of what we know about detailed cue-trading and coarticulatory phenomena in natural language. For example, the perceptual pointer will be delayed in such a way that CV and VC transitions for a particular consonant will look different, even though the actual formant motions are usually mirror images in time; and the perceptual pointer overshoot idea is probably insufficient to discount large changes such as those in lax vowels followed by /l/; and the cue-trading relationships illustrated in figure 5 and listed in table 3 would be difficult to explain in this oversimplified framework. It is also far from clear that continuous speech contains the kind of acoustic changes that would permit decisions about locations and number of phonetic segments to be made on the basis of changes in the direction and the velocity of a perceptual pointer. I have argued elsewhere that segmentation criteria are language-dependent and signal-dependent in ways that prevent strategies wherein segmentation precedes phonetic labeling (Klatt 1977).

Speech Recognition: Implications for Speech Perception
This is not the appropriate place to describe and compare in detail the various speech-recognition strategies being pursued at research labo-

ratories and in commercial devices. I have compared several systems elsewhere (Klatt 1986a). In this subsection I will simply mention a few techniques that have proved to work well with real data and thus might be considered in the design of perceptual models.

Auditory Modeling

In a speech-recognition context, the choice of an initial spectral representation can be critical. It is desirable to find a representation in which no important information is lost but as many irrelevant spectral details are removed as possible. Efforts to simulate aspects of the encoding of speech in the peripheral auditory system have led to new representations with at least three desirable properties: a nonlinear warping of the frequency scale to reflect the decreasing perceptual importance of higher-frequency intervals (Zwicker and Terhardt 1980), a widening of the analysis bandwidth at higher frequencies to mimic the ear's inability to resolve details within a critical bandwidth (Moore and Glasberg 1983), and adaptation effects that accentuate sudden spectral changes and tend to whiten steady-state spectra (Smith 1979). The latter effect can interact badly with an inappropriate distance metric, but Cohen (1985) found significant improvement in the performance of the IBM system when this type of front end replaced the previous representation. Measures of neural synchrony to frequency components in the input signal have also been studied as possibly leading to a better representation of formants for speech recognition, especially in noise (Seneff 1986, 1988; Hunt 1987), but we still do not know whether the auditory system makes use of synchrony information when making judgments of phonetic quality.

Metrics

In most speech-recognition systems, spectral comparisons or classifications of spectra are performed using a distance metric. Spectral distance measures range from the very simple summation over frequency of the squares of differences in decibels between two spectra (the Euclidean metric) to highly data-dependent calculations that use weightings to place emphasis on differences observed near spectral peaks (Klatt 1982). Another notable technique is to represent a spectrum by a cosine series expansion (Rabiner 1987) and to employ a metric consisting of a weighted sum of the squares of coefficient differences, where the weighting of a coefficient is based on its estimated importance to phonetic decisions. Such a weighting can be made to largely ignore spectral tilt and rapid changes across adjacent spectral channels attributable to noise. Attempts to evaluate spectral distance measures according to recognition performance (Nocerino et al. 1985) have identified a few clearly suboptimal approaches, but have not established any one choice as significantly superior.

Theoretically, it is the *changes* in the spectrum over time that constitute the most important information during speech production. A long steady vowel provides little more information than the brief transients that occur at the release of a stop consonant. Efforts to quantify spectral change so as to either detect phonetic boundaries or attend to the most important intervals of the acoustic stream have been largely unsuccessful. The problem has been that taking the derivative of rather variable spectral data accentuates the noise components and thus provides an unreliable measure. Rabiner (1987) has shown that a particular highly smoothed estimate of spectral change can dramatically affect the performance of many speech-recognition algorithms—usually halving the overall error rate. Direct incorporation of this idea into models like LAFS would be straightforward and might be an important first step toward speaker-independent interpretation of spectra.

Dynamic Time Warping
When comparing an unknown word with a set of stored word templates, one problem has been how to align the time axis so that events in the unknown word optimally match corresponding events in the correct template. A very powerful alignment technique known as dynamic programming essentially tries all reasonable time warpings—which has the side effect of permitting a great deal of freedom in time alignment and thus effectively destroying duration cues during word recognition.[4] The success of dynamic time warping does not mean that duration information is useless, but it does suggest that relegating duration interpretation to a postprocessor may be an especially powerful method for dealing with the variability of timing in speech when trying to interpret spectral events. Network models like LAFS, with "self-loops" that can absorb any number of similar spectral frames in a row, are a computational equivalent of dynamic time warping. The Trace model has no comparable algorithm and must instead define multiple instantiations of a feature detector, each attached to a different time in the neural spectrogram, in order to allow for timing variability; this leads to difficulties in deciding which detectors to believe at any given time.

Speaker-Independent Word Templates
One brute-force method of transforming a speaker-trained recognition system into a speaker-independent one is to collect data from a very large sample of speakers and then pick out a small set of representative speakers

to provide spectral templates. Wilpon and Rabiner (1985) have described procedures for clustering speakers into groups and have shown that 10–20 speakers can represent very large populations very well. This is another example of an engineering solution involving enumeration rather than systematic discovery of rules to transform each new speaker into a standard form. It is a solution available to perceptual models as well.

Hidden Markov Models

There are three major competing strategies in the speech-recognition ballgame at the moment: whole-word templates (Rabiner and Levinson 1981), hidden Markov models of words or phonemes (Jelinek 1985; Averbuch et al. 1987; Chow et al. 1987), and knowledge-based approaches to phonetic recognition (Zue 1985; Cole et al. 1985). It appears that the hidden Markov model is winning the competition and may continue to do so for a very long time. The reason is not that the hidden Markov models are so appealing in structure, but rather that they can be optimized on the basis of vast amounts of training data. Furthermore, the structure of the hidden Markov model can be changed in response to new insights that might be gained via the other approaches to speech recognition (Chow et al. 1987), and the impact of training on performance pushes the Markov modeler back into first place very quickly. This has two possible implications for those of us interested in models of human perception: that any model of speech perception that does not address issues of tuning and learning is incomplete, perhaps in a very essential way, and that there is great power in certain probabilistic formalisms.

Other Issues Related to Speech Perception and Lexical Access

Psychologists have been interested in lexical access mechanisms for a long time. Much of the research in this area has been concerned with visual cues to lexical information, but some psychological experiments have used auditory probes.

The Cohort Theory

In an update of the cohort model, Marslen-Wilson (1987; see also chapter 1 of this volume) offers evidence in support of lexical access mechanisms that work from left to right on a narrow phonetic or featural representation, as opposed to a phonemic representation of the input. For example, in a gating task, listeners can make early use of rounding cues in the noise portion of an utterance to differentiate "scoop" from the unrounded vowel in "scout".

The cohort theory states that words are recognized by considering all words consistent with a given span of acoustic input, known as the cohort. When the cohort reduces to one word, a lexical decision is rendered, even if the acoustic end of the word has not been heard. Semantic probes of the lexicon begin very early in this process. Semantic-priming studies show that the gated "capt..." primes both "guard" and "ship" by activating the lexical items "captive" and "captain". Gating from the back end of a word, such as presenting "...attle" for "battle", does not activate "war". All these results are consistent with the left-to-right assumption of the cohort model (and with the structure of LAFS).

In an important recent experiment, Marslen-Wilson (1987) has obtained evidence that top-down syntactic/semantic/pragmatic mechanisms of speech understanding do not interact directly with the processing of acoustic input by the bottom-up lexical access module—rather, it is as if the two accessing mechanisms compete in parallel to determine which one will arrive at a unique lexical item first.

A Constraint-Satisfaction Model

Pisoni and Luce (1987) argue the case that some form of segmental representation is essential for gaining access to the processes involved in word recognition. The most compelling experimental evidence that they cite involves phoneme monitoring in nonwords (Foss and Blank 1980) and misperceptions that involve segments rather than alternative whole words (Bond and Garnes 1980; Bond and Robey 1983; Cole 1973). Even so, there may be several different processing strategies that work in parallel during normal sentence comprehension, and not all of them need perform segmental analysis (Klatt 1979).

When trying to account for differences in intelligibility of 300 words presented to subjects in a noise background, Hood and Poole (1980) noted that high-frequency words were not always more intelligible. Pisoni et al. (1985) compared the 25 most intelligible words with the 25 least intelligible words from the Hood-Poole study with respect to phonetic similarity and frequency of occurrence in a 20,000-word phonemic dictionary. They found that the words that were difficult to recognize in noise had more high-frequency phonetically similar competitors. The implication is that word recognition involves a search through a space of phonetically similar words (here defined as words differing in but one phoneme), and that the frequency of occurrence of competing words in this phonetically similar non-left-to-right "cohort" plays a role in recognition. Though tantalizing, these results do not establish all the parameters of phonetic similarity that lead to competition—for example, simple acoustic similarity may explain these results as well as phonemic similarity.

Pisoni, Luce, and Nusbaum (1985) go on to argue that word-recognition strategies based on strict left-to-right processing of phonetic segments fail to account for recognition when the initial part of a word is obscured. They propose a more flexible matching strategy ("constraint satisfaction") that makes use of a number of different sources of information, such as initial phonetic segments, final segments, syllable stress pattern, greater distinctiveness of segments in stressed syllables, and broad manner-of-articulation coding of the segment sequence. Pisoni et al. show that the search-reduction power of working from the front rather than the back of a word are about equal in a 125,000-word lexicon.

The Role of Lexical Stress

Anne Cutler (chapter 11, this volume) investigated the hypothesis that listeners locate word boundaries in continuous speech in part by stressed syllable anchoring, and by interpretation of general prosodic cues. She notes that over 90 percent of English words are stressed on the first syllable (excluding closed-class function words). Also, the majority of misperceptions involving a shift in word-boundary location tend to move the boundary to a location just before a metrically strong syllable. Surprisingly, a semantic-priming experiment by Cutler (1986) revealed that word pairs such as "insight"-"incite" and the noun/verb forms of "forearm" are actually homophones in that both semantic readings are primed even though only one stress form is heard. To the extent that the fundamental frequency contour, f_0, signals stress, this result is very nice for proponents of LAFS, because one of the most difficult unaddressed problems is how to incorporate f_0 interpretation directly in a LAFS network. This result suggests that f_0 may not be a part of initial lexical hypothesis formation—perhaps f_0 interpretation is relegated to a separate module (Fodor 1983). As Marslen-Wilson (1987) has proposed, the most parsimonious model of processing may be one in which lexical hypothesis formation is free running and retrieves all readings of ambiguous words. Postprocessing then tests the plausibility of each reading and selects the correct one on the basis of syntax, semantics, pragmatics, intonation, and any other factors that help.

3 Discussion

Several models of lexical hypothesis formation from acoustic data have been critically reviewed. The results of the review are disappointing in that no model stands out as defendably superior.

The revised motor theory of Liberman and Mattingly (1986) is theoretically quite attractive. At a philosophical level, it can account for multimodal speech perception, for duplex perception, for cue-trading relationships that make sense only in articulatory terms (Repp 1982), and for other peculiarities attributable to the encodedness of speech. However, at an engineering level many practical problems face the designer who wishes to implement such a philosophy. It is clearly worthwhile to attempt to do so, but we must await a more favorable result of such efforts before wholeheartedly embracing the theory.

The analysis-by-synthesis model of speech perception continues to be an appealing approach on theoretical grounds, but again suffers from pitfalls when translated into engineering terms. An initial analysis must be found that can reduce the set of lexical candidates to a manageable size without rejecting the correct word, and no practical system is yet able to do this in continuous speech.

The phonetic-feature model of perception advocated by Stevens (1986) incorporates the advantages of sophisticated new insights into the relationship between acoustics and phonetics. There is real hope that relational attributes can be defined that reduce the variability inherent in speech spectra. It is also clear that efforts to avoid segmental decisions (i.e., avoid having to temporally align the features that have been computed in parallel) are well motivated and in line with recent theoretical advances known as tiered phonology. However, it is too early to embrace this formalism; engineering implementation of high-performance feature detectors and a lexical matching strategy are an essential next step.

The LAFS model of Klatt (1979, 1986a) is attractive because processing is simple pattern matching. In fact, LAFS is probably the best candidate model of those considered here if the goal is to take an existing model of speech perception and recast it in pseudo-neural terms on a parallel machine. All the detailed knowledge about the relations between acoustics and word sequences is contained in a network of expected spectral sequences. However, it has not been proved that enumeration of alternatives is a feasible approach to the characterization of variability inherent in speech. Again, the only convincing argument is an engineering demonstration.

Why have engineering demonstrations been so slow in arriving? The answer seems to be that some very fundamental gaps exist in our understanding of perception, as well as in our understanding of the detailed nature of the speech acoustics. These gaps limit recognition performance to totally unsatisfactory levels. Surprisingly little work has been done on systematic comparisons of consonants and vowels spoken by men and women in continuous sentence environments. We simply do not know how to deal with the seemingly unreasonable variability that has been encountered. Fundamental unsolved problems include the following:

• how to achieve source/filter separation, extract formant frequencies, and recover vocal tract shapes (Is this what perceptual strategies are all about?)
• how to characterize acoustic variability in the manifestation of phonetic events, normalize out or minimize cross-speaker variability, and define metrics that mimic perception
• how to represent alternatives—especially those having to do with cue trading, relative timing variation in different articulators, and cross-word-boundary recodings.

Three models of quite different structure are attractive to me: some form of the motor theory that involves decomposing a speech signal into component articulatory gestures, a model involving a phonetic feature extraction process that takes advantage of the existence of natural classes of sounds with simple articulatory definition and distinctive relational acoustic manifestations, and an atheoretical enumerative approach like LAFS that specifies expected sequences of speech spectra for word sequences of the language. When wearing my engineering hat, I would probably choose to work on LAFS because of its obvious advantages as a practical solution, but as a scientist I find the less-well-charted waters of the other alternatives to be more intriguing.

Acknowledgments

I would like to thank Stefanie Shattuck-Hufnagel, Ken Stevens and William Marslen-Wilson for valuable comments. The research was supported in part by the NIH and in part by DARPA under contract N00039-85-C-0254, monitored through the Naval Electronic Systems Command.

Notes

1. And integrating acoustic cues with those provided by the visual sense. Lip-reading cues appear to be integrated into phonetic decisions in such an early stage that the process must be essentially amodal and articulatory in nature (Studdert-Kennedy 1985; Summerfield, in press).

2. For example, if one set $p\{voicing\} = 0.5, p\{labial\} = 0.5, p\{alveolar\} = 0.5$, and $p\{velar\} = 0.5$, then all of the consonants /p, b, k, g/ would have the same probability: $0.5 \times 0.5 = 0.25$. No adjustment of these probabilities can selectively favor /p/ and /g/ over /b/ and /k/.

3. In fact, Church (1987) argues for an intermediate representation in which allophonic details are used to derive syllable structure and stress patterns for continuous speech, after which allophones are converted to phonemic alternatives (because he argues from the nature of phonological rule systems that the lexicon as stored in the head of the listener must be phonemic).

4. Attempts to treat the frequency axis in a similar way, so as to optimally align formant-related spectral peaks, do not result in improved recognition performance.

References

Allen, J. 1985. Cochlear modeling. *IEEE ASSP Magazine*, January, pp. 3–29.

Atal, B. 1975. Towards determining articulator positions from the speech signal. In G. Fant (ed.), *Speech Communication*, volume 1. Uppsala: Almqvist and Wiksell.

Atal, B. 1983. Efficient coding of LPC parameters by temporal decomposition. In *ICASSP-83*.

Atal, B., J. J. Chang, M. V. Mathews, and J. W. Tukey. 1978. Inversion of articulatory-to-acoustic transformation in the vocal tract by a computer sorting technique. *J. Acoust. Soc. Am.* 63: 1535–1556.

Averbuch, A., et al. 1987. Experiments with the Tangora 20,000 word speech recognizer. In *ICASSP-87*.

Bell, C. G., H. Fujisaki, J. M. Heinz, and K. N. Stevens. 1961. Reduction of speech spectra by analysis-by-synthesis techniques. *J. Acoust. Soc. Am.* 33: 1725–1736.

Bladon, A. 1982. Arguments against formants in the auditory representation of speech. In R. Carlson and B. Granström (eds.), *The Representation of Speech in the Peripheral Auditory System*. Amsterdam: Elsevier.

Blomberg, M., R. Carlson, K. Elenius, and B. Granström. 1986. Auditory models as front ends in speech recognition systems. In J. Perkell and D. Klatt (eds.), *Invariance and Variability in Speech Processes*. Hillsdale, N.J.: Erlbaum.

Blumstein, S. E., and K. N. Stevens. 1979. Acoustic invariance in speech production: Evidence from measurements of the spectral characteristics of stop consonants. *J. Acoust. Soc. Am.* 66: 1001–1017.

Bond, Z. S., and S. Garnes. 1980. Misperceptions of fluent speech. In R. Cole (ed.), *Perception and Production of Fluent Speech*. Hillsdale, N.J.: Erlbaum.

Bond, Z. S., and R. R. Robey. 1983. The phonetic structure of errors in the perception of fluent speech. In N. Lass (ed.), *Speech and Language: Advances in Basic Research and Practice*, volume 9. New York: Academic.

Bradley, D. C., and K. I. Forster. 1987. A reader's view of listening. *Cognition* 25: 103–134.

Bregman, A. 1978. The formation of auditory streams. In R. Requin (ed.), *Attention and Performance VII*. Hillsdale, N.J.: Erlbaum.

Browman, C. P., and L. M. Goldstein. 1985. Dynamic modeling of phonetic structure. In V. A. Fromkin (ed.), *Phonetic Linguistics: Essays in Honor of Peter Ladefoged*. New York: Academic.

Bush, M., and G. Kopek. 1986. Network-based connected digit recognition using explicit acoustic-phonetic modeling. In *ICASSP-86*.

Chistovich, L. A. 1985. Central auditory processing of peripheral vowel spectra. *J. Acoust. Soc. Am.* 77: 789–805.

Chomsky, N., and M. Halle. 1968. *The Sound Pattern of English*. New York: Harper and Row.

Chow, Y. L., M. O. Dunham, O. A. Kimball, M. A. Krasner, G. F. Kubala, J. Makhoul, P. J. Price, S. Roucos, and R. M. Schwartz. 1987. BYBLOS: The BBN continuous speech recognition system. In *ICASSP-87*.

Church, K. W. 1987. Phonological parsing and lexical retrieval. *Cognition* 25: 53–69.

Clements, G. N. 1985. The geometry of phonological features. In *Phonology Yearbook*, volume 2. Cambridge University Press.

Cohen, J. R. 1985. Application of an adaptive auditory model to speech recognition. *J. Acoust. Soc. Am.* 78, Suppl. 1: S78 (A).

Cole, R. A. 1973. Listening for mispronunciations: A measure of what we hear during speech. *Perception and Psychophysics* 13: 153–156.

Cole, R., M. Phillips, B. Brennan, and B. Chigier. 1986. The CMU phonetic classification system. In *ICASSP-86*.

Cutler, A. 1986. Forbear is a homophone: Lexical prosody does not constrain lexical access. *Language and Speech* 29: 201–220.

Darwin, C. J. 1976. The perception of speech. In E. C. Carterette and M. P. Friedman (eds.), *Handbook of Perception*. New York: Academic.

Delgutte, B. 1986. Analysis of French stop consonants using a model of the peripheral auditory system. In J. Perkell and D. Klatt (eds.), *Invariance and Variability in Speech Processes*. Hillsdale, N.J.: Erlbaum.

Disner, S. F. 1980. Evaluation of vowel normalization procedures. *J. Acoust. Soc. Am.* 67: 253–261.

Elman, J. L., and J. L. McClelland. 1984. Speech perception as a cognitive process: The interactive activation model. In N. J. Lass (ed.), *Speech and Language: Advances in Basic Research and Practice*, volume 10. New York: Academic Press.

Elman, J. L., and J. L. McClelland. 1986. Exploiting the lawful variability in the speech wave. In J. Perkell and D. Klatt (eds.), *Invariance and Variability in Speech Processes*. Hillsdale, N.J.: Erlbaum.

Fodor, J. 1983. *The Modularity of Mind*. Cambridge, Mass.: MIT Press.

Foss, D. J., and M. A. Blank. 1980. Identifying the speech codes. *Cognitive Psych.* 12: 1–131.

Fowler, C. A., and M. R. Smith. 1986. Speech perception as vector analysis: An approach to the problem of invariance and segmentation. In J. Perkell and D. Klatt (eds.), *Invariance and Variability in Speech Processes*. Hillsdale, N.J.: Erlbaum.

Fromkin, V. 1971. The non-anomalous nature of anomalous utterances. *Language* 47: 27–52.

Fujisaki, H., and M. Ljungqvist. 1987. Estimation of voice source and vocal tract parameters based on ARMA analysis and a model for the glottal source waveform. In *ICASSP-87*.

Gibson, J. J. 1966. *The Senses Considered as Perceptual Systems*. Boston: Houghton Mifflin.

Glass, J. R., and V. W. Zue. 1987. Acoustic segmentation and classification. In *Proceedings of DARPA Program Review*, San Diego.

Goldhor, R. 1986. A model of peripheral auditory transduction using a phase vocoder with modified channel signals. In *ICASSP-86*. (See also *ICASSP-83*, pp. 1368–1371.)

Halle, M., and K. N. Stevens. 1962. Speech recognition: A model and a program for research. *IRE Transactions on Information Theory* IT-8: 155–159.

Halle, M., and J. R. Vergnaud. 1980. Three dimensional phonology. *J. Linguistic Research* 1: 83–105.

Harrington, J., and A. Johnstone. 1987. The effects of word boundary ambiguity in continuous speech recognition. In *Proceedings of XIth International Congress of Phonetic Sciences*, Tallinn, Estonia.

Hebb, D. O. 1949. *The Organization of Behavior*, New York: Wiley.

Hood, J. D., and J. P. Poole. 1980. Influence of the speaker and other factors affecting speech intelligibility. *J. Exper. Psych.* 65: 6–11.

Hunt, M. J., and C. Lefebvre. 1987. Speech recognition using an auditory model with pitch-synchronous analysis. In *ICASSP-87*.

Huttenlocher, D. P., and V. W. Zue. 1984. A Model of Lexical Access from Partial Phonetic Information. In *ICASSP-1984*.

Huttenlocher, D. P. 1986. A broad phonetic classifier. In *ICASSP-86*.

Jakobson, R., G. Fant, and M. Halle. 1963. *Preliminaries to Speech Analysis: The Distinctive Features and Their Correlates*. Cambridge, Mass. MIT Press.

Jelinek, F. 1985. The development of an experimental discrete dictation recognizer. *Proc. IEEE* 73: 1616–1624.

Jusczyk, P. W. 1986. Toward a model of the development of speech perception. In J. Perkell and D. Klatt (eds.), *Invariance and Variability in Speech Processes*. Hillsdale, N.J.: Erlbaum.

Klatt, D. H. 1975. Word verification in a speech understanding system. In D. R. Reddy (ed.), *Speech Recognition: Invited Papers Presented at the 1974 IEEE Symposium*. New York: Academic.

Klatt, D. H. 1976. A Digital Filter Bank for Spectral Matching. In *ICASSP-76*.

Klatt, D. H. 1977. Review of the ARPA Speech Understanding Project. *J. Acoust. Soc. Am.* 62: 1345–1366.

Klatt, D. H. 1979. Speech perception: A model of acoustic-phonetic analysis and lexical access. In R. A. Cole (ed.), *Perception and Production of Fluent Speech*. Hillsdale, N.J.: Erlbaum. (See also *J. Phonetics* 7, 1979: 279–312.)

Klatt, D. H. 1981. Lexical representations for speech production and perception. In T. Myers, J. Laver, and J. Anderson (eds.), *The Cognitive Representation of Speech*. Amsterdam: North-Holland.

Klatt, D. H. 1982. Prediction of perceived phonetic distance from critical-band spectra: A first step. In *ICASSP-82*.

Klatt, D. H. 1986a. The problem of variability in speech recognition and in models of speech perception. In J. Perkell and D. Klatt (eds.), *Invariance and Variability in Speech Processes*. Hillsdale, N.J.: Erlbaum.

Klatt, D. H. 1986b. Response to Elman. In J. Perkell and D. Klatt (eds.), *Invariance and Variability in Speech Processes*. Hillsdale, N.J.: Erlbaum.

Klatt, D. H. 1986c. Representation of the first formant in speech recognition and in models of speech perception. In P. Mermelstein (ed.), *Proceedings of the Montreal Satellite Symposium on Speech Recognition* (Twelfth International Congress on Acoustics).

Klatt, D. H. 1986d. Models of phonetic recognition I: Issues that arise in attempting to specify a feature-based strategy for speech recognition. In P. Mermelstein (ed.), *Proceedings of the Montreal Satellite Symposium on Speech Recognition* (Twelfth International Congress on Acoustics).

Klatt, D. H. 1987a. Review of text-to-speech conversion for English. *J. Acoust. Soc. Am.* 82: 737–793.

Klatt, D. H. 1987b. Acoustic correlates of breathiness. *J. Acoust. Soc. Am.* 82, Suppl. 1: S91 (A).

Klatt, D. H., and C. Cook. 1976. A speech synthesis-by-rule program for response generation and for word verification. In W. A. Woods. (ed.), Speech Understanding Systems Final Report. Cambridge, Mass.: Bolt, Beranek and Newman, Inc.

Klatt, D. H., and K. N. Stevens. 1973. On the automatic recognition of continuous speech: Implications of a spectrogram-reading experiment. *IEEE Transactions on Audio and Electroacoustics* AU-21: 210–217.

Klein, W., R. Plomp, and L. Pols. 1970. Vowel spectra, vowel spaces and vowel identification. *J. Acoust. Soc. Am.* 48: 999–1009.

Levinson, S. E., and L. R. Rabiner. 1985. A task-oriented conversational mode speech understanding system. In M. R. Schroeder (ed.), *Speech and Speaker Recognition*. Basel: Karger.

Liberman, A. M., F. S. Cooper, D. S. Shankweiler, and M. Studdert-Kennedy. 1967. Perception of the speech code. *Psychological Review* 74: 431–461.

Liberman, A. M., and I. G. Mattingly. 1986. The motor theory of speech perception revised. *Cognition* 21: 1–36.

Lippmann, R. P. 1987. An introduction to computing with neural nets. *IEEE ASSP Magazine*, April: 4–22.

Lisker, L. 1978. Rapid vs. rabid: A catalogue of acoustic features that may cue the distinction. In Status Report on Speech Research SR-65, Haskins Labs, New Haven.

Marcus, S. M. 1984. Recognizing speech: On the mapping from sound to word. In H. Bouma and D. G. Bouwhuis (eds.), *Attention and Performance X: Control of Language Processes*, Hillsdale, N.J.: Erlbaum.

Marcus, S. M. 1986. Decoding the Speech Code. Manuscript 513, Institute for Perception Research, Eindhoven.

Marslen-Wilson, W. D. 1987. Functional parallelism in spoken word recognition. *Cognition* 25: 71–102.

Marslen-Wilson, W. D., and A. Welsh. 1978. Processing interactions and lexical access during word recognition in continuous speech. *Cognitive Psychology* 10: 29–63.

Martin, J. G., and H. T. Bunnell. 1982. Perception of anticipatory coarticulation effects in vowel-stop consonant-vowel sequences. *J. Exp. Psychology: Human Perception and Performance* 8: 473–488.

Massaro, D. W. 1987. A fuzzy logical model of speech perception. In *Proceedings of the XIth International Congress of the Phonetic Sciences*, Tallinn, Estonia.

Massaro, D. W., and G. C. Oden. 1980. Evaluation and integration of acoustic features in speech perception. *J. Acoust. Soc. Am.* 67: 996–1013.

McClelland, J. L., and J. L. Elman. 1986. The trace model of speech perception. *Cognitive Psychology* 18: 1–86.

McGurk, H., and J. MacDonald. 1976. Hearing lips and seeing voices. *Nature* 264: 746–748.

Miller, J. D. 1982. Auditory-perceptual approaches to phonetic perception. *J. Acoust. Soc. Am.* 71: S112 (A).

Miller, J. D., A. M. Engebretson, and N. R. Vemula. 1980. Vowel normalization: Differences between vowels spoken by children, women, and men. *J. Acoust. Soc. Am.* 68: S33 (A).

Miller, J. D., and A. Jongman. 1987. Auditory-perceptual approaches to stop consonants. *J. Acoust. Soc. Am.* 82: S82 (A).

Minsky, M. L., and S. Papert. 1969. *Perceptrons: An Introduction to Computational Geometry*. Cambridge, Mass.: MIT Press.

Moore, B. C. J., and B. R. Glasberg. 1983. Suggested formulae for calculating auditory filter bandwidths and excitation patterns. *J. Acoust. Soc. Am.* 74: 750–753.

Morton, J., and D. E. Broadbent. 1967. Passive versus active recognition models, or is your homunculus really necessary?. In W. Wathen-Dunn (ed.), *Models for the Perception of Speech and Visual Form*. Cambridge, Mass.: MIT Press.

Nearey, T. 1983. Vowel space normalization procedures and phone-preserving transformations of synthetic vowels. *J. Acoust. Soc. Am.* 74, Suppl. 1: S17 (A).

Nocerino, N., F. K. Soong, L. R. Rabiner, and D. H. Klatt. 1985. Comparative study of several distortion measures for speech recognition. *Speech Communication* 4: 317–331.

Oden, G. C., and D. W. Massaro. 1978. Integration of featural information in speech perception. *Psych. Rev.* 85: 172–191.

Oshika, B. T., V. W. Zue, R. V. Weeks, H. Neu, and J. Aurbach. 1975. The role of phonological rules in speech understanding research. *IEEE Trans. ASSP* 23: 104–112.

Perkell, J., and D. H. Klatt. 1986. *Invariance and Variability in Speech Processes.* Hillsdale, N.J.: Erlbaum.

Pisoni, D. B. 1978. Speech perception. In W. K. Estes (ed.), *Handbook of Learning and Cognitive Processing*, volume 6. Hillsdale, N.J.: Erlbaum.

Pisoni, D. B. 1985. Speech perception: Some new directions in research and theory. *J. Acoust. Soc. Am.* 78: 381–388.

Pisoni, D. B., H. C. Nusbaum, P. A. Luce, and L. M. Slowiaczek. 1985. Speech perception, word recognition and the structure of the lexicon. *Speech Communication* 4: 75–95.

Pisoni, D. B., and P. A. Luce. 1987. Acoustic-phonetic representations in word recognition. *Cognition* 25: 21–52.

Rabiner, L. R. 1987. Use of Spectral Change Information Can Significantly Reduce the Error Rate in Speech Recognition. Oral presentation at DARPA meeting at Bolt, Beranek and Newman, Inc., Cambridge, Mass.

Rabiner, L. R., and S. E. Levinson. 1981. Isolated and connected word recognition: Theory and selected applications. *IEEE Trans. Comm.* COM-29: 621–659.

Repp, B. H. 1982. Phonetic trading relations and context effects: New experimental evidence for a speech mode of perception. *Psych. Bull.* 92: 81–110.

Repp, B. H. 1987. Integration and segregation in speech perception. In *Proceedings of the 12th International Congress of Phonetic Sciences*, Tallinn, Estonia.

Rumelhart, D. E., G. E. Hinton, and R. J. Williams. 1986. Learning internal representations by error propagation. In D. E. Rumelhart et al. (eds.), *Parallel Distributed Processing: Explorations in the Microstructure of Cognition.* Cambridge, Mass.: MIT Press.

Rumelhart, D. E., and J. L. McCelland. 1986. On the learning of past tenses of English verbs. In D. E. Rumelhart et al. (eds.), *Parallel Distributed Processing: Explorations in the Microstructure of Cognition.* Cambridge, Mass.: MIT Press.

Rosenblatt, F. 1962. *Principles of Neurodynamics.* New York: Spartan.

Sachs, M. B., E. D. Young, and M. I. Miller. 1982. Encoding of speech features in the auditory nerve. In R. Carlson and B. Granström (eds.), *The Representation of Speech in the Peripheral Auditory System.* Amsterdam: Elsevier.

Schwartz, R., Y. L. Chow, and F. Kubala. 1987. Rapid speaker adaptation using a probabilistic spectral mapping. In *ICASSP-87.*

Sejnowski, T. J., and C. R. Rosenberg. 1986. NETtalk: A Parallel Network that Learns to Read Aloud. Technical Report JHU/EECS-86/01, Johns Hopkins University.

Seneff, S. 1986. A synchrony model for auditory processing of speech. In J. Perkell and D. Klatt (eds.), *Invariance and Variability in Speech Processes.* Hillsdale, N.J.: Erlbaum.

Seneff, S. 1988. A joint synchrony/mean-rate response model of auditory speech processing. *J. Phonetics* 16: 55–76.

Shamma, S. 1988. The acoustic features of speech sounds in a model of auditory processing: Vowels and voiceless fricatives. *J. Phonetics* 16: 77–92.

Shattuck-Hufnagel, S. 1979. A model of sentence production based on speech error constraints. In W. E. Cooper and E. C. T. Walker (eds.), *Sentence Processing: Psycholinguistic Studies in Honor of Merrill Garrett*. Cambridge, Mass.: MIT Press.

Shattuck-Hufnagel, S., and D. H. Klatt. 1979. The limited use of distinctive features and markedness in speech production: Evidence from speech error data. *J. Verbal Learning and Verbal Behavior* 18: 41–55.

Smith, R. L. 1979. Adaptation, saturation and physiological masking in single auditory nerve fibers. *J. Acoust. Soc. Am.* 65: 166–178.

Stevens, K. N. 1960. Toward a model for speech recognition. *J. Acoust. Soc. Am.* 32: 47–55.

Stevens, K. N. 1972. The quantal nature of speech: Evidence from articulatory-acoustic data. In E. E. David and P. B. Denes (eds.), *Human Communication: A Unified View*. New York: McGraw-Hill.

Stevens, K. N. 1986. Models of phonetic recognition II: A feature-based model of speech recognition. In P. Mermelstein (ed.), *Proceedings of the Montreal Satellite Symposium on Speech Recognition*, Twelfth International Congress on Acoustics.

Stevens, K. N. 1988, Acoustic Phonetics. In preparation.

Stevens, K. N., and M. Halle. 1964. Remarks on analysis by synthesis and distinctive features. In W. Wathen-Dunn (ed.). *Proceedings of the AFCRL Symposium on Models for the Perception of Speech and Visual Form*. Cambridge, Mass.: MIT Press.

Studdert-Kennedy, M. 1974. The perception of speech. In T. A. Sebeok (ed.), *Current Trends in Linguistics*. The Hague: Mouton.

Studdert-Kennedy, M. 1980. Speech perception. *Language and Speech* 23: 45–66.

Studdert-Kennedy, M. 1985. Development of the Speech Perceptuomotor System. Status Report on Speech Research SR-82/83, Haskins Laboratories, New Haven.

Studdert-Kennedy, M., A. M. Liberman, K. S. Harris, and F. S. Cooper. 1970. Motor theory of speech perception: A reply to Lane's critical review. *Psych. Rev.* 77: 234–249.

Summerfield, Q. In press. Preliminaries to a comprehensive account of audio-visual speech perception. In B. Dodd and R. Campbell (eds.), *Hearing by Eye*. Hillsdale, N.J.: Erlbaum.

Syrdal, A. K. 1984. Aspects of a model of the auditory representation of American English vowels. *Speech Communication* 4: 121–135.

Waibel, A., T. Hanazawa, G. Hinton, K. Shikano, and K. Lang. 1987. Phoneme Recognition Using Time-Delay Neural Networks. Technical Report TR-1-0006, ATR Interpreting Telephony Research Laboratories, Tokyo.

Wickelgren, W. A. 1969. Context-sensitive coding, associative memory and serial order in speech behavior. *Psych. Rev.* 76: 1–15.

Wilpon, J. G., and L. R. Rabiner. 1985. A modified k-means clustering algorithm for use in speaker-independent isolated word recognition. *IEEE Trans.* ASSP-33: 587–594.

Zue, V. W. 1985. The use of speech knowledge in automatic speech recognition. *Proc. IEEE* 73: 1602–1615.

Zue, V. W. 1986. Models of speech recognition III: The role of analysis by synthesis in phonetic recognition. In P. Mermelstein (ed.), *Proceedings of the Montreal Satellite Symposium on Speech Recognition* (Twelfth International Congress on Acoustics).

Zwicker, E., and E. Terhardt. 1980. Analytical expressions for critical-band rate and critical bandwidth as a function of frequency. *J. Acoust. Soc. Am.* 68: 1523–1524.

Chapter 7

Connectionist Approaches to Acoustic/Phonetic Processing

Jeffrey L. Elman

It is a curious paradox that some of the tasks that humans carry out with the least conscious awareness and with the greatest facility are precisely those tasks that seem to be the most complex and have been most resistant to analysis. The acoustic/phonetic processing of speech is one such domain. Introspection yields little insight into how this processing is done, and most listeners fail even to recognize that the task might be difficult. Yet attempts to duplicate this processing in machines have not been very successful.

In fact, acoustic/phonetic processing is hard. All the different components of language—pragmatics, semantics, syntax, morphology, phonology, phonetics—must find their expression through a single channel: the sound wave. That single channel thus represents an enormous compression of information, and it is quite amazing that humans are able to unravel the many twisted and merged threads.

However, humans do, by and large, succeed in understanding speech. Without minimizing the task, I would like to suggest that some of our difficulties in understanding just how acoustic/phonetic processing is carried out stem largely from misconceptions about the fundamental nature of processing mechanisms. Human perceptual mechanisms do not work like digital computers. In this chapter I would like to describe some work that has been carried out within a different theoretical framework for understanding human cognition and perception. The approach involves parallel distributed processing, or what has been called connectionist or artificial neural systems.

1 Problems in Acoustic/Phonetic Processing

I would like to focus on four major problems that have challenged traditional models of acoustic/phonetic processing:

- variability in how speech sounds are encoded
- the need to integrate information over time and to deal with local ambiguity
- uncertainty about what the units of processing are
- the acquisition problem—how can the structures and mechanisms needed to accomplish the above be learned?

Understanding how it is that human listeners cope with the variability of speech has been one of the most vexing problems in speech perception. Listeners seem to perceive a wide range of sounds as identical, even when the sounds differ considerably in their acoustic form. This variability arises from a number of causes, including coarticulation, changes in rate of speech, differences in vocal-tract morphology across speakers, dialectal variation, and phonological processes. Much recent work has attempted to demonstrate that there do in fact exist ways of analyzing the signal such that invariant percepts can be correlated with acoustic invariants (Stevens and Blumstein 1981; Kewley-Port 1983). This work remains controversial, and it seems likely that there will always be significant variability under any transformation.

The second problem—the need to integrate information over time— exists because an utterance unfolds over time, and the identity of earlier parts of the signal may depend crucially on material that follows. Thus, listeners need some mechanism that allows them to interpret as much as possible as quickly as possible, but which at the same time permits later information to gracefully alter earlier hypotheses.

The third problem—uncertainty about what the units of processing are—has two aspects to it. First, it is not at all clear what the primary units of perception are. Good arguments have been marshaled in favor of the distinctive feature, the phoneme, the demi-syllable, the context-sensitive allophone, the diphone, and the syllable. Second, no matter what the units of perception are, locating these units in the speech signal is no easy matter. Indeed, a first visual approximation of speech waveforms reveals few discontinuities, and often those that can be found are not correlated with the boundaries of any hypothesized units. Thus, the question is not only what the units are, but also how (whatever they are) they can be located in the signal.

Finally, there is the problem of acquisition. The perception of speech is a complex process, and solutions to at least some of the above problems must be learned (because the specifics vary from language to language). The process of acquisition is even more mysterious than what is acquired.

To an extent, some of the problems of acoustic/phonetic processing can be sidestepped by simply allowing higher-level information to supply missing information, or correct misanalyses. This approach is taken explicitly in some speech-recognition systems. For instance, the HWIM (Hear What I Mean) system developed at Bolt, Beranek & Newman (1976) passes a "segment lattice" on to the lexical retrieval system. This lattice lists the several segmental parsings that are deemed alternate but acceptable descriptions of the input. The correct parse is determined by the best fit with the lexicon.

Nonetheless, while it is undoubtedly true that higher-level information can compensate for errors in initial analysis, it would be a mistake to underestimate the ability of listeners to successfully process speech input even with degraded or absent higher-level information. The acoustic/phonetic input is extraordinarily rich in information. As linguists and psychologists we may not understand how that information is extracted; but in our everyday lives we do it easily and without thought.

For indeed, people *are* able to use the acoustic/phonetic input to perceive nonsense in the absence of higher-level information (although they do better with normal prose; see Marslen-Wilson and Tyler 1980). Furthermore, there is compelling evidence that listeners are quite sensitive to the variations in speech and that they exploit these variations as sources of information (Elman and McCelland 1986). Subtle differences in pronunciation may signal word juncture (Nakatani and Dukes 1977). Rate of speech can be used to adjust some phoneme boundaries (Miller 1981). And phonetic context seems to be taken into account by listeners in judging stimuli whose identity may be have been "distorted" by coarticulation (Repp and Mann 1980). Thus, whatever benefit accrues from higher-level sources of knowledge, it assists rather than replaces humans' remarkable ability to process the extremely complex, variable, time-extended acoustic input.

The von Neumann Brain?
Most attempts at understanding how humans process and produce language have taken the standard digital computer as the metaphor for how the brain works. The metaphor is rarely explicitly acknowledged, but it is manifested in a number of important ways:

• It is often assumed that logical functions are confined to "boxes," which are connected by arrows.

• Information processing is subject to a "digital flow of control," i.e., a problem-solving strategy consisting of *hypothesize, test,* and *branch* (i.e., modify the current hypothesis, or choose another one); only one hypothesis is tested at a given moment.

• Memory is conceived of as essentially passive. Information is stored in "boxes." Efficient retrieval of information can be facilitated by some clever organizing scheme (e.g., alphabetic, by frequency of use, by semantic feature), but ultimately the access of memory is decoupled from its contents.

All these characteristics are true of the von Neumann machine. This computational model has had a profound influence on the way we think about human cognition.

What is wrong with such a model? It is not at first obvious that this metaphor is wrong, or, even if it is, that it matters. The problem becomes apparent only when one takes the theorizing seriously enough to try to build a system based on it. Then failures are apparent. The clearest example of this comes from the field of speech recognition. Here a variety of approaches have been tried, and many of them (e.g., Hearsay, HWIM) have attempted to bring findings from linguistics and psychology to bear on the goal of getting computers to at least recognize (if not understand) human speech. Such attempts have, in general, been quite disappointing. In the end, the most successful systems—from the viewpoint of giving real-time performance in a limited but well-defined domain—are those that eschew psychological or linguistic considerations. Rather than attempting to understand (and mimic) how humans deal with the problems of variability, lack of segmentation, and interaction over time, these systems are constrained in such a way as to minimize these problems. Since context is the source of most variability in speech, context is highly constrained, and types are abandoned in favor of many unrelated tokens.

This approach is expedient, and it works, but it is extremely limited. Because the approach is limited, and in ways that do not seem to be true of human speech perception, it is not likely to shed much light on human abilities. Nor is this approach likely ever to lead to a machine-based system that functions with the versatility and flexibility humans exhibit. In the long term, then, one can argue that there is a practical as well as a theoretical price to be paid for expediency.

Similar problems in modeling other aspects of cognition have led some workers in cognitive science to explore alternative computational frameworks. For many years it was thought that mental "programs" were like computer programs, and that, just as a program can be run on different hardware, cognitive processes could be studied without reference to the hardware on which they are implemented. Recently, a number of cognitive scientists have recognized that, although that may ultimately be true, different hardware may run different programs with differing ease and efficiency. The brain is not at all like the von Neumann computer. It certainly seems worthwhile to explore computational systems whose architecture might map more plausibly onto a neural foundation.

These alternative computational frameworks involve what is called *parallel distributed processing* (Rumelhart et al. 1986); they are also sometimes called *connectionist* or *artificial* neural systems). While those who work within these frameworks differ in the degree to which they take the neural model seriously, the neural inspiration is evident. This framework offers an approach to the modeling of memory, recognition, and representation that differs radically from those suggested by the von Neumann metaphor. In this chapter I would like to describe two different applications of the PDP approach to problems in speech perception.

2   The TRACE Model of Speech Perception

The TRACE model (Elman and McClelland 1984, 1986; McClelland and Elman 1986) was developed in an attempt to understand a number of specific problems in speech perception. Two versions of the model exist. One version, TRACE II, focuses primarily on lexical effects on speech perception; it is described in detail in McClelland and Elman 1986. The other version, TRACE I, is concerned primarily with problems in acoustic-phonetic processing. That version will be described here.

Description
TRACE I identifies three levels of representation: the *feature* level, the *phoneme* level, and the *word* level. To some extent, the model is neutral with regard to the question of whether these are the correct representations. Different types of units would undoubtedly affect the performance of the model, but the important aspects of its behavior would remain unchanged. (The model is, of course, not neutral with regard to the question of whether such discrete representations are correct in the first place; it presupposes that they are. Later in this paper it will be suggested that a more *distributed* form of representation may be better.)

Nodes
Processing is carried out within the model over a large number of very simple processing elements we call *nodes*. Nodes can be thought of as hypothesis detectors; there are feature nodes, phoneme nodes, and word nodes. Nodes have associated with them a numeric value that represents

their *activation level*; this value changes over time and indicates the relative strength of the hypothesis represented by a given node.

Connections

Nodes are connected to one another in nonarbitrary ways that represent mutual compatibility or incompatibility of their hypotheses. Nodes whose concepts are mutually consistent (e.g., that the word "pan" contains the phoneme /p/) have excitatory connections; those whose concepts are inconsistent (e.g., that the phonemes /p/ and /a/ are simultaneously present in the input) have inhibitory connections. These connections, in addition to being either excitatory or inhibitory, have weights that indicate the extent of (in)compatibility.

Time: The TRACE

So far what has been described is a network that allows us to represent words, phonemes, and features, and the relationships between these different units. Time is an important additional variable in speech. The same sound may occur many times in an utterance, and it is important to bind the processing of that sound to the moment in time in which it occurs. We also require a mechanism that will allow us to preserve the *independence* of the time-bound processes while allowing for the *interdependence* that arises when one portion of an utterance sheds light on the identity of another.

We accomplish this by representing time as a series of networks, each identical and resembling what is sketched above but each responsible for processing a given portion of the utterance. These networks constitute an active memory. Indeed, in this framework there is no real distinction between short-term memory and the basic mechanisms of perception. The difference is only in which network is receiving the current input; as time progresses, input is directed toward successive networks. The networks are called *traces*, because they provide a trace of the recent past.[1]

Processing

Processing begins with the trace networks quiescent. When speech comes in, it is directed toward the feature nodes in the first trace. These become activated to the extent that the features they stand for are found in the input. As time progresses, the input is directed toward later networks. (After some period of time, when the very early part of the utterance has been completely processed and its interpretation cannot change, the first networks are "reused".)

Within a given trace, feature nodes are arranged in groups of eight nodes; each group is responsible for detecting a certain feature, and nodes within a group have different ranges of sensitivity to the feature (from strongly present to strongly absent). Nodes within a bank have inhibitory connections, reflecting the fact that a feature cannot be at the same time strongly present and strongly absent. Feature nodes have excitatory connections to the phoneme nodes above them; the strength of the connection depends on the degree to which a feature is present or absent in a phoneme. Also, because phonemes are less labile and have greater durations in time than features, the windows over which they receive input are broader. There are three feature traces for every phoneme trace, and a phoneme trace may also receive input from feature nodes in neighboring windows.

Within a trace, phoneme nodes have inhibitory connections to one another; they also have excitatory connections to word nodes. Word nodes occupy the traces corresponding to the time at which they begin. Phoneme nodes excite word nodes, which contain them in that trace position. Thus, in a given trace, a /p/ node excites the word node for "pan" (which, since it begins in that trace, also is located in the same trace); it also excites the word node for "nap" (which is located in a prior trace, since the word itself must have begun earlier in time). Following the rule that inconsistent concepts compete with one another, word nodes in a trace are connected by inhibitory links.

Simulations

The TRACE I model has been implemented as a computer program in order that its behavior could be precisely studied. The model takes real speech (in digitized form) as its input and attempts to "perceive" the features, phonemes, and words that it knows. The current version of the model is implemented in C on a VAX 11/750 computer. It possesses 16 features, 15 phonemes, and 250 words.[2] The features and phonemes known to TRACE I are listed in table 1.

In the first simulation, speech input corresponding to the syllable "ba" was presented in digitized form to the model.[3] Presentation is sequential; the first 5 msec of the input are processed first by the first trace, the second 5 msec by the second trace, and so on. The input is thus presented sequentially to successive traces; processing, however, occurs simultaneously in all traces—those that have already received input, the one currently receiving input, and those yet to receive speech input. Since the presentation is under computer control, it is possible to halt at any point, freeze the system, and examine the state of all the traces at that instant in time.

This is what has been done in figure 1. In this and similar figures, activations of word nodes are indicated in the upper panel and activations

Table 1
The fifteen different dimensions used in coding the real speech inputs to
TRACE I.

Feature	Description
power	log rms power
pitch	fundamental frequency of source
alpha	total LPC error; distinguishes speech and silence
edr	error dynamic range; voiced from voiceless
abrupt	change in rms power over time; stops/vowel transitions
diffuse	second moment of LPC spectrum
acute	gross concentration of energy in spectrum
consonantal	smoothed euclidean spectral difference; detects stop bursts and consonantal transitions
spectrum (3)	total energy in each section of the spectrum divided equally in three on a log scale
formant (3)	the values of the first three formants
loci (2)	the hypothetical formant onsets, back-extrapolated from the actual formant onsets (at voicing) to the stop release

of phoneme nodes in the lower panel. Time is represented along the horizontal axis; to minimize clutter, activity is shown only within every third trace, or every 15 msec. Within a trace, if a node is active it is shown by a letter, whose height indicates the activation of that node. In figure 1 the input has been stopped after the first 30 msec of speech have been presented (the arrow to the right of the number 6 shows which trace is receiving current input). It is obvious that a large number of phoneme nodes have become slightly active, but that there is not yet a clear indication as to which phoneme is present.

In figure 2 the state of the various traces is shown after 60 msec of speech have been processed (i.e., trace 14). The situation is now different. The node for /b/ is very active in the initial traces. Processing continues in the initial traces after the input has been received, so that the state of a trace changes even after it has become "memory." The node for /a/ has achieved some dominance, and this occurs in traces that *are yet to receive speech input*. This is particularly interesting, since at this point in time the consonantal formant transitions are still prevalent. What this illustrates is that the model is sensitive to the fact that the precise form of these formant transitions varies with the following vowel. Although the later traces have not yet received speech input, they do receive input from nodes in earlier traces, and thus they are able to anticipate the speech they are about to

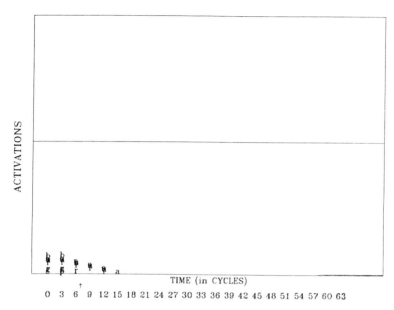

Figure 1
The state of TRACE after 30 msec of speech have been presented. Each 5 msec
is processed by a separate network; activity within 63 such networks is depicted
here. The bottom panel displays activations of phoneme nodes; the height of
a phoneme label indicates its relative activation. The upper panel displays
activations of word nodes.

hear. This way of looking at coarticulatory information is somewhat novel.
Rather than treating variation due to coarticulatory effects as noise in the
signal, TRACE I treats this information as a redundancy that can be
exploited to aid perception. I believe that this is what human listeners do,
and that it results in more efficient and accurate perception; recent experimental data support this view (Warren and Marslen-Wilson 1987).

Finally, in figure 3, we see the state of the traces after 120 msec of input
have been received (the input has reached trace 24). Not only is it clear
what phonemes have been heard, but we also see (in the upper panel) that
the model has identified the word as "ba" (see note 3).

Although TRACE I attempts to recover a level of representation where
there are discrete units (e.g., features, phonemes, and words), at no point
does the model attempt an explicit segmentation of the input into these
units. Instead, the node activations wax and wane smoothly as the continuously varying feature strengths in the signal change. Nonetheless, the
result of the competition between nodes is that, eventually, in most of the

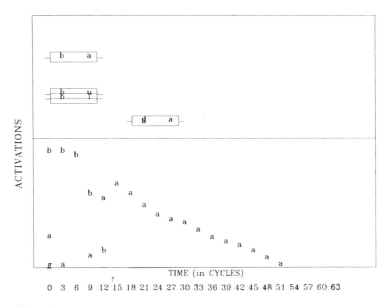

Figure 2
The state of TRACE after 60 msec of speech have been presented (trace 14).

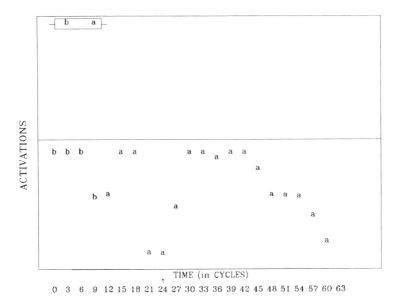

Figure 3
The state of TRACE after 120 msec of speech (trace 24).

traces a single phoneme is strongly active. *De facto* segment boundaries are defined as the points where one phoneme ceases to be dominant and another gains ascendancy. The point of view here is that segmentation should be understood as the *outcome* of the process of perception, rather than as a prerequisite for it.

The ability of the model to anticipate the identity of a sound well before it has been fully articulated results from a type of connection that has an important role in TRACE I. When phoneme nodes become active, they do more than activate nodes of words of which they are constituents. They also have the ability to adjust the mapping between features and other phonemes in adjacent time traces. They do this by connections that "hook onto" feature-to-phoneme connections in neighboring traces. These connections have a gating effect. When positive excitation flows along them, they increase the strength of the connections they hook onto; when they are at 0, they shut off the other connections.

It is useful to think of these modulatory connections as the model's way of adjusting the interpretation of featural input, given the coarticulatory effects that a speech sound may have. Thus, if a rounded vowel (e.g., [u]) is found to be present, there is reason to believe that the neighboring sounds share some of that rounding, because of coarticulation. The vowel is able to adjust the connections between the features that are sensitive to rounding (e.g., [ACUTE]), and the phonemes that might be so affected, in just such a way as to compensate for this coarticulation. This mechanism is one of the things that allow TRACE I to treat variability due to coarticulation as an additional source of information about the signal, rather than as unwelcome noise.

A somewhat more extreme example of the model's ability to use "hidden" coarticulatory information is seen in the next simulation. In this case the model was presented with the final 200 msec of a [gu]. Since this is well past the point where the consonantal formant transitions have finished, all that is left is the vowel portion of the syllable. Nonetheless, if we compare the running spectra of the vowel [u] extracted from the syllable [gu] with the same vowel extracted from the syllables [bu] and [du], as in figure 4, it is obvious that there are differences in pronunciation of the vowels which are due to the influence of the initial (deleted) consonant.

The model's response to the [u] from [gu] is shown in figure 5. At no point in time does the [g] node dominate a trace. This is reasonable, since the [g] is not fully present. Still, there is sufficient residual information that the [g] node is quite active. During many traces, it is the second most active

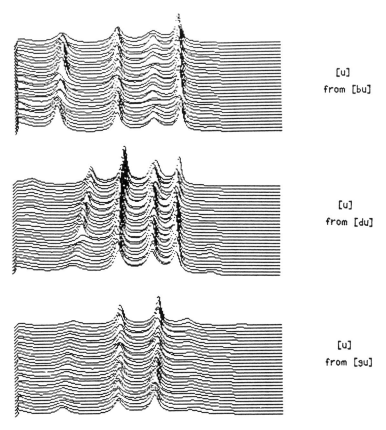

Figure 4
Running power spectra of the final 200 msec of the vowel [u], excised from the syllables [bu], [du], and [gu]. (Lower frequencies are displayed to the left of each plot; amplitude is indicated by height of traces.)

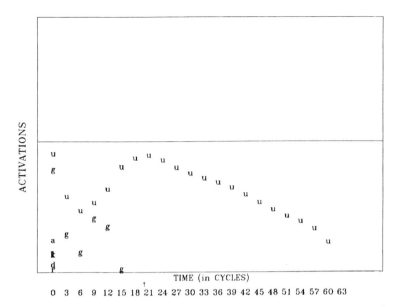

Figure 5
The state of TRACE after 100 msec of the [u] from [gu] have been presented
(see figure 4).

node. One can view this response as indicating a kind of "subliminal perception" on the part of the model.

Is this behavior of the model a fluke? Should it respond in this way? Or does it model a real ability possessed by human listeners? To test this, the vowels [a], [i], and [u] were extracted from the syllables [ba], [bi], [bu], [da], [di], [du], [ga], [gi], and [gu]. In all cases, the initial 175 msec were deleted, leaving approximately 200 msec of vowel. These vowel sounds were presented to listeners with the request that they guess which initial stop consonant was deleted. All subjects reported that this was a difficult task, since there was no obvious hint of the missing consonant. Yet table 2 shows that the pattern of "guesses" is consistent with the identity of the original consonant.

A more systematic illustration of the way in which TRACE exploits coarticulatory information is shown in the next simulation. Twenty-five tokens of each of the nine CV syllables ([ba], [bi], [bu], [da], [di], [du], [ga], [gi], and [gu]) were recorded. These syllables were chosen because they are a relatively confusable set, and because they exemplify much of the coarticulatory variability the model was designed to deal with.

Table 2
Response probabilities for identifying preceding consonant from steady-state portion of vowel.

Response	Original syllable		
	bu	du	gu
b	0.61	0.01	0.33
d	0.10	0.97	0.24
g	0.28	0.01	0.43

Table 3
Number of correct identifications in 25 trials: variable-weight and fixed-weight results (percentage correct given in parentheses).

[ba]		[bi]		[bu]	
variable	fixed	variable	fixed	variable	fixed
25	17	14	13	25	20
(100)	(68)	(56)	(52)	(100)	(80)
[da]		[di]		[du]	
variable	fixed	variable	fixed	variable	fixed
24	21	21	20	23	21
(96)	(84)	(84)	(80)	(92)	(84)
[ga]		[gi]		[gu]	
variable	fixed	variable	fixed	variable	fixed
22	21	24	22	25	24
(88)	(84)	(96)	(88)	(100)	(96)

Overall percentage correct for variable weight condition: 90
Overall percentage correct for fixed weight condition: 79

The tokens were presented to the model under two separate conditions. In the first condition, the model was able to use the modulatory connections described above in order to dynamically adjust the feature-to-phoneme mappings in accord with coarticulation. In the second condition, these connections were disabled. The model "listened" to the first 135 msec of each token. Then the processing was halted, and the dominant phoneme node during the initial portion of the syllable was taken to be the model's identification. The model's performance under the two conditions is presented in table 3. In each cell two sets of numbers are reported. The first gives the number of correct responses (out of 25) in the "variable-weight" condition (i.e., weight modulation between features and phonemes enabled); the percentage of correct responses is given in parentheses below. The second set gives the number of correct responses in the "fixed-weight" condition (i.e., weights between features and phonemes fixed and unmodulated), with percentage correct in parentheses below. In all cases the performance benefited from the active use of coarticulatory information, and in some cases the improvement was quite dramatic. Overall, the use of this variability yielded a 90% correct response rate, compared with 79% in the fixed-weight condition. Thus, it seems fair to say that TRACE I demonstrates that this processing architecture not only deals with coarticulatory variability but actually benefits from it.

Another type of phenomenon reported in the literature is what appears to be a perceptual restoration of missing or degraded acoustic input, resulting from higher levels of processing. One form this takes is the *phoneme restoration effect* (Warren and Sherman 1974). Another form is the *lexical effect* in phoneme identification (Ganong 1980). The latter effect consists of a perceptual bias toward hearing an ambiguous phoneme in a way that is consistent with an interpretation that allows a word to be perceived.

TRACE I permits interactions between levels of processing, and these interactions account for top-down effects in a very natural way. In the first three simulations, we saw how contextual (i.e., coarticulatory) information at the same level of processing could interact with perception. Now let us consider how TRACE I might allow contextual information at higher stages to guide perception at lower stages.

We presented input corresponding to a feature sequence[4] that specified /b/ and /p/ equally (that is, the input was ambiguous with regard to voicing), followed by feature specifications for /l/, then /a/, then /d/. Figures 6–8 show the phoneme and feature activations that resulted at several points during the input. Figure 6 shows the activation of the phoneme nodes (bottom panel) and word nodes (upper panel) roughly at the point where the information for the initial stop consonant has arrived, but before the liquid has been completed. The /b/ and /p/ nodes are equally activated (and thus overprint in the figure), since the input specifies them equally. The only node active in the upper panel (which displays word activity) is a dash, which corresponds to silence. In Figure 7, almost all of the word has been presented, and the input is at the final stop. Figure 8 shows the effect of allowing processing to continue after the input has been received. Whereas initially the system was unable to decide between a /b/ and /p/, by the end the /p/ dominates. Why is this? It is because the model has a node for the real word "plod" ([plad]) but none for the nonword "blod". Although the bottom-up information is somewhat degraded, it is sufficiently close to the word "plod" that that node becomes most active. Once active, the "plod" node provides input to its constituent phoneme nodes, so that they are

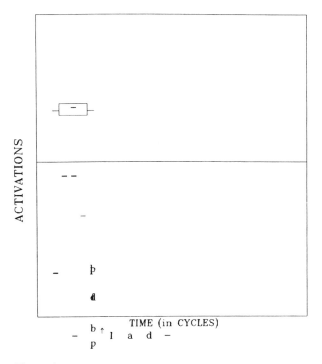

Figure 6
The state of TRACE after the initial bilabial stop of [b/p] [lad] has been presented. The bilabial stop is ambiguous for voicing.

activated not only by featural input but also by input from the lexical level. This additional input gives /p/ a slight edge over /b/. This is consistent with the effect reported by Ganong (1980).

One question that naturally arises, however, is whether the behavior elicited in the lexical-bias and phoneme-restoration experiments really reflects top-down processing interactions. It is entirely possible that the bias (or restoration) occurs at high levels. That is, one can imagine that information flows in one direction only (bottom-up). In cases where the input is ambiguous, some post-perceptual mechanism makes a decision about the identity of the ambiguous or missing information. By this account, the post-perceptual mechanism would have access to context but the lower perceptual processes would be informationally encapsulated from the results of high stages. In principle, TRACE I could accommodate such an account. There is, after all, no reason why TRACE I needs to allow top-down feedback. However, the version of the model we have adopted does permit this kind of interaction. Interestingly, a very specific prediction

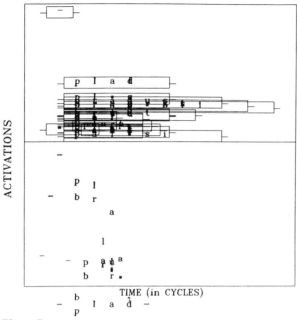

Figure 7
The state of TRACE after all the input has been received.

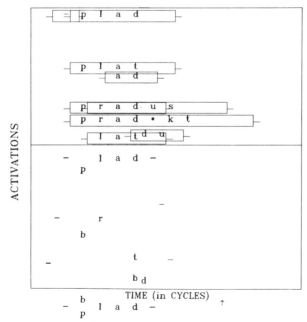

Figure 8
The state of TRACE approximately 1 sec after all the input has been received.

follows if one allows top-down feedback from the lexical level to phonemic processes: If the lexical level can in fact influence processing at the phoneme level, then it should be possible to produce effects which are entirely intraphonemic but which are triggered by a top-down input. Examples of intraphonemic phenomena are the perceptual compensations for co-articulation, which seem to be uncontroversially occurring at the level of phoneme perception (or lower; in any event, they are not lexical). The question arises: Can compensation for coarticulation be triggered from above?

For instance, consider what happens when an [s] or an [š] is followed by a sound that is perceptually intermediate between [t] or [k]. Repp and Mann (1980) have shown that listeners will judge the ambiguous sound to be more like a [t] if it follows an [s], and more like a [k] if it follows an [š]. This reflects a compensation for (i.e., it "undoes") certain coarticulatory effects that arise when these sounds are pronounced together. This effect is clearly sublexical, since it can be demonstrated for nonsense syllables. What happens if the sound that triggers the effect—the initial fricative—is itself ambiguous and between [s] and [š], in different lexical contexts which might bias perception one way or another? TRACE I predicts that if top-down interactions are present, the lexical bias on [s] or [š] occurs at the level of phoneme perception; once that has happened, TRACE I will be able to trigger the adjustment for coarticulation with the following stop. Thus, if one imagines sequences such as "Christma[s/š] [t/k]apes" or "fooli[s/š] [t/k]apes", in which both the fricative and the stop are am-biguous, the lexical bias will cause the fricative in the first sequence to be perceived as an /s/ and that in the second sequence to be perceived as an /š/; then compensation for coarticulation will cause listeners to hear the stop in the first sequence as /k/ and in the second as /t/. If the processing of phonemes is insulated from the results of lexical processing, however, the differential perception of the fricative in the first word will be only apparent (not real) and will not be able to trigger perceptual compensation at the level of phonemic perception. When this was tested in series of experiments (Elman and McClelland 1987), the outcome was that listeners actually did show compensatory behavior; thus, it seems that lexical pro-cessing is able to reach down and affect basic perceptual processing in just the way that is predicted by the model.

Discussion

We have considered two issues that have been problematic for models of speech perception (as well as for many machine-based systems). One is the question of how to deal with variability in the signal. This variability is usually taken as an impediment to speech perception, and it is true that if one attempts to unravel the speech wave using von Neumann architecture, the processing requirements grow exponentially as additional factors interact (because each new factor can interact with every other factor). On the other hand, TRACE I's use of a PDP architecture turns a problem into an advantage; inasmuch as variability represents an interaction of information, it can be exploited to make perception easier and more robust. Another problem for many conventional approaches to speech perception is that, on the one hand, speech input rarely has obvious indications as to segmental boundaries, yet on the other hand it seems likely that listeners are able to retrieve a representation consisting of discrete units. TRACE I offers a solution to this and allows us to see segmentation as the result of perception rather than as a prerequisite for it.

Of course, although TRACE I and TRACE II account for a wide variety of phenomena observed in speech perception, by no means do they solve all the problems of speech perception. The models are far from complete, and they do not attempt to deal with a large number of important and difficult sources of variability. Aside from their restricted scale, however, there are other more basic deficiencies with the current models. One is that the traces proliferate many tokens of the same type of node, and the tokens are totally independent. Not only is this inelegant, it fails to account for the common observation that occurrence of an item can prime recognition of the same item at a later point in time. There thus must be some way in which the tokens are bound together. A possible solution to this dilemma is to use McClelland's (1985) CID mechanism, in which information about types is kept in a separate structure that has the ability to "program" temporary copies of itself as needed. Thus, one might envision the traces as unprogrammed networks that are available to the perceptual mechanism to be used as short-term memory.

Such an approach would be useful for modeling other types of phenomena in speech perception. Consider the adjustment listeners make when listening to speech at different rates. Suppose that the information about feature/phoneme/word relationships were represented in a single network, and that there existed a means for these relationships (represented by connections between nodes) to be duplicated as needed in time-bound traces. Suppose also that there were a "rate detector" (sensitive, for example, to rate of change of certain features which correlate with syllabic nuclei). This rate detector might interact with the mechanism by which the central information is instantiated in the traces; this interaction would modify the feature/phoneme/word mappings in just such a way as to accommodate the changes brought about by the current rate of speech. In essence, this allows us to employ the same technique by which phonemes modify feature-to-phoneme connections to adjust for coarticulation, but to the more global phenomena resulting from rate changes. One could imagine that similar adjustments might be made for the normalization of vocal-tract acoustics that occurs when we listen to different speakers. It would be a mistake to minimize the difficulties associated with discovering the content of the normalization processes; however, the TRACE architecture does offer a mechanism by which they could be computed once discovered.

There are other shortcomings to the TRACE model. As Dennis Klatt has pointed out (comment on Elman and McClelland 1986), there are a number of cases where a featural description of phonemes requires second-order predicates (e.g., the logical exclusive-or function). The two layers which TRACE makes available for features and phonemes are not sufficient to encode such relationships (Minsky and Papert 1969). Another question is how the very rich set of relationships modeled by the intricate connections could be acquired by a language learner. And finally, there is the question of what the correct levels of representation are. TRACE chooses features, phonemes, and words, but it is by no means clear that these choices are correct.

These latter considerations lead to a somewhat different sort of approach than that used by TRACE. This other approach also employs a PDP framework, but there are important differences. The two basic ones are the use of distributed rather than local representations and the use of intermediate layers of nodes in mapping from one representation to another. The notion is not to reject some of the insights embodied in TRACE, but to look for ways of enriching its representations and processing capabilities.

3 Acquisition and Distributed Representations

Of the four questions raised at the outset of this chapter, two are very much concerned with the question of representation: What are the units of processing, and how do language learners come to learn their significance?

There have been many debates within linguistic theory about the levels of representation in language. At least eight different levels of representation have been proposed to intervene between the speech wave and the representation "word": spectral templates (Lowerre 1976), features (Cole, Stern, and Lasry 1986), diphones (Dixon and Silverman 1976; Klatt 1980), context-sensitive allophone (Wickelgren 1969), phonemes (Pisoni 1981), demisyllables (Fujimura and Lovins 1978), syllables (Mehler 1981), and morphemes (Aronoff 1976; Klatt 1980). *Word* itself is difficult to define. Are "telegraph" and "telegraphs" both entered in the lexicon? "Library" and "Congress" are words; is "Library of Congress" also a word? Or how is the notion *word* to be defined such that it will serve both for languages like English and for agglutinative languages like Turkish? Beyond the word, the situation is perhaps even more confusing. Though it is possible that all these processing levels lie between speech and word, such a proliferation of representational forms might make one a bit uneasy. One begins to have the sensation that the representational system might be far richer than any of these proposal suggest, and sufficiently flexible that it can accommodate a wide variety of processing demands. For modeling purposes, one would like to be able to start with no (or minimal) *a priori* assumptions about internal representations, teach a system to perform a set of behaviors, and then study the internal representations that are acquired by the system in order to carry out the behaviors; this approach might suggest new hypotheses about the representations humans use in performing the same behaviors. As we shall see, a new learning algorithm has recently been developed that makes this approach feasible.

In TRACE I, concepts are represented by single nodes. Thus, there are distinct nodes for features, phonemes, and words. The activation of a node is correlated with the certainty that the concept it represents is true. Another possibility would be to represent concepts as patterns of activation across a set of nodes, with no single node identifiable with any concept. In fact, the same set of nodes would participate in the representation of a large number of different concepts; what would differ would be the configuration of activation levels across the ensemble.

This approach has a number of interesting characteristics. Distributed representations allow for more graceful and gradual degradation of performance as units are lost from the system. Partial damage would result in a generalized deficit, and not in the loss of specific concepts (such as features, phonemes, or words). Another attractive feature is that distributed representations offer a representational flexibility that is simply not possible with the "one concept, one node" approach. Because patterns are represented over shared pools of elements, classes of patterns can be loosely defined, with shared similarities among those patterns exerting an effect on processing. Such functional coalitions can arise spontaneously and need not be pre-wired.[5]

But even if representations have this form (and the specific content of this counterproposal is still unclear), are they learnable or must they be innately specified? In this regard, the recent discoveries about how PDP networks can organize themselves using a simple but powerful learning algorithm are relevant. There are some preliminary findings that illustrate how one of these learning algorithms—back-propagation of error (Rumelhart, Hinton, and Williams 1986)—can be applied to acoustic/phonetic processing, and what it suggests about both the problems of representations and learning.

This work, which has been carried out by David Zipser and myself in our laboratories at the University of California, has concentrated primarily on discovering the underlying structure of similarities and differences hidden in the acoustic-phonetic input. Our hypothesis—as yet untested—is that human listeners will also be sensitive to this hidden structure, and that it will be reflected in human perceptual representations and processes. I will begin by giving a simple explanation of how the learning algorithm works. I will then present the results of several experiments we have carried out using this technique.

Learning in a Connectionist System

In general, knowledge in connectionist models is contained in the connections between processing elements (what is connected to what, and what is the strength of the connection). Thus, it seems natural that learning should consist of changing these connections (rather than, for instance, creating new nodes). During learning, the network is exposed to a large number of pairs of patterns. These patterns are supposed to exemplify some to-be-discovered relationship; the learning algorithms specify a method of altering the network in such a way that it "learns" what this relationship is. One can think of this as "extensional programming" (Cottrell, Munro, and Zipser 1987), in which the networks learn to compute an unknown function by being given many examples of the ways in which the function maps an input pattern to an output pattern. Some of the learning algorithms that have been applied to PDP models are very powerful. They also are interesting, in that they often yield novel and not intuitively obvious solutions to difficult problems. One particularly powerful learning algorithm has been recently developed by Rumelhart, Hinton, and Williams (1986). In what follows I will demonstrate how that algorithm can be applied to investigate some of the problems that have been raised here.

Imagine a network which is partitioned into three layers: an *input* layer, an *intermediate* (or *hidden*) layer, and an *output* layer. The nodes of the input layer receive input from the outside world; each of the nodes connects (unidirectionally) to each node in the intermediate layer. The nodes in the hidden layer receive input only from the input layer, and send their output connect to the output layer. The connections are initially assigned random weights (of both positive and negative sign), and the nodes start off with no activation. At this point, the network is "unprogrammed."

The process of learning consists of the following sequence of events: Our goal is to teach the network to associate many pairs of patterns, such that when we present one pattern to it, it responds with the appropriate pattern that is paired with it. Presumably, these pairs are related in some interesting or useful way, and provide an extensional definition of the function (rule, transformation, etc.) that is to be learned by the network. That function may in fact be unknown to us, in the sense that we—like children learning language—know what output is produced by what input but cannot precisely say what the transformation is that relates the two. Thus we have at our disposal a number of pattern pairs. We begin by randomly selecting one pair, and present one member of the pair to the input layer. The nodes in the input layer are activated by this pattern, and send excitatory and inhibitory output to the nodes in the hidden layer. Because the connection weights are initially random (reflecting the fact that at the outset the network "knows" nothing), the input received by the hidden layer is meaningless. The hidden units send excitatory and inhibitory output to the nodes in the output layer, and this too is meaningless. Thus, the pattern that results on the output layer is, on this first trial, most probably quite erroneous, given the goal that eventually we wish the network to produce the appropriate output for a given input.

The teaching occurs in the following way: We compare the output pattern we have obtained against the correct output. The difference between the two patterns provides us with a measure of error. That error is used to adjust the weights of the connections between the hidden units and the output units in just such a manner as to move toward a set of weights that would produce the desired output. The error signal is then propagated downward through the network and used to modify the weights between the input units and the hidden units.[6] The changes made on any given learning trial are incremental. Eventually, the connections are modified so that the network is able to reproduce reliably (with minimal error) the desired output pattern in response to a given input pattern. Furthermore, this can be done for a large number of pattern pairs. At this point, the network has learned the training data. The question of interest is whether it can generalize what it has learned to new data; if it can, we then try to analyze the network's solution to see how it has solved the problem.

This simple algorithm has proved to be quite powerful. Small networks can be taught to perform the exclusive-or function, to classify input strings as to whether they are symmetric about their center, to perform binary addition, to discriminate T from C, and to solve a number of other non-trivial problems.

Discovering an Acoustic Representation for Speech

We first attempted to teach a three-layered network of the sort described above to correctly associate a speech input with a phonetic characterization. The input was generated from about 56 tokens each of 9 different CV syllable types formed by combining the three voiced stops [b], [d], and [g] with the three vowels [a], [i], and [u]. From each token of these 9 syllable types we extracted the consonantal portion (the first 64 msec of each syllable) and a vocalic portion (also 64 msec in duration). This yielded 9 context-sensitive consonant types and 9 context-sensitive vowels, for a total of approximately 1,000 tokens. A Fourier transform was applied to each token, and the resulting power spectrum was then used as the input for the learning system.[7] Finally, each token was assigned a random 12-bit binary code representing its phonetic label (e.g., [b], [d], [g], [a], [i], or [u]). This phonetic label for each token provides us with the other pattern we need in teaching.

The network itself consisted of an input layer of 320 input nodes, a single hidden layer of 6 nodes, and an output layer of 12 nodes. The network is shown schematically in figure 9. Teaching proceeds as described above. On a single learning trial, one of the 1,000 tokens was randomly selected and was used to set the activation levels of the input layer. Nodes in the hidden layer were then activated by the input nodes, and output nodes were activated by the hidden nodes. The 12-bit output pattern was compared with the correct phonetic code for that token, and the error was used to modify the connections in the network. Then another one of the 1,000 tokens was presented.

The process was carried out for about 100,000 iterations; at that point the network had achieved perfect performance. When any of the 1,000 tokens was presented, the network correctly identified it by generating the 12-bit binary pattern corresponding to the phonetic label for that token. This same network was also able to generalize its behavior to unfamiliar data with only a small loss of accuracy; an increase in error rate of 2–3% was typical in generalization tests.

Now that we have taught the network to phonetically recognize these sounds, it is of interest to look at the behavior of the hidden units. These

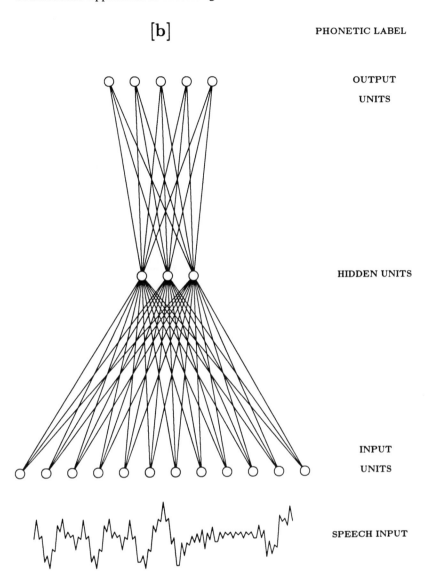

Figure 9
A schematic diagram of the network used for phonetic classification. The actual network consisted of 320 input nodes, 6 hidden nodes, and 12 output nodes. The flow of activation is from bottom to top.

are the intermediate units whose job it is, via their connections to both the input layer and the output layer, to carry out the mapping from power spectra to phonetic code. These hidden units are quite important, for they allow the network to alter the similarity structure of the inputs so that nonlinear relationships can be learned. In order to examine the behavior of the hidden units, we created a display matrix with hidden units heading the columns and token types heading the rows. After an input pattern had been presented, the activation of each hidden unit was used to determine the probability of placing a dot in the column of that hidden unit and in the row corresponding to the phonetic type of the token on that particular learning trial. For example, when a token of [b] from the syllable [ba] was presented, a dot was placed in that row, and in the column of each hidden unit with a probability equal to that unit's activation in response to that token. Thus, the more active a given hidden unit is when a specific token is presented, the darker the square for that hidden unit.

Figure 10 shows the results of several hundred thousand such iterations. The hidden units are numbered 0 through 5, and the 18 types are shown along the vertical axis. Upper-case letters indicate which portion of the CV syllable have actually been presented as input. Thus, in the first row we see results for /b/ tokens that were excised from the syllable /ba/; in the second row we see results for /b/ tokens excised from /bi/; in the tenth row the A indicates tokens of /a/ excised from /ba/; and so on.

The results are quite interesting in several respects. First, we see that one hidden unit (unit 4) is always on for the first 9 types and off for the last 9 types. It thus serves as a Consonant/Vowel detector. Note that the learning task did not explicitly require that the distinction be drawn. The network was required to learn 18 different phonetic labels without any clue as to their structure or their similarities. It so happens (reasonably) that the Consonant/Vowel distinction is a useful dimension along which to classify the 18 types, and this dimension is implicit in the stimuli.

In other cases, it is not as easy to interpret single hidden units. When both unit 2 and unit 4 are on, a velar stop (Ga, Gi, Gu) is signaled; otherwise, the vowel [i] is indicated.

One very striking result is the response pattern for unit 1. This unit always came on for the alveolar stops (Da, Di, Du), and was only minimally active at all other times. What makes this so surprising is that the alveolar stops exhibit a great deal of acoustic variability across different vowel contexts. The task simply requires that the network learn labels for the three different alveolar allophones. It was not required to group these together in any way (and indeed there was no feedback to inform the

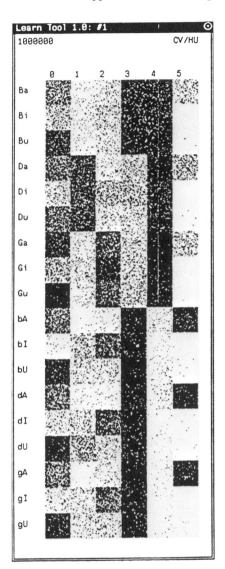

Figure 10
Graphic representation of average activation of 6 hidden units (labeled 0 through 5) in response to the 18 different phonetic tokens. Tokens are labeled with upper-case letters; the lower-case letters indicate the phonetic context in which the tokens were originally produced. Activation is indicated by shading; more active hidden units thus appear as dark squares.

network that any relationship existed among these three types). Nonetheless, the network spontaneously opted for a representation in which these allophones were grouped together, in just the same way as humans hear these acoustically different tokens as different forms of the same phonetic type.[8]

What this simulation illustrates is that in the course of learning to categorize a set of acoustic patterns—represented in a raw, relatively unanalyzed manner—there are aspects of the inputs that, for this task, cause them to be grouped together in various ways. Some of the groupings are intelligible within phonological-feature theory (e.g., the Consonant/Vowel distinction, or the grouping of alveolar sounds). Other groups are more difficult to interpret, and often are signaled by the activation of several hidden units in concert (in other words, they rely on distributed representations). We have just begun to try to analyze the acoustic basis for these latter groups, in order to see whether they have any correlate within human behavior.

One important thing to realize is that the groupings that evolve during the course of learning are highly sensitive to the input data. The learning algorithm minimizes error in the task at hand and distributes the variance equally across all the hidden units. If the input is sufficiently restricted, there is no need for something like unit 4's Consonant/Vowel feature to be developed. The elaboration of the internal representation is very much controlled by the data which the network is being asked to learn.

However, there is a shortcoming with the simulation just described: One might very reasonably ask where the phonetic labels have come from. In order to discover the feature set, we have had to tell the network what the abstract name of the sound is. Obviously they come from somewhere outside the network, and so it would seem that some prior learning (not yet illuminated by this simulation) has been done. Suppose we do not have available an abstract characterization for the input. Furthermore, suppose that speech is presented in a continuous fashion (as if it were "slid" slowly through the input layer of the network), and that the digitized speech samples were used as input rather than the results of a Fourier analysis.

In this simulation, the simple sentence "This is the voice of the neural network" was digitized. The network was modified so that it consisted of 50 input nodes, 20 hidden units, and 50 input units. The task in this case is for the network to simply "auto-encode" the speech patterns it is given. That is, the goal is to produce on the output units the same pattern received by the input units. A schematic picture of this network is shown in figure 11.

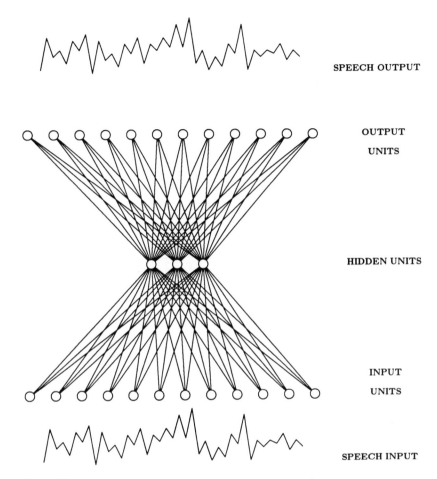

SPEECH OUTPUT

OUTPUT
UNITS

HIDDEN UNITS

INPUT
UNITS

SPEECH INPUT

Figure 11
A schematic diagram of the network used for identity mapping. The actual
network consisted of 50 input nodes, 20 hidden nodes, and 50 output nodes.

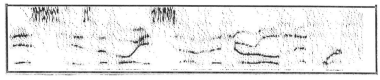

INPUT

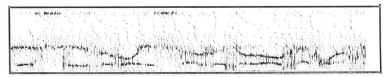

OUTPUT

Figure 12
Spectrograms of the input to the identity mapping network (upper panel) and the output produced by the network (lower panel). Input was the sentence "This is the voice of the neural network".

On the first learning cycle, the first 50 samples of the speech (corresponding to the first 5 msec of speech) were presented to the network, and it attempted to reproduce the input. On the next learning cycle, samples 2 through 51 were presented; on the next, samples 3 through 53; and so on. In this way, the network attempted to learn (where learning is now defined as simply the ability to reproduce) all overlapping 5-msec stretches of the speech.

After a million learning cycles, the weight values were frozen and the network was tested. The whole set of training data was passed through the network as a sequential stream of (now) nonoverlapping 50-sample inputs. The output was converted to analog form and replayed. The result was high-quality speech, with a correlation of 0.96 between the input and the output. Spectrograms of the input and the output are shown in figure 12.

As occurred in the previous simulation, the hidden units represent a kind of featural encoding of the input. Interpreting their content is more difficult than before (in part because there are more features), and the analysis at this point is preliminary. However, it is interesting that we are able to apply the learning procedure in a situation in which there are far fewer constraints on what must be presupposed for the procedure to work.

Conclusions

At the outset of this paper, four problems in the area of acoustic/phonetic processing were identified. These are surely not the only problems in acoustic/phonetics, but they are particularly interesting because it is not evident that they can be readily resolved within traditional processing frameworks. I have tried to suggest that the PDP approach offers a fresh and fruitful way of thinking about these problems.

The TRACE I model addresses the problem of *variability* and the problem of *processing over time*. Its basic premise is that variability in speech makes perception more robust. Speech rarely varies randomly, and TRACE I attempts to provide an account for what human listeners do exquisitely well: process the complex interactions among the many factors that shape the sound wave. The simulations described here show that the computational demands necessary to do this are best met by a highly parallel and interactive architecture. The model also suggests that there may not be a hard and fast distinction between the processing structures that mediate on-line perception and those that subserve short-term memory.

The second set of models address the problems of *acquisition* and *representation* using the "back-propagation of error" learning algorithm. These models illustrate a way in which representations can be built up gradually during the course of learning, and suggest that distributed representations offer an interesting alternative to the kinds of discrete categorial representation that are more common in linguistics.

PDP models of this sort have characteristics that help us understand human language behavior. For one thing, these models demonstrate that it is possible to take a relatively raw input and a simple learning rule, and to develop a highly complex and efficient internal representation with little *a priori* representational apparatus. Second, the learning rule often results in representations that are far more flexible and elaborate than those that require fixed and discrete categories. Though these representations are closely tied to the training data and the training task, they may also encode important and plausible distinctions not overtly required for the task (such as the Consonant/Vowel and alveolar groupings noted above). Third, much of the motivation for supposing that internal representations in perception are innate has come from the apparent poverty of data and the weakness of learning algorithms. The recent results with PDP learning algorithms have demonstrated that a surprisingly small amount of data may contain sufficient cues to the intrinsic structure in the data so that rather simple learning rules can be used to induce this structure. It is highly unlikely that the human perceptual system is as impoverished as the PDP networks described in this chapter, and I do not wish to suggest that these networks are adequate models for resolving the innateness issue. On the other hand, these models suggest different ways of understanding this thorny issue. Innate knowledge comes in many forms. In PDP models, it is the processing architecture and the learning algorithm that are innate, not the conceptual categories *per se*.

Notes

1. The treatment of time in TRACE is not entirely satisfactory. The reduplication of connections is hardly elegant. What is more serious, the many tokens (of features, phonemes, and words) are not bound together in any way by units that stand for types independent of their instantiation. Thus, priming is not expected. McClelland's (1986) Connection Information Distribution (CID) scheme suggests one approach to solving both these problems. The CID model allows for a central knowledge base, in the form of canonical connections. This central store represents knowledge of unit types. The model makes it possible to program additional connections on the fly, instantiating context-sensitive tokens of the types (only) as needed.

2. The lexicon is kept small only to speed up simulations; simulating a highly parallel processing system on a serial computer is time-intensive. Although the vocabulary is small, it was deliberately constructed so as to contain highly confusable items, a large number of minimal pairs (many of them pseudo-words), and phonetic contexts that produce a large number of coarticulatory effects. There is little question that if the model were implemented on suitable parallel hardware, the lexicon could be significantly expanded and could run very quickly.

3. "ba" is a lexical item for TRACE I, as are a number of other phonetically similar CV syllables. This was done so that we could examine the model's ability to make very fine distinctions among acoustically similar inputs.

4. In this simulation, artificial speech-like inputs were used. These were precomputed in order to create feature inputs that would share many of the overlapping, coarticulated properties of speech. The point of these simulations was to look at effects from the lexical level to the phoneme level, not to address problems of coarticulation. Thus, it is not critical that the input was pseudo-speech.

5. This approach does not directly address the question of how time should be represented. In TRACE, the network was replicated for different moments in time, so that time was represented spatially. A similar technique will be used in the simulations reported below. However, a more promising approach to the representation of sequential inputs is that described in Jordan 1986.

6. The algorithm and its derivation are described in detail in Rumelhart, Hinton, and Williams 1986.

7. More precisely, the input was actually represented as a matrix of 16 × 20 floating-point numbers. The 16 rows represented 16 frequency bins from 0 to 5 kHz, and the 20 columns represented 20 3.2-msec time intervals. In this form, the temporal aspect of the input was equated with its spatial position within the input vector. This does not mean that temporal structure cannot be discovered; however, there are serious limitations with this spatial metaphor of time (see Jordan 1986).

8. We have run this particular simulation many times, starting with different sets of initial random connections. The results are almost always the same. It is not the case that (for instance) unit 4 is always on when a consonant is presented; but almost always some unit will take on the role of discriminating consonant from vowel. The functions are robust; which unit assumes a specific function varies randomly.

References

Aronoff, M. 1976. *Word Formation in Generative Grammar.* Cambridge, Mass. MIT Press.

Bolt, Beranek, and Newman. 1976. Speech Understanding Systems: Final Technical Progress Report. BBN Report 3438.

Cole, R. A., Stern, R. M., and Lasry, M. J. 1986. Performing fine phonetic distinctions: Templates vs. features. In J. S. Perkell and D. H. Klatt (eds.), *Invariance and Variability in Speech Processes.* Hillsdale, N.J.: Erlbaum.

Cottrell, G. W., Munro, P. W., and Zipser, D. 1987. Image compression by back propagation: A demonstration of extensional programming. In N. E. Sharkey (ed.), *Advances in Cognitive Science*, volume 2. Chichester: Ellis Horwood.

Dixon, N. R. and Silverman, H. F. 1976. The 1976 modular acoustic processor (MAP). *IEEE Transactions in Acoustics, Speech, and Signal Processing* 25: 367–378.

Elman, J. L., and McClelland, J. L. 1984. The interactive activation model of speech perception. In N. Lass (ed.), *Language and Speech.* New York: Academic.

Elman, J. L., and McClelland, J. L. 1986. Exploiting lawful variability in the speech wave. In J. S. Perkell and D. H. Klatt (eds.), *Invariance and Variability in Speech Processes.* Hillsdale, N.J.: Erlbaum.

Elman, J. L., and McClelland, J. L. 1987. Cognitive Penetration of the Mechanisms of Perception: Compensation for Coarticulation of Lexically Restored Phonemes. Manuscript, Center for Research in Language, University of California, San Diego.

Fujimura, O., and Lovins, J. B. 1978. Syllables as concatenative phonetic units. In A. Bell and J. B. Hooper (eds.), *Syllables and Segments.* Amsterdam: North-Holland.

Ganong, W. F. 1980. Phonetic categorization in auditory word perception. *Journal of Experimental Psychology: Human Perception and Performance* 6: 110–125.

Jordan, M. I. 1986. Serial Order: A Parallel Distributed Processing Approach. Report 8604, Institute for Cognitive Science, University of California, San Diego.

Kewley-Port, D. 1983. Time varying features as correlates of place of articulation in soft consonants. *Journal of the Acoustical Society of America* 73: 322–335.

Klatt, D. H. 1980. Speech perception: A model of acoustic-phonetic analysis and lexical access. In R. Cole (ed.), *Perception and Production of Fluent Speech.* Hillsdale, N.J.: Erlbaum.

Lowerre, B. T. 1976. The Harpy Speech Recognition System. Ph.D. thesis, Department of Computer Science, Carnegie-Mellon University.

Marslen-Wilson, W., and Tyler, L. K. 1980. The temporal structure of spoken language understanding. *Cognition* 8: 1–71.

McClelland, J. L. 1985. Putting knowledge in its place: A scheme for programming parallel processing structures on the fly. *Cognitive Science* 9: 113–146.

McClelland, J. L. 1986. The programmable blackboard model of reading. In McClelland et al. 1986.

McClelland, J. L., and Elman, J. L. 1986. The TRACE model of speech perception. *Cognitive Psychology* 18: 1–86.

McClelland, J. L., Rumelhart, D. E., and the PDP Research Group. 1986. *Parallel Distributed Processing: Explorations in the Microstructure of Cognition.* Volume 2. Cambridge, Mass.: MIT Press.

Mehler, J. 1981. The role of syllables in speech processing: Infant and adult data. *Philosophical Transactions of the Royal Society* B 295: 333–352.

Miller, J. L. 1981. Effects of speaking rate on segmental distinctions. In P. D. Eimas and J. L. Miller (eds.), *Perspectives on the Study of Speech.* Hillsdale, N.J.: Erlbaum.

Minsky, M., and Papert, S. 1969. *Perceptrons.* Cambridge, Mass.: MIT Press.

Nakatani, L. H., and Dukes, K. D. 1977. Locus of segmental cues for word juncture. *Journal of the Acoustical Society of America* 62: 714–719.

Pisoni, D. B. 1981. In Defense of Segmental Representations in Speech Processing. Paper presented to meeting of Acoustical Society of America, Ottawa.

Repp, B. H., and Mann, V. A. 1980. Perceptual assessment of fricative-stop coarticulation. *Journal of the Acoustical Society of America* 69: 1154–1163.

Rumelhart, D. E., Hinton, G. E., and Williams, R. J. 1986. Learning internal representations by error propagation. In Rumelhart et al. 1986.

Rumelhart, D. E., McClelland, J. L., and the PDP Research Group. 1986. *Parallel Distributed Processing: Explorations in the Microstructure of Cognition.* Volume 1. Cambridge, Mass.: MIT Press.

Stevens, K., and Blumstein, S. 1981. The search for invariant acoustic correlates of phonetic features. In P. D. Eimas and J. L. Miller (eds.), *Perspectives on the Study of Speech.* Hillsdale, N.J.: Erlbaum.

Warren, P., and Marslen-Wilson, W. 1987. Continuous uptake of acoustic cues in spoken word-recognition. *Perception and Psychophysics* 41: 262–275.

Warren, R. M., and Sherman, G. 1974. Phonemic restorations based on subsequent context. *Perception and Psychophysics* 16: 150–156.

Wickelgren, W. A. 1969. Context-sensitive coding, associative memory and serial order in (speech) behavior. *Psychological Review* 76: 1–15.

Chapter 8

Parafoveal Preview and Lexical Access During Eye Fixations in Reading	Keith Rayner and David A. Balota

Lexical access is a topic of considerable interest to psycholinguists, and a great deal of research on auditory and visual word identification has been carried out over the past couple of decades. Much of the research on lexical access processes has focused on the identification of individual words that are isolated from the rest of the linguistic context in which they normally appear during listening and reading. Although the results of experiments dealing with lexical access processes for isolated words have yielded some important clues to the structure of the mental lexicon, contextual influences play an important role in how words are processed in listening and in reading. The processing of words during reading will be discussed in this chapter.

During reading, not only can prior context exert influences on how words are identified, but *parafoveal* processing of words can also influence how words are accessed in the lexicon. Whereas studies in which subjects must respond to a target word presented in isolation can effectively manipulate the preceding context (Morton 1964; Tulving and Gold 1963; Schuberth and Eimas 1977; Stanovich and West 1979), it is considerably more difficult to manipulate the amount of parafoveal information available for processing. Moreover, one can easily question the generalizability of studies in which words are responded to in isolation after either an appropriate, an inappropriate, or a neutral context has been presented, because the timing relationship between the processing of the context and the target word is often at variance with the timing relationships found in normal reading.

We will deal here with research concerning the relationship between lexical access processes and eye movements during reading. Our primary argument will be that lexical access processes (or word identification) typically serve to trigger eye movements in reading. In addition, we will argue that parafoveal processing on fixation n can influence this lexical-access process on fixation $n + 1$.

1 Defining Lexical Access

Our discussion of lexical access processes does not rely heavily on any particular model of lexical access. At one level, lexical access simply refers to the fact that the reader has made contact with lexical-level information. In this sense, lexical access is more a process than a completion of a stage. Consider, for example, the McClelland-Rumelhart (1981) model of word recognition. Within this model one might assume that the lexical access process begins when activation begins to accumulate at the lexical level. Clearly, there are many different levels in this access process, reflecting varying degrees of activation accumulation. Moreover, the levels tapped are defined in some sense by the tasks used to investigate them. For example, those who believe that lexical-decision performance is a good reflection of lexical access must rely on the notion that lexical access is the point at which the subject has obtained sufficient information to discriminate words from nonword letter strings. Likewise, those who use pronunciation tasks to measure lexical access apparently believe that lexical access is the point at which the subject has obtained sufficient information to determine a pronunciation code for the word.

When one considers normal reading, neither a discrimination between words and nonwords nor the assembly of a pronunciation code seems necessary. Then what do we mean by lexical access? We could begin by assuming that lexical access is the process whereby the reader accumulates sufficient information to make the decision to leave the currently fixated word. Like others investigating lexical access processes, we would then be defining lexical access by the task used to measure it. Obviously, such a definition is somewhat circular. The more important question is: What are the characteristics of the word that influence the decision concerning when to move the eyes from the currently fixated word? We will argue that the trigger that determines when to move the eyes is the speed with which a lexical-level representation reaches threshold (i.e., word identification). Within this vein, it is important to realize that we do not see word identification as the major holdup in normal skilled reading. Rather, factors associated with the programming of the eye movements represent the bottleneck in reading, since the motor aspects of programming a saccade take at least 150–175 msec (Rayner, Slowiaczek, Clifton, and Bertera 1983; Salthouse and Ellis 1980). Since the average fixation duration is around 225 msec, the programming of the saccade takes a considerable amount of time during a typical fixation. Once word identification has taken place, the programs still have to be set in motion to move the eyes to the next location in the text. We know that the visual information necessary for reading can be obtained within the first 50 msec or so of a fixation (Rayner, Inhoff, Morrison, Slowiaczek, and Bertera 1981), and reading is certainly possible under RSVP (Rapid Serial Visual Presentation) conditions wherein a new word is presented every 50 msec (Forster 1970; Potter, Kroll, and Harris 1980). Hence, we will argue that the process of lexical access takes place very quickly during an eye fixation and serves as the primary trigger to propel the eyes forward through text.

We are by no means arguing that higher-level comprehension processes never play a role in the decision to leave the currently fixated word. The notion is that breakdowns in the comprehension process signal the eye-movement system to abort the decision to move the eyes. For example, such situations might occur when the reader is garden-pathed (and misparses to string of words), or cannot find a referent of a currently fixated pronoun, or is having difficulty integrating the currently fixated word with the rest of the text representation. The point that we will be making is that in normal skilled reading the signal to move the eyes is determined *primarily* by word-identification processes. In addition, we will argue that this process can be influenced by the use of parafoveal information.

There is an alternative account of the decision concerning when to move the eyes: Since higher-order processes can influence how long the reader fixates a word, it may be that these comprehension processes *always* play a role in the decision to move from the currently fixated word. That is, the decision concerning when to move the eyes could be based on the combined effects of a number of levels of the language-processing system (including lexical-level analyses, syntactic analyses, and text-integration analyses). Unfortunately, the research to date has not discriminated clearly between this alternative and the previous alternative. In the present discussion we will attempt to force the more simplistic earlier account while also mentioning evidence that could be seen as consistent with the alternative account.

The primary evidence we will discuss consists of eye-movement data collected as subjects read text. In order to provide a framework for this discussion, we will provide in section 2 a brief overview of eye movements and the size of the perceptual span (or area of effective or useful vision) in reading. The major point that will be made in that section is that readers utilize varying levels of parafoveal information to the right of fixation. In addition, section 2 addresses the basic eye-movement characteristics typically found in reading. This will be critical in our discussion of parafoveal effects on lexical access. In section 3 we will discuss the cognitive processes in reading that may be reflected in fixation times on words. There we will argue that there is a rather tight link between the eye and the mind, so that how long a reader looks at a word reveals information about the ease or difficulty associated with the processing of that word. The research described in section 3 clearly indicates that the decision concerning when to leave a word can be influenced by higher-order comprehension processes.

In section 4 we will discuss the parafoveal-preview effect: If a reader has a preview of a word before looking directly at it, the processing time associated with that word is facilitated. Elsewhere (Balota and Rayner 1989) we have discussed the range of lexical-processing effects for foveal and parafoveal vision, emphasizing both the similarities and the dissimilarities. In sections 4 and 5 we will sketch the findings concerning the parafoveal-preview effect. These sections are important because we are going to end up arguing that lexical-access processes on fixation n can be modified by parafoveal information acquired on fixation $n - 1$.

2   Eye Movements and the Perceptual Span During Reading

Specifying the Eye-Movement Parameters

When we read, our eyes do not move smoothly across the page, as it seems phenomenologically. Rather, we make a series of left-to-right eye movements called *saccades*, separated by fixational pauses that last about 200–250 msec each. About 15–20 percent of the saccades in reading are *regressions* in which the reader makes a right-to-left saccade back to material that has already been traversed by the eyes. It is important to distinguish regressions from return sweeps, which are also right-to-left saccades but which place the eyes at the beginning of the next line rather than back to material already traversed. It is commonly believed that the two most common reasons for regressions are (1) that the reader failed to understand some part of the text and (2) that a saccade was a bit longer than intended and the reader had to make a corrective movement.

New information is extracted from text only during the fixational pauses. Saccades take 20–40 msec, and no information is obtained from the text as the eyes are moving. This was clearly demonstrated in an experiment by Wolverton and Zola (1983), who replaced text with different words, random letters, or strings of Xs for a 20-msec period either during the saccade or at some point during a fixation. Although such changes interfered with reading when presented during the fixation period (including the first 20 msec), they were not noticed and did not interfere with reading if presented during the saccade.

The average saccade length in reading is 7–9 character spaces, or a bit over one word. Number of character spaces is clearly the appropriate metric to use in assessing how far the eyes move, since the number of character spaces traversed by a saccade is relatively invariant when the same text is read at different distances even though the character spaces subtend markedly different visual angles (Morrison and Rayner 1981; O'Regan 1983).

The primary function of a saccade is to bring a new region of text into foveal vision for detailed analysis; reading on the basis of only parafoveal and peripheral information is difficult or impossible (Rayner and Bertera 1979; Rayner et al. 1981). Foveal vision represents the 2° of visual angle in the center of vision (about 6–8 letter spaces for normal-size text) and acuity is markedly better than in parafoveal vision, which in turn is better than peripheral vision. Since for English orthography the perceptual span is asymmetric to the right of fixation (McConkie and Rayner 1976; Rayner, Well, and Pollatsek 1980), our discussion of parafoveal and peripheral vision will deal with information to the right of fixation; parafoveal vision extends 5° to the right of fixation (or out to about 15 letter spaces from fixation), and peripheral vision includes the rest of the line.

Although a majority of the words in a text are fixated during reading, many words are skipped, so foveal processing of each word is not necessary. Roughly 80 percent of the content words in text and 40 percent of the function words are fixated. Of course, function words tend to be shorter on average than content words, and it is clearly the case that word length dramatically influences the probability that a word will be fixated (Rayner and McConkie 1976). Between 5 and 20 percent of the content words in a text receive more than one fixation. The values that have been cited are all influenced by text difficulty; thus, as the test becomes more difficult, the average fixation tends to get longer, the average saccade gets shorter, and the frequency of regressions increases. Therefore, the probability that a word will be fixated also increases, and fewer words are skipped, as the text gets more difficult.

The most striking aspect of both fixation duration and saccade length is the variability. Fixations can range from under 100 msec to over 500 msec within a given reader, although typically only a small percentage of fixations are under 100 msec and most fixation durations are between 150 and 350 msec. Even this restricted range indicates a considerable amount of variability. Saccades range from one character space to over 15. In fact, when a left-to-right saccade follows a regression or a series of regressions, saccades may exceed 15 character spaces, as the eyes typically do not fixate again on material read before the regression.

Lately, a number of researchers have begun to exploit the variability that exists in eye-movement records to study cognitive processes in reading. The basic idea is that eye-movement measures can be used to study moment-to-moment cognitive processes during reading. This is not to say that there is not a purely motoric component to the variability. For example, even when spatial and temporal uncertainty about when and where to move are eliminated, there is still variability in the latency of eye movements (Rayner et al. 1983). Similarly, there is variability in where the eye lands, even when a fixed target location is given (Coeffe and O'Regan 1987). Though this *noise* of motoric variability makes it difficult to interpret the cognitive *signal* in the eye-movement record, it is now clear that the signal is there, and great strides have been made in understanding reading via examination of eye-movement records.

The Perceptual Span in Reading
As was mentioned above, it is during the eye fixations that new information is obtained from text. Research on the size of the perceptual span during an eye fixation in reading has clearly demonstrated that the span is relatively small (for reviews, see Rayner 1978a and Rayner and Pollatsek 1987). This evidence has accumulated from experiments using the *moving-window* paradigm (McConkie and Rayner 1975; Rayner 1986; Rayner and Bertera 1979) or a variation of it called the *boundary* paradigm (Rayner 1975; Pollatsek, Rayner, and Balota 1986). As we shall see, both of these paradigms provide important information concerning the impact of parafoveal information on lexical access processes. Thus, we shall provide a brief description of each of them.

In the moving-window paradigm, readers move their eyes as they normally do in reading, but the amount of information available for processing on each fixation is controlled by the experimenter. Thus, within an experimenter-defined window, the normal text is available for the reader to process. However, the text outside the window is mutilated in some fashion. For example, all original letters (and sometimes the spaces between words) might be replaced by *X*s or other letters. The size of the window is sometimes equal to a certain number of character spaces to the right (and left) of fixation and sometimes coincides with word boundaries. Figure 1 shows examples of each. Figure 1 also shows an example of the boundary

```
The fluent processing of words during silent reading    Normal Text

XXXXXXXXXXprocessing ofXXXXXXXXXXXXXXXXXXXXXXXXXXXX      13- character window
                     .                                  (spaces filled)
XXXXXXXXXXXXXXXXXssing of wordXXXXXXXXXXXXXXXXXXXXXXXX
                       .

XXX XXXXXX processing of XXXXX XXXXXX XXXXX XXXXXXX      13-character window
                    .                                   (spaces preserved)
XXX XXXXXX XXXXXssing of wordX XXXXXX XXXXX XXXXXXX
                     .

XXX XXXXXX processing of XXXXX XXXXXX XXXXX XXXXXXX
                   .                                    2-word window
XXX XXXXXX XXXXXXXXXX of words XXXXXX XXXXX XXXXXXX
                    .

The fluent processing of green during silent reading    Boundary
                    .                                   technique
The fluent processing of words during silent reading
                     .
```

Figure 1
Examples of the moving-window and boundary paradigms. The top line represents a line of normal text. Examples of 13 character windows and a two-word
window are shown on two consecutive fixations. Fixation location is marked by
the dot in each example. The bottom rows show an example of the boundary
paradigm. In the example, the word *green* is initially presented, but when the
reader's saccade crosses over the boundary location (the letter *o* in *of*) it is
replaced by *words*.

paradigm in which a word (or a nonword) initially presented in text is
replaced by another word when the reader's eye crosses a boundary location. By examining how long the reader fixates on the target word as a
function of the relationship between the initially displayed word and the
target word, one can make inferences about the type of information acquired
at various distances from fixation.

Research using these eye-movement-controlled display-change paradigms suggests that the perceptual span extends from the beginning of the
currently fixated word, or about 3–4 character spaces to the left of fixation,
to about 15 character spaces to the right of fixation. However, within the
perceptual-span region, different types of information appear to be obtained at different distances from the fixation point. Figure 2 shows a line
of text on three consecutive fixations to illustrate the different types of
information acquired on each fixation. From the area closest to fixation
(extending to about 4–8 character spaces to the right of fixation), informa-

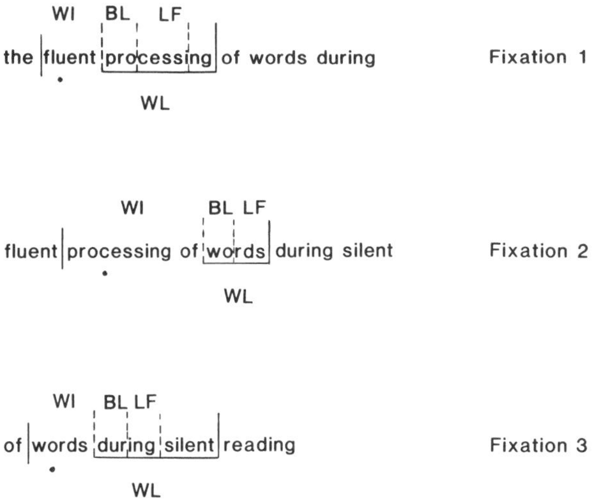

```
      WI    BL   LF
       |    |    |
the |fluent |processing| of words during          Fixation 1
     •
            WL


            WI          BL  LF
             |           |   |
fluent |processing of |words| during silent       Fixation 2
         •
              WL


   WI    BL LF
    |     |  |
of |words |during| silent| reading               Fixation 3
    •
         WL
```

Figure 2
An example of the different types of information obtained within the perceptual span on three successive fixations. The dot marks the location of fixation. WI: word identification; BL: beginning letters; LF: letter features; WL: word length.

tion used to identify the word on the current fixation is obtained. The region within which words are identified is variable because, depending on word length, on some fixations one word can be identified whereas on others two words can be identified (or possibly three when a number of short words occur together in text). Further to the right of fixation than the region of word identification, beginning-letter information and letter-feature information is obtained. Word-length information appears to be acquired over the largest range. Note that the total perceptual span region is about twice as large as the distance that readers typically move their eyes on each saccade. In essence, readers move their eyes to the next unidentified word. In addition, word-length information acquired on fixation n is used not only to program the next saccade but also to program the length of the saccade from fixation $n + 1$. That is, Rayner and Pollatsek (1981) showed that information acquired on fixation n was the primary determinant of how far the next saccade moved, but that length information acquired on fixation $n - 1$ also influenced the distance of that saccade.

When readers move their eyes, where they land on words is not haphazard (Rayner 1979; O'Regan 1981; McConkie and Zola 1984). A reader tends to fixate on the *preferred viewing location* (Rayner 1979), which is about halfway between the beginning and the middle of a word (although there is some variability in where the eye lands). This makes sense, since it is well known that the beginnings of words are more informative than the ends of words. That readers typically fixate between the beginning and the middle of the word is probably also related to the amount of partial information they obtained parafoveally on the prior fixation.

In essence, work on the perceptual span suggests that varying levels of information are obtained during a fixation depending upon the distance of that information from the fovea. By our present definition, lexical access clearly would occur for the fixated word. That is, readers obviously leave the currently fixated word. Also, because words are sometimes skipped, it appears that lexical access can occur for parafoveal words. Thus, we already have a modification of our definition of lexical access. That is, not only does lexical access influence the reader's decision when to move the eyes, but it can also influence the decision to skip words in the parafovea. Before we turn to a more detailed discussion of the impact of parafoveal information on lexical access processes, it is necessary to briefly discuss research that indicates that higher-level comprehension processes can also influence the decision to leave the currently fixated word. This research is particularly important because it suggests that word identification is not always the only determinant of the reader's decision to move the eyes.

3   What Processes Do Eye Fixation Times Reflect?

There is now abundant evidence that the amount of time a reader fixates on a word reflects something about the ease or difficulty of processing that word. However, before turning to this research it is important to note that there is an active debate concerning the most appropriate measure of processing time on a word (Rayner and Pollatsek 1987). The two primary measures that have been used are *first fixation duration* and *gaze duration*. Gaze duration represents the sum of all fixations on a word prior to a saccade out of that word to a new word. First fixation duration represents the duration of only the first fixation on a word. When a reader makes only one fixation on a word, then gaze duration and first fixation are the same. The fact that readers sometimes fixate more than once on a word has led to the debate concerning these two measures. Some researchers appear to use the first fixation duration on a word as a measre of lexical access (Inhoff 1984; McConkie, Zola, Blanchard, and Wolverton 1982). The reasons are not always explicit, but the assumption appears to be that what goes on beyond the first fixation reflects higher-order processing (Inhoff 1984) or is noise. However, the opposite assumption appears to have been made by

O'Regan, Levy-Schoen, Pynte, and Brugaillera (1984), who believe that refixations are often caused by landing in a "bad" place on a word and moving to more informative spot. Thus, according to O'Regan and colleagues, the second fixation on a word may be more informative than the first. (In their study, words were presented in isolation; it remains to be seen to what extent the mechanism they propose accounts for many of the refixations on words in text.)

The argument about which measure is best depends partly on what processes one is interested in measuring. For example, Inhoff (1984) argued that the duration of the first fixation on a word and the gaze duration reflect different processes. In his data, both first fixation duration and gaze duration were affected by word frequency, but only gaze duration was affected by the predictability of the word in the context. He thus posited that first fixation duration was the measure of lexical access, whereas gaze duration reflected text-integration processes as well. However, this distinction apparently does not hold up well when examined in light of a number of studies (see Rayner and Pollatsek 1987). As Rayner and Pollatsek (1987) have suggested, it is quite plausible that there is only a quantitative difference between the two measures, namely that the decision to refixate on a word can be made later in a fixation than the decision when to move the eyes. Thus, if a cognitive operation is really fast, it will affect the first fixation duration; if it is a bit slower, it may still affect gaze duration. In the present discussion, we will use gaze duration as our indicant of lexical access while noting any discrepancies in the data provided by the two measures.

In arguing for the utility of fixation time on a word, Just and Carpenter (1980) spelled out two important theoretical arguments: the eye-mind assumption and the immediacy assumption. The eye-mind assumption states that there is not a significant lag between processing of information by the eye and processing by the mind; thus, how long someone looks at a word while reading will directly reflect the ease or difficulty associated with processing that word. The immediacy assumption states that all processing associated with a given word is completed while the eyes are still fixating on that word; when the processing is completed, the eyes move on. Recent research has tended to suggest that the eye-mind assumption is quite reasonable (Rayner and Pollatsek 1987). However, with respect to the immediacy assumption, there is evidence that processes initiated on one fixation *spill over* onto the next word or words on subsequent fixations (Balota, Pollatsek, and Rayner 1985; Ehrlich and Rayner 1983; McConkie, Underwood, Zola, and Wolverton 1985). Thus, a strict interpretation of the immediacy assumption does not appear to be warranted. Of course, the important question for the present discussion is: What types of processes are completed before the eyes move on?

One variable that has a strong impact on fixation time on a word is word frequency (Just and Carpenter 1980; Inhoff 1984; Inhoff and Rayner 1986; Kliegl, Olson, and Davidson 1982; Rayner 1977; Rayner and Duffy 1986). When words are matched on word length (and number of syllables) and are equally likely in a sentence frame, readers look at low-frequency words about 90 msec longer (when measured by gaze duration and 40 msec longer when measured by first fixation duration) than high-frequency words (Inhoff and Rayner 1986; Rayner and Duffy 1986). We believe that this impact of word frequency most likely plays a role in both (1) the speed of identifying the currently fixated word and (2) the text-integration processes. Further evidence that fixation times reflect word-identification processes comes from work by Lima (1987) demonstrating that pseudo-prefixed words (e.g. *rescue*) receive longer fixations than prefixed words (*revive*) matched on word length and word frequency and from work by Inhoff (1987) showing that compound words (*cowboy*) are fixated longer than pseudo-compound words (*carpet*) and neutral words (*mirror*). Clearly, variables that one would *a priori* expect to influence lexical access processes do influence fixation times.

Priming effects from related words earlier in a sentence have also been demonstrated recently. Carroll and Slowiaczek (1986) asked subjects to read sentences containing a category name (e.g. *bird*) or a neutral prime word (e.g. *thing*), which was then followed by a target exemplar. The category prime word facilitated processing for both high-typicality (*sparrow*) and low-typicality (*vulture*) exemplars. However, high-typicality exemplars were processed more quickly than low-typicality exemplars in both primed and unprimed conditions. In a second experiment, Carroll and Slowiaczek extended the priming effect to primary associates. They also found that the priming effect was influenced by the syntactic structure of the sentence. When both the prime and the associated target word were in the same clause, semantic priming occurred. However, when the prime and the target were in different clauses, no associative priming was observed. Of course, such associative-priming effects could be totally intralexical.

Recently, there have also been many demonstrations that fixation times on words can be reduced by the relationship of the prior text to the currently fixated word. For example, words that are relatively predictable from the prior text receive shorter fixations than words that are not predictable from the context (Balota et al. 1985; Ehrlich and Rayner 1981; Inhoff 1984; Zola 1984). There is also a higher probability that predictable words will be skipped over than words that are not predictable from the prior context (Balota et al. 1985; Ehrlich and Rayner 1981; O'Regan 1979). Effects such as these appear to be accounted for by two factors. First, when words are predictable from prior context, readers can better utilize parafoveal information than when words are not predictable. Hence, they are able to skip over predictable words more frequently than over unpredictable words, because they can be identified on the prior fixation (Balota et al. 1985). Second, predictable words appear to be easier to integrate into the discourse structure that the reader constructs to comprehend text (Balota et al. 1985; Ehrlich and Rayner 1981). Thus, both levels of information may figure in the decision concerning when to leave a word.

In addition to priming effects and context effects, there are other effects that appear to reflect higher-order comprehension influences. That is, one finds variations in fixation times on target words as a function of (1) lexical ambiguity (Rayner and Duffy 1986; Duffy, Morris, and Rayner 1988) and (2) the distance between a target word and a prior mention of that word (Schustack, Ehrlich, and Rayner 1987) or a related referent (Ehrlich and Rayner 1983). In addition, research on syntactic parsing strategies that are employed by readers has shown that the record left by the eyes is a good reflection of the ease or difficulty readers have parsing sentences and recovering from misanalyses (Frazier and Rayner 1982, 1987; Ferreira and Clifton 1986; Rayner, Carlson, and Frazier 1983; Rayner and Frazier 1987).

All of the results discussed in this section are quite consistent with the idea that lexical access processes are reflected in fixation times on a target word in text. However, as we have noted, most of the results are also consistent with the idea that fixation times on words reflect both lexical access processes and text-integration processes (Balota et al. 1985; Carroll and Slowiaczek 1986; Ehrlich and Rayner 1981; Rayner and Duffy 1986; Schustack et al. 1987). To date it has not been easy to tease these two alternatives apart. Perhaps words that are relatively easy to access in the lexicon are also easier to integrate into an internal discourse representation that is constructed by the reader to comprehend the text.

Hopefully, it is clear from the research that has been discussed in this section that lexical access processes are reflected in fixation times on words. While other higher-order cognitive processes undoubtedly influence how long the reader remains fixated on a word, our argument is that much of the decision involved in deciding to move the eyes to another word is influenced by whether or not the fixated word has been identified. In fact, our suggestion is that the higher-order effects primarily exert their influence when the comprehension process breaks down. This would suggest that higher-order processes typically play a relatively minor role in determining when the eyes move next during normal fluent reading. Of course, the alternative suggestion is that they *always* play a role. As was noted above, the research to date cannot discriminate between these two possibilities. The important point for the present discussion is that lexical variables clearly play a role in the decision to leave the currently fixated word.

We shall now turn to the impact of parafoveal information on the decision to move the eyes. As we shall see, the research in this area provides information regarding the impact of identification processes on the decision when to move the eyes.

4 The Parafoveal Preview Effect

There are basically two ways in which parafoveal information can be utilized during an eye fixation in reading. First, as we indicated earlier, on some fixations the fixated word and the word to the right of fixation can both be identified. In such cases, the word to the right of fixation is generally skipped over by the ensuing saccade (Ehrlich and Rayner 1981; O'Regan 1979; Pollatsek et al. 1986; Schustack et al. 1987) and the duration of the fixation prior to skipping the word is increased (Hogaboam 1983; Pollatsek et al. 1986). Second, partial information acquired about the word to the right of fixation on fixation n could be integrated with information about that same word (in foveal vision) following the saccade on fixation $n + 1$.

A recent experiment by Blanchard, Pollatsek, and Rayner (1988) demonstrates that both things happen in reading. In their experiment, subjects read text with alternating one- or two-word windows; if on fixation n they received a two-word window, on fixation $n + 1$ they received a one-word window, and vice versa. An analysis including as a factor the length of the word to the right of fixation revealed that if readers received a two-word window (the fixated word and the word to its right) and if a short word was to the right of fixation, there was a much higher probability of skipping over the word than if the reader had a one-word window. On the other hand, if the word to the right of fixation had six letters or more, the probability of fixating the word was not influenced by whether or not the reader had a preview of that word. However, fixation times on that word were significantly shorter when there was a preview than when there was not. The results of the study by Blanchard et al. thus suggest (1) that short words to the right of fixation are sometimes identified and (2) that when words are not identified partial information is obtained and used on the next fixation. In the remainder of this section, the focus will be on cases in which the word to the right of fixation is not skipped (which are more frequent than instances in which the word is skipped). Under such circumstances, a parafoveal preview of the word to the right of fixation leads to faster processing of that word (we will henceforth refer to this as the *parafoveal preview effect*).

It has been known since the classic work of Dodge (1906) that a parafoveal preview of a word facilitates processing of that word. More recently, a number of experiments have verified this result and attempted to determine the locus of the effect (Balota and Rayner 1983; McClelland and O'Regan 1981; Rayner 1978b; Rayner, McConkie, and Ehrlich 1978; Rayner, McConkie, and Zola 1980). In these experiments, subjects were asked to fixate on a fixation cross and a letter string was presented parafoveally. When the subject made an eye movement to the letter string, it was replaced by a word, which the subject named (or categorized). The amount of time taken to name the target word was influenced by how far from fixation the string was initially presented and by the similarity between the string and the target word. If the initially presented string and the target word shared the same two or three beginning letters, the naming was faster than if they did not. While these experiments do not address an actual reading situation, experiments in which subjects are reading have yielded very similar results. For example, Rayner, Well, Pollatsek, and Bertera (1982) compared reading performance when (1) only the fixated word was available on each fixation and all letters to the right of fixation were replaced with other letters (Xs or other letters), (2) both the fixated word and the word to the right of fixation were available on each fixation (with letters further to the right replaced), and (3) the fixated word was available and partial information about the word to the right of fixation was available. In the third condition, either one, two, or three letters of the word to the right of fixation were available on each fixation. When the first three letters of the word to the right of fixation were available and the remainder of the letters were replaced with visually similar letters, the reading rate was not much different from when the entire word to the right of fixation was available. These data, like the naming-time experiments discussed above, show quite clearly that when readers are given a parafoveal preview of the beginning letters of the next word they read faster than when no such preview is provided.

That the parafoveal preview effect is not simply due to the perceptual salience of the beginning letters of a word is clear from a recent experiment by Inhoff (1987). Inhoff asked subjects to read sentences with the word order going from left to right (normal English text), or with the words printed from right to left but with the letter order within words going from left to right. Subjects read the sentences with either (1) a one-word window (the fixated word), (2) a two-word window (the fixated word plus the next word in the sentence), (3) a one-word window plus the first three letters of the next word, or (4) a one-word window plus the last three letters of the next word. Inhoff then examined the fixation time on target words (all of which were six letters long). Because the first three letters of a word are closer to fixation than the last three letters when one is reading from left to right but further away when one is reading from right to left, Inhoff's experiment provides a good test of the extent to which the parafoveal preview effect is due merely to the fact that the beginning letters of the next word are closer to fixation. Inhoff found that having the last three letters of the six-letter target word parafoveally available provided no facilitation in comparison with the one-word window. However, a preview of the first three letters provided significant facilitation for both right-to-left and left-to-right reading. Thus, simple perceptual salience does not appear to be an adequate explanation of the parafoveal preview effect.

Although a number of experiments have demonstrated a parafoveal preview effect in reading, the results of one experiment (McConkie et al. 1982) are inconsistent with the conclusion that partial word information is obtained parafoveally. McConkie et al. had subjects read sentences with the letters in specific target locations alternating with each eye movement. For example, *bears* changed to *peaks* after a saccade and then back to *bears* after the next eye movement. After reading, subjects were required to make forced choices indicating which words they identified as they read. Subjects generally indicated that they had read only one of the target words, and they did not combine the beginning letters of the target word (when it was parafoveally available) with other letters following the saccade. That is, in our present example, subjects never reported seeing *beaks* or *pears*. McConkie et al. also compared fixation durations on the target word in the alternating condition against a control condition in which the letters in the target location did not alternate back and forth. In the alternating condition, fixation duration was 10 msec longer than in the nonalternating condition (a nonsignificant difference). On the basis of the results, McConkie et al. concluded that partial word information is not obtained parafoveally and that information used to identify a word is obtained only on the fixation in which the word is completely identified. According to their conclusion, words can be identified parafoveally or they can be identified foveally, but partial word information is not obtained.

However, a more recent experiment (Balota et al. 1985) provides evidence that partial word information is obtained parafoveally and clarifies the results reported by McConkie et al. (1982). Balota et al. asked subjects to read sentences in which a target word was either predictable from the prior context or unpredictable (but not anomalous) from prior context. They used the boundary technique described previously, and they initially presented visually similar or dissimilar nonwords which changed to the target word when the reader's saccade crossed the invisible boundary. Comparing the visually similar and dissimilar conditions, Balota et al. found that first fixation durations were 15 msec shorter (which was significant) when the initially presented stimulus was visually similar to the target word than when it was dissimilar. When gaze duration was examined, the difference between visually similar and dissimilar conditions was much greater. Notice that the procedure of McConkie et al. only allowed them to examine first fixation on a word; each time the reader made an eye movement, the letters changed, so that a subject who fixated twice on the target word would see two different words. Balota et al. (see also Balota and Rayner 1989) discussed in detail some other issues that may have led McConkie et al. to prematurely reject the notion that readers can use partial word information from parafoveal vision.

The extraction of useful partial word information from parafoveal vision implies that it must be integrated in some way with the foveal information from the subsequent fixation. How that information is integrated may provide an important tool for understanding which codes are important in lexical access as well as for understanding the skilled performance of reading. In particular, it seems important to know whether the codes being extracted from words in parafoveal vision are visual features, sound codes, morphemes, abstract (case-independent) letters, or something else.

The evidence against the use of visual codes in integration across saccades is quite strong. McConkie and Zola (1979) asked subjects to read text presented in alternating (i.e., upper and lower) case. During each saccade, all the letters on a line of text changed case (e.g., *cHaNgE* to *ChAnGe*). McConkie and Zola found that the change of case was not noticed by subjects and, furthermore, that subjects read as rapidly when the case changed after each saccade as when there were no case changes. It could be argued, however, that the difficulty of reading alternating-case text may have prevented the extraction of any parafoveal information. To guard against this, Rayner, McConkie, and Zola (1980) investigated case changes using the naming paradigm described earlier. Subjects were asked to fixate on a cross, and a letter string was presented parafoveally. When the subject made an eye movement to the letter string, it was replaced by a word that the subject named. Rayner et al. found that case changes (even of the form *change* to *CHANGE*) had no effect on naming time and, more important, did not modulate the parafoveal preview effect. Thus, it appears that abstract letter codes extracted parafoveally influence lexical access for the to-be-fixated word.

Although the naming paradigm is more artificial than reading, it allows the experimenter somewhat greater control than when the subject is reading text; in fact, the results from the two paradigms are in almost perfect agreement. The typical size of the naming-facilitation effect (about 30 msec) agrees quite well with the reduction in mean gaze duration observed in reading. The parafoveal naming paradigm also allows for a test of whether sound codes are important in information integration. If they are, then the amount of facilitation should be less in a case like *write-walks* (where the first phoneme changes) than in *write-rough* (where the first phoneme stays the same). In fact, there was no facilitation in either case (Rayner et al. 1980). Other results reported by Rayner et al. (1980) are consistent with the conclusion that sound codes do not form the basis of the parafoveal preview effect.

Another candidate for a code conveying partial information is the morpheme. To test this possibility, Lima (1987) constructed sentence frames that could include either a true prefixed word (e.g. *revive*) or a pseudo-prefixed word (e.g. *rescue*) in the same target location. If extracting morphemes is a significant part of the benefit of parafoveal preview, then one should observe a larger parafoveal-preview benefit for the prefixed words. In fact, there was equal benefit in the two cases, suggesting that morphemes (or at least prefixes) are not active units in integration across saccades. However, Lima acknowledged that her results do not eliminate all possible models of parafoveal morpheme extraction.

A related candidate for the parafoveal access code is semantic information. It has been hypothesized that an unidentified parafoveal word is semantically preprocessed, which aids later identification of the word (Underwood 1980, 1981). Results testing this hypothesis are mixed (Bradshaw 1974; Inhoff 1982; Inhoff and Rayner 1980; Stanovich and West 1983), with at best small effects indicating such preprocessing, and with possible methodological problems. For example, Bradshaw (1974) reported results supporting a semantic-preprocessing model, but when certain potential methodological problems were eliminated no support for the model was obtained (Inhoff 1982; Inhoff and Rayner 1980). However, all these studies relied upon tachistoscopic exposures of pairs of words, which may be quite unlike normal reading. A more direct test of the semantic-preprocessing hypothesis was carried out by Rayner, Balota, and Pollatsek (1986) using the boundary technique described above. Each sentence contained a single target word (e.g. *tune*), and the parafoveal preview was either visually similar (*turc*), semantically similar (*song*), or unrelated (*door*). (The semantically similar pairs were shown to produce the standard foveal priming effect in a separate naming experiment.) Gaze durations on the target word were appreciably shorter when the preview was visually similar to the target word, but there was no difference between the semantically similar and unrelated conditions. Thus, semantic preprocessing or extraction of semantic features is not a viable explanation for the parafoveal-preview benefit in reading.

Thus, by exclusion, the experiments discussed so far suggest that the only units active in integration across saccades appear to be abstract letter codes. However, a different approach to the use of parafoveal information is to ask whether constraint can influence the use of such information. There have been two approaches to investigating constraint, one of which has addressed intralexical constraint and one of which has addressed the impact of sentential constraint.

With respect to the issue of intralexical constraint, Lima and Inhoff (1985) presented sentences in which one of two words appeared in a target location (e.g., "The weary *dwarf* ..." or "The weary *clown* ..."). The target words (such as *dwarf* and *clown*) were selected to have equal frequency in the language and to be equally predictable in the context, but were chosen so that the first three letters (e.g. *dwa*) of one word are shared by few words in the lexicon whereas the first three letters of the other (*clo*) are shared by many words. Since prior studies had demonstrated that seeing the first three letters of the parafoveal word produced a large benefit, Lima and Inhoff reasoned that, if lexical constraint were a potent variable in parafoveal processing, the preview benefit for *dwarf* should be greater than that for *clown*. In fact, there was an equal preview benefit in the two cases, indicating that lexical constraint does not operate on parafoveal information. Lima and Inhoff did find that the fixation time on *clown* was actually less than that on *dwarf*, regardless of whether there was a preview or not. They argued that the familiarity of a word's initial letter sequence affects the time required to process a word foveally.

The effect of sentential constraint on parafoveal processing was examined by Balota et al. (1985), who varied both the predictability of a target word and the availability of parafoveal information using the boundary technique. Two findings of interest emerged. First, earlier findings that a more predictable target word is more likely to be skipped than a less predictable target word (Ehrlich and Rayner 1981) were replicated. Thus, sentential constraint, unlike lexical constraint, does appear to influence the usefulness of parafoveal information. Of greater interest are those occasions when the target word was not skipped. The gaze duration on the target word was shorter when the word was more predictable, which again replicated an earlier result (Ehrlich and Rayner 1981). More important, the benefit of a parafoveal preview was greater when the target word was more predictable, indicating that (in some sense) extraction of parafoveal information is more efficient when guided by sentential context. Additional analyses indicated that more letters were extracted from the parafovea when context was high. Both of these findings run counter to a modular view of lexical access and are consistent with more interactive views (see, e.g., Paap, Newsome, McDonald, and Schvaneveldt 1982; McClelland and Rumelhart 1981). Balota and Rayner (1983), McClelland and O'Regan (1981), and Paap and Newsome (1981) have reported similar superadditive interactions between contextual constraint and the use of parafoveal information.

In this section, we have reviewed research that has attempted to determine the locus of the parafoveal-preview effect in reading. The evidence points to the conclusion that primarily letter-code information is being abstracted from the to-be-fixated parafoveal word. We prefer to interpret this effect as suggesting that lexical-level representations accumulate activation via letter-code information in the parafovea. Thus, when the reader brings the parafoveal word into fixation, there is already some activation for the lexical representations consistent with the first two or three letters of the target word. It is noteworthy that a simple extension of this framework can nicely handle the superadditive interaction between contextual constraint and parafoveal information. Our argument is based on a suggestion by McClelland and O'Regan (1981; see also Balota and Rayner 1983). The notion is that on some trials there is insufficient parafoveal activation for any single lexical representation to stand out from the other candidates. In these situations, all lexical candidates that are consistent with the parafoveal information receive some activation. However, there is no net influence on performance on such trials, because of an inhibitory influence that each partially activated lexical representation exerts on each other one. Likewise, on some trials, contextual constraint produces insufficient lexical activation for any single lexical representation to stand out among the potentially constrained candidates. On these trials, all constrained lexical representations receive some activation, which is again quickly reduced via an intralexical inhibitory mechanism. However, when the two sources of information combine there is sufficient lexical activation for a single representation such that it stands out from the other candidates. In this case, a single lexical representation can dominate the potential candidate set. McClelland and Rumelhart (1981) discussed a similar phenomenon, referred to as the "rich-get-richer" effect.

The important point for the present discussion is that such a framework can account for both the main effects of parafoveal information and contextual constraint, and also for the superadditive interaction between these two variables. The main effects of these variables reflect those trials in which there is sufficient lexical activation (due to contextual constraint and/or to parafoveal information) for a lexical representation to stand out from the other candidates. For the remainder of this chapter, we will be emphasizing the main effect of parafoveal preview and its relationship to lexical access and to movements of the eyes. Again, the parafoveal-preview effect simply reflects those situations in which the lexical representation for the currently fixated word is already activated via its earlier parafoveal preview.

5 Lexical Access and Eye Movements

When a reader has a parafoveal preview of the word to the right of fixation, reading proceeds more efficiently than when no preview is provided. What is the relationship between parafoveal preview, lexical access, and eye movements? In an attempt to be more specific about the relationship between parafoveal-preview effects, lexical access, and eye movements, let us consider the sequence of events that occurs when a reader is fixated on a particular word. From the example shown in figure 2, assume that the reader is fixated on the word *fluent* and that the word *processing* is to the right of fixation. When the reader fixates on *fluent*, visual feature information is encoded at the outset of the fixation and, as indicated earlier, it appears that the initial visual encoding processes takes about 50 msec (Rayner et al. 1981). During this initial encoding, two processes are initiated simultaneously and independently: the reader begins lexical access processes for the fixated word, while at the same time a preliminary target location for the next saccade is computed (Pollatsek and Rayner 1982). This determination of where to look next is based on word-length information, and the computation is generally to send the eyes to the *preferred viewing location* (Rayner 1979) in the next word.

At some point, the processes associated with lexical access for the foveally fixated word (*fluent*) will be completed and attention will shift to the word to the right of fixation (*processing*). Morrison (1984) has suggested that this shift of attention to the word to the right of fixation serves as an impetus or trigger for an eye movement that follows the attention shift in a time-locked manner. As noted, in most cases the saccade will take the reader to the preferred viewing location in the next word; in the example, this would be the letter *o* or *c*. Because of acuity limitations, in most situations the reader will not be able to identify the parafoveal word prior to the saccade. However, the first two or three letters (*p-r-o*) will be identified and coded in an abstract form. After the saccade, the reader will complete the lexical access process. Thus, the preview of the parafoveal word enables the reader to identify that word more quickly than when a preview was not available. The parafoveal preview enables the reader to get a head start into the lexicon. However, should the beginning letters of the parafoveal word change during the saccade (which can only happen in the laboratory, through the use of eye-contingent display-change techniques), the letters at the beginning of the word are reprocessed and the reader does not misread the word (McConkie et al. 1982; Rayner et al. 1980).

In some cases, the reader completely identifies the word to the right of fixation after the attention shift. If identification occurs early enough, the reader can cancel the saccade programmed to the next word and move to word *n* + 1 (as in moving from *processing* to *words*). However, if identification of the word to the right of fixation occurs sufficiently late in the fixation, the reader may not be able to cancel the next saccade. In such cases, one of two things may happen: The reader may move to the word to the right of fixation, but with a very short duration on that word followed immediately by a saccade to the right, or the reader may make a saccade that ends somewhere between the word to the right of fixation and the word after it. Figure 3 shows examples of these scenarios. The idea in each of these examples is that parallel programming of saccades (Becker and Jurgens 1979; Morrison 1984) occurs when the word to the right of fixation is identified and the reader is not able to cancel the saccade already programmed. If the word to the right is identified early enough in the fixation, the reader can cancel the saccade programmed to move to that word. In this case the reader will reprogram the saccade to skip that word. However, if the program for the next saccade has passed the point of no return, the reader can begin programming another saccade while the already programmed saccade is in the process of preparation. In this case the reader might program a very short fixation on the first word (word *n* + 1) followed by a fixation in the normal range on the second word (word *n* + 2). Alternatively, the saccade might land midway between the first and the second word.

These examples demonstrate that there is a close relationship between lexical access processes and when the eyes move. While the arguments may

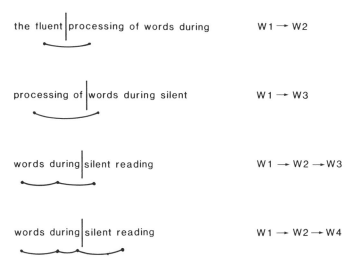

Figure 3
Examples of four different eye-movement patterns. In the top example, W1 was
identified on fixation 1 and W2 on fixation 2. In the second example, W1 and
W2 were both identified on fixation 1 and the eye moved to W3. In the third
example, W1 was identified on fixation 1 and attention shifted to W2. However,
W2 was identified prior to the saccade with a short fixation on W2 followed by
a saccade to W3. In the fourth example, the same sequence occurred as in the
third example; however, fixation 3 was halfway between W2 and W3, with the
next saccade going to W4.

be regarded as somewhat speculative, they do provide a principled account
of (1) why there are fixations in the range of 50–100 msec in reading (which
should not occur, given that the minimal oculomotor reaction time of the
eyes is around 150–175 msec) and (2) why there is some variability in where
readers fixate (most fixations are around the preferred viewing location,
but some are at the ends of words and on the blank spaces between words).
Although the arguments presented above based on Morrison's model
(1984) can thus account for two previously puzzling aspects of eye movements during reading (very short fixations and fixations not near the
preferred viewing location), the model cannot be complete since it does not
explain why a reader would ever fixate a word more than once or why
regressions would ever occur. It thus appears that some additional mechanism is needed, one that can interpose relatively late in a fixation to cancel
and/or alter the decision of where the eye is to move (i.e., to remain on the
current word or to move back). Our suggestion is that "higher-order"
cognitive operations, such as text-comprehension processes, express them-

selves through this additional mechanism. Thus, when the reader encounters some type of comprehension difficulty (garden-path effects, text-integration problems, or when something simply does not make any sense), the normal process is aborted and either the eyes are held in place, or the word is refixated, or a regression is programmed. Of course, if the program to make the next saccade is already too far along, the next fixation ($n + 1$) will then be longer (or there might be an immediate regression launched from fixation $n + 1$). Many studies have demonstrated that words that are difficult to process often have a second fixation on them. In such instances, it appears that the decision to refixate a word can be made later in a fixation than the decision of when to terminate the fixation.

A recent experiment by Pollatsek et al. (1986) provides some evidence concerning refixations on words. They used a boundary technique in which initially presented words or nonwords were replaced by the target word when the saccade crossed the boundary. As in a previous experiment by Rayner (1975), they examined fixation time on a target word as a function of where the reader was fixated on the prior fixation and as a function of the relationship between the initially presented stimulus and the target word. They found that visual similarity of the initially presented stimulus to the target word had an effect on the first fixation duration of the target word when the reader had been fixated close (3–5 characters from the beginning of the target) to the target word, but only had an effect on gaze duration (through the probability of refixating the word) when the reader had been fixated far (9 or more character spaces) from the target word.

Pollatsek et al. argued that these results suggest that refixation decisions are made later than decisions about when to terminate the fixation. The notion is that the visual similarity of the preview to the target word appears to influence the time needed to process the target word. Most of the effect is probably due to the fact that letter information has been extracted from the preview which aids lexical access (Balota et al. 1985; Rayner, McConkie, and Zola 1980). When the preview information is good (i.e., when fixation $n - 1$ is near the target word), lexical access is rapid enough to affect the decision of when to move the eyes. However, when fixation $n - 1$ is further from the target word, poorer preview information will be extracted and lexical access is likely to be slower. Thus, the most plausible explanation for the fact that first fixation duration is not affected when fixation $n - 1$ is at the far distance (in the study of Pollatsek et al.) is that letter information extracted parafoveally from the target location does not speed lexical access sufficiently to be able to beat the decision to move the eyes. The fact that letter information influences the probability of refixating the word at the far distance indicates that some letter information has been acquired, and that this information is unable to influence the decision to terminate the first fixation but is able to influence the later decision of where to fixate next. (It is important to remember here that our operationalization of lexical access is *when* the eyes leave the word, not simply the termination of the first fixation.) The same conclusion follows from an analysis of an experiment by Inhoff and Rayner (1986).

Inhoff and Rayner (1986) varied both the frequency of a target word (holding the number of letters constant) and whether there was a parafoveal preview of the word. They measured both the mean first fixation duration and the mean gaze duration on the target word when it was fixated. The results indicated that word frequency affected both first fixation duration and gaze duration when there was a parafoveal preview of the target word, but affected only gaze duration when there was not a parafoveal preview. This pattern of data is easily explained by making the same two assumptions we used to explain the data of Pollatsek et al.: (1) that lexical access is slower if there is poorer parafoveal information (in this case none) and (2) that the decision to refixate can be made later than the decision of when to terminate the first fixation. Thus, when there is no parafoveal preview, lexical access—even for the high-frequency words—is not fast enough to influence the decision to end the first fixation; however, lexical access for the high-frequency words is fast enough to influence the decision of whether to refixate the word and can affect gaze duration. On the other hand, when there is a parafoveal preview, lexical access for high-frequency words is fast enough to influence both decisions and can therefore affect both measures.

Thus, the experiments of Pollatsek et al. and Inhoff and Rayner suggest that first fixation duration on a word is unlikely to be affected by the time of lexical access unless a healthy dose of parafoveal information has been acquired on the prior fixation. Accordingly, both experiments also suggest that gaze duration may in many cases be a more sensitive measure of processing than first fixation duration, since the gaze duration may reflect processing events later in the first fixation than the duration of the first fixation. The argument also implies that the decision to move the eyes is made before lexical access is complete under conditions in which good parafoveal previews are not obtained. However, in such cases, the reader does not typically leave the word but rather refixates that same word to ensure the completion of the identification process. Further work is needed to determine whether the decision to move the eyes before lexical access is, in some cases, "automatic" and unaffected by ongoing cognitive processes or whether there are processing stages short of full lexical access that trigger the decision to move the eyes ahead in reading.

Conclusions

The major goal of the chapter was to provide a framework for discussing the complex relationship among lexical access, parafoveal processing, and eye movements in reading. In providing a tentative operationalization of lexical access in reading, we have suggested that lexical access is reflected by the decision when to move the eyes from the currently fixated word. Clearly, this is not all that is going on during a fixation on a given word. The data reviewed earlier indicate that readers utilize varying levels of parafoveal information during a given fixation. Moreover, we have argued that whether or not there has been a healthy dose of parafoveal preview on the prior fixation can modulate the eye-movement behavior.

The data reviewed converge nicely on a model of parafoveal processing, lexical access, and eye movements according to which the completion of lexical access on the current word triggers a shift in attention to the parafoveal word to the right of fixation. The work by Morrison suggest that this shift in attention triggers the programming of a saccade to that word. Moreover, it appears that, as the reader is fixating a given word, parafoveal information is accumulating about the to-be-fixated word. The research addressing the type of information that is accumulating indicates that it is primarily abstract letter code information. Thus, parafoveal information utilization facilitates the lexical access process on the next fixated word, thereby influencing both the shift of attention and its accompanying eye-movement process.

Although this sequence of lexical access, attention shift, and eye movement is the most typical sequence in reading, there are exceptions to this normal sequence. These include (1) the abortion of the decision when to leave the currently fixated word because of some disruption in higher-order comprehension processes and (2) sufficient analysis of a parafoveal word that leads to the identification of that word. Although there is little doubt that these exceptions often occur, we believe that, because of the oculomotor processes involved in reading and the temporal characteristics found in normal reading, lexical access of the currently fixated word is the *main* driving force for the decision concerning when to leave a word.

Acknowledgments

The preparation of this chapter was supported by Grant BNS86-09336 from the National Science Foundation. Much of the chapter was written when both of the authors were Fellows at the Netherlands Institute for Advanced Study, and we express our appreciation to that organization. We also would like to thank William Marslen-Wilson and an anonymous reviewer for their very helpful comments on an earlier version of the chapter. We would especially like to acknowledge our collaborations with Sandy Pollatsek and Bob Morrison, both of whom played major roles in the development of many of the ideas presented herein.

References

Balota, D. A., and Rayner, K. 1983. Parafoveal visual information and semantic contextual constraints. *Journal of Experimental Psychology: Human Perception and Performance* 5: 726–738.

Balota, D. A., and Rayner, K. 1989. Word recognition processes in foveal and parafoveal vision: The range of influence of lexical variables. In D. Besner and G. Humphreys (eds.), *Basic Processes in Reading: Visual Word Recognition.* Hillsdale, N.J.: Erlbaum.

Balota, D. A., Pollatsek, A., and Rayner, K. 1985. The interaction of contextual constraints and parafoveal visual information in reading. *Cognitive Psychology* 17: 364–390.

Becker, W., and Jurgens, R. 1979. An analysis of the saccadic system by means of double-step stimuli. *Vision Research* 19: 967–983.

Blanchard, H. E., Pollatsek, A., and Rayner, K. 1988. Parafoveal processing during eye fixations in reading. Manuscript in preparation.

Bradshaw, J. L. 1974. Peripherally presented and unreported words may bias the meaning of a centrally fixated word. *Journal of Experimental Psychology* 103: 1200–1202.

Carroll, P., and Slowiaczek, M. L. 1986. Constraints on semantic priming in reading: A fixation time analysis. *Memory and Cognition* 14: 509–522.

Coeffe, C., and O'Regan, J. K. 1987. Reducing the influence of non-target stimuli on saccade accuracy: Predictability and latency effects. *Vision Research* 27: 227–240.

Dodge, R. 1906. Recent studies in the correlation of eye movement and visual perception. *Psychological Review* 13: 85–92.

Duffy, S. A., Morris, R. K., and Rayner, K. 1988. Lexical ambiguity and fixation and fixation times in reading. *Journal of Memory and Language* 27: 429–447.

Ehrlich, K., and Rayner, K. 1983. Pronoun assignment and semantic integration during reading: Eye movements and immediacy of processing. *Journal of Verbal Learning and Verbal Behavior* 22: 75–87.

Ehrlich, S. F., and Rayner, K. 1981. Contextual effects on word perception and eye movements during reading. *Journal of Verbal Learning and Verbal Behavior* 20: 641–655.

Forster, K. I. 1970. Visual perception of rapidly presented word sequences of varying complexity. *Perception and Psychophysics* 8: 215–221.

Ferreira, F., and Clifton, C. 1986. The independence of syntactic processing. *Journal of Verbal Learning and Verbal Behavior* 25: 75–87.

Frazier, L., and Rayner, K. 1982. Making and correcting errors during sentence comprehension: Eye movements in the analysis of structurally ambiguous sentences. *Cognitive Psychology* 14: 178–210.

Frazier, L., and Rayner, K. 1987. Resolution of syntactic category ambiguities: Eye movements in parsing lexically ambiguous sentences. *Journal of Memory and Language* 26: 505–526.

Hogaboam, T. 1983. Reading patterns in eye movement data. In K. Rayner (ed.), *Eye Movements in Reading: Perceptual and Language Processes*. New York: Academic.

Inhoff, A. W. 1982. Parafoveal word perception: A further case against semantic preprocessing. *Journal of Experimental Psychology: Human Perception and Performance* 8: 137–145.

Inhoff, A. W. 1984. Two stages of word processing during eye fixations in the reading of prose. *Journal of Verbal Learning and Verbal Behavior* 23: 612–624.

Inhoff, A. W. 1987. Lexical access during eye fixations in sentence reading: Effects of word structure. In M. Coltheart (ed.), *Attention and Performance* 12. London: Erlbaum.

Inhoff, A. W., and Rayner, K. 1980. Parafoveal word perception: A case against semantic preprocessing. *Perception and Psychophysics* 27: 457–464.

Inhoff, A. W., and Rayner, K. 1986. Parafoveal word processing during eye fixations in reading. *Perception and Psychophysics* 40: 431–439.

Just, M. A., and Carpenter, P. A. 1980. A theory of reading: From eye fixations to comprehension. *Psychological Review* 87: 329–354.

Kliegl, R., Olson, R. K., and Davidson, B. J. 1982. Regression analyses as a tool for studying reading processes: Comments on Just and Carpenter's eye fixation theory. *Memory and Cognition* 10: 287–296.

Lima, S. D. 1987. Morphological analysis in reading. *Journal of Memory and Language* 26: 84–99.

Lima, S. D., and Inhoff, A. W. 1985. Lexical access during eye fixations in reading: Effects of word-initial letter sequences. *Journal of Experimental Psychology: Human Perception and Performance* 7: 272–285.

McClelland, J. L., and O'Regan, J. K. 1981. Expectations increase the benefit derived from parafoveal visual information in reading words aloud. *Journal of Experimental Psychology: Human Perception and Performance* 7: 634–644.

McClelland, J. L., and Rumelhart, D. E. 1981. An interactive activation model of context effects in letter perception: Part 1. An account of basic findings. *Psychological Review* 88: 375–407.

McConkie, G. W., and Rayner, K. 1975. The span of the effective stimulus in reading. *Perception and Psychophysics* 17: 578–586.

McConkie, G. W., and Rayner, K. 1976. Asymmetry of the perceptual span in reading. *Bulletin of the Psychonomic Society* 8: 365–368.

McConkie, G. W., Underwood, N. R., Zola, D., and Wolverton, G. S. 1985. Some temporal characteristics of processing during reading. *Journal of Experimental Psychology: Human Perception and Performance* 11: 168–186.

McConkie, G. W., and Zola, D. 1979. Is visual information integrated across successive fixations in reading? *Perception and Psychophysics* 25: 221–224.

McConkie, G. W., and Zola, D. 1984. Eye movement control during reading: The effects of word units. In W. Prinz and A. F. Sanders (eds.), *Cognition and Motor Processes*. Berlin: Springer-Verlag.

McConkie, G. W., Zola, D., Blanchard, H. E., and Wolverton, G. S. 1982. Perceiving words during reading: Lack of facilitation from prior peripheral exposure. *Perception and Psychophysics* 32: 271–281.

Morrison, R. E. 1984. Manipulation of stimulus onset delay in reading: Evidence for parallel programming of saccades. *Journal of Experimental Psychology: Human Perception and Performance* 10: 667–682.

Morrison, R. E., and Rayner, K. 1981. Saccade size in reading depends upon character spaces and not visual angle. *Perception and Psychophysics* 30: 395–396.

Morton, J. 1964. The effect of context on the visual duration threshold for words. *British Journal of Psychology* 55: 165–180.

O'Regan, J. K. 1979. Eye guidance in reading: Evidence for the linguistic control hypothesis. *Perception and Psychophysics* 25: 501–509.

O'Regan, J. K. 1981. The convenient viewing position hypothesis. In D. F. Fisher, R. A. Monty, and J. W. Senders (eds.), *Eye Movements: Cognition and Visual Perception*. Hillsdale, N.J.: Erlbaum.

O'Regan, J. K. 1983. Elementary perception and eye movement control processes in reading. In K. Rayner (ed.), *Eye Movements in Reading: Perceptual and Language Processes*. New York: Academic.

O'Regan, J. K., Levy-Schoen, A., Pynte, J., and Brugaillere, B. 1984. Convenient fixation location within isolated words of different lengths and structures. *Journal of Experimental Psychology: Human Perception and Performance* 10: 250–257.

Paap, K. R., and Newsome, S. L. 1981. Parafoveal information is not sufficient to produce semantic or visual priming. *Perception and Psychophysics* 29: 457–466.

Paap, K. R., Newsome, S. L., McDonald, J. E., and Schvaneveldt, R. W. 1982. An activation-verification model for letter and word recognition: The word superiority effect. *Psychological Review* 89: 573–594.

Pollatsek, A., and Rayner, K. 1982. Eye movement control in reading: The role of word boundaries. *Journal of Experimental Psychology: Human Perception and Performance* 8: 817–833.

Pollatsek, A., Rayner, K., and Balota, D. A. 1986. Inferences about eye movement control from the perceptual span in reading. *Perception and Psychophysics* 40: 123–130.

Potter, M. C., Kroll, J. F., and Harris, C. 1980. Comprehension and memory in rapid, sequential reading. In R. S. Nickerson (ed.), *Attention and Performance 8.* Hillsdale, N.J.: Erlbaum.

Rayner, K. 1975. The perceptual span and peripheral cues in reading. *Cognitive Psychology* 7: 65–81.

Rayner, K. 1977. Visual attention in reading: Eye movements reflect cognitive processes. *Memory and Cognition* 4: 443–448.

Rayner, K. 1978a. Eye movements in reading and information processing. *Psychological Bulletin* 85: 618–660.

Rayner, K. 1978b. Foveal and parafoveal cues in reading. In J. Requin (ed.), *Attention and Performance 7.* Hillsdale, N.J.: Erlbaum.

Rayner, K. 1979. Eye guidance in reading: Fixation locations within words. *Perception* 8: 21–30.

Rayner, K. 1986. Eye movements and the perceptual span in beginning and skilled readers. *Journal of Experimental Child Psychology* 41: 211–236.

Rayner, K., Balota, D. A., and Pollatsek, A. 1986. Against parafoveal semantic preprocessing during eye fixations in reading. *Canadian Journal of Psychology* 40: 473–483.

Rayner, K., and Bertera, J. H. 1979. Reading without a fovea. *Science* 206: 468–469.

Rayner, K., Carlson, M., and Frazier, L. 1983. The interaction of syntax and semantics during sentence processing: Eye movements in the analysis of semantically biased sentences. *Journal of Verbal Learning and Verbal Behavior* 22: 358–374.

Rayner, K., and Duffy, S. A. 1986. Lexical complexity and fixation times in reading: Effects of word frequency, verb complexity, and lexical ambiguity. *Memory and Cognition* 14: 191–201.

Rayner, K., and Frazier, L. 1987. Parsing temporarily ambiguous compliments. *Quarterly Journal of Experimental Psychology* 39A: 657–673.

Rayner, K., Inhoff, A. W., Morrison, R. E., Slowiaczek, M. L., and Bertera, J. H. 1981. Masking of foveal and parafoveal vision during eye fixations in reading. *Journal of Experimental Psychology: Human Perception and Performance* 7: 167–179.

Rayner, K., and McConkie, G. W. 1976. What guides a reader's eye movements? *Vision Research* 16: 829–837.

Rayner, K., McConkie, G. W., and Ehrlich, S. F. 1978. Eye movements and integrating information across fixations. *Journal of Experimental Psychology: Human Perception and Performance* 4: 529–544.

Rayner, K., McConkie, G. W., and Zola, D. 1980. Integrating information across eye movements. *Cognitive Psychology* 12: 206–226.

Rayner, K., and Pollatsek, A. 1981. Eye movement control during reading: Evidence for direct control. *Quarterly Journal of Experimental Psychology* 33A: 351–373.

Rayner, K., and Pollatsek, A. 1987. Eye movements in reading: A tutorial review. In M. Coltheart (ed.), *Attention and Performance 12*. London: Erlbaum.

Rayner, K., Slowiaczek, M. L., Clifton, C., and Bertera, J. H. 1983. Latency of sequential eye movements: Implications for reading. *Journal of Experimental Psychology: Human Perception and Performance* 9: 912–922.

Rayner, K., Well, A. D., and Pollatsek, A. 1980. Asymmetry of the effective visual field in reading. *Perception and Psychophysics* 27: 537–544.

Rayner, K., Well, A. D., Pollatsek, A., and Bertera, J. H. 1982. The availability of useful information to the right of fixation in reading. *Perception and Psychophysics* 31: 537–550.

Salthouse, T. A., and Ellis, C. L. 1980. Determinants of eye fixation duration. *American Journal of Psychology* 93: 207–234.

Schubert, R. E., and Eimas, P. D. 1977. Effects of context on the classification of words and nonwords. *Journal of Experimental Psychology: Human Perception and Performance* 3: 27–36.

Schustack, M. W., Ehrlich, S. F., and Rayner, K. 1987. The complexity of contextual facilitation in reading: Local and global influences. *Journal of Memory and Language* 26: 322–340.

Stanovich, K. E., and West, R. F. 1979. Mechanisms of sentence context effects in reading: Automatic activation and conscious attention. *Memory and Cognition* 7: 77–85.

Stanovich, K. E., and West, R. F. 1983. The generalizability of context effects on word recognition: A reconsideration of the roles of parafoveal priming and sentence context. *Memory and Cognition* 11: 49–58.

Tulving, E., and Gold, C. 1963. Stimulus information and contextual information as determinants of tachistoscopic recognition of words. *Journal of Experimental Psychology* 66: 319–327.

Underwood, G. 1980. Attention and the non-selective lexical access of ambiguous words. *Canadian Journal of Psychology* 34: 72–76.

Underwood, G. 1981. Lexical recognition of embedded unattended words: Some implications for the reading process. *Acta Psychologica* 47: 267–283.

Wolverton, G. S., and Zola, D. 1983. The temporal characteristics of visual information extraction during reading. In K. Rayner (ed.), *Eye Movements in Reading: Perceptual and Language Processes*. New York: Academic.

Zola, D. 1984. Redundancy and word perception during reading. *Perception and Psychophysics* 36: 277–284.

Chapter 9

| Reading and the Mental Lexicon: On the Uptake of Visual Information | Derek Besner and James C. Johnston |

How do experienced adult readers identify words? The answer to this question may appear so obvious to the intelligent layman that research is beside the point. As one of our physicist colleagues put it, "Well, you just see the word, and then you know it." There is nothing wrong with this answer as far as it goes; the catch is that we would like to understand how the "seeing" and the "knowing" are accomplished. This goal has challenged psychologists, educators, and neuropsychologists since Cattell (1886), but no consensus has yet emerged. A variety of theoretical controversies have arisen, and a fairly complete discussion is now a matter for entire books (e.g. Henderson 1982). In this chapter we focus on a small part of the larger question, which we believe is nevertheless quite fundamental: What is the nature of the visual information that observers use when reading words? As we shall see, even this limited inquiry will require us to consider in some detail how information is represented in the mental lexicon and how that information can be accessed.

In what follows we briefly review the types of visual information that might plausibly be used to identify words. We focus on the question of whether the skilled adult reader relies solely upon preliminary letter identification or also makes use of visual cues for units larger than letters (supra-letter cues) or units other than letters. We review a number of lines of evidence that have been offered in support of the use of supra-letter cues, as well as evidence for the claim that word recognition relies only upon preliminary letter identification. We then report four new experiments which attempt to further clarify the question. Finally, we try to make sense out of the complicated pattern of results in the literature by proposing the framework of a process model. According to this model, different tasks elicit different mixtures of processing paths, which are in turn differentially influenced by various types of visual information.

1   The Visual Information Used to Identify Words: Three Views

The types of visual information that might be used in word identification can be divided into three classes. First, there is the outline (or envelope) of the shape of a word (Cattell 1886; Crowder 1982; Erdmann and Dodge 1898; Monk and Hulme 1983; Haber and Haber 1981; Haber, Haber, and Furlin 1983). Second, there is the entire set of visual features in a word, which collectively constitute a word-specific visual pattern or WSVP. Variants of this second class have been proposed by Wheeler (1970), Rumelhart and Siple (1974), Coltheart and Freeman (1974), Rudnicky and Kolers (1984), Masson (1986), Howard (1987), and Smith (1969). Third, there is the sequence of the identities of the component letters in a word (Adams 1979; McClelland 1976; Rumelhart and McClelland 1982; Johnston 1981). It is clear that the first two types of information depend to a considerable degree on the case and the font used to display a word. Recent advocates of the third type of information have argued that what matters are *abstract* letter identities—i.e., representations that are indifferent to the specific case or font (Allport 1979; Saffran 1980; Rayner et al. 1980; Coltheart 1981; Evett and Humphreys 1981; Besner 1983; Besner et al. 1984; Besner and McCann 1987; Paap, Newsome, and Noel 1984; Henderson 1982).

The use of word-shape cues or WSVPs cannot be *necessary* for word identification, because words displayed in formats that destroy these cues (e.g. cAsE alternation or vertical presentation) can still be read rather easily (Coltheart and Freeman 1974). Nevertheless, the different types of visual information that could be utilized are not mutually exclusive. Thus it is possible that, when reading normally oriented lower-case text (hereafter *normal text*), readers rely upon preliminary letter identification in *conjunction* with outline shape and/or WSVPs. It is even logically possible that, when reading normal text, people abandon preliminary letter identification and rely solely upon word shape and/or WSVPs.

2   Outline Word Shape

Since the literature on the possible contribution of outline word shape to word identification has been cogently reviewed by Henderson (1982) and Paap et al. (1984), we will only touch upon the highlights here. The basic argument is that the evidence advanced for use of outline-shape cues is open to alternative explanation in terms of letter-level processes, whereas the best recent direct investigations have not provided any evidence for the use of word shape.

The observation that text can be read slightly more quickly in lower case than in upper case is often cited as evidence for the use of outline-shape information, since words written entirely in upper case do not have distinctive outlines. This observation can also be explained, however, by the hypothesis that lower-case letters in a word are more discriminable than upper-case letters, or by the hypothesis that readers have more practice reading in lower case.

The observation that proofreading errors are more numerous when word shape is preserved by a substitute letter (e.g. tesf for test) rather than altered by it (e.g. tesc for test) has often been used as evidence for a role of outline shape (Haber and Schindler 1981; Monk and Hulme 1983). This interpretation is problematic because a substitute letter that misspells a word but preserves word shape is often more confusable (in terms of letter features) with the letter it replaces than a substitute that alters word shape. An experiment by Paap et al. (1984) that varied both letter confusability and word shape found that all the apparent effects of word shape were due to the confounding factor of letter confusability.

In another approach, Haber, Haber, and Furlin (1983) had subjects read short passages in which one or two lines of computer-generated text terminated randomly in the middle of a sentence. Subjects were instructed to guess the next word on the basis of the prior context alone, or with various additional cues. Haber et al. found that guessing improved by about 20 percent when information about word length and word shape was provided. The main problem in interpreting this result is that the subjects were allowed essentially unlimited time to generate a guess; it is not clear what the relationship is between this type of guessing and word identification at normal reading speeds. It is also possible that the subjects could have generated a word hypothesis from previous context alone and then matched it against the subsequent shape information, rather than using the shape information to constrain the guess.

Paap et al. (1984) manipulated the number of words associated with a particular outline shape. If word shape makes a contribution to word identification, it would seem that unique shapes should provide much better cues than shapes that are common to many words. Paap et al. found that shape frequency made no contribution to word identification in either tachistoscopic-report or lexical-decision experiments. In a third experiment designed to maximize the possibility that word shape would be used, Paap et al. had subjects make lexical decisions to stimuli that were preceded by either a related or an unrelated single-word context. If expectations about forthcoming stimuli include specifications of their shapes, then words with rare shapes ought to be identified faster than words with common shapes. No effect of shape frequency was found in either the related or unrelated priming conditions.

It seems to us that the best conclusion at the present time is that there is no convincing evidence that word shape plays any role in word identification under conditions approximating normal reading by adults.

3   Word-Specific Visual Pattern Information

The idea that word identification is mediated by what we are calling a word-specific visual pattern is actually quite simple. It amounts to the claim that a word can be identified in the same way as other simpler forms—that is, on the basis of its component visual features. These features might simply be the set of all component individual strokes in the proper arrangement (Smith 1969), or they might be more exotic aspects, such as junctions between strokes, the shape of spaces between letters (Wheeler 1970), or any other property of the pattern. What is critical for our purposes is that the set of these features is used "directly" to access word identities, rather than accessing letter identities as an intermediary.

The best evidence that WSVPs might be *sufficient* to identify words comes from the neuropsychological literature. Howard (1987) describes a patient (T.M.) with an acquired dyslexia consequent to a cerebral vascular accident. T.M. cannot orally read nonwords, can name virtually no letters (1/20), and is extremely poor at pointing to a letter from four visually displayed alternatives when the target letter is presented auditorily (7/20). He is also very poor at cross-case matching of single letters (e.g. A/a-yes; A/r-no). Howard concludes that T.M.'s letter-identification abilities are very poor indeed.

In contrast, T.M.'s oral reading of single words, while far from perfect, seems to exceed what might be expected if word identification depended only upon preliminary letter recognition (32 percent of a set of 1,002 words were correctly read, and a further subset of errors were semantically related to the target). Further experiments found that inserting plus signs between letters (e.g. p + 1 + u + s) drastically impaired T.M.'s oral reading of single words (4 percent correct, vs. the 32 percent with normal presentation). Case alternation also impaired performance, although less severely (14 percent correct). T.M. was also completely unable to correctly read abbreviations.

His error responses were, however, semantically related to the target on 14 of 30 trials when the stimulus was displayed in familiar visual format (FBI; RSPCA), versus 1 of 30 trials when the stimulus was visually unfamiliar (fbi; rspca).

Howard suggests that T.M. has no abstract knowledge of the identity of component parts of words (i.e., letters). He concludes that "as far as it is possible to be an ideographic reader of an alphabetic script, T.M. is one; it appears that he recognizes words with no knowledge of their component letters." Howard also argues that T.M. does not make use of contour information (outline shape, in our terms), since he can identify words printed in all upper-case letters just as well as words printed entirely in lower case. It appears that T.M. must, by elimination, identify words (albeit not very well) on the basis of what we have called their WSVPs.

Howard's study of T.M. seems to provide support for the hypothesis that WSVPs are used in word identification. Two reservations are in order, however. The first reservation is that Howard may have underplayed the usefulness of T.M.'s residual letter-identification skills for word identification. If T.M. were reading on the basis of WSVPs with *no* contribution from letter identification, then it would be expected that his oral reading would drop to zero when words were either case-alternated or multilated by intermingled plus signs. This did not happen; with both of these manipulations, T.M.'s reading on various sets of stimuli was well above the floor (17 percent, table 7; 14 percent, table 8; 47 percent, table 9). The second reservation is that, even if it is granted that these results mean that T.M. identifies words on the basis of WSVPs, they do not compel the conclusion that normal readers do so. The critical fact is that T.M. is not merely slow in his oral reading but *excruciatingly* slow. In one of the experiments, his mean time to name individual words (varying in length from 3 to 9 letters) was over 3 seconds. Normal readers can identify a word in a fraction of a second. Surely the mechanism used by normal readers ordinarily generates a result long before the mechanism used by T.M. could get very far.[1]

Many of the problems with the work reviewed so far can be avoided by performing a different type of experiment: one in which the identification of words by normal subjects is tested under conditions where WSVPs cannot be used. A number of studies adopting this logic in conjunction with a great variety of paradigms—including tachistoscopic report, lexical-decision latency, same-different latency, and naming latency—have been reported. The results obtained so far from these different paradigms conflict in a rather complex way. In the remainder of the present chapter we will describe these results, report some new experiments of our own, and try to reconcile the various results using a single coherent model framework.

Death by Tachistoscope

Coltheart and Freeman (1974) performed one of the earliest experiments in which normal readers were tested under conditions that prevented the use of WSVPs. They found that reports of words from a brief display were impaired when the component letters appeared in alternating cases rather than entirely in either upper or lower case. Coltheart and Freeman concluded that there exist features larger than single letters which contribute to word identification. This conclusion was based on the implicit assumption that case alternation must disrupt processing at the level of word identification *per se*. It is possible, however, that case alternation disrupts the preliminary letter-identification process. Exactly how this might occur is open to speculation. Among the plausible possibilities are that case alternation requires frequent swapping of letter-identification routines and that it simply requires the consideration of a greater number of alternative letter shapes. Whatever the precise mechanism suspected, we need a way to control for the effects of case alternation on preliminary letter identification. The most straightforward control is to measure how much impairment, if any, case alternation produces with nonword letter strings. If case alternation only disrupts the use of WSVPs in word identification, performance should be impaired only with words and not with nonwords. If, on the other hand, case alternation has its effects at the letter level, we might expect both words and nonwords to be impaired by about the same amount. These comparisons, although easy to propose, are tricky to carry out, because the absolute levels of performance on words and nonwords are very different; under these circumstances one can ask what constitutes an equal degree of impairment. The results of the two most thorough studies with this design (McClelland 1976; Adams 1979) make it clear that nonword processing is, in fact, substantially disrupted by case alternation (except, possibly, in McClelland's study, at levels of nonword performance that are so low that multiple letters are rarely seen correctly on a trial). Adams (1979) argues from her data that words and nonwords are actually *equally* impaired, supporting the conclusion that WSVPs are not used in word identification at all. Given the problems inherent in assessing the additivity of factor effects when accuracy is the dependent variable, we are skeptical about the strength of this conclusion. It does seem clear to us, however, that these results totally undermine the force of Coltheart and

Freeman's claim to have positive evidence *supporting* the use of WSVPs in word identification.

Same-Different Comparisons and Lexical Decision

The results from simultaneous same-different matching tasks provide a different picture. A number of experimenters have found that, at least for "same" responses, words are more impaired by case alternation than are nonwords (Pollatsek et al. 1975; Bruder 1978; Taylor et al. 1977). Results from the lexical-decision task show a similar pattern; Besner (1983, experiment 1) and Besner and McCann (1987, experiment 1) found that case alternation impaired performance more with words than with nonwords. On the face of it, these results appear to support the hypothesis that WSVPs play a role in visual word recognition.

A potential problem with both same-different tasks and lexical-decision tasks is that they are yes-no tasks, requiring subjects to make judgments along a "goodness" axis (i.e., one responds "same" or "word" to the "good" items and "different" or "nonword" to the "bad" items). Tasks of this kind have been shown in a number of cases to be sensitive to any contaminating properties that also fall along a "goodness" axis (Balota and Chumbley 1984). For instance, it has been found that "yes" judgments that a letter string is a word (a "good" property) are slowed if the word forms an anomalous sentence (a "bad" property). Besner and his colleagues (Besner 1983, 1984; Besner, Davelaar, Alcott, and Parry 1984; Besner and McCann 1987) have specifically suggested that the visual familiarity of letter sequences may have a "goodness" dimension (i.e., same-case words look "good"; case-alternating strings do not), which contaminates word-nonword and same-different judgments.[2] The problem for theories of word identification is that the process of visual-familiarity discrimination need not be associated with the actual *identification* of any particular word; it can be likened instead to the common experience of recognizing a face as familiar (recognition memory) without retrieving who the person is. Thus, the evidence that WSVPs influence "yes" response latencies in lexical-decision tasks and same-different tasks need not mean that WSVPs have an input into word identification *per se*. Instead, WSVPs might be activating a sense of the familiarity of the item, and thereby facilitating the (positive) response to words. On the basis of the discussion so far, it may appear that we are giving this reservation more weight than it deserves, but it turns out to be critical for making sense of the larger pattern of evidence across a variety of tasks.

Naming

In order to bypass these problem, we can pick a different task which does not require yes-no judgments. One appealing choice is the *naming-latency task*, in which subjects read aloud single words and in which the time until voice onset is the dependent variable. This task requires subjects to produce a nonarbitrary, natural, well-learned response. Since a specific response is required for each word rather than a binary classification response, there is no reason to suspect contamination from implicit visual-familiarity judgments.[3] Thus, if we were to find in the naming task that words are more impaired by case alternation than nonwords, we would be much more confident that WSVPs play a role in word identification. Besner (1983, experiment 2) carried out such an experiment; he found, however, that case alternation did not impair words more than nonwords, despite reliable main effects of both lexical status and case alternation. This result, unlike the data from the same-different tasks and lexical-decision tasks, fails to support the predictions that arise from the hypothesis that WSVPs are used in word identification.

The question we now wish to address is whether the negative implications of this line of evidence can be strengthened. The fact that the result in question is essentially a null result is a special cause for concern; perhaps we are only dealing with a classic type 2 error—failing to reject an incorrect null hypothesis. In order to address this issue we attempted to replicate the essentials of Besner's (1983) experiment. To improve sensitivity, more items were included (32 per condition, versus 16 in the original experiment), and the letter strings were, on average, slightly longer. The results from this experiment are shown in table 1. Clearly, the results support Besner's conclusions.

Not only is the effect of case alternation not bigger for words than for nonwords, as is predicted by the WSVP hypothesis; it is significantly smaller ($p < .01$). For present purposes what is important is that the 95 percent confidence interval does not leave room for a true case-alternation

Table 1
Reaction times (RT) and error rates (%E) to name words and nonwords in experiment 1 ($n = 32$).

	Lower case		Case alternated	
	RT	%E	RT	%E
Words	484	2.1	528	6.2
Nonwords	562	10.8	648	23.8

effect that is larger for words. The obtained *smaller* effect of case alternation for words than for nonwords is not entirely anomalous. It forms a consistent pattern with the recent finding that, in the naming-latency task, case alternation also has a smaller effect for high-frequency words than for low-frequency words (Besner et al. 1984; Besner and McCann 1987). Possible explanations for both these results are discussed in more detail later.

If naming latency is the appropriate task with which to assess the WSVP hypothesis, then under the conditions we have been testing there is no evidence that readers use such information. At least one other caveat needs to be dealt with, however. In both the present experiment and the one by Besner (1983), subjects were tested under mixed list conditions such that they did not know from one trial to another whether the next stimulus would be a word or a nonword, and whether it would be in lower case or in mixed cases. The present design included half nonwords and half mixed-case stimuli, so only 1/4 of the trials consisted of words written in lower case. Perhaps under these conditions there was insufficient payoff, on the average, for subjects to bother trying to use WSVPs for word identification. Preliminary letter identification, in contrast, was usable on all trials, and so may have been favored under mixed-list conditions. This hypothesis is based upon the assumption that people have some strategic control over the word-identification process. The obvious test way to test this hypothesis is to compare the effects of case alternation under blocked and mixed conditions. If WSVPs are used only under favorable conditions, then naming latencies to words printed in lower case should be faster with blocked presentation than with mixed. We carried out a reasonably powerful experiment (32 subjects with 32 observations per condition) with this design; results are shown in table 2. The data are remarkably clear: Blocked and mixed conditions produced virtually identical results. The absence of a significant effect of blocking or mixing stimuli means that, at least in the present case, we do not have to worry about strategic control over the use of WSVPs in word identification.

Table 2
Reaction times (RT) and error rates (%E) to name words in experiment 2 ($n = 32$).

	Lower case		Case alternated	
	RT	%E	RT	%E
Blocked	497	0.78	554	2.1
Randomized	498	0.28	550	2.3

Table 3
Reaction times (RT) and error rates (%E) to name words in experiment 3
($n = 64$).

	Lower case		Case alternated	
	RT	%E	RT	%E
Associated	510	0.26	526	1.2
Unassociated	531	0.78	557	1.4

4   The Use of Context

So far, in experiments with isolated words, we have failed to find evidence for the use of WSVPs. Is it possible that WSVPs might nevertheless be used to identify words in connected prose? Perhaps WSVPs cannot be used to good advantage when all possible word candidates must be considered but can be used successfully when context permits the reader to generate expectations for upcoming words. Such context-generated expectations are presumably the basis for whatever effects sentence context has on word processing. It is still hotly debated, however, whether sentence context ever directly affects the process by which words are identified from visual information, or whether it only has an influence after lexical access has been completed (see Seidenberg 1985, Becker 1985, and Norris 1986 for different perspectives). In the absence of any resolution of this issue, it remains possible that, when sufficient context is available, WSVPs facilitate word identification. In testing this possibility, it seemed desirable to use a context manipulation that provided at least as much information as a typical sentence context. We chose to use single-word associative priming, with a relatively long stimulus-onset asynchrony (SOA) between prime and target (1,250 msec). Under these conditions there is evidence suggesting that priming might influence lexical access (Meyer et al. 1975). If substantial use of WSVPs occurs only when word-specific expectations can be generated (e.g. with long-SOA priming), then case alternation should be more disruptive under these conditions. Thus, we would expect case alternation to reduce the magnitude of the priming effect. Thirty-two subjects served in a naming-latency experiment in which the subject named single target words preceded by related or unrelated priming words. There were 32 observations per subject per condition. Half the stimuli, chosen randomly, appeared in lower case; the other half appeared in case-alternated form. The results of this experiment can be seen in table 3. A significant interaction was found, but it was in the direction opposite to that predicted by

Table 4
Reaction times (RT) and error rates (%E) to name words in experiment 4
($n = 32$).

	Lower case		Case alternated	
	RT	%E	RT	%E
Associated	485	0.29	503	0.29
Neutral	523	0.29	562	1.2

the WSVP hypothesis—the priming effect (related prime versus unrelated prime) was significantly larger for case-alternated stimuli, not smaller.

Not wanting to give up too easily, we tried one final experiment that attempted to maximize the likelihood that the subjects would actually use the prime word to generate word expectations and test these expectations using WSVPs. To maximize the incentive to use the primes, on unassociated trials we used a neutral prime (consisting of asterisks) instead of an unrelated word as in the previous experiment; thus, all prime words were now valid primes. To further increase the incentive to use WSVPs, we also now blocked trials by stimulus format (lower case versus case alternation); thus, on blocks with all lower-case stimuli, subjects could reply on a predictable relation between word candidates and WSVPs. The stimulus set and the procedure were otherwise the same. The results of this experiment can be seen in table 4. Once again we obtained a significant interaction in the wrong direction for the WSVP hypothesis—the priming effect was larger with case alternation, not smaller.

5 General Discussion

The naming-latency experiments reported here and in Besner 1983 failed to turn up any evidence for the use of WSVPs in word identification. We have come up emptyhanded, in spite of having deliberately explored circumstances which we hoped might be most favorable to the hypothesis. Still, the history of psychology is replete with premature rejections of promising hypotheses. The results of any one line of research are necessarily open to question, and, as we shall argue below, the naming-latency task we used is not without its pitfalls. There are also numerous loose ends that remain to be explained. In the remainder of the discussion we will sketch the framework of a model that provides an integrated account of the effects of case alternation on word identification.

The following are the most important phenomena which we believe need to be handled by an integrated account:

• in the simultaneous same-different matching task, a larger effect of case alternation on "same" responses to words than to nonwords (Bruder 1978; Pollatsek et al. 1975; Taylor et al. 1977)

• in the lexical-decision task, a larger effect of case alternation on words than on nonwords (Besner 1983, experiment 1; Besner and McCann 1987, experiment 1)

• in the lexical-decision task, equal effects of case alternation on high- and low-frequency words (Besner and McCann 1987, experiment 1)

• in the naming-latency task, a larger effect of case alternation for nonwords than for words (experiment 1)

• in the naming-latency task, a larger effect of case alternation for low-frequency words than for high-frequency words (Besner et al. 1984; Besner and McCann 1987, experiment 2)

• in the naming-latency task, a bigger effect of case alternation for unassociated words than for associated words (experiments 3 and 4).

6 The Processing Model

The processing model we propose is shown in figure 1. The kernel of the diagram consists of processing routes 1, 2 and 3. The fate of the WSVP

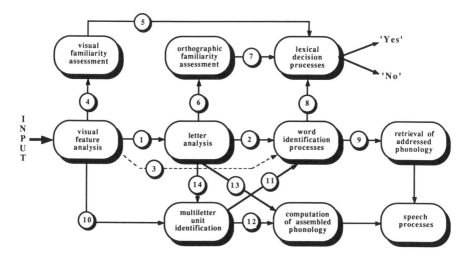

Figure 1
A processing model for aspects of visual word recognition, identification, and production.

hypothesis depends upon whether there is any substantial use of route 3. Routes 8 and 9 are shown to acknowledge that further processing is necessary for, respectively, making lexical decisions and retrieving the stored pronunciations of words (addressed phonology; see Patterson 1982). In principle, route 8 only needs to transmit whether contact with some lexical entry has been made; the particular entry activated need not be specified. Route 9, in contrast, must include information specific to the particular word that has been identified.

The processing path for familiarity judgments through route 4 and route 5 has previously been hypothesized by Besner and his colleagues (Besner 1980, 1983, 1984; Besner et al. 1984; Besner and McCann 1987). The key assumption is that there exists a system capable of *recognizing* a pattern, after assessing the pattern's degree of familiarity, without *identifying* it— that is, without retrieving what the pattern is, or even a pointer to that information. Such a mechanism might underlie the sense one gets of having seen a person before, but not knowing who the person is. Besner and colleagues have argued that such a mechanism may be activated by the *visual* familiarity of words, contributing a strong bias via route 5 toward a "yes" response in the lexical-decision task, and a "same" response in the same-different task. Route 6 is shown to acknowledge the possibility that a familiarity mechanism might also be activated by letter-level codes (Balota and Chumbley 1984).

Routes 10, 12, and 13 show the path for naming letter strings by what has been called the *assembled* route (Patterson 1982). Such a path is needed to provide an account of how people can pronounce nonwords with English-like structure. While it is not logically necessary for assembled pronunciations to be built upon the visual detection of multi-letter units, we think that this possibility is highly plausible. Detection of multi-letter units is especially likely for consonant clusters, like "ch" and "sh", that map onto a single phoneme (Pring, 1981); more generally, use of such units would help to avoid the co-articulation problems that make it difficult to implement spelling-to-sound rules on a letter-by-letter basis. Route 14 is shown to acknowledge the possibility that multi-letter units may sometimes be identified on the basis of letter codes rather than directly from features. Route 11 acknowledges the possibility that multi-letter units may some-times contribute directly to word identification, although McClelland and Johnston (1977) and Johnston (1978), among others, have failed to find evidence for this route.

In order to explain the phenomena at issue, we believe that it is sufficient to assume that case alternation affects three routes that tap the output of feature analysis: routes 1, 4 and 10. We will try to show that there is no need to invoke the disputed route 3, which links feature analysis directly to word identification. Clearly, case alternation should be expected theoretically to disrupt route 4 (to visual familiarity assessment) and route 10 (multi-letter unit detection), because they involve identifying the visual features of familiar units larger than a single letter. Since people have little or no experience with case-alternated stimuli, the familiarity of these units has to be reduced. In instances where upper-case and lower-case letters differ substantially in their features (e.g., e-E, g-G, or r-R), the reduction in familiarity of supra-letter features should be substantial. Even in other instances considerable disruption could be caused by the size mismatch, by the associated use of different spatial-frequency bands (i.e., more use of high spatial-frequency bands for lower-case letters), or by the distortion of features such as the shape of between-letter spaces (Wheeler 1970).

The logic by which case alternation is assumed to disrupt routes 4 and 10 is the same logic by which we were led to test whether case alternation would disrupt route 3: Whenever familiar units larger than a single letter are identified directly from visual features, case alternation should be disruptive. We do not wish to challenge the assumption that if route 3 were used it would also be disrupted by case alternation; instead we will argue that the observed phenomena can be explained without assuming that route 3 is used.

It is not so clear on *a priori* grounds whether case alternation should impede route 1. Logically, the identification of single letters does not depend on patterns of visual information extending across letters. On the other hand, there are various reasons why case alternation might slow down the process of identifying single letters, as Paap et al. (1984) have discussed. One simple reason is that twice as many patterns need to be considered. Another possible reason could be decreased psychophysical distinctiveness of lower-case letters because of increased lateral masking against a background of larger upper-case characters. (It would be interesting to know whether a simple increase in the spacing between letters would decrease the size of the case-alternation effect.). Still another possibility is a loss of distinctiveness of ascenders and descenders in lower-case letters because of the presence of numerous straight vertical lines in upper-case letters. We do not feel that any of these particular ways of motivating a case-alternation effect on route 1 is overwhelmingly compelling. On the other hand, the main effect of case alternation is typically not very large, and the residue not attributable to routes 4 and 10 may be quite small indeed. In any event, it turns out that the assumption that route 1 is harmed by case alternation is particularly helpful in explaining the phenomena at issue.

7   Explaining the Phenomena

Before getting to the detailed account of the six phenomena listed above, let us sketch the outline of the argument. The key assumption we make is that none of the tasks used so far provides a pure measure of word identification. We argue that the same-different task and the lexical-decision task are contaminated by effects of the familiarity-assessment mechanism (which recognizes words without identifying them), whereas the naming task is contaminated by effects of the assembled-pronunciation mechanism (which can pronounce *regular* words without having identified them). Since we argue that case alternation affects both the familiarity-assessment mechanism (via route 4) and the assembled-pronunciation mechanism (via route 10), each attempt to measure the effects of case alternation on word identification is contaminated by at least one extraneous processing path. We argue that, after adjustment for the effects of these contaminating paths, the only residual effect of case alternation is to slow letter analysis via route 1, with a concomitant slowing of the arrival of letter identities downstream at the word-identification mechanism via route 2. We therefore conclude that all observed effects of case alternation can be explained without recourse to the assumption that WSVPs mediate word identification via route 3.

We turn now to a detailed account of the six phenomena listed above.

The Same-Different Task: Word-Nonword Differences

We need to explain the finding that "same" responses to matching words are more affected by case alternation than are "same" responses to matching nonwords. This phenomena, by itself, is consistent with the use of WSVPs. Our alternative explanation depends upon the idea that the same-different task, like many other yes-no binary judgment tasks, is subject to contamination from other stimulus dimensions with unavoidable positive or negative associations. Such arguments have become commonplace in recent years. For instance, Besner (1984) has shown that contamination of this general form occurs for the same-different task in particular. The contaminating property was, in fact, familiarity, which is just the property that distinguishes words from nonwords. For present purposes we need to assume that familiarity assessment can also be based upon visual features (via route 4) rather than solely upon letter identities (via route 6). Besner's

(1984) experiment's showed that interference due to familiarity of items like FBI was specific to the upper-case form in which such items usually appear. Thus, Besner's results support our claim that route 4 provides for a source of case-alternation effects that is stronger for words than for nonwords.

The Lexical-Decision Task: Word-Nonword Differences

A second finding that would appear to support the use of WSVPs is that case alternation has a bigger effect on lexical-decision responses for words than for nonwords (Besner 1983; Besner and McCann 1987).

According to the WSVP hypothesis, this effect of case alternation is mediated by route 3. We prefer the assumption that most of the difference is due to the effects of case alternation on the familiarity assessment process via route 4. Because words are familiar and nonwords are not, words should produce a substantial output from the familiarity assessment mechanism, facilitating "word" responses. The assumption that case alternation disrupts route 4 thus produces a bigger case-alternation effect for words than for nonwords.

The Lexical-Decision Task: Word-Frequency Effects

A finding that appears perplexing for the WSVP hypothesis is that in the lexical-decision task, word frequency and case alternation can have approximately additive effects (Besner and McCann 1987; Fredriksen 1978). One might have thought that people would be most able to use route 3 for highly familiar words, whose visual patterns had been learned (P. A. Kolers, personal communication, 1984). This line of reasoning would lead naturally to the expectation that high-frequency words would be more impaired by case alternation that low-frequency words. (We will call this a pattern of underadditivity, since the added time for mixed-case plus low-frequency is less than the sum of the two separate effects.) Similar reasoning would appear to make sense for the effects of case alternation on the familiarity-assessment mechanism. High-frequency words are the ones that have the highest familiarity, so they are the ones for which case alternation should produce the biggest drop in assessed familiarity. We assume that route 4 is, in fact, used, and that, as this argument implies, the slowdown in its functioning should be underadditive with word frequency.

We now need to examine whether any interaction of case alternation and word frequency can be expected along the "main line" to word identification via identification of component letters (routes 1 and 2). Our processing framework assumes that case alternation slows letter analysis (via route 1), leading necessarily to a slowing in the arrival of letter identities to the

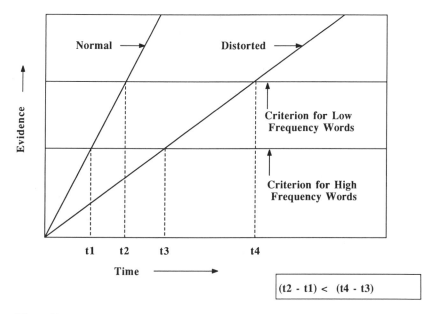

Figure 2
Evidence collection over time as a function of word frequency and format.

word-identification process (via route 2). At this point in the argument, we need to specify in slightly greater detail how the word-identification process works.[4] We assume that information about possible word identities accumulates over time; figure 2 shows information for a particular word accumulating at a linear rate (a simple first-order assumption that is not unreasonable as an approximation).

The first word to exceed its decision threshold will be identified. We now need to specify how case alternation and word frequency influence the process. We assume that case alternation lowers the rate of information accumulation for a word candidate (through slowing the rate at which letter identification proceeds, as described above). We also assume that higher word frequency is associated with lower decision thresholds. All that is left is to determine what happens when we combine the two factors that slow processing: case alternation and low word frequency. Since the ramp of information accumulation is assumed to be shallower (slower) with case-alternated stimuli, differences in threshold will have a bigger effect than with normal stimuli. Thus, the "main line" to word identification via routes 1 and 2, if we could observe it alone, is hypothesized to produce *overadditive* effects when case alternation and low frequency are combined. A similar "ramp effect" logic has previously been used (Becker and Killion, 1977) to predict an overadditive pattern for combining the effects of stimulus degradation (contrast reduction) and word frequency, but empirically an additive relationship was obtained (Stanners et al. 1975; Becker and Killion 1977; see below for further discussion). Our analysis, unlike the earlier analysis, includes the idea that the overadditive pattern produced by the ramp effect (routes 1 and 2) is roughly balanced by an underadditive pattern produced by the familiarity-assessment mechanism (route 4). We argue that the roughly additive observed effects of case alternation and word frequency are due to offsetting trends working in opposite directions. A corollary to our argument can be derived if we assume that the function relating the output of the familiarity-assessment mechanism to word frequency is negatively accelerated (that is, going from very high frequency to medium frequency has a big effect, whereas going from medium frequency to low frequency has little further effect). Given this assumption, if we examine only the lower frequency range, the familiarity-assessment mechanism will be affected very little, allowing us to observe more directly the underlying *overadditivity* of case alternation and frequency due to the ramp effect. Just such an effect can be seen in Frederiksen's (1978) data: Over the high to medium range of word frequency, case alternation and frequency has the usual additive effects; as word frequency decreases further, an overadditive interaction between case alternation and word frequency emerges.[5]

This type of claim that apparently additive effects are due to two offsetting underlying trends in opposite directions may seem unparsimonious, but we will show that it is useful in explaining other phenomena. Furthermore, its plausibility has been strengthened by Norris's (1984) finding that the additivity between contrast reduction and word frequency is not exact and can be statistically rejected under some circumstances.

The Naming-Latency Task: Word-Nonword Differences
In experiment 1 we used a naming-latency task to test the simple prediction from the WSVP hypothesis that words should be more impaired by case alternation than nonwords. Not only did we fail to confirm this prediction, but we found a significant effect in the opposite direction—a bigger effect of case alternation for nonwords. Although Besner (1983, experiment 2) failed to find any difference in a similar comparison, our experiment had substantially greater power, so we shall suppose that the true case-alternation effect is larger for nonwords than for words.

This result is in the opposite direction from the effects of case alternation for the lexical-decision tasks and same-different tasks discussed earlier. The apparent perversity of this pattern is one of the motivations for us to assume substantial differences between the tasks. In applying our model framework to the naming-latency task, the first thing to note is that there is no reason for the familiarity mechanism to play any role. This mechanism has its influence on the process of making a lexical decision or a same-different judgment, which is unrelated to word identification *per se*, and not on the path leading to naming responses. Naming does not require any other type of binary decision, so there is no reason to expect it to be subject to contamination by the "goodness" of the stimulus.

A further difference in the naming-latency task is that it *is* subject to contamination by the assembled pronunciation route. This is not much more than common sense when the stimuli are regular words, as most of our stimuli are. Figure 1 includes a processing path in which multi-letter units are identified on the basis of visual-feature information (route 10). Since this route identifies letter clusters directly from their visual configuration, it should be strongly disrupted by case alternation. To the extent that letter analysis is used as a basis for identifying letter clusters (route 14) or as input to assembling the pronunciation (route 13), a further effect of case alternation will be introduced, since we have already assumed that it slows letter analysis (via route 1).

We now come to the question of what the net effect of case alternation will be for naming words versus nonwords. According to our model framework, case alternation will, via the assembled pronunciation path (which effectively treats words as nonwords), have the same effect on naming both words and nonwords. The naming of words will also depend on the addressed-pronunciation path. Should the effects of case alternation via the computed path be increased or decreased by mixing in further effects via the addressed path? What is critical is whether adding the addressed path mixes in computations that are more affected by case alternation or less affected by case alternation. Figure 1 shows that case alternation interferes with the addressed route only via route 1, whereas assembled pronunciation also has a strong component via route 10 (the identification of multi-letter units directly from visual features). The question whether assembled pronunciations should be more affected by case alternation than addressed pronunciations therefore hinges upon whether route 10 is more affected than route 1. In view of the nature of the two routes, a larger effect for route 10 should clearly be expected. Route 1 is hypothesized to identify single letters individually, so case alternation is merely an incidental nuisance. Route 10 identifies familiar clusters of letters which are known as a unit, so case alternation should severely disrupt these entities (Pring 1981).

Working back through our chain of logic: If word naming mixes the effects of the addressed-pronunciation path (which should be only mildly disrupted by case alternation) with the effects of the computed-pronunciation path (which should be severely disrupted), the effects of case alternation on the mixture should be diluted. Thus, our framework offers a reasonable account of how naming latency can be disrupted by case alternation more for nonwords than for words. Furthermore, our model provides a principled account of how this can be true while the converse is true for lexical-decision and same-different tasks.

The Naming-Latency Task: Associated-Unassociated Word Differences
In experiments 3 and 4 we tested the prediction from the WSVP hypothesis that case alternation would have a bigger effect after associated primes than after unassociated primes. Not only was the WSVP hypothesis not supported, but we found that case alternation had a significantly smaller effect on associated words. This result can be explained quite straightforwardly on the basis of the same principles used to explain other phenomena. Since the familiarity-assessment mechanism is assumed to have no effect on the naming-latency task, we need not consider the impact of case alternation on route 4. The effect of case alternation on routes 1 and 2 should follow the earlier ramp-effect logic in which case alternation slows the rate at which information about word candidates accumulates (see figure 2). If we assume that associated words have temporarily lowered thresholds relative to unassociated words, then the rate change will operate over a shorter distance. Thus, the ramp effect produces an interaction in the direction observed: smaller case-alternation effects for associated words than for unassociated words. We also need to consider how this explanation is affected by the assembled pronunciation path, since our model framework allows it to contaminate word naming. There is no reason we can see why there should be any main affect of word association on this route (which has no knowledge of words), or any interaction with case alternation. The fact that priming will speed up the addressed-pronunciation path via route 2 does, however, mean that (by race-model logic) the reliance on that path rather than on the assembled pronunciation path will be somewhat increased. Since we have just argued that case alternation has a larger effect on the assembled-pronunciation route, reduced reliance on this route with associated primes should have an effect in the direction of reducing the case-alternation effect. Thus, both the direct and the indirect effects of priming should work in the same direction to reduce the predicted size of the case alternation effect on word naming.

The Naming-Latency Task: Word-Frequency Effects

Besner et al. (1984) and Besner and McCann (1987) have found that in the naming-latency task, case alternation has a larger effect on low-frequency than on high-frequency words. Our explanation for this overadditive results parallels in all respects our comments on the overadditive effect of case alternation and associative priming. Within the computed-pronunciation path, the logic of the ramp effect (assuming that high-frequency words have lower thresholds) will lead to a smaller case-alternation effect for high-frequency words. Furthermore, the fact that high-frequency words make less use of the assembled route (which is more impaired by case alternation than the computed-pronunciation path mediated by word identification) will reduce the size of the case-alternation effect.[6]

Concluding Comment: On Hypothesizing Multiple Processing Paths

We know of no evidence that makes a strong case that accomplished adult readers use word-specific visual patterns to identify words displayed normally (i.e., upright and in consistent lower-case print). To explain the complex pattern of results found in case-alternation experiments, we have set forth the framework for a multi-path processing model. This model assumes that the "main line" of word identification proceeds from visual features to abstract letter identities to word identities; past this point, the word identities are available for guiding naming or for lexical-decision judgments. In order to explain the complex dependence of case-alternation results on the task used, we found it necessary to hypothesize two additional processing paths: a familiarity-discrimination path that recognizes words without identifying them (which contaminates the lexical-decision task) and an assembled-pronunciation path that can derive the pronunciation of regular letter strings without identifying them (which contaminates the word-naming task). These three major processing paths together allow us to explain the otherwise distressing fact that case-alternation affects the word-naming task and the lexical-decision task in very different ways.

Perhaps it is useful to pull back from the details and consider whether we should be dismayed at having to invoke such complexities. Experimental psychology has traditionally had a limited tolerance for highly complicated explanations; while tastes may be changing a bit, complexity continues to arouse suspicions, and it should. We especially agree with the bias against theories that require a new *ad hoc* proviso for every new piece of data that is found, and with the bias against massive models with a multitude of free parameters that satisfy the sufficiency test (that is, the model will produce the obtained results) but give no sign of how many competing models of equivalent complexity would also fit (Johnston, van Santen, and Hale 1986). We do wish to advance reasons why the complexities we have invoked here should arouse less suspicion. First, none of the possible processing paths hypothesized was invented *de novo* solely to explain the phenomena under consideration here. Second, each path actually has a function that can be separately observed. The assembled-pronunciation path can name pseudo-words, and the familiarity-assessment path can recognize objects without identifying them. Third, we argue that, in view of the complex pattern of six types of results we tackled, the complexity of the model is not disproportionate. We certainly welcome attempts to develop alternative models and attempts to provide further converging tests of the present framework.

Moving to a more general level, we would like to close with two further overarching reasons why it is quite likely that experimental psychologists will have to learn to live with complexity. The first reason is that the brain is complicated. It is not unparsimonious to suppose that there are about as many different processing paths and mechanisms as there are demonstrably different functional areas in the brain. Also, the slowness of the components in the brain makes it likely that these paths are allowed to proceed at least partly in parallel, rather than only serially. The second reason is that even if we knew nothing about the brain, we might already suspect that complexity will be found, just from knowing that humans are biological systems with a long evolutionary development while occupying a diversity of ecological niches. A rich complexity of mechanisms available to deal simultaneously with one task is the natural consequence of the development of different ways of dealing with a rich variety of alternative demands. It is perhaps instructive to consider the amazing variety of partially redundant systems that birds can use for navigation; no matter what the weather, the locale, etc., a bird is unlikely to be bereft of processing possibilities. In complexity lies the competence to deal with diversity.

Even with these motivating background arguments on the table, we still believe that one should not lightly and without good reason proliferate paths and processes. But we feel that the literature we have surveyed and the data we have collected—especially the radically different patterns of factor effects on different tasks—virtually compel us to develop a moderately complicated story, with multiple processing paths. No one promised that science would be easy.

Notes

1. Masson (1986) has presented good evidence that under unusual circumstances WSVPs can be used in word identification. We would merely note that his stimuli are inverted à la P. A. Kolers; people have very little practice at reading in this way. Our suspicion is that, with sufficient practice, preliminary letter recognition comes to serve as the primary basis for word identification.

2. We are primarily concerned about the possibility that the visual familiarity or unfamiliarity of a specific word might contaminate yes-no judgments. There is a second form of contamination of "goodness" judgments when mixed-case stimuli are used that are not specific to an individual familiar word: Subjects may notice that mixed-case words have an alternation in the size of strokes unlike normal text; for this reason, mixed-case items might tend to look "bad" without regard to which word they do or don't look like. In fact it is reasonable that mixed-case nonwords may even look "bad" for this reason, which might conceivably make it easier to say "no" to them.

3. As we will see below, we are admittedly exchanging one set of problems for another, because the naming task does not logically require lexical access.

4. The word-identification system could be thought of as having a logogen-like structure (Morton 1969). Such an assumption causes no problems for our analysis here, but neither is it necessary for it. We have deliberately avoided using the term "logogen" so that our analysis can be considered independent of the particular theoretical assumptions of the rest of the logogen model.

5. In particular, see figure 12 in Fredriksen 1978. We assume that word frequency is an individual difference variable; if good readers were exposed to words that are as low in frequency for them as these items are for poor readers, the overadditivity of case alternation and word frequency should again be manifest.

6. We are currently looking to see whether case alternation impairs low-frequency words more than high-frequency words in naming when all the stimuli are irregular in terms of spelling sound correspondences. This experiment has the advantage that, according to most theories, the use of irregular words prevents a pronunciation from being based solely on the output of the assembled route.

References

Allport, D. A. 1979. Word recognition in reading: A tutorial review. In P. A. Kolers, H. Bouma, and M. Wrolstad (eds.), *Processing of Visible Language*, vol. 1. New York: Plenum.

Balota, D. A., and Chumbley, J. I. 1984. Are lexical decisions a good measure of lexical access? The role of word frequency in the neglected decision stage. *Journal of Experimental Psychology: Human Perception and Performance* 10: 340–357.

Becker, C. A. 1985. What do we really know about semantic context effects during reading? In D. Besner, T. G. Waller, and G. E. MacKinnon (eds.), *Reading research: Advances in Theory and Practice*. New York: Academic.

Becker, C. A., and Killion, T. H. 1977. Interaction of visual and cognitive effects in word recognition. *Journal of Experimental Psychology: Human Perception and Performance* 3: 389–401.

Besner, D. 1983. Basic decoding components in reading: Two dissociable feature extraction processes. *Canadian Journal of Psychology* 37: 429–438.

Besner, D. 1984. Specialized processors subserving visual word recognition: Evidence of local control. *Canadian Journal of Psychology* 38: 94–101.

Besner, D., and McCann, R. S. 1987. Word frequency and pattern distortion in visual word identification and production: An examination of four classes of models. In M. Coltheart (ed.), *Attention and Performance XII: The Psychology of Reading*. Hillsdale, N.J.: Erlbaum.

Besner, D., Coltheart, M., and Davelaar, E. 1984. Basic processes in reading: Computation of abstract letter identities. *Canadian Journal of Psychology* 38: 126–134.

Besner, D., Davelaar, E., Alcott, D., and Parry, P. 1984. Wholistic reading of alphabetic print: Evidence from the FDM and the FBI. In L. Henderson (ed.), *Orthographies and Reading*. Hillsdale, N.J.: Erlbaum.

Bruder, G. A. 1978. Role of visual familiarity in the word-superiority effects obtained with the simultaneous-matching task. *Journal of Experimental Psychology: Human Perception and Performance* 4: 88–100.

Cattell, J. M. 1886. The time taken up by cerebral operations. *Mind* 11: 220–242, 377–392, 524–538. Reprinted in Poffenberger, A. T. (ed.), *James McKeen Cattell*. New York: Basic Books, 1973.

Coltheart, M., and Freeman, N. 1974. Case alternation impairs word identification. *Bulletin of the Psychonomic Society* 3: 102–104.

Crowder, R. G. 1982. *The Psychology of Reading*. Oxford University Press.

Erdmann, B., and Dodge, R. 1898. *Psychologische Untersuchungen über das Lesen*. Halle: Niemeyer.

Evett, L., and Humphreys, G. W. 1981. The use of abstract graphemic information in lexical access. *Quarterly Journal of Experimental Psychology* 33A: 325–350.

Frederiksen, J. R. 1978. Assessment of perceptual decoding and lexical skills and their relation to reading proficiency. In A. M. Lesgold, J. W. Pellegrino, S. D. Fokkema, and R. Glaser (eds.), *Cognitive Psychology and Instruction*. New York: Plenum.

Haber, R. N., and Haber, L. R. 1981. Visual components of the reading process. *Visible Language* 15: 147–182.

Haber, R. N., and Schindler, R. M. 1981. Errors in proof-reading: Evidence of syntactic control of letter processing? *Journal of Experimental Psychology: Human Perception and Performance* 7: 573–579.

Haber, L. R., Haber, R. N., and Furlin, K. R. 1983. Word length and word shape as sources of information in reading. *Reading Research Quarterly* 18: 165–189.

Henderson, L. 1982. *Orthography and Word Recognition in Reading*. New York: Academic.

Howard, D. 1987. Reading without letters. In M. Coltheart, G. Sartori, and R. Job (eds.), *The Cognitive Neuropsychology of Language*. London: Erlbaum.

Johnston, J. C. 1978. A test of the sophisticated guessing theory of word perception. *Cognitive Psychology* 10: 123–153.

Johnston, J. C. 1981. Understanding word perception: Clues from studying the word superiority effect. In C. J. L. Tzeng and H. Singer (eds.), *Perception of Print: Reading Research in Experimental Psychology*. Hillsdale, N.J.: Erlbaum.

Masson, M. E. J. 1986. Identification of typographically transformed words: Instance-based skill acquisition. *Journal of Experimental Psychology: Learning Memory and Cognition* 12: 479–488.

McClelland, J. L., and Johnston, J. C. 1977. The role of familiar units in perception of words and nonwords. *Perception and Psychophysics* 22: 249–261.

McClelland, J. L., and Rumelhart, D. E. 1981. An interactive activation model of context effects in letter perception: Part 1. An account of basic findings. *Psychological Review* 88: 375–407.

Meyer, D. E., Schvaneveldt, R. W., and Ruddy, M. G. 1975. Loci of contextual effects on visual word recognition. In P. M. A. Rabbitt and S. Dornic (eds.), *Attention and Performance V*. New York: Academic.

Monk, A. F., and Hulme, C. 1983. Errors in proofreading: Evidence for the use of word shape in word recognition. *Memory and Cognition* 11(1): 16–23.

Morton, J. 1969. Interaction of information in word recognition. *Psychological Review* 76: 165–178.

Norris, D. 1984. The effects of frequency, repetition and stimulus quality in visual word recognition. *Quarterly Journal of Experimental Psychology* 36A: 507–518.

Norris, D. 1986. Word recognition: Context effects without priming. *Cognition* 22: 93–136.

Paap, K. R., Newsome, S. L., and Noel, R. W. 1984. Word shapes in poor shape for the race to the lexicon. *Journal of Experimental Psychology: Human Perception and Performance* 10: 412–428.

Patterson, K. E. 1982. The relation between reading and phonological coding: Further neuropsychological observations. In A. W. Ellis (ed.), *Normality and Pathology in Cognitive Function*. London: Academic.

Pollatsek, A., Well, A. D., and Schindler, R. M. 1975. Familiarity affects visual processing of words. *Journal of Experimental Psychology: Human Perception and Performance* 1: 328–338.

Pring, L. 1981. Phonological codes and functional spelling units: Reality and implications. *Perception and Psychophysics* 30: 573–578.

Rayner, K., McConkie, G. W., and Zola, D. 1980. Integrating information across eye movements. *Cognitive Psychology* 12: 206–226.

Rudnicky, A. I., and Kolers, P. A. 1984. Size and case of type as stimuli in reading. *Journal of Experimental Psychology: Human Perception and Performance* 3: 1–17.

Rumelhart, D. E., and McClelland, J. E. 1982. An interactive activation model of context effects in letter perception: Part 2. The contextual enhancement effect and some tests and extensions of the model. *Psychological Review* 89: 60–94.

Rumelhart, D. E., and Siple, P. 1974. Process of recognizing tachistoscopically presented words. *Psychological Review* 81: 99–118.

Saffran, E. 1980. Reading in deep dyslexia is not ideographic. *Neuropsychologia* 18: 219–223.

Seidenberg, M. S. 1985. The time course of information activation and utilization in visual word recognition. In D. Besner, T. G. Waller, and G. E. MacKinnon (eds.), *Reading Research: Advances in Theory and Practice*, Vol. 5. Orlando: Academic.

Smith, F. 1969. Familiarity of configuration vs. discriminability of features in the visual identification of words. *Psychonomic Science* 14: 261–262.

Stanners, R. F., Jastrzembski, J. E., and Westbrook, A. 1975. Frequency and visual quality in a word-nonword classification task. *Journal of Verbal Learning and Verbal Behavior* 14: 259–264.

Taylor, G. A., Miller, J. J., and Juola, J. F. 1977. Isolating visual units in the perceptions of words and nonwords. *Perception and Psychophysics* 21: 377–386.

Wheeler, D. 1970. Processes in word recognition. *Cognitive Psychology* 1: 59–85.

PART III
Lexical Structure and
Process

Chapter 10

Understanding Words and Word Recognition: Does Phonology Help?

Uli H. Frauenfelder and Aditi Lahiri

The primary objective of any model of spoken-word recognition is to explain how a listener is able to access the information stored in the mental lexicon on the basis of an acoustic signal. In this process of lexical access, the listener is generally assumed to extract information from the sensory input in order to construct some internal representation(s) of the input. This input representation is mapped onto the internally stored representations of lexical form to determine what word the speaker has actually produced.

The properties of the speech signal, while creating few apparent difficulties for the listener, make this mapping process challenging for psycholinguists to explain. First, speech is *variable*, and for a variety of reasons. Each phoneme manifests itself with different acoustic properties every time it is produced. Among the multitude of factors contributing to this variability, the phoneme's local environment (e.g., vowels are nasalized in English when followed by a nasal consonant) and its position within higher-order structural units (e.g., the underlying /t/ in the sequence *tote it* can have one of three surface forms—aspirated, flapped, and unexploded—depending on whether it occurs in syllable-initial, foot-internal, or syllable-final position [Ladefoged 1982]) are of special interest here.

Furthermore, any given word may be produced in many different ways by the same speaker, depending upon the speech rate and the environment of this word. Phonological processes triggered by appropriate phonological contexts result in varied pronunciations in which phonetic material is deleted, added, or substituted. For instance, as Cutting and Harrington (1986) point out, the word *actually* can be pronounced in many different ways, including [æktʃuəli], [æktʃuli], [æktʃəli], [æktʃli], [ækʃəli], and [ækʃli]. Accounting for the recognition of such surface variants is problematic for most theories of lexical access.

In addition to being variable, speech is *continuous*. Unlike written text, it has no "spaces" or periods of silence to indicate systematically where one sound or word ends and the next begins. Furthermore, the acoustic information corresponding to successive phonemes is not ordered in a strictly linear fashion but is *overlapping*. As a consequence, the same short stretch of speech may contain information corresponding to several different phonemes. Phonological processes of assimilation can accentuate this overlap by spreading a feature from one segment to another (for instance, the process of umlaut spreads the feature [−back] to the preceding vowel: *not, nötig*). The continuous and overlapping character of speech creates the problem of a continuous-to-discrete mapping, that is, of associating the continuous speech wave with discrete units such as phonemes or words.

Psycholinguists studying spoken-word recognition have tended to avoid or ignore the complexity of the sensory input and its analysis. More important, they have generally simplified the problem by restricting their research to the recognition of isolated monomorphemic words pronounced in their citation form. This narrow focus has led to the development of models in which many of the issues associated with understanding the continuous and varying speech input have not been dealt with. In particular, the question of how listeners recognize different surface variants of the same word having undergone phonological processes has not received sufficient attention.

We will argue here that *regular* phonological processes are at the origin of much of this variability. It is essential, therefore, in trying to explain the listener's ability to process fluent speech, to get a better understanding of these phonological processes. A number of important developments in phonological theory have, in fact, led to a good characterization of these processes. Unfortunately, psycholinguists have paid relatively little attention to these developments and consequently have not considered seriously the ways in which listeners might bring their phonological knowledge to bear on lexical processing. This is somewhat ironic, as Frazier (1987) points out, since we tend to accept without question the idea that listeners perceive unfamiliar languages with reference to the phonology of their native language.

The psycholinguists' ignorance of basic phonological concepts is reflected by their view of input and lexical representations and by the way they have ignored problems posed by phonological processes. Until recently most models of lexical access have assumed extremely simple input representations consisting of linearly concatenated segments with no internal structure. These segments were often implicitly assumed to be phonemes; however, unlike the normal assumptions in the phonological literature, these phonemes were seen as wholes rather than as composed of features. Lexical representations were similarly conceived of as unstructured strings of segments. Lexical access was assumed to consist in a sequential mapping between these two representations, starting with the beginning of each.

Although models making these simplistic assumptions might account for the recognition of isolated words spoken in citation form, it is evident that they cannot explain how listeners recognize words in fluent speech. Phonological processes leading to the alteration of the input (via deletion, substitution, or addition of phonetic material) obscure the relationship between the input and lexical representations, thereby complicating the mapping from one onto the other. Moreover, speech does not contain clear word boundaries indicating where such a mapping process should be initiated.

In this chapter we will attempt to show (as the title suggests) that listeners use their phonological knowledge to understand continuous speech, and that, by paying more attention to the descriptions provided by phonological theories, psycholinguists can develop a better picture of speech understanding. In section 1 we will present a brief account of some recent developments in phonological theory and then examine three basic types of phonological processes with the objective of identifying properties that have psychological implications. In section 2 we will examine three alternative psychological accounts of how listeners deal with these phonological processes.

1 Characterization of Phonological Representations and Processes

In the last decade, phonological theory has witnessed two major developments: one toward the use of hierarchical structures in phonological representations and one toward distinguishing between phonological rules on the basis of their conditioning context (e.g. morphophonemic or purely phonological). We will discuss briefly the main features of these two developments.

Nonlinear Representations
Phonological descriptions developed in the tradition of Chomsky and Halle's *Sound Pattern of English* (1968) used strictly linear representations.

Recognizing the inadequacies of such linear representations, phonologists have moved increasingly toward representations with a multi-dimensional (i.e., multi-level) organization. These representations include a hierarchical structure of *prosodic* levels and the nonlinear representation of *melodic* features.

Prosodic Levels

Phonological research has shown that hierarchically structured prosodic units like syllables and feet are necessary to characterize in a systematic fashion phonological processes whose structural contexts would otherwise be entirely arbitrary. As Kahn (1976) pointed out, unless the syllable is used as a phonological unit to describe the domain of application of the English aspiration rule (as merely syllable initial), this rule must be stated in a much more complicated and unmotivated fashion (voiceless stops become aspirated when followed by a stressed vowel with an optional intervening liquid or glide, and when not preceded by [s]). The need for prosodic structure can also be illustrated by an example from Old English, where rules of high-vowel deletion are best expressed in terms of foot structure (i.e., delete when in the weak branch of a foot [Dresher and Lahiri 1986]). The same rule without foot structure takes approximately the following cumbersome and arbitrary form: A high vowel is deleted when preceded by either a long vowel and a consonant, a short vowel and two consonants, or two sequences of a short vowel and a single consonant. In addition to syllables and feet, other prosodic constituents can serve as the domain of application of phonological rules (e.g., phonological words and phrases [Nespor and Vogel 1986]).

Melodic Levels

Another move toward nonlinear representations has been made at the level of features. Instead of defining segments as unordered lists or undifferentiated bundles of features, a multi-tiered representation attributes features to different tiers and allows the relationship between these features to be expressed in terms of links between the tiers. Within such a framework (which is an outgrowth of autosegmental phonology; see Clements and Keyser 1980, Clements 1985, McCarthy 1986, and Hayes 1986), there exists a separate tier, called the CV tier or the skeletal tier, which contains "slots" which are only specified for syllabicity (where C is [−syllabic] and V is [+syllabic]). Thus, the property of syllabicity is represented on its own auto-segmental tier.[1] This CV tier is linked both to the prosodic tier and to the *melodic* tier, where segmental features such as voice or nasality are also separately represented. In this perspective, a single feature on the melodic tier can be linked to more than one skeletal slot and a skeletal slot can be linked to more than one feature.

Example

A multi-dimensional representation of the word *pony* illustrates how different tiers are linked and how both the prosodic and melodic tiers can separately condition distinct phonological processes:

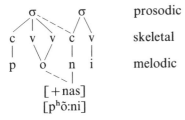

The syllables in the prosodic tier are built on the skeletal tier, and the association lines indicate the relationship between the syllables and the melodic tier via the skeletal representation.[2] The associations between tiers are not necessarily one-to-one but can also be one-to-many. For instance, the vowel /o/ represents a single set of features linked to two V slots indicating that it is a long vowel. The ambisyllabic character of the segment [n]—it closes the first syllable and begins the second—is expressed by the many-to-one association lines between the prosodic and the skeletal tier.

The relative independence of each of the tiers means that phonological rules can refer to any tier separately. For example, the two phonological processes applying on this word—syllable-initial aspiration and vowel nasalization—refer to the melodic and the prosodic tier, respectively. The consonant /p/ is syllable-initial and therefore becomes aspirated. The vowel /o/ is followed by a nasal consonant, and hence the feature [+nasal] is spread to it from the nasal consonant (as is shown by the linking of the vowel to the nasal tier).

In sum, although linguists still disagree about the exact details concerning these hierarchical representations, there is a clear consensus that multi-tiered structures are required to accurately account for phonological processes in natural language. Most psycholinguists, on the other hand, have retained a more traditional view of the representations involved in lexical access. As already mentioned, both the input and the lexical representation are generally assumed to consist of a string of concatentated segments. As will become apparent from the discussion below, a better characterization of phonological representations allows us to develop more explanatory models of lexical processing.

Lexical Phonology

Another major development in linguistic theory (now known as Lexical Phonology [Kiparsky 1982, 1985; Mohanan 1986]) has been the division of the phonological component into two separate modules: lexical and postlexical. The rules applying in the lexical component are sensitive to word-internal morphology, whereas postlexical rules are not since morphological structure is no longer available at this level. Postlexical rules are generally phonologically conditioned and apply across the board— that is, not only within words but also across word boundaries. Moreover, unlike lexical rules, they are not structure-preserving, and they can therefore create segments and sequential configurations that are not present in the underlying representation.

Velar softening and flapping in English illustrate the difference between lexical and postlexical rules. The American-English rule of flapping is postlexical. It applies anywhere in the phonological phrase, both within words and across morpheme and word boundaries: better → be[D]er, writer → wri[D]er, at a meeting → a[D] a mee[D]ing, and so on. Velar softening, on the other hand, is conditioned by word-internal morphology, since the statement of its context refers to nonback vowels of specific suffixes such as -*ize*: critic–criti[s]ize, public–publi[s]ize. The important consequence of these two rule types is that lexical rules create new "words" whereas postlexical rules generate word variants.

Our characterization of the lexical and postlexical rule components is, by necessity, oversimplified. Nonetheless, for the present purposes, we only want to suggest that these distinctions, which psycholinguists for the most part have ignored, are helpful in understanding lexical access. Indeed, psycholinguists have focussed their attention on phonological alternation resulting from lexical rules and not on the more productive domain of postlexical rules. In this chapter we will concentrate on the neglected postlexical phonological processes, since they create phonetic variants of a single word. Most current models of word recognition have not addressed the recognition of these forms.

Postlexical Phonological Rules

Phonological rules can delete, insert, and permute segments; they can also change features. The most common postlexical phonological processes change features (feature-changing rules being traditionally classified as either allophonic or neutralizing) or delete segments. We will consider each of these rule types in turn.

Feature-Changing Processes

Allophonic rules create nondistinctive contextual phonetic variants. The underlying phonemes represent the distinctive sound units of a language, and the allophones that are derived from them contain redundant phonetic information that is predictable from a given context. English, as we saw in the *pony* example above, nasalizes a vowel that is followed by a nasal consonant. The nasal vowels are allophonic in English, since they are always predictable in their distribution. Since allophonic rules create nondistinctive variants and do not refer to any word-internal structures, they are by definition postlexical.

Phonological processes that are neutralizing erase distinctions between phonemes in specific prosodic or melodic environments. Underlying feature contrasts are lost, and this leads to the identical surface realization of distinct phonological segments. Palatalization in English, for example, changes a /d/ to [dʒ] when followed by a glide [j], so that the word *could* would be realized as cou[dʒ] when followed by *you*. In this case, the resulting segment [dʒ] is identical to any other [dʒ] derived from a /dʒ/ phoneme. The consequence of this neutralizing processes is an ambiguous segment ([dʒ]) on the surface whose underlying form (either /dʒ/ or /d/ + /j/) cannot be determined merely on the basis of the signal.[3]

The simple segment ambiguity resulting from neutralization leads to different degrees of lexical ambiguity, ranging from partial ambiguity to total homophony. The neutralization in *did + you* (*did* becoming [dɪdʒ] when followed by a front glide) illustrates how ambiguous segments will frequently produce partial lexical ambiguity. Although [dɪdʒ] is not an English word, *digit* is; the syllable [dɪdʒ] from *did you* overlaps with the first part of *digit*. It is possible, moreover, that neutralization leads to a sequence that already exists in the lexicon of the language. For example, palatalization can change *hit* to [hɪtʃ] when followed by *you*. However, in contrast with the case for *did*, there already exists a lexical item (*hitch*) that is identical to the sequence [hɪtʃ] derived from *hit you* by neutralization.[4] When neutralizing rules apply *within* a word, the isolated surface form of the lexical item is always neutralized. We find the most extreme cases of ambiguity when such rules lead to lexical homophony, as in the case of syllable-final devoicing in German. Voiced consonants are devoiced in syllable-final position, thereby neutralizing the voicing distinction in this prosodic context. For example, in the German word *Rad* ("wheel"), the underlying /d/ is devoiced in word-final position; this makes it indistinguishable from another German word: *Rat* ("advice").

There is a fundamental difference between allophonic and neutralizing feature-changing rules: Only the latter create ambiguity. Contextual neutralization processes lead to identical surface realizations of distinct phonological segments, whereas the allophones resulting from allophonic processes are not ambiguous since it is possible to recover the underlying phoneme from them. Furthermore, allophones always appear in predictable environments. In terms of conditioning context, however, both neutralizing and allophonic rules can have as their domain of application a *prosodic* and/or a *melodic* level of representation.

Deletion Rules

Deletion rules, as the name suggests, delete segments entirely. Generally, such rules are simultaneously conditioned by both the prosodic and the melodic tier; very rarely does the melodic tier alone provide a context for deletion. In English, the loss of word-final [t] between consonants is an example of a deletion rule that is conditioned by both prosodic and melodic contexts. The consonant is retained when the following word begins with a vowel: *past three* (without [t]) as compared to *past eight* (with [t]).

Like neutralizing rules, deletion rules lead to differing amounts of ambiguity. When the application of a deletion rule results in a sequence that remains phonotactically legal, it can create homophones. For instance, in certain contexts in English, deletion of [t] can lead to ambiguity of the following kind:

interstate → [inerstate], as compared with *inner state.*

We have distinguished several types of phonological processes that produce varying surface forms of a word as a function of prosodic and melodic contexts. This characterization has been primarily linguistic. We have, however, discussed an important psychological consequence of phonological processes: the amount of resultant surface ambiguity. We will now consider further the psycholinguistic consequences of these processes for word recognition and examine some recent psycholinguistic efforts that have begun to appeal to phonological theory. Our discussion will focus on the types of phonological representations and processes that we have presented so far.

2 Psychological Approaches to Phonological Processes

We want to suggest that psycholinguists should pay more attention to phonological theory. Although it is unreasonable to assume a direct one-to-one correspondence between linguistic and processing models, phonological distinctions are clearly useful in guiding empirical investigations of human processing mechanisms. Phonological theory has not been used sufficiently in this fashion in research on word recognition, where phonological processes, when discussed at all, have been assumed to uniformly complicate the word-recognition process. Our intent is to illustrate the dangers in generalizing about phonological processes as a class and to show the need for examining each process individually. Listeners may not deal with these phonological processes in identical fashion, but instead handle them differently as a function of their specific properties. Futhermore, there is the danger of generalizing about lexical processing on the basis of the phonology of a few select languages. Typological studies of diverse phonological systems are helpful in that they provide information about the universality or the language-specificity of certain phonological processes. Clearly, experimental results for the processing of an idiosyncratic feature of a particular language should not be taken to reflect language processing in general.

There have been some new developments in the area of word recognition that recognize the importance of phonological distinctions. In this section we will focus on three ways in which the issue of phonological processes has been addressed. The emphasis in each of these approaches is slightly different. The basic assumption of the first approach is that listeners actively use their phonological and prosodic knowledge in analyzing the sensory input during lexical access. The result of this analysis is a rich, phonologically structured input representation, which is used to access the lexicon. The second approach involves pre-compiling phonological knowledge by applying the phonological rules of the language to the underlying forms and by including all the generated surface forms in the lexicon. Finally, connectionist models express phonological regularities in terms of connections between and within the different levels of representation.

Phonological Structuring of the Input Representation
Models within this general approach often take the form of a parser in which the analysis of the input is guided by an explicit knowledge source, the grammar. Some recent examples of phonological parsers can be found in Church 1987, Dogil 1987, Frazier 1987, and Grosjean and Gee 1987. These parsers appeal to different parts of grammar, such as the phonological principles defining the organization of segments into syllables and of syllables into larger prosodic units. For the most part, these parsers have not been constructed to handle word variants resulting from phonological processes.

In contrast to the phonologist, whose ultimate goal is determine the underlying representations and to derive the surface forms from these representations via a set of rules, the listener is assumed in this approach to recognize word variants by reversing such rules to recover the appropriate underlying representation. As we noted above, this is not always straightforward, since ambiguous surface forms may be derivable from several different underlying forms. To handle such cases, listeners are assumed to have phonology-based heuristics that lead them to prefer, initially at least, a certain analysis of the surface form. This analysis would be tested against the lexicon to determine whether there are any matching lexical entries. If this turned out not to be the case, this analysis would be abandoned and an alternative analysis tested. In this approach, the lexicon is assumed to contain only the underlying forms (one per word); the burden is on the listener to recover this lexical entry from its diverse surface manifestations.

In the following subsections, we will examine individually the phonological processes distinguished above, since each has different consequences for the parsing approach. Of all these phonological processes, allophonic variation (conditioned either prosodically or melodically) is most suited to this approach and therefore will be discussed first.

Prosodically Conditioned Allophonic Processes
Church (1983, 1987) has developed a chart parser that makes use of both prosodically conditioned allophones and phonotactic constraints to parse a phonetic input into a limited set of well-formed syllable structures. The prosodic context conditioning each allophone (e.g., the presence of aspiration, indicating that the voiceless stop is in syllable-onset position) is identified and is used to segment the input into syllabic units. Once the information concerning the syllabic structure has been derived from the allophones, the nondistinctive features are stripped away, leaving only a phonological input representation with syllable structure marked. This canonical or phonemic representation is then mapped onto the lexicon, which itself is also made of lexical entries with phonemic representations.

A major advantage of this parser is that it is able to reduce the number of comparisons or matches that have to be made with the lexicon. By incorporating syllabic structure in the input representation, it is possible to limit the lexical comparisons to those between syllable onsets and word onsets. This leads to a considerable saving over approaches where every phoneme must be tested as a potential word onset. However, syllable-based comparisons are successful only when words and syllables share the same boundary. Although this is often the case, resyllabification can produce syllables that straddle word boundaries. Such cases (perhaps rarer for English than for languages in which word boundaries have virtually no allophonic consequences) are clearly problematic for a purely syllable-based approach.

Melodically Conditioned Allophonic Processes

Although the parser proposed by Church exploits prosodically conditioned allophones, it fails to make use of melodically conditioned allophones (which also provide valuable information). These allophones can be used by the listener to predict the partial specification of upcoming segments (or, in the case of progressive assimilation, to confirm the identity of the preceding segments). In the case of nasal assimilation, since nasalization for vowels is not distinctive in English, the nasal consonant is entirely predictable. Listeners can, at least in principle, use the nasal feature associated with the vowel to anticipate the arrival of a nasal consonant without having to wait to identify its other distinctive features (such as its place of articulation).

Although little research has specifically investigated the predictive use of such allophonic information in word recognition, some experimental evidence (Martin and Bunnell 1982; Whalen 1982) suggests that listeners can use co-articulatory information in an immediate fashion to accelerate the identification of upcoming phonetic segments. Furthermore, the results obtained by Warren and Marslen-Wilson (1987) suggest that listeners exploit such allophonic information to constrain lexical hypotheses. Subjects performing in a gating task used coarticulatory information in the vowel to anticipate the following consonant. They were particularly successful in predicting a nasal consonant on the basis of the nasalized portion of the preceding vowel. Listeners appear to exploit featural information in accessing the lexicon without necessarily computing phonemic representations. These results suggest that psycholinguists should view phonemes not as monolithic units but—more as linguists do—as internally structured units that are divisible into features.

Neutralizing Phonological Processes

Neutralization causes the loss of underlying feature contrasts, leading to identical surface realizations of distinct phonological segments. The resulting ambiguity—ranging from local segmental ambiguity to total homophony—poses serious problems for models of lexical access, since it is impossible just on the basis of the signal to recover the intended underlying segment. As Klatt (1977) points out, neutralizing rules are irreversible since there is usually no unique inverse rule. He suggests that this ambiguity can be resolved only by appealing to syntactic and semantic contextual information.

We will explore here the possibility that principles within phonological theory can play a role in processing neutralized forms. There may be linguistic distinctions in the phonological component of grammar (e.g., the status of features that undergo neutralization) that lead the listener to prefer one reading of a homophone over the other.

To illustrate how listeners might use phonology-based strategies to interpret ambiguous segments, let us consider the case of nasality in Bengali. The feature [nasal] is distinctive in Bengali not only for consonants but also for vowels. Nasal and oral vowels contrast in word-final position or when followed by an oral consonant, as can be seen in such minimal pairs as /šak/ and /šãk/. Furthermore, Bengali also has a neutralizing rule of regressive assimilation, which nasalizes underlying oral vowels when followed by nasal consonants: /ban/ → [bãn]. Surface nasal vowels are therefore ambiguous; they can be nasal either underlyingly or through assimilation.

What do Bengali listeners do when they encounter an ambiguous surface nasal vowel? We suggest that they adopt a linguistically based strategy and initially interpret *all* surface nasality as derived from underlying nasal vowels. Accordingly, the vowel [ã] of both [bãn] and [bãd] would be interpreted as the underlying nasal vowel /ã/. Alternatively, listeners might show nonlinguistic preferences in interpreting the surface nasal vowels on the basis of extra-linguistic factors such as frequency, or they might even show random behavior. Finally, listeners could wait until they heard the following consonant and interpret the vowel on the basis of the identity of the consonant.

To examine these predictions (and to prevent subjects from taking the last option), Lahiri and Marslen-Wilson (1988) conducted a gating study in which subjects' performance was tested on word triplets containing (a) CṼCs with an underlying nasal vowel (as in [bãd]), (b) CVNs in which an underlying oral vowel surfaces as nasalized (as in [bãn]), and (c) CVCs in which an oral vowel is followed by an oral consonant (as in [bad]). These words were presented to the subjects in successively larger increments, starting with an initial presentation that included the initial consonant and the first four glottal pulses of the vowel and continuing with further presentations that increased in 40-msec steps until the offset of the vowel and then on until the end of the word. The subjects were asked to say at each increment what word they thought they were hearing. The result of interest was the response that the subjects gave for the vowel and the word-final consonant after having heard only part of the (nasalized) vowel.

Bengali listeners adopted the first linguistic strategy and interpreted nasality on the surface as coming from an underlying nasal vowel; that is, they overwhelmingly responded with CṼC words to both CVN and CṼC words. Their responses changed from CṼC to CVN only when the nasal murmur of the nasal consonant in CVN words became identifiable. The results from this study indicate a clear preference for initially interpreting a nasal vowel as underlyingly nasal.

It is instructive now to compare the performance of these Bengali listeners with that of English listeners in their interpretation of surface nasality. Nasality in English is nondistinctive for vowels, so that the feature nasal is not represented underlyingly. Consequently, surface vowel nasalization due to assimilation provides unambiguous information that there is an upcoming nasal consonant. Listeners have been shown (Warren and Marslen-Wilson 1987) to exploit this information in predicting the nasal consonant. Surface nasalization in Bengali, however, is interpreted not as the consequence of an assimilation rule but as an underlying nasal vowel followed by an oral consonant. Thus, listeners interpret nasalized vowels in radically different ways depending upon the phonological structure of their respective native language.

Deletion

Psycholinguistic research has either ignored the phenomenon of segment deletion or dealt with it uniformly by assuming that listeners cannot recover the appropriate underlying forms altered by deletion. In fact, deletion rules vary in the degree of ambiguity they cause on the surface. This depends largely upon the phonetic or phonological traces they leave behind. The success of a parsing approach in dealing with deletion will depend on the types of cues available on the surface.

Similar to neutralization of features, deletion of segments can cause lexical ambiguity when the deletion leads to homophony. If the output of a deletion rule is identical to an already existing lexical item, it will be impossible to reconstruct its underlying form with absolute certainty. Our previous example of *interstate* becoming *[iner]state* is a case of such lexical ambiguity, since the word *inner* already exists and *inner state* is a legitimate sequence in the language. But deletion of [t] does not always lead to an already existent word; the word *center* becomes ce[n]er, which is unambiguous, making the recovery of the deleted [t] easier in a phrase like *center field* than in *interstate*.

We can distinguish at least two classes of traces that are left behind by deletion rules:

1. a sequence of segments which violates the phonotactic constraints of the language

2. altered features of neighboring segments, compensatory lengthening of an adjoining segment, or the introduction of a new segment indicating that a segment has been deleted.

Examples of different types of traces will be provided below.

1. Phonotactic violations: Every language has a set of constraints that restrict the occurrence of sequences of segments in specific contexts. English, for instance, does not allow two successive stop consonants to occur in the same syllable. When the deletion of a vowel leads to such an illegal sequence, this is information that there must be a missing segment. Sometimes, in connected speech, the initial reduced vowel in a word like *potato* is deleted, producing the illegal syllable-initial cluster [pt]. This illegal sequence, together with the aspirated [p] (which shows that it is syllable-initial and cannot be followed by another stop), indicates that a vowel has been deleted.

2a. Altered segments: The segments preceding or following the deleted segment are often changed in the deletion process. Unstressed vowels in word-final syllables are frequently deleted in English when followed by a liquid or a nasal (consider *African* and *channel*). However, since the final cluster created (e.g., [kn] or [nl]) is illegal in English, the final nasal or liquid becomes syllabic. A listener hearing a syllabic nasal or a liquid can, in principle, infer that a vowel has been deleted, since syllabic consonants do not occur elsewhere.

2b. Added segments: The introduction of a glottal stop after the deletion of a medial [t] or [d], when followed by a nasal in words like *beaten*, is an example of a new segment indicating that a deletion has taken place. Here, the alveolar consonant leaves a trace in the form of a glottal stop before the [n] producing the surface form [biʔn] and not [bin].

2c. Compensatory lengthening: Another type of phonological trace is the compensatory lengthening of a contiguous sound. For instance, consonant deletion often leads to compensatory lengthening of the previous vowel. In casual speech, Turkish speakers frequently drop [v] when it is followed by a labial consonant or a vowel. This loss is compensated for by lengthening the vowel—[ovmak] alternates with [oːmak] ("to rub") (Sezer 1986).

The preceding discussion suggests that deletion should not be treated as a homogeneous process, since its consequences are varied. There appear to be instances of deletion, such as those leading to lexical homophony, from which listeners are unlikely to recover underlying forms. Nevertheless, many surface forms resulting from deletion retain phonological or phonetic traces of the missing segment. The success of a parsing approach depends critically upon the listeners' ability to actively use these traces to recover deleted segments.

It remains an open empirical question to what extent it is actually feasible for the listener to recover underlying forms when there is no transparent relationship between these forms and their surface manifestations. An obvious way of avoiding many of the problems associated with recovering underlying representations is simply to include the different word variants in the lexicon. In the next subsection we will examine how an approach that precompiles phonological knowledge in the lexicon deals with these phonological processes.

Precompiling Phonological Knowledge in the Lexicon

A strategy for dealing with variability that is shared by many speech-recognition algorithms is to include more than one template for the same word type. When the acoustic properties of an input deviate sufficiently from the existing templates, a new template is created. The innovation in a pre-compiling approach is to include templates or lexical entries for variants of a given word type only when they are called for by the phonological rules of the language. A set of phonological processes is assumed to apply to initially specified underlying representations. Word variants are thus generated and stored as lexical templates.

The effectiveness of this pre-compiling approach depends critically upon the quality of both the underlying phonological representations and the phonological rules applying to these representations; a pre-compiled lexicon can be only as good as the phonological theory upon which it is based. Unfortunately, most attempts at pre-compiling phonological knowledge have not exploited the recent advances in phonological theory described above.

It is instructive to examine an example of pre-compiling phonological knowledge into the lexicon that is found in the Lexical Access From Spectra or LAFS model (Klatt 1979; Klatt, this volume). We will examine which of the phonological processes distinguished above are pre-compiled in this model and how this pre-compilation is achieved. Models such as LAFS can be extended to cover additional phonological processes if a nonlinear approach to phonology is adopted.

LAFS precompiles phonological processes in the following fashion: First, every word to be included in its branching lexical decoding network is defined in terms of phonemic states and transitions between these states. Words having the same initial phonemes share the initial phoneme states and transitions but branch into different transitions and phoneme states where they diverge. Once a linear path through the network has been defined for each word, the final phoneme state of every word is connected by a transition to the initial phoneme state of every other word. A set of phonological rules are applied to these newly generated phonemic sequences (i.e., those crossing word boundaries). The application of these rules produces as output a phonetic lexical network in which phonemes either are replaced by appropriate allophones (allophonic rules) or by other phonemes (neutralizing rules) or are deleted altogether (deletion rules). Finally, a new network is created by replacing every transition between phonetic states with the corresponding mini-network of spectral states. These mini-networks of 10-msec spectral states are produced by another decoder, SCRIBER, as we will see below. The resulting lexical decoding network is made up of paths of spectral templates, each of which represents lexical hypotheses.

In recognizing a fluent utterance in the LAFS framework, the listener is assumed to follow a continuous path through the decoding network, moving smoothly in spectral template steps from one lexical hypothesis to another. Thus, LAFS is especially designed to pre-compile into the lexicon diverse phonological processes that apply across word boundaries. Klatt, in his description of LAFS, is much less explicit as to how within-word phonological processes are precompiled. The burden of pre-compiling these processes falls upon SCRIBER, the automatic phonetic transcriber that complements LAFS. SCRIBER generates a phonetic transcription of the acoustic input. In order to capture the context-dependent acoustic properties of these segments, phonetic sequences are converted into a sequence of concatenated diphones. Diphones represent the acoustic information corresponding to the transition between segments (i.e., from the midpoint of one phone to the midpoint of the next phone). These diphones are subsequently replaced by the same mini-network of spectral states used in LAFS.

By appealing to representations in which diphones are represented by a sequence of spectral states, LAFS and SCRIBER acquire some noteworthy properties. Such sequences allow these models to pre-compile co-articulatory effects between adjacent segments as well as phonological processes that operate between these segments. Furthermore, networks can be constructed so as to allow the variable amounts of feature spreading between the affected segments that are evident in vowel nasalization.

LAFS is, nonetheless, restricted in the types of phonological process that it can precompile. Specifically, it is restricted to those applying at word boundaries between word-final and word-initial segments and those applying within words between two adjacent segments. Both of these processes depend upon a strictly local melodic conditioning context. All other processes, however, including those that depend upon nonadjacent melodic contexts (like umlauting in German) or prosodic contexts (like reduction, which depends upon prominence relations between syllables), are not pre-compiled into LAFS. Such pre-compiling would require a richer underlying representation than the string of phonemic states used in LAFS. Some prosodic structure should be included in the initial phonologic representation.

A step in this direction can be found in the LEXGEN (Harrington, Laver, and Cutting 1986) program. Here, a large number of phonological processes apply to underlying forms which have syllable structure marked. In this way, word variants having undergone reduction or deletion processes—typical of fast speech—can also be pre-compiled. What is important to note is that the representation serving as the point of departure for the precompilation cannot be a simple concatenation of phonological units as in LAFS but must include prosodic structure.

An approach that pre-compiles phonological processes into the lexicon avoids the difficult problem of recovering a single underlying representation from ambiguous surface forms. Nonetheless, it does have some potentially negative consequences. First, it leads to a dramatic increase in the number of lexical entries that must be stored.[5] Second, such an approach is incapable of capturing the very generalizations that it is using to determine the pre-compiling. For example, as Klatt (1986) himself points out, LAFS reduplicates phonological processes for every word-to-word transition, which leads to the generation of an extremely large number of different between-word transitions.[6] The connectionist framework, as we will see in the following subsection, appears to present an alternative that can better express underlying phonological generalizations.

Connectionist Models
Since models developed within the connectionist framework have received considerable treatment in this volume (see the chapters by Elman and

Seidenberg), we will only mention briefly the ways in which such models incorporate phonological knowledge or regularity.

Prosodically Conditioned Allophonic Rules

The most explicit interactive activation model of spoken-word recognition, TRACE (Elman and McClelland 1984; McClelland and Elman 1986), distinguishes three different levels of representation: distinctive feature, phonemic, and lexical. Thus, TRACE does not include any prosodic structure and therefore cannot make use of prosodically conditioned allophonic information. Other models developed in the connectionist tradition (Dell 1986; MacKay 1987) can do so because they have nodes representing both syllables and their component parts. As a consequence, a model like that of MacKay differentiates between allophones as a function of their position in the syllable. For example, an aspirated stop in English would activate the phonological nodes that are connected to the onset of the syllable and not those connected to the coda.

Melodically Conditioned Allophonic Rules

Melodically conditioned allophonic processes are quite naturally exploited in TRACE, since featural information (both distinctive and nondistinctive) can activate several different phonemes simultaneously. Thus, TRACE allows allophonic featural information about an upcoming segment to pre-activate this phoneme; the nasal feature associated with the vowel could begin immediately to activate the following nasal consonant.

Neutralizing and Deleting Processes

There has been little discussion of how these models handle neutralizing and deleting phonological processes. There appear to be at least two ways in which word variants resulting from these processes could be recognized. First, they should be recognized when they provide the best fit with the appropriate lexical entry—that is, when the surface variant matches its canonic entry better than any other word in the lexicon. An alternative solution along the lines of the pre-compiling approach would involve adding new entries once the surface variant has been encountered with sufficient frequency. Clearly, additional work is required in this tradition to make more explicit how word variants are recognized.

Conclusion

In this paper we have been concerned with the neglected area of phonological processes and their effect upon lexical access. We claimed that psycholinguists have not paid sufficient attention to the role that phonological structure plays in the listener's remarkable ability to recognize words in their variable phonetic shape. Since phonological theory aims to account for linguistically significant variability in word forms, phonological descriptions (both in terms of structure and in terms of rules) are potentially valuable in investigating lexical processing. In our discussion of phonological theory, we appealed to recent developments in which phonological representations have hierarchical structure and in which rules are distinguished by their domain of application (lexical versus postlexical or melodic versus prosodic). We described several types of postlexical phonological processes (allophonic, neutralizing, and deleting) within this framework, and we identified properties of these rules having psycholinguistic consequences.

Focusing on these phonological processes, we then examined several alternative psychological accounts of how listeners deal with the variability in the phonetic shape of words. These approaches appear to be differentially suited to handle the types of phonological processes distinguished. According to the first approach, listeners reverse phonological processes to derive the underlying form. The success of this approach clearly depends upon the *recoverability* of this form. Our analysis has revealed that it is not equally feasible for listeners to recover the underlying representations of surface forms resulting from allophonic, neutralizing, and deletion processes. Listeners can easily recover an allophone's underlying representation (since it retains its distinctive featural content) and can productively exploit the allophone to identify its prosodic or melodic context.

It is less obvious, however, how listeners can recover the underlying representation of a word that has undergone neutralization or deletion, since the resulting surface form is often ambiguous. Here, the amount of ambiguity—ranging from local (segmental) to more global (lexical) ambiguity—depends upon factors such as the coincidental existence in the lexicon of identical but unrelated word forms and the presence of phonological and phonetic traces in the signal. Empirical studies examining the extent to which listeners can and do exploit surface cues to undo phonological processes are needed. However, on this view, the listeners' behavior is not based exclusively upon what is in the signal; their preferences in the analysis of ambiguous phonetic sequences also depend upon their phonological system, as was shown to be the case for the perception of Bengali nasal vowels.

Alternative approaches in which phonological knowledge is pre-compiled by storing surface variants in the lexicon have been proposed to avoid the difficulty presented by ambiguous surface forms. We examined one such proposal—the LAFS model of Klatt—which deals specifically with phono-logical processes that apply at word boundaries. This model can efficiently pre-compile phonological processes applying at word boundaries, but has not yet been extended to handle other types of prosodically conditioned processes, such as reduction rules. Pre-compiling these additional phono-logical variants requires a richer phonological representation.

It has not been our objective here to decide between the rough psycho-logical sketches that we have provided. A great deal of experimental research in this largely untouched domain is required to determine to what extent these approaches are successful in accounting for the listener's recognition of phonetic variants. Rather, our aim here has been to convince the reader that the two questions posed in the title of this chapter deserve affirmative answers. First, listeners do use their phonological knowledge in understanding spoken language, as is illustrated by the differences in the way English and Bengali listeners interpret nasalized vowels as a function of their grammar. Second, if listeners use their phonological knowledge in interpreting the sensory input, then psycholinguists should probably do the same in studying listeners. Linguistic distinctions between different types of phonological processes and levels of representation provide a useful basis for empirical research into listeners' ability to recognize words despite their variable phonetic shape.

Acknowledgments

We would like thank William Marslen-Wilson, Lyn Frazier, and Bruce Hayes for their helpful comments on earlier versions of this chapter.

Notes

1. These timing slots can also be represented as X's where the consonants and vowels can be distinguished by their location in the syllable structure (Levin 1982). Since this issue is not strictly relevant to our discussion, we will continue to use C's and V's for expository simplicity.

2. Principles of well-formedness constrain the associations between tiers; association lines, for instance, are not allowed to cross. A representation such as the following would therefore be ill-formed.

*C   V   C

3. Within phonological theory it is undisputed that such contextual neutraliza-tion is a productive phenomenon in natural language. Recent work in acoustics (Dinnsen 1985), however, has led to a controversy concerning the *completeness* of

neutralization in the acoustic signal. It has been claimed that neutralization is often not complete—that is, that there are acoustic differences which preserve the underlying distinction. Thus, for example, experimental studies on the final devoicing of obstruents in German and Catalan have suggested that the underlying voicing contrast is acoustically preserved (O'Dell and Port 1983; Dinnsen and Charles-Luce 1984; Dinnsen 1985). Clearly, if this were the case, the problem of disambiguating neutralized segments would not arise as acutely. However, studies on the neutralization of length contrasts (vowels in Dutch and consonants in Turkish and Bengali) demonstrate that no significant acoustic differences are observable in the appropriate neutralizing contexts (Lahiri, Schriefers, and Kuijpers 1987; Lahiri and Hankamer 1986). For the purposes of this chapter we assume that, at least in some instance, no surface cues exist to disambiguate neutralized phonemes.

4. As Hayes has pointed out to us, both *hitch you* and *hit you* can further merge to [hɪtʃu] when [j] deleted after palato-alveolars by a different rule.

5. Although English has a relatively simple morphology and consequently is a good candidate for pre-compilation, there are other languages (such as Turkish; see Hankamer, this volume) whose morphologies generate so many forms for any given lexical item that one might wonder whether the storage capacity of the human brain would be surpassed.

6. As a remedy to this problem, Klatt (1986; this volume) had recently changed his model to include a single separate network of cross-word-boundary spectral sequences that specifies every possible transition between words only once.

References

Chomsky, N., and M. Halle. 1968. *Sound Pattern of English*. New York: Harper and Row.

Church, K. 1983. Phrase-Structure Parsing: A Method of Taking Advantage of Allophonic Constraints. Dissertation, MIT (also distributed by Indiana University Linguistics Club).

Church, K. 1987. "Phonological parsing and lexical retrieval." *Cognition* 25(1–2): 53–69.

Clements, N. 1985. "Geometry of phonological features." In *Phonology yearbook 2*. New York: Academic.

Clements, G. N., and S. J. Keyser. 1983. *CV Phonology*. Cambridge, Mass.: MIT Press.

Cutting, D., and J. Harrington. 1986. "Phonogram: An interpreter for phonological rules." *Proceedings of the Institute of Acoustics* 8.

Dell, G. 1986. "A spreading activation theory of retrieval in sentence production." *Psychological Review* 93(3): 283–321.

Dinnsen, D. A. 1985. "A re-examination of phonological neutralization." *Journal of Linguistics* 21: 265–279.

Dinnsen, D. A., and J. Charles-Luce. 1984. "Phonological neutralization, phonetic implementation and individual difference." *Phonetica* 12: 49–60.

Dogil, G. 1986. Phonological Pivot Parsing. Presented at the 11th International Conference on Computational Linguistics, Bonn.

Dresher, B. E., and A. Lahiri. 1986. Metrical Coherence in Germanic. Presented at LSA annual meeting, New York.

Elman, J. L., and J. L. McClelland. 1984. "Speech perception as a cognitive process: The interactive activation model." in N. Lass (ed.), *Speech and Language*, volume 10. New York: Academic.

Frazier, L. 1987. "Structure in auditory word recognition." *Cognition* 25(1–2): 157–187.

Grosjean, F., and J. P. Gee. 1987. "Prosodic structure in spoken word recognition." *Cognition* 25(1–2): 157–187.

Harrington, J., J. Laver, and D. Cutting. 1986. "Word-structure reduction rules in automatic, continuous speech recognition." *Proceedings of the Institute of Acoustics* 8.

Hayes, B. 1986. "Inalterability in CV Phonology." *Language* 62(2): 321–352.

Kahn, D. 1976. Syllable Based Generalizations in English Phonology." Dissertation, MIT (also distributed by Indiana University Linguistics Club).

Kiparsky, P. 1982. "Some consequences of lexical phonology." *Phonology Yearbook* 2: 85–138.

Kiparsky, P. 1985. "From cyclic to lexical phonology." In H. van der Hulst and N. Smith (eds.), *The Structure of Phonological Representations, Part I*. Dordrecht: Foris.

Klatt, D. H. 1977. "Review of the ARPA speech understanding project." *Journal of the Acoustical Society of America* 62: 1345–1366.

Klatt, D. H. 1980. "Speech perception: a model of acoustic-phonetic analysis and lexical access." In R. A. Cole (ed.), *Perception and Production of Fluent Speech*. Hillsdale, N.J.: Erlbaum.

Klatt, D. H. 1986. "Problem of variability in speech recognition and models of speech perception." In J. S. Perkell and D. H. Klatt (eds.), *Invariance and Variability in Speech Processes*. Hillsdale, N.J.: Erlbaum.

Ladefoged, P. 1982. *A Course in Phonetics*. New York: Harcourt Brace Jovanovich.

Lahiri, A., and J. Hankamer. 1986. The Timing of Geminate Consonants. *Journal of Phonetics*, in press.

Lahiri, A., and W. D. Marslen-Wilson. 1987. The Mental Representation of Lexical Form: A Phonological Approach to the Recognition Lexicon. In preparation.

Lahiri, A., H. Schriefers, and C. Kuijpers. 1987. "Contextual neutralization of vowel length: Evidence from Dutch." *Phonetica* 44: 91–102.

Levin, J. 1985. A Metrical Theory of Syllabicity. Dissertation, MIT.

McCarthy, J. 1986. "OCP effects: Gemination and antigemination." *Linguistic Inquiry* 17(2): 207–263.

McClelland, J. L., and J. L. Elman. 1986. "The TRACE model of speech perception." *Cognitive Psychology* 18(1): 1–86.

MacKay, D. G. 1987. *The Organization of Perception and Action: Fundamentals of Theoretical Psychology.* New York: Academic.

Martin, J. G., and H. T. Bunnell. 1982. "Perception of anticipatory coarticulation effects in vowel-stop consonant-vowel sequences." *Journal of Experimental Psychology: Human Perception and Performance* 8: 473–488.

Mohanan, K. P. 1986. *The Theory of Lexical Phonology.* Dordrecht: Reidel.

Nespor, M., and I. Vogel. 1986. *Prosodic Phonology.* Dordrecht: Foris.

O'Dell, M. L., and R. F. Port. 1983. "Discrimination of word final voicing in German." *Journal of the Acoustical Society of America* 73: S1.

Sezer, E. 1986. "An autosegmental analysis of compensatory lengthening in Turkish." In L. Wetzels and E. Sezer (eds.), *Studies in Compensatory Lengthening.* Dordrecht: Foris.

Warren, P., and W. D. Marslen-Wilson. 1987. "Continuous uptake of acoustic cues in spoken word-recognition." *Perception and Psychophysics* 41(3): 262–275.

Whalen, D. H. 1982. "Subcategorial mismatches in lexical access." *Perception and Psychophysics* 35: 49–64.

Chapter 11

Auditory Lexical Access: Where Do We Start?	Anne Cutler

The lexicon, considered as a component of the process of recognizing speech, is a device that accepts a sound image as input and outputs meaning. Lexical access is the process of formulating an appropriate input and mapping it onto an entry in the lexicon's store of sound images matched with their meanings.

This chapter addresses the problems of auditory lexical access from continuous speech. The central argument to be proposed is that utterance prosody plays a crucial role in the access process. Continuous listening faces problems that are not present in visual recognition (reading) or in noncontinuous recognition (understanding isolated words). Aspects of utterance prosody offer a solution to these particular problems.

1 Lexical Access in Continuous Speech Recognition

There is, alas, no direct auditory equivalent of the little white spaces that so conveniently segment one word from another in continuous text. Speech is truly continuous. There are, admittedly, certain phonological cues to segmentation; for instance, the phonetic sequence [tb] must span a syllable boundary. But equally there are phonological effects that mask boundaries; the sequence [dj] can be affricated, irrespective of whether it belongs to one word (as in British English *duty*) or two (as in *did you*). There is no reliable cue marking every word boundary in speech, as there is in text.

Thus, in continuous auditory recognition there is a problem of *segmentation* that is absent in visual recognition (where spaces between words provide explicit word-boundary markers) and in the recognition of words in isolation. Segmentation is necessary because lexical access must operate with discrete units, since the lexicon must store discrete units. The number of potential utterances is infinite; no recognizer could possibly store in memory, for eventual match against a possible future input, every complete utterance that might conceivably be presented. Only the discrete meanings from which utterances are combined can reasonably be stored. When a recognizer is presented with continuous speech, therefore, it cannot begin the process of lexical access until it has taken some decision about how the stream of continuous speech should be segmented into units that one might reasonably expect to be matched in the lexicon.

The segmentation issue is closely connected with the question of the formulation of the lexical access code, i.e., the precise nature of the input to the lexicon. For instance, suppose that input representations in the lexicon were in the form of minimally normalized acoustic templates. Computation of the lexical access code would be trivial; however, attempts at lexical access would have to be initiated at vastly many arbitrarily determined points, leading to a huge imbalance of wasted versus successful access attempts. At the other extreme, suppose that the access code were a string of syllables. Then one might simply assume each syllable boundary to be a word boundary. This strategy would successfully detect each word boundary at relatively little cost in false alarms, but the computational cost of deriving the access code representation would be considerable—especially in English and other stress languages, where syllable boundaries are frequently unclear. Moreover, there is evidence that syllabic segmentation is not used in the recognition of English words (Cutler, Mehler, Norris, and Segui 1986).

The present chapter proposes a strategy for segmentation of continuous speech and for access of lexical forms in languages like English. The strategy is based on prosody. However, as the next section will describe, prosody may not be exploited in the most superficially plausible way.

2 Lexical Prosody and Metrical Prosody

Words and sentences both have prosodic structure. Word prosody, in lexical-stress languages such as English, consists of stress pattern: What is the stress level of each syllable of a word? Take, for instance, the words *generate*, *general*, and *generic*. All have different lexical prosody. *Generate* and *general* both have primary stress on the first syllable; *generic* is stressed on the second syllable. However, *generate* has secondary stress on the third syllable and hence is further distinguished from *general*, which has no secondary stress.

The prosodic structure of sentences embraces intonation contour and rhythm. The rhythm of an utterance is the pattern of strong and weak syllables in the words that make up the utterance. Metrical prosody is another name for this system. Thus, metrical prosody is in one sense a simpler system than lexical prosody, since it has only two levels: strong and weak. A strong syllable is any syllable containing a full vowel; a weak syllable contains a reduced vowel (usually a schwa). The citation form of *generate*, in terms of metrical prosody, has the pattern strong-weak-strong; the citation form of *general* is strong-weak-weak; and the citation form of generic is weak-strong-weak. Thus, although in terms of lexical prosody *generate* and *general*—both having initial stress—might seem more like each other than like *generic*, in terms of metrical prosody it is reasonable to consider *general* and *generic*—with only one strong syllable each—as in a sense more like each other than like *generate* (which has two strong syllables).

However, the difference between lexical prosody and metrical prosody is not just that the metrical prosodic system allows only two levels whereas the lexical prosodic system has more. The important difference is in the domain of each system. Lexical prosody, as the name suggests, refers to words. Lexical stress patterns are defined upon canonical pronunciations of words. Importantly, lexical stress patterns of words in citation-form pronunciations may not always be fully realized in actual utterances. (*General*, for example, is often pronounced with two syllables.) The metrical prosodic system, on the other hand, refers to the rhythmic pattern of longer stretches of speech. Again, citation-form rhythms may differ from the rhythms of the same forms produced in conversational context; however, actual rhythms and citation-form rhythms can equally well be described as a sequence of strong and weak syllables.

It might seem most likely that the relevant dimension of prosody for lexical representation, and hence lexical access, should be lexical prosody. As the next sections will demonstrate, such an assumption seems not to be justified.

3   Does Lexical Prosody Play a Role in Lexical Access?

In order to know the lexical prosodic structure of a word, the recognizer must know how many syllables the word has; in order to know how many syllables a word has, it is necessary to know where the word begins and ends. This dependence in itself suggests that lexical prosody may not be a crucial component of the lexical access code, at least in continuous speech recognition. If lexical prosodic information is useful for word recognition, then prior awareness of such information should facilitate lexical access; Cutler and Clifton (1984), however, found that lexical decision responses were not in fact facilitated when subjects were given prior knowledge of stress via a grouping of materials according to stress pattern.

Some pairs of words differ in stress pattern but are otherwise pronounced identically. *FOREarm* and *foreARM*, for instance, each have full vowels in both syllables, despite their stress-pattern opposition. If lexical prosody is entirely irrelevant to the lexical access code, then identical codes should be computed for each member of such pairs. That is, *FOREarm* and *foreARM* should, before the lexical-access stage of recognition, be effectively homophonous. And they are: Cutler (1986) tested such pairs in a cross-modal priming study. In this case the cross-modal priming task, developed by Swinney (1979), served as a diagnostic test for homophony. Swinney showed that homophones prime associates to each of their meanings; when a subject hears the homophone *bug*, for instance, lexical-decision responses to a simultaneously presented visual probe are faster if the probe is related to either the "insect" or the "listening device" meaning of *bug*. That is, both *ant* and *spy* are responded to faster than the matched control word *sew*. Similarly, when a subject hears a sentence containing either *FOREarm* or *foreARM*, in both cases the subject responds to visual probes related to either word (*elbow* versus *prepare*) faster than to matched control words. That is, pairs of words differing only in lexical prosody—such as *FOREarm* and *foreARM*—behave just like other homophones. Presentation of the sound sequence representing either one leads to access of the lexical representation of both. This result is not due simply to partial priming via partial phonetic overlap, since phonetically similar words do not prime one another (Slowiaczek and Pisoni 1986). The homophony of *FOREarm* and *foreARM* shows that differences of lexical prosody alone are not sufficient to produce differences in the lexical access code. Lexical prosody—i.e., the fact that *FOREarm* is stressed on the first syllable and *foreARM* on the second—appears to be irrelevant in lexical access.

This conclusion offers a way out of what would appear to be a dilemma produced by apparently contradictory results from investigations of a related phenomenon, namely the effects of erroneous lexical prosody. Some studies have suggested that misstressed words are harder to recognize. For example, Bansal (1966) found that Indian English, in which stress is signaled in a manner that is unconventional to British English ears, led British English listeners to misperceive stress placement and consequently to misinterpret the speaker's utterance so as to conform with the erroneous stress pattern—even though the chosen interpretation at times conflicted with the phonetic segmental structure of the utterance. Thus, one speaker pronounced *yesterday* with a pitch peak on the second syllable, and signaled the placement of lexical stress on the first syllable by lengthening only. In British English, pitch peaks and lengthening co-occur in the signaling of lexical stress. Listeners reported hearing *or study* rather than *yesterday*; that is, the stress was perceived as occurring where the pitch peak occurred, and the utterance was interpreted as one with lexical stress properly on that syllable even though this required interpretation of the reduced vowel [ə] as the full vowel [ʌ]. Similarly, Bond and Small (1983) found that misstressed words were infrequently restored in shadowing; with the number of times a mispronounced word was neither repeated verbatim nor restored to its proper form used as an index of disruptiveness of the mispronounciation, misstressing proved about three times as disruptive as mispronunciation of a single vowel or consonant. Cutler and Clifton (1984), using a semantic-categorization task, also found that misstressed words were disruptive; they were responded to more slowly than their correctly stressed versions.

The latter study, however, also made an explicit comparison between the prosodic and segmental attributes of stress. Cutler and Clifton compared the effects of misstressing words having two full syllables (such as *canteen* or *turbine*) against the effects of misstressing words with one weak syllable (such as *lagoon* or *wallet*). In the latter case, misstressing necessarily resulted in a segmental change as well (i.e., a change from a schwa to a full vowel), whereas in the former case it did not. Only in the latter case did misstressing necessarily inhibit recognition—*LAgoon* and *walLET* were responded to significantly more slowly than *laGOON* and *WALlet*, respectively. But when no segmental change was involved, the effect of the misstressing depended on the direction of the stress shift. Rightward shifts were harmful; *turBINE* was harder to recognize than *TURbine*. Leftward shifts, however, were harmless; recognition of *CANteen* and *canTEEN* did not differ significantly.

Taft (1984) also failed to find effects of misstressing on phoneme-monitoring response time. Detection of phoneme targets was not significantly slowed if the word immediately preceding the target was misstressed. In fact, responses were actually faster if the misstressing involved a leftward shift; *CHAMpagne* produced faster responses than the correct version *chamPAGNE*.

The apparent contradiction between these results disappears, however, with consideration of the distinction between lexical prosody and metrical prosody. All misstressings necessarily alter lexical prosodic structure. As Cutler's study of cross-modal priming showed, however, lexical prosody is irrelevant in lexical access. Only some misstressings appear to inhibit lexical access. Only some misstressings alter metrical prosody as well as lexical prosody—specifically, when a full vowel is reduced or a reduced vowel becomes full, the metrical structure of the word is altered.

The overall result of the misstressing studies can be summarized as follows: Changes in metrical prosodic structure necessarily inhibit recognition; changes only in lexical prosodic structure do not. Thus, Bansal's Indian speakers were *perceived* as giving full vocalic value to vowels that in British English would normally be reduced; Bond and Small's misstressings all resulted in reduced vowels becoming full; and Cutler and Clifton's *lagoon-wallet* condition similarly produced full vowel quality where reduction was expected. All these misstressings therefore altered the metrical prosody (via alteration of the vocalic segments), and they all produced significant decrements in recognition performance.

Taft, on the other hand, manipulated lexical prosody without altering metrical prosody. The words she used (e.g., *afghan* and *champagne*) had full vowels in both syllables, so shifting stress from one syllable to another left vowel quality intact and the metrical structure unchanged. Cutler and Clifton's *canteen-turbine* condition also left metrical structure intact. Taft found no effect of lexical prosodic shift under these conditions; Cutler and Clifton found no effect for leftward shifts. Rightward shifts, it is true, did inhibit recognition in Cutler and Clifton's study. However, they included several words like *whisky*, with an open final syllable. Bolinger (1981) suggests that the second syllable of such a word is in fact metrically weak. If that is the case, then rightward shifts in the Cutler-Clifton study may actually have altered metrical structure (whereas leftward shifts did not). Thus, the picture may be perfectly consistent: Misstressing only inhibits recognition when metrical prosody is changed, not when only lexical prosody is changed.

This implies that the role of prosody in the lexical access process is by no means a direct one. It is possible to describe the prelexical representations computed for lexical access purely in segmental terms; lexical prosody does not need to be marked in these codes. This is fully consistent with a view of lexical representations such as that proposed by Bolinger (1981), in which lexical entries have no stress patterns but have only segmental representations (in which full vowels are represented as full and reduced vowels as reduced) plus a marker indicating which syllable should receive primary accentuation in citation form. An accurate segmental representation will be all that is needed to access a lexical entry. Reducing a full vowel or giving full value to a reduced vowel (even when, as in the second syllable of *whisky*, the reduced form can be described as a very short version of the full form) results in an inaccurate segmental representation and hence in poorer recognition performance. The prosodic structure of words is not coded for lexical access; only the segmental structure is relevant.

However, the importance of the distinction between full and reduced vowels in this prelexical segmental representation suggests an indirect role for prosody in the lexical access process. That is, it may be reasonable to claim that there is a sense in which metrical prosody plays a role in lexical access even if lexical prosody does not. Some specific investigations of this issue will be considered in the next section.

4   Does Metrical Prosody Play a Role in Lexical Access?

Speakers assume that metrical prosody is more important to listeners than lexical prosody. This conclusion can be drawn from further consideration of misstressings. Sometimes speakers misstress a word quite by accident. Here are four examples of such errors in lexical stress (from Cutler, 1980):

(1) ... from my PROsodic-proSODic colleagues.

(2) ... each of these acoustic property detectors perhaps being subJECT— perhaps being SUBject to ...

(3) You think it's sarCASm, but its not.

(4) We're only at the early stages of it, we're still enTHUSiastic.

Sometimes the misstressing produces a change in vowel quality and hence an alteration in metrical prosody—as in (1), where the reduced vowel in the first syllable became a full vowel in the error, or as in (2), where the full vowel in the first syllable was reduced in the error. But sometimes a misstressing produces no metrical change at all—as in (3) and (4), where stress has shifted from one strong syllable, or full vowel, to another.

Speakers do not always correct their slips of the tongue; in fact, the correlation rate for lexical-stress errors (34 percent in the author's corpus) is noticeably lower than the mean correction rates for phonemic (75 percent) or lexical (57 percent) slips cited by Nooteboom (1980). When speakers do correct lexical-stress errors, however, they correct them significantly more often if the metrical prosody has been altered (61 percent) than if only the lexical prosody has changed (21 percent) (Cutler 1983). That is, errors like (1) and (2) are far more likely to be corrected than errors like (3) and (4). Speakers appear to assume that changes in metrical prosody will threaten listeners' reception of the message more than changes in lexical prosody.

Table 1
Slips of the ear: juncture misperception.

Spoken	Perceived
it was illegal	it was an eagle
assistant	his sister
a Coke and a Danish	a coconut Danish
my gorge is...	my gorgeous
she's a must to avoid	she's a muscular boy
fornication	for an occasion
paint your ruler	paint remover

Suppose, however, that a slip is made by a listener. Studies of slips of the ear show that prosodic misperceptions are very rare indeed. Metrical prosody, particularly, is resistent to distortion—the parts of the speech signal that are least susceptible to distortion are the vowels in stressed syllables (Bond and Garnes 1980; Browman 1978). The only way in which metrical prosody is distorted in slips of the ear is that weak syllables may be lost or duplicated.

Table 1 presents some slips of the ear. They are all errors in which juncture has been misperceived—that is, word boundaries have been added, lost, or shifted. It can easily be seen that, as with slips of the ear in general, metrical structure is preserved—strong syllables are perceived as strong, weak ones as weak. But what is interesting about these slips is the direction of the boundary mislocations: Boundaries tend to be perceived at the onset of strong syllables rather than weak. When "she's a must to avoid" is perceived as "she's a muscular boy", a boundary has been added prior to the final strong syllable, while boundaries before the two weak syllables preceding it have both been deleted. Similarly, when "a Coke and a Danish" is perceived as "a coconut Danish", boundaries before two weak syllables have been deleted, and when "it was illegal" is perceived as "it was an eagle", a boundary has been moved from the onset of a weak syllable to the onset of a strong syllable.

Sometimes the reverse is true, as in the final two examples in the table. Perception of "paint your ruler" as "paint remover", for instance, deletes a boundary before a strong syllable. However, such examples are in the minority. Sally Butterfield and I examined all the juncture misperceptions we could find in my own collection of slips of the ear and in published collections such as Bond and Garnes 1980 and Browman 1978. More than two-thirds of them (roughly the proportions in the table) conformed to the generalization that boundaries were perceived at the onset of strong syllables rather than weak ones. The effect was statistically significant (Butterfield and Cutler 1988).

This suggests a specific way in which metrical prosody may be exploited in lexical access: Strong syllables may be taken to be word onsets. Thus, metrical prosody may provide a way of dealing with the crucial segmentation problem in continuous speech recognition. Some further recent work from our laboratory offers strong support for this hypothesis.

Cutler and Norris (1988) investigated the detection of words embedded in nonsense matrices with differing metrical structures. For example, the word *mint* was embedded either in *mintayf* [mintef], in which the second syllable was strong, or *mintef* [mintəf], in which the second syllable contained a schwa (i.e., was weak). Cutler and Norris reasoned that, if segmentation were guided by metrical prosody such that boundaries were hypothesized prior to each strong syllable, then *mintayf* would be segmented (min-tayf), whereas *mintef*, with a weak second syllable, would not. A word spread across two segmentation units should prove more difficult to detect than the same word in an unsegmented string. Indeed, detection of *mint* in *mintayf* was significantly slower than detection of *mint* in *mintef*. Further experiments ruled out several confounds. For instance, it was not the case that *mint* in *mintayf* was spoken in such a way that it was less like some canonical lexical template for *mint* than *mint* in *mintef*. Cutler and Norris demonstrated this by presenting subjects with the same strings from which the final vowel-consonant sequence had been removed. If the actual articulation of the *mint* token were responsible for the difficulty of detecting *mint* in *mintayf*, then *mint* from *mintayf* should still be harder to recognize than *mint* from *mintef*. However, both tokens were detected equally rapidly.

Again, it was not the case that the greater difficulty of detecting *mint* in *mintayf* than in *mintef* was simply due to the nature of the second syllables. It could be that subjects waited till the end of the item to initiate a response, and they had to wait longer in *mintayf* than in *mintef* because the second syllable is longer. Alternatively, it could be that the louder a second syllable is, the more it interferes with processing of the first syllable, so that the second syllable of *mintayf*, being louder than the second syllable of *mintef*, interfered more with the processing of *mint*. But Cutler and Norris disposed of these possibilities by comparing detection of *mint* in *mintayf* versus *mintef* with detection of *thin* in *thintayf* versus *thintef*. The second syllable of *thintayf* is just as much longer and louder than the second syllable of *thintef* as the second syllable of *mintayf* versus *mintef*. If simple loudness or duration of the second syllable were responsible for the difficulty of *mint* in *mintayf* versus *mintef*, then detection of *thin* in *thintayf* should similarly be harder than detection of *thin* in *thintef*. On the other hand, if Cutler and Norris' interpretation of the difficulty of detecting *mint* in *mintayf* were correct, namely that it was due solely to the difficulty of detecting a word spread over two segmentation units, then detection of *thin* should be equally easy in both *thintayf* and *thintef*; although *thintayf*, with a strong second syllable, would be segmented (thin-tayf), the word *thin* belongs only to the first segmentation unit, so that segmentation should not hamper its detection in any way. Cutler and Norris' prediction was supported: Although *mint* was again harder to detect in *mintayf* than in *mintef*, *thin* was detected equally rapidly in both *thintayf* and *thintef*.

The conclusion drawn by Cutler and Norris was that metrical prosody is indeed exploited in word recognition. Specifically, it forms the basis of a strategy of segmentation, whereby boundaries are postulated at the onset of strong syllables.

5 Metrical Prosody of the English Vocabulary

The rationale for positing boundaries prior to strong syllables, it may be assumed, is that such boundaries are likely to be lexical unit (i.e., word) boundaries. Taft (1984) has direct evidence in support of this suggestion. She presented listeners with phonetically ambiguous strings, such as *lettuce/let us* (which is metrically strong-weak) and *invests/in vests* (which is metrically weak-strong). For the strong-weak strings, listeners greatly preferred the one-word interpretation; two-word interpretations were chosen more often for the weak-strong strings. That is, boundaries were inserted prior to strong rather than weak syllables. Thus, English listeners appear to segment speech on the working hypothesis that words will begin with strong syllables. However, this strategy will obviously not succeed with all words. In many English words the first syllable's vowel is weak—*appear, begin,* and *succeed* are three examples from the present paragraph. Why should listeners adopt a strategy that may often fail?

Closer consideration of the characteristics of the English vocabulary, however, suggests that a working hypothesis that words begin with strong syllables will fail surprisingly seldom in the recognition of everyday spoken English. First, there are in fact many more words beginning with strong than with weak syllables; second, words beginning with strong syllables have a higher frequency of occurrence than words beginning with weak syllables.

All the most common lexical prosodic patterns in English have a full vowel in the first syllable (Carlson, Elenius, Granstrom, and Hunnicutt 1985). However, more detailed information is available in the metrical statistics which David Carter and I compiled from a 30,000-word dictionary of British English. Seventy-three percent of all words (and 70 percent of polysyllabic words) were listed with a phonetic transcription in which the first vowel was full. (A 20,000-word corpus of American English shows an almost identical distribution: 78 percent of all words, and 73 percent of polysyllabic words, begin with a strong syllable.[1]) However, in a subset of the larger British English corpus, consisting of the 13,000 most common words, it was possible to examine the metrical structure of the vocabulary as a function of word class and frequency of occurrence. We assumed that all monosyllabic closed-class (grammatical) words, irrespective of their phonetic transcription in the dictionary, would be metrically weak in continuous speech. Using this assumption, we found that 72.32 percent of the whole of this 13,000-word subset, and 73.46 percent of the open-class (lexical) words, consisted of or began with strong syllables. But when the mean frequency with which each type of word occurs is taken into account, about 85 percent of open-class words in average speech contexts have full vowels in their (only or) initial syllables.

Of course, many of the words in an average utterance will be grammatical words, such as determiners, conjunctions, and pronouns, and nearly all of these will be monosyllabic and metrically weak. The mean frequency of grammatical words is very high indeed. The proportions of strong and weak onsets are exactly reversed in comparison with the open-class case: Only about 25 percent of grammatical words are polysyllables with strong onsets. (Another 25 percent are polysyllables with weak onsets; the remaining 50 percent are monosyllabic.) Thus, of all words in the average utterance, both grammatical and lexical, it may be that only a minority will have strong initial syllables. But it is highly debatable whether the process of *lexical access* as it was outlined at the beginning of this chapter applies in the same sense to grammatical words—i.e., whether grammatical words have lexical representations of the same kind as lexical words, and whether the process of converting sound to meaning in speech recognition is of the same nature and complexity for grammatical words (especially those that are monosyllabic and metrically weak) as for lexical words. Meaning itself is, after all, not of the same nature for grammatical as for lexical words; the meaning of grammatical words is context-dependent to a far greater degree (consider, for example, *to* in "to swim", "to Cambridge", "to John", "to arms", and "to a far greater degree").

Whatever the lexical model, however, it is clear that the metrical distribution of the English vocabulary allows listeners to extract considerable information from metrical structure. Wherever there is an open-class word there will be at least one strong syllable, and the likelihood is that open-class words will be or begin with strong syllables.

6   The Beginnings of Words and the Beginnings of Lexical Access

The thesis proposed in this chapter has been that the pattern of occurrence of strong and weak syllables offers the basis of a strategy for initiating the lexical access process in the recognition of continuous speech: Start a potential lexical access procedure whenever a strong syllable occurs. If word boundaries were reliably marked in continous speech, there would be no need to invoke such a strategy. This strategy is tailored to the specific problems of recognition in the auditory modality, of continuous speech rather than isolated words.

As the previous section described, the strategy will successfully locate the onsets of the majority of lexical words in the average communication. The strategy will not, as was also pointed out, locate the onsets of words beginning with weak syllables—*appear, begin, succeed*, and the like. However, it is at least conceivable that the strategy of treating strong syllables as if they were onsets is supplemented by an ancillary strategy whereby lexical words beginning with weak syllables can, under appropriate circumstances, be successfully accessed via their strong syllables. That is, may not the phonetic strings [piə], [gɪn], and [sid] serve as one potential access code for, respectively, the words *appear, begin*, and *succeed*? In fact, precisely such a model of lexical access for this type of word has been postulated independently by several authors (Cutler 1976; Bradley 1980; Grosjean and Gee 1987). In such a model, the lexical access process for words like *appear* might be somewhat more complicated than the lexical access process for lexical words that actually do begin with strong syllables. There is evidence that this may indeed be so. This evidence comes from recent work with the gating task (Grosjean 1980), in which successively larger fragments of a word are presented to listeners, who are asked to attempt to identify the word. Studies using this task have investigated how much of a word must actually be heard before the listener can be reasonably sure of what the word is. When words are presented in isolation, recognition of words with strong versus weak initial syllables is not significantly different (William Marslen-Wilson, personal communication). This is also true of the recognition of words in continuous speech, but only if the speech has been carefully read; if natural spontaneous speech is recorded and used in a gating task, then recognition of words with strong first syllables is significantly facilitated in comparison with recognition of words with weak first syllables (MacAllister, in preparation).

The one problem with postulating lexical access via strong syllables for words that begin with weak syllables is that there exists considerable evidence that auditory lexical access proceeds "left to right"—i.e., that the beginnings of words are always accessed before later portions. This evidence underlies the cohort model of auditory word recognition (see, e.g., Marslen-Wilson 1980 and this volume), in which, for instance, a word-initial phonetic string [piə] will activate the words *pierce*, *peerage*, *pianist*, etc. (but not *spear*, not *impious*, and not *appear*).

However, there is a conflict only if one assumes that lexical access must always be based on one and the same access code. This is of course not true of lexical access in language production (i.e., of the access of sound via meaning); any of a number of semantic specifications (e.g., "the originator of the cohort model", "Lolly Tyler's husband", "the editor of this book", "that tall chap in Room 155") will suffice to call up a particular sound pattern (e.g., [wIljəmazlənwIlsən]). In lexical access in perception it is certainly possible that a given meaning could be accessed via any one of several alternative access codes (e.g., the phonetic strings [piə] and [əpiə]), and if the starting point of a lexical string is specified it may well be optimally efficient to process it strictly left to right irrespective of how it begins. However, as was stressed at the beginning of this chapter, the major problem for lexical access in natural speech situations is that word starting points are *not* specified. The evidence presented here has shown how prosodic structure, in particular metrical prosodic structure, can offer a way out of this dilemma. Where do we start lexical access? In the absence of any better information, we can start with any strong syllable.

Acknowledgments

Some of the work described in this chapter was supported by grants from the Alvey Directorate and British Telecom. Thanks to the colleagues with whom collaborative work described here was performed: Sally Butterfield, Chuck Clifton, and Dennis Norris. Thanks to Carol Fowler, William Marslen-Wilson, and Dennis Norris for helpful comments on the manuscript.

Note

1. I am grateful to Uli Frauenfelder for compiling the American statistics.

References

Bansal, R. K. 1966. The Intelligibility of Indian English. Ph.D. thesis, London University.

Bolinger, D. L. 1981. Two Kinds of Vowels, Two Kinds of Rhythm. Indiana University Linguistics Club, Bloomington.

Bond, Z. S., and Garnes, S. 1980. Misperceptions of fluent speech. In *Perception and Production of Fluent Speech*, ed. R. Cole. Hillsdale, N.J.: Erlbaum.

Bond, Z. S., and Small, L. H. 1983. Voicing, vowel and stress mispronunciations in continuous speech. *Perception and Psychophysics* 34: 470–474.

Bradley, D. 1980. Lexical representation of derivational relation. In *Juncture*, ed. M. Aronoff and M.-L. Kean. Saratoga, Calif.: Anma Libri.

Browman, C. P. 1978. Tip of the Tongue and Slip of the Ear: Implications for Language Processing. UCLA Working Paper in Phonetics 42.

Butterfield, S., and A. Cutler. 1988. Segmentation errors by human listeners: Evidence for a prosodic segmentation strategy. In *Proceedings of SPEECH '88: Seventh Symposium of the Federation of Acoustic Societies of Europe*. Edinburgh.

Carlson, R., Elenius, K., Granstrom, B., and Hunnicutt, S. 1985. Phonetic and orthographic properties of the basic vocabulary of five European languages. *Speech Transmission Laboratory (Stockholm): Quarterly Progress and Status Report*, issue 1: 63–94.

Cutler, A. 1976. Phoneme monitoring reaction time as a function of preceding intonation contour. *Perception and Psychophysics* 20: 55–60.

Cutler, A. 1980. Errors of stress and intonation. In *Errors in Linguistic Performance: Slips of the Tongue, Ear, Pen and Hand*, ed. V. A. Fromkin. New York: Academic.

Cutler, A. 1983. Speakers' conceptions of the functions of prosody. In *Prosody: Models and Measurements*, ed. A. Cutler and D. R. Ladd. Heidelberg: Springer.

Cutler, A. 1986. *Forbear* is a homophone: Lexical prosody does not constrain lexical access. *Language and Speech* 29: 201–220.

Cutler, A., and Clifton, C. E. 1984. The use of prosodic information in word recognition. In *Attention and Performance X*, ed. H. Bouma and D. G. Bouwhuis. Hillsdale, N.J.: Erlbaum.

Cutler, A., J. Mehler, D. Norris, and J. Segui. 1986. The syllable's differing role in the segmentation of French and English. *Journal of Memory and Language* 25: 385–400.

Cutler, A., and Norris, D. G. 1988. The role of strong syllables in segmentation for lexical access. *Journal of Experimental psychology: Human Perception and Performance* 14: 113–121.

Grosjean, F. 1980. Spoken word recognition processes and the gating paradigm. *Perception and Psychophysics* 28: 267–283.

Grosjean, F., and J. Gee. 1987. Prosodic structure and spoken word recognition. *Cognition* 25: 135–155.

MacAllister, J. Lexical stress and lexical access. Ph.D. thesis, University of Edinburgh (in preparation).

Marslen-Wilson, W. 1980. Speech understanding as a psychological process. In *Spoken Language Generation and Understanding*, ed. J. C. Simon. Dordrecht: Reidel.

Nooteboom, S. G. 1980. Speaking and unspeaking: Detection and correction of phonological and lexical errors in spontaneous speech. In *Errors in Linguistic Performance: Slips of the Tongue, Ear, Pen and Hand*, ed. V. A. Fromkin. New York: Academic.

Slowiaczek, L. M., and Pisoni, D. B. 1986. Effects of phonological similarity on priming in auditory lexical decision. *Memory and Cognition* 14: 230–237.

Swinney, D. A. 1979. Lexical access during sentence comprehension: (Re)considerations of context effects. *Journal of Verbal Learning and Verbal Behavior* 18: 645–659.

Taft, L. 1984. Prosodic Constraints and Lexical Parsing Strategies. Ph.D. thesis, University of Massachusetts.

Chapter 12

On Mental Representation of Morphology and Its Diagnosis by Measures of Visual Access Speed

Leslie Henderson

The hope of finding a literature that is less taxing to study has propelled me back through the recent history of psychological work on visual word recognition. In order to justify this sort of retreat from the front, it is well to invent some kind of historical discovery. Hitherto, I have attempted to dine out on the meager coinage of a discovery that there is a node in history, in the late 1960s, at which juncture students of word recognition passed quietly and undemonstratively from the field of pattern recognition into that of language perception.

The preoccupations of the earlier tradition are nicely captured, at its culmination, in the title of Neisser's (1967) chapter reviewing work on reading: "Words as Visual Patterns." Nothing revolutionary marks the passage of word recognition into the depths of psycholinguistics. To be sure, some fairly obvious signs are evident on the surface of this new venture. In the literature, the term "mental lexicon" began its ascent of the word-frequency table. In the laboratory, the mysterious lexical-decision task became the instrument of choice. More subtly, the very notion of laboratory task as *diagnostic device* became more explicit. Within the previous tradition—that of pattern recognition—it could be said that task performance was, itself, the explicandum. Tachistoscopic report was a segment of the process of reading, in this view. "Word recognition" was construed as encompassing whatever the subject did to form a reportable percept of the written form.

As word recognition came to be regarded as the marriage of the perceptual domain to the domain of language, it began to seem more appropriate to take the experimental task not as a model of what was to be explained, but rather as a diagnostic device, conveniently applied to certain purposes that were themselves entirely cast in theoretical terms. In consequence, an increasingly elaborate structure of assumptions was required to harness task performance to theoretical conclusions. Hence, the lexical-decision task was licensed by the supposition that it obliged the reader to journey exactly as far as the portals of the lexicon, to ring the bell, and, if someone answered, to run home without further ado to report this happy domestic circumstance.

As for the parvenu concept of a *lexicon*, to some extent this merely provided a new vehicle for existing ideas. The postulation of word detectors supplied a language for referring to whatever underlies recognition, and the assertion that these word detectors interface the sensory system to the lexicon was reduced to the status of a reminder that words have meaning and grammatical significance and that all this must somehow be stored. Even this crude mitosis of the recognition system into components concerned with preliminary analysis, detector units at the lexical interface, and a lexicon with complex and indescribable contents did, however, allow the refinement of some traditional questions. To take a hackneyed example, the ancient problem of inner speech during reading could be reformulated in terms of two possibilities: a requirement that written words be translated into a phonological code in order to activate lexical detectors and, alternatively, some purpose served by word phonology that is retrieved as a consequence of lexical access.

Two other aspects of this limited cell division within the recognition system are worthy of comment. Both seem to attest to the fact that, although words might enter the lexicon, students of word recognition were reluctant to follow them in.

The first of these observations is that theorists, even when addressing the issue of how word phonology is retrieved from the lexicon, were inclined merely to posit a direct connection between orthographic and phonological word nodes, as it were, on the surface of the lexicon (rather than postulating, say, some intervening generative machinery).

The second is that most of the fashionable experimental variables in word-recognition studies (I have in mind especially word frequency, legibility, repetition, and associative priming) were interpreted as converging in their effects upon the activation of lexical detectors. When it appeared expedient, in face of certain local difficulties with this account, to permit a little more cell division in the access model (Becker 1976), this was done by simply dividing the preliminaries to lexical access into two stages.

If one seeks experiments on word recognition in this era that violate the monadic fastness of this hypothetical lexicon, one is obliged to look to studies that are frankly semantic, such as those manipulating lexical ambiguity.

All this brings me expeditiously to a second node in history, and to the beginning of this essay.

1   Lexical Decisions, Access Speed, and Inferences about Lexical Organization

The guiding principle that we are concerned with here is the notion that the form of lexical representation acts as a fundamental constraint on the procedure for gaining access to the lexicon. Given this accommodation of process to representation, it is reasonable to surmise that measures of access speed may be made to yield information about the functional architecture of the lexicon.

It is a commonplace observation about English spelling that it sometimes deviates from direct phonemic mapping to conserve the orthographic shape of a morph,[1] whereas the corresponding spoken forms exhibit allomorphic variation. Weir and Venezky (1968) had suggested that these spelling invariances might be of some use to the reader, but the most influential celebration of this feature of English spelling was Chomsky and Halle's (1968). They suggested that English orthography was a near-optimal representation of the underlying forms posited in generative phonology. As Klima (1972) has observed, this can be taken to imply that the reader uses the orthography to address the abstract lexical base forms and then proceeds to generate the phonetic realizations of these.

Chomsky and Halle's claim holds good over some allophonic variation in English inflectional endings and for phonemic alternations consequent on derivational suffixation, but as a general synchronic characterization of English writing it is highly exaggerated. (see, for example Sampson 1985.) Nevertheless, the view that the reader treats English orthography as in some way morphographic is, in a quite different interpretation, central to our concern here with the claim that the nature of lexical representations governs the perceptual procedure for gaining access to them. I refer, of course, to the invigorating proposal, first set out explicitly by Taft and Forster (1975), that lexical business is conducted wherever possible in the currency of morphemes and that consequently the orthographic input has to be parsed into morphs as a preliminary to gaining access to a lexicon composed in this way.

Recently (Henderson 1986), I have attempted to decompose Taft and Forster's (1975) theory into its elementary assumptions. A summary of this analysis is shown in table 1. The following points are noteworthy: It is the proposals about lexical representation that motivate the entire system. The

Table 1
A formulation and interpretation of the main assumptions of the model of Taft and Forster (1975), with particular reference to polymorphemic forms. (Adapted from Henderson 1986.)

Parsing assumptions

P1   All possible affixes are detected and marked.

P2   Parsing solutions are tested serially and recursively, beginning with the most fully stripped-down solution.

P3   All parsing attempts operate on an orthographic representation of the word, prior to and as a mandatory preliminary to lexical search.

Access assumptions

A1   The lexical entry code is an orthographic description of the root.

A2   After a root entry has been located, some unspecified process of affix checking takes place.

Lexical-representation assumptions

LR1 All words that share a root are represented in the lexicon under that single, root heading.

LR2 Root entries are created for bound as well as free roots, including some monogamous (i.e. unique combination, unproductive) roots.

LR3 The manner in which a particular complex form (e.g. root + affixes) is represented under the root heading is not specified. Presumably complex forms may be fully listed in some modality or merely represented as the conjunction of a root with a set of affixation rules.

Developmental assumptions

D1   The means by which analytical lexical representations are acquired is unspecified. The crucial question is: What are the necessary conditions for the creation of a root entry?

decomposed state of the entry necessitates the parsing of the orthographic input description into morphs in order for lexical verification to take place. Yet, curiously, the assumptions about the precise nature of the lexical representation are inexplicit, especially in comparison with the very specific assumptions made about parsing and verification.

2   Morphological Representation

Let us consider the four sets of assumptions about morphological representation that are caricatured in table 2. The notation of type 1 merely remind us that for some purposes it may be useful to regard *unlucky* as comprising three morphs that signal an underlying morphological constitution. In other words, the importance of this sort of segmented representation lies

Table 2
Four types of morphological representation for the word *unlucky* in the lexicon.

Type 1

un-luck-y, *luck-i-ness*, etc.

Type 2

luck

un-

-y

-ily

-less

-ier

-iness

(etc.)

Type 3

luck

[derivational rules D2, D17, D38, D87, etc. apply]

[inflectional rule I3 (plural) is blocked]

Type 4

luck

in the possibility of connecting the individual segments to different linguistic addresses at which further semantic, phonological, or grammatical information can be found. Thus, even though the representation does not allow economy at this access-node stage, it offers a prospect of a more parsimonious description of the word at a deeper level.

Taft and Forster (1975) considered such a representation as an alternative account of their early experiments. (See also Taft 1979b.) They employed an ordered bracketing notation, so *unlucky* would be represented as *un (luck (y))*. Taft and Forster do not explain how such a representation could be used to provide an account of their experimental results, but it seems evident from the context that the general form of the answer they have in mind is that the bracketed segments can be addressed independently, so that, for example, **relucky* will partially engage the representation.[2]

What I think we learn from Taft and Forster's passing reference to the Type 1 representation is that, although it might appear to imply some proposal about the representation of linguistic information in the lexicon (perhaps through mapping of the morphic units onto word-formation rules), in fact the entire focus of interest is on *the perceptual addressing of word detectors*; the notation merely serves to provide a summary (a very compressed one, in this instance) of various effects obtained in lexical-decision experiments.

The proposal that Taft and Forster preferred in their 1975 paper is the one designated Type 2 in figure 1. This representation can be translated into the assertion that regular complexes must be analyzed into their component morphs as a preliminary to access. (Butterworth [1983] refers to this as the denial of the Full Listing Hypothesis.) This is coupled with the assumption that the access code is the irreducible root morph. Although on this view it is true that complex words are not fully listed, the composite entry contains all the information from which an orthographic description of the input word can be directly reconstructed. Hence, a particular affixation pattern, such as adjectival -y, has to be replicated within the lexical entry of each root to which it may be affixed.

Taft and Forster claimed that this arrangement allows storage economy (1975, p. 645). However, such economy is severely limited. The lexicon is merely relieved of the burden of replicating the stem for each formation in which it participates. The only other property of the arrangement on which they comment is that the stem-headed entry captures in its organization the semantic relatedness of words that share a common stem.

On closer analysis, this seems a very peculiar claim. First, the phenomenon of automatic, unfocused associative priming (Neely 1977) suggests that the retrieval of semantic relatedness may be rapid and effortless even when uncorrelated with morphology. Second, *any* method by which morphological relationships are represented will serve to capture incidental semantic relatedness. What Taft and Forster add to this is a spatial metaphor ("allows for semantically related words to appear near each other ..." [p. 645]), the import of which is unclear. Third, root-sharing is a very *unreliable* way of signaling semantic relatedness.

Taft and Forster do not provide details of the manner in which affix information is stored within the stem-headed entry. All they assert is that those conjunctions of root with affix that form actual words are represented. This hierarchical arrangement allows the reader/listener to be tormented in the lexical-decision task, where he may be required to affirm that *unlucky* is truly a word but deny that comfortable status to *relucky* or *unlacky*, but it does not immediately seem to serve any larger linguistic or computational purpose. We might, I suppose, attempt to construct a computational rationale based upon the assumption that a processing bottleneck exists such that it is desirable to limit the number of access ports to the lexicon. However, I can think of no independent grounds for such an assumption. Moreover, even were grounds to present themselves, it is

not clear that underlying morphological structure would serve as an efficient basis for grouping words so as to facilitate passage through such a
perceptual bottleneck. Perhaps a more fruitful line of speculation might be
one that would lead us to suppose that this circuitous procedure for the
recognition of familiar formations arises out of the needs of the language
learner, who is continually faced with novel word constructions. A roughly
equivalent assumption is made in most models of oral reading, where it is
assumed that the machinery for spelling-sound translation, which in the
accomplished reader may serve largely to complicate pronunciation decisions about irregular words, is an inevitable vestige of the acquisition
process.

With regard to linguistic motivation, a mere listing of affixal conjunctions fails to express word-formation rules that govern surface factors such
as the order of application of affixes, any phonological and orthographic
interactions between stem and affix, and restriction upon conjunctions, as
well as underlying factors. If such rules are not represented, then we require
a lexical representation of each *combination* of affixes that may conjoin with
the root (e.g., *un-luck-iness*). However, this inelegant arrangement does have
the advantage that each composite word has a unique lexical address,
expressed as the conjunction of the stem with an affix pattern, and therefore
that node can be connected to any semantic interpretation that is peculiar
to the derivational form.

What if we attempt to eliminate the duplication of affixal information
across stem-headed entries? This objective is realized with marvelous
directness in the Type 4 representation. One could not wish for more
parsimony. Unfortunately, however, to interpret this terse representation
we are obliged to consider certain activities that are going on just out of
the frame. It might seem that we have dispensed with affix information
entirely. Clearly this would be absurd, since affixes do convey information
that is not reliably recoverable from other sources. What, then, has become
of the affixes? Recall, first, that in the Taft-Forster (1975) model of decomposition affixal spelling patterns are detected and removed as a preliminary
to the attempt to gain lexical access via the root code.[3] Whether or not we
want to call such affix detectors "affix representations," it is clear that there
has to be a node for each affix morph. What the Type 4 representation
requires us to assume, therefore, is that the affixal-morph detector is connected to some extra-lexical set of rules serving its interpretation.

The Type 4 representation is predicated upon the extreme form of the
transformationalist position on lexical representation. Chomsky (1970) and
Jackendoff (1975) have attempted to show that this position is not tenable

from a linguistic viewpoint. Part of Chomsky's argument concerns internal inconsistencies in syntax that result from the wholesale eviction of derivational forms from the lexicon. These attempted refutations seem controversial (Bauer 1983, pp. 75–78), and I shall not pursue them here. The remaining criticisms of the transformationalist position are not contestable. They draw attention to structural and syntactic idiosyncrasies of derivation. For example, in English nominalization, whether a verb may take a nominalizing suffix, and if so what suffix it should be, and what precise sense it imparts to the noun are all highly (though not totally) unpredictable matters.

The untenability of the radical transformationalist position may lead to a variety of compromises in which the linguist's obsession with evicting from the lexicon anything that can be treated by rule is pursued to a greater or a lesser extent. The general form of the solution is exhibited in the Type 3 representation; however, it is important to bear in mind that this is intended to refer to an entire species of solutions in which each derived formation is represented in the lexicon by those derivational rules that compose its orthographic and phonological structure and its meaning, together with any selectional restrictions that apply.

The particular version of Type 3 shown is one in which economy is pursued by listing within the entry pointers to derivational rules that apply. However, inflectional rules, which are almost universally productive, are referred to in the lexicon only on those rare occasions where their application must be blocked.[4]

This is an appropriate point at which to pause and consider the terrain in which we find ourselves. We have left psychological concerns with the perceptual recognition of words far behind. This is true both in terms of the empirical preoccupations of psychological students of "lexical access" and in terms of the content of theories in which morphological factors are held to influence word perception. Apart from a few experiments involving a gross comparison of inflectional and derivational formations (Stanners et al. 1979a) and assessments of the effects of various sorts of compositional transparency (Bradley 1980), psychologists have simply not concerned themselves with the sort of linguistic factors that enter into word-formation rules. Moreover, to the extent that questions of lexical representation and its possible role as a determinant of the access procedure have been attended to theoretically, this concern with representation has looked outward toward perceptual factors rather than inward toward linguistic factors. In sum, as far as extant work goes, the attempt to identify a central concern with lexical representation that is common to psychological and linguistic approaches amounts to the pursuit of a chimerical creature.[5] Accordingly, we shall examine these two strands separately in what follows, dealing first with the linguistic approach.

3 Linguistic Attitudes

In this section I shall review some examples of word-formation rules. Then I shall consider the implications these might have for the representation of morphological information in the lexicon. The section concludes with a brief, general examination of the motivation of linguistic proposals about the lexicon.

Word-Formation Rules

Consider the very productive and semantically transparent rule for the formation of causative verbs by adding the suffix *-ize*. This suffix may be employed to form verbs from nouns or adjectives. Among the regularities characterizing its usage are the following[6]: It may be added to nouns and adjectives only. Adjectives suffixed with *-al, -an, -ar,* and *-ic* require *-ize* if they are to form verbs. In the case of forms taking *-ic*, the predominant pattern is straightforwardly concatenative (as in *romantic-romanticize*) but a subset show an *-ic/-ize* alternation (*hypnotic-hypnotize*). Lexical stress usually does not change as a consequence of suffixation with *-ize* (e.g. *capital-capitalize*), although there exist a few neo-latinate exceptions (*hypnotic-hypnotize*). In terms of concatenative ordering, *-ize* is "primary"; that is, it belongs to a class of suffixes that are placed closer to the stem than the "secondary" ones (Kiparsky 1983)—for example, one could not say **feminismize*. However, unlike most other primary suffixes, *ize* does not trigger stress shift (*theory: theorize* but *theoretic*). Forms taking *-ize* can invariably (?) be nominalized by subsequent addition of *-ation* (*nominalization*).

Although *-ize* derivations are sometimes regarded as entirely semantically transparent, Marchand (1969) lists five types of transitive semantic composition—'make' (*legalize*), 'convert' (*dramatize*), 'subject to' (*hospitalize*), causatives from proper names (*bowdlerize*), and 'combine chemically' (*oxidize*)—plus a few intransitive formations (*theorize*). There are also some frank exceptions (*womanize; realize* in the sense of "become aware").

In sum, despite a tendency toward productivity and structural additivity, the rules for forming causative verbs with *-ize* must be supplemented with some specification of the forms to which the rule may be applied (and of the forms to which it *must* be applied). Unpredictable phonological or orthographic effects on the shape of the stem must be noted (e.g., in *hypnotize*, the deletion of *-ic* and the stress shift). Finally, idiosyncratic semantic compositions must be described.

What economies might be achieved in the representation of this information? Even though *-ize* is the predominant verb-forming suffix in English, it does not seem at all feasible to represent it by a default rule in which *-ize* may be applied save when the lexicon blocks its application. Can we, then, retreat to the intermediate state of parsimony in which the applicability of the rule is noted in the lexicon under a stem-headed entry (i.e., a Type 3 representation)? This would allow us to list subordinate rules within the lexical entry, stating any systematic variant of the semantic composition rule that applied. However, as we anticipated earlier, a number of structural (orthographic and phonological) problems arise when we attempt to list particular affixation rules as they apply to the irreducible stem (root).

Before we turn to these difficulties, it is worth reviewing some possible advantages to be found in the application of word-formation rules to the root. Perhaps the most widely remarked-upon morphological constraint imposed by English roots is that arising from the distinction between native and latinate forms. Certain phonological rules are restricted to latinate forms. Bound stems are largely peculiar to the latinate vocabulary. However, what concerns us here is the fact that most of the general affixation constraints in English morphology involve restrictions of affixes such as *-ity* to latinate roots. Unfortunately, despite the tendency of linguists (see, e.g., Chomsky and Halle 1968) to treat the native/latinate distinction as a synchronic feature of English, there is an almost total lack of evidence that the distinction has psychological reality for the average language user (but see Smith 1980 for an exploratory study). I shall therefore assume that, as far as morphology is concerned, roots are not tagged for some general feature such as (+latinate), and that the applicability of a restricted affix such as *-ity* would have to be specifically noted for each stem.

The primary difficulty with the Type 3 representation is that it requires some device for expressing the ordering of affixes. This problem was brutally solved in the Type 2 representation by simply listing all word-forming affixation patterns. Hence, the entry for *luck* would contain listings of both *-y* and *-ness*, for instance. Surely we can conceive of a more elegant arrangement. After all, adjectival *-y* and nominal *-ness* are applied in an invariable sequence. *Lucknessy* is inconceivable. This restriction is not due to a general prohibition on the formation of a noun from a noun or on the formation of an adjective from the product of that union. A *hostessless* evening is acceptable, at least grammatically.

There does exist one general principle for ordering affixes. This is the dichotomy between primary affixes (marked with a + boundary in phonological notation) and secondary (# boundary) affixes. Primary affixes are positioned closer to the stem and may interact with it phonologically. Thus, the primary suffix -ian causes stress shift in *hereditarianism* and precedes the secondary suffix -ism.

The distinction between primary and secondary suffixes has been of interest to generative phonologists because of the prospect of dividing suffixation into two stages harnessed to different phonological rules. Whatever the merits of this approach, it leaves a great many sequencing questions unresolved. For example, within the category of secondary suffixes, -er invariably precedes -ism (as in *consumerism*). However, sequencing rules cast in terms of particular affixes are difficult to formulate (Aronoff 1976, pp. 56–61; Bauer 1983, pp. 67–71). One problem is that within a set of suffixes more than one ordering may be permissable (*operationalize, nationalization*). Moreover, recursions are possible (*sensationalization*). Considerations such as these imply that the order of attachment of affixes to a particular root cannot be left to a set of word-formation rules that are ordered among themselves.

So far we have established that the mere listing of root-affix conjunctions is not in itself adequate to specify the positioning of affixes in multiply suffixed forms. This requires us to specify the order of application of affixes to the root. Two other sorts of evidence have been adduced in support of this conclusion, one phonological and one semantic. I shall discuss these in turn.

The phonological argument rests on the phenomenon of cyclicity: When an affix is added to an already complex form, it is the properties of this complex, and not simply those of the root, that determine the phonology of the new formation. Segui and Zubizarreta (1985) provide a number of examples of this principle, pursuant to the argument that each derived formation must in some sense be represented in the lexicon. A form of cyclicity also holds for semantic composition; the difference in sense between *unredoable* and *reundoable* reflects the order of attachment of the prefixes.

Quite a different argument is advanced by Aronoff (1976). He propounds the fundamental principle that all regular word-formation processes work by adding to an existing word. Only by this means, he claims, can their semantic composition be transparent. He considers coining by the unconstrained repermutation of bound morphemes (he gives the hypothetical example of *transfer* and *promote* being spliced and fused to coin *transmote*) as unpredictable and unproductive as blends such as *smoke* + *fog* → *smog*. However, Aronoff is prepared to allow that latinate bound stems such as *-mit* are represented as morphemes, while denying that they may serve as input to word-formation rules. Their reality as morphemes he grants on purely phonological grounds, since they are governed by morphophonological rules (e.g., *transmit-transmission*). (This has never seemed to me persuasive grounds for conferring morphemehood.)

Elimination of Redundancy

Linguistic treatments of English morphology serve to illustrate with particular vividness theoretical objectives that set at least some approaches to linguistics apart from psychology and lead to subtly different employment of shared terms like "lexicon." What I have in mind here is the relentless search for regular patterns, for example in word formation, harnessed to the attempt to embody these regularities in structured systems of rules. Here we find an unmarked frontier where purely descriptive statements get smuggled into the psychological domain dressed up as processing theories. In this context, the lexicon becomes a sort of "marc"—the ireducible pulp of arbitrary facts about words that remains in the linguist's press when the last, limpid drop of redundancy has been squeezed out. We can examine this approach by considering the notion of Lexical Redundancy Rules.

Chomsky noted in *Aspects* (1965) that the lexicon was required to store all idiosyncratic information that could not be derived from a universal rule, and that therefore *subcategorization features* needed to be recorded within a word's lexical entry. These features specify certain syntactic restrictions on the use of a lexical item. For example, the verb *put* has severe restrictions on the kind of complement it can take such that

*John put the X

is inadmissible whereas

John put the X in the Y

can be allowed. Chomsky noted that listing such restrictions within a lexical entry can lead to very clumsy entries. He suggested that the knowledge that is required to sustain grammatical utterances could achieve its most compact expression if a listing of permissible complements within individual entries was supplemented by a superordinate rule of lexical functioning, asserting that unless a type of complement was specified as permissible it should be assumed to be prohibited. Such rules have come to be known as *Lexical Redundancy Rules*, since they are motivated by a desire to purge the lexicon of information that is duplicated across several entries, thus achieving maximum compactness of representation. Further economies in lexical representation can be achieved where the tendency is for positive subcategorization features to co-occur by inventing a redundancy rule of the form "If A applies, then B applies."

Once again, information duplicated across lexical entries has been abstracted from these entries and expressed in the form of a general rule. One way in which this might be made to work is for the entries to contain a pointer to the general rule (in the manner of the Type 3 representation in figure 1). However, it is important to realize that this editing of lexical entries has not been motivated by processing considerations. It therefore seems fruitless to inquire how these restructurings might simplify or abbreviate the on-line computations required for the selection of terms in constructing an utterance. If this is so, then it is even more irrelevant to speculate psychologically as to whether what little we know about the salient mental limitations of processing and storage fits comfortably such a principle of compact lexical representation.

This sort of attempt to systematize lexical information has given rise to the term *Lexical Grammar*. Moreover, such attempts have progressed far beyond the realm of syntactic restrictions, exploring the scope for eliminating lexical redundancy in respect of orthographic, phonological, and semantic information. The principal domain in which this economy has attracted interest is that of derivationally related forms. It is probably fair to say that this attention to derivational relationships has revealed a surprising amount of idiosyncrasy in word formation, especially in semantic aspects. One focus of endeavor has been the search for derivations that are fully productive and semantically predictable. Thus, for instance, Levi (1978) has postulated a class of denominal adjective (i.e., an adjective derived by affixing a noun stem) that is entirely semantically predictable (e.g., *traumatic*). Such a derivational process that changes form class while leaving meaning unaffected amounts, it is suggested, to a syntactic rule. However, these formations are not structurally (i.e., orthographically or phonetically) predictable. For example, *trauma* and *saliva* bear different adjectival affixes, and *marine* bears a zero affix. The word form itself therefore requires lexical representation.

A case where this structural variation might be thought to be absent is adverb-forming -ly. This affix is almost universally productive when applied to adjectives. One systematic exception is the case of adjectives that already end in -ly (Bauer 1983). What remains are cases where a zero affix converts an adjective into an adverb (e.g., *fast*). This circumstance has, in turn, led linguists to propose an important sort of redundancy-eliminating strategy:

the *blocking* rule. This is a compact and powerful creature, but alas an untidy one. Blocking works fairly well as an account of how adverbial *fast* comes to prevent the formation of **fastly*. However, Aronoff (1976) has attempted to extend the device. For example, he argues that, despite the regularity of (e.g.) *curious-curiosity*, **gloriosity* is blocked by the availability of *glory*. Now, of course, there are cases where a single adjective may take more than one nominalized form. Aronoff deals with this by postulating what Clark and Clark (1979) have called "preemption by synonymy." That is, an alternative nominalization is blocked unless it carries some special sense. "But," you may interject, "are not *variousness* and *variety* both acceptable as well as synonymous?" Aronoff's response would be: "Why, yes, but that is because -*ness* is fully productive and therefore is not lexically specified."

However, there are limits on the productiveness of -*ness*. It cannot be used to form deverbal nouns, and this base-restriction requires specification. Moreover, even some de-adjectival formations are questionable (*worseness*, *nearestness*). It might be that the productivity of -*ness* is better accounted for by the phonological transparency of its formations (Cutler 1981) than by its putative status at a level of generality above that of particular lexical entries.

What is the psychologist to make of this relentless pursuit of islands of regularity? To this alien observer, it seems that the transformationalists have lost the high ground from which they sought to discover whole continents of morphology governed by grammatical rule. With the field conceded (at least broadly) to the lexicalists, scholarly attention has been diverted toward the discovery of an affix here or there that is wholly (well, almost) productive and yields a form that is entirely semantically predictable. As a last resort, the morpheme may be shorn of all its burdensome semantic commitments and justified in terms of its obedience to phonological rule. This is what Aronoff (1976) proposes for the vexatious class of latinate stems bound to unstressed prefixes (*refer*, *remit*, *receive*, etc.).

Is the relationship here between linguistics and psychology like that between natural history and biology, where the marvelously painstaking observations of the natural historian lead to inductive generalizations of the form *most rabbits eat lettuce*—which, though not hypotheses about scientific law, undoubtedly inform the scientific study of *Lagomorpha*?

It seems evident that linguistic propositions have a different and stronger form than generalized descriptions. They are in some sense *theoretical*. Thus, the constant attempt to arrive at an economical description of a language amounts to more than the documentation of regularities. For

Chomsky (1972), the pursuit of rules serves two objectives: the search for linguistic universals and the attempt to construct a theory of language acquisition. In the morphological domain, Berko's (1958) classic work is often cited in support of the general position that children's language competence depends upon the acquisition of rules. Indeed, it is not difficult to see in inflectional morphology a closed system governed by very general rules of agreement. Lexical-redundancy rules, however, have a less imperative character. As we have seen, redundancy rules governing subcategorization features of verbs that take the form "If A applies, then B applies" have no general motivation other than economy. In contrast, it might seem that Word-Formation Rules (WFRs) can be given a general justification insofar as they allow the language user to transcend his limited familiarity with particular word forms. However, this motivation is not captured by regarding WFRs as a species of Lexical Redundancy Rule. The extent to which the formulation of WFRs is influenced by the desire to eliminate redundant storage is most clearly evident in the proposed treatments of exceptions, for example by postulating a *blocking* rule. In this regard, it is necessary to distinguish between *blocking* as an informal psychological postulate, asserting a tendency for the individual not to use WFRS to synthesize a form when a familiar one can be retrieved that will serve the purpose, and *blocking* as a formal linguistic device for reconciling the economy of representation achieved by WFRs with the almost inevitable existence of exceptions. My own view is that the psychological thesis is weak. It is not difficult to get individuals to affirm the "reality" of *variousness* (*variety*) or even *astrologist* (*astrologer*). Such demonstrations are usually met by arguing that *-ness* is a special case of an unblocked WFR (see below) or that alternative derivations of a root are not "truly" synonymous. (Before entering such a dispute, it is well to agree on criteria for synonymy in advance.) However, it does seem that alternative derivations of a root with highly coextensive meanings are less common than equally synonymous derivations of different roots (*unable/incapable*; *objectionable/unacceptable*; *fearless/unafraid*), and this is a problem for a formulation of the blocking rule that accords it a status superordinate to individual WFRs. In any case, Bauer (1983) may be closer to the mark when he argues that blocking, when it occurs, results not so much from a prohibitory rule within the individual mind as from a failure of redundant derivations to gain institutional acceptance.

Another economizing strategy is to step down from an unconditional word-formation rule to a *Lexically Governed Rule* when the proportion of exceptions to be accommodated exceeds some criterial quantity. Thus, the very productive nominalization -*ness* might be applied at the stage of lexical insertion to transform any adjective not specifically marked as an exception, whereas the moderately productive nominalization -*ment* would be lexically governed (a verb that can take -*ment* would list within its lexical entry a pointer to that WFR). That is, it is assumed that there exists some critical ratio of exceptions to rule-bound instances beyond which it is less costly to list within lexical entries the fact that the rule applies rather than that it does not.

All this requires, of course, a considerable amount of accountancy, although there appears to be some debate among linguists as to what measure of economy is most appropriate (Jackendoff 1975). Like many other aspects of redundancy elimination, this lexical bookkeeping is based on the implicit assumption that storage is costly whereas processing is cheap.

Another assumption that seems to be implicit in the attempt to avoid Full Listing is that the individual does not—indeed cannot—distinguish between forms that are occurrent and those that, although legal, are unfamiliar. Indeed, Bauer (1983) goes so far as to deny the utility of this distinction.

4 Psychological Models Reconsidered

It is by now evident, I hope, even after this superficial examination of some of the issues concerning the representation of morphological information in the lexicon, that these linguistic issues are simply not addressed in current psychological models of morphological factors in word-perception experiments. Thus, in returning to the psychological assertions that I referred to at the beginning of this essay, I am able to echo the Delphic claim made in *Artemus Ward's Lecture*: "One of the principal features of my Entertainment is that it contains so many things that don't have anything to do with it."

What I want to suggest is that statements that hold lexical entries to be decomposed and stem-headed (Taft and Forster 1975), or decomposed and BOSS-headed (Taft 1979a), or intact but interconnected (Stanners et al. 1979a, 1979b), or intact and organized in interconnected nuclear form (Lukatela et al. 1980), are not really proposals about lexical representation that are strongly motivated by detailed linguistic considerations of the sort that we have just sampled. They do nothing so exciting as show that access speed may be used diagnostically like some mental equivalent of techniques for imaging the intact brain, allowing the form of our mental representations of words to be mapped.

Consider, for example, the nuclear representation of Serbo-Croatian inflected nouns advanced by Lukatela et al. (1980). These authors suggest that each grammatical case of a noun has a separate entry in the lexicon, which is directly addressable perceptually; that the various oblique cases are all connected to the nominative singular, as the nucleus, and this nucleus acts as the frequency counter for the entire paradigm through its reciprocal connections with each satellite entry; and that the recognition threshold sensitivity of the nucleus is set as some function of the collective paradigm frequency and the threshold of the satellite entries is set as the nuclear value plus a constant.

This nuclear model expresses the linguistic requirement that the various noun cases be distinguishable. It also captures the intuition that base or "citation" forms[7]—in this case the nominative singular—enjoy some special status. But beyond that, it does not represent (nor is it intended to) any significant linguistic information, such as the basis of the distinction between dative and locative cases. It is not a lexical representation in this sense. It does not pretend to be about how we understand text. Rather, the model may be translated back into propositions about performance on the lexical-decision task. As a model, it is motivated by assumptions about what subjects do to arrive at a lexical decision, how this process is affected by frequency, and so on. On this view, the fact that the pattern of access time is consistent with the model is not an indication that access time is diagnostic of representation, in some linguistically deeper domain. It merely reflects the fact that the model is an interpretation of the access-time data. The accommodation of the model to linguistic intuitions does not extend beyond the fact that nominative formations yield the swiftest decisions, and this gives the model its geometry.

Elsewhere (e.g. Henderson 1986), I have remarked on the tendency for the Taft-Forster (1975) model to discard its linguistic motivation in subsequent revisions. The primary stage of this development was evident in Taft and Forster's (1976) suggestion that the access code for all polysyllabic words is the first *syllable* encountered in a left-right search, once the prefixes have been set aside. Lexical verification has thus become a three-stage process in which only the earliest step is morphologically significant. In stage 1, any prefix-shaped spelling patterns are removed. In stage 2, the first syllable of the residue is used to activate its corresponding detector. This permits access to the lexical entry. Information about the remainder of the word is retrieved from the entry in stage 3, and checked against the stimulus input.

This arrangement has radical consequences for the view taken of lexical representation, since we must now speak not of stem-headed entries but, using the terminology introduced by Taft (1979a), of BOSS-headed entries. The BOSS ("Basic Orthographic Syllabic Structure") is a refinement of the initial-syllable access code proposed by Taft and Forster (1976), in which the syllable is given orthographic form.

The notion of a BOSS access code carries with it the startling implication that, for example, *candle, candid, candelabra, candidate, candy,* and *candor* share the same "entry," headed by CAND. Now, it seems rather peculiar to call this a lexical entry. Taft (1979a, p. 36) is careful to observe: "What I have previously termed 'lexical representations' can now be considered as the representations in the orthographic access file."

As a result of these theoretical developments, we now have two processes that require some deeper motivation—viz., prefix stripping and the subsequent division of the analysis of the "body" of the word into two stages: BOSS activation and verification of the remainder of the word. It seems fruitless to seek some linguistic motivation of the BOSS-headed entry, and I do not have time to consider alternative computational motivations. None have, to my knowledge, been proposed, although I have assumed that they would lie in the perceptual domain.

The conclusion that the morphic[8] effects obtained in current word-perception experiments do not reflect the process of gaining access to linguistically rich lexical representations is mildly reinforced by the apparent lack of linguistic patterning of the effects.

One curious feature of the effects of morphic structure on purported measures of recognition time is the greater tendency to detect effects of prefixation than of suffixation. Investigations of derivational complexity that involve simple comparisons between affixed and unaffixed forms have consistently shown no cost attached either to prefixation or to suffixation (Bergman, Hudson, and Eling, 1988; Henderson, Wallis, and Knight 1984). Costs have been reported for inflected vs. base forms (Gunther, Gfroerer, and Weiss 1984; Stanners et al. 1979a), but these effects are complicated by a number of incidental factors, such as lexical citation form (Gunther et al. 1984).

A rather more subtle factor has been pseudoaffixation, for which costs are predicted by the Taft-Forster model. There appears to be no simple cost to pseudosuffixation (Bergman et al. 1988; Colé et al., cited in Segui and Zubizaretta 1986; Henderson et al. 1984; Manelis and Tharp 1977).

However, Colé et al. and Manelis and Tharp found slower lexical decisions to pairs of words when truly suffixed and pseudosuffixed forms were intermixed. (The precise import of this result seems to me somewhat obscure.) In contrast to these findings on suffixation, some studies do find a cost associated with pseudoprefixation (Bergman et al. 1988; Rubin et al. 1979; Taft 1981). However, the conditions that are hospitable to this effect seem unclear (Rubin et al. 1979), and other studies have failed to find an effect (Colé et al. 1986; Henderson et al. 1984; Jordan 1986).

Perhaps the most refined technique for investigating morphic factors has been that utilizing repetition priming. I have reviewed this literature at length in Henderson 1985, and so I shall confine myself to a brief resumé and some updating. The seminal work was that of Stanners et al. (1979a,b), which suggested that morphologically related forms (i.e., ones sharing the same root but differing inflectionally or derivationally) exhibited facilitatory priming of the later-coming form. This effect survived when the two related forms were separated by many trials. Only in the case of forms related within a regular inflectional paradigm was the magnitude of the priming effect as great as that engendered by repetition of identical forms. Forms related by irregular inflection or by derivation showed a reduced, but still detectable, amount of facilitation. The significance of these findings in the present context is twofold. First, it appeared that a perceptual distinction could be found, corresponding to the underlying linguistic distinction between derivation and inflection. Second, the differing response to regular and irregular inflectional relationships suggested that these effects occurred at a morphic locus, that is, at a stage of processing sensitive to signs of morphological structure that are evident in the spelling of the surface forms.

A number of important recent methodological developments have suggested that the interpretation of priming effects in the lexical-decision task is likely to be much more complicated than was originally thought. Priming can have episodic components that are not necessarily lexically mediated (Feustel, Shiffrin, and Salasoo 1983; Jacoby and Dallas 1981; Monsell 1985). Priming relationships may create expectations that lead to special processing strategies (Forster and Davis 1984). Moreover, some priming effects, at least, seem to occur at processing stages other than that of lexical access (Seidenberg, Waters, Sanders, and Langer 1984).

When an attempt is made to eliminate effects that are clearly not located at the lexical-access stage, the pattern of results that remains seems to invite a quite different interpretation from that proposed by Stanners et al. This conclusion emerges from a careful series of experiments by Fowler, Napps,

and Feldman (1985). They found that when episodic factors were minimized, a base form was primed as effectively by inflectional or derivational
relatives as by itself.

Another linguistic variable that has attracted experimental attention is
structural transparency, the degree to which a stem is modified by vowel
or consonant alternation or stress shift when it accommodates a suffix.
Orthographically, there is a continuum of stem changes, from perfect
transparency (*destructive-destructiveness*) through slight modification
(*conclude-conclusion*; *hang-hung*) to radical change (*shake-shook*; *destroy-
destruction*). Some authors have referred to this dimension as "degree of
irregularity" (e.g., Fowler et al. [1985]), but it seems worth preserving the
distinction between how *great* the orthographic modification is and how
predictable it is. We might want to argue, say, that *hung* is unpredictable
whereas *conclusion* conforms structurally to a derivational rule.

The Taft-Forster model of prelexical morphic parsing is surprisingly
mute about the expected consequences for recognition of deviations from
transparency, whether rule-governed or capricious, but it is very difficult
to see how parsing could handle rule-governed alternations without time
cost. Stanners et al. (1979a) reported effects of orthographic transparency
that were consistent across three experiments but not statistically reliable
in any one of them. Subsequent studies by Downie, Milech, and Kirsner
(1985) and by Fowler et al. (1985) found no qualification of stem-priming
by transparency.

This lack of sensitivity of stem-priming to variation in transparency is
actually a bit of a puzzle,[9] since it might seem to imply that these priming
effects occur deeper in the system, beyond the point at which particular
orthographic shape is influential. This view is persuasively argued by
Downie et al. and by Fowler et al. Unfortunately, a different set of experiments suggests quite the opposite conclusion. In these latter studies, priming
seems to involve shared orthographic constituents that play no role in the
lexical representation of the target—e.g., *cart-cartridge* (Monsell 1985);
expire-pirate (Jordan 1986). An extreme case of such nonlexical priming
through shared components can be found in Jakimik, Cole, and Rudnicky's
(1985) report that lexical decisions about spoken words were faster if a
preceding word shared a component having both the same sound and the
same spelling (e.g., *mess-message*).

What seems clear is that most of these priming effects cannot be accounted for in terms of repeated activation of a stem detector that functions
as the head of the target's lexical entry.

The fundamental problem of interpretation that confronts us in these priming studies concerns the stage of processing at which the target's analysis is influenced by the foregoing primer. Until quite recently, there was broad agreement that long-lag repetition priming effects were due to repeated stimulation of a modality-specific lexical detector. Drastically simplified, and without citing in detail the sources of evidence, the argument ran as follows: Longer-lag effects must be located at or beyond a word (or at least "lexical") detector stage, because nonword repetition yields only slight and transient effects. On the other hand, some limits are set on the possible depth of the effects within the lexical system, since most (perhaps even all) of the facilitation is modality-specific. Moreover, in bilinguals, cross-language priming occurs only for synonyms that are cognates (structurally similar translations, such as Spanish *Obedienca* and English *Obedience*). Finally, "full" stem-priming seemed to hold only for forms that were regularly related. Irregularly related forms, which could not gain access to the lexicon through the same stem detector, appeared to yield reduced facilitation (Stanners et al. 1979a) or even none at all (Kempley and Morton 1982).

A substantial volume of evidence has accumulated since 1985 that is inconsistent with this last conclusion. The study by Fowler et al. (1985), referred to above, found full priming for irregularly related forms. Using a very different procedure, with a masked primer immediately preceding the target, Forster, Davis, Schoknecht, and Carter (1987, experiment 7) found full priming when the target and the prime were different members of an irregular inflectional paradigm (*WEEP-WEPT*). Feldman and Fowler (1987) used the conventional long-lag priming technique to study lexical decision in Serbo-Croatian, a highly inflected language. Decisions about nominative singular targets were facilitated as much by Oblique Case primers that undergo a spelling change of the stem as by those that have unchanged stems.

Taken together, these findings suggest that priming by morphological relatives occurs at a stage beyond that of the word detectors. If this is bad news for those who hoped to find support for the thesis that (regular) morphological relationships are established at a stage where prelexical morphological parses are tested against the lexicon's store of orthographic descriptions, it is rather better news for those who fear that the repetition priming technique harnessed to the lexical-decision task is hopelessly linguistically shallow as a diagnostic probe. Instead, the bad news for those individuals is that the technique may vacillate between telling us about earlier and later processes. Certainly the "late-stage" account we have just considered cannot comfortably accommodate priming effects that occur between orthographically similar but morphologically unrelated words. Here again, there are seemingly inconsistent findings. On one hand, Henderson et al. (1984), Murrell and Morton (1974), and Napps and Fowler (in press) found no effects of purely orthographic similarity. On the other hand, Evett and Humphreys (1981), Forster and Davis (1987), Jakimik et al. (1985), Jordan (1986), and Monsell (1985) did obtain such facilitation. It is not yet clear whether a systematic account can be given of the necessary and sufficient conditions for such "pseudomorphic" priming to obtain. Certainly, most of the evidence comes from short-lag studies. Where positive evidence can be found using long lags, the primer was a free morpheme and the target could usually be parsed as a compound of this with another morpheme (Monsell's *ridge-cartridge* effect).

Forster et al. (1987) resolve some other inconsistencies with the proposal that purely orthographic priming may be peculiar to targets that are "lexical hermits" (words with few orthographic neighbors). These tend to be long words. However, their explanation that the neighbor used as primer is mistaken for the target (the best-match hypothesis) cannot be extended to cover the findings of Jakimik et al., those of Jordan, or those of Monsell.

So far we have concentrated on morphic and pseudomorphic effects, that is, aspects of word structure that are *perceptible*. What of morphological factors that are not signaled in the orthography or in the phonology? This is the domain in which we might expect linguistic and psychological approaches to converge. The difficulty here, I suspect, is the apparent lack of a standard task that probes those deeper layers. This notwithstanding, there are very recent signs that a second generation of psycholinguistic studies of morphology is developing. This work centers on such "postperceptual" aspects as the inflectional/derivational distinction and a number of correlated factors: semantic predictability (variously termed "compositionality," "semantic transparency," etc.), productivity, and syntactic significance.

There are a number of hints that the inflection/derivation distinction may capture at least an aspect of some psychologically real, underlying factor. Although stem-priming studies have been equivocal (Stanners et al. 1979a,b; Fowler et al. 1985), Taft (1985) refers to unpublished data suggesting an inflectional/derivational distinction in the effects of pseudosuffixation. In a number of recent papers, Hartmut Günther has suggested that inflected forms—but not derived forms—engender longer lexical decisions than their base forms (Günther 1988). Unfortunately, however, most of the evidence that Günther adduces involves comparisons across different studies. In view of the possible limitations of the lexical-decision task for work at this "depth," it is not surprising to find neuropsychological attempts at demonstrating a dissociation. Miceli and Caramazza (1987) have described an aphasic, Italian-speaking patient who made a large number of morphological errors in producing or repeating polymorphemic words. Over 96 percent of these were inflectional errors. However, we clearly need to find a patient with the converse dissociation (derivational but not inflectional errors) before we can draw any strong conclusions about the distinctness of the underlying representations.

On the whole, studies of semantic predictability have failed to detect reliable effects. Of course, this may show only that the techniques were inappropriate. Monsell (1985) reported that priming of a compound by one of its component morphemes was as substantial in predictable compounds (e.g., POLE-BEANPOLE) as in unpredictable ones (e.g., TAIL-COCKTAIL). On the other hand, there is a hint in the data that predictable compounds are intrinsically easier to recognize. In contrast, Bergman et al. (1988) found no effect of semantic predictability on recognition speed for Dutch prefixed forms.

Osgood and Hoosain (1974) and Wilson (1984) reported that transparent but not opaque compounds would prime their individual constituents if these appeared subsequently; but this may only reflect memory processes.

Outside the rather special realm of compounds, an extreme case of semantic opacity is to be found in those latinate formations that may be viewed, at least from a diachronic standpoint, as prefix + bound stem (*commit, permit,* etc.). Many linguists (e.g. Marchand [1969]) have argued from grounds of semantic unpredictability and lack of productivity that these forms are monomorphemic. Others have suggested that the obedience of putative stems like -*mit* to morpho-phonological alternations gives them the status of morphemes (Aronoff 1976), though why these rules must be applied to -*mit* rather than directly to, say, *commit* is unclear to me. What little evidence exists concerning such forms suggests that they are no less susceptible to stem-priming (Stanners, Neiser, and Painton 1979), that they exhibit stem-frequency effects (Taft 1979b), and that they behave like prefixed rather than pseudoprefixed items (Taft 1981; Bergman, Hudson, and Eling [1988] draw a different conclusion for Dutch).

It appears, then, that neither ease of recognition nor primability of constituents can readily be used to distinguish complex words that are semantically opaque. Other avenues that may yield more conclusive findings about semantic composition are just beginning to be explored. These include neuropsychological investigations (Kay 1987) and studies of pre-fixedness judgments (Smith 1987).

"Productivity" of a Word-Formation Rule has been the subject of con-trasting definitions (Henderson 1987). My own view is that it is essentially a dispositional, and hence psychological, concept, which refers to the contemporary language user's preparedness to employ a WFR creatively in production or comprehension. This factor leads us naturally into a very detailed sort of investigation that takes as its focus particular affix systems. Already, Bradley (1980) and Anshen and Aronoff (1987) have suggested that the exceptionally productive suffix -*ness* differs in its mental represen-tation from other, more restricted affixative systems. This finding is scarcely secure as yet, but I suspect that it points the way to a fruitful marriage of linguistic analysis to psychological investigation.

"Syntactic force" is the somewhat clumsy label I have applied to affixa-tion that changes form class while leaving meaning scarcely disturbed. This property is correlated with others that we have already discussed in that inflection has maximum syntactic force, and within the derivational field, suffixation more often has syntactic force than does prefixation. Little investigative attention has so far been directed toward this variable, but this has not deterred some theorists from taking up a firm position. In an engagingly wide-ranging discussion, Cutler, Hawkins, and Gilligan (1986, p. 747) have asserted that the more an affix's function is purely syntactic, "the more its processing will be distinct from the way its stem is processed." In this, they develop a line of thought that can be discovered in Morton's (1968) early ruminations on logogens.

Cutler et al. present a set of arguments that are elegant and very general. They also differ from most of the proposals we have considered in attempt-ing to build a bridge that is strongly anchored both in linguistics and in experimental psychology. I shall therefore briefly review their argument.

Cutler et al. start from the fact that there is a very strong tendency for languages to prefer suffixation to prefixation, with infixation being ex-ceeding rare. They then show that although this asymmetry is correlated with left-right asymmetry in syntax, the bias is stronger in morphology, suggesting the need for some other supplementary account. Such an account, they suggest, is to be found in the processes underlying word recognition. The essence of this is that individual words are analyzed in a left-to-right order. A primary objective of this analysis is to recover con-tentive information that is usually to be found in the stem. This information must be separated from syntactic information, so that the two can undergo independent processing. In general, the lexical content takes precedent in comprehension; thus, it would be efficient to locate it first. All of this argues for the stem to be situated leftward in the word.

The assumption that a visually presented word is analyzed in left-to-right order is one that many students of reading may find uncongenial. Most of the evidence that Cutler et al. present refers to speech perception and production. Though they seem to have little hesitation about importing the left-to-right premise into visual word recognition, their basic thesis does not require this. Since their objective is to provide an account for an evolutionary tendency across languages, it would suffice to argue that this arises from processing constraints that are reflected in the nature of the perception of *spoken* words.

The assumptions that Cutler et al. ask us to make about morphological representation are minimal; they scarcely extend beyond the assertion that most morphological boundaries are marked at some stage of processing and that this is especially likely to be true the greater the contrast between semantic and syntactic function across the boundary.

Despite their disarming protestation that they wish to claim no more than that stem and affix are partitioned *at some stage* of processing, their association of this segmentation with the left-to-right prelexical analysis of words seems to draw us unavoidably toward the conclusion that morphemic segmentation takes place at a very early stage. This, in turn, confronts us with a puzzle, since (in English, at least) affix information is, on its own, extraordinarily ambiguous concerning syntactic class. Thus, we have *rival* (V), *hospital* (N), and *tidal* (Adj.); *shorten* (V), *oxen* (N), and *wooden* (Adj.); and *clatter* (V), *baker* (N), and *faster* (Adj.).

It is only fair to point out that Cutler et al. explicitly focus on inflectional morphology, and that the import of their comments for lexical morphology is not developed in detail. Thus, although their arguments are well grounded in the larger arena of cross-language comparisons, the application of these arguments to English derivational morphology are indeterminate. What they seem to have in mind is a distinction between contentive and grammatical morphemes like that to which aphasiologists (e.g. Garrett [1982]) have appealed when offering double-dissociation accounts of agrammatic and jargonaphasic speech disorders.

Conclusions

My primary concern in this chapter has been to use morphology as the arena in which to examine the employment of the concept of lexical representation by linguists and by psychologists. In particular, I have hoped to show that it is quite misguided to suppose that much of this work converges on a central core of common issues, although a linguist and a psychologist might differ somewhat in types of evidence adduced and in forms of argument.

Much linguistic work in this area seems indubitably to be about lexical representation but cannot usefully be regarded as making explicit assertions about *mental* representation. There are, I think, two simple but important points to be made here. First, the economy of lexical representation, which is a motivating principle for many linguistic proposals, has the status of a criterion by which many linguistic theories seek to be judged. In psychology, the economy-of-storage principle is no more than a particular hypothesis about the nature of mental representation, which must compete on equal terms with other hypotheses and be subject to adjudication by external (i.e., explanatory) criteria. Second, it must be appreciated that representational claims are psychologically empty unless accompanied by a processing model.

Nowhere is the complexly interacting duality of process and representation more evident than in the postulation of linguistic rules. Much of the linguistic ingenuity that has gone into constructing elegant and compact descriptions of the lexical knowledge the language user is required to have takes the form of law-like statements accompanied by parsimonious devices for limiting their application. Thus, for example, rule application may be qualified by ordering the rules, by tagging exceptions to which the rule does not apply, by tagging those entities to which the rule does apply, or even by formulating at a secondary level another rule that obstructs the application of the original rule. We have considered examples of each of these above.

It seems unreasonable to deny that such organized systems of rules and their qualifiers offer a cogent description of the regularities of a language, but it is clearly a quite different matter to establish that this form of representation is one that is felicitously matched to the characteristics of the human processor and therefore provides a satisfactory account of acquisition, the quality of expert performance, the resistance of the processor to corruption due to component failure, and the pattern of impaired performance that sufficient damage yields.

People exhibit skill in solving problems in a variety of domains which are governed by formal, abstract rules. Until quite recently it has seemed natural, perhaps even unavoidable, to assume that they succeed to the extent that their behavior is controlled by mental representations of these abstract rules. However, attempts to establish the psychological reality of these rules have been largely unsuccessful in areas as diverse as syllogistic reasoning and transformational syntax. This has led psychologists to explore the possibility that alternative cognitive processes might underlie rule-like behavior—processes that might also give a more satisfactory account of systematic deviations from the rules. Perhaps the most concerted attempt of this sort has been that of Johnson-Laird (1983), who has used the notion of mental models. Another, less systematic, approach has explored the notion of analogies in problem solving and in language. For example, the traditional view that creativity in print-to-sound translation (that is, the ability to assign a plausible pronunciation to an unfamiliar word) depends upon the reader's employment of the most frequent elementary spelling-sound correspondences has been challenged by the suggestion that, instead, the reader decides on a pronunciation by on-line lexical activation of word analogies (see Henderson 1985b, Humphreys and Evitt 1985, and Patterson and Morton 1985 for recent reviews).

Fortunately, a detailed examination of these questions lies outside the scope of this chapter. Nevertheless, it is worth taking note here of the distinction between asserting that behavior largely conforms to the abstract rules governing a system and the much stronger proposition that performance is controlled by mental representations of these abstract rules. Moreover, as Butterworth (1983) has astutely observed, there are interesting parallels between the problem of formulating morphological rules and that of formulating print-to-sound rules. To his comments I would add the following observations.

Most theories of the creative process in oral reading have assumed that it plays some role even in pronunciation decisions for familiar words. This is true both of abstract rule-based approaches (Coltheart 1978) and of analogy-based views (Glushko 1979). Presumably the major reason for this assumption is that effects of regularity are found for all but the most common words (Seidenberg, Waters, Barnes, and Tanenhaus 1984). The mechanism for dealing with novel stimuli is therefore held to operate in parallel with the attempt to retrieve the entire phonological solution from the lexicon, rather than being assigned a fall-back role.

A second feature of all theories of oral reading until very recently was that conformity to rule was regarded as a strictly dichotomous property of words. That is, a word was held to be regular if and only if each of its component spelling-sound correspondences was the most common translation in a type count of words containing that letter (or sometimes a multi-letter pattern treated as a graphic unit). Hence, on account of the pronunciation assigned to the EA, *veal* was classed as regular and *head*, *steak*, and *react* were classed as irregular, without further distinction. The motivation for this assumption was to allow "regular" forms (and unfamiliar forms) to be successfully translated by nonlexical rules without lexical verification. However, evidence has begun to accumulate that degree of regularity influences performance (Brown 1987; Rosson 1984; Shallice and McCarthy 1985), and this has posed difficulties for theorists intent on preserving the sharp distinction between lexically retrieved pronunciation and pronunciation assembled from universal nonlexical rules. Though it seems feasible to give some sort of account of graded regularity effects by assuming that translation rules are lexically governed, with varying scope, by analogy with lexically governed morphological rules, to the best of my knowledge no one has attempted such a formulation.

Another lesson that might be learned from the postulation of translation rules in oral reading is that the *processing* questions concerned with retrieval and decision making tend to be underestimated. Consider the naive employment of "horse-race" models that lack a decision-making component (Henderson 1982; Patterson and Morton 1985).

Perhaps the most direct challenge to the rule-based approach to representational issues comes from "connectionist" modeling, in which the boundary between process and representation is, in any case, peculiarly difficult to define. An especially germane example of the parallel distributed processing approach is to be found in the attempt by McClelland and Rumelhart (1986) to model the learning of English strong verb forms. However, the question of whether, when we are concerned with the microstructure of processing (in terms, say, of the connections and their weightings, in an associative network), we require explicitly to postulate rules, or whether these arise as mere epiphenomenal "global" characterizations of the behavior of the entire system, is an open one (Pinker 1987).

Turning now to the portion of the psychological approach that makes least contact with linguistic analyses, we are confronted with the lexical-decision task—an ingenious piece of 1960s technology, mass-produced and readily transportable, guaranteed to be pre-focused so as to permit a sharply detailed view of the very surface of the lexicon.

The positive virtues of the instrument are far from negligible. It seems to pose to the subject a standard question that does not vary in ways determined by the target (as happens in the category-verification task). The task decision is mapped onto a binary response, which lacks the idiosyncratic production features of the word-naming task.

Above all, the task seems to yield to a simple logical analysis of its content, in that it appears to require processing up to but no farther than the point of lexical access. However, these assumptions are not unproblematical. It has to be assumed that the processing path taken by the task stimulus retraces the early steps taken by a word in a sentence that we are bent on understanding. Obviously, some of the processing stages will be abbreviated in sentence comprehension. Nevertheless, it is reasonable to seek assurance that the pathway through those stages is not deviant in the experimental model of access. We also need assurance that the very idea of lexical access as a determinate and punctiform event holds good.

The apparent precision with which psychologists focus on the point of access to the lexicon might suggest that the lexicon is circumscribed by clearly marked boundaries, a fashion of speaking that is reinforced by decisive talk of pre-access and post-access locations. Furthermore, linguists and psychologists often frame important-sounding theoretical questions in terms of whether X or Y is held to be "in the lexicon." For example, some linguists have asserted that -*ness* formations are not listed in the lexicon. Conversely, at least one psychologist has been reproached for assuming that letter-sound correspondence rules are to be found "in the lexicon."

For the most part, these metaphors offer a harmless enough shorthand for referring to difficult abstractions. The danger lies in assuming that they furnish a common language for comparing theories. In particular, it is perilous to presume that the boundaries of the linguist's hypothetical "lexicon" are congruent with that of the psychologist. This becomes evident as soon as we notice that in most linguistic discussion the boundaries of the lexicon are supplied *by definition*. Thus, for Chomsky as for Bloomfield, it is the job of the lexicon to contain linguistic information that cannot be derived by rule. As we have seen, much linguistic energy has gone into the eviction from the lexicon of predictable regularities. Now, the form of words that I have just employed is itself foreign to the psychologist. If he should tell us that he passed his day devising an ingenious strategy for evicting material from the lexicon, we would suspect him of exercising the black arts (ECT or worse). This serves to illustrate the fact that the lexicon of linguistics enjoys a different ontological status than psychology. Furthermore, it is a widely held assumption in the psychological study of oral reading that the lexicon of an English reader contains mappings at the word level between written and spoken forms, even when the words are regular in the sense of having spelling-sound relationships that are entirely predictable by "nonlexical" rule. Whether this hypothesis is correct is irrelevant. What matters is that it is a proposition that is only interpretable in terms of psychological data. Of course, some will hold that if the lexicon postulated by a linguist is not a set of assertions about the organization of knowledge that people have in their heads, then it is not about anything at all. In this view, linguistics amounts to the pursuit of psychology by other means.

Whatever position we arrive at on the ultimate objectives of linguistic and psychological theory, it seems evident that much recent psychological work that purports to be about the mental representation of morphological information does not, in fact, refer to underlying features of words that enable them to do their work in sentences. It is for this reason that I have pedantically insisted on distinguishing between "morphs" and "morphemes." The danger, as I have previously expressed it, is that psychologists may mistake models of lexical-decision performance for statements about lexical grammar.

However, it would be wrong to portray linguistic and psychological approaches as ventures that are incapable of touching at any point. Even if the lexical decision task affords too narrow a field of view to take in much of the organization of our knowledge about words in their various lexico-semantic and lexico-syntactic aspects, there are signs of convergence between linguistic and psychological approaches. Nowhere is this more evident than in the search for a better formulation of the underlying dimension that is summarized in the inflectional/derivational dichotomy.

Acknowledgments

This research was supported by the Economic and Social Research Council. I am grateful to Hartmut Günther for helpful discussion and to Brian Butterworth, Carol Fowler, and William Marslen-Wilson for stimulating comments on an earlier draft.

Notes

1. I believe that considerable confusion results from use of the term "morpheme" to refer both to an abstract grammatical element and to its particular realizations in spoken or written words. The latter job I have tried, no doubt inconsistently, to reserve for the somewhat neglected term "morph" (whence "allomorphic" arises naturally).

2. Actually, there are many puzzles about this alternative to the prefix-stripping account. For example, it is very unclear how *relucky activates a portion of the entry for unlucky whereas plucky does not. However, it is not my purpose here to conduct investigative surgery on a mere passing suggestion.

3. This is not a strictly necessary corollary of the notion of decomposition as a preliminary to lexical access. The written form might be immediately searched for stem morphs, so that, for example, with a Type 2 lexical representation, the parsing *p-luck-y* is only rejected after consultation of the contents of the *luck*-headed entry. Such a system would yield pseudostem effects rather than the pseudoaffix effects that have been the focus of experimental attention provoked by the original Taft-Forster formulation (but see Monsell 1985 for an apparent facilitatory pseudostem effect).

4. The representations in table 2 have been simplified to the point of caricature. The problem of how and at what stage form class is specified has been neglected. Moreover, by simply listing address codes for affixation rules without attempting to formulate the rules, problems in ordering the application of the rules have been evaded.

5. However, very recently there have been some developments in this direction (see, for example, Henderson 1987).

6. Information culled from Marchand 1969 (pp. 318–321).

7. I am indebted to Hartmut Günther for the idea that saliency of the citation form might be responsible for some seemingly morphological parsing effects.

8. I fastidiously eschew the deeper implications of "morphological." Widespread recent use of the terms "morphological" and "morpheme" in this context may lead to confusion between lexico-syntactic and orthographic/phonological aspects.

9. Transparency may be an effective variable in other sorts of tasks not relevant here.

References

Anshen, F., and Aronoff, M. 1987. Accessing Morphologically Complex Words. Paper presented at International Workshop on Linguistic and Psychological Approaches to Morphology, Selwyn College, Cambridge.

Aronoff, M. 1976. *Word Formation in Generative Grammar*. Cambridge, Mass.: MIT Press.

Bauer, L. 1983. *English Word-Formation*. Cambridge University Press.

Bergman, M. W., Hudson, P. T. W., and Eling, P. A. T. M. 1988. How simple complex words can be: Morphological processing and word representations. *Quarterly Journal of Experimental Psychology* 40A: 41–72.

Berko, J. 1958. The child's learning of English morphology. *Word* 14: 150–177.

Bradley, D. C. 1980. Lexical representation of derivational relation. In M. Aronoff and M.-L. Kean (eds.), *Juncture*. Saratoga, Calif.: Anma Libri.

Brown, G. D. A. 1987. Resolving inconsistency: A computational model of word naming. *Journal of Memory and Language* 26: 1–13.

Butterworth, B. 1983. Lexical representation. In B. Butterworth (ed.), *Language Production*, volume 2. London: Academic.

Chomsky, N. 1965. *Aspects of the Theory of Syntax*. Cambridge, Mass.: MIT Press.

Chomsky, N. 1970. Remarks on nominalization. In R. Jacobs and P. Rosenbaum (eds.), *Readings in English Transformational Grammar*. Waltham, Mass.: Ginn.

Chomsky, N. 1972. *Language and Mind*. New York: Harcourt Brace Jovanovich.

Chomsky, N., and Halle, M. 1968. *The Sound Pattern of English*. New York: Harper and Row.

Clark, E. V., and Clark, H. H. 1979. When nouns surface as verbs. *Language* 55: 767–811.

Coltheart, M. 1978. Lexical access in simple reading tasks. In G. Underwood (ed.), *Strategies of Information Processing*. London: Academic.

Cutler, A. 1981. Degrees of transparency in word formation. *Canadian Journal of Linguistics* 26: 73–77.

Cutler, A., Hawkins, J. A., and Gilligan, G. 1985. The suffixing preference: A processing explanation. *Linguistics* 23: 723–758.

Downie, R., Milech, D., and Kirsner, K. 1985. Unit definition in the mental lexicon. *Australian Journal of Psychology* 37: 141–155.

Evett, L., and Humphreys, G. W. 1981. The use of abstract graphemic information in lexical access. *Quarterly Journal of Experimental Psychology* 33A: 325–350.

Feldman, L. B., and Fowler, C. A. 1987. The inflected noun system in Serbo-Croatian's lexical representation of morphological structure. *Memory and Cognition* 15: 1–12.

Feustel, T. C. Shiffrin, R. M., and Salasoo, A. 1983. Episodic and lexical contributions to the repetition effect in word identification. *Journal of Experimental Psychology: General* 112: 309–346.

Forster, K. I., and Davis, C. 1984. Repetition priming and frequency attenuation in lexical access. *Journal of Experimental Psychology: Learning Memory and Cognition* 10: 680–698.

Forster, K. I., Davis, C., Schoknecht, C., and Carter, R. 1987. Masked priming with graphemically related forms: Repetitions or partial activation? *Quarterly Journal of Experimental Psychology* 39A: 211–251.

Fowler, C. A., Napps, S. E., and Feldman, L. 1985. Relations among regular and irregular morphologically related words in the lexicon as revealed by repetition priming. *Memory and Cognition* 13: 241–255.

Garrett, M. F. 1982. Production of speech: Observations from normal and pathological language use. In A. W. Ellis (ed.), *Normality and Pathology in Cognitive Functions*. London: Academic.

Glushko, R. J. 1979. The organization and activation of orthographic knowledge in reading aloud. *Journal of Experimental Psychology: Human Perception and Performance* 5: 674–691.

Günther, H. 1988. Oblique word forms in visual word recognition. *Linguistics* 26: 583–600.

Günther, H., Gfoerer, S., and Weiss, L. 1984. Inflection, frequency and the word superiority effect. *Psychological Research* 46: 261–281.

Henderson, L. 1982. *Orthography and Word Recognition in Reading*. London: Academic.

Henderson, L. 1985a. Issues in the modelling of pronunciation assembly in normal reading. In K. Patterson, J. C. Marshall, and M. Coltheart (eds.), *Surface Dyslexia*. London: Erlbaum.

Henderson, L. 1985b. Toward a psychology of morphemes. In A. W. Ellis (ed.), *Progress in the Psychology of Language*, volume 1. London: Erlbaum.

Henderson, L. 1986. From morph to morpheme: The psychologist gaily trips where the linguist has trodden. In G. Augst (ed.), *International Research in Graphemics and Orthography*. Berlin: de Gruyter.

Henderson, L. 1987. Linguistic and Psychological Approaches to Morphology. Final Report to the Economic and Social Research Council on Grant C0026 2075.

Henderson, L., Wallis, J., and Knight, D. 1984. Morphemic structure and lexical access. In H. Bouma and D. Bouwhuis (eds.), *Attention and Performance X*. London: Erlbaum.

Humphreys, G. W., and Evett, L. J. 1985. Are there independent lexical and nonlexical routes in word processing? *Behavioral and Brain Sciences* 8: 689–740.

Jackendoff, R. 1975. Morphological and semantic regularities in the lexicon. *Language* 51: 639–671.

Jacoby, L. L., and Dallas, M. 1981. On the relationship between autobiographical memory and perceptual learning. *Journal of Experimental Psychology: General* 3: 306–340.

Johnson-Laird, P. 1983. *Mental Models*. Cambridge University Press.

Jordan, T. R. 1986. Testing the Boss hypothesis: Evidence for position-insensitive orthographic priming in the lexical decision task. *Memory and Cognition* 14: 523–532.

Kay, J. 1987. On the Origin of Morphological Errors in Acquired Dyslexia. Paper presented at International Workshop on Linguistic and Psychological Approaches to Morphology, Selwyn College, Cambridge.

Kempley, S. T., and Morton, J. 1982. The effects of priming with regularly and irregularly related words in auditory word recognition. *British Journal of Psychology* 73: 441–454.

Klima, E. S. 1972. How alphabets might reflect language. In J. F. Kavanagh and I. G. Mattingly (eds.), *Language by Eye and by Ear*. Cambridge, Mass.: MIT Press.

Levi, J. N. 1978. *The Syntax and Semantics of Complex Nominals*. New York: Academic.

Lukatela, G., Gligorijevic, B., Kostic, A., and Turvey, M. T. 1980. Representation of inflected nouns in the internal lexicon. *Memory and Cognition* 8: 415–423.

McClelland, J. C., and Rumelhart, D. E. 1986. On learning the past tense of English verbs. In J. L. McClelland et al. (eds.), *Parallel Distributed Processing*, volume 2. Cambridge, Mass.: MIT Press.

Manelis, L., and Tharp, D. A. 1977. The processing of affixed words. *Memory and Cognition* 5: 690–695.

Marchand, H. 1969. *The Categories and Types of Present-Day English Word Formation*. Munich: Beck.

Miceli, G., and Caramazza, A. 1987. Dissociation of Inflectional and Derivational Morphology. Report 23, Cognitive Neuropsychology Laboratory, Johns Hopkins University.

Monsell, S. 1985. Repetition and the lexicon. In A. W. Ellis (ed.), *Progress in the Psychology of Language*, volume 2. London: Erlbaum.

Morton, J. 1968. Considerations of Grammar and Computation in Language Behavior. C.R.L.L.B. Progress Report VI, University of Michigan.

Murrell, G., and Morton, J. 1974. Word recognition and morphemic structure. *Journal of Experimental Psychology* 102: 963–968.

Napps, S., and Fowler, C. A. The effect of orthography on the organization of the mental lexicon. *Journal of Psycholinguistic Research*, in press.

Neely, J. H. 1977. Semantic priming and retrieval from lexical memory: Roles of inhibitionless spreading activation and limited-capacity attention. *Journal of Experimental Psychology: General* 106: 226–254.

Neisser, U. 1967. *Cognitive Psychology*. New York: Appleton-Century-Crofts.

Osgood, C. E., and Hoosain, R. 1974. Salience of the word as a unit in the perception of language. *Perception and Psychophysics* 15: 168–192.

Patterson, K., and Morton, J. 1985. From orthography to phonology: An attempt at an old explanation. In K. Patterson, J. C. Marshall, and M. Coltheart (eds.), *Surface Dyslexia*. London: Erlbaum.

Pinker, S. 1987. Paper presented to Experimental Psychology Society, Oxford, July 1987.

Rosson, B. 1984. The interaction of pronunciation rules and lexical representations in reading aloud. *Memory and Cognition* 13: 90–99.

Rubin, G. S., Becker, C. A., and Freeman, R. H. 1979. Morphological structure and its effect on visual word recognition. *Journal of Verbal Learning and Verbal Behavior* 18: 757–767.

Sampson, G. 1985. *Writing Systems*. London: Hutchinson.

Segui, J., and Zubizarreta, M. L. 1985. Mental representation of morphologically complex words and lexical access. *Linguistics* 23: 759–773.

Seidenberg, M. S., Waters, G. S., Barnes, M. A., and Tanenhaus, M. K. 1984. When does irregular spelling or pronunciation influence word recognition? *Journal of Verbal Learning and Verbal Behavior* 23: 383–404.

Shallice, T., and McCarthy, R. 1985. Phonological reading: From patterns of impairment to possible procedures. In K. Patterson, J. C. Marshall, and M. Coltheart (eds.), *Surface Dyslexia*. London: Erlbaum.

Smith, P. T. 1980. Linguistic information in spelling. In U. Frith (ed.), *Cognitive Processes in Spelling*. London: Academic.

Smith, P. T. 1987. How to Do Experiments with Morphologically Complex Words. Paper presented to International Workshop on Linguistic and Psychological Approaches to Morphology, Selwyn College, Cambridge.

Stanners, R. F., Neiser, J. J., Hernon, W. P., and Hall, R. 1979a. Memory representation for morphologically related words. *Journal of Verbal Learning and Verbal Behavior* 18: 399–412.

Stanners, R. F., Neiser, J. J., and Painton, S. 1979b. Memory representation for prefixed words. *Journal of Verbal Learning and Verbal Behavior* 18: 733–743.

Taft, M. 1979a. Lexical access via an orthographic code: The Basic Orthographic Syllabic Structure (BOSS). *Journal of Verbal Learning and Verbal Behavior* 18: 21–39.

Taft, M. 1979b. Recognition of affixed words and the word frequency effect. *Memory and Cognition* 7: 263–272.

Taft, M. 1981. Prefix stripping revisited. *Journal of Verbal Learning and Verbal Behavior* 20: 284–297.

Taft, M. 1985. The decoding of words in lexical access: A review of the morphographic approach. In D. Besner, T. G. Waller, and G. E. Mackinnon (eds.), *Reading Research: Advances in Theory and Practice.* New York: Academic.

Taft, M., and Forster, K. I. 1975. Lexical storage and retrieval of prefixed words. *Journal of Verbal Learning and Verbal Behavior* 14: 638–647.

Taft, M., and Forster, K. I. 1976. Lexical storage and retrieval of polymorphemic and polysyllabic words. *Journal of Verbal Learning and Verbal Behavior* 15: 607–620.

Weir, R., and Venezky, R. L. 1968. English orthography—More reason than rhyme. In K. S. Goodman (ed.), *The Psycholinguistic Nature of the Reading Process.* Detroit: Wayne State University Press.

Wilson, M. D. 1984. Composition of the Mental Lexicon. Ph.D. thesis, University of Cambridge.

Chapter 13

Morphological Parsing and   Jorge Hankamer
the Lexicon

Much discussion in recent psycholinguistic literature on the processing of morphologically complex words has focused on the following two questions[1]:

1. What is listed in the mental lexicon?[2]
2. To what extent is parsing involved in word recognition?[3]

These questions are interrelated, since the answer to one may limit the range of possible answers to the other. In fact, investigators who have taken a particular position on one of these questions have always adopted some position on the other as well.

Taft and Forster (1975) proposed that prefixed words in English are recognized by a process of prefix stripping followed by lexical lookup of the root. Such a model gives a clear role to parsing in recognition, and presumes that roots (even when the root is a bound morpheme) are listed in the lexicon whereas the affixed forms are not. This model was refined and extended in Taft 1979; see also Taft 1981. Stanners et al. (1979) suggested a similar treatment for inflectional suffixes. At the opposite end of the scale, Butterworth (1983) defended the Full Listing Hypothesis (FLH), according to which each word has its own lexical entry and there is no need for parsing in normal word recognition.[4]

Two important variants of the FLH have dominated in recent years: FLH-A (full listing with morphologically complex entries) and FLH-B (full listing with nucleus and satellite organization). The A version was suggested as an alternative by Taft and Forster (1975), and has been accepted by numerous investigators since. The basic idea of FLH-A is that complex words have their own lexical entries, but the entries include a representation of morphological structure. Thus, the word *unties* would have a lexical entry of its own, but that entry would contain a morphological analysis of the word: ((un(tie))s). The B version has been adopted even more widely

(Bradley 1978, 1980; Lukatela et al. 1978, 1980; Segui and Zubizarreta 1985). Here the idea is that every word has its own entry, but all entries for complex words are linked in the organization of the lexicon to a basic entry for the uninflected or root word. Thus, *unties* would have its own entry in the lexicon, which would be linked (as would the entries for *ties*, *untie*, *tied*, *retie*, etc.) to the basic entry *tie*. The basic entry is called the *nucleus* of the cluster of entries, and all the others are called *satellites*.

There are apparently infinite variations on these basic themes. Bybee (1987) proposes a model that incorporates the connectionist assumptions of model B, along with its notion of special status for "basic" forms, and at the same time a version of the structured entries of model A (though the structure is expressed in terms of connections between affixes). Segui and Zubizarreta (1985) propose a full-listing model in which prefixed forms are accessed via the entry for the prefixed form, and suffixed forms are accessed via the entry for the root, which has pointers to the entries for suffixed forms. Laudanna and Burani (1985) propose a full-listing model in which there are entries for whole words and also entries for morphemes; a word is accessed via its full entry, and its morphological composition is given by pointers from the word entry to the component morpheme entries, providing in effect a model of type A.

Further, most proponents of full-listing models follow Butterworth in proposing listing for common or known forms and parsing as a "backup" device to be called on for uncommon or previously unknown forms.

In the psycholinguistic literature, where parsing is contemplated as playing a role in word recognition it is usually assumed that the basic parsing operation is affix stripping, as proposed by Taft and Forster. In this kind of model, affixes are first stripped off and then the remaining root is accessed by lookup in a lexicon of roots.[5]

It is the purpose of this chapter to argue that all versions of the FLH are untenable as hypotheses about speakers of human languages in general. The argument is based on an examination of morphological complexity in agglutinative languages (with Turkish as the central example) and on a demonstration that the number of forms corresponding to a single noun or verb root is considerably larger than would be consistent with the assumption that all forms are listed in a mental lexicon.

I will argue in addition that the parsing model that is required in the face of such languages cannot be an affix-stripping model (at least where suffixes are concerned), but must rather allow for recognition of the root before suffixes are recognized.

1 Stark Models

The following are three possible assumptions regarding the lexical representation of morphologically complex words:

A. List all forms of all words in the lexicon without representation of internal structure and without representation of connections to morphologically related entries.

B. List all forms in the lexicon together with some representation of internal structure or some representation of connection to morphologically related entries (or both).

C. List only atoms (roots, affixes) in the lexicon.

These three assumptions are mutually incompatible as stated, though it is possible to formulate mixed or intermediate positions of various kinds under which some complex forms are listed in the lexicon and others are not. One position that has been contemplated is that forms involving derivational affixes are listed and forms involving inflectional affixes are not; another is that irregular forms are listed and regular forms are not; a third is that very common forms are listed and uncommon ones are not.

Let me first dispense with a straw man. Nobody has seriously proposed a model like A, which would allow no explanation for numerous observed effects. (For reviews, see Cutler et al. 1985; Butterworth 1983; Stemberger and MacWhinney 1986 and in press.) The arguments I am about to present are directed against all versions of the FLH, and *a fortiori* against position A.

Position C may also be a straw man. It is the strongest form of the Taft-Forster hypothesis, and it is consistent with positions taken by a very small minority of investigators in this area. It is, however, not a position that has firmly been espoused by anyone, to my knowledge, unless we count theoretical linguists who have no concern for psychological reality.

I myself particularly do not want to espouse position C. There seems to be plenty of evidence that morphologically, semantically, and syntactically complex forms may be listed in the mental lexicon. I argue here only that all versions of the FLH, except those too weak to really count as versions of the FLH, are inadequate as theories about human lexicons. My position will be consistent with theories that allow full listing for some morphologically complex forms, such as those involving prefixes and perhaps those involving derivational morphology. It will not be consistent with any theory that requires full listing of all words known to and readily usable by competent adult speakers of a language.

All the psycholinguistic work on the lexical representation of morphologically complex words that I could find was confined to investigations of European languages (English, French, Italian, German, Dutch, Spanish, Serbo-Croatian); in fact most of it was on English. In the broad spectrum of languages, this is a very skewed sample. These languages have in common, among other things, a rather stunted morphological structure within words. It is easy for investigators, as many did apparently unthinkingly and a few (see Cutler et al. 1985, p. 748) thinkingly, to restrict attention to cases where the most complex word consists of just one root[6] and one affix.

When attention is restricted to this group of languages, and to the very simplest complex words in them, it is easy enough to believe that "the enormous storage capacity of the human brain" (Bybee 1987, p. 27, note 1) would provide plenty of room to house an entry for every word. I will argue in what follows that agglutinative languages, and in general languages that provide for words of significant complexity, are not amenable to any account consistent with the FLH.

2 Agglutination

Many languages (e.g. Turkish, Finnish, Hungarian, Quechua, Swahili) are characterized by what is called "agglutinative" word structure. What characterizes agglutinative languages is that stem formation by affixation to previously derived stems is extremely productive, so that a given stem, even though itself quite complex, can generally serve as the basis for even more complex words. A not particularly extreme example, from Turkish, is the word

indirilemiyebilecekler,

which has as a root *in* ('descend'). From this root the affixation of the causative suffix *dir* derives the stem *indir* ('lower'); to this stem the passive suffix *il* is attached to derive a stem meaning 'be lowered'; the affix *e* attaches to this stem, giving a new stem meaning 'be able to be lowered', which in turn forms the base to which the negative affix *me* can be attached, yielding a stem meaning 'not be able to be lowered'; the affix *yebil* creates a new stem from this, meaning 'able to not be able to be lowered'; the future affix *ecek* may be attached to this to produce a stem meaning 'will be able to not be able to be lowered'; finally (in this case) the agreement affix *ler*, signifying agreement with a third-person plural subject, may be attached to yield a word meaning '[they] will be able to not be able to be lowered', or 'they will be able to resist being brought down'.

In nominals, word formation by agglutination is equally prolific. An example:

ceplerimizdekilerdenmiş

The root is *cep* ('pocket'). To this is affixed the plural suffix *ler*, producing a stem meaning 'pockets'. The first-person plural possessive suffix *imiz* affixes to that, producing a stem meaning 'our pockets'. The locative case suffix *de* yields a stem meaning 'in our pockets'. The "relativizer" suffix *ki* yields a stem meaning 'the one that is in our pockets'. The plural suffix *ler* pluralizes that to yield 'the ones that are in our pockets'. The ablative suffix *den* yields a stem meaning 'from (among) the ones that are in our pockets'. And the dubitative suffix *miş* makes from this a predicate meaning '[it] is/was supposedly/reportedly from (among) those that are/were in our pockets'.

From these examples, it is clear that Turkish words can be composed of quite a few morphemes. There are, of course, some limitations on the order and combination of these morphemes. A complete description of the permissible combinations—a morphotactics for the language—requires the definition of over 40 stem categories and at least 150 suffix categories (Hankamer 1986, 1988). Here I will only sketch some of the more interesting aspects of the verbal and nominal morphotactics.

In all forms, the root comes first. (I am excluding discussion of several interesting reduplicative prefixation processes; see Demircan 1987.) A partial description of the affix order in verbs is as follows:

root-RFL-RCP-CAUS*-PASS-POT1-NEG-POT2-ASP-TNS-AGR

Here each affix symbol represents a category of affixes (possibly containing only one member).[7] The asterisk means that the causative suffix can iterate. Here is an example, adapted from Lewis 1967 (p. 153):

daya   -n -ış -tır -t   -ıl -a   -mı -yabil-ecek-ti -k

prop up-RFL-RCP-CAUS-CAUS-PASS-POT1-NEG-POT2-ASP-TNS-AGR

'we might not have been able to be made to make someone else practice mutual aid'

The description is only partial, because at various points there are other possible continuations than the one shown. For example, after POT2 (second potential), instead of an ASP (aspect) suffix an infinitive or verbal noun suffix may be chosen. The form is then a nominal, and may receive further suffixation according to the rules for nominal morphotactics. Alternatively, any of several adverbial or participial suffixes may be chosen, each leading to further (and different) suffixing possibilities. After the ASP suffix, it is possible to choose an AUX (auxiliary) suffix, which yields a stem that undergoes further suffixation according to the morphotactics for non-verbal predicates.

The nominal morphotactics is no less complex. The basic pattern is

root-DER*-PL-POSS-CASE

where DER is a category of derivational affixes that take nouns to nouns, PL is the plural affix, POSS is a category of possessive markers, and CASE is a set of case affixes. I will discuss just two of the complications.

Among the derivational affixes are two (-ci, 'person for', and -lik, 'thing for') that can form an iterative loop:

göz	'eye'
gözlük	'glasses'
gözlükçü	'seller of glasses (oculist)'
gözlükçülük	'the occupation of oculists'
gözlükçülükçü	'a lobbyist for the oculist profession'
gözlükçülükçülük	'the occupation of being a lobbyist for the oculist profession'

After this point Turkish speakers and hearers tend to get confused, but it is clear that this derivational suffixation is a very productive process.

Another loop is introduced by the "relativizer" suffix *ki*, which may be affixed to certain stems formed by case suffixes:

ev	'house'
evler	'houses'
evlerimiz	'our houses'
evlerimizde	'in our houses'
evlerimizdeki	'the one in our houses'

The effect of the *ki* suffix is to create a stem that is effectively of the same category as a simple noun root like *ev*; then the cycle of suffixation may begin again:

evlerimizdekiler	'the ones in our houses'
evlerimizdekilerin	'of the ones in our houses'
evlerimizdekilerinki	'the one of (belonging to) the ones in our houses'

This cursory and incomplete description of Turkish morphotactics is intended to bring home the fact that agglutinative languages contain words of considerable morphological complexity. Indeed, the morphotactic principles allow for iterative loops that, in principle, produce words of indefinite length. I will now try to head off two possible objections.

Possible objection number 1: "Those can't be words." They most certainly are words. Turks recognize them as words. The affixes are bound morphemes and cannot stand in isolation. Phonological rules sensitive to word boundaries (stress placement, vowel harmony, final stop devoicing) treat them as words.

Possible objection number 2: "Turks don't really use words that long." But they do, and quite frequently. I counted words and morphemes in a small sample (several thousand words) of Turkish text (journalistic prose, which tends to be morphologically more complex than natural speech but considerably less complex than technical writing), counting morphemes very conservatively—i.e., counting as distinct morphemes only the roots and the clearly productive suffixes. The average number of morphemes per word was 3.06, despite the fact that many of the most common words (articles, particles, conjunctions) are always monomorphemic. Words of five morphemes or more made up 19.8 percent of the sample.[8]

In the following section I will briefly review recent computational research concerned with morphological parsing in agglutinative languages.

3 Morphological Parsing

Morphological parsing has attracted relatively little attention in computational linguistics until recently. There has been considerable attention paid to syntactic parsing over the past two decades, but almost all syntactic-parsing models assume either that there is no real need for morphological parsing or that any such morphological parsing will be trivial (such as the recognition of a few suffixes at the ends of words). This attitude is predictable from the fact that virtually all syntactic-parsing research has been concerned with English, or with languages morphologically very like English.

Before reviewing the main lines of recent work in morphological parsing, it will be useful to note some differences in the problems faced by morphological parsers as opposed to syntactic parsers as typically conceived. The discussion to follow assumes an orthographic input stream, in which word boundaries are marked but morpheme boundaries within words are not.

Morphological parsing poses a different set of problems than syntactic parsing, at least as it has been conceived in connection with the analysis of written text. A syntactic parser for English can be designed with the assumption that the boundaries between the words are marked in the input, and with the assumption that (with virtually no exceptions) the shapes of the words are not affected by context.[9] The input to a morphological parser is the surface form (rather, an orthographic representation of the surface form) of a word, in which the morpheme boundaries are not marked and the shapes of the morphemes in general vary with context. It is not trivial in general to determine from the surface character string how many morphemes there are in the word and which surface segments are to be assigned to which morpheme.

A morphological parser thus requires a morphophonological component that mediates between the surface form of a morpheme as encountered in the input text and the lexical form in which the morpheme is stored in the morpheme inventory.[10]

In addition to a means of recognizing variant forms of morphemes as the same, the parser requires a morphotactic component that specifies which combinations of morphemes are permitted. Without such a specification, the number of false parses that would have to be considered is astronomical. This is not so easily seen in morphologically impoverished languages like English, but it becomes quite clear upon consideration of the morphological complexity of agglutinative languages, as will be shown in the next section.

Given these two requirements, there are various possible approaches to the actual analysis of words. Morphological-parsing algorithms may be divided into affix-stripping models and root-driven analysis models. For suffixing languages, this equates to right-to-left versus left-to-right algorithms. Both approaches have been taken from very early on in the history of morphological parsing.

Packard's (1973) parser for ancient Greek proceeds by stripping affixes off the word, and then attempting to look up the remainder in a lexicon. Only if there is an entry in the lexicon matching the remainder and compatible with the stripped-off affixes is the parse deemed a success.[11]

Sagvall (1973), on the other hand, devised a morphological analyzer for Russian that first looks in a lexicon for a root matching an initial substring of the word. It then uses grammatical information stored in the lexical entry to determine what possible suffixes may follow.

In the early 1980s, three different approaches to morphological parsing of agglutinative languages were developed independently: one for Quechua (Kasper and Weber 1982a,b), one for Finnish (Koskenniemi 1983), and one for Turkish (Hankamer 1984). These three approaches differ in their treatment of morphophonemic alternation, but they are essentially identical in the way they treat morphotactics. They all proceed from left to right, in the fashion of Sagvall's parser. Roots are sought in the lexicon that match initial substrings of the word, and the grammatical category of the root determines what class of suffixes may follow. When a suffix in the permitted class is found to match a further substring of the word, grammatical information in the lexical entry for that suffix determines once again what class of suffixes may follow. If the end of the word can be reached by iteration of this process, and if the last suffix analyzed is one that may end a word, the parse is successful.

So far as I know, this approach to morphotactics for agglutinating languages was first proposed by Weber (1976). The essential principle on which all three models agree is the representation of the morphotactics in terms of a finite-state transition network in which suffix morphemes sanction transitions between stem categories.

A simple example will serve to illustrate how it works. The Turkish parser's lexicon contains the following entries[12]:

ev	00N0	'house'
lar	N0N1	PL
ımız	N1N2	1plPOSS
da	N2N3	LOC
ki	N3N0	REL

The categorial notation in the middle field represents the category transition associated with the morpheme. The notation 00N0 for *ev* means that that morpheme combines with nothing on the left and yields a stem of category N0, i.e. a nominal root. The notation N0N1 for *lar* means that that morpheme combines with a stem of category N0 on the left and yields a stem of category N1. The third field in each entry is a gloss.

Now, given the word *evlerimizdekiler* ('the ones that are in our houses'), the analysis proceeds as follows:

1. A substring-matching routine detects a match between the lexical-entry form *ev* and an initial substring of the word. This routine returns a pointer to the first segment in the unanalyzed portion of the word.

2. Since the lexical entry for *ev* designates it as yielding a stem of category N0, the next search is for a suffix that can attach to N0. One such suffix is *lar*, which matches *ler* in the surface string.[13] Hence the stem *evler* is recognized, and it has the category N1.

3. Similarly, *ımiz* is a suffix that can attach to a stem of category N1, yielding a stem of category N2, and it matches the substring *imiz* in the word.

4. The locative suffix *da* matches *de* in the surface string, yielding a stem of category N3.

5. The relative suffix *ki* can attach to a stem of category N3, yielding a stem of category N0.

6. Given a stem of category N0, the plural suffix *lar* can be recognized, yielding a stem of category N1.

7. Stems of category N1 can stand as words; and the end of the surface form has been reached, so it is recognized as a word.

To summarize: First the root is recognized, by matching a lexical form to an initial substring of the surface word. Then suffixes are recognized iteratively; each suffix match yields a new stem, which determines a class of permissible successor suffixes. Recognition of suffixes is mediated by a routine that allows for influence of phonological and grammatical context on suffix shape.

All three of the current approaches to morphological parsing in agglutinative languages proceed essentially in this fashion. The reasons why none of them adopt the suffix-stripping approach will be discussed in the next section.

4 Consequences

In this section I will first argue that if morphological parsing is to play a role in human word recognition, it must be imagined as proceeding from left to right (as in the three computational approaches described in the previous section), at least for languages with agglutinative suffixation. A suffix-stripping approach is not viable. Second, I will argue that the FLH cannot be seriously maintained for such languages, because of the size, the complexity, and the sheer number of words. The conclusion will then be that, for agglutinative languages at least, human word recognition does involve parsing, and this parsing proceeds from left to right in roughly the fashion of the computational models discussed above.

As was noted in the previous section, all three of the independently developed computational approaches to morphological parsing for agglutinative languages adopt a root-first strategy rather than a suffix-stripping approach. Although the motive in each case was surely computational efficiency rather than a conscious attempt to mimic human word recognition, I believe that the computational considerations can in this case be translated directly into psycholinguistic considerations, and that a careful examination of these considerations will provide a telling argument against suffix stripping as a human word-recognition process.[14]

It was noted above that the method of left-to-right morpheme recognition is common to all three of the current models for parsing words in agglutinative languages. One reason it has been universally adopted, even though the models were developed independently, is that the left-to-right recognition approach narrows the choice of possible suffixes at every step to suffixes that can combine with a stem of the current stem category. It might be thought that a suffix-stripping strategy enjoys the same advantage, since the recognition of a suffix would narrow down the set of possible stems to which it could be attached; there is a significant asymmetry, however, for the set of suffixes determined by a stem is a finite (and always very small) set, whereas the set of stems determined by a suffix is always very large, and not necessarily even finite.

Every time a suffix is stripped off, the remaining part of the word must be analyzed as one of the stem categories that the morphotactics allows preceding the suffix just removed. Since most suffixes can attach directly to roots, this means that at almost every step in the stripping process the lexicon must be searched to see if the current remainder is a root. Most initial substrings of a word will not be roots, so most of these searches will be futile. The larger the lexicon, of course, the more wasteful this process becomes.[15]

To fully appreciate how bad the explosion of false analyses is, consider that in Turkish any final low vowel could be the dative suffix attached to a nominal stem (simple or complex), and any final high vowel could be the accusative suffix or the third-person singular possessive suffix. Thus, for any word ending in a vowel, the vowel would have to be stripped and a search of the lexicon made to see if the remainder were listed as a noun. If not, further attempts would have to be made to strip further suffixes; if any such attempt were successful, another lexical search would have to be made. Thus, every successful suffix strip requires a lexical search, most of which will be futile. About a quarter of all roots and a third of all suffixes end in vowels. Because of the relative frequency of some of the vowel-final suffixes, approximately half of the words in running text end in vowels. The vast majority of these, of course, are not nouns in the dative, the accusative, or the possessive.

It seems clear, then, that if morphological parsing is involved at all in word recognition in suffixing languages, it must proceed from left to right, as in the computational parsing models developed for these languages.

I will now argue that parsing must be involved in normal word recognition in such languages.

The first point to observe is that under a full-listing hypothesis the individual entries would have to be much larger than for simple words in languages like English. A speaker who understands a word like *ceplerimizdekilerdenmiş* knows a good deal more than that it is a word. That speaker must have access to a very complex semantic representation, which, if it is not produced by parsing, must be a part of the stored lexical entry. The longer the word, of course, the more information will have to be contained in the lexical entry. And since there are far more words at the complexity level of five morphemes than at the level of one morpheme, the average complexity of lexical entries would have to be very high.[16]

The second point is that the number of lexical entries would have to be very high. Since the morphotactics for a language like Turkish allows for loops, as was illustrated in section 2, the number of entries would have to be infinite, which is high indeed. It is interesting, however, to contemplate the number of entries required even if looping is suppressed.

A common estimate of the number of forms for a given Turkish verb root is 2,000. A study of the morphotactics underlying the morphological parser for Turkish reported by Hankamer (1986), however, indicates that the number of forms associated with a given verb root, even with looping suppressed, is far higher than that. The morphotactics was incorporated into a generator program, which was instructed to count all forms generated from one root in accord with the morphotactics, discounting any recursions. The results were surprising: Without any recursions, the morphotactics accepts 1,830,248 forms from one verb root. If one level of recursion is allowed, the number jumps to 26,664,190. The figures for nouns are even more impressive. The number of forms generated from one noun root with no recursion is 9,192,472. When one level of recursion is allowed, the number jumps to 216,618,444.

It seems that agglutinative morphology is even more productive than has been thought. Given a lexicon containing 20,000 noun roots and 10,000 verb roots, which does not seem unreasonable for an educated speaker of Turkish, the FLH would require over 200 billion entries. Furthermore, most of the entries would necessarily be complex, and thus would take up significant storage space in the human brain.

It might be interesting to think about how much of the storage capacity of the human brain would be taken up by such a full lexical listing. Sagan (1985) estimates the storage capacity of the human brain, based on an estimate of the total number of connections among the neurons, to be about 10^{14} bits—the equivalent of about 12,500,000,000,000 bytes. If we assume it takes 100 bytes to store a very basic lexical entry (and remember that most of the words in Turkish will require far more than that), it would be possible to store just 125 billion words in a human brain that was dedicated to such storage and nothing else whatever. On the much more reasonable assumption that one knows one or two orders of magnitude more about each word than 100 bytes' worth, the figure drops to 12.5 billion or 1.25 billion. And of course, most of the brain is not used for storing words.

It seems quite clear that the FLH cannot be maintained for languages with agglutinative morphology.

Conclusion

I have tried to bring together two lines of research that have heretofore been conducted in isolation from each other, and to show that both linguistics and computational research can have clear consequences for psychological models.

A careful examination of morphological complexity in agglutinating languages shows clearly that the full-listing model cannot be an adequate model of general natural-language word recognition. In such languages, parsing must be involved in human word recognition, and not just for rare or unfamiliar forms (unless one wants to call the majority of words occurring in ordinary text rare and unfamiliar). Study of the morphological properties of such languages shows, in addition, that the parsing mechanism employed by their speakers must proceed "from left to right," recognizing the root first and then successive suffixes. For these languages, affix stripping is not a reasonable general parsing theory.

What are the consequences for a theory of human word recognition in general? In particular, what are the consequences for languages with a lot less morphological complexity?

The existence of languages with agglutinative morphology indicates that the human mind has, or is capable of acquiring, a parsing mechanism that allows the recognition and understanding of words of impressive complexity. We have no proof that users of languages like English make use of this ability, but I wonder if there is any reason to think that they do not. Since the computational considerations for a language like Turkish indicate that hearers must recognize a root well before recognizing the last suffix at the end of the word, it should be possible to devise experiments to track morpheme recognition as words are processed, perhaps by means of something so simple as a morpheme-recognition task. If such experiments can be devised and turn out to be reliable for a language like Turkish, perhaps they can then be adapted to languages like English.

A number of further questions remain open, and I will briefly mention some of the ones that might reward investigation.

Since there is both typological (Cutler et al. 1985) and experimental (Segui and Zubizarreta 1985) evidence that prefixes are treated differently from suffixes, it is possible that human word recognition relies on different strategies in the two cases. This possibility should be investigated, perhaps by studying the asymmetries between prefixation and suffixation within and across languages.

The possibility also remains open that there is a difference in treatment between derivational and inflectional affixation, or between regular and irregular morphology. The arguments that agglutinative languages require morphological parsing in word recognition depend on the existence of words with long sequences of morphemes following the root. It is fair to say that it is the suffixes farthest away from the root that provide the arguments, since the farther a suffix is from the root the less plausible it is that it is part of a listed form. Perhaps it is not an accidental correlation that the suffixes nearest the root are the derivational ones and are the ones most likely to show irregularity. It may be possible to investigate these differences, if we can devise some sufficiently delicate morpheme-monitoring techniques.

What I claim to have shown is just that the full-listing hypothesis cannot stand as a universal model of human word processing. This leaves open the possibility that the correct model for all languages is a mixed model in which some morphologically complex forms are listed while others are understood via parsing; it also leaves open the possibility that morphologically simple languages like English and the other Indo-European languages are full-listing languages, whereas agglutinative languages are lexical-parsing languages. Only careful experimental research will resolve these questions.

Acknowledgments

This research was supported by grants from the Institute for Turkish Studies, the American Council of Learned Societies, and the UCSC Academic Senate. Facilities and research assistance were provided by the Max-Planck-Institut für Psycholinguistik, in Nijmegen, the Netherlands, and by the UCSC Syntax Research Center. I am grateful to William Marslen-Wilson and to Geoffrey K. Pullum for suggestions and comments.

Notes

1. See, for example, the thorough review by Butterworth (1983). See also more recent discussions by Segui and Zubizarreta (1985), Stemberger and MacWhinney (1986), Stemberger and MacWhinney (in press), and Bybee (1987).

2. By "lexicon" I mean, as do the authors mentioned here, a language speaker's internal representation of knowledge about particular forms (morphemes, words, fixed phrases).

3. I will use "word recognition" instead of "word processing" or "word understanding," though I assume that what happens during word recognition involves far more than the decision that the input constitutes a word. In particular, in the case of morphologically complex words, a (possibly quite complex) semantic interpretation must somehow be constructed or accessed.

4. Butterworth acknowledges that human language users have word-parsing ability, but suggests that it is resorted to only in unusual circumstances (in the recognition of previously unheard words, during language acquisition, etc.).

5. As with full-listing models, there are innumerable variations: Prefixes may be treated differently from suffixes (Cutler et al. 1985), or derivation may be treated differently from inflection (ibid., p. 744).

6. Most writers in the psycholinguistic literature use the word "stem" where a linguist would say "root." This follows naturally from the restriction of attention to at most bimorphemic words.

7. For a descriptive treatment, see Lewis 1967, pp. 143–153; for a more complete description of the morphotactics, see Hankamer 1986.

8. Here and in all other references in this chapter to frequency counts in Turkish text or lexicon, the source is a small corpus of texts, including fiction and journalistic prose, collected, entered, and verified as part of a Turkish text library development program supported by the UCSC Syntax Research Center.

9. In the case of a real human parser taking auditory input rather than written text, these differences between morphological and syntactic parsing would probably disappear.

10. In full-listing models, perhaps the problem will be to relate the several listings of possible forms for a stem + affix with one another in such a way that the common contribution to meaning of the several forms of the affix is explicitly represented. This very interesting problem, which has been largely ignored in all psychological studies of human word processing, will not be dealt with in any depth in the present chapter.

11. Brodda and Karlsson (1980) apply a similar method to the analysis of Finnish, an agglutinating language, but without any lexicon of roots. Suffixes are stripped off from the end of the word until no more can be removed, and what is left is assumed to be a root. Since nobody has proposed that in normal word recognition humans do without a lexicon, I will not discuss this model further.

12. This is oversimplified somewhat. For a more complete description of the Turkish morphotactics, see Hankamer 1986.

13. The reason the lexical-entry form *lar* matches *ler* in the surface form is that a morphophonological rule of vowel harmony intervenes to adjust the shape of the morpheme to suit its surface context. The treatment of morphophonemic alternation will not be discussed in any detail in this chapter. However, I will point out that it is on this point that the three current morphological parsing models differ. The Koskenniemi model makes use of two-level rules that mediate between surface forms and lexical representations, the Hankamer model uses generative-style rules in an analysis-by-synthesis fashion, and the Kasper-Weber model for Quechua lists all allomorphs together with environmental conditions on their occurrence. Consult the cited references for details of these treatments.

14. The question whether prefix stripping plays any role in human word recognition remains open.

15. Even for a morphologically impoverished language like English, an affix-stripping model leads immediately to intolerable consequences. If potential affixes are stripped before lexical lookup, then lexical-decision time (in auditory mode) for a word like *fix* should be even longer than for a nonword. I don't know whether anyone has thought to test this, but I am sure such an effect has not been reported.

16. Because most suffixes produce stems that can accept further suffixation, the number of possible forms increases with each instance of suffixation. If there is a stem category containing N stems, and M suffixes can attach to stems of that category, the next higher level of complexity contains $N \times M$ stems.

References

Bradley, D. C. 1978. Computational Distinctions of Vocabulary Type. Dissertation, MIT.

Bradley, D. C. 1980. Lexical representation of derivational relation. In M. Aronoff and M.-L. Kean, eds., *Juncture*. Saratoga, Calif.: Anma Libri.

Brodda, B., and F. Karlsson. 1980. An Experiment with Morphological Analysis of Finnish. Papers from the Institute of Linguistics, University of Stockholm, Publication 40.

Butterworth, B. 1983. Lexical representation. In *Language Production*, volume 2. London: Academic.

Bybee, J. L. 1987. Morphology as Lexical Organization. Working Paper in Linguistics, State University of New York, Buffalo.

Cutler, A., J. Hawkins, and G. Gilligan. 1985. The suffixing preference. *Linguistics* 23: 723–758.

Demircan, Ö. 1987. Emphatic reduplication in Turkish. In *Studies on Modern Turkish*, Proceedings of the Third Conference on Turkish linguistics, ed. H. E. Boeschoten and L. T. Verhoeven. Tilburg University Press.

Hankamer, J. 1988. Parsing nominal compounds in Turkish. In *Morphology as a Computational Problem*, ed. Karen Wallace. Occasional Paper No. 7, UCLA.

Hankamer, J. 1986. Finite state morphology and left to right phonology. In Proceedings of the West Coast Conference on Formal Linguistics, Vol. 5, Stanford University.

Hankamer, J. 1984. Turkish Generative Morphology and Morphological Parsing. Presented at Second International Conference on Turkish Linguistics, Istanbul.

Kasper, R., and D. Weber. 1982a (revised 1986 by Stephen McConnel). User's Reference Manual for the C Quechua Adaptation Program. Occasional Publication in Academic Computing No. 8, Summer Institute of Linguistics, Inc.

Kasper, R., and D. Weber. 1982b (revised 1986 by Stephen McConnel). Programmer's Reference Manual for the C Quechua Adaptation Program. Occasional Publication in Academic Computing No. 9, Summer Institute of Linguistics, Inc.

Koskenniemi, K. 1983. Two-Level Morphology. Department of General Linguistics Publication No. 11, University of Helsinki.

Laudanna, A., and C. Burani. 1985. Address mechanisms to decomposed lexical entries. *Linguistics* 23: 775–792.

Lewis, G. 1967. *Turkish Grammar*. Oxford University Press.

Lukatela, G., B. Gligorijevic, A. Kostic, and M. T. Turvey. 1980. Representation of inflected nouns in the internal lexicon. *Memory and Cognition* 8: 415–423.

Lukatela, G., Z. Mandic, B. Gligorijevic, A. Kostic, M. Savic, and M. T. Turvey. 1978. Lexical decision for inflected nouns. *Language and Speech* 21: 166–173.

Packard, D. 1973. Computer-assisted morphological analysis of ancient Greek. In A. Zampolli and N. Calzolari, eds., *Computational and Mathematical Linguistics: Proceedings of the International Conference on Computational Linguistics*. Florence: Leo S. Olschki.

Sagan, C. 1985. *Cosmos*. New York: Ballantine.

Sagvall, A.-L. 1973. *A System for Automatic Inflectional Analysis Implemented for Russian*. Stockholm: Almqvist and Wiksell.

Segui, J., and J. Zubizarreta. 1985. Mental representation of morphologically complex words and lexical access. *Linguistics* 23: 759–774.

Stanners, R. F., J. J. Neiser, W. P. Hernon, and R. Hall. 1979. Memory representation for morphologically related words. *Journal of Verbal Learning and Verbal Behavior* 18: 399–412.

Stemberger, J., and B. MacWhinney. 1986. Frequency and the lexical storage of regularly inflected forms. *Memory and Cognition* 14(1): 17–26.

Stemberger, J., and B. MacWhinney. In press. Are inflected forms stored in the lexicon? In M. Hammond and M. Noonan, eds., *Theoretical Morphology*. San Diego: Academic.

Taft, M. 1979. Recognition of affixed words and the word frequency effect. *Memory and Cognition* 7: 263–272.

Taft, M. 1981. Prefix stripping revisited. *Journal of Verbal Learning and Verbal Behavior* 20: 289–297.

Taft, M., and K. Forster. 1975. Lexical storage and retrieval of prefixed words. *Journal of Verbal Learning and Verbal Behavior* 14: 638–647.

Weber, D. 1976. Suffix-as-operator analysis and the grammar of successive encoding in Llacon (Huanuco) Quechua. Documento de Trabajo No. 13, ILV, Peru.

Chapter 14

| Psycholinguistic Issues in the Lexical Representation of Meaning | Robert Schreuder and Giovanni B. Flores d'Arcais |

In this chapter we approach the problem of the lexical representation of meaning from a psycholinguistic perspective. In sections 1 and 2 we will briefly review some of the main issues and work on the lexical representation of meaning from a psychological perspective; in section 3 we will discuss some of our own work on lexical semantic representation.

One of the unique and essential properties of the acoustic or visual objects called "words" is that they provide, either directly or indirectly, access to both linguistic and nonlinguistic knowledge. The connection is bidirectional. Linguistic and/or conceptual representations can be connected with word representations that subsequently can be produced (that is, transformed into some physical realization). These physical events can be transformed by the perceiver's sensory transducer systems into the appropriate code, which in turn can access the perceiver's knowledge systems. Those who have tried to explain and describe these phenomena have traditionally assumed something like a "mental lexicon." Simply stated, this would be the store of all our knowledge related to words. The notion of a mental lexicon is useful in directing theorizing and guiding empirical research, even if it might eventually turn out that the mental lexicon is not something fundamentally separate from other knowledge systems (that is, not a separate submodule within the language module). We will assume here the current view of the mental lexicon as an important relay station connecting certain specific sensory events or motor (output) patterns with mentally represented knowledge structures.

In particular, we will consider the question of how lexical entries are connected with other knowledge systems. Other questions that we will deal with are these: What is the nature of lexical semantic representations? What is the role of thematic structures (see Tanenhaus and Carlson, this volume)? Do certain connections between related lexical entries exist? How can the mental lexicon be accessed by information from the outside world other than written or spoken words? Some of these questions are not independent, as we will show.

After discussing some general goals of a theory of meaning in the mental lexicon, we will briefly review two different approaches to lexical meaning within cognitive psychology. We will start by discussing the work that has concentrated on the general properties of the representation of meaning within the lexicon. The structure of lexical meaning itself was not studied directly; the hope was, by studying patterns of relatedness between lexical items, to find evidence for some general structural properties. Second, we will briefly review work that has used a more direct approach to the study of lexical meaning, in which specific suggestions are made about substructures *within* the semantic representation of lexical entries. This concerns the representation of various types of information within a single lexical entry—in other words, the structure of a single lexeme in the mental lexicon. Different approaches, touching upon notions of components and decompositionality, structured descriptions of lexical semantic information, and fixedness of meaning, will be reviewed. In section 3 we concentrate on our own work on the connections of the lexicon with knowledge representations and the outside world.

We conclude this introduction with some remarks on the general goal of a theory of lexical semantic information. First, such a theory should explain a number of *intensional* phenomena. Among these are traditionally counted synonymy, ambiguity, antonomy, entailment, polysemy, and vagueness. These phenomena all deal with *senses* of words. Second, the theory should be able to describe the *form* of the mental representation of meaning. A third goal would be to explain *extensional* relations between words and the world as human beings conceive it (Johnson-Laird, Herrman, and Chaffin 1984). An additional goal is the explanation of a large number of experimental findings dealing with categorization and typicality, property verification, judgments of semantic similarity, interpretation of metaphors and idioms, and so on. As is already apparent from this brief discussion of goals and questions to be answered, it is difficult to determine the boundary between the representations in the mental lexicon and other knowledge representations (sometimes called the mental encyclopedia; see Clark and Clark 1975). There is as yet no principled way to determine what kind of information should be called lexical semantic information and what kind of information should be called "knowledge of the world."

1 Semantic Relations between Lexical Entries

Network Models

Within cognitive psychology and artificial intelligence there has been broad interest in the general properties of the representation of meaning within the mental lexicon. The general idea underlying the various theories and approaches is that the various lexical units, and/or the underlying concepts, are represented mentally as a set of elements or entries bearing some relations to one another. All theories make, implicitly or explicitly, some assumptions about the organization of the units. For example, in many theories lexical units are taken to be related to one another by some form of associative relation. Perhaps the most important contributions come from the area that is generally referred to as "semantic memory."

Within the field of sementic-memory research there are several models, with different characteristics. The main idea, however, is that the various units in semantic memory are organized according to an associative network. The single entries are related to one another by means of labeled associative connections. In Quillian's (1968) theory, for example, words are stored in memory as configurations of pointers to other words, and each configuration of pointers gives a representation of the meaning of a word. The various units in the configuration have mutual labeled connections. Still very influential within this approach is the model of Collins and Loftus (1975), in which the meaning of a word is represented as a concept node which is connected to other nodes. When a node is accessed, activation *spreads* to contiguous conceptual nodes in the network. This excitation spreads out in a decreasing gradient; nodes that are closer to the node that has been addressed will be activated more strongly than more distant nodes. Together, the various concepts that underlie words form a semantic network, organized in terms of semantic similarity. This semantic network should be distinguished from the *lexical* network made up by the *names* of the concept; the latter network is taken to be organized along lines of phonemic similarity.

Johnson-Laird et al. (1984) provide an in-depth discussion of network models. They conclude that network models fail on two accounts: First, as a class of theories they are too powerful to be refuted by empirical evidence; second, there are too many problems in explaining certain semantic phenomena. These problems are caused by the fact that network models deal exclusively with *intensional* relations between words. That is, they can explain relations between *words*, but they do not deal with the relations of words to their referents in the world.

Scaling Semantic Relatedness

Another approach to the mental lexicon is based on the similarity of meaning between words. Studies within this approach have taken as a point of departure intuitions of similarity in meaning, systematically collected for subsets of the lexicon that form specific semantic domains (e.g., cooking terms, animal names, or kinship terms). The basic assumption is that the structure of the internal representations will be reflected in these intuitive judgments. Informants express these intuitions in the form of judgments of similarity—for example, by sorting words into groups with similar or dissimilar meanings (see Miller 1969 for an overview). A number of different mathematical procedures can then be employed to produce a metric of similarity. Ultimately each word of the set comes to be assigned a position in a dimensional semantic space or as a point in a cluster. In the case of spatial representations, the positions of the words are defined by sets of coordinates on a number of dimensions. These dimensions can sometimes be interpreted in terms of semantic properties.

The results of these procedures can be viewed as an end in themselves, telling us something about the general properties of semantic representations in the mental lexicon (Fillenbaum and Rapoport 1971). Alternatively, they can be used as a heuristic device guiding further theorizing (Miller 1972). But although this scaling research has had some success in establishing general notions about the kinds of semantic information that underlie intuitions of meaning similarity, it has been less successful in specifying constraints on the structure of meaning representation in the mental lexicon. For words referring to animals, for instance, Henley (1969) has shown that size and level of ferocity are primary variables in the judgment of similarity. However, there is much more to the semantics of words referring to animals than size and ferocity. This kind of work helps in determining the relative salience of certain information, but it does not help in solving the much more difficult question about the representation of this information in the lexicon.

2   Representation of Meaning within a Single Lexeme

The second issue we want to address concerns the structure of representations of semantic information *within* a single lexeme in the mental lexicon. There have been remarkably few attempts to face this issue in recent theoretical and experimental psycholinguistic research. The groundwork for research of this sort, provided by Miller and Johnson-Laird (1976), has had surprisingly little follow-up. We will return to this work shortly.

Decomposition Revisited

The idea that word meanings can be described as a set of necessary and sufficient conditions has had a long history in philosophy, linguistics, and psycholinguistics. According to this view, word meanings can be decomposed into a set of more basic primitive elements. Within cognitive psychology these necessary and sufficient conditions are often called *defining attributes*. In addition to this, often the assumption of *characteristic attributes* is made (Smith, Shoben, and Rips 1974). These are attributes that are not necessary but seem to hold for so-called prototypical members of the set of possible referents for a given word (Rosch 1975).

The componentiality assumption is useful in describing a number of linguistic and psycholinguistic phenomena that deal with properties and relations like synonymy, ambiguity, anomaly, and entailment. The degree of synonymity between words can be analyzed, for example, in terms of the amount of overlap in their componential representations. Subjective similarity in meaning, substitutability in paraphrase, and confusability in long-term memory can thus be accounted for in one framework (Gentner 1981).

Decompositional theories come in many varieties. The simplest ones are those that represent meaning as an unordered collection of atomic predicates (Katz 1972). Another approach is (or was) procedural semantics. Miller and Johnson-Laird (1976) investigated the hypothesis that meaning components could be defined as mental computational procedures that were tightly related to sensory transducer systems. These procedures were assumed to be used in verification procedures, in which tests were carried out to check whether a certain word could be used as a description of an object in the outside world. This approach (especially the verificationist part of it) was vehemently attacked by Fodor (1978, 1979). Finally, many theories in linguistics, AI, and psycholinguistics try to assign complex, static semantic structures to lexical entries, often concentrating on verbs (Gentner 1981; Jackendoff 1976, 1983; Schank 1972; Talmy 1985). Common to all approaches is the assumption of the existence of a certain number of innate conceptual primitives, among them categories like THING, PLACE, DIRECTION, ACTION, EVENT, MANNER, AMOUNT, CAUSE, and MOVE. In recent years the assumption of certain primitives has become more and more linguistically motivated, and less *ad hoc* than in (e.g.) Schank 1972. This work has not received the attention it deserves from psycholinguists, owing partly to the difficulty of testing proposals for representational structures dealing with meaning for their processing consequences.

The opposite position (no decomposition of words; a word is represented by a not-further-analyzable symbol) is most often associated with the additional assumption of so-called meaning postulates or rules of inference (Fodor 1975). According to this view (using the classic examples), the word *bachelor* is represented not as (MALE, ADULT, NOT MARRIED) but as an unanalyzable whole. The system has, however, rules of inference, such as BACHELOR → MALE and BACHELOR → ADULT. The symbols in these meaning postulates are always directly associated with a word in the language. How these symbols are connected to objects and events in the world remains a question, but this is also a question for decompositional theories. For primitive terms like MALE or ADULT the same questions hold, and, in the view of nondecompositional theory, "Why postpone the problem?" (Fodor 1975; Fodor, Fodor, and Garrett 1975; Fodor, Garrett, Walker, and Parks 1980)

Empirical Evidence

We turn now to some of the empirical evidence bearing on the issue of decomposition, restricting ourselves to empirical tests that actually try to settle the question. There are many experimental results that are described using a decompositional terminology but that do not address the problem directly.

The general idea behind the experiments to be discussed here is that words are decomposed into their meaning components during comprehension and that the process of building a semantic representation takes more time for sentences using complex words. One line of support for decomposition comes from experiments in which so-called inherent negatives are used. The assumption is that the meaning of a word like "absent" is represented as (NOT(PRESENT)). In picture-sentence matching tasks a systematic and complex pattern of latencies is found, where pairs such as "present"/"isn't present" behave similarly to pairs such as "present"/"absent" (Carpenter and Just 1975; Clark 1974; see Clark and Clark 1977 for an overview). In another, related line of research, simple and complex words were compared. Perhaps the best definition of complexity (see Kintsch 1974 for some ways *not* to define complexity) so far proposed is one-way entailment. The proposal that word A is more complex than word B is defined as "A entails B but not the other way around" (*rise/move, kill/die, bachelor/man*).

In experiments related to this approach, simple and complex words were used in verification or memory tasks. Generally this line of research has shown negative results, finding no differences between simple and complex verbs in processing time or memory retrieval (Fodor et al. 1975, 1978;

Kintsch 1974; Thorndyke 1975). Schreuder (1978) presented a case where complex words actually took *less* time to process in a picture-word verification task—although these results could also be explained by the fact that the more complex verbs gave a better description of the event than the simpler verbs used.

Should this failure to find differences between simple and complex words lead us to conclude that word meanings are processed holistically? Even though Fodor and his co-workers (1975, 1978, 1980) would disagree, the issue is not yet settled. One problem involves the assumptions about the processing consequences of complexity that underlie the assumption that more components entails more processing and a higher memory load. However, though complexity effects can be *explained* by decomposition, they are by no means a *necessary consequence* of decomposition. That is, it could be the case that meaning components are processed in parallel, without any increase in processing load for words with more components than others. There is another way to look at the issue, and that is not by counting the number of primitives but by looking at the way these primitives are connected in a given structure.

Much linguistically oriented work has been done in recent years on specifying the semantic structure of lexical entries, and surprisingly little empirical psycholinguistic testing has been done on these proposals. One exception is the research by Gentner (1981), who tested the "connectivity hypothesis." This hypothesis views verb semantic structures as frames for sentence representations and predicts that memory strength between nouns in a sentence increases with the number of underlying verb subpredicates that connect the nouns. In Gentner's experiments, subjects were given subject nouns as cues to recall SVO sentences. General verbs with relatively few subpredicates (*damage/clean*) were compared with more specific verbs (*smash/scrub*) whose additional subpredicates either did or did not provide additional connections between the nouns in the sentence. She found that it was not the number of subpredicates as such that predicted performance (level of recall of the object noun) but the number of connecting sub-predicates in the verbs. The problem with these experiments is that different, non-matched sets of verbs were used, and that the predictions hinged rather critically upon properties of the LNR model of verb meaning (Norman, Rumelhart, and LNR Research Group 1975).

Schreuder (1978) took a more general approach in which the only assumption was that in the structure of verbs describing human locomotion one part deals with a change of place and another part deals with the motion of the body. Schreuder paired up verbs with adverbial phrases that gave information either about the part dealing with change of place or about the part dealing with motion of the body. The pattern of results indicated that the link between the two aspects of verb meaning structures could be severed, suggesting that the two meaning structures have an independent status. Like Gentner, then, Schreuder provides evidence for decomposition, although in both cases they are using rather off-line taks. One could still argue, therefore, that these structures were the result of inferential processing going on *after* comprehension. This, however, is also the case for the careful study of Fodor et al. (1980), who employed scaling measures that gave no evidence at all for a definitional structure of lexical entries.

The issue, therefore, still seems open. The empirical results are equivocal. Since even Fodor relies not only on logical arguments but also on empirical ones, there is still work to do. The problem for the non-decompositionalists is that so far they have been trying to prove the null hypothesis. What is needed is a test where the non-decompositional account could predict differences and the decompositionist would not.

Within psycholinguistics, there has been little recent progress in research on lexical semantic representation. Although papers reporting on lexical priming must number in the hundreds by now, the issues of decomposition and (more generally) lexical semantic structure have simply been ignored. Most psycholinguists and cognitive psychologists continue to think of word meaning in terms of a decompositional framework. Componentiality is usually assumed without question, especially within psychological and psycholinguistic models (see McNamara and Sternberg 1983 or Stemberger 1985).

The global problem of decomposition deserves renewed attention. One possibility for a new approach would be to study in detail the timing with which semantic knowledge becomes available during word and sentence processing, and what kind of knowledge it is, depending on the word and its context (Barsalou 1982; Whitney, McKay, Kellas, and Emerson 1985). In this type of research, no sharp distinction between lexicon and en-cyclopedia is made. The strong version of the decompositional theory (a lexical entry is replaced by its *full* definition during comprehension) becomes very implausible if one assumes that lexical entries are connected with *all* relevant information in the encyclopedia. The amount and the kind of information that becomes available during understanding could then be dictated by its saliency and/or its usefulness during comprehension.

Fixed Meanings?

The componential approach, whether in terms of atomic predicates or in terms of more structured descriptions of semantic content, often suggests that the meaning of a lexical entry is in some way fixed. The meaning-postulate approach also has difficulties in explaining the notion of "uncertainty." In fact, all current accounts of semantic representation have problems with three aspects of meaning—vagueness, polysemy, and lexical creativity—all of which reflect the non-fixedness of word meaning.

Vagueness

There is much evidence that the boundary of referential application of a lexical term is never a sharp discontinuity, but rather is a region where the term gradually moves from being applicable to being inapplicable. We will present some examples here.

Labov (1972) presented subjects with pictures of containers that differed in the ratio of width to height, and asked them to label the pictures "bowl", "cup", or "vase". At the more extreme ratios the responses were nearly uniform, but at intermediate ratios different responses were equally probable. Thus, there was no sudden discontinuity in the application of these words. Some properties were related to a specific class. For example, having a handle is typical for cups. As a result, instances with a wider range of height-to-width ratios were labeled as cups if they had a handle than if they didn't. However, the extreme cases could not be made into cups by adding a handle. Similar vagueness can be found with category labels. Very often inconsistencies between and within subjects are apparent with intermediate typicality terms (e.g., do bookends belong to the category of furniture? [McCloskey and Glucksberg 1978]). In some cases fuzzy set theory has been applied to model the degree of appropriateness of labeling, but this application is not without problems (Roth and Mervis 1983). Another point where considerable vagueness crops up is with quantificational terms like "some" and "several". For this type Hormann (1983) has shown that interpretation is dependent upon the particular objects that are quantified (e.g., a few mountains are judged to be smaller in quantity than a few crumbs).

One last example of vagueness can be found in temporal adverbs like "soon", "recent", and "just", which are used to locate situations in time but which do not set clear boundaries to the time interval between the reference point and the time at which the situation referred to occurs. Van Jaarsveld and Schreuder (1986) showed that the frequency and duration of everyday human acts expressed by verbal phrases in sentences had a systematic effect on the estimated length of the time interval denoted by a given temporal adverb (compare 'John has just thrown his cigarette away' and 'John has just married'). Note that vagueness in all these examples is intimately connected with the effects of context; it is the combination of different sources of knowledge that determines the more precise meaning of the particular terms used.

The conclusion from this type of research is generally that, given a componential framework, the various components of meaning are differentially important. In addition, no subset of components can conclusively be said to be both necessary and sufficient (Hersh and Caramazza 1976). How to *model* vagueness within the lexicon is an unsolved problem, since the approach usually taken (the fuzzy-set approach) can only adequately *describe* experimental results because it does not make any explicit suggestions about the nature of semantic representations.

Polysemy
A classic issue for a semantic theory is polysemy. Psycholinguistic research has very often explored polysemy, but has nonetheless paid very little attention to it as a problem in semantic theory (for an exception see Miller 1986). Polysemous words are often used interchangably with homonyms and homographs, and are used as semantic "ambiguities" to test theories and models of lexical access. The main questions asked here are whether both senses of a lexically "ambiguous" word are accessed simultaneously and whether the disambiguating role of the context is to be located before or after the ambiguous word has been accessed.

Traditional linguistics defines polysemy as a major shift in the meaning of a word (Fodor 1980; Lyons 1977; Ullmann 1962), the result of which is a number of different but interrelated meanings. Polysemy is distinguished from homonymy, which refers to the phenomenon of different meanings that do not have any apparent connection: homonyms have developed historically from distinct lexemes which for various reasons have acquired the same form. There is still a lack of agreement among lexicographers and linguists on the way polysemous words should be represented and listed in a dictionary—whether each meaning should have a separate entry in the lexicon (Weinreich 1966) or whether all senses should be listed under one single entry (Fillmore 1971).

Psycholinguistic work on polysemy is almost nonexistent. One attempt to study polysemy was the investigation by Caramazza and Grober (1976) of the polysemous word *line*.

The basic notion of this approach is that underlying the different senses of a word there is a very general abstract conceptual representation, a single *core meaning*. The various senses a polysemous word can take in different sentences are contextually dependent and are not part of this core meaning. They would be derived from this core meaning by the use of rules corresponding to what linguists have called construal rules or production rules. Caramazza and Grober call these *instruction rules*, to emphasize their procedural character.

Thus, in order to produce a specific sense of a word, we would first access in memory the core meaning and then apply the appropriate instruction to generate the requested sense. For example, the core meaning of the word *line* (Caramazza and Grober 1976) could be defined as UNIDIMENSIONAL EXTENSION. The sense of *line* in the sentence "We built a fence along the property line" would be realized by picking up this core meaning and applying to it the instruction "REALIZE CONCRETE BOUNDARY CONCEPT". The approach taken here is much in line with Jackendoff's (1976) work.

Lexical Creativity

No language has the words to cover all possible concepts that speakers may want to express. When the lexicon does not provide a term for a given concept related to a situation, an object, or an event, a *lexical gap* exists. Such gaps can be general in the language (the dictionary does not provide a lexical item) or individual (a person does not know a given word in the language). Momentary lexical gaps may of course also arise for a given speaker when the access to the appropriate term in the mental lexicon is blocked because of memory failure. When such situations arise, the speaker may find it necessary to create a new lexical item. This process has come to be studied under the term *lexical creativity* or *lexical innovation*.

Language allows enormous flexibility in innovations. Denominalizing verbs and compounding nouns or adjectives are among the devices a language such as English can provide. Some of these types of constructions have been studied extensively. For example, nominal compounds have been investigated both linguistically (Downing 1977) and psycholinguistically (Gleitman and Gleitman 1970).

The types of meaning carried by a nominal compound vary enormously. An ice machine is a machine to make ice, an ice-box is a box containing ice, and an iceberg is a berg made of ice. In some innovations the meaning of the elements is transparent in the compound; in others, the original meaning of the individual parts of the compound, or of the word that has been transformed, have lost some or all of their original meaning.

At first sight, lexical innovation should provide some problems—after all, how does a listener know what a speaker means when confronted with a never-before-heard lexical item? But apparently not only do speakers not seem to have substantial problems in creating new lexical items, but listeners do not seem to have problems in understanding them.

The interpetation of some compounds is, however, not always easy, and people show a variety of interpretations when confronted with them. Is a *black house bird* a bird that lives in a black house, or a black bird of a domestic species? Is a *black bird house* a house suitable for a black bird (or a house where black birds live), or a house for a bird, painted in black (Livant 1961)? Stress and intonation are important cues for the listener, but they are not always sufficient to uniquely determine one meaning. When people are asked to provide paraphrases of this type of expression (Gleitman and Gleitman 1970), they provide a variety of interpretations based on diverse cues and articulated on different principles, among which semantic plausibility and prior familiarity are only two of the more important ones.

Newly created nominal compounds can carry a considerable amount of ambiguity. When they became frozen in language, this ambiguity disappears, and these items may even be represented as complete units in the mental lexicon. In fact, it could be argued that they have been stored as unitary lexical items. But what happens when they are true innovations? How do we interpret a new compound? Is a *computer-house* a house suitable to keep computers in, a house where computer companies are located, a house that contains computers, or a house designed by computers? The way in which a speaker chooses to lexicalize a particular type of relation between the two elements of a compound is by no means uniform, and the principles governing this are hard to specify. For example, the assignment of the meaning "house designed by a computer" to the compound *computer-house* is dependent on our knowledge that a computer is a device that can be used to design projects. *Dog-house* can be interpreted as a house suitable for dogs, or in which dogs live (notice that these interpretations are equivalent to two of the possible interpretations of *computer-house* as "house to put computer in" or "which contains computers"), but the interpretation of "a house designed by dogs" would be bizarre indeed.

The available theories proposed to account for the way innovations are created and interpreted point to different aspects of the process of lexical innovations, such as the way the meanings of two nouns come to be combined in the meaning of the compound (Downing 1977), or the pragmatic conventions governing the use and interpretation of innovations. Given the ambiguity of most innovations, a correct interpretation has to rely on factors of this type. Such factors have been studied by Clark and Clark (1979) in their investigation of innovation phenomena with denominal verbs (i.e., nouns used as verbs, such as *to wrist* in "He wristed the ball over the net" [Clark and Clark 1979, p. 767]).

How are the meanings of such words determined and interpreted? The theory proposed is that innovative denominal verbs have *shifting* (rather than fixed) sense and denotation. Innovative denominal verbs are neither denotational nor indexical, but are "contextuals," having a large number of potential senses and depending on context for their interpretation. The use of these verbs is regulated by a kind of pragmatic convention between speaker and listener according to which the speaker means to denote an event, a state, or a process which the listener can uniquely compute on the basis of mutual knowledge, of the verb itself, and of the linguistic context. Historically, the process though which certain nouns have come to be used as verbs is a process of *idiomatization*, which follows a series of stages.

Children's lexical innovations serve the same function as those of adults, but also compensate for the individual child's limitations in vocabulary (Clark 1981). Children's innovative meanings are often contextual, which means that understanding innovations requires (just as has been shown for adults) a considerable use of context and of knowledge of the world. In Clark's (1981) theory, the child's process of constructing lexical forms is accounted for by three principles: productivity, semantic transparency, and regularization.

Some Conclusions

It is sometimes argued that network models, feature models, and models that employ meaning postulates are formally equivalent (Hollan 1975; Johnson-Laird et al. 1984). Furthermore, procedural semantics seems to belong to the same class of models. One could argue, therefore, that one need not bother about differences between those formalisms. This may be correct, but it should be realized that formally equivalent representational systems can differ enormously in the constraints they impose on processing systems that operate on those representations (Newell and Simon 1972). Over and above this, it is important for models of language processing to have some idea about the nature and the time course of the information that becomes available after lexical access. And, finally, what all formalisms need is more constraints, since as a class they are too powerful (Johnson-

Laird et al. 1984). Some of these constraints might come from taking extensional aspects of lexical semantics into account. In the model to be presented in the next section, at least some attention is paid to the relation between lexical semantic information and the outside world.

3   Connecting Different Types of Lexical Information: A Model

In this section we will describe a model that belongs to the general class of interactive activation models (the "connectionist" approach). Activation models have been proposed in the domains of visual word recognition (McClelland and Rumelhart 1981), complex motor behavior like typing (Rumelhart and Norman 1982), and language production (Stemberger 1985).

Words are acoustic or visual patterns that have an arbitrary relation to knowledge representations. The human system is equipped with pattern recognizers for these acoustic or visual patterns. Let us assume that the endpoint of the pattern recognizer is a *word node*. This node collects evidence for the pattern it represents from the outside world, and perhaps from the system itself too. When a word node has reached a certain absolute level of activation (or a certain difference level compared with the other word nodes), the word has been "recognized"; it will now start to activate other nodes to which it is connected.

The word node has connections to (or is part of) networks that deal with syntactic, orthographic, phonological, articulatory, and morphological information. All this information concerns *words*. But there is also information about the things to which words refer, be this related to the external world or to internal states of the mind. Words can be seen as access codes or *pointers to knowledge structures*; after recognizing '... dog ...', knowledge about dogs can become available.

Let us now deal with the level of knowledge representation. At this level we assume something like a network organization. We will assume that the knowledge system can be described as a very complex network of nodes connected with (labeled) links. Again the nodes can be seen as "evidence collectors," and above a certain level of activation they start to activate other nodes. All nodes are connected, either directly or by way of intermediate nodes and links.

Different parts of this net—i.e., different knowledge representations—are assumed to form in their *ensemble* useful units of information. There are occasions on which the simultaneous activation of these different parts of the net presents some advantage for the system. One might call such a collection of parts of the total net a *concept.*

A node connecting different *substructures* of the total net—different pieces of the knowledge representation—is called a *conceptual node* in our model. Conceptual nodes are not directly connected with one another. A conceptual node functions as an evidence collector; it "receives" activation, and when its level of activation exceeds a certain level it starts activating other nodes. This means that when certain parts of the net become activated they may activate a concept node; if this node is sufficiently activated, it might start to activate other parts of the net that are connected to that concept node too. When a subset of the parts connected with a certain concept node is activated, the concept node helps to trigger the other pieces of information to which it is connected.

In our model, concept nodes are usually (but not always) linked to word nodes (these nodes are assumed to represent the word's *lemma*). Pre-lexical children do have concepts, and for both adults and children concept nodes that are not connected to word nodes form lexical gaps. When a concept node has been activated sufficiently by a part of the net, it not only triggers other substructures within the net; it may also start to activate a word node (maybe more than one in the case of synonyms). A sufficiently activated word node, in its turn, can activate other information, such as articulatory motor programs or orthographic knowledge.

At this point one could very well ask why concept nodes are really necessary, since parts of the semantic network could be connected directly with the word nodes. The arguments against this are the following: First, we want to be able to define a collection of parts of the semantic net as important to the system (i.e. as a concept), whether or not the language of the system has a word for that collection of information. Second, a concept can have a number of different lexicalizations; in this model there is no need to significantly increase the number of links in the system. Especially in multi-language systems, this feature of the model would save a large number of links.

Summarizing so far: We distinguish three types of units of representation (figure 1). First, there are *word nodes* or units. When a word is presented, the appropriate word unit is eventually activated within the mental lexicon. A second type of unit is the *conceptual unit* or *node*. Each word unit activates one conceptual unit (and sometimes more). Words that are synonyms activate the same conceptual unit. Third, this unit is taken to be a node connecting a set of *semantic* structures.

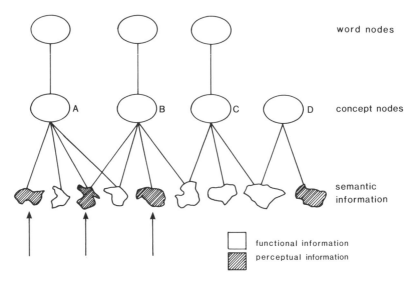

Figure 1
Three levels of representation in the mental lexicon.

The semantic information that becomes available when a conceptual node is activated consists of a series of semantic structures. For example, when the word *table* is seen or heard, and the conceptual node TABLE is accessed, the following pieces of semantic (or encyclopedic) information will also become available (though not necessarily at the same time):

(a) that it has a horizontal surface
(b) that in most cases it has four legs
(c) that it can be used to put objects on
(d) that it is a piece of furniture.

Some of these elements refer to physical characteristics, such as (a) and (b). Some other elements deal with functional properties of the objects, such as (c). Other elements identify category membership, such as (d). On the basis of our previous work on lexical priming (Flores d'Arcais, Schreuder, and Glazenborg 1985; Schreuder, Flores d'Arcais, and Glazenborg 1984), we propose a distinction between two classes of elements within these semantic structures:

(i) Elements which are based on *perceptual* data, directly corresponding to *physical* attributes. We will call these *P elements*. Since our research has restricted itself to the visual modality, these elements will be defined here primarily in visual terms. However, the same analysis should hold for other modalities as well.

(ii) Components or elements based on more abstract knowledge and corresponding to abstract and functional properties. We will call these *F elements*.

We know, for example, that coffee is *black*, that it is *liquid*, that it has a *bitter* taste, that it is a *stimulating* drink, that it is *produced* in warm climates, and that it is *made of* roasted seeds. Blackness, fluidity, taste, etc. are P elements of our semantic knowledge about coffee. That coffee contains caffeine, that it comes from warm climates, and other such facts constitute the F elements of the semantic knowledge.

Let us illustrate a few more features of the model.

Conceptual units can share semantic information. This notion is represented in figure 1 by the common links of the two conceptual units A and B to the same semantic elements. The larger the number of common links, the more the two conceptual units are related to each other.

As a consequence of these links, a concept node A can be activated either directly via presentation of a written or spoken word, or via the activation of the semantic elements which are shared by the concept nodes A and B and which become activated when the concept node B is accessed. When the concept node A is activated, the concept nodes of other objects sharing with A some perceptual and/or functional properties (P and F elements) are also activated to some extent. The amount of activation is a function of the number of the elements shared by the two concept nodes, but also of the strength with which a given element is activated. For example, P elements might be more or less strongly activated, depending on their perceptual saliency. F elements might be more or less activated, depending on the importance of the attribute within the concept (Barsalou 1982).

Finally, a very specific assumption is that perceptual pattern analyzers (other than word-recognition systems) are connected to P elements. These analyzers can activate structures that deal with information about shape, color, motion patterns, etc. In figure 1 these systems are represented by the upward-pointing arrows, indicating that pattern analyzers can activate semantic structures. This means that P elements can be activated "directly" by information from the outside world, but F elements can only be activated indirectly. An F element can only become activated via the activation of a concept node. Thus, once a concept node has been activated, either by P elements or by a word node, the F elements connected to that concept node are activated as well.

Another point concerns the exact nature of the P elements in our model. Consider, for example, the P elements related to the concept node RED. Not only is there a wide range of values in the color spectrum which is involved in the activation process of this concept node, but also the combinations of the concept RED with concepts such as HAIR, BEET, WINE, and SUNSET are related to the activation of a wide range of P elements, all of which are connected to the one concept node RED. These and several other issues will require further development and specifications of the model so far discussed.

Some Empirical Evidence for the Model

In this subsection we will briefly summarize some of the main results obtained in experiments using lexical priming, which have provided evidence for the existence of independent components within the semantic representation underlying words, and for different activation rates of these components.

The experiments we discuss here are reported in detail elsewhere (Flores d'Arcais and Schreuder 1987; Flores d'Arcais et al. 1985; Schreuder et al. 1984; Schreuder 1988). We will summarize here the main results. All the experiments used priming paradigms; in the first experiment we will discuss here we used a lexical decision task, and in the second we used a word-naming task (Schreuder et al. 1984). The respective response latencies were taken as indications of the relative ease of access to the word in the mental lexicon. In both experiments we used pairs of words, a prime and a target. The prime either was unrelated to the target, or was related to it in terms of perceptual properties (P elements) and/or in terms of abstract or functional properties (F elements). These pairs of words were generally not associatively related (Lupker 1984, 1985). For each target we constructed a quartet of word pairs, as in the following example:

table-cherry (unrelated pair)
ball-cherry (pair of words related on P elements)
banana-cherry (pair of words related on F elements)
apple-cherry (pair of words related on both P and F elements).

In this way the presence or absence of perceptual and functional relatedness were orthogonally varied. The words *ball* and *cherry* are perceptually related because their referents have the same spherical shape; *banana* and *cherry* both refer to the abstract/functional category of fruits but do not refer to objects of similar shape; *apple* and *cherry* refer to objects of the same category which have also a similar shape.

Table 1
Mean reaction times in milliseconds for lexical decision and naming with four different types of prime-target relatedness. (Data from Schreuder et al. 1984.)

	Lexical decision		Naming	
	Perceptually related	Perceptually unrelated	Perceptually related	Perceptually unrelated
Functionally related	654	670	600	619
Functionally unrelated	681	694	601	629

The stimulus material used in our experiments consisted of 20 such sets of four, giving a total of 80 word pairs. In the lexical-decision experiments we added 20 sets of prime-target pairs in which the target was a nonword in Dutch; in the word-naming experiment we used only the 80 pairs in which the target was a real word.

In the lexical-decision experiment the similarity between prime and target on F elements produced a significant and strong positive effect on the decision latency. Similarity on P elements had a much smaller but still nontrivial positive effect, being at the boundary of conventional significance values. The results can be seen in table 1.

No statistical evidence was found for an interaction between perceptual relatedness and functional relatedness; the two types of similarity showed independent effects on the time necessary to take lexical decisions. Thus, the often-reported semantic-priming effect was replicated in this lexical-decision experiment, but now using a type of relatedness not previously investigated: similarity of perceptual attributes independently varied from more abstract or functional similarity.

Our data, thus, showed that perceptual similarity of the referent of the pairs of words involved in the experimental trial influences word processing. The only semantic relation of the word *ball* to the word *cherry* is the fact that the referents of both words have a spherical form, and this seems to be sufficient to facilitate lexical decision on the second word, when the first is given as a prime.

In the word-naming experiment, with exactly the same stimulus-word pairs, only the P-element correspondence between prime and target significantly facilitated word naming. F-element relatedness had no significant effect. Again, in this experiment, no interaction was obtained.

The two experiments thus have shown that it is possible to experimentally separate two components of the semantic representation of referential words. These two components showed an independent contribution to semantic priming. Priming was obtained not only when the target word was related to the prime on F elements, as was already known, but also by a correspondence with it on *perceptually* based properties.

The two experiments have thus shown a theoretically interesting contribution of two different components of semantic representation to lexical processing. However, they have also opened an intriguing question: Why did we obtain a difference in the relative contribution of the two components to priming in the two tasks used, namely a stronger effect of relatedness on F elements in the lexical decision task and an effect only of similarity on P elements in the word-naming experiment? Why does the previous presentation of the word *football* facilitate the naming of the word *apple* more than the presentation of the word *banana*, whereas the opposite is true for the lexical decision task?

Our tentative explanation (Schreuder et al. 1984) ran as follows: Within the semantic information that becomes available when a word is presented, the P elements would have an earlier or an initially stronger activation than the F elements. In order to account for the difference found, we then only have to assume that in the relatively faster word-naming task the priming effect takes place at a time at which the perceptual component has an already high level of activation while the functional component is not yet sufficiently activated, and that in the lexical decision task (where reaction times are slower) the process of target activation takes place during the time in which the F elements have reached a sufficient level of activation.

In order to test whether the difference found was related to the different rates of activation of the two components isolated, we experimentally varied the response times in the two tasks used, speeding up the response in the lexical decision task and slowing down the response in the word-naming task. With faster lexical-decision responses we expected a stronger priming effect of the P elements, and with slower naming latencies we expected a stronger priming effect of F elements (Flores d'Arcais et al. 1985).

In a lexical-decision experiment the response time was speeded up by using a short deadline for the responses, and in a word-naming experiment the response times were slowed down by using visually degraded target words. These manipulations produced the predicted results (see table 2). Compared with the first two experiments, slowing down word naming produced a change in the priming effect: In "fast" naming the priming effect was stronger for prime words related to the target on a perceptual dimension, but in "slow" naming the F elements had a stronger effect. Thus, the P elements seem to be more effective at an earlier stage in lexical processing,

Table 2
Mean reaction time in milliseconds for sped-up lexical decision and slowed-down naming with four different types of prime-target relatedness. (Data from Flores d'Arcais et al. 1985.)

	Lexical decision		Naming	
	Perceptually related	Perceptually unrelated	Perceptually related	Perceptually unrelated
Functionally related	499	513	761	788
Functionally unrelated	503	529	799	806

and the F-elements seem to reach maximum effectiveness somewhat later. Conversely, by speeding up lexical decision we obtained a less strong effect of the F elements as compared with the "normal" lexical-decision condition. The data thus indicate again a differential point of maximum activation effect of P and F elements in lexical priming with a lexical decision task.

To conclude: We have been able to experimentally separate two components within the semantic information that becomes activated when a word is recognized, and we have been able to show, furthermore, that these components become activated at different rates. Perceptually based semantic information, which is probably acquired earlier in the process of the ontogeny of a word's meaning and which is based on direct experience with objects, seems to become available earlier or with a faster maximum activation than information based on abstract or functional properties of the objects to which the words refer.

Notice that the scope of our conclusions does not go beyond the class of referential words—namely, nouns having concrete, precise, and easy picturable referents. We do not want to suggest that the semantic representation of every word contains a perceptual component. On the other hand, the results are theoretically important in the sense that they have shown that it is possible to distinguish, within the representation underlying a word, separate structures which might become activated with different strengths and/or different rates.

Our claims so far are, therefore, the following:

(1) Certain "relatedness" effects in lexical processing arise because lexical entries are connected to the same pieces of knowledge representation; that is, some of this information is *shared* by lexical entries. In this sense, priming effects are seen as essentially similar to all repetition effects in lexical processing; in semantic priming the repetition takes place at the semantic

level, in word repetition the repetition takes place at more levels of lexical structure.

(2) Some of those pieces of knowledge representation have to do with sensory-specific information (for instance, information dealing with shape and color); other representations deal with more abstract, functional knowledge.

(3) These "perceptual" structures can also independently lead to relatedness effects similar to the ones obtained with more abstract, functional representations.

Further Empirical Evidence: Object Recognition and Object Naming

We will now discuss access to the system by routes other than printed or spoken words. Our model assumes that perceptual representations play a crucial role in semantic activation during object recognition, and that they influence lexical processing because they can be directly activated by perceptual analyzing systems. In accessing lexical entries from visual perceptual input, these structures will become available early compared with more abstract information that can only become available *after* object recognition (i.e., after concept node activation). Objects access general semantic structures, just as words do (this does not imply that they access exactly the same structures, but that there is an overlap among the two). Therefore, classical lexical priming effects should be obtained whether the prime or target is a word or a picture of an object to be named.

Our framework assumes that the same conceptual unit will ultimately be addressed when a word is presented or an object. In a series of experiments (e.g. Flores d'Arcais and Schreuder 1987) on object naming in an object-object priming paradigm, we have been able to show that the same type of decomposition between P elements and F elements applies as was suggested by our results using only word-word pairs.

The framework introduced in the present study also allows a convincing explanation of various results of studies on picture and word categorization. However, we need to introduce a distinction between "perceptual" and "conceptual" categories.

It is a well-known finding (Smith and Magee 1980) that pictures can be categorized faster than words. This is usually explained by assuming that pictures access semantic information faster than words. In terms of our model, this would be information that would be represented by P elements. Take, for example, the picture of a dog; it would usually show ears, legs, a tail, hairs, a certain outline, a shape of head, etc. This is all information represented by P elements. Furthermore, generally dogs eat meat, and this is some piece of knowledge connected with our concept of dog. In most cases, however, this information would not be present in the picture itself, but could be inferred once the object in the picture was recognized as a dog.

For a number of categories, it is possible to be unable to recognize a particular member of that category while at the same time being able to name the category (e.g., birds). Imagine that you are presented with a picture of a tapir. Many of us don't know the name of the animal, and don't know what specific animal it is, but it is easy for us to recognize it as an animal, and also as some kind of mammal. However, for a number of categories it is not at all clear which perceptual features would allow people to produce a category name without first recognizing the item itself. Is it possible, for instance, to recognize a tie as a piece of clothing before recognizing it as a tie? It seems that, although certain objects can be classified as members of a given category before or without being recognized as specific objects, for other categories certain objects cannot be classified as members of these categories before they are recognized at a specific level.

These arguments give us the basis for introducing the term *perceptual categories*, as opposed to conceptual categories. A perceptual category is a category that is defined predominantly in terms of perceptual attributes of its members, whereas a conceptual category is defined more by functional attributes of its members. There is, of course, no sharp boundary between these two types; it is more a matter of degree. An example of a perceptual category would be BIRD; an example of a conceptual category would be KITCHEN UTENSILS. Members of this last class mostly share conceptual features of a functional nature, whereas members of the category BIRD mainly share perceptual attributes. In terms of our model, a perceptual category is one for which the concept node has relatively more P nodes than F nodes; this entails that it can be triggered by visual perceptual information. Therefore, a picture of a sparrow activates directly the SPARROW node and also the BIRD node.

Consider now a conceptual category like KITCHEN UTENSILS. Here a picture of a spoon does not directly activate the concept KITCHEN UTENSIL; it activates that concept only indirectly, after the concept node SPOON has been sufficiently triggered. So, even if the objects (pictures) can be recognized equally fast at the specific level of sparrow or spoon, there should be a difference in ease of recognition at the category level.

Pictures of members from categories characterized more perceptually should be categorized faster than pictures of members of more abstract categories. This prediction was tested in an experiment (Schreuder 1988) in which subjects were presented with pictures of members of perceptual and conceptual categories, respectively, and category-verification time for each single picture was measured. In the experiment, a name-verification task was also used. Another group of subjects had simply to judge whether a given name could apply to a picture. Notice that the distinction between conceptual and perceptual categories does not apply for this task. Aside from possible effects on naming latency as a result of word frequency or amount of experience with the words, there is no reason why one should judge the correctness of the label "chicken" for a picture of a chicken faster than the label "tie" for a picture of a tie, provided that both are adequate pictures. By introducing this name-verification task, possible effects caused by different recognizability of the two sets of pictures of objects in the two categories for the main experiment could be controlled for.

The results showed that category verification was faster for objects belonging to what we have called perceptual categories than for objects belonging to conceptual categories. No significant difference was found for the two types of categories in the name-verification task with the same set of pictures. If we take these results as a base-line condition, then it is unlikely that the difference in the time requested to perform the categorization task in the two conditions could be attributed to differences in recognizability of the pictures used for the two types of categories.

The semantic information that a picture ultimately activates differs in its accessability. Semantic information that is "directly" present in the picture can be activated earlier than semantic information that depends for its activation on the activation of concepts at a more specific level. This also supports the notion that some concept nodes can be activated by perceptual elements in their semantic representations, these P elements in turn being directly activated by the object-recognition system.

In this section we have reviewed some evidence about certain aspects of the process of semantic activation underlying object naming. We have been able to obtain substantial support for specific aspects of our model. This support comes from experiments using a wide range of experimental tasks (word naming, lexical decision, object naming, object verification). The first series of experiments we summarized here showed that it is possible to differentiate the contribution of two different elements to lexical priming—namely, what we have called P elements and F elements. The second series of experiments offered additional evidence for this distinction on the basis of priming with object naming and in an object-categorization task, which showed a difference in categorization time between members of categories for which the critical cue for category membership can be defined in terms of perceptual characteristics, and members of "conceptual" categories.

Conclusion

We started our chapter with a short overview of work of the last twenty years on the lexical semantic representation of meaning. We concluded that no major new psycholinguistically oriented theory of representation has been developed, and that most psycholinguists are still tacitly assuming some form of semantic decomposition. Much of the work has concentrated on relations between lexical entries and has neglected the mapping between lexical entries and the objects and events in the world.

In our approach, we leave open the issue of representational format and concentrate instead on a broad distinction between different types of semantic information. The question how meaning is represented in the human cognitive system is too important, however, to leave unspecified, and our model must be made more specific in this respect. In general, the whole issue of semantic representation deserves much more attention within psycholinguistics.

We have made a broad distinction between those semantic structures that deal with perceptual information and those that deal with more abstract, functional information. Information dealing with perceptual matters (shape, form, color, etc.) can be triggered by modality-specific perceptual processing systems. This perceptually based information is similar to more abstract/functional information in the sense that classic lexical priming can be obtained via both types of information.

As we noted when introducing our framework, most of the issues are open, and the model will have to be specified much further. For the present, the evidence reported here represents a contribution toward a psychological theory of lexical representation.

References

Barsalou, L. W. 1982. Context-independent and context-dependent information in concepts. *Memory and Cognition* 10: 82–93.

Caramazza, A., and Grober, E. 1976. Polysemy and the structure of the subjective lexicon. In C. Rameh (ed.), *Semantics: Theory and Application. Georgetown University Round Table on language and linguistics.* Washington, D.C.: Georgetown University Press.

Carpenter, P. A., and Just, M. A. 1975. Sentence comprehension: A psycholinguistic processing model. *Psychological Review* 82: 45–73.

Clark, E. V. 1981. Lexical innovations: How children learn to create new words. In W. Deutsch (ed.), *The Child's Construction of Language*. New York: Academic.

Clark, E. V., and Clark, H. H. 1979. When nouns surface as verbs. *Language* 55: 767–811.

Clark, H. H. 1974. Semantics and comprehension. In T. A. Sebeok (ed.), *Current Trends in Linguistics, Vol. 12: Linguistics and Adjacent Arts and Sciences*. The Hague: Mouton.

Clark, H. H. 1983. Making sense of nonce sense. In G. B. Flores d'Arcais and R. J. Jarvella (eds.), *The Process of Language Understanding*. Chichester: Wiley.

Clark, H. H., and Clark, E. V. 1977. *Psychology and Language*. New York: Harcourt Brace Jovanovich.

Collins, A. M., and Loftus, E. F. 1975. A spreading activation theory of semantic processing. *Psychological Review* 82: 407–428.

Downing, P. 1977. On the creation and use of English compound nouns. *Language* 53: 810–842.

Fillenbaum, S., and Rapoport, A. 1971. *Structures in the Subjective Lexicon*. New York: Academic.

Fillmore, C. F. 1971. Types of lexical information. In D. D. Steinberg and L. A. Jakobovits (eds.), *Semantics: An Interdisciplinary Reader in Philosophy, Linguistics and Psychology*. Cambridge University Press.

Flores d'Arcais, G. B., and Schreuder, R. 1987. Semantic activation during object naming. *Psychological Research* 49: 153–159.

Flores d'Arcais, G. B., Schreuder, R., and Glazenborg, G. 1985. Semantic activation during recognition of referential words. *Psychological Research* 47: 39–49.

Fodor, J.A. 1975. *The Language of Thought*. New York: Crowell.

Fodor, J. A. 1978. Tom Swift and his procedural grandmother. *Cognition* 6: 229–247.

Fodor, J. A. 1979. In reply to Philip Johnson-Laird. *Cognition* 7: 93–95.

Fodor, J. A., Garrett, M. F., Walker, E. C. T., and Parkes, C. H. 1980. Against definitions. *Cognition* 8: 263–367.

Fodor, J. D. 1980. *Semantics: Theories of Meaning in Generative Grammar*. Cambridge, Mass.: Harvard University Press.

Fodor, J. D., Fodor, J. A., and Garrett, M. F. 1975. The psychological unreality of semantic representations. *Linguistic Inquiry* 6: 515–531.

Gentner, D. 1981. Verb semantic structures in memory for sentences: Evidence for componential representation. *Cognitive Psychology* 13: 56–83.

Gleitman, L. R., and Gleitman, H. 1970. *Phrase and Paraphrase. Some Innovative Uses of Language*. New York: Norton.

Henley, N. M. 1969. A psychological study of the semantics of animal terms. *Journal of Verbal Learning and Verbal Behavior* 8: 176–184.

Hersh, H., and Caramazza, A. 1976. A fuzzy set approach to quantifiers and vagueness in natural language. *Journal of Experimental Psychology: General* 105: 254–276.

Hollan, J. D. 1975. Features and semantic memory: Set-theoretic or attribute model? *Psychological Review* 82: 154–155.

Hormann, H. 1983. The calculating listener or how many are *einige, mehrere,* and *ein paar* (some, several, and a few)? In R. Bauerle, C. Schwartze, and A. von Stechow (eds.), *Meaning, Use, and Interpretation of Language.* Berlin: De Gruyter.

Jaarsveld, H. van, and Schreuder, R. 1986. Implicit quantification of temporal adverbs. *Journal of Semantics* 4: 327–339.

Jackendoff, R. 1976. Toward an explanatory semantic representation. *Linguistic Inquiry* 7: 89–150.

Jackendoff, R. 1983. *Semantics and Cognition.* Cambridge, Mass.: MIT Press.

Johnson-Laird, P. N. 1978. What's wrong with Grandma's guide to procedural semantics. A reply to Jerry Fodor. *Cognition* 6: 249–261.

Johnson-Laird, P. N., Herrmann, D. J., and Chaffin, R. 1984. Only connections: A critique of semantic networks. *Psychological Bulletin* 96: 292–315.

Katz, A. 1972. *Semantic theory.* New York: Harper & Row.

Kintsch, W. 1974. *The Representation of Meaning in Memory.* Hillsdale, N.J.: Erlbaum.

Labov, W. 1972. The boundaries of words and their meanings. In C.-J. N. Bailey and R. W. Shuy (eds.), *New Ways of Analyzing Variation in English, Vol. 1.* Washington, D.C.: Georgetown University Press.

Livant, W. H. 1961. Productive grammatical operations I: The noun compounding of 5-year-olds. *Language Learning* 12: 15–26.

Lupker, S. J. 1984. Semantic priming without association: A second look. *Journal of Verbal Learning and Verbal Behavior* 23: 709–733.

Lupker, S. J. 1985. Relatedness effects in word and picture naming: Parallels, differences, and structural implications. In A. W. Ellis (ed.), *Progress in the Psychology of Language, Vol. 1.* London: Erlbaum.

Lyons, J. 1977. *Semantics,* Vol. 1. Cambridge University Press.

McClelland, J. L., and Rumelhart, D. E. 1981. An interactive activation model of context effects in letter perception: Part 1. An account of basic findings. *Psychological Review* 88: 375–407.

McCloskey, M. E., and Glucksberg, S. 1978. Natural categories: Well defined or fuzzy sets? *Memory and Cognition* 6: 462–472.

McNamara, T. P., and Sternberg, R. J. 1983. Mental models of word meaning. *Journal of Verbal Learning and Verbal Behavior* 22: 449–474.

Miller, G. A. 1969. A psychological method to investigate verbal concepts. *Journal of Mathematical Psychology* 6: 169–191.

Miller, G. A. 1972. English verbs of motion: A case study in semantics and lexical memory. In A. W. Melton and E. Martin (eds.), *Coding Processes in Human Memory.* Washington: Winston.

Miller, G. A. 1986. Dictionaries in the mind. *Language and Cognitive Processes* 1: 171–185.

Miller, G. A., and Johnson-Laird, P. N. 1976. *Language and Perception.* Cambridge, Mass.: Belknap Press of Harvard University Press.

Newell, A., and Simon, H. A. 1972. *Human Problem Solving.* Englewood Cliffs, N.J.: Prentice-Hall.

Norman, D. A., and Rumelhart, D. E. 1975. *Explorations in Cognition.* San Fransisco: Freeman.

Quillian, M. R. 1968. Semantic memory. In M. L. Minsky (ed.), *Semantic Information Processing.* Cambridge, Mass.: MIT Press.

Rosch, E. 1975. Cognitive representations of semantic categories. *Journal of Experimental Psychology: General* 104: 192–233.

Roth, E. M., and Mervis, C. B. 1983. Fuzzy set theory and class inclusion relations in semantic categories. *Journal of Verbal Learning and Verbal Behavior* 22: 509–525.

Rumelhart, D. E., and Norman, D. A. 1982. Simulating a skilled typist: A study of skilled cognitive-motor performance. *Cognitive Science* 6: 1–36.

Schank, R. C. 1972. Conceptual dependency: A theory of natural language understanding. *Cognitive Psychology* 3: 552–631.

Schreuder, R. 1978. Studies in Psycholexicology with Special Reference to Verbs of Motion. Ph.D. thesis, University of Nijmegen.

Schreuder, R. 1988. The access of semantic information by pictures and words. Submitted for publication.

Schreuder, R., Flores d'Arcais, G. B., and Glazenborg, G. 1984. Effects of perceptual and conceptual similarity in semantic priming. *Psychological Research* 45: 339–354.

Smith, E. E., Shoben, E. J., and Rips, L. J. 1974. Structure and process in semantic memory: A featural model for semantic decisions. *Psychological Review* 81: 214–241.

Stemberger, J. P. 1985. An interactive activation model of language production. In A. W. Ellis (ed.), *Progress in the Psychology of Language*, vol. 1. Hillsdale, N.J.: Erlbaum.

Talmy, L. 1985. Lexicalization patterns: Semantic structure in lexical forms. In T. Shopen (ed.), *Language Typology and Syntactic Description, Vol. III.* Cambridge University Press.

Thorndyke, P. W. 1975. Conceptual complexity and imagery in comprehension and memory. *Journal of Verbal Learning and Verbal Behavior* 14: 359–369.

Ullmann, S. 1962. *Semantics: An Introduction to the Study of Meaning.* Oxford: Basil Blackwell & Mott.

Weinreich, U. 1966. Explorations in semantic theory. In T. A. Sebeok (ed.), *Current Trends in Linguistics*, Vol. 3. The Hague: Mouton.

Whitney, P., McKay, T., Kellas, G., and Emerson, W. A., Jr. 1985. Semantic activation of noun concepts in context. *Journal of Experimental Psychology: Learning, Memory, and Cognition* 11: 126–135.

PART IV
Parsing and Interpretation

Chapter 15

| The Role of Lexical Representations in Language Comprehension | Lorraine Komisarjevsky Tyler |

It is clear from recent work in linguistics, psycholinguistics, and computational linguistics that lexical representations play a central role in the process of integrating different types of linguistic and nonlinguistic knowledge. Not only do lexical representations provide the basic bridge between sound and meaning, linking the phonological properties of word forms with clusters of syntactic and semantic attributes; they also provide the basic structural framework in terms of which an utterance can be interpreted.

The syntactic and semantic properties of words become available once the sensory input has been mapped onto representations of lexical form. Other chapters in this volume discuss the nature of form-based representations and the processes involved in making contact with them. In this chapter, I will focus on representations of semantic and syntactic content. I will begin by summarizing the process by which the content of lexical representations becomes available for the construction of higher-level representations, arguing for the parallel activation of syntactic and semantic codes, with the early selection of the contextually relevant word sense and syntactic information (Marslen-Wilson 1987; Marslen-Wilson, this volume). In the main body of the chapter I will discuss how lexical representations are used in the interpretation of an utterance, and the implications this has for the structure of the language-comprehension system.

1 The Nature of the Activation Process

An important feature of the comprehension of spoken language is that words are recognized in utterance contexts before enough of the word has been heard to ensure correct identification on the basis of the sensory input alone (Marslen-Wilson and Tyler 1980a; Tyler and Wessels 1983). To account for this finding, it has been proposed that some initial portion of the sensory input is mapped onto all those representations of lexical form with which it is compatible. This makes available the syntactic and semantic properties of words, which can then immediately be evaluated, in parallel, against the specifications of the context (Marslen-Wilson and Welsh 1978; Marslen-Wilson 1984, 1987). This parallel evaluation process continues until a single lexical entry is selected which best matches both the context and the sensory input. The emphasis on parallelism in the lexicon is a crucial aspect of the model, since the early recognition of words in context cannot be explained without it (Marslen-Wilson 1987).

What is the evidence for this parallel activation of multiple codes and for the early selection of the contextually relevant codes? There are three types of evidence. The first is the evidence, mentioned above, that words are recognized earlier in context than they are when they appear in isolation. This robust finding is obtained by means of a variety of experimental techniques (Grosjean 1980; Marslen-Wilson and Tyler 1980a; Tyler and Wessels 1983, 1985). If words in isolation are identified at the earliest point at which there is sufficient sensory input to uniquely identify the word, then words in context must be being identified when the sensory input is still ambiguous as to the correct identity of the word. This means that the prior context in which the word is heard provides the necessary information to compensate for the ambiguous signal. This, in turn, means that information about the syntactic and semantic properties of words must become available very early in the word-recognition process; otherwise there would be no informational base upon which context could discriminate among different candidates.

The second type of evidence comes from lexical-ambiguity and gating studies. The ambiguity studies, typically using the cross-modal lexical-decision task (Swinney 1979; Onifer and Swinney 1981; Seidenberg, Tanenhaus, Leiman, and Bienkowski 1982), find that the syntactic (Seidenberg et al.) and semantic (Swinney) properties of words become available early in the processing of a word. These studies also show that context does not influence the early activation of this type of lexical information. Even when the meaning of a word or its syntactic form class is highly constrained by the context, all syntactic and semantic information is momentarily activated—even if it is contextually inappropriate.

In a different type of study—using the gating task, where subjects hear successively larger fragments of a word and are asked to say what word they think they are hearing—I also found evidence of the momentary activation of multiple lexical codes. Subjects frequently produced syntactically and semantically inappropriate words in response to the first few fragments—corresponding to the first 50–200 msec—of a word (Tyler 1984).

These types of studies also show that context does eventually function to assist in the selection of a unique candidate. In the ambiguity studies, for example, shortly after a word has been identified, only its contextually appropriate syntactic and semantic properties are available (Seidenberg, Tanenhaus, Leiman, and Bienkowski 1982). And in gating studies (Tyler 1985), semantically and/or syntactically inappropriate words are not produced by subjects after they have heard an average of 250 msec of a word.

The third type of evidence for the parallel activation of multiple lexical codes is perhaps the most direct and compelling. This is a study in which subjects heard spoken words and made lexical decisions to visual probes presented concurrently with these words (Marslen-Wilson 1987). Earlier research by Swinney (1979) has shown that lexical decisions to visual probes are facilitated when they are semantically related to concurrently presented spoken words. Marslen-Wilson's spoken stimuli consisted of words, such as *captain* and *captive*, that share the same initial sequence but diverge from each other at the onset of the vowel following the /t/ burst. The visual probes were semantically related to one or the other of the words. For example, *ship* is a semantic associate of *captain* and *guard* is an associate of *captive*. These visual probes were presented at two positions relative to the spoken word. The first position occurred just before the two words (*captain* and *captive*) diverged from each other. The second probe position occurred well after the point at which they diverged, toward the end of the word. Marslen-Wilson found that at the early probe position lexical decisions to both visual probes were facilitated, which suggests that the meanings of both spoken words (*captain* and *captive*) were activated. However, at the late probe position only the visual probe related to the actual word was facilitated, suggesting that by this point a single word had been selected.

This study was extended by Zwitserlood (1987) in order to examine the role of context in the activation process. The test items (*captain/captive* pairs) were similar to those used in the Marslen-Wilson study, but Zwitserlood presented them either in semantically biasing or neutral contexts. She found that context had no effect on the initial activation process. The meaning of both *captain* and *captive* were facilitated at the early probe positions (about 200 msec into the word), even when only one of them was contextually appropriate. At later probe positions, only the contextually relevant word was facilitated.

The weight of the experimental evidence, then, supports the claim that early in the processing of a word there is multiple activation of semantic and syntactic codes, which are evaluated in parallel against the representation of the prior context. The intersection of the accumulating sensory input and the context results in the eventual selection of the contextually appropriate lexical content. What are the implications of this early activation of lexical codes for the development of higher-level representations of an utterance?

2   How Do Lexical Representations Function in Language Processing?

If, as I have argued, the lexical processing system is structured so as to make available representations of lexical content early in the process of recognizing a word, then how and when is this information used in the development of higher-level representations?

A reasonable hypothesis to pursue is that early activation results in early use of the information that is activated. This is undoubtedly the case for form-based information. The phonological and orthographic properties of a word are used immediately to constrain the identity of the word in question (Warren and Marslen-Wilson 1986, 1987; Marslen-Wilson 1987). Is this also the case for representations of lexical content—for the syntactic and semantic attributes of words that have consequences for the construction of higher-level representations? The research that William Marslen-Wilson and I have carried out over the past 15 years suggests that it is. Much of this research has focused on the processing of verbs, although the claims we make about the function of lexical representations are not restricted to verbs. We have focused on verbs because of the important role they have in language comprehension and in current psychological and linguistic theorizing.

In linguistics, a number of theories (Gazdar 1982; Bresnan 1982; Chomsky 1965) have focused on the representation of verbs and on the structural implications of those representations for the interpretation of an utterance. These theories have moved lexical representations into a central position in determining the syntactic and semantic properties of an utterance. They closely link the subcategorization properties of a verb with its argument structure in a semantic interpretation. The argument frames associated with lexical items specify not only how these arguments might function in a purely syntactic representation of an utterance, but also how they might function in its semantic interpretation. This semantic interpretation determines how the utterance is projected onto a discourse model. The argument frames associated with verbs have consequences for linguistic analysis and for the construction of an interpretation in the nonlinguistic, conceptual domain (Tanenhaus and Carlson, this volume).

It is thus widely accepted that the representation of each verb includes a specification of its semantic and syntactic properties, although the exact definition of these properties differs. From a psychological perspective, we want to know how these lexical representations function in on-line processing. How are they used in the process of constructing a representation of an utterance?

Research on this issue falls into two broad camps. One body of work—primarily identified with the "Amherst group" (see e.g. Clifton, Frazier, and Connine 1984; Frazier 1987; Ferreira and Clifton 1986; Rayner and Frazier 1987)—claims that, although different types of lexical information might become immediately available to the perceiver (in their case, the reader), the parser makes use of only those that are relevant to the initial syntactic representation that it builds (i.e., major category and phrasal information). Since this initial syntactic parse is computed "blind" of either the meaning of the utterance or the semantics of the word being processed, the semantic specifications of a word have consequences for syntactic processing only after its syntactic properties have been exploited.

This model makes a number of very strong predictions about the time course with which different aspects of lexical information can be projected onto higher-level representations. The one that is of most concern to us here is the prediction that the processing system will generate syntactic structures that will be incompatible with the meaning of the utterance. Almost all the evidence suggesting that the processing system makes this type of error comes from the Amherst group.

If, in contrast, the processing system is able to make use of all types of lexical information in constructing higher-level representations, then such misparses will hardly ever occur. I would argue that the entire lexical specification of a word is momentarily activated *and* used when the word is recognized. This information is then assessed against the demands of the utterance-and-discourse context in which the word occurs. The contextually appropriate aspects of the word's representation then function to constrain the interpretation of subsequent words. Context does not operate in a top-down fashion to determine which aspects of lexical representations should be considered; rather, it selects the contextually appropriate reading of a word after its entire lexical specification has been assessed.

Take, for example the verb *claim*, which has as part of its syntactic specification the fact that it can take both a sentential complement and a noun-phrase complement. When *claim* is identified, this sentential comple-ment and this NP complement (and all other lexically specified informa-tion) are activated and assessed against the prior context. If the context prefers one or another type of complement (on syntactic or semantic grounds), then only that structure will be projected from the lexicon. This structure will then be part of the representation against which subsequent words are evaluated for their contextual compatibility. Structures projected from the lexicon do not place constraints on the identity of individual words. Rather, they constrain the type of structure that can be built and, therefore, the relations between words within a phrase.

On this view, there is no processing discontinuity in the use of different types of lexical information, since all are assessed in parallel against the context. In a number of studies, William Marslen-Wilson and I have ex-amined the immediate processing consequences of various types of lexical syntactic information—such as subcategorization and major category information—that accept only particular lexical categories in the struc-tures they initiate. We have also looked at the effects of two kinds of semantic information: information that is clearly lexically specified (i.e., selection restrictions such as *animate*, *human*, and *abstract*, which accept particular members of lexical categories in the phrase under construction) and information that cannot be directly lexically represented but rather is based on properties of lexical semantic representations (i.e., pragmatic information). The representation of a word cannot contain all the various and subtle interpretations that the word could have in different real-world contexts. Instead, we assume that the process of pragmatic inference is triggered by the activation of specific aspects of a word's meaning. When the semantic properties of a word are activated and assessed against the context, this involves more than just an assessment of intensional meaning. It also involves evaluating the pragmatic implications of that entity or event with respect to what the listener knows about how it functions in the world.

On-Line Use of Lexical Representations

What is the evidence for the claim that all these different types of information have immediate structural consequences? In a number of studies we have found no evidence that, for example, lexical semantic or pragmatic informa-tion is used much later than syntactic information to constrain the ways in which words are structurally combined. In one study (Marslen-Wilson, Brown, and Tyler 1988; Tyler 1985), we focused on verb-argument relations to ask whether both the syntactic and the semantic specifications of a verb function to immediately constrain the properties of its argument. In particular, we examined syntactic subcategory information, semantic selection restrictions, and pragmatic inference based upon the semantic specifications of the verb.

The idea behind the experiment was the following: If identification of a verb (such as *sleep*) includes accessing information about the kinds of arguments it selects, and if this acts as a structural constraint on the immediate processing of subsequent items, then the noun phrase *the house* in the sequence "He slept the house" would violate subcategorization constraints imposed by the verb. When the syntactic and semantic properties of *the house* are assessed (unsuccessfully) against the context, processing will be disrupted. Similarly, if either selection restrictions or the pragmatic implications of the verb place constraints on the particular words that can occur as its argument, then violating either type of constraint will also disrupt processing. So, for example, if the subject hears "The girl eats the brick", the selection restrictions on the verb *eats* will accept only edible substances as its argument. Since bricks are not edible, *brick* violates semantic constraints on acceptable verb-argument structures, and processing will be disrupted. The same logic applies to pragmatic inference generated by lexical representations. If the pragmatic plausibility of an argument is a factor influencing the appropriateness of a particular verb-argument combination, then processing should again be disrupted when an argument is pragmatically implausible.

To test these claims, we constructed materials of the following types:

(1a) The crowd was waiting eagerly. The young man GRABBED the *guitar* and ...

(1b) The crowd was waiting eagerly. The young man BURIED the *guitar* and ...

(1c) The crowd was waiting eagerly. The young man DRANK the *guitar* and ...

(1d) The crowd was waiting eagerly. The young man SLEPT the *guitar* and ...

In condition (a) the relationship between the verb (*grabbed*) and object noun (*guitar*) is normal. In condition (b) the object noun is pragmatically implausible; however, it is not linguistically anomalous, in view of the semantics of the preceding verb and the prior context. In condition (c) the object noun violates selection restrictions (Chomsky 1965) on the prior verb (*drank the guitar*), in that the argument slot for *drink* is restricted to liquid substances. In condition (d) the noun violates strict subcategorization restrictions on the verb (*slept the guitar*), because *sleep* is intransitive and cannot take a direct object. This means that the appropriate syntactic structure cannot be built and the semantic relations between verb and noun are not coherent. Conditions (c) and (d), then, violate constraints on permissable syntactic and semantic structural combinations of words.

To assess the effect of these various types of verb-argument violations on the process of developing an interpretation of an utterance, we had subjects perform a word-monitoring task. They were asked to press a response key as soon as they heard a target word (in this case, the word *guitar*) in the utterance, and their reaction times (from word onset) were recorded. The pattern of results was very clear. Subjects were significantly slowed down by all three types of violation. However, the amount by which their processing was disrupted varied according to the type of violation. The mean response time for the normal condition (a) was 241 msec. This increased by a small but significant amount in the presence of a pragmatic anomaly (268 msec), and by a larger amount in the presence of a word that violated selection restrictions (291 msec). The slowest RTs were in response to subcategorization violations (320 msec).

These results suggest that the lexical representation of a verb imposes immediate structural constraints—in the form of verb-argument frames—on the processing of the subsequent input. These constraints encompass many different aspects of a verb—its semantic as well as its syntactic specifications. The important point here is that all types of constraint affect the analysis of incoming words immediately.

Perhaps the most surprising result of this study was the immediate effect of the pragmatic implications of the verb. Response times increased significantly when the listener heard an utterance containing a pragmatically implausible verb-argument structure. This increase was smaller than for the two types of linguistic violation, reflecting the fact that pragmatic implausibility does not actually prevent the listener from developing a representation of an utterance (as subcategorization violations do), although it may increase the difficulty of doing so. What the increase in RT in the pragmatic-implausibility condition indicates is that listeners are attempting, as soon as they activate the lexical specifications of a verb, to evaluate these with respect to their model of the world on the basis of the utterances they have heard. This is evidence, then, that the argument frames associated with each verb have immediate consequences for the linguistic analysis of an utterance and for its interpretation within a nonlinguistic, conceptual domain.

Some research we started many years ago (Tyler and Marslen-Wilson 1977) and recently revived (Marslen-Wilson and Young, unpublished) is relevant to this issue. In our first study, we examined the effect of semantic context on the interpretation of category information. We presented subjects with syntactically ambiguous phrases, such as *landing planes*, which were preceded by a semantic context that biased toward either the adjectival reading ("If you walk too near the runway ...") or the verbal reading ("If you've been trained as a pilot ..."). We found that listeners' responses to a visual probe presented at the offset of the fragment were faster when the probe was consistent with the contextually appropriate reading of the fragment. This suggested that listeners' syntactic interpretation of the fragments was guided by the prior semantic context.

This study was criticized by Townsend and Bever (1982), Cowart (1983), and Cowart and Cairns (1987), who pointed out that the stimuli contained a number of confounds, the most serious of which was the presence of singular and plural cataphoric pronouns in the context sentences. The contexts biasing toward the adjectival reading tended to contain plural pronouns, whereas those biasing toward the verb reading often contained singular pronouns. For example, for the ambiguous phrase *cooking apples*, the adjectival context was "Although THEY may be very tart ..."; the verb context was "Although IT doesn't require much work ...".

Since the test sentences were heard in isolation, these pronouns could be interpreted as referring to an entity that has yet to be mentioned. They may lead the listener to believe that either singular or plural potential referents will occur later in the sentence. This could be construed simply as a syntactic bias, without involvement of the pragmatic properties of the discourse context. It is therefore important to determine whether a discourse effect can still be observed when the pronoun effect is neutralized.

For this reason, a further study was carried out (Marslen-Wilson and Young, unpublished) using pairs of context sentences with exactly parallel structures and the same pronouns. These context sentences differed only in their pragmatic implications. For example:

(2a) If you want a cheap holiday, visiting relatives ...

(2b) If you have a spare bedroom, visiting relatives ...

Visiting can be interpreted either as a verb form (a gerund), in which case the sentence will have a reading in which relatives are being visited by someone, or it can be interpreted as an adjectival form modifying the noun *relatives*. The two cases will generate different structural implications. If *visiting* is interpreted as a verb, it will project onto a verb-phrase construction. If it is interpreted as an adjective, it will project onto an adverbial phrase.

My claim is that both of these possibilities are activated when the word *visiting* is recognized, and that they are assessed in parallel against the prior semantic and syntactic context. At this point the context cannot determine which reading (verb or adjective) is preferred, since both are possible. Therefore, both syntactic frames (verb phrase and adjectival phrase) are projected from *visiting*. It is only when the listener hears *relatives* and can assess its syntactic and semantic specifications against the context that a single reading can be selected. This, in turn, has structural implications for the interpretation of the subsequent input.

If the lexical specifications of *visiting relatives* are assessed in parallel against the context so that only the contextually appropriate reading generates structural constraints on the subsequent input, then processing of the subsequent word ought to be affected by the extent to which it is consistent with the contextually appropriate structure. For example, the word *are* is consistent with the verbal reading of fragment (a) but not with the adjectival reading. Therefore, it should take subjects longer to process *are* when it follows (2b) than when it follows (2a). Similarly, the word *is* is an appropriate continuation for the adjectival reading but not for the verbal one. Marslen-Wilson and Young found, just as in the original experiment, that subjects named appropriate probes significantly faster than inappropriate probes.

These results confirm that nonlinguistic context affects the assignment of a syntactic analysis, and they tell us that it does so very early. The probe word comes immediately after the end of the fragment, at the point where the ambiguity of the fragment first becomes fully established. The ambiguity of these fragments depends on hearing both words. Sequences like *visiting houses* are not ambiguous in the same way. This means that we are finding significant context effects at what is effectively the earliest point at which we can measure. This supports the claim that both the syntactic and the semantic properties of *visiting relatives* were evaluated immediately and in parallel against the context.

Finally, there is additional evidence that the pragmatic implications of a verb are immediately assessed against the existing discourse representation to constrain the analysis of the utterance being heard. In various studies (Marslen-Wilson and Tyler 1980b, 1987; Tyler and Marslen-Wilson 1982a), we presented subjects with short stories which were followed by a continuation fragment. The fragment always had the same structure: a noun phrase followed by an incomplete verb phrase. What varied was the nature of the initial noun phrase. It could be a definite description (e.g., *the man*), a proper name (e.g., Philip), or an unambiguous pronoun, or it could take the form of a zero anaphor (i.e. it was not lexically realized). For example:

3. After the surgeon had examined the 12-year-old girl with the badly broken leg, he decided he would have to take immediate action. He'd had lots of experience with serious injuries. He knew what he had to do next.

(a) The surgeon quickly injected ...

(b) He quickly injected ...

(c) Quickly injecting ...

Each of the fragments (a)–(c) contains an anaphoric device linking the fragment to the preceding discourse. In fragment (a) the device is a description of some individual previously mentioned. In (b) it is an unambiguous personal pronoun. In (c), an example of *zero anaphora*, there are no explicit lexical cues at all.

In each case, to interpret the fragment, the listener has to determine who is the agent of the action denoted by the verb and to evaluate this with respect to the preceding discourse. In (a) and (b) the agent is directly lexically specified ("the surgeon", "He"), and can be unambiguously related to possible antecedents just on the basis of this lexical information. It is case (c) that concerns us here. The only way that agency can be assigned is on the basis of a differential pragmatic inference that matches the properties of "Quickly injecting ..." to the properties of potential antecedents in the discourse. It is necessary to infer who is most likely to be injecting whom.

To measure the timing of anaphoric linkage in these three conditions, we used the naming technique described above. Subjects heard the short story together with one of the three continuation fragments. At the offset of the fragment (i.e., at the end of "injecting") a visual probe word was presented, which the subjects had to name as rapidly as possible. In the example above, the probe would have been either HIM or HER. For each case, HER is a more appropriate continuation than HIM. The critical experimental question was whether the size of the expected preference (faster naming of the appropriate probe) would be the same in the zero-anaphor case (where the linkage depends entirely on pragmatic inference) as in the other two conditions (where there are explicit lexical markers). If the appropriateness effect is as strong in the zero-anaphor case as in the other two, then we would claim that the missing subject of the verb will have been filled in, on-line, on the basis of a process of differential pragmatic inference, triggered by the meaning of the verb in relation to the context.

We found a marked appropriateness effect in each condition, and its size did not differ significantly for different types of fragment. Moreover, the effect remained unchanged by various additional factors—whether or not, for example, the subject of the continuation sentence was the focus of the discourse (see Karmiloff-Smith 1980). We can contrast example 3, where "the surgeon" is both the agent of the action denoted by the verb and the main focus of the story, with the following example:

4. Mary lost hope of winning the race to the ocean when she heard Andrew's footsteps approaching her from behind. The deep sand was slowing her down. She had trouble keeping her balance. *Overtaking* ...

Here Mary is the focus of the discourse, although Andrew is the appropriate agent of the verb in the continuation fragment. We found that when we set up this type of conflict situation, the pragmatic implications of the verb always determined the assignment of agency. They were much stronger than the discourse focus.

What these results suggest is that the listener develops a discourse model of the story as it unfolds over time. This discourse model might or might not establish a particular protagonist as the focus of the story. When the listener hears a continuation fragment containing a zero anaphor, the lexical specifications of the verb are immediately assessed against the discourse model. Whether or not the discourse model contains a specific discourse focus, the pragmatic implications of the verb in relation to the discourse will determine which protagonist is chosen as the agent of the continuation fragment. The important point is that the agent is selected just as rapidly on the basis of pragmatic inferencing based on the semantics of the verb as on the basis of a direct anaphoric device (such as a definite noun phrase).

The view I have been developing here is supported by some recent work by Tanenhaus and Carlson (this volume). In contrast with the Amherst view that syntax is the central component in the language-processing system, Tanenhaus and Carslon stress the centrality of various non-syntactic aspects of lexical representations—in particular, the thematic roles associated with verbs. They propose that when a verb is identified, all the different senses of the verb, together with the sets of thematic roles (agent, theme, etc.) associated with each sense are made available to the processing system. Provisional assignments of thematic roles to the verb are made immediately, and this provides a mechanism for enabling the arguments of a verb to be semantically interpreted. This also means that pragmatic inference and discourse context are immediately brought into play so that they can affect the initial interpretation of the sentence.

Selective Use of Lexical Representations

On the view I have been outlining, all types of lexical information are immediately activated and exhaustively evaluated with respect to the discourse context. They all have immediate consequences for the representation that is under construction. Elsewhere (Marslen-Wilson and Tyler 1981, 1987; Tyler and Marslen-Wilson 1982b) we have argued that there is no evidence that different types of lexical information are used to construct different types of higher-level structures. Rather, all types of lexical information seem to constrain the development of a single representation.

This approach is very different from that proposed by the Amherst group. Frazier (1987), Clifton, Frazier, and Connine (1984), and Rayner, Carlson, and Frazier (1983) claim that as each word is perceived, it is incorporated into a constituent-structure representation by the syntactic parser, using only lexical category information. Other types of syntactic information that are assumed to be associated with lexical items, such as lexical preferences for particular syntactic structures, are not used for this initial parse.

There are several important facts about this parser: It can construct only one analysis at a time, it is organized so as to construct a representation that involves the fewest additional nodes in the phrase marker, and it operates under time pressure and therefore prefers to attach new items to the current phrase marker. These conditions on its structure result in the two general parsing strategies—minimal attachment and late closure—that guide the initial syntactic analysis of a sentence. These strategies are impervious to item-specific structural preferences and to lexical meaning.

In parallel with the parser's activities, a thematic processor chooses the most plausible thematic frame for each head of phrase, using discourse and real-world knowledge. Since the thematic processor knows only about the thematic roles and argument structures associated with verbs and other heads of phrases, it builds its own independent representation solely in these terms (Rayner, Carlson, and Frazier 1983).

Moreover, neither processor can directly affect the operations of the other. The only communication between them is initiated by the parser, which is allowed to submit its analysis to the thematic processor. If the thematic processor doesn't like the proposed structure, it can ask the parser to reanalyze the sequence, but it cannot suggest alternate analyses. This model is, in many respects, a direct descendant of Bever's (1970) language-processing model, which also has parallel but independent representations constructed by autonomous subcomponents of the language-comprehension system.

On the Amherst account, all the syntactic information within a lexical entry becomes available when a word is identified, but only the information that is relevant for the syntactic representation the parser prefers to construct is used immediately. To illustrate how this model works, consider the following example of the parsing strategy of late closure:

(5a) Even before the truck stopped the driver was getting nervous.

(5b) Even before the police stopped the driver was getting nervous.

According to the Amherst group, the parser pursues its strategy of late closure, irrespective of any structural preferences that might be associated with the verb *stopped* and irrespective of the pragmatic context (i.e., the fact that in (5a) trucks are less likely to stop something than to be being stopped). This means that readers will treat (5a) and (5b) alike. They will delay closing off the subordinate clause as long as possible, and will assume that the NP following the verb is its object, rather than closing off the subordinate clause early and taking the NP as the subject of the main clause.

At the same time, the thematic processor will be constructing its own representation based on the thematic frames associated with the verb. In (5a), this will result in a different interpretation of the sentence from the one the syntactic parser is constructing, because of the thematic relationship between *truck* and *stopped*. When the parser submits its analysis to the thematic processor, a mismatch will be detected. It is at this point that readers will realize that their initial parse of the sentence is incorrect, and the parser will have to reinterpret the sentence.

The second parsing principle, minimal attachment, can be illustrated with the following example:

(6) The spy saw the cop with the revolver.

When the parser encounters this type of sentence, it follows the principle of postulating the fewest additional nodes and incorrectly attaches the PP "with the revolver" to the verb phrase "saw". For the sentence to make sense, the parser should attach the PP to the NP "the cop". The thematic processor, however, constructs the correct interpretation. Thus, the syntactic parse and the thematic representation conflict, and the parser has to attempt a second analysis of the sentence.

An important aspect of the Amherst claim is that these structural biases affect the *first* parse through a sentence, whereas lexical preferences and pragmatic context come into play only at a later stage of the interpretation process. To test this claim it is necessary to use tasks that probe the representation the perceiver constructs *as it is being constructed* rather than at some later point in time. "On-line" tasks are assumed to probe the initial representation of a sentence (Marslen-Wilson and Tyler 1980a; Tyler and Marslen-Wilson 1982b). These are tasks in which the subject's response is closely tied in time to relevant aspects of the sentence. If we want to know whether, for example, verb preferences affect the initial parse, then we have to probe immediately after the verb has been encountered. Probing at some later point in the sentence runs the risk that the response will be influenced by processes that occurred after the first structure was assigned. It is, therefore, critical to use an appropriate experimental task when attempting to address issues concerning *when* particular types of analysis are carried out. Unfortunately, this has often not been done in parsing research. A few studies have employed some type of on-line task (e.g. Clifton, Frazier, and Connine 1984; Ferreira and Clifton 1986), but many have not (e.g. Crain and Steedman 1985; Mitchell 1987). This has added to the difficulty of interpreting the often contradictory experimental results (e.g. Stowe, in press; Ferriera and Clifton 1986).

The model developed by the Amherst group has been tested in a number of studies, most of which have been carried out by Frazier, Rayner, Clifton, and colleagues, who claim solid empirical support for their model. However, this and related research has not been completely convincing, because it has tended to conflate a number of issues that need to be treated separately. The Amherst claim is that there are purely structural biases corresponding to the parsing principles of minimal attachment and late closure. What must be established is whether these biases ignore the specific syntactic and semantic preferences of a verb, whether they are affected by the meanings of the other words in the sentence, and whether they ignore the pragmatic context of the sentence. To show that there are parsing preferences that are independent of any other source of information, we need to examine separately the effects of all these: lexical preferences, parsing principles, and pragmatic context. This has not been done systematically.

Verb Preferences
The issue of whether the initial syntactic parse of a sentence is developed solely on the basis of parsing principles, without taking into account specific lexical preferences, has barely been investigated. Frazier's (1987) position is that lexical preferences associated with particular verbs do not guide the initial parse (although they may be used later), but she presents no data to support her claim. The closest she came to testing this hypothesis was in a study (Rayner and Frazier 1987) in which the experimental sentences were divided into two groups—those with and those without

lexical preferences associated with the verb—on the basis of the experimenters' intuitions rather than any objective criteria. Rayner and Frazier found that readers parsed the sentences according to the principle of minimal attachment, irrespective of lexical preferences. This is not, however, a very compelling test of the role of lexical preferences, in view of the lack of any objective assessment of preferences prior to the experiment.

A few other studies have examined the role of lexical preferences in parsing. For example, Ford, Bresnan, and Kaplan (1982) and Clifton et al. (1984) show that lexical information about preferred subcategorization frames is used very rapidly during reading, and Holmes (1987) and Mitchell and Holmes (1985) find that readers make use of the structural biases of complement verbs in assigning structure to a sentence. However, Frazier (1987) claims that these studies do not show unequivocally that lexical preferences guide the initial decisions of the parser as opposed to providing some type of later filtering mechanism, because of limitations in the tasks and materials used in the various studies.[1] It should be clear from the above brief description of research on the role of lexical preferences in initial parsing decisions that this still remains an open issue.

So far, I have only discussed the structural preferences some verbs may have. There is also the question of whether the thematic preferences some verbs have (for animate agents, for example) affect the initial parse. Ferreira and Clifton (1986) explored this issue by contrasting sentences containing reduced or unreduced relative clauses, where the verb required an animate agent in some cases but not in others. They found that the animacy of the agent did not affect the reader's first parse of the sentence, which was always based on a minimal attachment strategy. But what they failed to do in this study was to determine whether the verbs they used had syntactic preferences in addition to their assumed (and untested) semantic preferences. It is a mistake to look in detail at the role of any one factor without also controlling for the potential effects of others.

Noun Preferences

It is insufficient just to examine the role of verb preferences (both semantic and syntactic) in parsing decisions. We also need to know whether the meaning of the various NPs around the verb affects the operations of the parser. There is very little research on this aspect of sentence interpretation. Stowe's (in press) recent study is relevant here. She asked whether readers could use thematic information (in the form of the animacy or inanimacy of subject NPs) in assigning a syntactic analysis to a sentence. She used sentences of the type I discussed earlier:

(7a) Even before the police stopped the driver was getting nervous.

(7b) Even before the truck stopped the driver was getting nervous.

According to the principle of late closure, readers should assume that the NP (*the driver*) following the verb (*stopped*) is its object, rather than closing off the subordinate clause and assuming that the NP is the subject of the main clause. This should lead to a garden path in (7a). This strategy should be followed regardless of the animacy of the subject of the subordinate clause. However, Stowe found that when the subject was inanimate and therefore unlikely to be the agent of the action denoted by the verb, as in (7b), readers tended to close after the verb. In the presence of an animate subject, as in (7a), the verb was taken as transitive, which led to a garden path in the main clause. Thus, Stowe found that animacy affects the initial syntactic interpretation of the sentence.[2] Clearly, the relationship between lexical preferences (both syntactic and semantic) and syntactic parsing decisions is an important issue in parsing, and much more research is needed to clarify it.

Pragmatic Context

The role of the meaning and syntactic preferences of individual words must be established independently of the issue of whether the parser is influenced by the pragmatic context of an utterance—an issue that has been investigated numerous times and in different ways. The results from Amherst suggest that the first structure attempted by the parser is not affected by any aspect of the pragmatic context (Ferreira and Clifton 1986; Rayner, Carlson, and Frazier 1983). However, as Taraban and McClelland (1987) point out, in these studies weak pragmatic constraints tend to be pitted against strong syntactic ones, so that it is not surprising that syntactic principles should win. In support of this point, other studies have explicitly manipulated various aspects of the pragmatic context—presuppositional information (Crain and Steedman 1985; Altmann and Steedman 1987) and lexical semantics (Stowe, in press)—and have found that they all affect the syntactic representation which is constructed.

Frazier (1987) tends to dismiss such results on the grounds that either the materials used in an experiment do not contain the appropriate linguistic structures to test the theory (Tyler and Marslen-Wilson 1977) or the tasks used do not probe the initial representation which the parser develops (Crain and Steedman 1985; Stowe, in press; Altmann 1987; Mitchell and Holmes 1987). Since Frazier claims that pragmatic context has an effect only after the parser submits its analysis to the thematic processor, she predicts that there will be an effect of pragmatic context—but only in tasks that tap late stages of processing. She claims that most of the studies that purport to show an effect of pragmatic context on syntactic structure use tasks (such as whole-sentence reading times) that tap late stages of processing.

However, recent results reported by Altmann and Steedman (in press) are hard to refute on these grounds. They presented subjects with sentences containing either complement clauses (such as "The psychologist told the woman that he was worried about her marital problems") or relative clauses (such as "The psychologist told the woman that he was worried about to visit him again"). These were preceded by a semantic context that induced either the complement reading or the relative-clause reading. On the Amherst model, subjects should always attempt the complement reading first (minimal attachment), and therefore should be garden-pathed in the sentences where the correct reading is the relative-clause reading. However, if pragmatic context is used immediately to guide the initial parse, subjects should not be garden-pathed. Altmann and Steedman found that when the pragmatic context biased against the minimal-attachment reading, it was the syntactic structure that was consistent with the pragmatic context which was developed first. Since they used a word-by-word reading task, their results cannot be dismissed on the grounds that the task does not tap the early stages of processing.

Moreover, the Amherst group's own research on this topic suffers from a serious methodological flaw: They have never systematically evaluated the strength of the semantic biases in their materials. Ferreira and Clifton (1986) and Rayner et al. (1983) construct sentences which they assume provide semantic/pragmatic biases against the minimal-attachment reading— for example (from Rayner et al. 1983),

(8) The spy saw the cop with a revolver but the cop didn't see him.

Rayner et al. assume (but never establish empirically) that the semantics of the prepositional phrase (*with a revolver*) requires that it be attached to the noun phrase (*the cop*), therefore creating a bias toward the non-minimal-attachment reading. In spite of this assumed bias, they still found evidence of garden-pathing, indicating that the initial parse of the sentence had not been affected by pragmatic plausibility (although pragmatic plausibility did have an effect later).

These results have recently been challenged by Taraban and McClelland (1987), who argue that, since the materials used by Rayner et al. had not been pretested, there is no way of knowing whether they contained a bias toward the minimal-attachment reading in the sequence up to the prepositional phrase (*a revolver*). To check this, they asked subjects to read sentences like (8) above, up to and including the preposition at the beginning of the critical VP, as in (9).

(9) The spy saw the cop with ...

Subjects were asked to generate a completion for the incomplete sentence. They then saw the completed sentence and rated how well it matched their expectations. Subjects rated VP completions (minimal attachment) significantly closer to their expectations than NP completions. In other words, the context preceding the prepositional phrase biased toward minimal attachment. What we cannot be sure about is the nature of the biases. Taraband and McClelland did not try to determine to what extent they resulted from verb preferences or from such variables as the meaning of the subject or object noun phrases.

Taraban and McClelland then constructed a new set of materials which had not been included in the original Rayner et al. experiment. These materials generated an NP (non-minimal attachment) completion, and subjects subsequently rated these sentences as closer to their NP expectations. Finally, these two sets of items (one set containing a VP bias and the other containing an NP bias) were used in a word-by-word reading-time task. Subjects were significantly faster at reading the sentences where the bias was consistent with the continuation. That is, they were faster to read sentences that were biased either toward minimal attachment or to NP attachment, as long as the prepositional phrase was consistent with this bias. This study demonstrates the subtle interplay among the various sources of information within a sentence and suggests that they all contribute to the initial interpretation.

An additional problem with the study by Rayner et al. (1983) is that the materials were not pretested to ensure that pragmatic factors were actually strong enough to override putative syntactic biases. When experimental materials are pretested to ensure that they do indeed provide appropriately strong pragmatic constraints, then they clearly affect the initial structural interpretation of an utterance (Tyler and Marslen-Wilson 1977; Marslen-Wilson and Young, unpublished). Similarly, in the anaphora studies discussed earlier (Tyler and Marslen-Wilson 1982a; Marslen-Wilson and Tyler 1987), we objectively established the strength of contextual constraints and found that they could determine the assignment of predicate-argument relations in logical form. Recall that the pragmatic implications of a verb, in relation to the discourse context, were sufficient to assign agency to the subject of the continuation sentence (see example 4). Such influence would be explicitly excluded by the Amherst group. Context (in the form of the thematic parser) can tell the syntactic parser whether the representation it has constructed is compatible with the context, but it can never directly tell the parser what the content of its analyses should be.

A slightly different aspect of the anaphora data supports my position. When we generated stories in which the verb exerted no pragmatic biases (as in example 10 below), then discourse focus alone could effectively and rapidly determine the assignment of agency.

(10) As Bill was buying popcorn at the movies, he saw an old girlfriend get in line for a ticket. He had arrived at the movies especially early. He wanted to be sure of getting a good seat. *Waving at ...*

Here the pragmatics of the verb are neutral, and designed to be equally compatible with both potential antecedents, but the discourse sets up *Bill* as its focus. These results showed that discourse focus on its own could also control the on-line interpretation of utterance fragments—and to the same extent as the pragmatic implications of the verb and definite noun phrases. Once again, we see agency being assigned under conditions where the parser could have no basis for doing so purely on linguistic grounds. It is only in the representation of the discourse that any basis exists for choosing one actor or another as the subject of the verb in the continuation fragment.

Conclusion

I would argue that these various results suggest that the research of the Amherst group does not conclusively establish that syntactic parsing is independent either of semantic bias or of the semantic and syntactic specifications associated with individual words. Since these factors have been conflated in most studies, further research is needed to evaluate their role in syntactic parsing. Indeed, there is considerable evidence from a variety of sources that the interpretations of the syntactic implications of verb are immediately constrained by the semantic context in which it occurs.

The view I have developed here suggests that representations of lexical content become available early in the process of recognizing a word, and certainly well before all of the word has been heard. These representations are evaluated, in parallel, against the demands of the context, and those that fit contextual specifications then form part of the higher-level representation against which upcoming words are assessed. The on-line processing data I have presented suggest that this holds for all types of lexical representation (both semantic and syntactic). There was no evidence from these studies that only specific types off syntactic information are used immediately in the process of interpreting an utterance.

Acknowledgments

I wish to thank William Marslen-Wilson for his helpful comments on an earlier draft of this paper. Part of this work was supported by an MRC programme grant to myself and William Marslen-Wilson.

Notes

1. It is sometimes difficult to see what kind of data the Amherst group would take as evidence of lexical preferences affecting parsing decisions. For example, Clifton et al. (1984) found an effect of lexical preferences using a task that is generally considered to reflect immediate processing (lexical decision). Nevertheless, the authors proposed alternate explanations rather than taking this as evidence of lexical preferences affecting initial parsing decisions.

2. These results are in direct conflict with those of Ferreira and Clifton (1986), and there is no obvious way of resolving the discrepancy at present (Stowe, in press). This is always a problem when materials and tasks vary so much between experiments.

References

Altmann, G. 1987. Modularity and interaction in sentence processing. In J. Garfield (ed.), *Modularity in Knowledge Representation and Natural-Language Understanding*. Cambridge, Mass.: MIT Press.

Altmann, G., and Steedman, M. 1987. Interaction with context during human sentence processing. *Cognition*, in press.

Bever, T. 1970. The cognitive basis for linguistic structures. In J. Hayes (ed.), *Cognition and the Development of Language*. New York: Wiley.

Bresnan, J., ed. 1982. *The Mental Representation of Grammatical Relations*. Cambridge, Mass.: MIT Press.

Chomsky, N. 1965. *Aspects of the Theory of Syntax*. Cambridge, Mass.: MIT Press.

Clifton, C., Frazier, L., and Connine, C. 1984. Lexical expectations in sentence comprehension. *Journal of Verbal Learning and Verbal Behavior* 23: 696–708.

Cowart, W. 1983. Reference Relations and Syntactic Processing: Evidence of a Pronoun's Influence on a Syntactic Decision that Affects Word Naming. Doctoral dissertation, City University of New York.

Cowart, W., and Cairns, H. 1987. Evidence for an anaphoric mechanism within syntactic processing: Some reference relations defy semantic and pragmatic constraints. *Memory and Cognition* 15(4): 318–331.

Crain, S., and Steedman, M. 1985. On not being led up the garden path. In D. Dowty, L. Kartunnen, and A. Zwicky (eds.), *Natural Language Parsing: Psycholinguistic, Computational and Theoretical Perspectives.* Cambridge University Press.

Ferreira, F., and Clifton, C. 1986. The independence of syntactic processing. *Journal of Memory and Language* 25: 348–368.

Ford, M., Bresnan, J., and Kaplan, R. 1983. A competence based theory of syntactic closure. In J. Bresnan (ed.), *The Mental Representation of Grammatical Relations.* Cambridge, Mass.: MIT Press.

Frazier, L. 1987. Theories of sentence processing. In J. Garfield (ed.), *Modularity in Knowledge Representation and Natural-Language Understanding.* Cambridge, Mass.: MIT Press.

Gazdar, G. 1982. Phrase structure grammar. In G. Pullum and P. Jacobson (eds.), *The Nature of Syntactic Representation.* Dordrecht: Reidel.

Grosjean, F. 1980. Spoken word recognition processes and the gating paradigm. *Perception and Psychophysics* 28: 267–283.

Holmes, V. 1987. Syntactic parsing: In search of the garden path. In M. Coltheart (ed.), *The Psychology of Reading.* London: Erlbaum.

Holmes, V., Kennedy, A., and Murray, W. 1987. Syntactic structure and the garden path. *Quarterly Journal of Experimental Psychology* 39A(2): 277–295.

Karmiloff-Smith, A. 1980. Psychological processes underlying pronominalisation and non-pronominalisation in children's connected discourse. In J. Kreiman and A. Ojeda (eds.), Papers from the Parasession on Pronouns and Anaphora. Chicago Linguistic Society.

Marslen-Wilson, W. D. 1984. Function and process in spoken word recognition: A tutorial review. In H. Bouma and D. Bouwhuis (eds.), *Attention and Performance X: Control of Language Processes.* Hillsdale, N.J.: Erlbaum.

Marslen-Wilson, W. D. 1987. Functional parallelism and spoken word recognition. *Cognition* 25: 71–102.

Marslen-Wilson, W. D., Brown, C., and Tyler, L. K. 1988. Lexical representations in language comprehension. *Language and Cognitive Processes* 3.

Marslen-Wilson, W. D., and Tyler, L. K. 1980a. The temporal structure of spoken language understanding. *Cognition* 8: 1–71.

Marslen-Wilson, W. D., and Tyler, L. K. 1980b. Towards a psychological basis for a theory of anaphora. In J. Kreiman and A. Ojeda (eds.), Papers from the Parasession on Pronouns and Anaphora. Chicago Linguistic Society.

Marslen-Wilson, W. D., and Tyler, L. K. 1981. Central processes in speech understanding. *Philosophical Transactions of the Royal Society* B 295: 317–332.

Marslen-Wilson, W. D., and Tyler, L. K. 1987. Against modularity. In J. Garfield (ed.), *Modularity in Knowledge Representation and Natural-Language Understanding.* Cambridge, Mass.: MIT Press.

Marslen-Wilson, W. D., and Welsh, A. 1978. Processing interactions and lexical access during word recognition in continuous speech. *Cognitive Psychology* 10: 29–63.

Marslen-Wilson, W. D., and Young, A. 1984. Unpublished manuscript, University of Cambridge.

Mitchell, D. 1987. Lexical guidance in human parsing: Locus and processing characteristics. In M. Coltheart (ed.), *The Psychology of Reading.* London: Erlbaum.

Mitchell, D., and Holmes, V. 1985. The role of specific information about the verb in parsing sentences with local structural ambiguity. *Journal of Memory and Language* 24: 542–559.

Onifer, W., and Swinney, D. 1981. Accessing lexical ambiguities during sentence comprehension: Effects of frequency-of-meaning and contextual bias. *Memory and Cognition* 9: 225–236.

Rayner, K., Carlson, M., and Frazier, L. 1983. The interaction of syntax and semantics during sentence processing: Eye movements in the analysis of semantically biased sentences. *Journal of Verbal Learning and Verbal Behavior* 22: 358–374.

Rayner, K., and Frazier, L. 1987. Parsing temporarily ambiguous complements. *Quarterly Journal of Experimental Psychology* 39A(4): 657–675.

Seidenberg, M., Tanenhaus, M., Leiman, J., and Bienkowski, M. 1982. Automatic access of the meanings of ambiguous words in context: Some limitations of knowledge-based processing. *Cognitive Psychology* 14: 489–537.

Stowe, L. Thematic structures and sentence comprehension. To appear in G. Carlson and M. Tanenhaus (eds.), *Linguistic Structure in Language Processing.* Dordrecht: Reidel.

Swinney, D. 1979. Lexical access during sentence comprehension: (Re) consideration of context effects. *Journal of Verbal Learning and Verbal Behavior* 18: 645–660.

Taraban, R., and McClelland, J. Constituent attachment and thematic role assignment in sentence processing: Evidence for content-guided processing. Submitted for publication.

Townsend, D., and Bever, T. 1982. Natural units of representation interact during sentence comprehension. *Journal of Verbal Learning and Verbal Behavior* 21: 688–703.

Tyler, L. K. 1984. The structure of the initial cohort. *Perception and Psychophysics* 36(5): 417–427.

Tyler, L. K. 1985. Real-time comprehension processes in agrammatism: A case study. *Brain and Language* 26: 259–275.

Tyler, L. K., and Marslen-Wilson, W. D. 1977. The on-line effects of semantic context on syntactic processing. *Journal of Verbal Learning and Verbal Behavior* 16: 683–692.

Tyler, L. K., and Marslen-Wilson, W. D. 1982a. The resolution of discourse anaphors: Some on-line studies. *Text* 2: 263–291.

Tyler, L. K., and Marslen-Wilson, W. D. 1982b. Speech comprehension processes. In J. Mehler, E. Walker and M. Garrett (eds.), *Perspectives on Mental Representation*. Hillsdale, N.J.: Erlbaum.

Tyler, L. K., and Wessels, J. 1983. Quantifying contextual contributions to word-recognition processes. *Perception and Psychophysics* 34: 409–420.

Tyler, L. K., and Wessels, J. 1985. Is gating an on-line task? Evidence from naming latency data. *Perception and Psychophysics* 38(3): 217–222.

Warren, P., and Marslen-Wilson, W. D. 1987. Continuous uptake of acoustic cues in spoken word recognition. *Perception and Psychophysics* 41(3): 262–275.

Warren, P., and Marslen-Wilson, W. D. 1988. Cues to lexical choice: Discriminating place and voice. *Perception and Psychophysics* 43: 21–30.

Zwitserlood, P. 1987. The Locus of the Effects of Sentential-Semantic Context in Spoken Word Processing. Manuscript, Max-Planck-Institut für Psycholinguistik.

Chapter 16

Grammar, Interpretation, and Processing from the Lexicon	Mark J. Steedman

It seems intuitively obvious that our comprehension of sentences is "incremental," in the sense that each successive word seems to contribute to a gradual accumulation of meaning more or less as soon as it is encountered. Not only the "sense," or language-internal meaning, but also the referential identity of individuals and entities in the domain of discourse seems to become available immediately. That is, we feel that it is not merely semantic interpretation that is incremental, but reference itself.[1]

If interpretations are available at every turn in sentence processing, then there is every reason to suppose that the local syntactic ambiguities that abound in natural-language sentences may be resolved by taking into account the appropriateness to the context of utterance of those interpretations, even when the rival analyses are incomplete. Indeed, the possibility that human language processors are able to draw on the full power of their inferential mechanism to resolve ambiguities seems to offer the only possible explanation of the fact that human languages tolerate such an astonishing profusion of local and global ambiguities, and of the fact that human language users are so rarely aware of them.

The "Strong Competence Hypothesis" of Bresnan and Kaplan (Bresnan 1982) embodies the attractive assumption that rules of natural grammar may be expected to correspond directly to the steps that a processor goes through in assembling a given analysis. Under this hypothesis, the only additional components of a processor besides the grammar itself are a mechanism for building interpretable structures according to the rules of the grammar, and a mechanism for coping with local and global ambiguities as to *which* rule of the grammar to apply (that is, a mechanism for deciding which analysis or analyses to pursue at any give point in a sentence). The property that the Strong Competence Hypothesis postulates is, of course, not a necessary property for a language processor, as Berwick and Weinberg (1983) have pointed out, although its psychological appeal is obvious.

However, when taken in conjunction with our overwhelming intuition that comprehension is incremental, it immediately leads to a paradox. Almost nothing else that we know about natural-language grammar seems to be as we would expect if the hypothesis held.

Take surface structure, for example. There is no particular problem about constructing a grammar that corresponds in this direct fashion with an incremental processor. Any left branching context-free (CF) grammar, generating trees of the form illustrated in (1), provides an example.

(1)

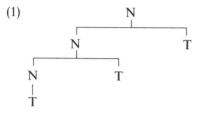

(N stands for nonterminal symbols or phrases, and T stands for terminal symbols or words.) If in addition we assume a rule-to-rule compositional semantics, then for each terminal in a left-to-right pass through the sentence, as soon as it is syntactically incorporated into a phrase, the interpretation of that phrase can be provided. And since the interpretation is complete, it may also be evaluated—for example, if the constituent is a noun or a noun phrase, then its extension or referent may be found. In contrast, a right-branching CF grammar, giving rise to trees like that in (2), does not have this property for a left-to-right processor.

(2)

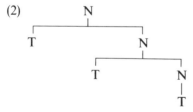

In the absence of some further apparatus going beyond rule-to-rule processing and rule-to-rule semantics, all comprehension (as opposed to purely syntactic structure-building) must wait until the end of the string, when the first complete constituent is built and can be interpreted.

If human grammars are indeed incrementally interpreted, as our intuitions suggest, and if the Strong Competence Hypothesis does indeed hold, then we might expect left-branching structures to be the norm among the languages of the world. For example, on the slightly chauvinistic assumption that many or most languages include a category of transitive verbs whose semantics defines them as first combining with objects to yield predicates which in turn combine with subjects to yield sentences, then the clause structure shown in (3) should be common.

(3)

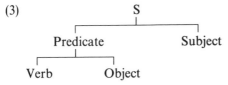

But of course, VOS languages are not at all common. Nor are OVS languages, which would have the same property. The most common order is SOV, followed closely by SVO. Neither seems as suited to incremental left-to-right interpretation under the Strong Competence Hypothesis.[2]

(4)

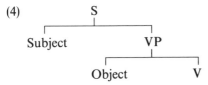

English is an obvious example of a predominantly right-branching language, apparently ill-matched under the Strong Competence Hypothesis to the manifest intuition that incremental interpretation is available to its users.

There are a number of ways out of this apparent paradox. Perhaps the easiest is to assume that the Strong Competence Hypothesis is simply wrong, and that steps in processing are not in fact related rule-to-rule with the grammar. This tactic has been popular among linguists, because it does at least leave them with a coherent research program. The competence hypothesis is no more than a heuristic device, for the questions of the psychological reality of incremental interpretation and of the nature of grammar are logically independent. Demonstrating the reality of the former could not disprove orthodox generative grammar; there is no necessity for such a relation. Processors, including incrementally interpreting ones, can be quite independent of what we think of (say on semantic grounds) as "the" syntax of a language. As Berwick and Weinberg (1983) have pointed out, compilers frequently parse programming languages according to a "covering grammar" which is quite different from the grammar that appears in the reference manual. However, in the case of human language there is a price to pay in terms of parsimony of the theory, for to abandon the Strong Competence Hypothesis is to abandon the possibility of plasticity in development. The explanatory burden is merely shifted onto the theory of acquisition, and hence (by arguments familiar from Chomsky 1968, passim) onto the theory of evolution.

A second way of escaping the paradox is to deny the validity of our intuition that incremental interpretation is available. This tactic has been widespread among experimental psychologists, who have tended, not surprisingly, to be more reluctant to abandon the attractions of the Strong Competence Hypothesis. The claim has been that the sensation of incremental interpretation is an artefact, brought about either by the extreme rapidity and predictive nature of syntactic processing itself, or by the way in which the context makes the message itself redundant, or by processes of semantic interpretation that are supposed to proceed entirely autonomously, without benefit of syntactic analysis. As a result, experiments claiming to investigate the mechanism that resolves local ambiguities during syntactic processing have neglected to control for the possibility that an important factor in this process may be incremental comprehension. This neglect is the more surprising in view of the fact that a few studies have in fact demonstrated such effects. These include Carroll et al. 1978, Tanenhaus 1978, Marslen-Wilson et al. 1978, and the experiments considered in sections 3 and 4 below.

It is less often remarked that there is a third and potentially less disadvantageous way out of the paradox: to retain the Strong Competence Hypothesis, and to continue to respect our intuitions concerning incremental semantics, but to reject the standard theories of grammar. One group who have advocated a move of this kind are the Lexical-Functional Grammarians (Bresnan 1982—cf. Steedman 1985b), who coined the term "competence hypothesis" and who claim that the unification component of their theory is capable of incremental semantics. Another theory of grammar that is claimed to be directly compatible with incrementation is put forward in Ades and Steedman 1982 and in Steedman 1985a, 1987a, and 1988. The theory consists in an augmentation or extension of the Categorial Grammars of Ajdukiewicz (1935), by including rules of grammar corresponding to the "combinators" used by Curry and Feys (1958) to define the foundations of all applicative systems, including the λ calculus.

Combinatory Grammar fragments have been developed for a number of notoriously problematic constructions involving single and multiple unbounded dependencies and coordinate constructions in more than one language. One interesting consequence of the theory lies in its radical implications for the concept of surface structure (Steedman 1985a, pp. 538–540), which it implies can be analyzed as predominantly *left*-branching. It also allows an appropriate semantic interpretation to be compositionally assigned to each of the nonstandard constituents that result. It is thus directly compatible with incremental comprehension under the Strong Competence Hypothesis.

Section 1 of the present chapter sketches the combinatory theory of grammar, concentrating on its relation to incrementally interpretative processing and referring the reader elsewhere for detailed linguistic argumentation and language-specific details. This is followed by a review of an experimental paradigm that has been claimed to support the view that human sentence processing is "knowledge-rich" and that it draws on the results of incremental comprehension to resolve local ambiguities during parsing, in contrast to the "knowledge-free" structural techniques that have usually been proposed. This paradigm is then used to illustrate in some detail the various possible architectures for incremental and interactive sentence processors. The chapter concludes that there is really only one such architecture that is theoretically, empirically, and computationally reasonable. This architecture is of a kind called "parallel weakly interactive," and it conforms strictly to the modularity hypothesis of Fodor (1983).

1 Combinatory Grammars

Applicative systems define the notion of the *application* of a function to an argument and the notion of the *abstraction*, or definition, of a function. The idea of a function is akin to the everyday notion of a "concept," and natural-language semantics could hardly be any less than a system in which concepts can be applied and new concepts defined. Many natural-language constructions are strongly reminiscent of abstractions. For example, the relation of the "topicalized" sentence (a) in (5) to the canonical sentence (b) is both semantically and structurally similar (apart from the order of function and argument) to the application of a λ expression to an argument in (c) to yield (d):

(5) a. Harry, I know you like!

    b. I know you like Harry

    c. $\lambda x[\text{know}'(\text{like}' \text{ x you}')I']$ Harry

    d.   know$'($like$'$ Harry$'$ you$')$ I$'$

However, the absence in (a) of any explicit linguistic realization of a variable binding operator like λ or a bound variable like x in (c) makes it interesting to ask whether some less familiar variety of applicative system might bear a more direct relation to natural language than the λ calculus. Such a system offers the interesting possibility that we might thereby explain the notorious "constraints" on the unbounded dependencies or "extractions" illustrated by sentence (a) above, and the related idiosyncracies of coordinate constructions. The interest of Curry and Fey's (1958) work in this connection is that their combinators allow the definition of applicative systems using operations that are entirely local and operate on adjacent entities, entirely without the use of bound variables.[3]

Categorial Grammar

Categorial grammars consist of two components. The first is a categorial lexicon, which associates each word of the language with at least one syntactic and semantic *category*. This category distinguishes between elements like verbs, which are syntactically and semantically *functions*, and elements like NPs and PPs, which are syntactically and semantically their *arguments*. The second component is a set of rules for *combining* functions and arguments, which are here called *combinatory rules* because of their close relation to Curry's combinatory logic. In the "pure" categorial grammar of Bar Hillel (1953), this component was restricted to rules of functional application, and it made the grammar context-free, equivalent to more familiar phrase-structure grammars. Later versions, starting with those of Lambek (1958, 1961) and Geach (1972), have included more abstruse combinatory operations (see Steedman 1987a for a more detailed bibliography). Many of these extensions conform to the following limiting principle, as does the original operation of functional application:

(6) Principle of Adjacency:
    Combinatory rules may only apply to entities that are linguistically realized and adjacent.

This principle embodies the central assumption of the present theory. It expressly excludes the postulation of "empty" categories, and it embodies a very strong form of localism. We are thereby already committed to some class of combinators. Unbounded operations, such as abstraction operators, movement, and coindexing, are excluded under the Principle of Adjacency.

The Categorial Lexicon

Some syntactic categories (such as nouns) which are naturally thought of as arguments, bear straightforward categories such as N. Others (like verbs) are naturally thought of as functors. In the present theory, functions that combine with arguments to their right bear a category of the form X/Y, denoting a rightward-combining function from category Y into category X. For example, determiners are NP/N and transitive verbs are VP/NP.

Other functions that combine with their arguments to the left are distinguished by the use of a backward slash, and bear categories of the form $X \backslash Y$, denoting a leftward-combining function from Y into X.[4] For example, VP-adverbial phrases, such as quickly, bear the category $VP \backslash VP$, and predicate phrases, such as *arrived*, bear the category $S \backslash NP$.[5]

Both types of function may of course have more than one argument, and may mix the two types of slashes, combining with different arguments in different directions. However, all function categories are unary or "curried." For example, the ditransitive verb *give* will bear the category $(VP/NP)/NP$— a (rightward-combining) function from (indirect) objects into (rightward-combining) functions from (direct) objects into VPs. This restriction has no great significance. Unary nth-order curried functions are equivalent to n-ary first-order functions, as was first noted by Schönfinkel (1924). Where convenient, I shall assume this equivalence without comment, referring to a function like $(VP/NP)/NP$ as "binary" and to VP as its "range."

The categories of all expressions, including the lexical categories, conform to the following principle, which embodies an assumption of the strongest possible "type-driven" relationship between syntax and semantics (cf. Klein and Sag 1985):

(3) Principle of Transparency:
    The information in the syntactic type of an expression includes the
    information in its semantic type.

In other words, if an expression bears the syntactic category of a function from objects of syntactic type α into those of type β, then it is also semantically a function over the corresponding semantic types. The syntactic type will also of course determine a number of additional factors, such as linear order and agreement, which are not represented semantically. Such categories can be represented by a single data structure uniting syntactic type and semantic interpretation in unification-based implementations like those of Zeevat, Klein, and Calder (1986), Pareschi and Steedman (1987), and Pareschi (in preparation). (See Karttunen 1986, Uszkoreit 1986, Shieber 1986, and Wittenburg 1986 for related approaches.) However, the principle embodies some strong assumptions about the nature of semantic representations in the present grammar. For example, if we wanted to follow Montague in accounting for ambiguities of quantifier scope by changing the type of NP arguments into functions, then we would probably have to do it at some other level of semantic representation. (See Kang 1988 for an interesting discussion of this point.)

The combinatory rules govern the combination of function categories with other adjacent categories to yield new categories conforming to the above principle. The simplest such rules are the ones that apply a function to an argument.

Functional Application

Because of the assumption enshrined above in the Principle of Transparency, we can write the syntactic and semantic combinatory rules as one, associating each syntactic category in a rule with the semantic interpretation that it transparently reflects. Indeed, the only point of distinguishing the two at all is to make explicit the relation that the interpretation of the result bears to that of the inputs. The following obvious rules are required:

(8) a. $X/Y{:}F \ Y{:}y \Rightarrow X{:}Fy \quad (>)$

    b. $Y{:}y \ X\backslash Y{:}F \Rightarrow X{:}Fy \quad (<)$

In this and the other combinatory rules that follow, X and Y are variables that range over any category, including functions, so X/Y is any rightward-combining function and $X\backslash Y$ is any leftward-combining function. Uppercase F, G, etc. are used for the interpretations of functions; lower-case x, y, etc. are used for the interpretations of arguments. The application of a function F to an argument x is represented by left-to-right order; e.g., Fx. Semantic interpretations appear to the right of the syntactic category that identifies their type, separated by a colon.

The first of these rules, called Forward Application, allows rightward-combining functions such as transitive verbs to combine with arguments to their right. Its application in a derivation is indicated by underlining the operands and indexing the underline with the symbol $>$. The second instance of the rule of functional application allows a leftward-combining function to combine with an argument to its left, and is indicated in derivations by an underline indexed by $<$. Both rules determine the interpretation of the result, whose type is written underneath. It seems natural to assume that tensed verb phrases bear the category $S\backslash NP$, so that tensed transitive verbs such as *eat* are $(S\backslash NP)/NP$, ditransitives are $((S\backslash NP)/NP)/NP$, and so on, giving rise to derivations like the following:

(9) Harry   eats   apples
    -----   ----------   ------
     NP   (S\NP)/NP   NP
           ----------------->
                  S\NP
           ----------------------<
                   S

This derivation assigns an interpretation of type S, which we might write as eat' apples' harry', where functional application "associates to the left," so that the result is equivalent to ((eat' apples') harry'). It is the interpretation of the verb, eat', that determines the grammatical relations of the first argument (harry') and the second (apples') as subject and object, respectively.[6]

The above two rules are the only two rules of functional application that the theory allows. In particular, application of a function to an argument is by definition subject to their left-to-right order being consistent with the directionality of the function, because that is what the slashes mean. Obvious though this restriction is, it will be useful to enshrine it under the title of the principle of Directional Consistency, as follows:

(10) Principle of Directional Consistency:
    All syntactic combinatory rules must be consistent with the
    directionality of the principal function.

The "principal" function is the one whose range is the same as the range of the result. (Since there is only one function concerned in functional application, the adjective is redundant in the case at hand.)

The above principle is not a stipulation, for it could be shown to follow from the semantics of the metalanguage in which the grammar is couched. Informally, directionality is a property of the argument of a function. The direction of a slash on a particular argument of a function denotes the relative position of the entity with which it may combine. The consistent rules are limited by the categories themselves.

Combinators, Right Node-Raising, and Leftward Extraction
The two central problems for any theory of natural-language grammar are posed by "deletions" and "extractions" in coordinate and other constructions, exemplified in (11).

(11) a. [I know Harry will cook] and [I think Betty might eat] the
        mushrooms we picked in the dank meadows behind the Grange.
    b. These mushrooms, I think Betty might eat.

Both constructions appear to separate elements like objects and verbs which belong together in semantics. Both may separate them by unbounded amounts, including clause boundaries. They therefore appear to force us to abandon simple assumptions like the Principle of Adjacency (3), or the assumption that rules of grammar should apply to constituents. According to the present theory, however, both of these phenomena can be explained without abandoning either assumption, under some simple extensions to the combinatory rules and a consequent extension of the concept of a constituent to include entities corresponding to strings like *might eat* and *I think Betty might eat.*

Coordination

Coordination can be accommodated in a categorial grammar using the following syncategorematic schema, inherited from Dougherty (1970) via Gazdar (1981), which can be paraphrased as "Conjoin like categories." [7] For the present purposes, the semantics of the rule can be ignored, except to note that it is obtained from that of the conjuncts by applying some functional Φ to the notoriously problematic interpretation of the conjunction (here written as "&") and the conjuncts themselves:

(12) Coordination:
$$\text{X:F conj X:G} \Rightarrow \text{X:}\Phi\text{\&FG}$$

Using such a rule schema, transitive verbs could coordinate as follows:[8]

```
(13)   I     cooked     and      ate      the beans
       ---   ----------  ----   ---------  ---------
       NP  (S\NP)/NP  çonj (S\NP)/NP    NP
           ----------------------- coord
                  (S\NP)/NP
                  -------------------->
                       S\NP
           ------------------------------<
                        S
```

Functional Composition

The following sentence will block in a pure categorial grammar:

```
(14)   I    will    cook   and    might    eat    the mushrooms we picked
       ---  ---------- ------ ----  --------- ------- ----------------------
       NP (S\NP)/VP VP/NP conj (S\NP)/VP VP/NP              NP
```

Functional application will not help us here, but the earlier papers propose a comparably simple rule that will. It is the following (we will ignore the question of how the interpretations are related for the moment, and just treat it as a rule relating syntactic/semantic categorial types):

(15) Forward Functional Composition
$$\text{X/Y Y/Z} \Rightarrow \text{X/Z}$$

This rule, which has the appearance of the "cancellation" rule of fractional multiplication, for reasons that will be apparent directly, will be indexed " $> \mathbf{B}$ ". It allows the following derivation for the coordinate sentence (14):

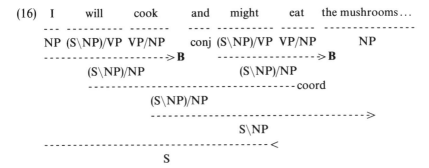

The categories of the adjacent functors $will_{(S\backslash NP)/VP}$ and $cook_{VP/NP}$ match the rule, as do the parallel categories *might* and *eat*. The result has the same type—$(S\backslash NP)/NP$—as the transitive verb in (9), so the rest of the derivation is the same as the earlier one.

Semantically, this rule is almost as simple as functional application. It is, in fact, functional *composition*. The combinator that composes two functions F and G was called **B** by Curry, and can be defined by the following equivalence:

(17) **B**FGx = F(Gx).

A convention that application associates to the left is again followed, so that the left-hand side is equivalent to ((**B**F)G)x. It follows that we can consider the application of **B** to F and G as producing a new function equivalent to abstracting on x in the above expression, thus:

(18) **B**FG = [x]F(Gx).

(Curry's "bracket abstraction" notation "[x] ⟨expression⟩" means much the same as the λ notation λx ⟨expression⟩. It is used here to remind us that the combinators are the primitives, not the abstraction operator.) We can therefore write the forward composition rule more completely as follows:

(19) Forward Functional Composition
   X/Y:F Y/Z:G ⇒ X/Z:**B**FG

The fact that semantics of the rule is functional composition ensures that the interpretation of the result will be the one we want.[9] The fact that composition is an *associative* operation ensures that such will be the case for any order of composition of the component functions.

Repeated application of Forward Composition to the verb sequences in examples like (20) will allow coordination of indefinitely long strings of verbs, on the assumption that each is a function over the result of the one to its right.

(20) She [may have seemed to have wanted to meet,]$_{(S \backslash NP)/NP}$ but
      [actually turned out to dislike,]$_{(S \backslash NP)/NP}$ the man you brought to
      the party at Harry's

On the other hand, violations of the "across the board" condition on right node-raising and all other movement out of coordinate structures are still disallowed as a consequence of the composition mechanism and the assumption that coordination is an operation on adjacent constituents of like type. Thus, sentence 21 is not accepted, because $(S \backslash NP)/NP$ and $S \backslash NP$ are not of the same category.

(21) * I   will cook   and   might eat beans   potatoes
         ---- ----------   ----   --------------   --------
         NP   (S\NP)/NP   conj   S\NP   NP
               ----------------------------------*

From what general class of rules is the Forward Composition rule chosen? For the purpose of answering this question, it will be convenient to distinguish the two functions F and G in the above example as the "principal" and the "subsidiary" function, respectively. Like the rule of Functional Application (8), this rule is subject to the Principle of Directional Consistency (10): The subsidiary function must occur to whichever side is consistent with the slash on the principal function. The rule is also subject to a less obvious principle, which is claimed in Steedman 1987 to limit all combinatory rules in Universal Grammar that produce a function as their output, as follows[10]:

(22) Principle of Directional Inheritance:
      If the category that results from the application of a combinatory
      rule is a function category, then the slash defining directionality for
      a given argument in that category will be the same as the one
      defining directionality for the corresponding argument(s) in the
      input function(s).

(There is only one argument of the function that results from composition, and it is only inherited from one input function, so we can ignore the plural possibilities for the present purposes.)

The functional composition rule therefore potentially gives rise to four instances, distinguished by the left-to-right order and directionality of the principal and subsidiary functions, as follows:

(23) a. $X/Y{:}F$ $Y/Z{:}G \Rightarrow X/Z{:}BFG$ $(>\mathbf{B})$

   b. $X/Y{:}F$ $Y\backslash Z{:}G \Rightarrow X\backslash Z{:}BFG$ $(>\mathbf{B}x)$

   c. $Y\backslash Z{:}G$ $X\backslash Y{:}F \Rightarrow X\backslash Z{:}BFG$ $(<\mathbf{B})$

   d. $Y/Z{:}G$ $X\backslash Y{:}F \Rightarrow X/Z{:}BFG$ $(<\mathbf{B}x)$

As with all combinatory rules, natural languages are free to include rules on any of the four patterns, to restrict variables in any given rule to certain categories (such as S or maximal categories), or even to entirely exclude some of them. All four rules have been used to account for various phenomena in English.[11]

Type-Raising

The following examples require more than functional composition alone:

(24) a. [I will cook] and [Betty may eat] the mushrooms we picked in the dismal glens above the Grange.

   b. [I think I will cook] and [you think that Betty may eat] the mushrooms etc.

The problem with examples like these is that the subject(s) cannot combine with the tensed verb(s) or the composed verb group(s), whose categories dictate that they have to combine with something else first:

(25)   I   will   cook   ...
   --- ---------- ------
   NP (S\NP)/VP VP/NP
       ----------------->**B**
          (S\NP)/NP
   --------------------*

Functional composition alone does not help—composition is for combining *functions*, not arguments. However, there is an operation of "type-raising," which is widely used in the Montague Grammar literature to map arguments (such as subjects) into functions over functions-that-take-such-arguments (such as predicates).[12] Type raising is indexed $\mathbf{C}_*$, for reasons given below, and the instance of the rule that is relevant here is the following "forward" version:

(26) Subject Type-raising:

   $NP \Rightarrow S/(S\backslash NP)$ $(>\mathbf{C}_*)$

It will permit the following derivation for (25):

(27)   I   will   cook and Betty   might   eat   the mushrooms ...

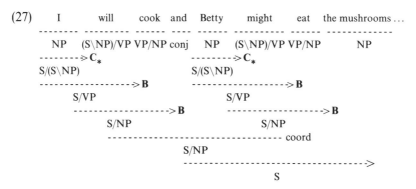

The subject NP in the example raises into the category $S/(S\backslash NP)$. This category can, in turn, compose with the verb by the standard forward composition rule. Further iteration of composition and application completes the derivation. No other raised category for the subject NP will allow this or any other derivation. The more complex unbounded across-the-board right node-raised example (24b) is accepted in a parallel manner, since the embedded subjects can also raise under the rule, and repeated composition can again assemble two constituents of type S/NP. However, violations of the across-the-board condition are still not permitted, because the grammar does not yield categories of like type:

(28)   *[I will cook]$_{S/NP}$ and [Betty might eat potatoes]$_S$
      [the mushrooms ...]$_{NP}$

Even across-the-board extraction may not combine subject and object extraction, for the same reason:

(29)   *[I will meet]$_{S/NP}$ and [will marry Mary]$_{S\backslash NP}$ [your best friend]$_{NP}$

And of course, the following example is excluded, because only adjacent categories can coordinate:

(30)   *[I will cook]$_{S/NP}$ [the mushrooms]$_{NP}$ and [Betty will eat]$_{S/NP}$

Like composition, the type-raising rules have a simple and invariant semantics. The semantics corresponds to another of Curry's basic combinators, called C_*, defined by the following equivalence:

(31) $C_* xF = Fx$.

It follows that C_* applies to an argument creates the following abstraction over the function (again, Curry's "bracket abstraction" notation is used):

(32) $C_* x = [F]Fx$.

Type raising is here assumed to be subject in English to a "direction-preserving" property proposed by Dowty, such that arguments may only raise into *rightward*-looking functions over leftward-looking ones, or into *leftward*-looking functions over rightward ones. (I assume that this restriction would follow from a formal statement of the Principles of Inheritance and Consistency.) There are therefore just two possible direction-preserving type-raising rules, of which (26) is one special case, and which can be written as follows:

(33) Direction-preserving Type-raising

  a. $X{:}x \Rightarrow \Sigma/(\Sigma\backslash X){:}\mathbf{C}_* x \quad (> \mathbf{C}_*)$

  b. $X{:}x \Rightarrow \Sigma\backslash(\Sigma/X){:}\mathbf{C}_* x \quad (< \mathbf{C}_*)$

The rule uses a polymorphic type variable Σ, and must be restricted, if only for the purposes of the parser. I shall assume for the present purpose that X must be the sort of thing that is subcategorised for by a verb, and that the functions that X raises over are (finite, nonfinite, participial, or whatever) *verbs*—that is, functions of any arity into (finite, nonfinite, participial, etc.) S.[13] In derivations, the variable Σ will be expanded to the category that instantiates it, as in (27).

Nonstandard Constituent Coordination

As is pointed out in Steedman 1985a and in Dowty 1988, Combinatory Grammars offer an account not only of coordinations of verb groups but also of the "nonconstituent" coordination of sequences of arguments, because arguments are allowed to type-raise into functions, and then to compose, as in the following example, adapted from Dowty:

(34)

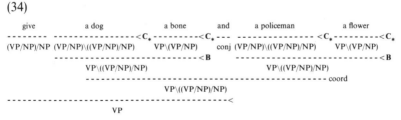

While this derivation invokes the second instance, $< \mathbf{C}_*$, of type-raising, and another instance, $< \mathbf{B}$, of composition, the constraints of Adjacency, Consistency, and Inheritance will not permit rules that would allow the following examples to yield the same interpretation:

(35) a. #Give a bone a dog and a flower a policemen

b. *A policemen a flower and give a dog a bone

Dowty points out that a combinatory grammar also allows such right node-raised nonstandard constituents to "strand" prepositions, just as standard constituent coordinates can, as in (36).

(36)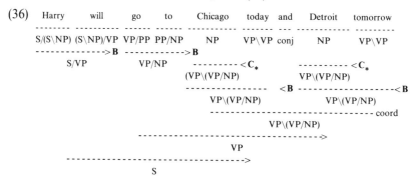

Dowty also points out that the acceptability of such strandings appears to be precisely parallel to island constraints on leftward extraction, as would be predicted on the present model, in which both rightward and leftward extraction depend on the possibility of assembling the residue into a single entity via the composition rule.

Leftward Extraction

The two combinatory syntactic rules of functional composition and type raising provide almost all that we need in order to solve the second problem exemplified in example (11) namely that of leftward extraction in *wh*-movement constructions. Thus, in example 37 the subject NP can again raise over the predicate category, and iterated composition can again assemble the subject and all the verbs in the entire sequence *Harry must have been eating* to compose into a single function.

(37)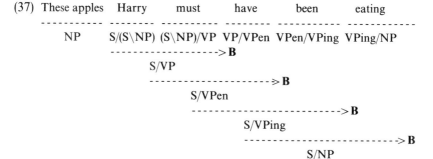

The important result is that the entire clause has been assembled into a single function adjacent to the extracted argument. Technically, this function still cannot combine, because the directionality of the slash forbids it. There are a number of ways of handling this detail in a manner consistent with the Principle of Adjacency, and we will pass over the matter here.[14]

The rules of functional composition and type-raising provide a general mechanism for unbounded extraction. On the assumption that one category for the tensed verb *believe* is (S\NP)/S′, and that the complementizer *that* is S′/S, repeated application of the forward composition rule allows extractions across clause boundaries:

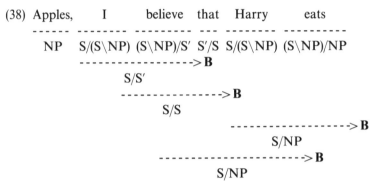

(38) Apples,   I   believe   that   Harry   eats

       NP   S/(S\NP) (S\NP)/S′ S′/S S/(S\NP) (S\NP)/NP

                  --------------->**B**

             S/S′

            --------------->**B**

             S/S

                        --------------->**B**

                       S/NP

             --------------------->**B**

                S/NP

The corresponding subject extractions can be excluded on the assumption that the slash-crossing instance > **B**x of forward composition is excluded from English, thus capturing the Fixed Subject Constraint or *that*-trace filter of Bresnan (1972) and Chomsky and Lasnik (1977) and excluding sentences like (39) from English.

(39) *Harry, I believe that eats apples.

Other parametrically related properties of English, in particular its fixed word order, depend upon the exclusion of this rule (Steedman 1987a). The possibility of exceptional subject extraction in examples like (40)

(40) Harry, I believe eats apples

is captured by assigning a special lexical category to bare-complement verbs like *believe* (Steedman 1987a, section 3.2.2). Once again, such details are passed over here.

At this point, the question naturally arises whether any other combinatory operations than these two are implicated in natural-language grammars. The construction in (41) is of a type that Taraldsen (1979) and Engdahl (1981, 1983) have talked of as including a "parasitic" gap or empty category.

(41) (articles) which I will file _ without reading _ₚ

The important properties of the sentence are that it has more than one gap corresponding to a single extracted item (*which articles*) and that one of these gaps (indicated by subscript p) is in a position from which extraction would not normally be allowed. In Steedman 1987a it is proposed to accommodate this construction by including rules corresponding to one more of Curry's combinators, the one he called S. The possible rules are again correctly limited by the principles of Consistency and Inheritance. The implications of such rules for the grammar of English are explored more fully there.

2   Syntactic Processing and Incremental Interpretation in Combinatory Grammar

The introduction of functional composition and other combinatory rules into the grammar has radical implications for the concept of surface structure, and for syntactic processing. Most important, in return for a simple account of coordination, we are forced to conclude that the surface syntax of natural sentences is much more ambiguous than under traditional accounts. It will be recalled that many strings that in classical terms would not be regarded as constituents have that status in the present grammar. For example, the unbounded extraction in example 38 implies that the surface structure of the sentence "Those cakes I can believe that she will eat" includes constituents corresponding to the substrings *I can, I can believe, I can believe that, I can believe that she, I can believe that she will,* and *I can believe that she will eat.* In fact, since there are other possible sequences of application and composition that will accept the sentence, the theory implies that such sequences as *can believe that she will eat, believe that she will eat, that she will eat, she will eat,* and *will eat* may also on occasion be constituents. Since these constituents are defined in the grammar, it necessarily follows that the surface structure of the canonical "I can believe she will eat those cakes" may also include them, so that (42) represents only one of several possible surface-structure alternatives to the orthodox right-branching tree:

(42)

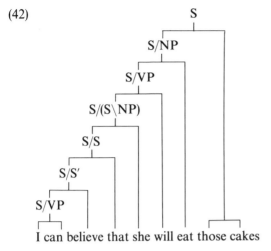

I can believe that she will eat those cakes

The proliferation of possible analyses that is induced by the inclusion of function composition seems at first glance to have disastrous implications for processing efficiency, because it introduces an explosion of what Wittenburg (1986) has called "spurious" ambiguities—that is, of alternative surface analyses that do not differ in interpretation. I will pass over this problem, noting that Pareschi (forthcoming) and Pareschi and Steedman (1987) argue that an efficient solution to this problem is offered by two properties of combinatory categorial grammar. The properties in question are the *associativity* of functional composition and the *procedural neutrality* of combinatory rules. The first property means that, as already noted, all these derivations yield identical results. The second property means that the constituents of any derivation can be directly recovered from the interpretation that results from any other derivation in the same equivalence class of "spuriously ambiguous" derivations. These properties suggest that unification-based parsers can thereby cope with both "spurious" and genuine attachment ambiguities with a uniform chart-based apparatus with no significant additional overheads to those engendered by more traditional grammars.

It is more important for present purposes to note that the effect of the Functional Composition rule has been to convert the right-branching structure that would result from simple functional application of the categories in the above example into a *left*-branching structure. It was remarked in the introduction that left branching allows incremental interpretation of sentences by left-to-right rule-to-rule processors under the Strong Competence Hypothesis. In the example, such a processor could, as it encountered each word of the sentence, build a single constituent corresponding to the prior string up to that point. And since the composition rule corresponds to semantic as well as syntactic composition, each of these constituents can immediately be interpreted. Indeed, as the earlier papers point out, there is no reason for any autonomous syntactic representation, as distinct from the interpretation itself, to be built at all.[15] And if such fragments can be interpreted, then the results of evaluating them with respect to the context can be used to resolve local syntactic ambiguities. Thus, combinatory grammars seem to offer to formalism for natural-language grammar that is directly compatible with such processing, under the Strong Competence Hypothesis, without the addition of any extra apparatus.

Adopting the weak version of the interaction hypothesis, in turn, suggests a variety of processing strategies that will reduce the proliferation of semantically equivalent analyses induced by the combinatory rules. For example, in an implementation of the present grammars as "shift and reduce" parsers (Ades and Steedman 1982), a (nondeterministic) "reduce first" strategy will tend to produce left-branching derivations of the kind illustrated above. Such derivations have the property that, at any given point in the left-to-right pass of the processor, an interpretation for each analysis for the entire prior string is produced, which can then be evaluated with respect to the context (Steedman 1985a, p. 539). Moreover, this reduce-first strategy, by choosing the left-branching analyses that are permitted by the combinatory grammar over the right-branching ones that are proposed under traditional accounts of surface grammar, has the further desirable property of minimizing the depth of the shift-reduce processor's stack, thus countering Kimball's (1973) and Frazier and Fodor's (1978) objections to bottom-up parsing. Such strategies are under investigation by Pareschi (forthcoming) and Haddock (1986, 1987, forthcoming).

3 Evidence for Incremental Semantics and Interactive Processing

There is a well-established psycholinguistic tradition of accounting for the resolution of local syntactic ambiguities by purely structural criteria, rather than by any appeal to semantics. Much of this work can be summarized as having identified two main families of structural criteria. The first is a criterion that amounts to choosing the analysis that produces fewest nodes. For example, the VP *see the boy with a telescope* has (given some assumptions about constituent structure) the following two analyses, because of the ambiguity of the PP *with a telescope* between a VP argument and a Chomsky-adjoined NP modifier:

(43) a.

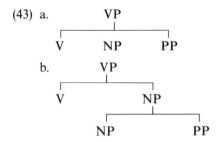

b.

Under a criterion that has been most succinctly defined by Frazier (1978) under the name "Minimal Attachment," analysis (a) is supposedly preferred to (b) by the human sentence-processing mechanism, because it has one fewer node.[16]

The second strategy applies to the case where a category such as a VP modifier could attach to more than one VP in the sentence structure, as in the ambiguous VP *say Harry died last Saturday*, where the unambiguous adverbial modifier *last Saturday* could modify the saying or the dying:

(44) a.

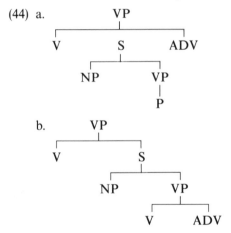

b.

The two analyses do not differ in complexity, but there is general agreement that the preferred reading is for the dying to have occurred last Saturday— that is, for attachment as low down and far to the right of the structure as possible, an observation variously enshrined in strategies of "right association" (Kimball 1973), "late closure" (Frazier 1978), and "final arguments" (Ford et al. 1982).

The unacceptable effect of sentences like

(45) The horse raced past the barn fell

is commonly attributed to purely structural properties of the two structures that are locally possible at the word *raced*, arising from its ambiguity between a transitive verb and a past-participial NP modifier, coupled with a limit on human ability to recover from the ensuing "garden path" (Bever 1970; Kimball 1973; Frazier 1978). The preference for the garden-path-inducing VP reading of the substring *raced past the barn* over the non-garden-pathing participial-phrase reading is argued by these authors to arise from one or other of the "Minimal Attachment" strategies.

It has always been known that semantics can on occasion override such effects. Bever himself noted that the garden-path effect in (46) could be overridden by sense-semantic effects arising from the involvement of different kinds of arguments, as in (47):

(46) The authors read in the garden stank

(47) The articles read in the garden stank

It is important to be clear from the start that this purely sense-semantic effect turns out to be comparitively weak; Crain (1980), reported in Crain and Steedman 1985, found a rather slight effect of lexical materials, and Rayner, Carlson, and Frazier (1983) found no effect.

However, the weakness of the sense-semantic effect should not be taken to imply a similar ineffectiveness for all effects of meaning and context upon sentence processing. Crain and Steedman (1985) pointed out that complex NPs differ from simple ones not only in structural complexity but also in presuppositional complexity—that is, in the assumptions that they embody concerning the entities that are established in the context of utterance, and by virtue of which the NPs actually refer.[17] In particular, postmodifiers (such as participial phrases, prepositional phrases, and restrictive relative clauses) all presuppose that there is a *set* of entities of the type denoted by the head noun, which the modifier restricts.

A second experiment (Crain 1980, reported in Crain and Steedman 1985) will help to make the point. Consider the following pair of sentences:

(48) a. Complement Target Sentence:
          The psychologist told the wife that he was having trouble with *her husband.*

      b. Modifier Target Sentence:
          The psychologist told the wife that he was having trouble with *to leave her husband.*

Each of these sentences contains a local ambiguity at the word *that* between an analysis of the following string as a complement clause, as in (a), or as a relative clause, as in (b). In the "neutral" or "null" context, readers resolve the ambiguity in favor of the complement analysis, so that version (b), which demands the relative-clause analysis, engenders a garden-path effect. Frazier has argued that this garden path is a consequence of the Minimal Attachment strategy, just as the earler *horse raced* examples are. However, the use of a restrictive relative clause modifier in (b) presupposes that there is more than one wife in the context of discourse, and that one of these wives is distinguished by being troublesome to the psychologist.[18] By contrast, the absence of a modifier in (a) presupposes that just one wife is established in the context of discourse. Crain argued that if incremental comprehension were indeed characteristic of human processors, then a context supporting the presuppositions of either the simple or the complex NP analyses of the locally ambiguous substrings in the earlier examples could make the processor favor that analysis, overriding the classic garden-path effect or creating novel garden paths where there were none before. Moreover, he argued, the fact that the so-called null context supports the presuppositions of neither analysis did not mean that it would be neutral with respect to the two analyses.

To demonstrate that garden-path effects could be controlled by referential context, Crain preceded the presentation of "complement" and "modifier" target sentences like (48a) and (48b) above with contexts that supported the presuppositions of the respective analyses. For the "psychologist" sentences, such contexts were the following:

(49) a. Complement-supporting context:
     A psychologist was counseling a married couple. One member of the pair was fighting with him but the other one was nice to him.

   b. Modifier-supporting context:
     A psychologist was counselling two married couples. One of the couples was fighting with him but the other one was nice to him.

These contexts were claimed by Crain to constitute a minimal pair, differing only in the number of participants, and in particular in the number of wives that could be inferred to be involved. The first of these contexts supports the presupposition of sentence 48a that there is one wife in the context, and therefore demands the complement-clause analysis. It fails to support the presuppositions of the relative sentence 48b that there are several wives under discussion. If the classic garden-path effect is under the control of context, then that effect should be unaffected or even exacerbated. By contrast, the second of these contexts supports the presuppositions of the relative-clause sentence 48b and denies those of the complement-clause target 48a. On the same assumption, this second context should therefore reduce or even eliminate the classic garden-path effect. The two types of contexts illustrated in (49) can be crossed with the corresponding pairs of target sentences illustrated in (48) to yield four conditions: complement-supporting context, complement target (CC); complement-supporting context, modifier target (CM); modifier-supporting context, modifier target (MM); and modifier-supporting, complement target (MC). The prediction is that the "crossed" conditions CM and MC should engender garden paths, whereas the "uncrossed" conditions CC and MM should not. Although some details of Crain's actual experiment have been criticized by Altmann, a number of experimental studies on a pattern closely related to the above (Crain 1980; Crain and Steedman 1985; Altmann 1986, 1987; Altmann and Steedman 1988), using either grammaticality judgments (Crain), global reading times, or subject-paced reading times (Altmann), show the effect of context on local syntactic attachment ambiguities of the kind whose processing characteristics have been claimed to support Minimal Attachment and related structural strategies. Crain's and Altmann's experiments have used a wide variety of presuppositionally loaded grammatical parameters and constructions, including definiteness (Crain), participial modifiers (Crain), restrictive relatives (Crain, Altmann) and prepositional-phrase post-modifiers (Altmann).

Ferreira and Clifton (1986) have claimed that Crain's result does not appear when a measure more related to on-line processing, namely eye movements, is used. They claim that Crain's and Altmann's results arise from *post hoc* reanalysis, an argument which is criticized at length on theoretical grounds in section 4 below. The materials and methods of Ferreira's study have been criticized by Altmann and Steedman (1988), on the grounds that their materials do not constitute minimal pairs of contexts and targets. An experiment controlling for these factors and using subject-paced phrasal reading time as an on-line measure is reported by Altmann and Steedman (1988, expt. II). This experiment replicates the earlier results in all relevant respects, and shows that there is a substantial effect of context on reading time within the critical phrase. Indeed, this experiment suggests that, once the materials and the context are properly controlled, any residual effect is in the direction opposite to that predicted by the minimal-attachment hypothesis.

Crain and Steedman proposed a mechanism for such context-based decisions of local syntactic ambiguities that invoked a "Principle of Referential Success," according to which successfully referring analyses were to be selected in favor of unsuccessful ones. Altmann (1986, p. 201) and Altmann and Steedman (1988) have reformulated this principle in terms of partial NP analyses and the failure of their presuppositions in an incremental constraint-satisfaction model suggested by Haddock (1987). The principle can be defined informally as follows:

(50) Principle of Referential Support:
A (possibly incomplete) NP analysis whose referential presuppositions are supported by the context will be favored over one whose referential presuppositions are not supported by the context.

We will return to the important question of how such processors might actually be organized, and to what architectures are possible or sensible for them. It is more important for the moment to note that this proposal also has implications for the processing of such sentences in the so-called null context, typical of the psycholinguistic sentence-processing experiment, in which no analysis refers. We have been very vague so far about what exactly we mean by saying that a referent or set of referents is present in the context. But it clearly means much more than mere prior presence or representation of the entities in question in some model which we may think of as some variety of propositional database in the hearer's mind, to which expressions refer anaphorically. We often encounter definite referring expressions whose referents are not previously established in the recipients mind—for example, in fictions such as novels, or in intensional contexts as in (51).

(51) Did you see *the man who just walked past the window*?

Such definites refer to entities which the speaker regards as established. But for the hearer they may or may not be so. If they are not, then the hearer must introduce appropriate representations in their database. If a referring expression not only denotes a novel entity but also carries additional presuppositions which are also not yet satisfied, then the corresponding modifications must also be made.

Arguments for the Parallel Weak Interaction

Strong and Weak Interaction

According to the strong interaction hypothesis, semantics and context can "prescribe" specific courses of action to syntactic processing, actively restricting the search space within which it operates—say, by affecting the order in which rules of grammar are to be tried, or even by entirely excluding some of them.

The weak version of the interaction hypothesis is much more restrictive. According to this version, syntax autonomously "proposes" analyses, whereas semantics and context merely "dispose" among the alternatives that it offers. The only interaction that is allowed is that interpretative processes may deliver judgment on the contextual appropriateness of the alternatives that are proposed by syntax, causing it to abandon some and continue with others. Some authors have since preferred to talk of "instructive" versus "selective" interaction rather than strong versus weak, but I will continue to use the latter terms.

Crain and Steedman (1985) argue that the only coherent form of interaction is the weak or selective one, according to which the results of evaluation can suspend a line of analysis on the grounds that its interpretation is contextually inappropriate but cannot predispose syntactic processing toward any particular construction, a proposal which is tentatively endorsed by Fodor (1983, p. 78n). This is the mechanism that we were tacitly assuming when arguing that the presence in a hearer's mind of several potential referents (say several wives in Crain's example) will cause a simple NP analysis (e.g. "the wife") to be rejected in favor of a complex NP analysis ("the wife that he was having trouble with"), whereas other contexts that do not support the presuppositions of restrictive adjuncts (including the so-called "null context") will support the simple NP analysis.

It will be convenient to refer to the two uses of definite referring expressions contrasted above as "given" and "new," respectively.[19] In the traditional psycholinguistic experiment, in which sentences are presented out of context, definite expressions are by definition of the new variety. However, they still carry their presuppositions, which must be supported or accommodated by the hearer. Crain and Steedman (1985) argued that in a case of local ambiguity of this kind, it was reasonable to assume that the reading carrying fewest presuppositions, and therefore requiring fewest modifications to the database, would be favored under a "Principle of Parsimony":

(52) Principle of Parsimony:
    A reading that carries fewer unsatisfied presuppositions will be
    favored over one that carries more.

It should be obvious that the above principle subsumes the earlier criterion of Referential Support as a special case: A reading that fails to refer by definition carries more unsatisfied referential presuppositions than one that does refer, since the latter carries no such unsatisfied presuppositions.

4 Architectures for Incrementally Interpreting Interactive Processors

We can identify a number of parameters that determine possible architectures for interactive processors of the kind that are implied by these experimental accounts. The first parameter concerns the nature of the interaction itself. Crain and Steedman distinguish two versions of the interactive hypothesis, which they call the "strong" and "weak" versions. Weakly interactive processors may be further divided into "parallel" and "serial" versions. A third parameter concerns the "intimacy" (or fineness of grain) of the interaction, that is, the question of whether the comprehension process can only adjudicate over large units, such as clauses, or whether appeal can be made at each successive word. This parameter has a rather different character than its predecessors. In a processor that is consistent with the Strong Competence criterion, it is a property of the grammar rather than the processor *per se*. A fourth parameter concerns the "top-down" or "bottom-up" direction of application of the rules of the grammar. Any advantages also depend on the particular grammars that are involved.

An early proposal for incremental semantics and the weak interaction in processing was made by Winograd (1972), who proposed to allow reference to the context or the database to decide ambiguities in NP analyses in examples like (53).

(53) Put the block in the box on the table.

Winograd's actual architecture was *serially* weakly interactive. That is, syntax proposed a single analysis for the NP (actually, the program started with the longest alternative, *the block in the box*. Only if that failed to refer—perhaps because there was no block in the box—would the processor backtrack for another analysis.)

This proposal appears to have influenced the work of Bobrow and Webber (1980, 1981) on the RUS parser, although the weak interactions that they allow from semantics are strictly sense-semantic and do not involve reference at all. More specifically, they allow information about the sense-semantic type of arguments such as NPs and PPs, and a rich form of case-frame/subcategorization information associated with verbs, to interact to disambiguate verb senses and grammatical relations in an incremental fashion. However, reference plays no part in this model, although some of the problems that Bobrow and Webber propose to handle purely on the basis of sense-semantics seem to be likely to require reference.

The program of Bobrow and Webber uses sense-semantics in the form of a rich set of semantic argument types and case frames—for example, to rule out a reading of *the door* as an agent in ergative sentences like (54).

(54) The door opened.

However (Bobrow and Webber 1980), such strategies will tend to yield no reading at all for sets of sentences like (55).

(55) a. I am wearing my birthday present.

   b. I am driving my birthday present.

("Apparel-NP" and "vehicle-NP" are among their sense-semantic categories subcategorized for by verbal case-frames.) They offer a generalization based on a hierarchically structured type system for the criterion of sense-semantic compatibility in order to handle this problem (as well as a number of other cases, including pronominals and NPs like *the thing* whose sense-semantics is underspecified). But they also point out that something more is needed. The type system will still not handle certain cases of metonymy that they mention, as when a customer in a restaurant is referred to as "the hamburger". A specific domain of reference seems to be inextricably involved in such cases.

Crain and Steedman (1985) argue on metatheoretical grounds against the alternative "strong" interaction hypothesis, according to which the referential context might predispose the processor toward certain constructions. However, they note (p. 326) that, while some versions of the strong interaction hypothesis are empirically distinguishable from the weak variety, some are not. A version that says that the presence in a hearer's mind of several wives predisposes them toward complex NP analyses in general—not just *the wife that he was having trouble with* but also *the horse raced past the barn*—certainly makes a strong prediction, although it is so absurd as to be hardly worthy of experimental investigation. But a version that says that on encountering the word *wife* the presence of several referent wives "switches on" the complex NP analysis and switches off the simple one could probably not be distinguished experimentally from the alternative weak hypothesis, according to which the analyses would be developed first and then adjudicated by appeal to the context. The arguments against this version of the strong hypothesis rest on its theoretical complexity, and its probable computational costliness, in comparison with the weak interaction. As Fodor has pointed out, there seem to be just too many ways to say what we mean for this effect to be very helpful, and it is noticeable that the strong interaction, though frequently advocated, has rarely if ever been implemented as a program.

Serial vs. Parallel Interaction

Once one is committed to the weak interaction, it is clear that there is a second parameter that must be fixed in specifying an interactive architecture, namely whether the proposal of alternative analyses by the syntactic component for disposal by the comprehension process occurs serially, one by one, or in parallel.

If the alternative analyses of ambiguous substrings were to be proposed in series, then a weakly interactive parser would have to specify the order on other than contextual grounds—say, by rule-ordering. If the simple analysis were to be ordered before the complex, then we would have something closely related to a parser embodying Minimal Attachment in the form of rule ordering, such as the ATN-based processor proposed by Wanner (1981). The only difference would be that the present theory would allow interpretation to precipitate reanalysis in the "two-wife" context, as opposed to the "one-wife" context, under the criterion of Referential Failure, thus predicting Crain's and Altmann's experimental results. In particular, we might still expect the increase in processing load for the nonminimal analysis predicted by the Minimal Attachment strategy, despite the avoidance of the garden path itself.

However, when it comes to the null context, for which the rival NP analyses are new rather than given and the ambiguity is resolved under the more general criterion of parsimony, it is clear that the mechanism must be parallel rather than serial. We cannot reject an innovating noun phrase merely because it carries a great many previously unsatisfied presuppositions, for it may be the only possible analysis.[20] We can only reject it in comparison with some other analysis carrying fewer unsatisfied presuppositions. In general, the same is true for the criterion of referential failure, since the alternative to a referentially failing "given" interpretation is always the "new" analysis. It follows that the mechanism implicit in the earlier informal account must be one in which syntax offers alternatives in parallel.

There is further evidence to suggest that alternative analyses must be developed in parallel by human sentence processors. This evidence is quite independent of whether these alternatives are disposed of by semantics or not. Consider the alternatives that a processor must consider in dealing with the following set of sentences[21]:

(56) a. Who do you want _?

   b. Who do you want to have _?

   c. Who do you want _ to have dinner?

   d. Who do you want to have dinner with _?

   e. Who do you want _ to have dinner with the president?

   f. Who do you want to have dinner with the president on behalf of _?

g. Who do you want _ to have dinner with the president on behalf of your government?

h. Who do you want to have dinner with the president on behalf of your government for _?

Sentences b, d, f, and h are "equi NP-deleted"; a, c, e, and g are not. Thus there is a local ambiguity in all members of the set after the word *want*. If either the equi or the non-equi analysis were consistently chosen first, say by ordering the respective lexical entries (Ford, Bresnan, and Kaplan 1982—see Steedman 1985b, p. 378, for a critique of this proposal), or by a "most recent filler" strategy (Frazier, Clifton, and Randall 1983), then we would expect the setences in the other set to show an increased processing load. What is more, we might expect this increased load to grow larger as the sentences grew longer. Intuitively this seems unlikely; there is no obvious difference in difficulty between the two sets, even for the longer examples. This kind of lexicl ambiguity is rather different from the attachment ambiguities considered above. The two analyses just seem to be maintained in parallel indefinitely, and neither leads to a garden path in the null context.[22]

Frazier, Clifton, and Randall (1983), who took the serial non-interactive proposal to extreme lengths, claimed to find experimental evidence in support of a two-stage parser in which all long-range dependencies, whether lexically determined (as in sentences with equi and control verbs) or not (as in the case of *wh*-dependencies), are determined after structural analysis is complete. They claimed that even when a verb does not permit an equi analysis (as in the case of *force*), the first, structure-building pass of the parser will construct an equi analysis with an empty category, under a strategy which they call the "most recent filler" strategy. That is, in a sentence like

(57) Everyone liked the woman who the little child *forced to sing those stupid French songs* last Christmas

the processor will incorrectly build a structure including

(58) ... the child$_i$ forced [PRO$_i$ to sing ...].

By contrast, when faced with

(59) Everyone liked the woman who the little child *started to sing those stupid French songs for* last Christmas

the processor will correctly build a structure including

(60) ... the child$_i$ started [PRO$_i$ to sing ...].

It is only at the later stage of associating fillers (e.g. subjects and relative pronouns) with gaps (e.g. empty categories) that the processor will access the lexical information that *force* does not permit this construction, forcing the first stage to restart.

We noted earlier that this proposal is surprising, and that it does not conform to our intuitions as to what goes on when we process such sentences. Nevertheless, it would constitute a very strong argument against the parallel model proposed here, were it robust. However, Crain and Fodor (1985) have pointed to a number of problems with the materials and method of this experiment. In an experiment with revised materials and a self-paced reading-time measure (as opposed to Frazier et al.'s measure of latency between the end of the sentence and a "got it" comprehension response), there was no evidence of increased processing time due to revision of anomalous equi analyses for unambiguously non-equi verbs such as *force*.

This result appears to contradict Frazier's two-stage parser. Crain and Fodor did find some evidence of a processing advantage of the equi analysis for ambiguous verbs such as *beg*, and admit the possibility of serial processing with a "most recent filler" strategy of some other kind. However, in the absence of an actual garden-path effect, or at least of some increase in the overhead when disambiguation points occur very late after the disambiguation point, the processor proposed here, using parallel processing with structure sharing, is not excluded. The mere fact that there is a preference for the equi analysis in the null context tells us nothing.

Intimacy of Evaluation in Incremental Semantics and Interactive Processing

A further parameter of incremental semantics and the architecture of a (serial or parallel) weakly interactive processor is the "intimacy" of the interaction, or the frequency with which syntax can appeal to interpretation for guidance. At one extreme, one might believe (as certain early psycholinguists who managed the considerable mental feat of believing that transformations corresponded to operations of the processor had to), that such interactions apply only to complete clauses or even sentences. Or one might believe that smaller units, such as noun phrases, can be evaluated as soon as they are complete, without waiting for the rest of the matrix clause. Such more intimate incremental semantics and interactive processing was a feature of Winograd's (1972) program. At the other extreme, one might believe that even more intimacy is possible. If, as our intuitions suggest, the most incomplete fragments of constituents can be interpreted, then an interactive parser could appeal very frequently indeed—perhaps as each new word is processed.

However, there is an important restriction on this aspect of the processor. If a rule-to-rule grammar and processor are to conform to the Strong Competence Hypothesis, then only *constituents*, as defined by the grammar, can receive an interpretation, or be evaluated, or be used to guide interactive processing. It is this corollary of the Strong Competence Hypothesis that makes the predominance in natural languages of right-branching constructions so surprising. But if one adheres to that hypothesis, then the limit on intimacy of incrementation and interaction is simply a question of grammar.

Top-Down vs. Bottom-up

A further parameter governing the architecture of any language processor, whether incremental and interactive or not, concerns the direction of application of the rules of the grammar. Does the processor work top-down and predictively through the rules of the grammar, starting from the distinguished symbol S, or does it work bottom-up, starting from the words in the string? There are potential advantages to both tactics, and it turns out that this parameter also depends on the particular grammar that the processor embodies.[23]

There is a considerable intuitive appeal to the bottom-up strategy. Data-driven perceptual models always have the psychological edge over top-down models, because they tie the mechanism to the properties of the domain, with obvious desirable consequences for theories of development and evolution. In the syntactic domain, part of their appeal also arises from the fact that almost any well-formed constituent—as well as many strings which are apparently non-constituents—counts as a complete utterance, not just complete sentences. Although nothing about this phenomenon is incompatible with top-down processing,[24] it is natural to think of this property as arising from a processor that starts from the words and builds whatever it can. A further intuitive appeal of such processors is that they appear more straightforwardly compatible with incremental semantic interpretation, allowing each successively larger constituent to be interpreted as soon as it is built.

A more practical advantage of bottom-up processors is that they are not necessarily vulnerable to the special problems which (left) recursive rules of grammar create for (left-to-right) top-down processors.[25] Such rules, in the absence of special mechanisms (which, though simple enough, compromise the Strong Competence Hypothesis), cause infinite recursion. Nevertheless, they are widespread in natural languages.

However, bottom-up processors as models of human sentence comprehension have been criticized on a number of grounds. Kimball (1973) and Frazier and Fodor (1978) assert that they do not have the same "predictive" capacity as top-down processors, which alow the entire "left context," or the portion of the sentence to the left of the point in the string which the analysis has reached, to limit the search space for the remainder (but see Kimball 1975). They also make the predominance of right-branching structures puzzling for a second reason: Bottom-up processors such as those related to "shift-reduce" or LR parsers (Aho and Johnson 1974; Shieber 1983; Pereira 1985) require an indefinitely large stack for right-branching structures, whereas left-branching ones keep the stack depth constant.

These objections have been countered by Pereira (1985), who has also argued for bottom-up shift-reduce parsing, within a rather different framework than the one presented here. However, the combinatory grammars discussed in sections 1 and 2 of the present chapter provide a grammatical framework that avoids both problems, by embedding information equivalent to predictive "reachability tables" (Kay 1980) in the grammar itself and by inducing left-branching structures on what would, in pure categorial grammar, be right-branching sentences.

Modularity and Incremental Interactive Processing

Nothing in the proposal that human sentence processors are bottom-up, and weakly parallel-interactive, with as much intimacy as the grammar allows under the Strong Competence Hypothesis, conflicts in any way with the modularity hypothesis of Fodor (1983, pp. 78 and 135). Though an unusually high degree of parallel structure is here claimed to hold between syntax, processing, semantics, and even the inference system, with a consequent reduction of the theoretical burden upon innate specification, these components are all formally and computationally autonomous and domain-specific.

On a Supposed Alternative to Parallel Weak Interaction

The weakly interactive incremental model has received some support from the psychology and artificial intelligence communities (Bobrow and Webber 1980a,b; Carroll et al. 1978; Marslen-Wilson et al. 1978; Sanford and Garrod 1981; Steedman and Johnson-Laird 1978; Swinney 1979; Tanenhaus 1978; Winograd 1972). However, the dominant model of sentence processing in both the psychology and the AI literature has not been this one. Both groups have predominantly opted for a serial non-interactive architecture, driven by or embodying nonsemantic parsing "strategies" predominantly drawn from the two families of "Minimal Attachment" and "Right Associa-tion" (Bever 1970; Kimball 1973; Fodor and Frazier 1978; Frazir 1978; Wanner 1980; Ford, Bresnan, and Kaplan 1982; Marcus 1980). The realiza-tions of this model vary a great deal. Some are "one-stage" parsers; others operate in two stages, separating structure-building from assignment of dependencies (Frazier, Berwick). Some more or less explicitly include the strategies as rules (Frazier, Ford); others embody them directly in rule-orderings (Wanner) or less directly in other aspects of the parser (Marcus). However, for present purposes these distinctions are not as important as the fact that a number of crucial predictions arise from the comparison of these models with the one advocated here.

Serial Non-Interactive Architecture
By far the most commonly proposed alternative to the architecture we are proposing here has been the non-interactive or "autonomous" variety depending on parsing strategies or preferences (see the earlier references). Usually, the very existence of garden-path phenomena has been taken to indicate that, in cases of local ambiguity, analyses are proposed singly and in series, recovery from inappropriate analyses being on occasion impossible.

Of course, none of these parsers is entirely non-interactive. Everyone admits that, once syntactic analysis is complete and an interpretation can be obtained, the context may reveal an anomaly and precipitate a re-analysis. (This amounts to a very weak form of the weak interaction, with the clause or sentence as the unit.) It is often assumed (Ferreira and Clifton 1986; Frazier 1987) that Crain's and Altmann's results are compatible with such processors, since most of their results do not use on-line measures of processing difficulty, but only overall measures, such as reading times. (However, Altmann and Steedman [1988] replicated the earlier results with an on-line measure.) It seems not to be generally realized that, under any reasonable set of assumptions about how such a serially non-interactive processor could work, the proposal leads to a logical contradiction, since it immediately forces an evidently false prediction, as follows.

Consider the earlier examples of contextual control of garden paths. Crain showed that a context containing several wives would eliminate the classical garden-path effect of (61).

(61) The psychologist told the woman that he was having trouble with *
     to leave her husband.

The asterisk marks the first point at which the serially autonomous pro-cessor can detect an anomaly. Thanks to the new proposal, the processor can restart syntactic analysis when it detects the syntactic anomaly and the mismatch between the context and the presuppositions of the simple NP that it has produced via Minimal Attachment. It can therefore avoid the garden path, by reanalyzing at a cost in processing that we might hope would show up on some appropriate measure. All seems well with the serially non-interactive theory.

Unfortunately, it isn't. Without appealing to reanalysis, we wouldn't be able to explain how context can prevent the garden path. But now it is hard to see why the sentence should *ever* garden-path. Consider the information the processor has available at the end of its first, minimally attaching, pass through the sentence. It has blocked, grammatically, and it can presumably tell that the context does not support the NP analysis that it has produced. But what kind of serial autonomous processor can recover to autonomously produce a syntactic analysis just in the case when the context will in fact turn out to be consistent with the alternative analysis, but fails in this purely syntactic process when the context will not in fact support it (for example, when it is the null context)? It is a very strange serial autonomous processor indeed, for it appears to have foresight about the contextual compatibility of an analysis which it has not yet built because it is serial. And it appears to be able to allow the success of its purely syntactic processes to be determined by semantic and referential facts to which it can have no access because it is autonomous.

The serial non-interactive model therefore runs into a paradox when faced with Crain and Altmann's results showing that local syntactic-ambiguity resolution is under the control of context. There seem to be only two ways out of this paradox for those who wish to maintain the hypothesis of serial non-interactive processing. One is to assume that the effect on the serial autonomous processor of this kind of *post hoc* assessment of the context is to predictively affect the future operations of the processor when it restarts. However, such a proposal amounts to incorporating not only interaction, but the *strong* interaction. The difficulties of even seeing how this kind of interaction could work have already been noted, and presumably this is not what the proponents of serial autonomy intend. The only alternative appears to be to adopt the parallel weakly interactive theory, as being the only class of processor that is straightforwardly compatible with Crain's and Altmann's experimental results. Under the Strong Competence Hypothesis, the combinatory grammars discussed in sections 2 and 3 seem to be uniquely suited to this kind of processing.

Acknowledgments

This paper owes a lot to conversations and collaborations over a number of years with Gerry Altmann, Stephen Crain, Nick Haddock, Remo Pareschi, and Henry Thompson. Section 4 is an expanded cousin to some portions of the introduction to Altmann and Steedman 1988. Thanks to William Marslen-Wilson, Henry Thompson, and Bonnie Lynn Webber for reading and commenting on the draft. Part of the work was supported under a grant from ESPRIT (project 393).

Notes

1. By "reference", I mean something like "evaluation to the level of discourse entities," or to Webber's (1978) level 2 representations, rather than evaluation to the level of entities in the world or the model.

2. Mallinson and Blake (1981, p. 148) cite 2 VOS and 1 OVS languages in a sample of 100 languages. In the same sample there are 76 languages which are either SOV or SVO.

3. Some possible computational advantages of applicative systems that avoid the overheads of variable-binding via the use of combinators are discussed in Turner 1979a, and in Steedman 1987b.

4. The present theory follows Lambek and Steedman 1987a in this respect, and differs from the earlier versions in Ades and Steedman 1982 and Steedman 1985, which used nondirectional slashes, constraining order in the combinatory rules.

5. Some authors, including Lambek, use other conventions.

6. The last, subject, argument of the verb must be defined for plural or singular number by the inflection of the verb, and the subject argument must be compatible with this specification, to capture basic subject-verb agreement using an obvious unification-based mechanism of the kind proposed for this problem by Shieber (1986). See Steedman 1987a for further remarks on agreement, and Pareschi and Steedman for a discussion of unification-based combinatory grammars.

7. The notion of "like category" is of course problematic for any theory of syntax, as well-known examples like "Pat is a Republican and proud of it" (Sag et al. 1985) reveal. We shall not discuss such problems here, assuming that some finer-grained feature-based categorization of atomic categories like NP such as the one offered by them can be applied to the present theory.

8. It might appear more natural for a categorially based approach to eschew such syncategorematic rules, and drive coordination from the lexical category of the conjunct by associating the following categorial type with sentential conjunctions: and := $(\Sigma \backslash \Sigma)/\Sigma:\Phi\&$. However, such a category requires notationally tedious elaboration if overgeneration is to be prevented, so we will continue to use the syncategorematic rule as a convenient abbreviation.

9. Assuming a proper semantics for the conjunction rule.

10. Steedman (in press) argues that this principle follows from other principles of the theory, rather than by stipulation.

11. Besides the forward rule (a), Dowty (1988) has used the backward rule (c) in his account of English "non-constituent" coordination (see below). While Dowty suggested that "slash crossing" composition should be excluded, the slash-crossing backward rule (d) is introduced in Steedman 1987a, and has also been proposed by Moortgat (1985) and Morrill (1987) to account for right extraposition. A very restricted version of the forward crossing rule (b) is proposed for English "gapping" by Steedman (in press).

12. I do not intend to suggest that the present syntactic use of type raising is related in any way to Montague's (1973) account of quantifier scope phenomena. See Steedman 1987a for remarks on subject-verb agreement and type-raised subject category.

13. Different notations are used in Steedman 1985a and in Steedman 1987a, but they all amount to the same thing. The category of NPs in Karttunen 1986 is related to a type-raised category.

14. See Steedman 1987 for details, including the parallel treatment of relativization. See Szabolcsi 1987 for extensions to "pied piped" *wh*-items.

15. However, the interpretation in question must be intensional rather than extensional, and it should be thought of as a structural object, related to a traditional deep structure or "logical form."

16. In Kimball's (1973) account, the explanation is similar but arises under a number of his "principles," the most important being (early) "closure."

17. The question of what exactly is meant by an "entity" here, and of what is meant by its being "established in the context," is one to which we return below.

18. The possibility that this relative is non-restrictive is presumably excluded by the absence of punctuation, and by the fact that in most dialects *that*, unlike *who*(*m*), cannot introduce nonrestrictives anyway.

19. The terms are from Halliday 1967, although they are used informally here. Presumably the distinction is merely one example of the general tendency of referring expressions to depend for their effect upon the intensional characteristics of the context. Other related distinctions are referential and attributive definiteness and de dicto/de re.

20. If it is the only analysis, a serial processor is going to have to either reanalyze when it fails to find an alternative or save the analysis against the possibility of such failure. Either strategy amounts to simulating parallelism.

21. "Empty categories," indicated by _, are used (as usual) merely for expository clarity.

22. Of course, in order to avoid redundancy in the analyses of the remainder of the string, it follows that an efficient processor will have to resort to some trick such as "structure sharing" between the two analyses.

23. This use of the parsing term-of-art "top-down" should not be confused with the (unfortunately) widespread use of the phrase to describe what we call in this

chapter the "strong" or instructive interaction between high- and low-level processes such as semantics and syntax.

24. A top-down processor could simply define all the nodes in question as possible start symbols.

25. The word *necessarily* is important. Some ways of handling nondeterminism, such as chart parsing, may reintroduce the problem of left-recursion into a bottom-up parser.

References

Ades, A., and Steedman, M. J. 1982. On the order of words. *Linguistics and Philosophy* 4: 517–518.

Ajdukiewicz, K. 1935. Die syntaktische Konnexitat. *Studia Philosophica* 1: 1–27. English translation in *Polish Logic: 1920–1939*, ed. Storrs McCall (Oxford University Press).

Altmann, G. 1986. Reference and the Resolution of Local Ambiguity: Interaction in Human Sentence Processing. Ph.D. Thesis, University of Edinburgh.

Altmann, G. 1987. Modularity and interaction in sentence processing. In Garfield, J. (ed.), *Modularity in Knowledge Representation and Natural-Language Processing*. Cambridge, Mass.: MIT Press.

Altmann, G., and Steedman, M. J. 1988. Interaction with the context in human syntactic processing. *Cognition* 30: 191–238.

Berwick, R. C., and Weinberg, A. S. 1983. The role of grammars in models of language use. *Cognition* 13: 1–62.

Bever, T. G. 1970. The cognitive basis for linguistic structures. In Hayes, J. R. (ed.), *Cognition and the Development of Language*. New York: Wiley.

Bobrow, R. J., and Webber, B. L. 1980. Knowledge representation for syntactic/semantic processing. In Proceedings of the First Annual National Conference on Artificial Intelligence, Stanford.

Bobrow, R. J., and Webber, B. L. 1981. Some issues in parsing and natural language understanding. In Proceedings of the 19th Annual Meeting of the Association for Computational Linguistics, Stanford.

Bresnan, J., ed. 1982. *The Mental Representation of Grammatical Relations*. Cambridge, Mass.: MIT Press.

Bresnan, J., Kaplan, R. M., Peters, S., and Zaenen, A. 1982. Cross-serial dependencies in Dutch. *Linguistic Inquiry* 13: 613–635.

Carroll, J., and Bever, T. G. 1978. The perception of relations. In Levelt, W. J. M., and Flores d'Arcais, G. (eds.), *Studies in the Perception of Language*. New York: Wiley.

Chomsky, N. 1968. *Language and Mind*. New York: Harcourt, Brace.

Crain, S. 1980. Pragmatic Constraints on Sentence Comprehension. Ph.D. dissertation, University of California, Irvine.

Crain, S., and Fodor, J. D. 1985. How can grammars help parsers? In Dowty, D. R., Karttunen, L., and Zwicky, A. M. (eds.), *Natural Language Parsing: Psychological, Computational, and Theoretical Perspectives*. Cambridge University Press.

Crain, S., and Steedman, M. J. 1985. On not being led up the garden path: The use of context by the psychological parser. In Dowty, D., Karttunen, L., and Zwicky, A. (eds.), *Natural Language Parsing: Psychological, Computational, and Theoretical perspectives*. Cambridge University Press.

Curry, H. B., and Feys, R. 1958. *Combinatory Logic*, volume I. Amsterdam: North-Holland.

Dowty, D. 1988. Type raising, functional composition, and non-constituent conjunction. In Oehrle, R., Bach, E. and Wheeler, D. (eds.), *Categorical Grammars and Natural Language Structures*. Dordrecht: Reidel.

Engdahl, E. 1981. *Multiple Gaps in English and Swedish*. Trondheim: Tapir.

Engdahl, E. 1983. Parasitic gaps. *Linguistics and Philosophy* 6: 5–34.

Ferreira, F., and Clifton, C. 1986. The independence of syntactic processing. *Journal of Memory and Language* 25: 348–368.

Fodor, J. A. 1983. *The Modularity of Mind*. Cambridge, Mass.: MIT Press.

Ford, M., Bresnan, J., and Kaplan, R. M. 1982. A competence-based theory of syntactic closure. In Bresnan, J. (ed.), *The Mental Representation of Grammatical Relations*. Cambridge, Mass.: MIT Press.

Frazier, L. 1978. On Comprehending Sentences: Syntactic Parsing Strategies. Ph.D. thesis, University of Connecticut. Indiana University Linguistics Club.

Frazier, L. 1987. Theories of sentence processing. In Garfield, J. (ed.), *Modularity in Knowledge Representation and Natural-Language Processing*. Cambridge, Mass.: MIT Press.

Frazier, L., and Fodor, J. D. 1978. The sausage machine: A new two-stage parsing model. *Cognition* 6: 291–325.

Frazier, L., Clifton, C., and Randall, J. 1983. Filling gaps: decision principles and structure in sentence comprehension. *Cognition* 13: 187–222.

Gazdar, G. 1981. Unbounded dependencies and coordinate structure. *Linguistic Inquiry* 12: 155–184.

Geach, P. T. 1972. A program for syntax. In Davidson, D., and Harman, G. (eds.), *Semantics of Natural Language*. Dordrecht: Reidel.

Haddock, N. J. 1986. Incremental interpretation and noun phrase reference. In Haddock, N. J., and Klein, E. (eds.), Edinburgh Working Papers in Cognitive Science, volume 1: Categorial Grammar, Unification Grammar, and Parsing. Available from Centre for Cognitive Science, Edinburgh University.

Haddock, N. J. 1987. Incremental interpretation and combinatory grammar. In Proceedings of the Tenth International Joint Conference on Artificial Intelligence, University of Milan.

Haddock, N. J. Forthcoming. Incremental Semantic Interpretation and Incremental Syntactic Analysis. Ph.D. thesis, University of Edinburgh.

Halliday, M. A. K. 1967. Notes on transitivity and theme in English, Part 2. *Journal of Linguistics* 3: 199–244.

Kang, B. 1986. Functional Inheritance, Anaphora, and Semantic Interpretation. Ph.D. dissertation, Brown University.

Karttunen, L. 1986. Radical Lexicalism. Report CSLI-86-68, Center for the Study of Language and Information. Presented at Conference on Alternative Conceptions of Phrase Structure, New York.

Kay, M. 1980. Algorithm Schemata and Data Structures in Syntactic Processing. Technical Report CSL-80-12, Xerox Palo Alto Research Center.

Kimball, J. 1973. Seven principles of surface structure parsing in natural language. *Cognition* 2: 15–47.

Kimball, J. 1975. Predictive analysis and over-the-top parsing. In Kimball, J. (ed.), *Syntax and Semantics*, volume 4. New York: Academic.

Klein, E., and Sag, I. A. 1985. Type-driven translation. *Linguistics and Philosophy* 8: 163–201.

Lambek, J. 1958. The mathematics of sentence structure. *American Mathematical Monthly* 65: 154–170.

Lambek, J. 1961. On the calculus of syntactic types. In *Structure of Language and Its Mathematical Aspects*. Providence: American Mathematical Society.

Mallinson, G., and Blake, B. J. 1981. *Language Typology*. Amsterdam: North-Holland.

Marcus, M. P. 1980. *A Theory of Syntactic Recognition for Natural Language*. Cambridge, Mass.: MIT Press.

Marslen-Wilson, W. D., Tyler, L. K., and Seidenberg, M. S. 1978. The semantic control of sentence segmentation. In Levelt, W. J. M., and Flores d'Arcais, G. (eds.), *Studies in the Perception of Language*. New York: Wiley.

Montague, R. 1973. The proper treatment of quantification in ordinary English. In Hintikka, J., Moravcsik, J. M. E., and Suppes, P. (eds.), *Approaches to Natural Language*. Dordrecht: Reidel. Reprinted in R. H. Thomason (ed.), *Formal Philosophy: Selected Papers of Richard Montague* (New Haven: Yale University Press, 1974).

Pareschi, R. 1986. Combinatory Grammar, Logic Programming and Natural Language Processing. Unpublished paper, Centre for Cognitive Science, University of Edinburgh.

Pareschi, R. Forthcoming. Type-Driven Natural Language Analysis. Ph.D. thesis, University of Edinburgh.

Pareschi, R., and Steedman, M. J. 1987. A lazy way to chart-parse with extended categorial grammars. In Proceedings of the 25th Annual Meeting of the Association for Computational Linguistics, Stanford.

Pereira, F. 1985. A new characterization of attachment preferences. In Dowty, D., Karttunen, L., and Zwicky, A. (eds.), *Natural Language Parsing: Psychological, Computational, and Theoretical Perspectives*. Cambridge University Press.

Rayner, K., Carlson, M., and Frazier, L. 1983. The interaction of syntax and semantics during sentence processing. *Journal of Verbal Learning and Verbal Behavior* 22: 358–374.

Sag, I. A., Gazdar, G., Wasow, T., and Weisler, S. 1985. Coordination and how to distinguish categories. *Natural Language and Linguistic Theory* 3: 117–171.

Sanford, A. J., and Garrod, S. C. 1981. *Understanding Written Language.* Chichester: Wiley.

Schönfinkel, M. 1924. Über die Bausteine der mathematischen Logik. *Mathematische Annalen* 92: 305–316.

Shieber, S. 1983. Sentence disambiguation by a shift-reduce parsing technique. In Proceedings of the 21st Annual Meeting of the Association for Computational Linguistics, Massachusetts Institute of Technology.

Shieber, S. M. 1986. *An Introduction to Unification-Based Approaches to Grammar.* University of Chicago Press.

Steedman, M. 1985a. Dependency and coordination in the grammar of Dutch and English. *Language* 61: 523–568.

Steedman, M. J. 1985b. LFG and psychological explanation. *Linguistics and Philosophy* 8: 359–385.

Steedman, M. J. 1987. Combinatory grammars and parasitic gaps. *Natural Language and Linguistic Theory* 5: 403–439.

Steedman, M. 1988. Combinators and grammars. In Oehrle, R., Bach, E., and Wheeler, D. (eds.), *Categorial Grammars and Natural Language Structures.* Dordrecht: Reidel.

Steedman, M. J. (in press) Constituency and coordination in a combinatory grammar. In Baltin, M., and Kroch, A. (eds.), *Alternative Conceptions of Phrase Structure.* University of Chicago Press.

Steedman, M. J., and Johnson-Laird, P. N. 1977. A programmatic theory of linguistic performance. In Smith, P. T., and Campbell, R. N. (eds.), *Advances in the Psychology of Language: Formal and Experimental Approaches.* New York: Plenum.

Swinney, D. A. 1979. Lexical access during sentence comprehension: (re)consideration of context effects. *Journal of Verbal Learning and Verbal Behavior* 18: 645–660.

Szabolcsi, A. 1987. Bound variables in syntax. In Proceedings of the Sixth Amsterdam Colloquium, Institute for Language, Logic and Information, University of Amsterdam.

Tanenhaus, M. K. 1978. Sentence Context and Sentence Perception. Ph.D. thesis, Columbia University.

Taraldsen, T. 1979. The theoretical interpretation of a class of marked extractions. In Belletti, A., Brandi, L., and Rizzi, L. (eds.), *Theory of Markedness in Generative Grammar.* Scuole Normale Superiore di Pisa.

Wanner, E. 1980. The ATN and the sausage machine: Which one is baloney? *Cognition* 8: 209–225.

Webber, B. L. 1978. A Formal Approach to Discourse Anaphora. Ph.D. thesis, Harvard University.

Winograd, T. 1972. *Understanding Natural Language*. New York: Academic.

Wittenburg, K. W. 1986. Natural Language Parsing with Combinatory Categorial Grammar in a Graph-Unification-Based Formalism. Ph.D. thesis, University of Texas.

Chapter 17

Against Lexical Generation of Syntax

Lyn Frazier

Two views of the relation between lexical and syntactic information will be contrasted in this chapter. On one view, lexical knowledge, including information about the peculiarities of the current lexical item, guides the formation of a hypothesis about how an item should be incorporated into the syntactic structure assigned to preceding portions of the sentence. Since the constituent-structure analysis of an input item is itself based on the idiosyncrasies of this item, there is simply no opportunity for a conflict to arise between the initial constituent-structure analysis and the detailed properties of the particular lexical item. For example, given a verb such as *build*, which always takes a direct object, the parser should never even consider constructing an intransitive-verb phrase headed by this item; likewise, given an obligatorily intransitive verb such as *sleep*, the processor should never entertain the possibility that the following phrase is an object of this verb. On this view, syntactic hypotheses are lexically generated from item-specific information.

The lexical generation of syntax illustrated above may be compared with a system granting priority to item-independent information which defines the possible shape of syntactic phrases and the grammatically permissible relations between them. If this type of general (item-independent) information forms the basis for immediate syntactic hypotheses, then the idiosyncratic properties of a particular lexical item may prove to be incompatible with a syntactic analysis based on some general classification of that lexical item (e.g., the fact that it is a verb, or that it carries lexical stress). On this second view, it is most natural to assume that syntactic information is organized in a fashion permitting rather direct prediction about the sequence of permissible categories in the input. The major task of the parser, on this view, is to fit input items into those categories. On these assumptions, it could matter a great deal precisely where the cut is between lexical (item-specific) information and general syntactic (item-independent) information. For example, cast in terms of context-free rewriting rules (e.g., S is rewritten as NP followed by VP), the decision for nonterminals to correspond to predicates (as in generative semantics), to a major syntactic category ($+/-$ Verb) or to a strict subcategory (transitive verb) results in somewhat different grammars inviting quite different processing hypotheses. And, unless humans are simply strait-jacketed by their processing device, on this view we would expect syntactic information to be precompiled. Precompilation of syntactic knowledge will allow the knowledge to be organized in a fashion that reduces the length of the inference chain connecting the general classification of lexical items with the possible phrasal configurations of the language. Since this is precisely the information that will be needed to guide the early analysis of a linguistic input, precompilation would be economical.

If it were to turn out that syntactic processing involved the immediate computation of all possible syntactic structures of a sentence, then the above distinctions would amount primarily to details about the precise timing of processing operations. Under these conditions, all and only the analyses corresponding to successful lexical-syntactic matches would be computed and pursued. But many investigators have proposed processing systems in which the processor's first analysis is given special priority. See Kimball 1973, Wanner and Maratsos 1978, Frazier and Fodor 1978, Ford, Bresnan, and Kaplan 1983, Berwick and Weinberg 1984, and Abney 1986 for examples and discussions of serial-processing models in which only one syntactic analysis is considered in early stages of parsing; see Gorrell 1987 for a "staggered" serial-processing model. In this sort of system, both the behavior of the system and (more important) the principles underlying it may differ substantially depending on whether syntactic structure is lexically generated.

Even in this sort of serial system, however, the impact of the distinction between lexical and syntactic generation of structural hypotheses would be minimal if there were no lexical ambiguities in natural languages. But of course languages tend to be riddled with lexical ambiguities. Much of the difficulty involved in language analysis arises from the pervasive ambiguities at all levels of structure, including the lexical level, together with the impossibility of systematically resolving those ambiguities on the basis of any one type of information that can be specified in advance (see Frazier 1978 for discussion and supporting examples). Thus, to abstract away from lexical ambiguity in studies of the relation between lexical and syntactic structure is not a harmless idealization but rather a distortion of the basic problem.

Most of the available intuitive and experimental evidence can be interpreted in accord with either the lexically driven or the structurally driven view of parsing (for a contrasting view, see the chapter by Tanenhaus and Carlson in this volume). The evidence typically shows only that item-specific lexical information and item-independent structural information is integrated rapidly during sentence analysis. Thus, the preferred readings of ambiguous sentences conform to the preferred or most frequent use of lexical items (Ford, Bresnan, and Kaplan 1983; Fodor 1978). And sentences are processed more quickly when the actual syntactic analysis conforms to the lexical preferences of individual items than when it does not (Clifton, Frazier, and Connine 1984). But these findings are consistent with either a lexical or a structural genesis of syntactic hypotheses.

Here we will examine the issue from a slightly different perspective. First, we will look at the experimental literature to see what generalizations must be captured, and should be explained, in any theory of language processing. It will become apparent below that accounting for these generalizations is not problematic, on the assumption that syntactic hypotheses are generated structurally—e.g., through the use of phrase-structure rules or precompiled grammatical principles (perhaps all those referring to sisterhood; see Frazier 1985b). However, on the assumption that syntactic hypotheses are lexically generated, difficulties arise. This is true regardless of whether we assume a categorial grammar (in which case we will be entirely unable to state our processing generalizations in terms of independently required grammatical classes), a principle-based grammar (at least one in which we use the individual principles of X' theory to project syntactic structure), or a rule-based phrase-structure grammar.

To reiterate, the basic question addressed here is whether lexical (item-specific) information or syntactic (item-independent) information governs the formation of the processor's initial constituent-structure analysis of an input item. Most investigators seem to have concluded that lexical information determines syntactic analysis (Ford et al. 1983; Fodor 1978; Abney 1986; Holmes 1987; Stowe, in press; Tanenhaus and Carlson, this volume). I shall argue below that this conclusion is wrong—or that, at very least, it is an uncomfortable conclusion because it leaves many observations entirely unexplained.

As the discussion develops, I will try to emphasize why this apparently trivial descriptive detail of the processing system warrants so much attention. It will become apparent below that the answers to the question of whether syntax is lexically generated will, in large part, determine the grammatical systems which can easily be used to model the facts about human parsing. For example, if syntax *is* lexically generated, it becomes very attractive to consider the possibility that lexical information is "precompiled," permitting the lexical label of an item to directly encode its combinatorial possibilities. Categorial grammar provides perhaps the best example of this type of system, since all lexical labels directly encode the nature of the category the item may combine with, as well as the nature of the resulting category (see section 2 below). However, if syntax is not lexically generated, then this sort of system becomes rather unattractive. Similarly, especially if syntax is not generated directly from item-specific information, we must ask whether syntactic (item-independent) information is precompiled—presumably into something roughly like phrase-structure rules or templates. The alternative is for the parser to directly exploit the individual principles governing the (decomposed) relations which jointly result in the observable sequence of permissible syntactic categories. For example, the parser might use such principles as the requirement that noun phrases be case-marked, the requirement that arguments be assigned a thematic role, and the requirement that major phases (VP, NP, AP, PP) must be headed and must share the syntactic-category features of their heads (Chomsky 1986). Although it is logically possible to use these individual (uncompiled) principles predictively, it would be cumbersome to do so. Thus, it would be highly unexpected for the processor to repeatedly draw lots of inferences on-line in advance of receiving the items which the inferences are about. In short, issues concerning the precise form in which grammatical information is represented, and whether certain information is precompiled, are closely related to the issue of whether syntactic hypotheses are generated lexically or structurally.

We turn now to the experimental evidence.

1 Processing classes

Questions about the perceptual processing of a linguistic input—e.g., about how a phonological or orthographic description of an input is developed and matched (somehow) against the representations in the mental lexicon—will be set aside here. Focusing just on the later stages of lexical and syntactic processing, we will see that various generalizations seem to emerge.

Single vs. multiple analysis

We may begin by determining how many representations or analyses are entertained by the processor at a point of ambiguity, postponing for the moment questions about whether candidate representations are maintained only very briefly or until they are no longer of any conceivable use to the processor. If we consider various lexical representations, it appears that the processor follows a multiple-analysis strategy, and thus that all common representations of an input are considered simultaneously. For semantically ambiguous lexical items (e.g. *bank*) and categorially ambiguous items (e.g. *swing, rose*), cross-modal-priming studies indicate that multiple representations are considered even in strongly biased or disambiguating contexts (Seidenberg et al. 1982; Swinney 1979; Tanenhaus and Lucas 1987). With respect to thematic frames (or predicate argument frames), there are again various indications that all possible frames are considered (Tanenhaus and Carlson, this volume; Rayner, Carlson, and Frazier 1983; Shapiro, Zurif, and Grimshaw 1986).[1]

By contrast, when it comes to constituent-structure decisions, numerous studies indicate that—initially and essentially immediately—the human language processor assigns just a single analysis (by minimally attaching new items into the current phrase or clause; see examples and references below). Evidence for this view derives from several sources. Intuitions reveal systematic structural preferences across a wide range of disparate structures (where semantic and pragmatic plausibility are controlled, though see Crain and Steedman 1985 for discussion of presuppositional biases in certain specific structures)—see Kimball 1973 and Frazier and Fodor 1978. On-line measures of processing complexity also reveal a systematic asymmetry: The unpreferred structure takes longer to process than the initially computed structure; the complexity of the unpreferred structure can be observed immediately (e.g. on the first fixation in the disambiguating region of the sentence) and may give rise to actual disruption effects (e.g. regressive eye movements extending beyond immediately preceding characters); and the full perceptual complexity of the unpreferred structure cannot be attributed to its structure *per se*, since a disambiguated form of the same structure will not show comparable complexity or disruption effects (Frazier and Rayner 1982; Kennedy and Murray 1984; Rayner and Frazier, in press; Rayner et al. 1983).

For present purposes, we can illustrate the preferences as in (1)–(3).

(1)
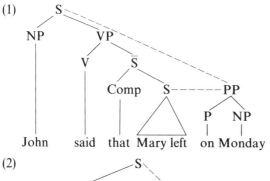
John   said   that Mary left   on Monday

(2)
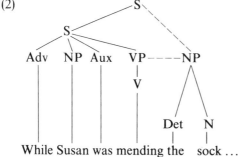
While Susan was mending the   sock ...

(3)
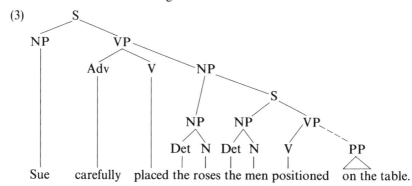
Sue   carefully   placed the roses the men positioned   on the table.

In each case, the ambiguous phrase (the final one) prefers attachment low down, where it is attached as a sister to the verb (as in (2) and (3)) or the verb phrase (as in (1)). Thus, if we simply consider whether on encountering a linguistic input more than one representation of it is considered simultaneously, the answer seems to be No for constituent-structure decisions, in striking contrast to stored lexical representations.

Immediate vs. Delayed Selection

For stored representations, multiple analysis at the lookup stage does not entail multiple analysis at later stages—e.g., the processor might immediately select and pursue just a single analysis from the set of items identified, even in cases of ambiguity. Indeed, in the case of semantically ambiguous items (homophones, e.g. bank) it appears that precisely this occurs. One meaning is immediately selected (either the semantically appropriate meaning, in biased contexts, or the most frequent one, in unbiased or null contexts).[2] Thus, in priming studies, priming of a word semantically related to the subordinate or inappropriate meaning of a homophone is observed if there is no delay before the presentation of the associate. However, after even a short lag of a few hundred milliseconds, it appears that only the selected meaning is active (Swinney 1979; Seidenberg et al. 1982; Rayner and Duffy 1986).

By contrast, several eye-movement studies (Frazier and Rayner, 1987) have furnished evidence that categorially ambiguous items are not processed according to a comparable (immediate-selection) strategy. Rather, the processor appears to wait for the occurrence of disambiguating material before committing itself to an analysis when it comes to choosing between different major syntactic-category labels. In one experiment testing the sentences in (4), we find that the target items (underlined) in the ambiguous (a and b) forms take less time to read than the disambiguated sentences (c and d forms); however, the following (disambiguating) items take longer to read in the ambiguous forms (a, b) than in the disambiguated forms (c, d). This is precisely what we would expect according to a delay stratetgy.

(4) a. The *warehouse fires* numerous employees each year.
        (Ambiguous, NV)

    b. The *warehouse fires* harm some employees each year.
        (Ambiguous, AN)

    c. That *warehouse fires* numerous employees each year.
        (Disambiguated, NV)

    d. Those *warehouse fires* harm some employees each year.
        (Disambiguated, AN)

(5) a. The *church pardons* very few people.   (Ambiguous, NV)

    b. The *church pardons* are difficult to obtain.   (Ambiguous, AN)

    c. This *church pardons* very few people.   (Disambiguated, NV)

    d. Those *church pardons* are difficult to obtain.   (Disambiguated, AN)

(6) a. Without a doubt, *ringing bells* is disturbing to everyone in the neighborhood.   (Ambiguous, VN)

    b. Without a doubt, *ringing bells* are disturbing to everyone in the neighborhood.   (Ambiguous, AN)

   c. Without a doubt, *ringing* loud *bells* is disturbing ...
     (Disambiguated, VN)

   d. Without a doubt, loud *ringing bells* are disturbing ...
     (Disambiguated, AN)

In fact, this general pattern was observed regardless of whether the ambiguity was unsystematic and thus involved unrelated meanings (as in (4)) or whether it was systematic (as in (5)). Similarly, in an experiment testing sentences like those in (6), where the order of prenominal adjectives disambiguates the target items, the evidence again supported the view that the selection of major syntactic category is delayed in cases of ambiguity.

One might object (as one reviewer did) to relying on a comparison across different techniques. Indeed, if the crucial difference between immediate selection and a delay strategy were determined by absolute time (e.g., 325 msec after offset), the difficulty of comparing results from distinct techniques might entirely invalidate the comparison. However, the point of interest here is not the absolute time involved in selection, but rather the underlying principles governing processing. In the eye-movement study, one could easily have found support for an immediate commitment strategy. Imagine, for example, that perceivers prefer to analyze an input item as the head of a phrase, or at least as an obligatory member of an independently required phrase. In this case, ambiguous NV forms should have taken no longer to read than their disambiguated counterparts (in any region), but the ambiguous AN forms should have taken considerably longer than any of the other ambiguous or disambiguated forms in the disambiguating region of the sentence. Thus, eye-movement recording certainly could, in principle, reveal the operation of an immediate-selection principle. Likewise, it is clear what would constitute evidence for a delay strategy in cross-modal priming. At whatever time lag selective access (priming only of targets related to one meaning) occurs in the presence of prior disambiguation, multiple access (priming of targets related to any of the meanings of an item) should occur in contexts lacking bias or disambiguation. Once we recognize that the comparison is of the principles underlying processing, there is no difficulty comparing across techniques simply because different absolute times may be involved; it is not the absolute times that are being compared.

At present we do not really know how strict subcategorization information is accessed (here I use subcategorization in the sense of Chomsky 1965). It is clear, however, that the processor does not delay analysis of the string (e.g. attachment into constituent structure of potential complements of the verb) until disambiguating information is encountered. For example, *know* may take either a noun phrase or a sentential complement. However, in a sentence like (7), there is clear evidence of processing difficulties when the disambiguating phrase "was correct" is encountered. This suggests that the processor goes ahead and assigns a syntactic analysis to potential complements of *know*—i.e., taking *the answer* as direct object—before subcategorization ambiguities are disambiguated.

(7) Karen knew the answer to the difficult problem was correct.

In short, the processor apparently does not delay analysis when it encounters strict subcategorization ambiguities, in contrast with the case of major syntactic-category ambiguities.

A recent self-paced reading study (Mitchell 1987) reinforces the idea that analysis of the string is not delayed until the subcategory of an item has been established. Examining reading times for the first (italicized) frames of sentences like those in (8), Mitchell finds a pattern of evidence suggesting that readers initially analyzed the postverbal noun phrase as a direct object even when it followed obligatorily intransitive verbs, as in (8b).

(8) a. *After the audience had applauded the actors*/sat down for a well deserved drink.

   b. *After the audience had departed the actors*/sat down for a well deserved drink.

To reiterate, we don't have definitive evidence about how subcategorization ambiguities are resolved. Quite possibly this occurs by some frequency-ordered check. The important point, however, is that constituent-structure analysis is not delayed until subcategorization is disambiguated; if it were, no incorrect analysis should occur in examples like (7) or (8).

The evidence suggests then that the cut between the phrasal syntax and the lexicon occurs at the "level" of major syntactic category. Things might have turned out otherwise. For example, the processor might have proceeded immediately with a syntactic analysis of the input even in the presence of ambiguities about the major syntactic category of the current input (just as it proceeds with an analysis in the face of constituent-structure ambiguities concerning phrasal attachment); but analysis of the input might have been delayed until the subcategory was disambiguated—e.g., in the sequence "talk about Reagan", analysis might depend on disambiguating the subcategory of "talk" (whether it takes "about Reagan" as an argument) with categorization of the item as a noun or verb being dictated by the processing principles that govern analysis of the phrasal syntax. Instead, the evidence suggests it is the major syntactic category $(+/-\text{Noun}, +/-\text{Verb})$ that defines the "lower boundary" of the phrasal syntax.

Summary

Constituent-structure analysis proceeds by a "single-analysis" strategy. By contrast, multiple lexical analyses are considered, at least in the case of prestored representations. Apparently, lexical-semantic ambiguities (e.g., *bank*) are resolved immediately on the basis of available information, whereas major category decisions—but not subcategory (e.g., transitive vs. intransitive) decisions—are delayed and are resolved only after disambiguating information has been encountered.

We will turn to the question of whether the processing decisions discussed are clustering together in a manner we might expect according to one or another grammatical framework. But first it should be emphasized that there is no logical necessity for any of the above processing decisions to be accomplished in the particular way it is. For example, it is probably not at all irrelevant that multiple analysis occurs with pre-stored representations (e.g., alternative meanings, categories, or thematic frames of individual lexical items). But, of course, there is no logical reason why lexical lookup must involve multiple analysis; there is nothing incoherent about a single-analysis (self-terminating) lookup strategy.

Similarly, in principle at least it would be entirely possible for multiple constituent-structure representations to be computed simultaneously, for category decisions to occur immediately, or for selection of one meaning of a homophone to be delayed in cases of ambiguity.

2 Categorial Grammar

We will now examine the relation between the classes implicated in a processing description and the grammatical classes of categorical grammar. In the psycholinguistic literature, categorial grammar has been claimed to offer a solution to the problem of how people semantically interpret sentences on an essentially word-by-word basis (Ades and Steedman 1982; Steedman, this volume). How semantic interpretation occurs on line (or at all) is an important outstanding problem, and thus the potential solution offered by a categorial-grammar approach deserves to be evaluated seriously. In its most radical form (Steedman, this volume), this proposal has attributed to all sentences a left-branching structure (among others), permitting bottom-up on-line assembly of phrases. (A strictly bottom-up compositional interpretation runs into trouble in right-branching structures, since interpretation must be delayed until the most deeply embedded— i.e., the rightmost—constituent is encountered.)

Since proponents of this radical form of categorial grammar have not (to my knowledge) even shown how this idea could be reconciled with the linguistic or psycholinguistic evidence concerning constituent structure, I will simply assume this proposal cannot be maintained. I will further assume that any attempt to claim that children acquire a more standard grammar but then parse with the left-branching grammar will be not only undesirable on theoretical grounds but also empirically false (e.g., it will be incapable of accounting for the evidence concerning constituents in various experimental paradigms; see chapter 5 of Fodor, Bever, and Garrett 1974). Nevertheless, more standard uses of a categorial grammar are of considerable interest.

In particular, it may be possible to recast certain grammatical conditions that have usually been assumed to be syntactic in terms of function-argument structure (Bach and Partee 1980). Other things being equal, there may be parsing reasons to prefer the function/argument approach. It is known that memory for semantic information or "gist" is superior to memory for surface syntactic information. If semantic information must or will be retained under any circumstances, but syntactic information need only be retained until an interpretation has been assigned (see discussion in Frazier 1985a), casting constraints like anaphoric and pronominal restrictions in terms of function argument structure could reduce the memory burden in language comprehension—i.e., it would not be necessary to retain a syntactic structure until secure "coreference" or binding relations could be established.

In a categorial grammar, there are three types of category, as illustrated in (9).

(9) a. A.

 b. A/B (A ≠ B)

 c. A/A

Basic categories (A in (9a)), such as common nouns or noun phrases, typically serve as arguments. Functors typically look for something of one category (e.g., B) to make something of a different category (e.g., A). For example, a determiner looks for a common noun to make a noun phrase. Since in this system the category label determines how items may combine, intransitive, transitive, and ditransitive verbs will typically be assigned distinct categories—for example, the transitive will amount to "(S/NP)/NP", i.e., something that combines with a noun phrase to form something that combines with a noun phrase to form a sentence. Modifiers will be of the category A/A, since they combine with a phrase of some type (e.g., a common noun phrase) to form a phrase of the same type. Of course, categorial grammar just provides a framework within which different analyses might be proposed, so category labels may differ somewhat, depending on the particular categorial theory at issue.

On the above view, categorial selection will subsume major-category assignment and subcategory assignment, together with all syntactic attachments that follow from these assignments. Thus, the general framework provides no straightforward means for distinguishing between major syntactic category (where analysis is delayed in cases of ambiguity) and subcategory (where analysis proceeds even in the absence of disambiguating evidence).

Further, within a categorial framework, sentence processing has been discussed in terms of "parsing from the lexicon" (see Steedman, this volume) using semantic and discourse factors to adjudicate in cases of ambiguity (see Crain and Steedman 1985), implying that there is no role for structural factors in language processing. Indeed, it has been proposed that no structural representation of a sentence is constructed or maintained (Ades and Steedman 1982). This view (embodying a radical form of the hypothesis that sentence analysis is lexically based) engenders several problems in addition to the difficulties associated with the failure to distinguish between subcategory and major category.

Consider the attachment preferences above, for example. It is simply an accident that arguments abide by the same principles as nonarguments. In the case of arguments, attachment preferences must result from category selection; in the case of nonarguments, some "structural" principle is needed to choose between the grammatically possible analyses of a categorially unambiguous item. The preference for low attachment in an example like (2) must follow from categorial selection, whereas in (1) it is a "modifier" (adjunct PP) that is preferentially attached low (no categorial ambiguity is involved). In other words, (1) is the case where the attachment of a phrase (presumably of type "S/S") is not uniquely determined by its category. Some new principle will be needed to handle such cases, and it will only be an accident that this principle favors the same analyses (viewed in terms of phrase-structure geometry) as the category-selection principles.

Sentence 3 above is a particularly interesting case, since it would appear that low attachment must follow from a category preference for the verb "position" to be analyzed as ditransitive (if the locative phrase is an argument). However, the initial preference still seems to be for low attachment, even if we exchange the position of the verbs "position" and "place". This is problematic because there seems no way to escape the conclusion that syntactic configuration is determining preferred (not obligatory!) category selection.

In conclusion, the natural classes of the general categorial grammar framework are simply not what we need for stating parsing generalizations. To talk about which processing decisions are governed by which principles, we must refer to what appear to be arbitrarily chosen members of several distinct grammatical classes. Though difficulties arise given either lexically driven or structurally driven parsing, the problems are particularly acute on the assumption that parsing is lexically based (i.e., that the preferred category of an input item determines the analysis of a sentence).

3   Principle-Based Grammar

Imagine that the ongoing attempt to derive phrase-structure rules from independent principles of grammar is entirely successful (Stowell 1981; Chomsky 1981, 1986). If so, independently required principles will explain all details of the phrase-structure rules of a language. For example, in English case is assigned to the right, under adjacency with the case assigner. From this it follows that the object of a case-assigner (verb or preposition) must occur to its right. One needn't stipulate such facts in a phrase-structure rule enumerating the possible shapes of a verb phrase or a prepositional phrase.

Imagine further that each of the individual principles of theta theory, X′ theory, and case theory is used directly to parse sentences, without being precompiled into a form representing their joint consequences for a string of constituents. In this kind of system, several problems will arise.

It is natural (though by no means necessary; see Abney 1986) for phrase structure to be postulated by projecting the properties of lexical items, if the parser is exploiting a principle-based grammar. The principles of X′ theory specify that the categorial features of a phrasal node are determined by its head. If this type of principle is used directly when the processor constructs phrase structure, we would expect a maximal projection (e.g., verb-phrase node) to be postulated by projecting the properties of its head. This head-projection hypothesis makes a clear prediction that the postulation of phrasal nodes will be delayed in head-final phrases.

At present, there is very little evidence concerning the processing of head-final constructions. The only relevant experimental evidence that

I'm aware of runs counter to the prediction. In a self-paced reading study of head-final verb phrases in Dutch relative clauses, Frazier (1987b) argues that analysis of such phrases is not delayed—as indicated by the existence of misanalyses that would be precluded by information carried by the head.

One final piece of evidence derives from investigation of syntactic parsing strategies in Dutch. Frazier (1987b) presents both intuitive and experimental evidence in support of the operation of the Minimal Attachment strategy in Dutch, i.e., a strategy of attaching new items into a phrase marker using the fewest nodes consistent with the grammar. In English, it appears that we can attribute perceivers' constituent-structure strategies to the parser simply pursuing the first available syntactic analysis. In the case of Minimal Attachment, we need only assume that it takes more time to postulate more nodes (whether this is due to the time needed to access phrase-structure rules, as proposed in Frazier and Fodor 1978, or whether it is due, say, to node postulation *per se*). The tendency for perceivers to follow "Late Closure" and thus attach new items low, into the current phrase or clause, can also be attributed to the parser pursuing the first available constituent-structure analysis on the assumption that more recently encountered material is more readily accessible in memory than more distant material.

But now what will happen in Dutch if we assume that the processor follows the first analysis strategy? If we maintain the assumptions we have made for English—that the processor builds up the phrase structure as each word is encountered—there are no problems that I am aware of. We simply replace the grammar of English with the grammar of Dutch and make the correct predictions about parsing preferences and perceptual complexity (Frazier 1987b). However, if we assume the head-projection hypothesis we make the wrong predictions. For example, in (10) the preposition *van* can either mark the internal argument of the verb *houden* ('like') or introduce a prepositional phrase modifying the subject noun phrase. Taking the first available analysis of the phrase "van Holland" ('from Holland') will lead to the VP-attachment analysis illustrated in (10a) if the VP has already been postulated at this point in the analysis of the sentence. This is due to Minimal Attachment, as may be seen by comparing (10a) and (10b). However, if the processor has postulated only those phrasal nodes whose heads have been encountered, then clearly the first available analysis of the PP will be as a modifier of the preceding NP, as illustrated in (11).

(10) a.

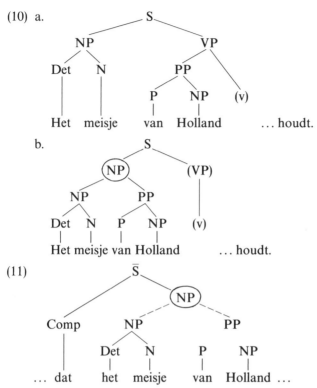

(11)

There is no evidence of difficulty in processing the sentence in (10). This is expected on the view that the predictable S and VP nodes have already been entered in the phrase marker when the PP is encountered. There is, however, evidence of difficulty in (12), where the non-minimal-attachment analysis of the PP "van Holland" turns out to be required. In short, the parsing preferences in Dutch provide further evidence against the head-projection hypothesis (as a processing claim).[3]

(12) ... dat het meisje van Holland van Spanje houdt
  (= "that the girl from Holland liked Spain")

Let us now return to the correspondence between grammatical and processing classes. It turns out that here too there is a problem for attempts to directly exploit the uncompiled principles of the grammar. The distinction between (general) phrase structure and structure projected from the strict subcategorization of a particular lexical item evaporates if phrase structure is projected directly from lexical items. This makes it extremely difficult to account for a finding like Mitchell's (see above) where it appears that the parser has misanalyzed a noun phrase as a direct object of an obligatorily intransitive verb. This error could arise only if the processor mistook the verb for an entirely different verb which permitted a direct object. This is not the type of error we would expect many subjects to make, even under conditions where an intransitive verb is displayed in the same frame as a noun phrase.

In sum, if lexical information and general grammatical principles are used to project syntactic structure, we again face difficulties due to the failure to distinguish between general phrase structure, category, and sub-category. Further, if the joint consequences of the grammatical principles are not considered, then this sort of lexically based parsing system will (apparently incorrectly) predict the existence of delayed phrase-structure analysis of head-final phrases.

4   Traditional Phase-Structure Rules

Pretend it's 1980. Consider the general framework of the Revised Extended Standard Theory, which is giving way to a modular grammar with separate principles governing case assignment, binding, and so forth. Assume, crucially, that the grammar contains phrase-structure rules, even if principles of various modules explain the properties of these rules (e.g., principles of case, theta assignment and X′ theory; see Stowell 1981).

This view too will run into difficulties given any principle that guarantees priority of lexical over syntactic information in generating hypotheses (e.g., the "lexical preference principle" of Ford et al., a principle granting priority to more specific information over more general information, or priority to bottom-up information over predictive, global, or top-down information). Any of these principles would lead the preferred or most frequent subcate-gorization of a head of phrase to determine the initial syntactic analysis.

Mitchell's results will be difficult to explain on this view, since we must assume that the parser constructs an analysis (e.g., "departed the actors" must be taken as a phrase) that has already been determined to be ungram-matical, since it will have been constructed on the basis of lexical informa-tion about *depart*. Further, if we assume that lexical information is given priority in all languages, in head-final languages we will encounter the same problems encountered by the head-projection hypothesis, since it is the head of the phrase that carries information about item-specific lexical preferences.

Alternatively, we might assume that lexical preferences are granted pri-ority over general syntactic factors only when the relevant lexical information (the head) occurs phrase-initially. But then we would expect a considerable processing advantage for head-initial languages over head-final ones (where lexical preferences would not be available to guide phrase construction). Hence, we might have expected head-initial languages to outnumber head-final ones. But they do not—contrary to what we would expect if there really were a striking processing advantage to using lexically specific information before general phrase-structure information.

If we give up the assumption that syntactic hypotheses are lexically generated, there is no problem at all in accounting for the processing or language generalizations considered above. Single analysis applies to all constituent-structure decisions (i.e., the output of the phrase-structure rules defines the class of constituent structure decisions). The decisions that are subject to the delay strategy are simply lexical category (major syntactic category) decisions. Since strict subcategorization is viewed as a within-category distinction (unlike in categorial grammar), delayed category selection will not entail a delay until strict subcategorization has been disambiguated. And if major category and general phrase-structure information are used to immediately structure an input, with item-specific information used rapidly to evaluate or filter syntactic analyses, no delay of analysis is predicted in head-final phrases. In short, at least descriptively, everything is fine.

5 Implications

More evidence is needed about some of our processing generalizations—especially evidence on the analysis of syntactic category ambiguities, on the "Mitchell effect," and on the processing of head-final constructions. However, numerous everyday experiences and experimental demonstrations attest to our ability to parse (automatically, without practice) in the absence of any information about lexical heads of phrases or their item-specific preferences—consider the case of unknown words, or the parsing of grammatically inflected nonsense (Epstein 1961), or the syntactic effects observed in the anomalous conditions in standard experimental paradigms (Forster 1979). This would be a difficult cognitive task if normal parsing depended on lexical information and not on general phrase-structure configurations.

In any case, current evidence at least favors a structural source for early syntactic analysis. Problems arise (on all views considered here) for proposals granting item-specific lexical information priority over structural factors in early syntactic processing.[4] This in turn implies that we should be skeptical of any theory of language processing that grants an absolute across-the-board priority to bottom-up information (over "top-down" predictive information), to specific information (over general information), or to local (over more global) information.

In terms of grammar, there are also interesting implications of our findings. We saw above that a rule-based grammar could readily accommodate the parsing generalizations of section 1 so long as item-specific information was used to evaluate or filter syntactic analyses. But so far we have only considered the descriptive adequacy of the rule-based approach. And we have ignored questions about whether the advantages of this approach were intrinsic to a rule-based system. Once we consider this question, it is obvious that the advantages of this system derive from other factors (namely, the particular type of information packaged together). A rule-based system in which subcategorization information is captured by phrase-structure rules (as was suggested in early transformational frame works and early generalized phrase-structure frameworks; see Chomsky 1965 and Gazdar 1982) would fail to distinguish category and subcategory, leaving a rule-based grammar open to one of the objections leveled against the other proposals considered here. Moreover, a rule-based approach is not very explanatory; it hides or disguises questions about why grammatical information should be organized in one fashion rather than another.

If instead of a rule-based approach we consider a principle-based approach, these questions are highlighted. Thus, rather than assuming that the grammar organizes information into "packages" (phrase-structure rules), we might assume that grammatical principles are organized for purposes of language processing—e.g., that they are precompiled into something like phrase-structure rules. On this view, one maintains the explanatory advantage of a principle-based grammar, but the parsing predictions depend on the precise organization of the principles. If we assume that all principles that exploit sisterhood as their basic structural relation are precompiled or organized together (Frazier 1985; Freedman and Forster 1985), then the parsing predictions are very similar to a view based on phrase-structure rules. However, unlike an approach that stipulates the existence of phrase-structure rules, we must now explain *why* grammatical principles should be organized in this fashion for purposes of parsing. (The fact that the principle-based grammar forces us to ask this question is, of course, one major advantage of the approach.)

Basically, then, we have three questions to answer:

(i) Why are grammatical principles organized at all for purposes of parsing?
(ii) Why aren't more syntactic principles organized together; why just those referring to sisterhood? Why not precompile all syntactic principles, resulting in something like a generalized phrase-structure grammar?
(iii) Why isn't lexical information included, i.e., why is the cut between syntactic principles and lexical information made in the precise way it is?

I think the answer to all three questions is the same, namely, parsing speed. Numerous factors indicate that the parser is designed to be able to quickly assign structure to an input item. Indeed, this seems to explain the parsing strategies found in natural languages (see discussion above and in Frazier 1987a). Further, in view of the limits on immediate memory for unstructured material, it is not clear that language comprehension could take place if the parser were not designed to quickly assign structure to an input.

If grammatical principles were not organized for parsing, the same syntactic inferences would have to be drawn over and over again. Presumably this would (at least at times) result in delays of analysis due to the interaction of the computations (syntactic inferences) with capacity limitations. Hence, precompiling the consequences of at least some grammatical principles will facilitate quick analysis. However, if all syntactic inferences were precompiled (e.g., those involving binding and other relations based on c-command, in addition to those based on sisterhood), the advantage of precompiling certain principles would evaporate because the search set of "rules" or phrasal sequences would simply become too large.[5]

Question iii is perhaps best addressed by considering the possibility that subcategory, rather than major syntactic category, defines the cut between lexical information and syntactic information, so that the delay strategy applies at the level of subcategory rather than at the level of major category. (I assume here that parsing must be based on some property of the input, on any view.) In this case, syntactic analysis of phrasal relations could not proceed until the subcategory of an item had been determined, i.e., disambiguated by later context. But now disambiguation will depend, for example, on details of the complement of a verb. This may require analysis of a long stretch of input. For example, consider (7), where choosing the right subcategory of *know* depends on identifying the category of an item occurring seven words later, as well as identifying the correct structure of all intervening items. This would be a long time to delay analysis. Thus, by basing analysis on lexical information at the level of major syntactic category, the parser may proceed immediately, or shortly after an input is encountered, rather than having to wait to determine which subcategory of the item is appropriate for the input sentence.

Principle-based grammars force theories of performance to account for any organization of grammatical principles evidenced in language processing.[6] In the present case, processing theories seem capable of meeting the challenge.

Acknowledgments

The first part of this paper was originally presented as comments on Mark Steedman's talk "Sentence processing from the lexicon" at the Max-Planck-Institute in Nijmegen, in July 1986. The paper was expanded, and written, while I was a Visiting Scientist at the MIT Center for Cognitive Science. I would like to thank both institutions for their support. I am grateful to Steve Abney, Josef Aoun, Bob Berwick, Janet Fodor, Jim Higginbotham, John Limber, Michael Rochemont, and William Marslen-Wilson for comments on various parts of this work.

Notes

1. The evidence of Rayner, Carlson, and Frazier (1983) for multiple access of thematic frames is indirect and turns on the hypothesized role of thematic frames in identifying initially overlooked analyses of a string. By contrast, the evidence of Shapiro et al. is more directly linked to the access of multiple lexical-semantic frames (thematic frames or the selectional frames of Grimshaw [1979]). The analysis of data presented by Tanenhaus and Carlson in this volume also seems to require the access and continued availability of multiple thematic frames.

2. At present it remains unclear precisely when selection occurs for a single meaning of an equi-based item in a neutral context.

3. Here we have examined only the most straightforward instantiation of a principle-based parser using X' theory to directly postulate phrasal nodes. Existing principle-based parsers actually use alternative methods of phrase postulation, and thus escape the predictions examined here. For example, in Berwick 1985 those features common to a phrase-initial item and the head of the phrase are projected or percolated to provide a partial specification of a phrasal node before its head is encountered. This is an interesting idea, but it certainly does not count as a direct instantiation of X' theory (i.e., head projection), since it permits nonheads to determine the categorial specification of their mother nodes. Abney (1986) suggests a different approach within his principle-based parser. He considers the use of templates to capture local dependencies between adjacent items; the system (in one version, at least) simply parses with these nongrammatical templates instead of the conventional phrase-structure rules.

In sum, one might sidestep the delay prediction of a principle-based parser that uses head projection to identify phrases. But then it really isn't all that clear whether one is still using the principles of the grammar in an uncompiled fashion. In more recent work, Abney suggests using the principles of grammar as licensing conditions that apply rapidly to assign structure. Though it might appear that rapid use of all uncompiled principles leads to the same effect as precompiling the (joint) consequences of those principles, this is not quite true, because of the lack of separation of structure from properties of individual lexical items and because of inferences warranted only by right context, assuming that "accidental gaps" in the phrase structure of a language are possible.

4. In addition to the problems discussed in the text, there is the problem of how, given any lexically based parsing system, conflicts between the preferred lexical form of one item and the preferred form of another are resolved and how lexical parsing principles are integrated with syntactic ones. The only explicit account of this type that I am aware of is that of Ford, Bresnan, and Kaplan (1983). This proposal, at least, needed to resort to arbitrary syntactic strategies (e.g., the Final Arguments Principle, Invoked Attachment). And, to resolve conflicts between the preferences of different lexical items, it was at times necessary to compute the logical entailments of the various possible global syntactic structures. Both the arbitrariness of the parsing strategies (what evidence could children use to learn parsing strategies?) and the implausibility of this general sort of resolution mechanism argue against the only explicit lexically generated parsing hypothesis available (apart from those that abstract away from problems of lexical ambiguity). See Frazier 1983 for discussion.

5. Robert Berwick (personal communication) informs me that the problem of searching the fully expanded rule set for generalized phrase-structure grammar is not even NP-complete. Parsing with a generalized phrase-structure grammar (Gazdar 1981; Gazdar et al. 1984) provides a good analog for parsing with a principle-based grammar in which the consequences of all syntactic principles are precompiled or organized together.

I assume in the text that the option of precompiling (or organizing together) arbitrarily selected principles is simply excluded on general grounds. In Frazier 1985b it is proposed that only coherent sets of principles, e.g. those exploiting the same representational vocabulary, constitute potential processing modules.

6. The hypothesis that the grammar provides a strictly simultaneous definition of well-formed structures places interesting constraints on the grammar, i.e., prohibiting principles from applying at one "level" of representation but not at another. By casting generalizations in terms of chains and by stating grammatical laws over "heads," "tails," or "all members" of chains, it appears to be possible to maintain that all grammatical laws apply to all grammatical representations. This both restricts the notion of possible grammar and opens the door for performance explanations of the organization of linguistic knowledge. Unfortunately, pursuing the consequences of this approach would take us far beyond the scope of this chapter.

References

Abney, S. 1986. A New Model of Natural Language Parsing. Manuscript, MIT.

Ades, A., and Steedman, M. 1982. On the order of words. *Linguistics and Philosophy* 4: 517–558.

Bach, E., and Partee, B. 1980. Anaphora and semantic structure. *Chicago Linguistic Society* 16.

Berwick, R. 1985. *The Acquisition of Syntactic Knowledge*. Cambridge: MIT Press.

Berwick, R. 1986. Principle-based parsing. MIT manuscript.

Berwick, R., and Weinberg, A. 1985. Models for deterministic parsing. In Proceedings of NELS 12.

Chomsky, N. 1965. *Aspects of the Theory of Syntax*. Cambridge, Mass.: MIT Press.

Chomsky, N. 1981. *Lectures on Government and Binding: The Pisa Lectures*. Dordrecht: Foris.

Chomsky, N. 1986. *Knowledge of Language: Its Nature, Origin and Use*. New York: Praeger.

Clifton, C., Frazier, L., and Connine, C. 1984. Lexical expectations in sentence comprehension. *Journal of Verbal Learning and Verbal Behavior* 23: 696–708.

Crain, S., and Steedman, M. 1985. On not being led up the garden path: The use of context by the psychological parser. In D. Dowty, L. Kartunnen, and A. Zwicky (eds.), *Natural Language Parsing*. Cambridge University Press.

Epstein, W. 1961. The influence of syntactical structure on learning. *American Journal of Psychology* 74: 80–85.

Fodor, J., Bever, T., and Garrett, M. 1974. *The Psychology of Language: An Introduction to Psycholinguistics and Generative Grammar*. New York: McGraw-Hill.

Fodor, J. D. 1978. Parsing strategies and constraints on transformations. *Linguistic Inquiry* 9: 427–474.

Fodor, J. A. 1981. Does performance shape competence? *Philosophical Transactions of the Royal Society, London* 295: 285–295.

Ford, M., Bresnan, J., and Kaplan, R. 1983. A competence-based theory of syntactic closure. In J. Bresnan (ed.), *The Mental Representation of Grammatical Relations*. Cambridge, Mass.: MIT Press.

Forster, K. 1979. Levels of processing and the structure of the language processor. In W. E. Cooper and E. C. T. Walker (eds.), *Sentence Processing*. Hillsdale, N.J.: Erlbaum.

Frazier, L. 1978. On Comprehending Sentences: Syntactic Parsing Strategies. Doctoral dissertation, University of Connecticut.

Frazier, L. 1983. Review of Bresnan's *Mental Representation of Grammatical Relations*. *Natural Language and Linguistic Theory* 1: 281–310.

Frazier, L. 1985a. Syntactic complexity. In D. Dowty, L. Kartunnen, and A. Zwicky (eds.), *Natural Language Parsing*. Cambridge University Press.

Frazier, L. 1985b. Modularity and the representational hypothesis. In Proceedings of NELS 12.

Frazier, L. 1987a. Sentence processing: A tutorial review. In M. Coltheart (ed.), *Attention and Performance XII*. Hillsdale, N.J.: Erlbaum.

Frazier, L. 1987b. Syntactic processing: Evidence from Dutch. *Natural Language and Linguistic Theory* 5: 519–560.

Frazier, L., and Fodor, J. 1978. The sausage machine: A new two-stage parsing model. *Cognition* 6: 291–328.

Frazier, L., and Rayner, K. 1982. Making and correcting errors during sentence comprehension: Eye movements in the analysis of structurally ambiguous sentences. *Cognitive Psychology* 143: 178–210.

Frazier, L., and Rayner, K. 1987. Resolution of syntactic category ambiguities: Eye movements in parsing lexically ambiguous sentences. *Journal of Memory and Language* 26: 505–526.

Freedman, S. E., and Forster, K. I. 1985. The psychological status of overgenerated sentences. *Cognition* 19: 101–132.

Gazdar, G. 1982. Phrase structure grammar. In P. Jacobson and G. K. Pullum (eds.), *The Nature of Syntactic Representation*. Dordrecht: Reidel.

Gazdar, G., Klein, E., Pullum, G., and Sag, I. 1984. *Generalized Phrase Structure Grammar*. Cambridge, Mass.: Harvard University Press.

Gorrell, P. 1987. Studies in Human Syntactic Processing: Ranked Parallel versus Serial Models. Doctoral dissertation, University of Connecticut.

Grimshaw, J. 1979. Complement selection and the lexicon. *Linguistic Inquiry* 10: 279–326.

Holmes, V. M. 1987. Syntactic parsing: In search of the garden path. In M. Coltheart (ed.), *Attention and Performance XII*. Hillsdale, N.J.: Erlbaum.

Kennedy, A., and Murray, W. 1984. Inspection times for words in syntactically ambiguous sentences under three presentation conditions: Eye movements in the analysis of semantically biased sentences. *Journal of Experimental Psychology: Human Perception and Performance* 10: 833–847.

Kimball, J. 1973. Seven principles of surface structure parsing in natural language. *Cognition* 2: 15–47.

Mitchell, D. 1987. Lexical guidance in human parsing: Locus and processing characteristics. In M. Coltheart (ed.), *Attention and Performance XII*. Hillsdale, N.J.: Erlbaum.

Rayner, K., Carlson, M., and Frazier, L. 1983. The interaction of syntax and semantics during sentence processing: Eye movements in the analysis of semantically biased sentences. *Journal of Verbal Learning and Verbal Behavior* 22: 358–374.

Rayner, K., and Duffy, S. 1986. Lexical complexity and fixation times in reading: Effects of word frequency, verb complexity, and lexical ambiguity. *Memory and Cognition* 14: 191–201.

Rayner, K., and Frazier, L. In press. Parsing temporarily ambiguous complement structures. *Quarterly Journal of Experimental Psychology.*

Seidenberg, M., Tanenhaus, M., Leiman, J., and Bienkowski, M. 1982. Automatic access of the meanings of ambiguous words in context. *Psychology* 14: 489–537.

Shapiro, L., Zurif, E., and Grimshaw, J. 1986. Sentence processing and the mental representation of verbs. Manuscript, Brandeis University.

Stowe, L. In press. Thematic structures and sentence comprehension. In G. Carlson and M. Tanenhaus (eds.), *Linguistic Structure in Language Processing.* Dordrecht: Reidel.

Stowell, T. 1981. Origins of Phrase Structure. Doctoral dissertation, MIT.

Swinney, D. 1979. Lexical access during sentence comprehension: (Re)consideration of context effects. *Journal of Verbal Learning and Verbal Behavior* 18: 645–660.

Tanenhaus, M., and Lucas, M. 1987. Context effects in lexical processing. *Cognition* 25: 213–234.

Wanner, E., and Maratsos, M. 1978. An ATN approach to comprehension. In M. Halle, J. Bresnan, and G. A. Miller (eds.), *Linguistic Theory and Psychological Reality.* Cambridge, Mass.: MIT Press.

Chapter 18

Lexical Structure and Language Comprehension	Michael K. Tanenhaus and Greg N. Carlson

Much of the richness of lexical representation comes from semantic and syntactic information that becomes apparent only when one considers how lexical representation interfaces with the syntactic and semantic structure of a sentence. In this chapter we will be concerned with the representation and processing of such "higher-level" lexical structure. We will be examining the time course with which different types of lexical knowledge are accessed and used during comprehension, and we will be developing some preliminary proposals about lexical representation.

It is generally agreed among linguists that the lexical representation of a word contains all the linguistically relevant information about the word that is not predictable from general rules. This includes the specification of the word's pronunciation, its spelling, its morphological characteristics, its meaning or meanings, and its membership in a major syntactic category. Lexical representation also includes certain more "combinatory" aspects of the meaning and of the syntactic characteristics of the lexical item. This information is of two main types: "argument-structure information" and "control information." By "argument-structure information" we intend any information concerning the types of immediate complements a word may take. (Verbs take a rich variety of complements, but other categories take them as well.) Syntactic subcategorization (Chomsky 1965), which is a specification of the types of constituents that can serve as complements of a lexical item, is one kind of such information. Another kind of "argument information" that has been proposed, which we will examine in some detail later, is the verb's thematic structure—the "roles" or "modes of participation" that characterize how the arguments of the verb partake in the event denoted by the verb.

"Control information" refers to the way the particular verb influences the interpretation of empty categories, chiefly the empty subjects of infinitival complements. (The phenomenon of control can, in fact, be accomplished by a number of different means, some doing without empty categories.) For example, the subject of the verb *promise* controls the interpretation of the infinitive ("John promised Mary _ to wash himself/*herself"), whereas the object (and not the subject) of the verb *persuade* controls its interpretation ("John persuaded Mary _ to wash *himself/herself").

There is extensive psycholinguistic evidence that the noncombinatory aspects of lexical representation are immediately accessed and used in comprehension. However, much less is known about the access and use of argument and control information; whether this type of information is accessed and used immediately remains controversial.

Information about the role of lexical knowledge in comprehension is crucial to the understanding of the nature of linguistic processing. Our conscious experience of sentence comprehension is that it is immediate and effortless. This seems paradoxical in light of some basic facts about language and language processing. Input into the comprehension system, whether it is spoken or printed, is basically sequential, whereas the structure of language results in massive local indeterminacy. One way of dealing with this indeterminacy is to delay making commitments until enough input has accumulated to reduce ambiguity. However, this view of language processing as a "catch-up" game is now generally considered untenable in light of empirical evidence about the immediacy of comprehension (Marslen-Wilson 1975; Marslen-Wilson and Tyler 1987).

Although there is currently little debate about the immediacy of comprehension, two very different views of the comprehension process dominate the current literature. One tradition, stemming from Kimball (1973) and developed in most detail by Lyn Frazier and colleagues, assumes that much of comprehension involves rapidly building a syntactic skeleton by making primary use of phrase-structure rules and some simple decision principles (e.g., Minimal Attachment) with syntactic-category information as the primary input. A system like this will necessarily make mistakes as a result of ignoring other sources of information, including lexical knowledge. Consistent with this, Frazier and colleagues (most notably Rayner and Clifton) have marshaled a large body of experimental data suggesting that small "local garden paths" are quite common in language processing. A central problem in this framework is to specify how the comprehension system is able to rapidly arrive at the correct interpretation when revisions are necessary (Frazier 1987).

In contrast, other researchers (Crain and Steedman 1985; Marlsen-Wilson and Tyler 1987) see the comprehension system as rapidly and optimally integrating lexical, syntactic, and contextual information in some form of a mental-models representation (Johnson-Laird 1983). Researchers in this tradition have not said much about the nature of the representation, nor have they said much about the specific mechanisms involved. However, they have provided an impressive body of evidence that the system can make rapid use of available information to immediately resolve, or perhaps even avoid, the problem of indeterminacy.

Information about the role of lexical knowledge in comprehension is likely to be decisive in choosing among (or perhaps reconciling) these different perspectives on language processing. Whereas a "compute and revise" parser can ignore certain types of lexical knowledge (temporarily, at least), an "optimal uptake" system must immediately exploit the full range of potentially available lexical knowledge in order to reduce the local indeterminacy problem and to provide rapid communication among the different types of knowledge to be integrated.

It is easy to see that more and more of local indeterminacy can be eliminated by decreasing the time lag between the operations of the parser and the availability of the relevant lexical information. Immediate access to argument-structure information and control information about a verb could allow the parser to "project" structure yet to be encountered on the basis of information in the verb's lexical entry, thereby "guiding" the parse.

Making all relevant lexical information available immediately does not, however, eliminate the local indeterminacy problem. For example, consider a sentence that begins "Bill gave the puppy ...". This could be continued in at least two distinct ways: "... a bath" and "... to Roberta". But if lexical representation can make the alternative possibilities and information about how they are to be evaluated available in parallel, the indeterminacy problem may well be more tractable.

We will first review the results of some of our recent research on sentences with long-distance dependencies. These studies, we will conclude, demonstrate that the language processing has immediate access to the lexical information discussed above. We will then develop some explicit representational and processing assumptions about how a particular type of lexical information—thematic roles—is used in comprehension, and we will review some experimental evidence that provides preliminary support for the framework that we have been developing. Our interest in exploring thematic roles is motivated by several considerations. First, under certain assumptions, thematic roles can provide much of the lexical parallelism that we have suggested would be extremely useful in parsing. Second, as Frazier and colleagues have argued persuasively (see Frazier 1987), thematic relations are the only vocabulary shared by the parser, the discourse model, and the world knowledge. On the proposal we will develop, the parallel access of thematic roles helps guide parsing decisions and mediates among discourse structure, world knowledge, and parsing.

1 Lexical Structure and Long-Distance Dependencies

During the last few years, we have been mapping out the time courses with which various types of lexical information are accessed and used in the parsing of sentences with long-distance dependencies. We will refer to these types of sentences as *filler-gap* sentences, following Fodor (1978). In a filler-gap sentence, the "filler" must be associated with an empty category, or "gap," that occurs later in the sentence. For example, in the sentence illustrated in (1), the questioned phrase, "Which book", must be semantically interpreted as the direct object of *read*.

(1) *Which book* did the little boy read _ in school?

Much of current syntactic theory has focused on sentences with empty categories, and there is a growing psycholinguistic literature on the processing of these sentences, which we will not attempt to review here (see Clifton and Frazier 1987 and Fodor 1987 for recent reviews). Our primary interest has been in using these sentences to provide a window on the processing of verbs. Filler-gap sentences are well suited for this purpose because the location of a possible gap often depends on the specific lexical properties of the verb that follows the filler. Consider for example, the fragments in (2).

(2) a. Which girl did the boy hope ...

b. Which girl did the boy persuade ...

c. Which girl did the boy hurry ...

In (2a) the filler "which girl" cannot be the object of the verb *hope*, because *hope* does not allow a direct object (although it does take complements, as in "Which girl did the boy hope would win the prize?"). In contrast, the filler in (2b) can be the object of *persuade* (although it need not be, as in "Which girl did the boy persuade the teacher to punish?"). In (2c) the filler may or may not be the object of *hurry*, depending on whether *hurry* is being used transitively or intransitively. Our research strategy has been to see how different lexical properties of verbs influence when a filler is associated with a verb. The logical possibilities range from limited use of lexical information (e.g., gaps might initially be posited after all verbs regardless of the particular properties of the verb) to the immediate use of all possible lexical knowledge.

We have been using an "embedded-anomaly" technique developed in collaboration with Laurie Stowe. The idea is to look for increases in processing load that result from a filler's being associated with a gap that results in an implausible interpretation. Plausibility effects can then be used to diagnose when gaps are posited and filled.

In the first set of experiments (Stowe, Tanenhaus, and Carlson 1985; Tanenhaus, Stowe, and Carlson 1985), we investigated the comprehension of embedded *wh*-questions which contained an optionally transitive verb (e.g., *asked*). Clifton, Frazier, and Connine (1984) had demonstrated that filler-gap sentences with optionally transitive verbs are comprehended more rapidly when the verb is used with its preferred subcategorization. We were interested in testing Fodor's (1978) hypothesis that the preferred subcategorization of the verb, or lexical preference, determines whether a gap is initially posited at the verb.

We will review one of our experiments here. We constructed filler-gap sentences in which an optionally transitive verb was used intransitively. An example is "The physical therapist wasn't sure which doctor the orderly hurried rapidly toward _". The filler is the object of the preposition *toward*. There is a decoy (possible) gap following the verb *hurried*, because the filler could have been the object of hurried, as in the sentence "The physical therapist wasn't sure which doctor the orderly hurried _ to the operating room". We wanted to see whether readers initially posit and fill the possible gap at the verb.

We constructed plausible and implausible fillers for each sentence. The implausible filler for the example sentence was "The orderly wondered which bed the nurse hurried quickly toward _". The fillers differed in plausibility only with respect to the decoy gap; they were equally plausible as objects of the preposition—an orderly can more plausibly hurry a doctor than hurry a bed, but an orderly could hurry toward a bed as plausibly as toward a doctor. In addition to varying the plausibility of the filler, we also used two types of verbs: verbs that subjects prefer to use transitively and verbs that subjects prefer to use intransitively. Lexical preference was determined by norms collected by Connine et al. (1984). All together, then, there were four conditions, illustrated in table 1. The sentences were presented one word at a time on a CRT in a self-paced reading task in which subjects pressed a button to receive the next word. The logic of the experiment was as follows: Sentences with implausible fillers should become incongruous only if subjects posited and filled the decoy gap after the verb. Thus, plausibility effects, reflected in longer reading times, serve as a diagnostic for when gaps are posited and filled.

Table 1

Transitive preference verb with plausible filler

The district attorney found out which witness the reporter asked anxiously about.

Transitive preference verb with implausible filler

The district attorney found out which church the reporter asked anxiously about.

Intransitive preference verb with plausible filler

The physical therapist wasn't sure which doctor the orderly hurried rapidly toward.

Intransitive preference verb with implausible filler

The physical therapist wasn't sure which bed the orderly hurried rapidly toward.

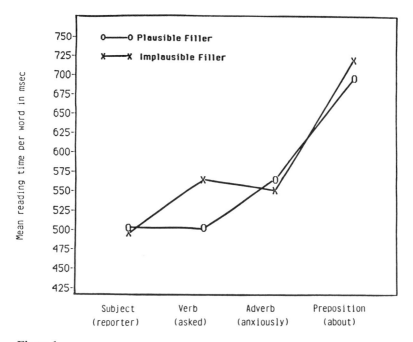

Figure 1

Reading times for critical words in sentences with late gaps and transitive expectation verbs (e.g., "The district attorney found out which witness/church the reporter asked anxiously about").

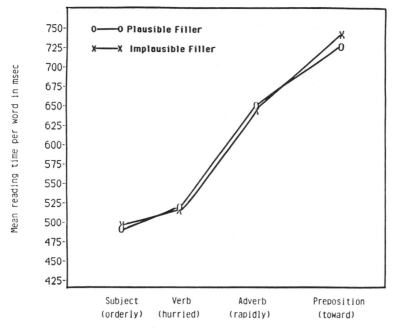

Figure 2
Reading times for critical words in sentences with late gaps and intransitive expectation verbs (e.g., "The physical terapist wasn't sure which doctor/bed the orderly hurried rapidly toward").

The results for the transitive preference verbs are presented in figure 1. The data of interest are the reading times for the words beginning with the verb (*hurry*) that marks the first possible gap location. Reading times for the implausible fillers were significantly longer than reading times to the plausible fillers beginning at the verb. Thus, a gap is posited, filled, and semantically interpreted immediately at the verb. This result has since been replicated behaviorally (Tanenhaus, Boland, and Garnsey 1987) and with cortical evoked potentials (Garnsey, Tanenhaus, and Chapman in press). The conclusion that gaps are posited and filled immediately upon encountering a verb is consistent with results obtained by Stowe (1984, 1986), Crain and Fodor (1985), and Swinney et al. (1987).

The data for the intransitive preference verbs are presented in figure 2. In contrast to the transitive preference verbs, there was no hint of a plausibility effect at the verb. The most straightforward interpretation is that readers did not posit a gap following the intransitive preference verbs, although it is possible that a gap was posited and quickly rejected using subcategorization information as a filter (Clifton and Frazier, in press). We will offer a possible explanation for these data in terms of "thematic roles" in section 2; for now, the important point is that the lexical properties of the verb determined whether the readers semantically interpreted the filler as the object of the verb.

A recent series of experiments (Tanenhaus, Boland, and Garnsey 1987; Boland et al., forthcoming) has found an important qualification to the early-filling strategy for transitive expectation verbs. These experiments compared verbs like *remind*—which are obligatorily used transitively, and typically used with a complement, as in (3)

(3) Bill reminded John to go to a movie.

—with verbs like *read*, which are typically used transitively but do not allow infinitive complements. Our previous studies had used mostly verbs, like *read*, that do not allow infinite complements.

The subject's task was to continue reading the sentences one word at a time by pressing a "Yes" button, and to press a "No" button if the sentence stopped making sense. The sentences accumulated across a CRT screen. The test sentences were intermixed with a large number of filler sentences. About 10 percent of the filler sentences were semantically anomalous. The instructions and practice sentences gave subjects some examples of sentences that they should judge to not make sense; for example, in the sentence "The bathroom is located at the top floor of the yellow chair", subjects were instructed that they should respond No at *chair*). Subjects rarely responded No during a plausible sentence, and word-by-word reading times averaged about 350 msec. The conditions of interest here are illustrated in (4).

(4) a. Which child did Bill remind to watch the show?

b. Which movie did Bill remind to watch the show?

c. Which book did the child read in bed at night?

d. Which food did the child read in bed at night?

In sentence (4a) *child* is a plausible object of *remind*, whereas in sentence (4b) *movie* is an implausible object. In (4c) *book* is a plausible object of read, whereas in (4d) *food* is not. At the verb *read*, subjects were more likely to reject the sentences with implausible fillers (i.e., to press the No button) than the sentences with plausible fillers. When subjects did press the Yes button to continue the sentence, response latencies were significantly longer for the sentences with implausible fillers. This condition replicates our previous "early-filling" results. In contrast, there were no differences between the plausible and implausible filler conditions for sentences with the verb *remind*. Plausibility effects did not occur until the preposition *to* provided unambiguous syntactic evidence that the questioned phrase had to be the direct object of the verb. Thus, for verbs that are likely to be followed by complements, readers do not seem to associate a filler with a possible role in which it is incongruous unless the structure of the sentence allows no other alternative.

The difference between *read* and *remind* suggests the following account of lexically driven gap-filling: In a filler-gap sentence, the comprehender is looking for a role for the filler. When a verb is encountered, the roles associated with its arguments become available. If the filler is implausible in all these roles, the sentence becomes incongruous, because no plausible readings remain temporarily under consideration. In our experiments, this would have been the case for verbs, like *read*, that do not take complements. However, for verbs like *remind*, the sentential complement in the lexical entry signals the likely availability of an upcoming role for the filler which could result in a plausible reading. Thus, on the basis of the lexical representations, readers can see how to construct a plausible reading even if the actual structures have yet to be encountered.

Our results complement the findings by Shapiro, Zurif, and Grimshaw (1987) that processing load as measured by a dual-task paradigm increases with the complexity of the argument structure of the verb, as was initially hypothesized by Fodor, Bever, and Garrett (1974). Shapiro et al. concluded that lexical access makes available the full argument structure of a verb.

We have also been using the embedded-anomaly technique to investigate the access of verb-control information. Some examples of verb control are illustrated in (5).

(5) a. The girl started _ to sing.

    b. The girl forced the woman _ to sing.

The verb *started* is an example of a subject-control verb. The terminology arises because its grammatical subject ("the girl", in example 5) serves as the implicit subject of the infinitive "to sing". In contrast, *forced* is an object-control verb. Its object, "the woman", controls the interpretation of the subject of the infinitive. Many verbs can be used as either subject-control or object-control verbs. For example, *beg* is used as a subject-control verb in (6a) and as an object-control verb in (6b).

(6) a. The girl begged _ to sing for her brother.

    b. The girl begged her brother _ to sing for her.

When verbs like *beg* are placed in filler-gap constructions, their control properties can remain ambiguous for several words or more, as is illustrated in (7a) and (7b).

(7) a. Which woman did the girl beg _ _ to sing some songs?
       (object control)

    b. Which woman did the girl beg to sing some songs for _?
       (subject control)

Frazier, Clifton, and Randall (1983) conducted an experiment in which subjects were presented with sentences one word at a time and then judged, at the end of each sentence, whether it made sense. They found that subjects were faster to say that they comprehended sentences like (7b) than sentences like (7a). They argued that this was because subjects followed a "recent-filler" strategy and assumed that "the girl" was the subject of the complement "to sing", resulting in a garden path for sentences like (7a), in which the more distant filler, "the woman", functions as the subject of the infinitive. Surprisingly, they also found the same pattern of results when ambiguous control verbs like *beg* were replaced by unambiguous control verbs like *hope* and *force*.

Frazier et al. (1983) argued that subjects use the recent-filler strategy on a first pass through a sentence, even when it violates verb-control information because access to verb-control information is delayed long enough so that it is not immediately available to guide initial filler-gap assignment. The recent-filler strategy works well for subject-control verbs. The subject of the verb is correctly interpreted as the subject of the infinitive clause. For example, in the sentence "Which woman did the girl hope to sing for?", the most recent filler, "the girl", would be interpreted as the subject of *sing*. However, the recent-filler strategy will result in a garden path for sentences with object-control verbs. In the sentence "Which woman did the girl force to sing some songs?", "the girl" will be mistakenly interpreted as the subject of *sing*.

Although argument and control information are somewhat different types of lexical information, there does not seem to be an obvious reason why one type of information should be rapidly accessed but not the other. Moreover, the evidence of Frazier et al. (1983) for delayed use of verb control information is indirect, and there are a number of possible alternative explanations for why sentences with object-control verbs might simply be more complex than sentences with subject-control verbs (see Fodor, in press), which do not require the assumption that verb control information has been ignored.

In a recent series of experiments, we (Boland, Tanenhaus, and Garnsey (forthcoming)) have used the embedded-anomaly technique to show that verb control information is, in fact, used immediately. We used materials like those in (8).

(8) a. Which frog/snake did the girl force _ _ to hop past the rock?

b. The girl forced the frog/snake to hop past the rock.

Fillers were either plausible (*frog*) or implausible (*snake*) as the subject of a verb like *hop* in an infinitive clause, as illustrated in (8a). Using a number of self-paced reading tasks, we found that readers detected the incongruity of a snake hopping immediately at the verb *hop*. This demonstrates that the control properties of *force*—an object-control verb—were used immediately. In fact, readers detected the incongruity just as rapidly in the filler-gap sentences as in non-*wh* sentences in which the plausible and implausible objects are in their normal grammatical positions, i.e., after the verb, as in (8b).

In sum, our studies of filler-gap sentences provide clear evidence that the language processor has rapid access to both argument-structure information and control information. These results complement the increasing body of evidence that lexical information plays an immediate role in guiding other types of parsing decisions, including attachment and closure decisions (Speer and Foss 1987; Mitchell and Holmes 1985; Tarraban and McClelland 1987).

However, our filler-gap studies do not specifically address the form of the lexical representations made available to the processing system when a verb is accessed. One possibility is that only the alternative syntactic subcategorizations for a verb are activated. However, it does not seem likely that readers gauge the potential congruity of a filler with respect to possible syntactic positions on the basis of syntactic representations alone. It seems more plausible that readers have access to the possible range of situations, including types of events and participants, that can occur with the verb. This type of semantic information specific to verb-argument relations is given by thematic roles.

2 Thematic Roles

Frazier and colleagues (Frazier 1986; Rayner, Carlson, and Frazier 1984) have argued that thematic relations are the only vocabulary shared by the parser, the discourse model, and knowledge of the world. They have proposed a special thematic processor that provides a channel of communication among these domains. On our view, which is quite similar in spirit to theirs, thematic roles themselves can do much of this work by virtue of the way they interact with other comprehension mechanisms.

The basic idea (Cottrell 1985) is that all the thematic roles (case roles) associated with a verb are activated in parallel when the verb is encountered. In addition, we propose that thematic roles are provisionally assigned to arguments of verbs as soon as possible, and that any active thematic roles that are not compatible with the assignment become inactive. Active thematic roles that are not assigned arguments within the sentence are entered into the discourse model as unspecified entities or addresses. On our proposal, thematic roles can enable the parser to make early semantic commitments yet to recover quickly from the inevitable misassignments that occur as a consequence of the local indeterminacy that is characteristic of natural language. We will further suggest that thematic roles can provide a mechanism for rapid interaction among the parser, the discourse model, and real-world knowledge. (See Cottrell 1984 and McClelland and Kawamoto 1986 for computational models in which parallel activation of case roles—roughly, thematic roles—plays an important part in resolving lexical and syntactic ambiguities.)

Parallel activation of thematic roles would be consistent with the large body of research on lexical processing demonstrating that multiple codes associated with a word are activated in parallel. For instance, multiple senses of ambiguous words are usually accessed even in the presence of biasing context (Onifer and Swinney 1981; Seidenberg et al. 1982; Swinney 1979; Tanenhaus et al. 1979; Burgess, Tanenhaus, and Seidenberg 1987). Moreover, a number of lexical and sublexical phenomena can be explained elegantly on the assumption that there is parallel bottom-up activation, with incompatible representations competing with one another (McClelland and Rumelhart 1981; Seidenberg 1985; Seidenberg, this volume). When representations are compatible, on the other hand, all remain active (Seidenberg and Tanenhaus 1979; Tanenhaus, Flanigan, and Seidenberg 1980).

Representational Assumptions

We now turn to three representational assumptions about thematic roles that have been guiding our recent work. The first is that the meaning of a verb is decomposable into two parts, one consisting of a set of thematic roles and one which we will call the *core meaning* of the verb. The second assumption is that the sets of roles associated with the verb are themselves associated with corresponding syntactic configurations in the verb's subcategorization information. Thus, thematic assignment has rapid and specific structural consequences. The third assumption is that not all the roles in a verb's entry must be assigned in any given sentence. The roles that remain unassigned we call *open* thematic roles. After reviewing these claims, we turn to a discussion of experimental support for these representational assumptions.

The general phenomenon of thematic roles goes under a number of different terms in the linguistics literature, including thematic relations, case roles (and relations), semantic roles, participant roles, deep cases, semantic cases, and theta-roles. Though many of these terminological distinctions carry with them particular views of their theoretical status, there is a shared underlying intuition that certain characteristic "modes of participation" in an event can be identified and generalized across a variety of verb or sentence meanings. The "modes of participation)" include such notions as Agent, Goal, Instrument, Source, Location, Benefactee, Patient, Theme, and Location. These are commonly viewed as roles assigned by a verb to its arguments, which are typically though not exclusively Noun Phrases.

There is currently little agreement on an exact inventory of thematic roles, and less yet on the status of thematic roles in linguistic theory. On the one hand, in Government-and-Binding Theory (Chomsky 1981) they are viewed as elements playing a critical role in the syntax, as they were in quite a different way in Fillmore 1968. At the other extreme, Ladusaw and Dowty (1988) argue that thematic roles are simply generalizations over entailments of verb meanings and are hence themselves without any special standing in a linguistic or semantic theory. Many take a position on thematic roles somewhere between these extremes; the most common understanding is that thematic roles are semantic or conceptual elements. However, thematic roles need not be viewed as conceptual primitives. Jackendoff (1987) identifies thematic roles with certain conceptual configurations. For example, the notion of agency is identified with the conceptual element functioning as the first argument of the concept of causation.

For present purposes, we will assume that thematic roles are primitive entities associated with arguments of verbs. It is possible that from the point of view of grammatical theory, thematic roles are derivative or even epiphenomenal, but that they function as primitives in the language-comprehension system (or, possibly, vice versa). However, for the sake of clarity we will begin with the assumption that thematic roles are fundamentally linguistic entities which are accessed during language comprehension.

Linguistic proposals about thematic roles are often guided by certain assumptions about how they are associated with the arguments of a verb. Bresnan (1982) uses the terms *coherence, completeness,* and *uniqueness* to designate these assumptions.

coherence: No argument of a verb is assigned more than one thematic role.
completeness: Every argument of a verb is assigned some thematic role.
uniqueness: No two arguments of a given verb may receive the same thematic role.

As a standard example, consider the verb *rent* in example 9.

(9) John rented Bill a summer cottage.

Here, we will assume that John functions in the role of Agent, Bill functions as Goal, and the summer cottage functions as Theme (or Patient).[1] In this case, each argument is assigned a role, each has a unique role, and each has just one role, satisfying the three principles listed above. Although each of these principles can be challenged (for instance, the principle of coherence may be violated in the example sentence itself, as one could argue that John functions as both Agent and Source), they form a reasonable starting part for further investigation.

In order to make predictions about the character of lexical access and language processing, it is necessary to present a view of how thematic roles fit into the organization of the system as a whole. We associate thematic roles with verb entries, leaving aside the question of whether other lexical categories, particularly nouns and adjectives, should be analyzed similarly. Each member of the set of syntactic "arguments" of a verb gets a thematic role from the lexical entry of the verb. The verb's "syntactic arguments" are the subject of the clause in which the verb appears and all the phrases subcategorized for by the verb (see Chomsky 1965, chapter 2), which are sister constituents of the verb under the immediately dominating VP node. We assume that the verb associates thematic roles with no constituents beyond these, such as modifiers and other adjuncts. By way of illustration, consider example 10 with the phrase structure indicated.

(10) $[_s[_{NP}\text{John}][_{VP}\text{rented}[_{NP}\text{Bill}][_{NP}\text{a summer cottage}]][_{PP}\text{in June}]]$

The subject of the sentence is the NP *John*. The verb *rent* subcategorizes for the two ensuing NPs, *Bill* and *a summer cottage*. So the verb associates a thematic role with each. Following Stowell (1981), we will call the set of thematic roles associated with a verb its *thematic grid*. The thematic grid associated with the verb *rent* in example 10 would be {Agent, Theme, Goal}. Of course, the roles in the grid need to be associated with the correct constituents. In the example, *John* would be associated with the Agent role, *summer cottage* with the Theme role, and *Bill* with the Goal role. However, we will leave aside the mechanics of how roles are to be associated with constituents.

The PP "in June" is not a subcategorized phrase, and thus does not receive a thematic role from the verb. When a PP is a subcategorized phrase, as in (11), it will be assigned a thematic role by the verb.

(11) a. John rented a summer cottage *to Bill*.

b. Max filled his gas tank *with water*.

c. Betty looked *at Fred* with a puzzled expression on her face.

Other types of subcategorized phrases, such as infinitives and sentential complements, will likewise be assigned thematic roles by verbs in sentences.[2]

Thus far we have not addressed the relationship between thematic roles and the other central aspects of lexical representation with which they interface, namely verb meaning and syntactic subcategorization. We have been assuming that thematic role assignment contributes to the meaning of a sentence and that there is a component of verb meaning that is independent of thematic assignments, which we will call the *core meaning* or *sense* of the verb. The meaning of a verb, then, is a combination of a core meaning and a thematic grid. This division allows for a distinction between two types of verb-based lexical ambiguitions. Contrast the ambiguity illustrated in (12) with the ambiguity illustrated in (13).

(12) John acted in the auditorium.

(13) a. John is cooking.

b. Fred is baking.

c. Sally is ringing.

On the favored interpretation of (12), John played a role in a play. However, the sentence could mean that he went about some purposeful activity, as in "John acted quickly to put out the fire". John is playing the same role, Agent, in both of these interpretations. Thus, the ambiguity associated with act illustrated in (12) can be reasonably analyzed as an ambiguity of sense.

Consider now the ambiguities of (13). One could treat these the same way as the ambiguity in (12); however, the close similarities in meaning and the apparent systematicity of the ambiguity have struck various researchers as calling for a slightly different analysis in which the ambiguity is explicable in terms of thematic roles. In each of these examples, a common analysis goes, there is an ambiguity as to the role that gets assigned to the subject of the sentence. If it is Agent, then the most likely reading is obtained; if it is Theme, then the less plausible readings emerge (Julie probably has a bell inside her, Fred is getting cooked, and Mary is being baked). On this analysis, then, ambiguities can arise in spite of a single core meaning, because the subject of the sentence can be assigned one of two thematic roles.

Verbs may have different subcategorizations associated with distinct thematic grids. Consider the very productive class of causative/inchoative (or causative/"ergative") verbs in English, where the intransitive version (e.g., "The butter melted") has the inchoative reading and the transitive version (e.g., "Mary melted the butter") has the causative reading.

(14) a. The butter melted/Mary melted the butter

    b. The window broke/Jimmy broke the window

    c. The rifle fired/Susan fired the rifle

The intransitive versions assign the same role (Theme) to their subjects that the transitive verbs assign to their objects; in addition, the transitive version assigns Agent to the subject. So the thematic grid associated with the intransitive would be {Theme}, whereas the grid associated with the transitive version would be {Agent, Theme}. In view of the analysis of verb meaning into the core and thematic components, it is possible to maintain that both versions of each verb have the same core meaning. For purposes of illustration, let us designate the core meaning of the verb *melt* with MELT. The analysis of the meanings of the transitive and intransitive versions would be as follows. (See Carlson 1984 for a formal presentation of this distinction in meaning.)

melt$_{intrans}$ melt$_{trans}$

MELT   {Theme}   MELT   {Agent, Theme}

Since different subcategorizations are associated with these thematic grids, no actual thematic ambiguities arise. However, let us return to the examples 13, where ambiguity does appear, and examine them a little more closely.

Consider the verb in (13a): *ring*. It has a transitive version in which the subject is Agent and the object is Theme, as in "Mary rang the doorbell", so this transitive sense has the associated grid {Agent, Theme}. One of the intransitive senses is clearly like the inchoative readings in (14), with a thematic grid {Theme}—this is the less likely reading of (13a) on which Mary must have a bell inside her. But what of the other intransitive reading, where Mary is functioning as Agent? One possible analysis is to associate the thematic grid {Agent} with this reading. However, this misses an important point about the meaning of this reading of the intransitive: that in order for Mary to be the Agent there must be something—a bell, or a telephone—that she is ringing. That is, there is understood to be a Theme in the situation, even though it is not explicitly mentioned in the sentence. We are suggesting, then, that (following Jackendoff 1972) one should analyze the more plausible readings of the intransitive examples of (13) as having the same thematic grid associated with them that the transitive version has associated with it, namely {Agent, Theme}. But this leaves a mismatch between the number of arguments in the intransitive version (one) and the number of thematic roles in the grid (two). If we are to maintain this analysis, then, we must assume that the Theme role remains unassigned in such examples. This is precisely what we wish to claim. We will refer to such unassigned thematic roles as *open thematic roles*. To illustrate, consider the following three examples, with the roles assigned as indicated.

(15) a. {Theme}

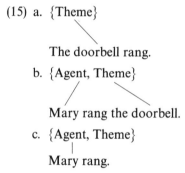

The doorbell rang.

  b. {Agent, Theme}

Mary rang the doorbell.

  c. {Agent, Theme}

Mary rang.

Example 15c exhibits an open thematic role—the Theme. The corresponding interpretation of the open role is much like an indefinite and not like a pronoun. The closest available paraphrase of (15c) would be "Mary rang something" rather than "Mary rang it". Thus, we are proposing that it is possible to have fewer syntactically realized arguments than thematic roles on a grid associated with that subcategorization of the verb, and that under these circumstances open roles arise.

Let us summarize the points of this section before we turn to discussion of comprehension processes. First, verb meanings are analyzable into (at least) two different components: a "core" meaning and the portion of the meaning contributed by the thematic grid. It is quite common to find the same verb with a constant core meaning but different thematic grids (as in the causative/inchoative alternatives) in different sentences. Thus, we would expect this class of ambiguities to show common processing characteristics, in contrast to the class of true sense ambiguities where more than one core meaning is associated with a common form.

Second, we also countenance unfilled or open thematic roles. It would have taken us too far afield to discuss the identification of these on the basis of linguistic evidence alone (see Carlson and Tanenhaus 1988). However, the open-thematic-roles analysis predicts an important distinction. We presented as an intuitive test for the presence of an open role the implication that something else is a necessary participant in the situation playing that role. Judgments of "likely" participation cannot arise from open roles, which require necessary participation. For instance, if John is running to catch a plane, he is very likely to be at or near an airport. However, one could just as easily use such an utterance to describe a situation in which there is no airport (the plane landed in a meadow), in spite of the fact that such situations usually do involve airports. In contrast, necessary participation is a requirement for implications arising from open roles.[3]

We have recently proposed (Carlson and Tanenhaus 1988) that open thematic roles are entered into the discourse model, or the semantic representation of the discourse, as addresses, or free variables. Later in the next section, we will return to some empirical consequences of this hypothesis.

Experimental Studies
We will now briefly review some recent experimental investigations of issues related to our hypotheses about thematic roles and language processing. We will focus on three areas corresponding to our main representation assumptions: the differences between proposed components of verb meaning involving thematic ambiguities and those involving ambiguities of core meaning ("sense ambiguities"), the influence of thematic assignments on parsing decisions, and the effects of open thematic roles on the creation and integration of local discourse structure.

Sense and Thematic Role Ambiguities
One of our central assumptions is that the core meaning or sense of a verb can be distinguished from the thematic roles associated with the sense. As a consequence, we predict a processing difference for sentences exhibiting temporary ambiguities such as those illustrated in (16) and (17).

(16) Bill *passed* the test to his friend.

(17) Bill *loaded* the truck onto the platform.

In (16), *passed* is ambiguous between two senses—roughly, to earn a passing grade and to hand over. The phrase that follows the ambiguous verb biases the sense of that verb. In (16), "the test" biases the *grade* sense.

Readers should experience a small garden path when this sense later turns out to be incorrect. This follows from the assumption that lexical access will make available multiple senses of such a word as *pass*, but only the contextually most appropriate sense (or, in the absence of biasing context, the most frequent sense) will remain active, whereas the others become increasingly deactivated. When a reader or hearer initially selects the wrong sense of an ambiguous verb, reinterpretation requires retrieving the alternative sense. This should take time and processing resources. In (17), the noun phrase "the truck" could be either the Location of the loading or what is being loaded (the Theme). When the wrong thematic assignment is initially made, thematic reassignment should be relatively cost-free because the core meaning of the verb remains constant; because the alternative thematic roles are generally active and available; and because the syntactic-thematic mappings provide explicit information about how roles are to be assigned, so only a limited domain of information needs to be reexamined.

The null hypothesis is that the ambiguities are both sense ambiguities, and that hence they are not fundamentally distinct. In an experiment conducted in collaboration with Curt Burgess (for details see Tanenhaus, Burgess, Hudson-d'Zmura, and Carlson 1987) we used experimental materials similar to those illustrated in (18) and (19), for sense and thematic-role ambiguities, respectively.

(18) a. Bill *passed* the test to his complete surprise.

b. Bill *failed* the test to his complete surprise.

c. Bill *passed* the test to the person behind him.

d. Bill *handed* the test to the person behind him.

(19) a. Bill *loaded* the truck with bricks.

b. Bill *filled* the truck with bricks.

c. Bill *loaded* the truck onto the ship.

d. Bill *drove* the truck onto the ship.

In (18a) and (19c), different senses of *pass* are selected by the final disambiguating phrase; disambiguation does not take place until after presentation of the direct object NP. The sentences in (18b) and (18d) are control sentences using unambiguous verbs that have core meanings related to the appropriate sense in the ambiguous version of the sentence. The sentences of (19) repeat that same pattern for the thematic ambiguities: (19a) and (19c) involve temporary ambiguity of thematic assignment to the direct object, to be disambiguated by the final constituent; (19b) and (19d) serve as

Table 2
Latencies (in msec) for sentences judged to make sense, with percentage judged to make sense in parentheses.

Ambiguity type	Ambiguous verb	Control verb
Sense	2,445 (77)	2,290 (94)
Thematic	2,239 (92)	2,168 (93)

unambiguous controls. The test sentences were intermixed with filler sentences that varied in structure, in order to discourage strategies.

The sentences were displayed on a CRT, and the subjects' task was to decide as quickly as possible whether the sentence made sense. We assumed that subjects would initially select the incorrect verb sense or thematic assignment on approximately half the trials where temporary ambiguity is possible. If incorrect sense selection results in a garden path once disambiguating information to the contrary arrives, this should be reflected either in fewer sentences with sense ambiguities being judged to make sense or in longer reaction times to comprehend these sentences, all relative to control sentences. In contrast, thematic-role ambiguities should result in much weaker garden paths. Filler trials included sentences that were incongruous, such as "Several people borrowed ideas under the bed."

The results are presented in table 2, which displays reaction time (in msec) to the sentences judged to make sense and percentage of sentences judged to make sense. The judgment data show the predicted interaction between verb type (sense or thematic) and ambiguity (ambiguous or control condition). The interaction obtained because sentences with sense ambiguities were less likely to be judged to make sense than their controls, whereas sentences with the thematic-role ambiguities were not. The reaction-time results for those sentences judged to make sense show the same pattern; however, the interaction was not reliable.[4]

Thematic Feedback to the Parser

The assumption that arguments are assigned thematic roles immediately (at least once the verb is encountered) suggests that provisional thematic-role assignment may provide a mechanism whereby pragmatic knowledge and processing context influence subsequent syntactic decisions. It seems plausible that the meaning of an argument, the core meaning of the verb, and general world knowledge are taken into account in making provisional thematic assignments (e.g., "pack the suitcases" prefers suitcases as Location, whereas "pack the clothes" prefers clothes as Theme, because of the nature of suitcases and clothes and not because of any grammatical properties of the nouns denoting these things). Since thematic assignments often have direct syntactic consequences, the nonsyntactic information used in assigning thematic roles might have immediate parsing consequences.

Some evidence in support of the hypothesis that initial thematic assignments can provide feedback to the parser has been obtained by Stowe (in press). In one experiment Stowe used verbs, such as *stopped*, that have a causative reading when used transitively and an ergative reading when used intransitively. For example, when *stop* is used transitively ("Frank stopped the car") the subject is Agent and the object is Theme; when it is used intransitively ("The car stopped") the subject is Theme. These verbs were placed in subordinate clauses preceding the main clause, as in "Even before the police stopped the driver was getting nervous". In the absence of punctuation the clause boundary in these sentences is temporarily ambiguous, because the NP after the verb could be either the object of the verb or the subject of the next clause. Frazier (1978) and Frazier and Rayner (1982) have shown that, in the absence of punctuation, readers initially assume that the NP following the verb is its object, rather than closing off the subordinate clause and taking the NP to be the subject of the main clause. This typically results in a garden-path effect. If, however, the subject of the subordinate clause is inanimate, and thus more likely to be a Theme than an Agent, then the reader may "close off" the subordinate clause after the verb, there being no remaining unassigned roles on the grid. To test this prediction, Stowe manipulated the animacy of the subject of the subordinate clause, using materials like those in (20).

(20) a. Even before the police stopped the driver was getting nervous. (animate ambiguous)

   b. Even before the truck stopped the driver was getting nervous. (inanimate ambiguous)

   c. Even before the police stopped at the light the driver was getting nervous. (animate control)

   d. Even before the truck stopped at the light the driver was getting nervous. (inanimate control)

Subjects read sentences such as these one word at a time, with a secondary task of pressing a button if and when the sentence became ungrammatical. Reading times were recorded, as were judgments of ungrammaticality.

The main finding was that when the subject of the subordinate clause was animate, as in (20a), the reading times for the main clause were longer by more than half a second than the reading times for controls, such as (20c) and (20d). On the other hand, there was no corresponding effect when the subject was inanimate, as in (20b). This provides evidence that the meaning of the noun was playing a role in determining parsing decisions, and we hypothesize that *animacy* is the key element. In the presence of an animate subject, the verb was taken as a transitive, leading to a garden path in the main clause. Our account is that animacy affects thematic assignment, which in turn has direct consequences for the syntax of the sentence being processed.

Whether animacy information can guide parsing decisions remains controversial. Stowe's experiment can be questioned on methodological grounds: Word-by-word reading times in her experiment were long—more than 700 msec per word. The likely explanation for the long reading times has to do with the task. Stowe provided subjects with feedback following grammaticality judgments. A subject who judged a sentence to be ungrammatical when garden-pathed—e.g., at *was* in the sentence "Even before the police stopped the driver was getting nervous"—would be told that he or she had made a mistake. This kind of feedback probably made subjects think carefully before responding. It will be important to replicate Stowe's experiment with a task that results in more normal reading rates.

A replication is particularly important because Ferreira and Clifton (1986) report results that seem to suggest that animacy information cannot guide parsing decisions. They examined eye-fixation durations in sentences such as "The defendant evidence (that was) examined by the judge ..." in which the subject NP was either animate or inanimate. They reasoned that if thematic assignment could provide feedback to the parser, then reading times for the postverbal *by* phrase, which unambiguously shows the verb to be a past participle (in a reduced relative) rather than a simple past tense, should be shorter when the subject is inanimate ("the evidence examined ...") than when it is animate ("The lawyer examined ..."). Reading times on the verb were longer when the subject was inanimate, which would be consistent with a thematically based revision. However, there was no significant animacy effect at the *by* phrase, which suggested that the parser was not able to use thematic feedback.

Although these results are certainly not encouraging for the thematic-feedback hypothesis, there are several reasons why they are not definitive. First of all, the mechanism for thematic feedback is not as straightforward for verbs that have a simple past/past participle ambiguity as it is for verbs that have a causative/inchoative ambiguity. On our view, accessing a verb such as *stopped* makes available both the thematic structure associated with the causative interpretation and that associated with the inchoative interpretation. After the verb has been recognized, both the Theme and the

Agent are active possible roles for the subject of the sentence. In contrast, the past tense/past participle ambiguity is a morphological ambiguity, with different thematic mappings (and not grids) associated with each tense. Since past participles are generally less frequent than simple past tenses, especially in the environment of a noun phrase, the more frequent past tense may rapidly inhibit the past participle. Thus, there may not be an active Theme role for the subject, depending on the character of lexical access for morphological ambiguities.

In addition, we have several concerns about Ferreira and Clifton's materials. It is not clear that it is appropriate to compare *by* phrases following full relatives and *by* phrases following reduced relatives. It is possible, for instance, that a *by* phrase is generally more felicitous after a full relative than after a reduced relative, even when there isn't a possible garden path. One way to rule out this possibility is to include a control condition with reduced relatives that have unambiguous past-participle forms (e.g., stolen, taken). A second concern is that many of Ferreira and Clifton's sentences have plausible continuations where the inanimate subject could be continued with a simple past form.

However, if our assumption that the processing system makes provisional thematic assignments is correct, we can offer a tentative explanation in terms of thematic-role assignment for the filler-gap study of Stowe et al., discussed earlier in this chapter. Recall that in this experiment we found evidence for a plausibility effect immediately at the matrix verb when the filler was an implausible object of the verb (e.g., "... which food the child read") for transitive preference verbs but not for intransitive preference verbs. Most of the intransitive preference verbs we used exhibited the same contrast exploited by Stowe (1986) in the animacy study discussed earlier. In sentences like "The physical therapist wasn't sure which bed the orderly hurried rapidly toward", subjects may have initially assumed that the subject of the embedded verb (*hurried*) was playing the role of Theme, because this is the thematic assignment associated with the intransitive preference. As a consequence, there would no longer be a possible role for the filler, and thus the implausible filler would not be associated with the verb. This explanation depends crucially on the assumption that the assignment of an argument to a thematic role deactivates incompatible thematic assignments.

Open Thematic Roles and the Discourse Model
In the preceding subsection, the verbs in question had different thematic grids associated with the different syntactic environments in which they

occurred. One of our central assumptions is that different subcategorizations are often associated with the same thematic grid. When this is the case, thematic roles can be left unfilled or open. Consider the well-studied class of "spray-load" verbs. In the sentence "John loaded the truck with bricks", *John* would be the Agent, *the truck* would be the Location, and *bricks* would be the Theme. In the sentence "John loaded the truck", *the truck* is also likely to be the Location. (Trucks are possible but unlikely Themes.) There is still something being loaded, however, and what is being loaded is not made explicit. Our proposal is that the Theme is an open role in this example. We have proposed (Carlson and Tanenhaus 1988) that open thematic roles are represented as unspecified entities in a discourse model or other conceptual representation of a discourse, and that they, like anaphors and presuppositions, can help create local discourse coherence (Grosz, Joshi, and Weinstein 1983).

We have recently conducted an experiment that demonstrates that open roles may indeed function as antecedents for definite noun phrases. In a classic study, Haviland and Clark (1974) showed that a sentence beginning with a definite phrase takes longer to comprehend when the context does not introduce an explicit antecedent for the noun phrase. Note that the discourse in (21) is awkward because (21a) does not introduce an antecedent for "the clothes" in (21b).

(21) a. Mary stopped to look in the window.

b. The clothes were beautiful.

Garrod and Sanford (1981) later showed that sentences with antecedentless definite noun phrases without prior antecedents do not complicate processing when the definite noun phrase is part of the meaning, or when it is logically entailed by the verb in a preceding sentence. For example the verb *dress* entails that clothes were being put on, and thus the discourse in (22) is felicitous.

(22) Mary tried to dress her child.

The clothes were too small.

If open thematic roles can create discourse addresses, a definite NP should be easier to integrate into a discourse if the previous sentence introduces an open role that can plausibly be "filled" by the NP than if the context does not create an open role. We tested this hypothesis in an experiment (Tanenhaus et al. 1987) for which we constructed sets of two-sentence discourses in which a target sentence beginning with a definite noun phrase, such as (23b), was preceded either by a context sentence that introduced an open thematic role that the NP could plausibly fill, as in (23b), or by a sentence that created a plausible context for the target sentence but that did not leave an open role, as in (23a).

(23) a. The miners were drilling a large tunnel. (open Location)

    a'. The miners were making a large tunnel. (no open roles)

    b. *The rock* was hard to remove.

The two sentences for each set were counterbalanced across two presentation lists. Subjects were presented with the context sentence on a CRT. When they pressed a button indicating that they had read and understood the context sentence, they were presented with the target sentence. Their task was to decide whether the target sentence made sense in view of the context. Target sentences were judged to make sense more often when the context sentence introduced a possible role than when it did not (97 percent versus 84 percent), and latencies to target sentences judged to make sense were shorter when the context introduced an open thematic role than when it did not (1,628 msec versus 1,847 msec).

Another situation where open roles may create discourse coherence is when a context sentence introduces a discourse entity that can fill an open Goal role in a following sentence. Consider cases of sentences giving the rationale for an action, keeping in mind that rationale is particularly keyed to the role of Goal (Jones 1985). If the second sentence contains an open Goal role that can plausibly be filled by an entity already introduced, intuition suggests that it is more easily integrated with the first sentence than when no open role occurs. For example, notice the contrast found in (24), between the (24b) continuation (which has an open Goal role) and the (24b') continuation (which lacks such a role).

(24) a. Her nephew's birthday was coming up, so ...

    b. Mary sent a book. (open Goal)

    b'. Mary bought a book. (no open Goal)

From a general conceptual point of view, if one knows that someone's birthday is coming up, buying a gift is certainly as common as sending a gift; thus, situational plausibility offers no straightforward account of this contrast. Similar results may be obtained by filling the role in the second sentence, so that no open Goal occurs but there is still the inference of some entity involved. For instance, *give away* and *donate* mean roughly the same thing, but in (25) we would analyze *give away* as having the Goal role "filled" (by *away*, it appears).

(25) a. The Salvation Army was having a Christmas drive, so ...

    b. John donated some toys. (open Goal)

    b'. John gave away some toys. (no open Goal)

There seems to be a marked contrast between the (b) and (b') continuations in these examples, with (25b') being more difficult to integrate with (25a) than (25b).

Open thematic roles may also provide a channel of communication between the discourse model and the parser. There is an increasing body of evidence demonstrating that some parsing preferences depend upon the choice of particular lexical items (Ford et al. 1982; Speer and Foss 1986; Mitchell and Holmes 1985). One possible explanation for these effects is that parsing biases are determined by a verb's most frequently used subcategorization. An alternative possibility is that some of these preferences are thematically mediated. Consider the verb *donate* again. *Donate* can occur either with two arguments, as is illustrated in (26a), or with three arguments, as in (26b).

(26) a. John donated some money.

    b. John donated some money to the library.

In the absence of context, intuition suggests that the three-argument sentence is more natural. This could be interpreted as a subcategorization preference effect, with *donate* occurring more frequently with an NP and a PP than with just an NP, or it could have a more conceptually based explanation (Kurtzman 1984). We propose a conceptual explanation, similar to that proposed by Kurtzman, but cast in terms of thematic roles. Upon encountering *donate*, people expect to be told both what is being donated and who or what will be the "Goal" of the donation. The three-argument sentence satisfies these expectations better than the two-argument sentence. Intuitive evidence in support of the conceptual explanation comes from placing sentences (26a) and (26b) in a context, like (27), that provides a plausible discourse entity for the Goal.

(27) The state library budget was slashed, so ...

    a. Bill donated some books.

    b. Bill donated some books to his local library.

Now, our intuitions suggest that the two-argument form (27a) is at least as natural as the three-argument form (27b). This contrasts with the examples in (28), which use a verb that does not leave an open role. (We assume that the *for* phrase is not subcategorized under the verb for benefactive verbs like *buy*.)

(28) The state library had its budget slashed, so ...

    a. Bill bought some books.

    b. Bill bought some books for his local library.

Now, the two-argument form (28a) is clearly less natural than the three-argument form (28b).

Intuition also suggests that plausible "fillers" for thematic roles provided by context may influence closure decisions. Earlier we discussed Stowe's "animacy" experiments with verbs exhibiting causative-ergative alternations, such as *stopped* and *finished*. When these verbs are placed in subordinate clauses with animate subjects, there is a parsing bias in favor of the causative reading. Thus, garden paths occur with sentences like (29).

(29) By the time the man finished the meal was cold.

However, a context like (30) seems to eliminate the garden path by providing a plausible conceptual filler for the Theme for *finished*.

(30) Although dinner was ready, the man was in the middle of
    varnishing his desk.

    By the time the man finished the meal was cold.

It is not the case, however, that the presence of a conceptual filler rules out late closure. The late-closure interpretation still seems perfectly natural when the NP following the verb is consistent with the interpretation provided by context, as in (31).

(31) a. Although dinner was ready, the man was in the middle of
       varnishing his desk.

    b. By the time the man finished the job the meal was cold.[5]

This example suggests that people assume, upon processing the verb *finish*, that the man finished varnishing his desk. When the following NP is consistent with that interpretation, as in (31), it is parsed as the object of the verb; if not, the NP is parsed as the subject of the next clause. Thus, open roles can allow information in the discourse model to guide attachment and closure decisions.

Summary and Conclusion

The issue that we have tried to address is the extent to which aspects of higher-level lexical structure—in particular, information about the argument structure of verbs—is made available and used during language comprehension. As we argued at the beginning of the chapter, this issue is crucial to distinguishing between very different views of sentence comprehension. The evidence we briefly reviewed in our discussion of the processing of sentences with long-distance dependencies suggests that both information about verb control and information about verb argument structure is rapidly accessed and used during parsing. These results complement other recent demonstrations of immediate lexical influences in parsing.

Much of our discussion was devoted to exploring some hypotheses about how the thematic roles associated with verbs might serve as a lexically based communication channel among different sources of knowledge that must be integrated during comprehension. One of the ideas motivating our proposals was that thematic roles might provide just the sort of mechanism to allow the comprehension system to make rapid "on-line" commitments, yet cope with the local indeterminacy presented to it because of the hierarchical structure of language. We presented some preliminary experimental evidence in support of two of our primary claims: that lexical representations of verbs can be divided into a core meaning and a set of thematic roles, and that thematic roles can play an important part in certain aspects of discourse integration and in communication between the discourse model and the parser.

It is also important to emphasize the preliminary nature of our explorations. Although we have presented a framework for exploring some basic issues about the role of higher-level lexical representation in language processing, a great deal more empirical and theoretical work needs to be done before our knowledge of higher-level lexical processing is rich enough to support the kind of detailed processing models that researchers are now developing for the recognition of spoken and written words.

Acknowledgments

The research reported here was partially supported by NSF grants BNS-8217378 and BNS-8617738, and by NIH grant HD-22271. Many of the ideas discussed here were developed in discussions with Susan Garnsey and Julie Boland.

Notes

1. We are going to use the term *Theme* to include what is also called *Patient*. We are using this terminology simply to avoid dealing with important issues that would take us too far afield to consider even superficially here (see Jackendoff 1987).

2. Whether a phrase is subcategorized can be determined by standard constituency tests. In Carlson and Tanenhaus (in press) we describe in some detail the phrases that are subcategorized for a range of verbs.

3. However, we do not wish to maintain that *all* instances of implied necessary participation arise from the presence of open thematic roles. One class of such implications comes from considering the microstructure of the event referred to. For instance, if Bill runs, it is implied that he has legs, or if Mary kisses her son, it is implied that Mary has lips; yet we would not provide an open role for Bill's legs or Mary's lips in the analysis of "Bill runs" or "Mary kisses her son". This in no way denies the validity of the implication, but it does provide a distinction in the way such implications arise: Only a subclass of the set of entailments of necessary participants in an event arise from open roles.

4. There are several potential shortcomings with this experiment. One is that we did not norm the materials to ensure that the noun phrase following the ambiguous verb was equally biasing in the sense-ambiguity sentences and the thematic-role-ambiguity sentences. Thus, it is possible to argue that our results do not clearly demonstrate a difference between sense and thematic role, but instead that they simply demonstrate that larger garden paths occur in more strongly biased contexts. A replication experiment that controls for degree of bias is in progress. A second problem is that the information that disambiguates a thematic ambiguity is syntactic, whereas the information that disambiguates a sense ambiguity is generally semantic or pragmatic. Since syntactic information tends to be more determinate than semantic or pragmatic information, it is possible that subjects took longer to abandon the initially biased reading in the sense-ambiguity conditions, because this interpretation was not completely ruled out until late in the sentence.

5. We are currently testing these hypotheses experimentally in collaboration with Bob Peterson and Susan Garnsey. The observation illustrated by the example in (38) is due to Peterson.

References

Boland, J., Tanenhaus, M. K., and Garnsey, S. M. Forthcoming. Lexical structure and parsing: Evidence for the immediate use of verb control information in parsing.

Bresnan, J. 1982. Polyadicity. In J. Bresnan (ed.), *The Mental Representation of Grammatical Relations*. Cambridge, Mass.: MIT Press.

Burgess, C., Tanenhaus, M. K., and Seidenberg, M. S. In press. Implications of non-word interference for lexical ambiguity resolution. *Journal of Experimental Psychology: Learning Memory* and *Cognition*.

Carlson, G. N. 1984. Thematic roles and their role in semantic interpretation. *Linguistics* 22: 259–279.

Carlson, G. N., and Tanenhaus, M. K. 1988. Thematic roles and language comprehension. In W. Wilkins (ed.), *Thematic Relations*. New York: Academic.

Chomsky, N. 1981. *Lectures on Government and Binding*. Dordrecht: Foris.

Chomsky, N. 1986. *Aspects of the Theory of Syntax*. Cambridge, Mass.: MIT Press.

Clifton, C., Jr., and Frazier, L. 1986. The use of syntactic information in filling gaps. *Journal of Psycholinguistic Research* 15: 209–224.

Clifton, C., and Frazier, L. 1988. Comprehending sentences with long-distance dependencies. In G. Carlson and M. K. Tanenhaus (eds.), *Linguistic Structure in Language Processing*. Dordrecht: Reidel.

Clifton, C., Frazier, L., and Connine, C. 1984. Lexical expectations in sentence comprehension. *Journal of Verbal Learning and Verbal Behavior* 23: 696–708.

Connine, C., Ferreira, F., Jones, C., Clifton, C., and Frazier, L. 1984. Verb frame preferences: Descriptive norms. *Journal of Psycholinguistic Research* 13: 307–319.

Cottrell, G. 1985. A Connectionist Approach to Word Sense Disambiguation. Doctoral dissertation, University of Rochester.

Crain, S., and Fodor, J. D. 1985. How can grammars help parsers? In D. Dowty, L. Kartunnen, and A. Zwicky (eds.), *Natural Language parsing*. Cambridge University Press.

Crain, S., and Steedman, M. 1985. On not being led up the garden path: The use of context by the psychological syntax processor. In D. Dowty, L. Kartunnen, and A. Zwicky (eds.), *Natural Language Parsing*. Cambridge University Press.

Ferreira, F., and Clifton, C. 1986. The independence of syntactic processing. *Journal of Memory and Language* 25: 348–368.

Fillmore, C. 1968. The case for case. In E. Bach and R. Harms (eds.), *Universals in Linguistic Theory*. New York: Holt, Rinehart, and Winston.

Fodor, J. D. 1978. Parsing strategies and constraints on transformation. *Linguistic Inquiry* 9: 427–474.

Fodor, J. D. In press. Modularity within the syntactic processor. *Journal of Psycholinguistic Research*.

Fodor, J. A., Bever, T. G., and Garrett, M. 1974. *The Psychology of Language*. New York: McGraw-Hill.

Ford, M., Bresnan. J., and Kaplan, R. 1982. A competence-based theory of syntactic closure. In J. Bresnan (ed.), *The Mental Representation of Grammatical Relations*. Cambridge, Mass.: MIT Press.

Frazier, L. 1978. On Comprehending Sentences: Syntactic Parsing Strategies. Ph.D. dissertation, University of Connecticut. Distributed by Indiana University Linguistics Club.

Frazier, L. 1987. Theories of sentence processing. In J. Garfield (ed.), *Modularity in Knowledge Representation and Natural-Language Processing*. Cambridge, Mass.: MIT Press.

Frazier, L., and Fodor, J. 1978. The sausage machine: A new two-stage parsing model. *Cognition* 6: 291–325.

Frazier, L., and Rayner, K. 1982. Making and correcting errors during sentence comprehension: Eye movements in the analysis of structurally ambiguous sentences. *Cognitive Psychology* 14: 178–210.

Frazier, L., Clifton, C. J., and Randall, J. 1983. Filling gaps: Decision principles and structure in sentence comprehension. *Cognition* 13: 187–222.

Garnsey, S. M., Tanenhaus, M. K., and Chapman, R. M. In press. Evoked Potentials and the study of Sentence Comprehension. *Journal of Psycholinguistic Research.*

Garrod, S. C., and Sanford, A. J. 1981. Bridging inferences and the extended domain of reference. In J. Long and A. Baddeley (eds.), *Attention and Performance IX.* Hillsdale, N.J.: Erlbaum.

Gazdar, G., Klein, E., Pullum, G., and Sag, I. 1984. *Generalized Phrase Structure Grammar.* Cambridge, Mass.: Harvard University Press.

Grosz, B., Joshi, A., and Weinstein, S. 1983. Providing a unified account of definite noun phrases in discourse. In Proceedings of the 21st annual Meeting of the Association for Computational Linguistics.

Hudson, S., and Tanenhaus, M. K. 1982. Lexical ambiguity resolution in the absence of contextual bias. In Proceedings of the Sixth Annual Cognitive Science Meeting.

Jackendoff, R. 1987. The status of thematic relations in linguistic theory. *Linguistic Inquiry* 28: 369–412.

Jackendoff, R. 1972. *Semantic Interpretation in Generative Grammar.* Cambridge, Mass.: MIT Press.

Jones, C. 1985. The Syntax and Thematics of Rationale and Purpose Clauses. Ph.D. dissertation, University of Massachusetts.

Kurtzman, H. 1984. Studies in Syntactic Ambiguity Resolution. Doctoral dissertation, MIT. Distributed by Indiana University Linguistics Club.

Ladusaw, W., and Dowty, D. 1988. Towards a non-grammatical account of thematic roles. In W. Wilkins (ed.), *Thematic Relations.* New York: Academic.

Marslen-Wilson, W. D. 1975. Sentence perception as an interactive parallel process. *Science* 189: 226–228.

Marslen-Wilson, W. D., and Tyler, L. K. 1987. Against modularity. In J. Garfield (ed.), *Modularity in Knowledge Representation and Natural-Language Understanding.* Cambridge, Mass.: MIT Press.

McClelland, J. L., and Kawamoto, A. 1986. Mechanisms of sentence processing: Assigning roles to constituents of sentences. In J. McClelland et al. (eds.), *Parallel Distributed Processing,* volume 2: *Psychological and Biological Models.* Cambridge, Mass.: MIT Press.

McClelland, J. L., and Rumelhart, D. 1981. An interactive activation model of context effects in letter perception: Part 1. An account of basic findings. *Psychological Review* 88: 375–405.

Mitchell, D. C., and Holmes, V. M. 1985. The role of specific information about the verb in parsing sentences with local structural ambiguity. *Journal of Memory and Language* 24: 542–559.

Onifer, W., and Swinney, D. A. 1981. Accessing lexical ambiguities during sentence comprehension: Effects of frequency of meaning and contextual bias. *Memory and Cognition* 9: 222–236.

Rayner, K., Carlson, M., and Frazier, L. 1984. The interaction of syntax and semantics in sentence processing: Eye movements in the analysis of semantically biased sentences. *Journal of Verbal Learning and Verbal Behavior* 22: 358–374.

Seidenberg, M. 1985. Constraining models of word recognition. *Cognition* 14: 169–190.

Seidenberg, M., and Tanenhaus, M. K. 1979. Orthographic effects in rhyme and monitoring. *Journal of Experimental Psychology: Human Learning and Memory* 5: 546–554.

Seidenberg, M., Tanenhaus, M. K., Leiman, J., and Bienkowski, M. 1982. Automatic access of the meanings of ambiguous words in context: Some limitations of knowledge-based processes. *Cognitive Psychology* 14: 489–537.

Shapiro, L., Zuriff, E., and Grimshaw, J. 1986. Sentence processing and the mental representation of verbs. Manuscript.

Simpson, G. 1984. Lexical ambiguity and its role in models of word recognition. *Psychological Bulletin* 96: 316–340.

Simpson, G., and Burgess, C. 1985. Activation and selection processes in the recognition of ambiguous words. *Journal of Experimental Psychology: Human Perception and Performance* 11: 28–39.

Speer, S., and Foss, D. 1986. Syntactic and thematic contributions to sentence complexity. Paper presented at 27th Annual Meeting of the Psychonomic Society, New Orleans.

Stowe, L. 1984. Models of Gap Location in the Human Language Processor. Dissertation. Distributed by Indiana University Linguistics Club.

Stowe, L. 1986. Parsing *wh*-constructions: Evidence for on-line gap location. *Language and Cognitive Processes* 2: 227–246.

Stowe, L. 1988. Thematic structures and sentence comprehension. To appear in G. Carlson and M. Tanenhaus (eds.), *Linguistic Structure in Language Processing*. Dordrecht: Reidel.

Stowe, L., and Tanenhaus, M. Forthcoming. Models of filler-gap assignment: The role of pragmatic and lexical information.

Stowe, L., Tanenhaus, M. K., and Carlson, G. 1985. Parsing Filler-Gap Sentences. Paper presented at 26th Annual Meeting of the Psychonomic Society, Amherst, Mass.

Stowell, T. 1981. Origins of Phrase Structure. Doctoral dissertation, MIT.

Swinney, D. A. 1979. Lexical access during sentence comprehension: (Re)consideration of context effects. *Journal of Verbal Learning and Verbal Behavior* 18: 645–659.

Swinney, D., Ford, M., Bresnan, J., Frauenfelder, U., and Nicol, J. 1987. Timecourse of Co-indexation during Sentence Comprehension. Paper presented at 28th Annual Meeting of the Psychonomic Society, Seattle.

Tanenhaus, M., Leiman, J., and Seidenberg, M. 1979. Evidence for multiple stages in the processing of ambiguous words in syntactic contexts. *Journal of Verbal Learning and Verbal Behavior* 18: 427–440.

Tanenhaus, M., Flanigan, H., Seidenberg, M. 1980. Orthographic and phonological code activation in auditory and visual word recognition. *Memory and Cognition* 8: 513–520.

Tanenhaus, M., Stowe, L., and Carlson, G. 1985. The interaction of lexical expectation and pragmatics in parsing filler-gap constructions. In Proceedings of the Seventh Annual Cognitive Science Society Meetings.

Tanenhaus, M. K., Boland, J., and Garnsey, S. M. 1987. Lexical Structure and Language Comprehension. Presented at 28th Annual Meeting of the Psychonomic Society, Seattle.

Tanenhaus, M. K., Burgess, C. Hudson-d'Zmura, S., and Carlson, G. 1987. Thematic roles in language processing. In *Proceedings of the Ninth Annual Cognitive Science Society Meetings*. Hillsdale, N. Erlbaum.

Tarraban, R., and McClelland, J. In press. The role of semantic constraints in interpreting prepositional phrases. *Journal of Memory and Language.*

Contributors

David A. Balota   Washington University, St. Louis

Derek Besner   University of Waterloo, Ontario

Brian Butterworth   University College London

Greg N. Carlson   University of Rochester

Anne Cutler   MRC Applied Psychology Unit, Cambridge

Gary S. Dell   University of Rochester

Jeffrey L. Elman   University of California, San Diego

Giovanni B. Flores D'Arcais   Max-Planck-Institut für Psycholinguistik, Nijmegen

Uli H. Frauenfelder   Max-Planck-Institut für Psycholinguistik, Nijmegen

Kenneth I. Forster   University of Arizona, Tucson

Lyn Frazier   University of Massachusetts, Amherst

Jorge Hankamer   University of California, Santa Cruz

Leslie Henderson   Hatfield Polytechnic

James C. Johnston   National Aeronautics and Space Administration

Dennis H. Klatt   Massachusetts Institute of Technology

Lorraine Komisarjevsky Tyler   University of Cambridge

Aditi Lahiri   Max-Planck-Institut für Psycholinguistik, Nijmegen

William Marslen-Wilson   MRC Applied Psychology Unit, Cambridge

Keith Rayner   University of Massachusetts, Amherst

Mark S. Seidenberg   McGill University

Robert Schreuder   University of Nijmegen

Mark J. Steedman   University of Pennsylvania

Michael K. Tanenhaus   University of Rochester

Index